APPLIED SPORT PSYCHOLOGY

SEVENTH EDITION

APPLIED SPORT PSYCHOLOGY

PERSONAL GROWTH TO PEAK PERFORMANCE

Jean M. Williams, Editor
University of Arizona, Emeritus

Vikki Krane, Editor
Bowling Green State University

APPLIED SPORT PSYCHOLOGY: PERSONAL GROWTH TO PEAK PERFORMANCE, SEVENTH EDITION
Published by McGraw-Hill, 2 Penn Plaza, New York, NY 10121 Copyright © 2015 By McGraw-Hill education. All rights reserved. Printed in the United States of America. Previous editions © 2013, 2010, 2006. No part of this publication may be reproduced or distributed in any form or by any means, or stored in a database or retrieval system, without the prior written consent of McGraw-Hill Education including, but not limited to, in any network or other electronic storage or transmission, or broadcast for distance learning.

Some ancillaries, including electronic and print components, may not be available to customers outside the United States

This book is printed on acid-free paper.

2 3 4 5 6 7 8 9 0 DOC/DOC 1 0 9 8 7 6 5 4

ISBN: 978-0-07-802270-8
MHID: 0-07-802270-3

Senior Vice President, Products & Markets: Kurt L. Strand
Vice President, Content Production & Technology Services: *Kimberly Meriwether David*
Brand Manager: *Gina Boedeker*
Executive Director of Development: *Lisa Pinto*
Manager Editor: *Sara Jaeger*
Associate Marketing Manager: *Alexandra Schultz*
Brand Coordinator: *Adina Lonn*

Director, Content Production: *Terri Schiesl*
Content Production Manager: *Faye Schilling*
Content Project Manager: *Judi David*
Buyer: *Nichole Birkenholz*
Cover Designer: *Studio Montage, St. Louis, MO.*
Cover Image: *Vikki Krane*
Compositor: *Laserwords Private Limited*
Typeface: *9/11 ITC Stone Serif–Medium*
Printer: *R. R. Donnelley*

Library of Congress Cataloging-in-Publication Data

Applied sports psychology: personal growth to peak performance/Jean M. Williams University of Arizona, Emeritus, Vikki Krane, Bowling Green State University.—Seventh edition.
    pages cm
    ISBN 978-0-07-802270-8 (alk. paper)
    1. Sports—Psychological aspects. 2. Coaching (Athletics) I. Williams, Jean M. (Jean Marie)
GV706.4.A66 2014
796.01'9—dc23

2013041275

www.mhhe.com

BRIEF CONTENTS

Preface xii

Contributors xvii

1 Sport Psychology: Past, Present, Future 1
   Jean M. Williams, University of Arizona, Emeritus; Vikki Krane, Bowling Green State University

PART ONE—LEARNING, MOTIVATION, AND SOCIAL INTERACTION

2 Motor Skill Learning for Effective Coaching and Performance 19
   Cheryl A. Coker, Plymouth State University

3 A Positive Approach to Coaching Effectiveness and Performance Enhancement 40
   Ronald E. Smith, University of Washington

4 The Motivational Climate, Athlete Motivation, and Implications for the Quality of Sport Engagement 57
   Joan L. Duda, The University of Birmingham, UK; Darren C. Treasure, Competitive Advantage International, USA

5 The Self-Fulfilling Prophecy Theory: When Coaches' Expectations Become Reality 78
   Thelma Sternberg Horn, Miami University; Curt L. Lox, Southern Illinois University; Francisco Labrador, Wittenberg University

6 Leadership in Sport: The Critical Importance of Coach and Athlete Leadership 101
   Julia D. Sterrett, Lehigh University; Jeff Janssen, Janssen Sports Leadership Center

7 The Sport Team as an Effective Group 124
   Mark A. Eys, Wilfrid Laurier University; Shauna M. Burke, Western University; Paul Dennis, High Performance Coach, York University; Blair Evans, Wilfrid Laurier University

8 Communicating Effectively 140
   David P. Yukelson, The Pennsylvania State University

PART TWO—MENTAL TRAINING FOR PERFORMANCE ENHANCEMENT

9 Psychological Characteristics of Peak Performance 159
   Vikki Krane, Bowling Green State University; Jean M. Williams, University of Arizona

10 Increasing Awareness for Sport Performance 176
    Kenneth Ravizza, California State University at Fullerton; Angela Fifer, United States Military Academy

11 Goal Setting for Peak Performance 188
    Daniel Gould, Michigan State University

12 Understanding and Managing Stress in Sport 207
    Sheldon Hanton, Cardiff Metropolitan University, UK; Stephen Mellalieu, Swansea University, UK; Jean M. Williams, University of Arizona, Emeritus

13 Understanding and Using Imagery in Sport 240
    Robin S. Vealey, Miami University; Samuel T. Forlenza, Michigan State University

14 Cognitive Techniques for Building
    Confidence and Enhancing
    Performance 274
    *Jean M. Williams, University of Arizona,
    Emeritus; Nate Zinsser, United States Military
    Academy; Linda Bunker, University of Virginia,
    Emeritus*

15 Concentration and Strategies for
    Controlling It 304
    *Jean M. Williams, University of Arizona,
    Emeritus; Robert M. Nideffer, Enhanced
    Performance Systems; Vietta E. Wilson,
    York University, Senior Scholar, Emeritus;
    Marc-Simon Sagal, The Winning Mind*

PART THREE—IMPLEMENTING TRAINING PROGRAMS

16 Integrating and Implementing a
    Psychological Skills Training
    Program 329
    *Robert S. Weinberg, Miami University; Jean M.
    Williams, University of Arizona, Emeritus*

17 Conducting Evidence Based Coach-Training
    Programs: A Social-Cognitive Approach 359
    *Frank L. Smoll, University of Washington;
    Ronald E. Smith, University of Washington*

18 Gender, Diversity, and Cultural
    Competence 383
    *Diane L. Gill, Ph.D., University of North
    Carolina at Greensboro; Cindra S. Kamphoff,
    Ph.D., Minnesota State University, Mankato*

PART FOUR—ENHANCING HEALTH AND WELL-BEING

19 When to Refer Athletes for Counseling
    or Psychotherapy 405
    *David Tod, University of the Sunshine Coast;
    Mark B. Andersen, Victoria University*

20 Drug Abuse in Sport: Causes and Cures
    421
    *Mark H. Anshel, Middle Tennessee State
    University*

21 Athlete Burnout: An Individual and
    Organizational Phenomenon 444
    *J.D. DeFreese, University of North Carolina at
    Chapel Hill; Thomas D. Raedeke, East Carolina
    University; Alan L. Smith, Michigan State
    University*

22 Injury Risk and Rehabilitation:
    Psychological Considerations 462
    *Jean M. Williams, University of Arizona,
    Emeritus; Carrie B. Scherzer, Mount Royal
    University*

23 Career Transition among Athletes: Is
    There Life after Sports? 490
    *David Lavallee, University of Stirling, UK;
    Sunghee Park, Kookmin University, South
    Korea; Jim Taylor, San Francisco*

24 Exercise Psychology 510
    *Rod K. Dishman, University of Georgia; Heather
    O. Chambliss, University of Memphis*

Index 541

CONTENTS

Preface xii

Contributors xvii

1 Sport Psychology: Past, Present, Future 1
Jean M. Williams, University of Arizona, Emeritus; Vikki Krane, Bowling Green State University

History of Sport Psychology 2

1965–1979: Birth of Sport Psychology and Supporting Organizations 3

The 1980s: Increased Research, Professional Growth, and Acceptance 5

1990–2013: Progress in Research, Application, and Professional Issues 7

History of Sport Psychology in Eastern Europe 10

Future Directions in North American Applied Sport Psychology 11

PART ONE—LEARNING, MOTIVATION, AND SOCIAL INTERACTION

2 Motor Skill Learning for Effective Coaching and Performance 19
Cheryl A. Coker, Plymouth State University

Motor Learning Defined 19

Phases of Motor Skill Learning 20

The Cognitive Phase 20

The Associative Phase 21

The Autonomous Phase 23

Whole versus Part Practice 24

Teaching Several Skills: Blocked versus Random Practice 26

Teaching Several Variations of a Skill: Variable Practice 28

Intervention Strategies 31

Case Study 33

Situation #1 Sample Response 34

3 A Positive Approach to Coaching Effectiveness and Performance Enhancement 40
Ronald E. Smith, University of Washington

Operant Conditioning: The ABCs of Behavior Control 41

Positive and Aversive Approaches to Influencing Behavior 42

Positive Reinforcement: Getting Good Things to Happen 44

Performance Feedback: Providing Information Needed to Improve Performance 50

4 The Motivational Climate, Athlete Motivation, and Implications for the Quality of Sport Engagement 57
Joan L. Duda, The University of Birmingham, UK; Darren C. Treasure, Competitive Advantage International, USA

Achievement Goals: The Importance of How We Judge Our Competence 58

Doing It for the Joy: The Determinants of Intrinsic Motivation and Self-Determination 66

5 The Self-Fulfilling Prophecy Theory: When Coaches' Expectations Become Reality 78
Thelma Sternberg Horn, Miami University; Curt L. Lox, Southern Illinois University; Francisco Labrador, Wittenberg University

The Expectation–Performance Process 79
Sport Applications 86

6 Leadership in Sports: The Critical Importance of Coach and Athlete Leadership 101
Julia D. Sterrett, Lehigh University; Jeff Janssen, Janssen Sports Leadership Center

7 The Sport Team as an Effective Group 124
Mark A. Eys, Wilfrid Laurier University; Shauna M. Burke, Western University; Paul Dennis, High Performance Coach, York University; Blair Evans, Wilfrid Laurier University

The Nature of Sport Groups 125
Group Cohesion 125

8 Communicating Effectively 140
David P. Yukelson, The Pennsylvania State University

Communication Defined 141
Communication in Sport 142
Communication and Groups 144
The Sport Psychologist as a Skilled Helper 152

PART TWO—MENTAL TRAINING FOR PERFORMANCE ENHANCEMENT

9 Psychological Characteristics of Peak Performance 159
Vikki Krane, Bowling Green State University; Jean M. Williams, University of Arizona

Overview of Peak Performance 160
Psychological Characteristics During Peak Experiences in Sport 160
Flow and Peak Performance 161
The Individualized Zone of Optimal Functioning 162
Psychological Attributes and Skills of Successful and Less Successful Athletes 164
A Profile of Mental Toughness 167
Team, Coach, Family, and Organizational Influences on Peak Performance 168
Conclusion: What It Takes to "Make It" 169

10 Increasing Awareness for Sport Performance 176
Kenneth Ravizza, California State University at Fullerton; Angela Fifer, United States Military Academy

The Importance of Awareness in Athletics 177
Awareness as It Relates to Skill Development 178
Techniques for Developing Awareness 183

11 Goal Setting for Peak Performance 188
Daniel Gould, Michigan State University

Goal-Setting Research and Theory 188
Examining Athletes' and Coaches' Uses of Goal Setting 191

Goal-Setting Guidelines 193

A Goal-Setting System for Coaches 198

Common Problems in Setting Goals 199

12 Understanding and Managing Stress in Sport 207

Sheldon Hanton, Cardiff Metropolitan University, UK; Stephen Mellalieu, Swansea University, UK; Jean M. Williams, University of Arizona, Emeritus

Cognitive-Behavioral Stress Management in Sport Psychology 207

Causes of and Responses to Stress 208

Measurement of Stress-Related Symptoms 211

Explaining the Relationship of Stress to Performance 212

Implications for Stress Management Interventions 216

13 Understanding and Using Imagery in Sport 240

Robin S. Vealey, Miami University; Samuel T. Forlenza, Michigan State University

What Is Imagery? 240

Does Imagery Work to Enhance Athletes' Performance? 243

How Does Imagery Enhance Athletes' Performance? 247

How Do You Set Up an Imagery Training Program? 249

Imagery Cookbook for Coaches and Practitioners 254

Case studies 262

14 Cognitive Techniques for Building Confidence and Enhancing Performance 274

Jean M. Williams, University of Arizona, Emeritus; Nate Zinsser, United States Military Academy; Linda Bunker, University of Virginia, Emeritus

Key Definitions: Confidence, Mental Toughness, Optimism, Self-Efficacy 275

Common Misconceptions about Confidence 276

Prerequisites for Gaining Confidence 277

Self-Talk 280

Identifying Self-Talk 284

Techniques for Controlling Self-Talk 286

15 Concentration and Strategies for Controlling It 304

Jean M. Williams, University of Arizona, Emeritus; Robert M. Nideffer, Enhanced Performance Systems; Vietta E. Wilson, York University, Senior Scholar, Emeritus; Marc-Simon Sagal, The Winning Mind

Attention Control Training Principles 306

Increasing Awareness of Types of Attention 312

External Factors: Strategies to Minimize External Distractions 315

Internal Factors: Strategies to Stay Focused 317

PART THREE—IMPLEMENTING TRAINING PROGRAMS

16 Integrating and Implementing a Psychological Skills Training Program 329

Robert S. Weinberg, Miami University; Jean M. Williams,University of Arizona, Emeritus

Are Psychological Interventions Effective in Improving Sport Performance? 330

Who Will Benefit from Psychological Skills Training? 331

Who Should Conduct the Psychological Skills Training Program? 332

When Should You Implement a Psychological Skills Training Program? 334

When Should Athletes Practice Psychological Skills? 334

How Much Time Should Be Spent in Mental Training? 335

Setting Up a Mental Skills Training Program 336

Determining What Skills to Include 342

Evaluation of Program Effectiveness 345
Practical Pointers for Teaching Mental Skills 346
Ethical Considerations for the Coach and Sport Psychology Consultant 351
Potential Problem Areas 351

17 Conducting Evidence Based Coach-Training Programs: A Social-Cognitive Approach 359
Frank L. Smoll, University of Washington; Ronald E. Smith, University of Washington

Developing Coach-Training Programs 360
Measurement of Coaching Behaviors 361
Implementing Sport Psychology Workshops for Coaches 367
A Final Word 373

18 Gender, Diversity, and Cultural Competence 383
Diane L. Gill, Ph.D., University of North Carolina at Greensboro; Cindra S. Kamphoff, Ph.D., Minnesota State University, Mankato

Overview and Framework 383
The Cultural Context of Sport 385
Gender and Sexuality 389
Race and Ethnicity 392
Cultural Competence in Sport Psychology 394

PART FOUR—ENHANCING HEALTH AND WELL-BEING

19 When to Refer Athletes for Counseling or Psychotherapy 405
David Tod, University of the Sunshine Coast: Mark B. Andersen, Victoria University

The False Dichotomy of Performance Enhancement Versus Problematic Personal Issues 406
How to Start the Referral Process 408
When Referrals Don't Go Smoothly 409
Some Specific Athlete-Related Issues 410
Professional Development Tasks for Practitioners and Students 415

20 Drug Abuse in Sport: Causes and Cures 421
Mark H. Anshel, Middle Tennessee State University

Review of Drugs Banned in Sport 423
Rationale for an Antidrug Policy in Sport 427
How Widespread Is Drug Abuse in Sport? 427
Likely Causes of Drug Abuse in Sport 429
Strategies for Controlling Drug Abuse 431

21 Athlete Burnout: An Individual and Organizational Phenomenon 444
J.D. DeFreese, University of North Carolina at Chapel Hill; Thomas D. Raedeke, East Carolina University; Alan L. Smith, Michigan State University

What Is Athlete Burnout? 445
What Is Not Athlete Burnout? 446
Why Does Burnout Occur? A Review of Theoretically Informed Burnout Antecedents 446
Overtraining 446
Integrating the Burnout Knowledge Base: How the Individual and Organization Fit 450
Preventing Athlete Burnout: Individual and Organizational Intervention Strategies 453

22 Injury Risk and Rehabilitation: Psychological Considerations 462
Jean M. Williams, University of Arizona, Emeritus; Carrie B. Scherzer, Mount Royal University

Factors That Predispose Athletes to Injury 462
Interventions to Reduce Injury Vulnerability 467
Athletes' Reactions to Injury 469
Teaching Specific Psychological Rehabilitation Strategies 478

23 Career Transition among Athletes: Is There Life after Sports? 490
David Lavallee, University of Stirling, UK; Sunghee Park, Kookmin University, South Korea; Jim Taylor, San Francisco

History and Background 490
Theoretical Perspectives on Career Transition 491
The Conceptual Model of Career Transition 492
Stage 1: Causes of Career Termination 493
Stage 2: Factors Related to Adaptation to Career Transition 495
Stage 3: Available Resources for Adaptation to Career Transition 498

Stage 4: Quality of Career Transition 500
Stage 5: Intervention for Career Transition 500

24 Exercise Psychology 510
Rod K. Dishman, University of Georgia; Heather O. Chambliss, University of Memphis 510

Exercise and Mental Health 511
Plausible Mediators or Mechanisms 516
Physical Activity Behavior Change 517
Social and Environmental Features 521
Index 541

PREFACE

Coaches and athletes have turned to applied sport psychology to gain a competitive edge—to learn, among other things, ways to manage competitive stress, control concentration, improve confidence, increase communication skills, and promote team harmony.

The first edition of *Applied Sport Psychology: Personal Growth to Peak Performance,* which was published in 1986, was one of the first books written specifically to introduce coaches and sport psychologists to psychological theories and techniques that could be used to enhance the performance and personal growth of sport participants from youth sport to elite levels. The book focused primarily on three dimensions: (1) techniques for developing and refining psychological skills to enhance performance and personal growth, (2) suggestions for establishing a learning and social environment that would enhance the effectiveness of coaches and maximize the skill and personal growth of athletes, and (3) special issues such as staleness and burnout, psychology of injury and injury rehabilitation, and retirement from athletics.

Later editions had the same focus but were expanded to cover more topics and to add a physical activity focus. New chapters were added on motivation, training youth sport coaches, improving communication, referring athletes for professional counseling, drug abuse in sport, cultural competence, and exercise psychology. The last chapter reflected the growing importance to applied sport psychology of understanding the psychological benefits and risks of exercise and the psychological and behavioral principles for enhancing exercise adoption and adherence.

New to this Issue

The same important topics, focus, and organizational structure have been retained for this seventh edition, but the revision reflects the latest research, practice, and anecdotal examples in applied sport psychology. In this edition, we have not added any new chapters, but we have taken new approaches to several of the topics. The chapter on sport leadership reflects more contemporary theoretical approaches to understanding leadership. It also now addresses how to develop leadership skills in athletes, as well as coaches. The coverage of stress, anxiety, and arousal have been updated and extended, including a broader coverage of theoretical approaches to the topic. And, in this edition, coverage of stress, anxiety, and arousal theory, and relaxation and energizing techniques have been combined into a single chapter. A new approach also has been taken in the coverage of athlete burnout in sport, reflecting the newest conceptualizations on this topic.

All of the chapters have updated reference lists and integrate the most recent research into the discussion of each topic. Also throughout all of the chapters, many new exercises and case studies have been added to help students think more critically about applied sport psychology and to apply the content to real-world situations. Current examples have been added to all chapters as well as additional discussion of practical applications reflecting today's coaches and athletes.

The Online Learning Center (http://www.mhhe.com/williams7e) provides additional resources for instructors and has been updated coinciding with the seventh edition of the book. Visit the site to fine helpful materials such as a test bank of questions, Powerpoint presentations, student learning experiences, and audio visual aids. All of these materials reflect the content changes throughout the book. The test questions, which can be used in quizzes and tests, have been reviewed to reflect the new information and all revisions in the chapters. The updated powerpoints highlight important concepts and summarize each the revised chapter. The student learning experiences and audio visual aids can assist instructors in bringing the content to life and applying it to real-life situations.

The same important topics, focus, and organizational structure have been retained for this seventh edition, but the revision reflects the latest research, practice, and anecdotal examples in applied sport psychology. In this edition, we have taken new approaches in the chapters on sport leadership and burnout in sport. We also updated and extended the coverage of stress, anxiety, and arousal theory and, in this edition, have combined these topics with relaxation and energizing techniques into a single chapter. Throughout the chapters, many new exercises, learning activities, and case studies have been added to help students think more critically and apply the content to real-world situations.

Written Specifically for Sport Psychologists and Coaches

Approximately 400 books have been published on mental skills for peak performance, but most of these books continue to be written primarily for the sport participant. Their coverage is not comprehensive enough for the sport psychologist or coach who needs to understand the rationale behind the psychological constructs and must know how to make application across a wide variety of situations and sport participants. Books written for sport psychologists and coaches are typically general textbooks that attempt to cover the entire field of sport psychology. Thus their coverage of applied issues—and particularly psychological interventions for enhancing sport performance, personal growth, and exercise participation—is superficial compared to the in-depth coverage this text provides. Other applied textbooks do not have the comprehensive coverage of this book, the expertise of the diverse contributors, or as clear a presentation of the theories and research that provide the foundation for application.

Based on the Latest Research and Practice

The knowledge and experiential base in applied sport psychology, particularly for science-based interventions, has greatly expanded since the initial publication of this book. Each new edition has reflected the latest research and cutting-edge practice in applied sport psychology. Although the primary focus of the seventh edition continues to be on application, each chapter provides theoretical and research foundations when appropriate. When using the book as a textbook for a graduate course, the instructor may want to supplement it with readings from the research studies cited by the contributors.

Comprehensive Coverage of Topics

No other text in applied sport psychology encompasses the comprehensive approach taken here. The first chapter discusses the past, present, and future of sport psychology. The remainder of the book is divided into four parts.

Part One covers learning, feedback, motivation, leadership, and social interactions that result in group cohesion and the development of effective groups and communication. For clarity and simplicity, some of these chapters have been written in the vernacular of the coach. These chapters are not only useful for coaches, however. Sport psychologists frequently find it necessary to work with coaches in areas such as improving communication skills, building team rapport, and fostering more effective leadership behaviors. Also, the same principles of learning, motivation, and social interaction that help to increase a coach's effectiveness apply to the sport psychologist teaching mental skills and interacting with athletes. Thus the knowledge and insight gained from reading the chapters in Part Two are as appropriate for current and prospective sport psychologists as they are for coaches.

Part Two of the book discusses mental training for enhancing performance. This section begins with a chapter on the psychological characteristics of peak performance; other chapters discuss identifying ideal performance states, setting and achieving goals, managing stress and energy levels, training in imagery, identifying optimal concentration and learning how to control it, and building confidence. Part Three deals with implementing training programs. The first chapter provides suggestions for integrating and implementing a psychological skills training program. The second chapter provides guidance on how to conduct sport psychology training programs with coaches. The final chapter provides guidance and suggestions for achieving cultural competence.

Part Four focuses on enhancing health and wellness. It contains chapters that address when sport competitors should be referred for professional counseling, causes and cures for drug abuse in sport, the occurrence and prevention of burnout, injury risk and rehabilitation, termination from sport competition, and the psychological benefits of exercise as well as interventions to increase exercise adoption and adherence. No sport psychology book has dealt with all of these issues, even though they are crucial to sport performance, personal development, and the enhancement of sport and exercise participation and benefits.

The appropriateness of these chapters for certain courses will depend on the students' backgrounds and interests. The book was planned to provide complete coverage of psychological theories, techniques, and issues relevant to enhancing personal growth, sport performance, and exercise participation. Instructors may select those chapters that are appropriate for their courses. For example, Chapters 2 and 3 concern motor skills learning and principles of reinforcement and feedback; this material might be redundant if students already have a thorough background in motor learning. Chapter 23, on termination from sport competition, may interest only individuals who work with athletes who are nearing retirement or dropping out of sport competition.

Written by Leading Experts in Sport Psychology

The contributors to this volume are leading scholars and practitioners in sport and exercise psychology. They work with sport participants from youth sport to Olympic and professional levels, and many have illustrious backgrounds as elite athletes or coaches.

Integrated Organization and Writing Style

The book has the major advantage of drawing on the diverse expertise and perspectives of 43 contributors, but it avoids the common disadvantage of disparate coverage and diverse writing styles frequently found in edited textbooks. The content and sequencing of chapters have been carefully coordinated to ensure comprehensive coverage and progressive development of concepts while eliminating undesirable overlap and inconsistency in terminology. Writing focus, styles, and organization have been standardized as much as possible. In addition, many of the chapters in this edition have been rewritten for even greater clarity and succinctness. Each chapter cites appropriate research and theory, applies this work to the world of sport and/or exercise, and provides examples and intervention exercises whenever appropriate. Each chapter also begins with an introduction that highlights the content of the chapter and ends with a conclusion or summary of the major psychological constructs and skills and study questions for students.

Application Examples and Teaching Resources

The numerous examples given throughout the book greatly facilitate the translation of psychological theory and constructs into everyday practice. Many of the examples involve well-known professional and amateur sportspeople. The examples cut across a wide variety of sports and provide important anecdotal evidence that can be used to motivate individuals to develop psychological and behavioral skills for their sport and exercise participation. These real-life examples are frequently supplemented with hypothetical examples, exercises, and case studies created by the contributors to clarify appropriate applications.

To further provide an optimal learning environment for students, instructors can visit the Online Learning Center http://www.mhhe.com/williams7e for a wealth of resources. Chapter lecture PowerPoints, an objective test bank, and an annotated list of audiovisual resources are available.

Applied Sport Psychology Provides Many Benefits

The rewards are many for those who choose to dedicate themselves to the pursuit of excellence and personal growth through use of the theories and techniques of applied sport and exercise psychology. Coaches and sport participants acknowledge the importance of mental factors in sport development and performance, yet the time individuals actually spend practicing mental skills belies this view. In publishing this book, we have made a serious effort to help abolish that inconsistency by supplying not only the necessary knowledge to improve performance, but also the knowledge to improve the psychological climate of a sport program. The benefits that can be derived from this text will arise not just in sport performance, but in overall performance outside of sport and, perhaps most important, in general personal growth and increased physical and mental health.

Acknowledgments

We wish to thank George Cunningham at Texas A&M University, Fred Green at Troy University, Michael Johnson at Kansas State University, Katrina Radke Gerry at Foothill College, Tucker Readdy at the University of Wyoming, Jennifer J. Waldron at the University of Iowa, and Amy S. Welch at Johnson State College for their insightful reviews of the sixth edition. We also thank Katie Sullivan Barak, Reed J. Kaus, and Campbell Query for their help updating the supplemental materials.

We are also indebted to the fine editorial staff at McGraw-Hill, most particularly we thank Carol Field, our developmental editor, for her efficiency and thoroughness during the development of this edition. Finally, we would like to thank Judi David, our project manager, and Susan Norton, our freelance copyeditor, for their attention to detail and guidance during the production process.

Jean M. Williams & Vikki Krane

CONTRIBUTORS

Jean M. Williams is a professor emeritus at the University of Arizona. She taught courses in stress and coping and psychology of excellence and did consulting with intercollegiate athletes and coaches and with top amateur and professional athletes. Earlier in her career she coached nationally ranked fencing teams. Dr. Williams has published nine books (seven are edited texts) and more than 100 research articles and book chapters. She is a past president, fellow, and certified consultant in the Association of Applied Sport Psychology and a fellow in the National Academy of Kinesiology.

Vikki Krane is a professor with the School of Human Movement, Sport, and Leisure Studies at Bowling Green State University. She is a former editor of *The Sport Psychologist* and the *Women in Sport and Physical Activity Journal*. Dr. Krane is on the editorial boards of the *Psychology of Sport and Exercise, The Sport Psychologist,* and *Qualitative Research in Sport & Exercise*. Dr. Krane is a fellow of AASP and a certified consultant and has consulted with a variety of athletes, including high school, rising elite adolescents, and college athletes.

Mark B. Andersen is a registered psychologist and professor at Victoria University, Melbourne, Australia. He is in the College of Sport and Exercise Science and coordinates the master and doctorate of applied psychology degrees (sport emphasis) in the College of Arts. He teaches in the areas of rehabilitation and the professional practice of psychology. He currently sits on four editorial boards. He has published seven books, more than 160 journal articles and book chapters, and has made over 100 national and international conference presentations Outside academia he has a private psychotherapy practice.

Linda K. Bunker is professor emeritus at the University of Virginia. She has worked extensively with professional golfers and tennis players. Dr. Bunker was selected as the 2000–2001 Alliance Scholar for the AAHPERD. She has written more than 100 articles and authored 15 books, including *Motivating Kids Through Play, Parenting Your Super-Star, Golf: Steps to Success,* and *Mind Mastery for Winning Golf*. She was on the Advisory Board of the Womens' Sports Foundation, *SHAPE* magazine, and the Melpomene Institute and was a nationally ranked tennis player and four-sport athlete at the University of Illinois.

Shauna M. Burke is an Assistant Professor in the School of Health Studies at Western University, Ontario, Canada. Her primary specialization is the psychology of health and physical activity, with a focus on child health and obesity. In addition to numerous presentations at national and international scientific conferences, Shauna has published her research in a number of peer-reviewed journals and co-authored a textbook and several book chapters. Shauna has also served as a sport psychology consultant for various organizations including the Ontario Hockey Federation and the Ontario Hockey League.

Heather O'Neal Chambliss received her MA in Counseling from Louisiana Tech University and her Ph.D. in Exercise Psychology from the University of Georgia. Dr. Chambliss was a research scientist at The Cooper Institute in Dallas, TX, where she was project director of a NIMH-funded trial examining exercise as an anti-depressant treatment and co-chair of the CI Physical Activity and Mental Health Conference. Her interests include exercise and mental health and health behavior change. Dr. Chambliss is a fellow of the American College of Sports Medicine and serves on the ACSM Behavioral Strategies Committee.

Cheryl Coker is a professor in the Department of Health and Human Performance at Plymouth State University. Dr. Coker is a motor learning specialist whose interest in skill acquisition and performance stems from her experiences as a teacher, coach, and athlete. She has given over 80 presentations throughout the United States and internationally on coaching and motor behavior, has contributed to numerous scholarly and practitioner journals, and is the author of the textbook *Motor Learning and Control for Practitioners,* which has been well received for its applications-based approach.

J. D. DeFreese is a postdoctoral research associate in the Department of Exercise and Sport Science at the University of North Carolina at Chapel Hill. His research examines the link of athlete psychological health, including outcomes of burnout and well-being, with athlete physical health and social functioning. DeFreese also serves as the assistant program coordinator for the Brain & Body Health Program at UNC's Center for the Study of Retired Athletes. This consultation service, in collaboration with UNC physicians, provides former athletes with a comprehensive evaluation of their cognitive and physical functioning.

Paul W. Dennis is the high performance coach at Toronto's York University. Prior to that, he was the Player Development Coach for Toronto Maple Leafs of the National Hockey League, a position that required applied sport psychology expertise. He has consulted with the NBA's Toronto Raptors and MLS's Toronto FC. In 2002 and 2003, he was the mental skills coach to Canada's World Junior hockey team, and to Canada's 2013 World Champion Sledge hockey team. He continues to teach a fourth-year sport psychology class at York. He received his doctorate from the University of Western Ontario under the supervision of Dr. Albert V. Carron.

Rod K. Dishman is a professor of exercise science and an adjunct professor of psychology at the University of Georgia. He advises graduate students studying behavioral neuroscience and interventions to increase physical activity. Dr. Dishman received his Ph.D. at the University of Wisconsin, Madison, and has focused his research on neurobiological aspects of the mental health outcomes associated with physical activity and on the behavioral determinants of physical activity. He is a fellow of the American College of Sports Medicine, the American Psychological Association, and the AAKPE. He has served as a consultant on exercise for the National Institutes of Health and the Sports Medicine Council for the USOC.

Joan L. Duda is a professor of Sport and Exercise Psychology in the School of Sport and Exercise Sciences at The University of Birmingham, UK. She is past president of the AASP and has been a member of the executive boards of several professional organizations in the field. Professor Duda has published over 300 research papers and book chapters on motivational processes in the physical domain and the psychological and emotional dimensions of sport, exercise, and dance. She also has been a mental skills consultant for over 25 years, working with athletes/dancers, coaches, and parents from the grassroots to the Olympic and professional levels as well as performing artists. For her contributions to the field, she received an honorary doctorate degree from the Norwegian School of Sport Sciences.

M. Blair Evans is a doctoral student in Psychology at Wilfrid Laurier University; he completed his Master's education at the University of Lethbridge. Blair's primary research interests include social influences in sport groups (e.g., group dynamics in individual sport teams) as well as social-cognitive determinants of exercise (e.g., exercise outcome proximity). Blair is an active member of professional organizations including SCAPPS and he was recently awarded the outstanding student paper award at the annual meeting for NASPSPA.

Mark A. Eys is the Canada research chair (Tier II) in Group Dynamics and Physical Activity and an associate professor at Wilfrid Laurier University (Canada) in the departments of Kinesiology/Physical Education and Psychology. His research focus is group dynamics in sport and exercise, with specific interests in cohesion and individual roles within a group environment. Mark is an Early Researcher Award recipient from the Ministry of Research and Innovation (Province of Ontario). He is also a former intercollegiate basketball player and has coached soccer at club and university levels.

Angela Fifer is a performance enhancement trainer at the United States Military Academy at West Point, where she provides performance excellence training to numerous varsity and club teams and individuals. Angie completed her Ph.D. in Kinesiology from Michigan State University. Her research has focused on recreational female marathoners and how they find life meaning through running. She won the 2009 AASP Distinguished Student Practitioner Award. Angie is an avid marathoner and recent Ironman finisher.

Samuel T. Forlenza is a doctoral candidate at Michigan State University, where he is completing his Ph.D. in Kinesiology with a specialization in Psychosocial Aspects of Sport and Physical Activity. Sam's primary research interests include the use of exercise video games—or exergames—to improve exercise duration and intensity, and imagery use in sport and exercise settings. He enjoys teaching and consulting, where he has worked with athletes at the youth, high school, and collegiate levels.

Diane L. Gill is a professor in the Department of Kinesiology and the Linda Arnold Carlisle Distinguished Excellence Professor in Women's and Gender Studies at the University of North Carolina at Greensboro. Her research emphasizes social psychology, with a focus on physical activity and psychological well-being. Her publications include the text, *Psychological Dynamics of Sport and Exercise,* and over 100 journal articles, and she has presented over 100 scholarly papers at national and international conferences. She is former editor of the *Journal of Sport and Exercise Psychology,* and former president of APA Division 47, the North American Society for the Psychology of Sport and Physical Activity, and the Research Consortium of AAHPERD.

Daniel Gould is the director of the Institute for the Study of Youth Sports and a professor at Michigan State University. His research focuses on competitive stress and coping, positive youth development through sport, and the effectiveness of psychological skills training interventions. He is also involved in coaching education and children's sports. Dr. Gould has been a consultant to elite international athletes in a wide variety of sports. Formerly a wrestler and football and baseball player, he remains an avid fitness enthusiast. Dr. Gould was the founding co-editor of *The Sport Psychologist.* He served as president of the AASP and held leadership positions with numerous organizations such as U.S.A. Wrestling and the U.S. Olympic Committee.

Sheldon Hanton is pro vice-chancellor for research at Cardiff Metropolitan University, UK, and professor of Sport Psychology. He is the editor of *The Sport Psychologist* and Advisory Board Member for the *Journal of Sports Sciences.* Dr. Hanton is a chartered psychologist with the British Psychological Society and practitioner with the Health and Care Professions Council. He also sits on the Economic and Social Research Council Peer Review College. His research interests focus on competition and organizational stress, positive organizational psychology, mental toughness, reflective practice and injury psychology amassing around 250 journal articles, edited texts, book chapters, and conference communications.

Thelma Sternberg Horn is an associate professor in the Department of Kinesiology and Health at Miami University (Ohio). Her research interests are focused on the social psychological factors that influence the psychosocial development of children, adolescents, and young adults in sport and physical activity settings. Dr. Horn is a former editor of the *Journal of Sport and Exercise Psychology,* and the third edition of her edited text, *Advances in Sport Psychology,* was published in 2008. She has coached at both interscholastic and intercollegiate levels and continues to work as a consultant with coaches in youth sport and interscholastic programs.

Jeff Janssen is one of the world's top experts on sports leadership and president of the Janssen Sports Leadership Center. Mr. Janssen's pioneering work on sports leadership has led to the creation of comprehensive and cutting edge leadership academies for student-athletes and coaches at North Carolina, Michigan, Illinois, Arkansas, LSU, NC State, Colorado, and many other schools. He also has authored *The Team Captain's Leadership Manual, Championship Team Building, How to Develop Relentless Competitors,* The Commitment Continuum™ System, and *The Seven Secrets of Successful Coaches.*

Cindra S. Kamphoff, Ph.D., is an assistant professor in the Department of Human Performance at the Minnesota State University, Mankato. She received her Ph.D. from the University of North Carolina at Greensboro. Her research has focused on gender and cultural diversity, including projects on women's issues in coaching, cultural competence, and diversity content in AASP conference programs. She received the 2006 NASPE *Sport and Exercise Psychology Academy Dissertation Award.* She is an active member of AAHPERD and AASP, and has presented over 30 papers at national and international conferences. She works regularly as a consultant teaching mental skills to athletes.

Francisco (Paco) Labrador received a bachelor's degree in psychology and exercise science from Hiram College in Ohio and a master's degree in sport studies from Miami University. Mr. Labrador has just completed his tenth season as the head volleyball coach of the women's

intercollegiate team at Wittenberg University in Ohio. During those years, his teams have reached the Final Four of the NCAA Division III national tournament several times. In 2011, they won the national championship, and Mr. Labrador was named national coach of the year. Several of his teams also have received national awards for academic achievement.

David Lavallee is a professor and head of the School of Sport at the University of Stirling in Scotland. He received a master's degree in counseling psychology from Harvard University and a doctorate in sport and exercise psychology from The University of Western Australia. Professor Lavallee is on the editorial board of *Sport, Exercise and Performance Psychology, International Review of Sport and Exercise Psychology, Journal of Clinical Sport Psychology* and *Qualitative Research in Sport, Exercise and Health.* He is also a former All-American soccer player.

Curt L. Lox is a professor and chair of the Department of Kinesiology and Health Education at Southern Illinois University Edwardsville. His research interests center around the psychological impact of exercise for special populations, including the elderly, overweight and obese children and adults, and individuals with brain injuries. Dr. Lox has coached at the youth and high school levels and has worked as a sport psychology consultant for players and coaches at the interscholastic, intercollegiate, national, and professional levels. He currently serves as the sport psychology consultant for the United States martial arts team. Dr. Lox is lead author of an exercise psychology text titled *The Psychology of Exercise: Integrating Theory and Practice.*

Stephen D. Mellalieu is an associate professor at Swansea University, UK. He has published over 70 research papers and co-edited several texts within the applied sport psychology field. His research interests lie in stress and performance, psychological skills, and the organizational environment of elite sport. He is associate editor of the *Journal of Applied Sport Psychology,* an editorial board member of *The Sport Psychologist,* and co-founder and network editor of the International Rugby Board Rugby Science Network. Stephen is also a British Psychological Society chartered sport and exercise psychologist with consultancy experience in a number of Olympic and professional sports.

Robert M. Nideffer has been a professor on the faculties of the University of Rochester, the California School of Professional Psychology, and San Diego State University. He has been involved in sport psychology since 1969 and is the founder of Enhanced Performance Systems. Dr. Nideffer has published extensively in the sport psychology and stress management areas, with 15 books and more than 100 articles to his credit. He has worked with Olympic-level and professional athletes in a wide variety of sports and has been a member of policy-setting committees in the United States, Canada, and Australia.

Sunghee Park is an assistant professor at Kookmin University in South Korea. She teaches courses in foundations of sport psychology and sport counseling. Formerly a professional tennis player, she participated two Olympic Games (Atlanta and Sydney). Based on her athletic and academic careers, she consults with professional tennis players and national team members and coaches. Dr. Park is a member of the board of directors in the Korean Society of Sport Psychology and a member of an International Society of Sport and Exercise Psychology.

Thomas Raedeke is a professor in Kinesiology at East Carolina University. Given his interest in motivation, stress, and well-being, one of his research specialties focuses on burnout. Currently, he is an associate editor for *Research Quarterly for Exercise and Sport* and on the editorial boards of the *Journal of Applied Sport Psychology* and *Sport, Exercise, and Performance Psychology*. Dr. Raedeke is a certified consultant through the Association of Applied Sport Psychology, has served as chair for the Sport and Exercise Psychology Academy, and was a recipient of the University of North Carolina Board of Governors Award for Excellence in Teaching. Prior to university employment, he was a research assistant at the American Coaching Effectiveness Program/Human Kinetics and the United States Olympic Training Center.

Kenneth Ravizza is a professor at California State University at Fullerton. His research examines the nature of peak performance in a variety of domains. He has developed and implemented performance-enhancement programs for business groups, health care and school staffs, cancer patients, police officers, and physicians. He has worked with his university's baseball, softball, and gymnastics teams; with Olympic athletes such as U.S. baseball, water polo, softball, and figure skaters; and with professional teams such as the Anaheim Angels and New York Jets. He also has consulted with numerous athletic departments in the area of coaching effectiveness (UCLA, Texas, L.S.U., Harvard). Ken enjoys working in his garden to recharge himself.

Marc-Simon Sagal is managing partner at Winning Mind LLC. He consults regularly with Olympic and professional athletes from around the world as well as with corporate clients and the military. Marc is widely published in the area of performance psychology and is co-author of the book *Assessment in Sport Psychology* with Dr. Robert Nideffer. Additionally, Marc played a key role in the development of the Athlete's Competitive Edge system, the world's first Web-based, sport-psychological assessment and training program. Marc is a former professional soccer player and coach.

Carrie B. Scherzer is an assistant professor of psychology at Mount Royal University in Calgary, Albert.She completed her doctorate at the University of Arizona in clinical psychology, with an emphasis in sport psychology. Dr. Scherzer received her BA in psychology (Honours) from Concordia University and her MS in athletic counseling at Springfield College. Her research interests include rehabilitation from injury, eating disorders, and professional training and development. She is a certified consultant of the AASP and a member of the student development and certification review committees. She has done performance enhancement, injury rehabilitation, and academic counseling with intercollegiate athletes.

Alan L. Smith is professor and chairperson in the Department of Kinesiology at Michigan State University. His research addresses the link of sport and physical activity involvement with young people's psychological and social functioning. This work includes issues surrounding peer relationships, motivational processes, and athlete burnout. Smith has served as associate editor of the *Journal of Sport & Exercise Psychology* and on the editorial boards of *Child Development, International Journal of Sport Psychology,* and *Journal of Applied Sport Psychology.* He is president of the North American Society for the Psychology of Sport and Physical Activity and is a fellow of the National Academy of Kinesiology.

Ronald E. Smith is Professor of Psychology and Director of Clinical Training at the University of Washington. He is a co-founder and past president of the Association of Applied Sport Psychology. His major research interests are in personality, stress and coping, and sport psychology research and interventions. Dr. Smith has directed performance enhancement programs for several professional baseball organizations, and his research team has developed widely used sport psychology measurement tools, including the Coaching Behavior Assessment System, the Sport Anxiety Scale-2, the Athletic Coping Skills Inventory-28, the Motivational Climate Scale for Youth Sports, and the Achievement Goal Scale for Youth Sports.

Frank L. Smoll is a professor of psychology at the University of Washington. His research focuses on coaching behaviors in youth sports and on the psychological effects of competition. He has published more than 130 scientific articles and book chapters, and he is co-author of 19 books and manuals on children's athletics. Dr. Smoll is a fellow of the APA, the AAKPE, and the AASP. He is a certified sport consultant and was the recipient of AASP's Distinguished Professional Practice Award. Dr. Smoll has extensive experience in conducting psychologically oriented coaching clinics and workshops for parents of young athletes.

Julia D. Sterrett is the director of the Lehigh Athletics Leadership Academy where she conducts comprehensive leadership training for student-athletes and coaches and participates in the review, evaluation, and development of Lehigh's 25 Division I sports programs. Julia played softball at Lehigh before earning her Master's degree in Intercollegiate Athletics Leadership from the University of Washington. She joined the Janssen Sports Leadership Center as an associate, and conducts leadership development seminars with student-athletes at high schools and colleges across the country.

Jim Taylor has worked with junior-elite, collegiate, world-class, and professional athletes for over 25 years. His consulting practice focuses on sports performance, parenting, and corporate training. He received his bachelor's degree from Middlebury College and earned his MA and Ph.D. in psychology from the University of Colorado. Dr. Taylor is the author of 10 books, has published over 500 popular and scholarly articles, and has given more than 600 workshops throughout North America, Europe, and the Middle East. He competed internationally as an alpine ski racer, holds a second-degree black belt in karate, and is a marathon runner and Ironman triathlete.

David Tod teaches in the Department of Psychology, Aberystwyth University, UK. He received his doctorate from Victoria University in 2006. His research interests include the training and supervision of practitioners, applied sport psychology service delivery, and the relationship between body image and health, particularly around perceptions of muscularity. Since 1993, David has provided applied sport psychology services to a range of athletes from juniors to Olympians across a variety of sports. He competed in rugby union, powerlifting, and ballroom dance.

Darren has held faculty positions at Arizona State University, Southern Illinois University, Edwardsville, and the University of Illinois at Urbana-Champaign. He has published over 60 scientific articles, book chapters, and an edited volume on motivation in sport and exercise. Treasure left full-time academics in 2004 to pursue a career in high performance sport. He has provided performance psychology support to Olympic and World Champions and athletes who have competed and won at the highest echelons of collegiate and professional sport. He is experienced working with high profile coaches and has driven cultural change programs with teams and whole organizations. Treasure is the author of the National Federation of State High School Associations "Fundamentals of Coaching" course that over 250,000 high school coaches have successfully completed since its launch in 2007. Dr. Treasure currently resides in Portland, Oregon where he provides performance psychology support for Nike's Oregon Project and consults with a select number of professional athletes (NFL, NBA) and organizations invested in pursuing high-level performance.

Robin S. Vealey is a professor in the Department of Kinesiology and Health at Miami University. She has authored two books: *Coaching for the Inner Edge* and *Competitive Anxiety in Sport*. She has served as a sport psychology consultant for the U.S. Ski Team, U.S. Field Hockey, elite golfers, and many college athletes and teams. Dr. Vealey is a fellow, certified consultant, and past president of the Association of Applied Sport Psychology and former editor of *The Sport Psychologist*. A former collegiate basketball player and coach, she now enjoys the mental challenge of golf.

Robert S. Weinberg is a professor in the Department of Kinesiology and Health at Miami University. He has published over 140 journal articles as well as 8 books and 30 book chapters. He was editor-in-chief of the *Journal of Applied Sport Psychology* and served as president of AASP and NASPSPA and chair of the AAHPERD Sport Psychology Academy. He is a certified consultant of AASP and a member of the U.S. Olympic Committee's Sport Psychology Registry. He has worked extensively with young athletes, developing their psychological skills. He has been a varsity athlete and coach in tennis, football, and basketball.

Vietta E. "Sue" Wilson is a retired professor of York University, where she taught sport psychology, coaching, and self-regulation courses. She is certified (BCIA) in biofeedback and neurofeedback. She has consulted with a variety of sports from novice to Olympic and world champion levels. Her BF/NF Performance-Enhancement Suite is used worldwide for the -assessment and training of athletes; she personally provides training via hands-on seminars or the Web. She was an athlete and coach in three sports, taught for the Canadian Coaching Association, and remains physically active.

David Yukelson is director of sport psychology services for the Penn State University Athletic Department. He provides counseling and support to coaches and athletes in the areas of mental training techniques for managing concentration and confidence under pressure, leadership effectiveness, communication and team cohesion, coping skill strategies for handling multiple demands and stress effectively, and issues pertaining to the personal development of intercollegiate student-athletes. He is a past president, fellow, and certified consultant in the Association of Applied Sport Psychology (AASP), has published numerous articles in professional refereed journals, and is a frequent invited speaker at national and international conferences.

Nate Zinsser is director of the Performance Enhancement Program at the United States Military Academy, and is responsible for a sport psychology curriculum currently being implemented throughout the U.S. Army. Dr. Zinsser is the author of *Dear Dr. Psych,* the first sport psychology guidebook for youth sport participants, and he contributed a sport psychology advice column to *Sports Illustrated for Kids* for five years. His formal training in sport psychology from the University of Virginia is complemented by his experience as a state wrestling champion, world-class mountaineer, and third-degree black belt in karate.

CHAPTER

1

Sport Psychology: Past, Present, Future

Jean M. Williams, *University of Arizona, Emeritus*
Vikki Krane, *Bowling Green State University*

Within the past 35–40 years, the academic community and the public have recognized the field of study called **sport psychology.** Sport psychologists study motivation, violence, leadership, group dynamics, exercise and psychological well-being, thoughts and feelings of athletes, and many other dimensions of participation in sport and physical activity. Among other functions, modern-day sport psychologists teach sport psychology classes, conduct research, and work with athletes, coaches, and exercise participants to help improve performance and enhance the quality of the sport and exercise experience.

Coaches showed interest in the psychological aspects of athletic competition even before there was a science called sport psychology. For example, in the 1920s Knute Rockne, the football coach of the fighting Irish of Notre Dame, popularized the pep talk by making it an important part of his coaching. We should note, however, that Rockne did not attempt to psych up his team for every contest. Coaching interest in contemporary sport psychology involves more than a mere concern for psyching up athletes for competition.

Applied sport psychology is concerned with the psychological factors that influence participation and performance in sport and exercise, the psychological effects derived from participation, and theories and interventions that can be used to enhance performance, participation, and personal growth. Applied sport psychology has grown tremendously in recent years, as evidenced by the number of coaches and athletes now looking to sport psychology for a competitive edge. These individuals have turned to various psychological training programs to learn, among other things, ways to manage competitive stress, control concentration, improve confidence, and increase communication skills and team harmony.

One goal of psychological interventions is to learn to consistently create the ideal mental climate that enables athletes to perform at their best. A goal for exercise psychologists is to use interventions to enhance physical and mental health by increasing exercise participation. Further, there are many specific intervention goals. What follows are a few situations that identify the diverse circumstances under which individuals might turn to the field of sport psychology for help.

When to use sport psychology

Val is only a third-year coach but already has the reputation of coaching players with excellent physical fundamentals and conditioning. Her team's poor play comes more from mental lapses and from not handling pressure. Val's goal this season is to increase her players' mental toughness.

Tim is a student athletic trainer. After taking a sport psychology workshop, he recognizes that he could be more effective in helping his injured athletes heal and be ready mentally to return to play if he incorporated psychological skills into their injury rehabilitation program.

Matt is a sport psychology consultant who was just hired by a professional team that rarely plays up to its potential because of internal dissention and too much concern with personal stats. His task is to help resolve the conflicts and enhance cohesiveness and team play.

Andrew is a fitness trainer at a health resort. Most of the guests either have led sedentary lives or have started exercise programs but quit within a few months. Andrew's job is to help the guests set fitness goals and plan strategies that will achieve those goals.

Brian arrives as a new wrestling coach at a major university. He discovers that some of his wrestlers are on steroids and others have eating disorders. What should he do?

Jennifer is a recreational golfer who has played for over 20 years. She loves golf but has become quite frustrated with her putting. Her normally excellent putting game has gone into a two-year slump. She knows it's mental but can't seem to correct it.

Kimberly is a first-year physical education teacher who is having difficulty motivating many of her students to actively participate in class. How can she improve her teaching?

The authors of subsequent chapters will present psychological principles and interventions that can be used to enhance performance, personal growth, and health. These principles and interventions provide the foundation for effectively dealing with the preceding situations as well as many others that athletes, coaches, sport psychology consultants, athletic trainers, fitness trainers, and physical educators might encounter.

But first, in this chapter we will provide a brief overview of the past, present, and future of sport psychology, with primary emphasis on sport psychology practices in North America and the role Eastern Europe played in the early development and use of sport psychology to enhance performance. The coverage is not all-inclusive but selective to the focus of the book. For a more comprehensive historical overview see Landers (1995) and Vealey (2006).

History of Sport Psychology

According to Mahoney (1989), sport psychology's conceptual roots lie in antiquity. For example, in early Greek and Asian cultures the interdependence of mind and body was not only acknowledged but also emphasized as central to both performance and personal development. However, most of the scientific foundation of modern sport psychology has developed since the 1970s. The roots for the emergence and acceptance of sport psychology as a discipline lie largely within the domain of kinesiology (the study of physical activity), but developments within the discipline of psychology also played a major role in its evolution and psychologists conducted some of the early influential sport psychology investigations.

Coleman Griffith, a psychologist considered by many to be the grandfather of sport psychology in North America, was the first person to research sport psychology over an extended period of time and then to apply it to enhance the performance of athletes and coaches (Gould & Pick, 1995). Griffith was hired by the University of Illinois in 1925 to help coaches improve the performance of their players. He wrote two books, *Psychology of Coaching* (1926) and *Psychology of Athletics* (1928); established the first sport psychology laboratory in North America; published over 40 articles (half dealt with sport psychology); and taught the first courses in sport psychology. (We should also credit Carl Diem in Berlin and A. Z. Puni in Leningrad (now St. Petersburg) for establishing sport psychology laboratories in Europe about this same time period.) Griffith also corresponded with Notre Dame coach Rockne about psychological and motivational aspects of coaching, and he was hired in 1938 to improve the performance of the Chicago Cubs baseball team.

Another pioneer practitioner and researcher from this historical era was Dorothy Yates (Kornspan & MacCracken, 2001). She taught at Stanford and San Jose State College and had a private practice in psychology. Yates wrote two books (1932, 1957) and a research article (1943) describing her mental training interventions with boxers and aviators. The intervention focused on mental preparation, particularly a relaxation set-method. Because of her success she was asked in 1942 to develop a psychology course at San Jose State for athletes and aviators. Some of her students became aviators flying during World War II, and letters from them testified to the effectiveness of her work and teaching.

Unfortunately, the pioneering efforts in sport psychology by Griffith and Yates were not followed in any systematic way, and therefore no recognizable discipline of sport and exercise psychology was established in the 1930s and 1940s (Vealey, 2006). In fact, up until the mid-1960s, very little writing occurred in sport psychology except for one book and occasional research studies that were, according to Landers (1995), typically atheoretical, unsystematic, and laboratory-based. This book, *Psychology of Coaching* (1951), was written by John Lawther, a psychologist who also headed the Pennsylvania State University basketball team. Coaches were particularly interested in Lawther's treatment of such topics as motivation, team cohesion, personality, feelings and emotions, and handling athletes.

1965–1979: Birth of Sport Psychology and Supporting Organizations

During the 1960s, two San Jose State University clinical psychologists, Bruce Ogilvie and Tom Tutko (1966), created considerable interest in sport psychology with their research and the book that resulted, *Problem Athletes and How to Handle Them*. According to Ogilvie, this book "moved the coaching world off dead center." After extensively researching the personality of athletes, Ogilvie and Tutko developed the controversial Athletic Motivation Inventory, which they claimed predicted success and problems in athletes. In actuality, sport is so complex that no inventory can predict performance, let alone one based on trait personality theory. For example, they advised one football team not to draft a highly successful college player because he did not have what it would take mentally to make it in the pros. The player went to another team and earned the Rookie of the Year award. Despite legitimate criticism of their prediction claims (see Fisher, Ryan, & Martens, 1976), Ogilvie and Tutko's considerable consulting with college and professional teams did much to foster public interest in applied sport psychology. Because of Ogilvie's numerous contributions in the 60s, and later, many in the field have called him the father of applied sport psychology in North America.

Establishment of Professional Organizations

The 1960s also witnessed the first attempts to bring together groups of individuals interested in sport psychology. Sport psychology first organized on the international level with the formation of the International Society of Sport Psychology (ISSP) in Rome in 1965. More than 400 attendees representing 27 countries came to Rome. Dr. Ferruccio Antonelli, an Italian psychiatrist, was elected the first president of the organization and provided leadership during the early years. ISSP continues to host worldwide meetings.

The second meeting of ISSP was hosted in 1968 in Washington, DC, by the newly formed North American Society for the Psychology of Sport and Physical Activity (NASPSPA). The first annual meeting of NASPSPA was held in 1967 prior to the American Alliance for Health, Physical Education, Recreation, and Dance (AAHPERD) conference in Las Vegas, Nevada. Dr. Arthur Slatter-Hammel of Indiana University was the first president. NASPSPA hosts annual meetings that focus on research in the subareas of motor learning and control, motor development, and sport and exercise psychology.

The late 1960s also saw the formation of the Canadian Society for Psychomotor Learning and Sport Psychology, also referred to as SCAPPS to reflect the French translation of the name. Founded by Robert Wilberg at the University of Alberta in 1969, SCAPPS was initially under the auspices of the Canadian Association for Health, Physical Education, and Recreation, but it became independent in 1977. The members and leaders of NASPSPA and SCAPPS were extremely influential in building the research base in sport psychology and gaining acceptance of the field. During this same time period, the equivalent can be said within Europe for sport psychologists who, in 1969, created the European Federation of Sport Psychology (FEPSAC—the acronym reflects the French translation of the name) and elected Ema Geron (then from Bulgaria, now Israel) as its first president.

Sport psychology's organizational growth continued in the 1970s, when it was added to the conference programs of the American College of Sports Medicine (ACSM) and AAHPERD. The Sport Psychology Academy, formed within AAHPERD in 1975, was the first group for which a major goal was to bridge the gap between the researcher and practitioner by providing an opportunity for sport psychologists to share their research and expertise with coaches and physical education teachers.

Table 1-1 Timeline for the Establishment of Professional Organizations and Journals*

1965	International Society for Psychology of Sport (ISSP)
1967	North American Society for the Psychology of Sport and Physical Activity (NASPSPA)
1969	Canadian Society for Psychomotor Learning and Sport Psychology (SCAPPS)
1969	European Federation of Sport Psychology (FEPSAC)
1970	*International Journal of Sport Psychology* (ISSP)
1975	Sport Psychology Academy (SPA) added to AAHPERD
1979	*Journal of Sport and Exercise Psychology* (NASPSPA) (its name was *Journal of Sport Psychology* prior to 1988)
1985	Association for Applied Sport Psychology (AASP) (its name was the Association for the Advancement of Applied Sport Psychology prior to 2006)
1987	Division 47 (Exercise and Sport Psychology) of the American Psychological Association (APA)
1987	*The Sport Psychologist*
1989	*Journal of Applied Sport Psychology* (AASP)
2000	*Psychology of Sport and Exercise* (FEPSAC)
2003	*International Journal of Sport and Exercise Psychology*
2007	*Journal of Clinical Sport Psychology*
2008	*International Review of Sport and Exercise Psychology* (ISSP)
2010	*Journal of Sport Psychology in Action* (AASP)
2012	*Sport, Exercise, and Performance Psychology* (APA Division 47)

*Initials in parenthesis after journals indicate sponsoring organization

Recognition Through Knowledge Base

In the decade of the 1970s, sport psychology in North America began to flourish and receive recognition within kinesiology as a subdiscipline separate from motor learning. Systematic research by ever-increasing numbers of sport psychologists played a major role in this coming of age. In fact, the primary goal of sport psychologists in the 1970s was to gain acceptance for the field by advancing the knowledge base through experimental research (largely lab-based). Although no agreement existed as to an appropriate knowledge base for the field, and research topics were varied and involved many target populations, most of the scholarship in this era was directed toward social psychological research (e.g., personality, social facilitation, achievement motivation, competitive anxiety, team cohesion, coach behaviors, coach–athlete relations).

The earlier interest in personality research declined in the mid-1970s because of heated debates about the validity of personality traits and the inventories used to assess them, most of which came from mainstream psychology. Many sport psychologists continued to believe that internal mechanisms (i.e., traits) govern behavior, but these psychologists also became concerned about the influence of environmental variables. The **interactionism paradigm**, which considers person and environmental variables and their potential interaction, surfaced and gained considerable credibility. Although not as extensive, research also began to focus on two other areas in the 70s: the study of women in sport from a feminist perspective, largely due to a conference hosted by Dorothy Harris (1972) and a book published by Carole Oglesby (1978), and exercise psychology, largely through Bill Morgan's research into exercise, fitness, and well-being. The growing volume of quality research in the 70s led in 1979 to the establishment of the *Journal of Sport Psychology*.

Discouragement of Applied Work

In addition, we should mention that applied work was discouraged during the 70s. Some of the negativity towards premature application came from the bad publicity stemming from Arnold Mandel's work with the San Diego Chargers. Mandel was a psychiatrist who was hired in 1973 to enhance performance, but an offshoot of his work was the discovery that many of the professional football players were taking steroids and "speed" purchased on the street. Mandel wrote them prescriptions for the drugs in an effort to get them off uncontrolled substances. Management would not acknowledge the drug problem, let alone try to help him resolve it. The end result was that, by court order, Mandel was banned from further contact with players and not even allowed within a certain geographical radius of the stadium. See Mandel's book, *The Nightmare Season* (1976), for an interesting description of his work with the Chargers.

Instead of forays into application, many in the field felt that sport psychology would be better served by first developing a research foundation upon which intervention work might be based. This goal influenced some of the research during the 70s, but provided an even greater influence on research in the 80s (which continues today). It also contributed to the emphasis within sport psychology research in the late 1970s and early 1980s on a more cognitive focus (see the next section) as this inquiry is particularly relevant to applied concerns.

The 1980s: Increased Research, Professional Growth, and Acceptance

In the 1980s, the emphasis on scientific credibility, including the development of a sufficient scholarly foundation to justify the practice of sport psychology, grew tremendously. That, in turn, led to consulting with athletes and to recognizing and addressing important professional issues.

Research

Perhaps the best reflection of the quality and volume of work in any academic area is the number of research journals devoted strictly to the discipline. By the 1980s, there were four sport psychology journals (see Table 1-1 on page 4).

Much of the research published in these journals was driven by cognitive theories from psychology and the desire to test their applicability within a sport and exercise setting (e.g., self-efficacy, motivational orientations, competence motivation, outcome attributions) and by topics of relevance to potential performance enhancement interventions (e.g., athletes' thoughts, images, and attention control). Straub and Williams' (1984) book *Cognitive Sport Psychology* propelled research in this area while Morgan (1984) highlighted the role of inner dialogue on marathon performance, supporting the need for attention to cognitive interventions in sport psychology.

Rainer Martens' 1979 article "About Smocks and Jocks" spawned another advancement in the field: an increase in field research. Martens chided the field for largely conducting laboratory-based research when more relevant questions and findings would result from field research. This focus on field research spurred more and better applied questions and results. Field research has been conducted on topics such as identifying coaching behaviors most effective in promoting learning and personal growth; discovering ways to enhance team harmony and coach–athlete communications; learning how to set and use goals; determining psychological characteristics of successful performers; and developing psychological and behavioral interventions for enhancing performance, personal growth, and exercise participation.

Two other important research developments occurred during the 1980s. One was better documentation of the effectiveness of psychological interventions at enhancing performance (see the meta-analysis by Greenspan and Feltz, 1989, for examples of research documentation from this era). The second was increased attention to exercise and health psychology issues such as the psychological effects of exercise and overtraining, factors influencing participation in and adherence to exercise programs, exercise addiction, the relationship of exercise to stress reactivity, and psychology of injury and injury rehabilitation (see Chapters 22 and 24). The end result was the establishment of a distinct knowledge base for exercise and health psychology and for applied work to enhance the performance of athletes.

Use by United States Olympic Committee (USOC) and others of sport psychology professionals   Considerable growth and recognition of the value of sport psychology interventions occurred because of publicity stemming from sport psychology professionals working with athletes, particularly Olympic athletes. In 1983, the USOC established an official Sport Psychology Committee and a registry of qualified sport psychologists and in 1985, the USOC hired Shane Murphy, its first fulltime sport psychologist. As a result of the USOC's development of its sport psychology program, sport psychologists played an increasingly prominent and visible role in the 1984 and 1988 Olympics (see Suinn, 1985, and *The Sport Psychologist,* no. 4, 1989). Television and written coverage of various sport psychology topics and interventions with Olympic athletes also created considerable interest among professionals and laypersons. Involvement by sport psychologists in the Olympic movement (see *Journal of Sport Psychology in Action,* no. 2, 2012) and on the professional level and intercollegiate level continues to grow.

Professional issues   The growing use of sport psychology practitioners during the 1980s led to important professional issues such as: Is there an adequate scientific base for the practice of sport psychology? What kinds of services should be offered? Who is qualified to provide these services? Almost 20 articles debating these issues were published in sport psychology journals during the 80s. In reference to the second question, an article by Danish and Hale (1981) was particularly influential. They advocated a human development and educational approach (e.g., teaching mental skills) for sport psychology interventions as opposed to the clinical and remedial model of correcting problems typically found in clinical psychology. This early clarification and distinction stemmed partly from tensions between sport psychologists trained in kinesiology-based versus clinical psychology–based programs. This debate is still relevant today, but less so as evidenced by the creation in 2007 of the *Journal of Clinical Sport Psychology*.

Formation of AASP and APA division 47   One important applied development during the 1980s was the formation in 1985 of the Association for Applied Sport Psychology (AASP, known as the Association for the Advancement of Applied Sport Psychology prior to 2006). John Silva played the primary role in forming AASP and served as its first president. The purpose of AASP is to promote applied research in the areas of social, health, and performance enhancement psychology; the appropriate application of these research findings; and the examination of professional issues such as ethical standards, qualifications for becoming a sport psychologist, and certification of sport psychologists. Another objective is to promote the field of sport psychology within mainstream psychology. Prior to this time relatively few people from psychology were involved in sport psychology. AASP has clearly met this last objective—approximately 55 percent of its more than 1,800 members received their highest academic degree in psychology.

Additional support for the growing recognition of sport psychology within mainstream psychology comes from the American Psychological Association (APA). In 1987 the APA officially recognized a sport and exercise psychology division, Division 47. Bill Morgan served as the first president. Division 47 provides APA members with an opportunity to share research and address relevant sport psychology issues.

1990–2013: Progress in Research, Application, and Professional Issues

The last 25 years have been characterized by exciting growth and diversification in knowledge and practice of sport psychology and considerable progress regarding professional issues in sport psychology.

Intervention research   Particularly impressive, and relevant to this book, is the continued research into the effectiveness of interventions to enhance the performance of athletes and to increase the physical activity levels of all types of individuals. Although more research is needed, the findings from this era should quiet critics who have questioned whether sufficient knowledge exists to justify ethical delivery of sport psychology services. For example, when this book was first published in 1986, its editor, Jean Williams, was criticized by several prominent colleagues because she had envisioned a book to promote applied sport psychology by exposing current and future coaches and sport psychologists to psychological theories and interventions they could use to enhance the performance and personal growth of athletes. One colleague even called her a charlatan.

Diversifying Research

In her overview of the historical development of sport and exercise psychology, Vealey (2006) describes 1993–2005 as a time of emerging diversity in methods, paradigms, and epistemology. For examples, she cites hermeneutic or interpretive approaches, feminist epistemology and methodology, a pragmatic research philosophy, an ecological meta-theoretical approach, and use of single-subject designs and qualitative methods. As Vealey notes, the use and promotion of such diverse approaches is promising because it leads to multiple ways to ask and address different questions.

Two of the preceding advances are particularly important. The use of single-subject designs has been particularly beneficial to intervention research (and practice) because it allows personalizing interventions based on qualities of the individual and it avoids the masking effect that sometimes occurs with nomothetic (group means) comparisons. Use of this methodology has grown since the 1990s (see *Barker, Mellalieu, McCarthy, Jones & Moran,* 2013 for a review of these studies). Qualitative studies are also noteworthy. They have the potential to add greatly to knowledge in applied sport psychology because rather than statistically analyzing numbers or ratings, researchers gain in-depth knowledge on a topic by observing and interviewing people. Before the 1990s, research consisted almost exclusively of quantitative methods, but during the 90s use of qualitative data collection techniques increased. During the 2000s, about one-third of the published studies in three North American sport psychology journals used qualitative methods (Culver, Gilbert, & Sparkes, 2012). Much of this growth can be attributed to Tara Scanlan's work and promotion efforts (Scanlan, Ravizza, & Stein, 1989; Scanlan, Stein, & Ravizza, 1989). She also was instrumental in using and advocating a mixed methods approach (combining qualitative and quantitative research methods in a single study or across a line of research) (Scanlan, Russell, Beals, & Scanlan, 2003).

Another indicator of diversity in the field during this era (1990–2013) was the call for more research into the influence of culture on psychological processes and behavior. First highlighted by Duda and Allison (1990), there is now a growing body of literature on cultural sport psychology (e.g., Schinke & Hanrahan) and application of cultural studies within sport psychology (Ryba, Schinke, & Tennenbaum, 2010). This work recognizes the importance of understanding the experiences of marginalized (i.e., minority) participants and how to best implement sport psychology interventions with diverse athletes (see Chapter 18).

Women Trailblazers in US Sport Psychology

Employing a feminist cultural studies perspective, Krane and Whaley (2010) pointed out the gap in our historical knowledge that overlooked the contributions of women in the field of sport and exercise psychology. They identified eight trailblazing women in U.S. sport psychology: Joan Duda, Deborah Feltz, Diane Gill, Penny McCullagh, Carole Oglesby, Tara Scanlan, Maureen Weiss, and Jean Williams. These trailblazers began their careers in sport

psychology prior to the passage of Title IX (the law that prohibited sex discrimination in U.S. public educational institutions), when lack of support and outright discrimination against women students and faculty was common. In spite of the challenges they faced, they were instrumental in moving the field forward. As Krane and Whaley stated, "Their legacy includes generations of students who have carved their own careers in sport and exercise psychology; lines of research that have established the field as rigorous, theory-based, practical, and relevant; and leadership in professional organizations that was and continues to be thoughtful, competent, and wise" (p. 369). While their contributions to the field spanned the 1970s through today, it took the current focus on diversity and cultural studies in sport and exercise psychology to open an avenue for acknowledging their contributions in the written history of the field.

Sport psychology books   Another reflection of the increase in knowledge in sport psychology and its application comes from the tremendous growth in the number of books dealing with applied sport psychology. In a 1991 critique of psychological skills training books in applied sport psychology, Sachs identified 48 books. By 2008 the list had grown to 391 (Burke, Sachs, Fry, & Schweghhardt, 2008) and it continues to expand.

Training of sport psychology consultants   What is the necessary minimum curriculum to produce the scholarly competencies and practitioner skills for the would-be sport psychology consultant? Answering that question, and then monitoring the impact on graduate programs, the training of graduate students, and the use of sport psychology consultants has been a professional focus during this era. In 1991, AASP established a curricular model for individuals to become certified to provide services such as performance enhancement interventions for athletes. See AASP's Web site (http://www.appliedsportpsych.org/Consultants/become-certified) for the specific criteria and process for becoming a certified consultant.

> *Areas of Competency Required for AASP Certification:*
>
> *Sport and Exercise Psychology*
> *Professional Ethics and Standards*
> *Biomechanical and/or Physiological Bases of Sport*
> *Historical, Philosophical, Social, or Motor Behavior Bases*
> *Psychopathology and Its Assessment*
> *Counseling Skills*
> *Research Design, Statistics, or Psychological Assessment*
> *Biological Bases of Behavior*
> *Cognitive-Affective Bases of Behavior*
> *Individual Behavior*
> *Competence within Skills/Techniques/ Analysis in Sport or Exercise*
> *Mentored Consulting Experience*

Tracking surveys of graduates with a specialization in sport psychology from 1989 to 1999 (Andersen, Williams, Aldridge, & Taylor, 1997; Williams & Scherzer, 2003) show that a high percentage of master's and doctoral degrees met the 14 certification criteria if consulting with athletes was one of their career goals. It appears that this curricular model has influenced the program of study of most graduate students in the United States who have an interest in consulting. Another indication of the acceptance of AASP's certification standards is that, starting in 1996, the USOC requires consultants who wish to work with Olympic programs to be AASP-certified. Unfortunately, it is unlikely that other consumers are equally aware of the importance of picking qualified consultants.

Ethical standards Another professional issue in which progress occurred in the 1990s is setting standards for ethical behavior. Although the growth in applied sport psychology led to a tremendous boon for individuals interested in consulting, negative by-products resulted, such as unqualified individuals providing services and unethical practitioners promising more than they could deliver. These concerns and others led AASP to approve ethical standards and guidelines for sport psychologists (see http://www.appliedsportpsych.org/about/ethics/ethics-code/). Individuals certified by AASP have to agree to observe these ethical standards.

Job Market

Four career tracks have been identified within applied sport and exercise psychology: (a) teaching and research in sport sciences, (b) teaching and research in psychology, (c) consulting with athletes and various other populations, and (d) applying sport psychology skills across diverse contexts (e.g., coaching, academic athletic counseling, health promotion) (APA Division 47, 2013). Many faculty in academic positions also consult with athletes and coaches. During the 1990s, there was tremendous growth in academic positions. For example, the graduate tracking studies showed that 58–61 percent of respondents with doctoral degrees in this decade obtained positions in kinesiology departments (Andersen et al., 1997; Williams & Scherzer, 2003). Unfortunately, we have no empirical information on what has happened in this job market since 1999. Anecdotally, we know that graduates are obtaining jobs in academic positions. Enthusiasm is tempered, however, by the fact that in the current economic climate, many universities also have slowed hiring of new faculty.

We are seeing growth in consulting opportunities for applied sport psychologists. Of the current AASP membership, 40 percent indicated that they spend at least a portion of their professional time in private practice. Yet, while these opportunities exist, consulting with university and elite athletes remains competitive. According to Voelker (2013), "at least 20 NCAA Division I universities have a sport psychologist on staff and another 70 to 100 contract with outside specialists." A recent study of 198 NCAA

Division I athletic directors and 58 university presidents found that while they perceive sport psychology services to be beneficial, they remain reluctant (or unable) to commit funds to hire a full-time consultant (Wrisberg, Withycombe, Simpson, Loberg, & Reed, 2012). Interestingly, one bright spot in the employment market is the U.S. military, who now is hiring civilians with applied sport psychology background to conduct mental skills training with military personnel, and who has become one of the largest employers of sport psychology graduates (Riccuti, Baird, & Clark, 2013). Further, consulting opportunities exist in domains outside of sport such as music, business, and health (e.g., injury rehabilitation in medical centers, cancer centers).

Growth in Exercise Psychology

Another important development during the last 20 years is that exercise psychology has become a highly viable area of specialization, particularly within the academic community. Although the content within this domain is meritorious in its own right and grew tremendously during this era, much of the growth has been driven by widespread grant support. For example, funding opportunities have occurred because of recent attention to the exercise goals in Healthy People 2000 and the position statements from the ACSM and Centers for Disease Control on the importance of exercise in reducing risk of disease and all-cause mortality.

History of Sport Psychology in Eastern Europe

Sport psychology in the former Iron Curtain countries of Eastern Europe is of particular importance to people interested in peak performance. These nations have a long history of giving a great deal of attention to the applied aspects of sport psychology—more specifically, to enhancing elite athletes' performance through applied research and direct intervention. As a consequence of this emphasis, sport psychologists in Eastern Europe played an active role in the selection, training, and competitive preparation of athletes.

Before the breakup of the Soviet Union and the fall of communist control, sport psychology in Eastern Europe was a highly esteemed field of academic and professional concern that received considerable state support and acceptance. In some nations, sport psychologists were even awarded the title of academician, a title that elevated the recipient to the level of a national hero. This high esteem occurred because the countries perceived sport excellence as an important propaganda tool in advancing the communist political system, and sport psychologists were viewed as central figures in facilitating the athlete's quest for excellence.

Vanek and Cratty (1970) reported that the first interest in sport psychology in Eastern Europe can be traced to a physician, Dr. P. F. Lesgaft, who in 1901 described the possible psychological benefits of physical activity. The first research articles were published by Puni and Rudik in the early 1920s. The Institutes for Physical Culture in Moscow and Leningrad also were established in the early 1920s, and the beginning of sport psychology can be traced to them.

Garfield and Bennett (1984) reported that "the extensive investment in athletic research in the communist countries began early in the 1950s as part of the Soviet space program" (p. 13). Russian scientists successfully explored the possibility of using ancient yogic techniques to teach cosmonauts to control psychophysiological processes while in space. These techniques were called **self-regulation training** or **psychic self-regulation** and were used to voluntarily control such bodily functions as heart rate, temperature, and muscle tension, as well as emotional reactions to stressful situations such as zero gravity. About 20 years later, these methods were systematically applied to the Soviet and East German sport programs. According to Kurt Tittel, then director of the Leipzig Institute of Sports (a 14-acre sport laboratory that during the 1970s employed 900 people, over half of whom were scientists), new training methods similar to psychic self-regulation were responsible for the impressive victories by East German and Soviet athletes during the 1976 Olympics (Garfield & Bennett, 1984).

Salmela (1984) reported that sport psychology research in Eastern European countries was more limited in scope than in North America because of greater governmental control. Rather narrowly focused five-year research plans were determined by the state with the advice of its sport psychologists. All sport psychology researchers within the country were required to coordinate and streamline their research efforts to accomplish the stated research objective. Salmela (1981) also indicated that this research focus tended to be of a field variety and applied primarily toward top-level achievement in sport. This focus is not surprising considering each state's heavy emphasis on sport excellence and the easy access by sport psychologists to elite athletes. Most of the Eastern European sport institutes where the athletes were trained had teams of sport psychologists. For example, on a visit to a major sport institute in Bucharest, Romania, Salmela (1984) reported meeting with a team of eight sport psychologists. A sport psychology faculty of that size is considered normal for that type of sport institute. In contrast, at that time in North America one or two people were the average faculty size.

Although most North American sport psychologists would find government-dictated research endeavors abhorrent, a large-scale, unified approach to a particular research topic does have advantages. Salmela (1984) cited one positive example: all Eastern European countries successfully implemented as many as 30 hours of training in self-control for all elite athletes.

The exact training techniques the Eastern European sport psychologists employed remain vague; however, a book by a Russian sport psychologist indicates that autogenic training, visualization, and autoconditioning (self-hypnosis) were key components (Raiport, 1988). Because of its government-funded research and widespread integration of sophisticated mental training programs with rigorous physical training, many authorities believed Eastern Europe was ahead of North America and the rest of the world in the development and application of applied sport psychology. Whatever gap initially existed has closed. As communist control in Eastern Europe ended and the Soviet Union broke up in the late 1980s and 1990s, the status of sport and sport psychology in Eastern Europe changed. With the considerable decline in state support, many sport psychology consultants who worked with elite athletes either lost their positions or moved to other countries. Another consequence of these changes is that interests among the remaining sport psychologists became broader (including, for example, noncompetition) (Kantor & Ryzonkin, 1993).

Future Directions in North American Applied Sport Psychology

Exciting challenges remain for applied sport psychology, both in terms of expanding its scientific foundation and professional practice and in dealing with professional issues. Vealey (2006) offers some good future directions for research. In line with the diversifying research theme identified earlier, she advocates that questions and methods be even more inclusive and diverse, which requires taking a problem-focused approach to scholarship and avoiding the traps of traditional insular paradigms. Further, she suggests asking questions such as, "How can we induce social-structural change in sport and exercise to enhance the psychological and physical well-being of participants? How do social-cultural factors influence mental processes and behavior related to sport and exercise psychology? . . . What types of sport experiences influence positive and negative psychological outcomes for participants?" (pp. 148–150).

When it comes to interventions, Vealey advocates the inclusion of a cultural praxis approach (Ryba & Wright, 2005). For example, interventions should be designed as tools for individual empowerment and social justice and they should help athletes understand how problematic subcultures may have enculturated negative self-perceptions and unhealthy behaviors. In other words, sport psychology interventions should do more than help athletes perform better.

We offer a few additional observations, suggestions, and predictions. One certainty is that both knowledge and interest in applied sport psychology will continue to grow and even larger numbers of individuals will seek the services of a sport psychology consultant or express interest in becoming a sport psychologist. The appropriate training of these future sport psychologists will depend on their career goals. For those who aspire to do consulting work, we believe AASP's certified consultant requirements will remain the dominant curricular model for their training. Because of a tremendous growth in the knowledge base within sport and exercise psychology, we predict even greater specialization in the training of future students. The growth in specialization will continue particularly within health and exercise psychology, driven largely by ever-increasing opportunities in external research funding and the resulting potential for academic positions.

We are hopeful the academic job market will expand, but it must be supplemented by greater growth in consulting and nontraditional career options. The most consulting opportunities in the future will probably come from applied sport psychologists who recognize the potential for using their training in sport psychology not just in sport settings but also to enhance performance in domains such as the performing arts, music, business, and the military. (See the December 2002 issue of the *Journal of Applied Sport Psychology,* which was devoted to moving beyond the psychology of athletic excellence, for articles regarding these types of consulting.)

Other less traditional realms for future career growth are areas such as youth life-skills development through sport, injury prevention and rehabilitation (e.g., hospitals, sports medicine, and physical therapy centers), exercise and wellness promotion (e.g., insurance companies, employee wellness programs, medical centers, and treatment centers for substance abuse), and the military. Good examples of programs in youth life-skills development are The First Tee (Petlichkoff, 2004; http://www.thefirst tee.org) and Play It Smart (Petitpas, Van Raalte,

Cornelius, & Presbrey, 2004; http://playitsmart. footballfoundation.com). Particularly exciting are the new career opportunities in the military. The United States Army has recognized the relevance of performance enhancement skills in military settings and has established programs in cognitive enhancement and performance, and comprehensive solider and family fitness. These military programs are expanding and new opportunities are emerging for graduates with postgraduate degrees in performance psychology, sport psychology, or related fields of study, as well as AASP certification.

In the future, we anticipate even greater acceptance of sport psychology within mainstream psychology. One continuing impetus comes from what sport psychology has to offer in response to the call for more emphasis on studying positive psychology, which seeks to understand positive emotion and build one's strengths and virtues (Seligman & Csikszentmihalyi, 2000). The field of sport psychology has been doing this since its inception. Greater acceptance will result in more research and professional practice cross-fertilization, and more sport psychology and psychology of excellence course offerings in psychology departments, but probably no appreciable increases in sport psychology appointments within psychology departments.

In conclusion, as great as the growth of applied sport psychology has been, the future looks even brighter. We are confident that the field of applied sport psychology has much to offer you, the reader of this book. We are hopeful that you will use the content in this book to enhance your own performance and personal growth.

Summary

Applied sport psychology is concerned with the psychological factors that influence participation and performance in sport and exercise, the psychological effects derived from participation, and theories and interventions that can be used to enhance performance, participation, and personal growth. Today many athletes and coaches look to sport psychology for a competitive edge by seeking psychological training programs to learn, among other things, ways to manage competitive stress, control concentration, improve confidence, and increase communication skills and team harmony.

The storied history of sport and exercise psychology shows the ebbs and flows of research trends (e.g., topics and methods used) and professional opportunities. Throughout, however, there has been a concerted research effort to develop the knowledge base and assess the application of applied sport psychology interventions. Today, professional organizations address educational, research, and professional issues while promoting and supporting consultants, faculty, and students.

Challenges remain for applied sport psychology, both in terms of expanding its scientific foundation and professional practice and in dealing with professional issues, but one certainty is that both knowledge and interest in sport psychology will continue to grow. A key future challenge will be growing the job market at a rate that parallels the increasing number of individuals interested in becoming a sport psychologist and then ensuring that these individuals are appropriately trained for the job market. We anticipate the academic job market will remain strong, particularly for individuals specializing in exercise psychology, but it must be supplemented by greater growth in consulting and nontraditional career options.

Study Questions

1. Define what is meant by applied sport psychology and when it might be used.

2. How are sport psychologists trained and what do they do?

3. Briefly describe the development of sport psychology in North America.

4. Contrast the development of sport psychology in Eastern Europe to that in North America.

5. If you conducted a really good study that might be publishable or given as a talk, what journals and organizations would you want to check out?

6. What progress has been made on the professional issues identified in this chapter?

7. What are some of the concerns and questions that sport psychologists must address in the future?

8. What relationship does sport psychology have to the call for psychologists to put more emphasis on positive psychology?

9. Describe some of the traditional and nontraditional job opportunities that sport psychology professionals might pursue.

References

Andersen, M. B., Williams, J. M., Aldridge, T., & Taylor, T. (1997). Tracking the training and careers of graduates of advanced degree programs in sport psychology, 1989 to 1994. *The Sport Psychologist, 11,* 326–344.

APA Division 47 (2013). *Graduate training and career possibilities in exercise and sport psychology.* Retrieved from http://www.apadivisions.org/division-47/about/resources/training.aspx.

Barker, J. B., Mellalieu, S. D., McCarthy, P. J., Jones, M. V., & Moran, A. (2013). A review of single-case research in sport psychology 1997–2012: research trends and future. *Journal of Applied Sport Psychology, 25,* 4–32.

Burke, K. L., Sachs, M. L., Fry, S., & Schwehhardt, S. (Eds.). (2008). *Directory of graduate programs in applied sport psychology* (9th ed.). Morgantown, WV: Fitness Information Technology.

Culver, D. M., Gilbert, W., & Sparkes, A. (2012). Qualitative research in sport psychology journals: The next decade 2000–2009 and beyond. *Sport Psychologist, 26,* 261–281.

Duda, J. L., & Allison, M. T. (1990). Cross-cultural analysis in exercise and sport psychology: A void in the field. *Journal of Sport & Exercise Psychology, 12,* 114–131.

Garfield, C. A., & Bennett, H. Z. (1984). *Peak performance.* Los Angeles: Tarcher.

Gould, D., & Pick, S. (1995). Sport psychology: The Griffith era, 1920–1940. *The Sport Psychologist, 9,* 391–405.

Greenspan, M. J., & Feltz, D. L. (1989). Psychological interventions with athletes in competitive situations: A review. *The Sport Psychologist, 3,* 219–236.

Griffith, C. R. (1926). *Psychology of coaching.* New York: Scribner.

Griffith, C. R. (1928). *Psychology of athletics.* New York: Scribner.

Harris, D. V. (Ed.). (1972). *Women in sport: A national research conference.* State College, PA: Pennsylvania State University.

Kantor, E., & Ryzonkin, J. (1993). Sport psychology in the former USSR. In R. N. Singer, M. Murphey, & L. K. Tennant (Eds.), *Handbook of research on sport psychology* (pp. 46–49). New York: Macmillan.

Kornspan, A. S., & MacCracken, M. J. Psychology applied to sport in the 1940s: The work of Dorothy Hazeltine Yates. *The Sport Psychologist, 15,* 342–345.

Krane, V., & Whaley, D. (2010). Quiet competence: Writing women into the history of sport and exercise psychology. *The Sport Psychologist, 18,* 349–372.

Landers, D. M. (1995). Sport psychology: The formative years, 1950–1980. *The Sport Psychologist, 9,* 406–417.

Lawther, J. D. (1951). *Psychology of coaching.* Englewood Cliffs, NJ: Prentice Hall.

Mahoney, M. J. (1989). Sport psychology. In I. Cohen (Ed.), *The G. Stanley Hall lecture series* Vol. 9 (pp. 97–134). Washington, DC: American Psychological Association.

Martens, R. (1979). About smocks and jocks. *Journal of Sport Psychology, 1,* 94–99.

Morgan, W. P. (1984). Mind over matter. In W. F. Straub & J. M. Williams (Eds.), *Cognitive sport psychology* (pp. 311–316). Lansing, NY: Sport Science International.

Ogilvie, B., & Tutko, T. (1966). *Problem athletes and how to handle them.* London: Pelham.

Oglesby, C. A. (1978). *Women in sport: From myth to reality.* Philadelphia: Lea & Febiger.

Petitpas, A. J., Van Raalte, J. L., Cornelius, A., & Presbrey, J. (2004). A life skills development program for high school student-athletes. *The Journal of Primary Prevention, 24,* 325–334.

Petlichkoff, L. M. (2004). Self-regulation skills in children and adolescents. In M. R. Weiss (Ed.), *Developmental sport and exercise psychology: A lifespan perspective* (pp. 273–292). Morgantown, WV: Fitness Information Technology, Inc.

Raiport, G. (1988). *Red gold: Peak performance techniques of the Russian and East German Olympic victors.* New York: Tarcher.

Riccuti, D., Baird, S., & Clark, C. (2013, June 26). *Performance psychology within the military.* Webinar, Association for Applied Sport Psychology.

Ryba, T. V., Schinke, R., & Tennenbaum, G. (Eds.) (2010). *The cultural turn in sport and exercise psychology.* Morgantown, West Virginia: Fitness Information Technology.

Ryba, T. V., & Wright, H. K. (2005). From mental game to cultural praxis: A cultural studies model's implications for the future of sport psychology. *Quest, 57,* 192–212.

Sachs, M. L. (1991). Reading list in applied sport psychology: Psychological skills training. *The Sport Psychologist, 5,* 88–91.

Salmela, J. H. (1981). *The world sport psychology sourcebook.* Ithaca, NY: Mouvement Publications.

Salmela, J. H. (1984). Comparative sport psychology. In J. M. Silva III & R. A. Weinberg (Eds.), *Psychological foundations of sport* (pp. 23–24). Champaign, IL: Human Kinetics.

Scanlan, T. K., Ravizza, K., & Stein, G. L. (1989). An in-depth study of former elite figure skaters: I. Introduction to the project. *Journal of Sport & Exercise Psychology, 11,* 54–64.

Scanlan, T. K., Stein, G. L., & Ravizza, K. (1989). An in-depth study of former elite figure skaters: II. Sources of enjoyment. *Journal of Sport & Exercise Psychology, 11,* 65–83.

Schinke, R., & Hanrahan, S. (Eds.) (2009). *Cultural sport psychology.* Champaign, IL: Human Kinetics.

Seligman, M., & Csikszentmihalyi, M. (2000). Positive psychology: An introduction. *American Psychologist, 55,* 5–14.

Straub, W. F., & Williams, J. M. (Eds.). (1984). *Cognitive sport psychology.* Lansing, N.Y: Sport Science International.

Suinn, R. M. (1985). The 1984 Olympics and sport psychology. *Journal of Sport Psychology, 7,* 321–329.

U.S. Olympic Committee. (1983). U.S. Olympic Committee establishes guidelines for sport psychology services. *Journal of Sport Psychology, 5,* 4–7.

Vanek, M., & Cratty, B. J. (1970). *Psychology and the superior athlete.* New York: Macmillan.

Vealey, R. S. (2006). Smocks and jocks outside the box: The paradigmatic evolution of sport and exercise psychology. *Quest, 58,* 128–159.

Voelker, R. (2013). Hot careers: Sport psychology. *GradPSYCH Magazine.* Retrieved from, http://www.apa.org/gradpsych/2012/11/sport-psychology.aspx.

Williams, J. M., & Scherzer, C. B. (2003). Tracking the training and careers of graduates of advanced degree programs in sport psychology, 1994 to 1999. *Journal of Applied Sport Psychology, 15,* 335–353.

Wrisberg, C., Withycombe, J., Simpson, D., Loberg, L. A., & Reed, A. (2012). NCAA division-I administrators' perceptions of the benefits of sport psychology services and possible roles for a consultant. *The Sport Psychologist, 26,* 16–28.

Yates, D. H. (1932). *Psychological racketeers.* Boston: Badger.

Yates, D. H. (1943). A practical method of using set. *Journal of Applied Psychology, 27,* 512–519.

Yates, D. H. (1957). *Psychology you can use.* New York: Crowell.

Learning, Motivation, and Social Interaction

Motor Skill Learning for Effective Coaching and Performance

Cheryl A. Coker, *Plymouth State University*

Most people get excited about games, but I've got to be excited about practice, because that's my classroom.

—Pat Summitt, Basketball

Effective coaching depends on many factors. Coaches must have excellent knowledge of their sport, be innovative strategists, skilled motivators, and effective personal counselors. However, at the core of successful coaching is an understanding of the motor learning process. First and foremost, effective coaches must be good teachers. Most sports comprise a diverse array of complex motor skills. Athletes enter the sporting arena with different abilities and prior experiences. The coach must understand both how the novice performer acquires brand-new skills and how the experienced athlete maintains, and possibly improves peak performance on well-learned skills. This understanding will enable the coach to structure effective practices and to provide clear, effective feedback to the athlete about performance errors. For the sport psychologist, this understanding serves as the basis for a more comprehensive assessment of athlete behavior and of potential intervention strategies that will enhance performance.

Motor Learning Defined

Motor skill learning should be understood as a set of internal processes, associated with practice or experience, leading to relatively permanent changes in the capability for skilled movement behavior. **Capability** means that once a skill has been learned, the potential, or likelihood, for exhibiting skilled performance is quite high, although we realize that even highly skilled athletes do occasionally make errors. Because motor learning is internal, taking place within the athlete's central nervous system, we cannot observe learning directly. We can, however, monitor an athlete's *performance*, which is observable behavior, and draw an inference about learning. For example, a beginning swimmer's first attempts at the butterfly stroke will likely proceed in an awkward, step-by-step manner. As the swimmer practices, form, timing, and coordination improve. By monitoring these changes in performance, we infer that the swimmer is learning. It is also important that the changes in performance are relatively permanent; that is, the athlete should be able to demonstrate the skill repeatedly, even after a period of no practice.

Phases of Motor Skill Learning

As athletes progress from the novice stage to an advanced level, they go through different phases or steps (see Figure 2-1). These phases commonly are characterized by the goal of the athlete in each (Gentile, 2000), as well as their behavioral tendencies (Fitts & Posner, 1967). Such information is useful, as it provides the coach a basis from which to make informed decisions that will optimize the learning of his or her athletes (see summary Table 2-1 following this section). It would, however, be misleading to think of these phases as distinct because, as learning progresses, one phase blends gradually into another so that no clear transition between them is evident (Christina & Corcos, 1988; Fitts & Posner, 1967). Thus, the phases of learning should be thought of as a continuum, with some overlap occurring between them. Coaches should also be aware that an athlete can be in one stage for a given skill and in a different stage for another skill. For example, a soccer player may be in the autonomous stage for dribbling but the cognitive stage for heading the ball because it is being introduced for the first time. Finally, it would also be

misleading to think of these stages as age dependent. Fourteen-year-old Guan Tianlang, who finished 58th at the 2013 Masters and was the youngest golfer ever to make the cut in a major tournament would be considered highly proficient yet adults who have skied all of their lives become novices when introduced to snowboarding for the first time.

The Cognitive Phase

In the cognitive or beginning phase of skill learning, athletes focus on gaining an understanding of how the skill is to be performed. The coach or instructor assists the athlete in this process by describing the skill's key elements. In addition, he or she will typically provide demonstrations, digital video, charts, or other visual cues to help the learners "picture" the new skill.

Based on the explanation and demonstrations provided by the coach, athletes begin to develop a **motor program** for that skill. A motor program is an abstract, internal representation of the skill, similar to a computer program that contains a set of instructions to guide the movement. At first the motor program may be very crude, containing just enough details to allow the athletes to make a "ballpark" response. There also are likely to be errors in the program. However, with practice and feedback, both from the athlete's sensory systems and from the coach, the motor program is revised and refined so that

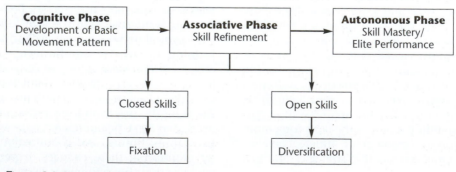

Figure 2-1 **Stages of learning**

it gradually becomes more effective at controlling performance.

Much conscious attention is directed toward the details of the movement in this phase and athletes are unable to attend to external events such as the positions of teammates or movements of defensive players. The movements produced in this phase will lack synchronization and appear choppy and deliberate. This phase is also characterized by inconsistency, and the production of numerous errors that are typically gross in nature. Athletes will be highly dependent on the coach at this point as they lack the capability to determine the specific cause of an error and its subsequent correction. Finally, the dominant sensory system in this phase is *vision* as is evident when a beginner learns to dribble a basketball, intently watching both the hand and the ball.

Role of the Coach

The role of the coach during the cognitive phase is to facilitate the athlete's development of a basic movement pattern by clearly communicating the critical aspects of the skill through verbal instructions and demonstrations. There is much truth in the saying "a picture is worth a thousand words," and a demonstration will help learners create a reference image of the skill so that practice can begin. However, a correctly performed demonstration does not necessarily ensure that the athletes' attention was focused on the most important part of the demonstration. Verbal cues should be used to direct athletes' attention in conjunction with the demonstration (e.g., Janelle, Champenoy, Coombes, & Mousseau, 2003). The coach must tell the athletes *specifically* what to look for, whether it is the pattern of racket movement in a looped tennis backswing, the position of the recovery elbow in the freestyle, or the entire pattern of coordination in a baseball swing. Magill (2004) further recommends that those cues be short and concise rather than providing "continuous verbal commentary while demonstrating the skill" (p. 259) to avoid overloading the athlete with information.

Once athletes have been exposed to several demonstrations, they must be afforded the opportunity to practice the skill. Accordingly, the role of the coach also entails the design of practice experiences for initial motor program development. This practice should allow for numerous repetitions (blocked practice) in which athletes can allocate their undivided attention to the details of the movement itself to encourage the discovery of effective performance strategies. Furthermore, the provision of feedback is important in this phase to reinforce, motivate, and guide athletes in modifying their performance.

Duration of the Cognitive Phase

The cognitive phase of learning is a relatively short period in the overall learning process. It may last only a few minutes or it may involve a longer period if the skill is complex. The cognitive phase is complete when the athletes can reasonably execute the skill the way it was demonstrated (Christina & Corcos, 1988).

The Associative Phase

The focus of the associative or intermediate phase of skill learning is refinement. Through practice, the learner moves from having a general idea of how to execute the movement to being able to perform the skill both accurately and consistently. The coach's role during this phase shifts to one that mainly involves planning and implementing effective practice conditions as well as providing feedback for skill enhancement.

During the associative phase of learning, the motor program is further developed and athletes gradually eliminate extraneous movements and make fewer, less gross errors. They improve their speed, accuracy, coordination, and consistency. Movements will become more automated, allowing for reallocation of attentional resources to performance factors such as monitoring the environment and planning game strategy. Visual control of movement is gradually replaced by **proprioceptive control,** or "feel," and dribbling a basketball can now be effectively executed without looking at the ball or hand and probably even with the eyes closed. Were pro-prioceptive cues not available during the early phases of learning? Yes, they were available but it takes many practice trials before athletes come to associate the feel of their movements with the outcomes that these movements produce. Schmidt (1975) referred to the generation of "expected sensory consequences," meaning that we expect our movements to feel a certain way, and we can use such sensory feedback to evaluate the correctness of our movements. In other words, using this information, the athlete not only learns to identify the cause of performance errors but, over time, will also develop the capability to generate strategies for their correction.

The Role of the Coach

During the associative phase, the coach must design effective practices to optimize skill refinement. Understanding the nature of the skill is the first step to accomplishing this objective. A skill can be categorized as falling on a continuum between being closed and open according to the predictability of the environment in which that skill is performed. Closed skills are those performed in a relatively stable, predictable environment such as bowling, target archery, free throw shooting, and tennis serving. Successful performance of such skills requires that the athlete be able to consistently and accurately replicate the movement pattern (*fixation*), and practice should reflect this objective. Some closed skills, however, involve intertrial variability. For example, each time a putt is attempted in a round of golf, it is from a different position in relation to the hole. For these types of skills, consistency in technique is important, but the performer also must be able to utilize that technique in a variety of situations. Accordingly, the athlete should practice on different greens, a variety of slopes, and from different locations and distances from the hole. Open skills are those in which the environment is changing and unpredictable. Examples include returning a punt in football, executing a breakaway in field hockey or soccer, and driving through heavy rush-hour traffic. Because the performer must constantly

conform his or her actions to those of the environment, the objective of practice is to *diversify* the movement pattern or teach the athlete to be able to quickly adapt to the demands of the performance situation. Practice should therefore be gamelike so that the athlete becomes better at anticipating changes in the environment.

As indicated earlier, athletes in the associative phase are increasingly able to direct their attention toward aspects of the performance environment. Given the nature of open skills, learning where to direct one's attention to locate appropriate cues is critical to successful decision making and performance. Research has shown that there are marked differences in visual search strategies between beginners and experts. For example, expert soccer players were found to fixate more often on the knee and hip regions of their opponents than their novice counterparts, suggesting that the information in these areas was important in anticipating the opponent's next move (Nagano, Kato, & Fukada, 2004). Research has also shown that these anticipatory skills can be acquired and enhanced through specific training in visual search strategies and decision making (e.g., Raab, Masters, & Maxwell, 2005; Vickers, 2007). In addition to directing athletes to focus toward the areas in which the critical cues for performance occur, coaches should provide a variety of practice experiences where they have to identify and respond to those cues (Magill, 1998). By manipulating task or practice variables within those experiences, such as imposing rule modifications, altering playing area dimensions, and manipulating situational factors such as the positioning of the defense (Passos, Araújo, Davids & Shuttleworth, 2010), coaches can create a learning environment that can shape visual search and decision-making behaviors through self-exploration and guided discovery (Williams, Jannelle, & Davids, 2004). This strategy will be discussed in more detail later in the chapter.

Finally, the provision of effective feedback continues to be an important role of the coach throughout this phase. That feedback not only should guide the athletes in correcting movement errors but should also help them develop their error detection and correction capabilities by teaching them to relate the feelings associated with a movement to the resulting performance outcome.

Duration of the Associative Phase

The associative phase of skill learning is a much longer period than the cognitive phase, ranging from perhaps a few hours for learning simple skills to several years for mastering complex ones. In fact, not all learners will transition to the final stage of learning as it represents the highest level of skill proficiency.

The Autonomous Phase

The autonomous or advanced phase of learning emerges when the learner can perform the skill at a maximal level of proficiency. As the term implies, performance is quite automatic; the learner seems to require very little conscious thought or attention to the details of movement. In fact, asking highly skilled performers to consciously focus on their movements will seriously disrupt performance, especially in high-speed activities such as performing a routine on the uneven bars in gymnastics or executing a dodge and kick for a goal in soccer.

Exercise 1: Automatic behavior

To experience what happens when elite athletes consciously focus on their movements, perform the following:

Everyone has a natural walking pace. Determine your natural pace by walking across the room several times. Describe your thought process during this activity as well as what happened to your gait.

In the autonomous phase, the athletes' motor program for generating the correct movements is highly developed and well established in memory. Free from having to concentrate on executing the skill, they can concentrate on other things besides technique. For example, the NBA's Rajon Rondo can dribble down court at full speed on a fast break and does this without looking at the ball and while planning the best strategy for getting the ball to the basket. During such a play, he considers the position and movements of his opponents and teammates and whether to pass, drive to the basket, pull up short and shoot, or set up a new play. Rondo does all this while dribbling the ball at full speed, giving no thought to the mechanics of dribbling.

Progressing from the cognitive through the associative and arriving at the autonomous phase of learning requires an amount of practice and a period of time that depends on the abilities of the individual, the complexity of the task itself, the learner's prior movement experiences, and the efficiency of the learning environment. Certainly high-speed dribbling requires more time and practice to master than does a vertical jump or a simple forward roll. In fact, some speculate that it requires a minimum of 10 years and over a million repetitions to produce high-level performance in major sports such as football, basketball, baseball, and gymnastics (Ericsson, Krampe, & Tesch-Römer, 1993).

Role of the Coach

Instruction during the autonomous phase of learning basically serves two purposes: first, to help athletes maintain their level of skill, and, second, to motivate the athletes to want to continue to improve. Once a consistently high level of skill is achieved, it must be maintained not only during a single season but also from season to season. Recall that our definition of motor learning referred to changes in the capability for skilled behavior that are relatively permanent. Also, it would be a mistake to assume that learning has ended in the autonomous phase and that performance cannot be improved. Although the level of competence an athlete may achieve in a skill has certain limits, and performance may be approaching some arbitrary standard of perfection, the progression to this point usually occurs so gradually that it is rarely possible to claim that athletes have reached their highest level of achievement. However, because of the difficulty in improving performance as one approaches the highest levels of skill, even though practice continues, athletes may lose motivation to strive for improvement. Thus, the role of the coach as a motivator becomes very important during this phase of learning. The use of goal setting and reinforcement can help skilled athletes maintain motivation. These topics will be discussed in detail in later chapters.

Error Correction and the Learning Process

An understanding of the motor learning process and the phases of skill learning is not only important for teaching new skills to novice athletes but also critical when a coach desires to *change* a highly skilled athlete's well-learned technique. Making a minor change in technique, such as widening a baseball player's batting stance, is simple and can usually be accomplished easily. Having a tennis player change from an Eastern forehand grip to the continental grip also should be accomplished with little difficulty. This is because changes such as these require very little relearning. However, when you ask athletes to make a major change in technique, such as going from a two-hand backhand in tennis to a one-hand backhand, you are essentially asking them to return to the cognitive phase of learning and progress through the associative to the autonomous phases again. The process of relearning a skill is therefore time intensive, and performance will initially suffer. Thus, major changes in technique should be undertaken during the off-season and athletes must be motivated to invest in the amount of practice necessary to see the change through.

Practice Considerations

Often considered the single most important factor in the control of learning is **practice.** In general, the greater the number of practice trials, the better the learning. Current knowledge suggests that the necessary conditions for reaching international-level performance in many different domains is at least 10 years of effortful practice under optimal training conditions (Ericsson, 2003; Ericsson et al., 1993). Such conditions require a well-defined task

of appropriate difficulty for the athlete, information feedback, and sufficient opportunities for repetition and correction of errors. Ericsson and his colleagues use the term *deliberate practice* to characterize training activities that contain all of these elements.

Deliberate practice by itself, however, is not enough to enable athletes to learn a skill correctly. For practice to be effective, the athletes must be motivated to learn. The old adage "practice makes perfect" is not necessarily true; athletes must practice with the *intent* to improve. This means that skill learning involves more than simply going through the motions physically. Without the goal to constantly improve the level of performance, practice can lead to a mediocre level of proficiency or, worse, a deterioration of skill.

Whole versus Part Practice

Many of the sport skills an athlete must learn are quite complex, such as a floor exercise routine in gymnastics, a reverse lay-up in basketball, or a forward double somersault with two twists in diving. Even a relatively simple skill, such as a 2-foot putt in golf, may seem very complex to the beginner. A coach must decide whether to present all aspects of such skills to the athlete at once for practice or to divide the skill into smaller, meaningful units that can be practiced separately and then combined into the whole skill.

The **whole** method requires that the athletes practice the activity or skill in its entirety, as a single unit. The **part** method requires that the athletes practice each component of the activity or skill separately and then combine the parts into the whole skill. Between these two extremes are two variations. In the first, the **progressive-part** method, the first two parts of a skill are practiced separately and then combined and practiced as a unit. The third part is practiced separately next and then combined with the first two, and so on until the skill is performed in its entirety. The second variation is known as the **repetitive-part** method. Using this method, the first part is practiced independently. Once

Table 2-1 Performer Characteristics and Role of the Coach for Each Stage of Learning

Stage of Learning	Performer Characteristics	Role of the Coach
Cognitive	High degree of cognitive activity	Motivate to want to learn the skill
	Use of self-talk	Provide verbal instructions and demonstrations to help learners gain a basic understanding of the skill
	Development of initial motor program	
	Much conscious attention to details of movement	Design experience for initial development of motor program
	Inability to attend to external events	Assist learner by providing feedback regarding errors and prescribing corrections
	Lack synchronization and appear choppy and deliberate	
	Inconsistent	Encourage
	Production of numerous errors	
	Errors are large	
	Lack capability to determine specific cause of errors and subsequent corrections	
	Vision is the dominant sensory system	
Associative	Fewer errors	Plan and implement appropriate practice opportunities (fixation vs. diversification)
	Improvements in speed, accuracy, coordination, and consistency	
	Attend less to physical execution of skill	Teach visual search strategies
	Can devote attention to environment	Continue to provide feedback to reinforce, motivate, and correct performance
	Proprioceptive control replaces visual	
	Refining motor program	Help athletes to develop error detection and correction capabilities
	Developing capability to identify errors and generate strategies for their correction	
Autonomous	Highly proficient	Continue to plan appropriate practice opportunities
	Performance is automatic	
	Focus completely directed to environment and decision making	Provide feedback when needed Motivate

a level of proficiency is obtained, the second is immediately added to it and the two parts are practiced together. The pattern continues until all parts have been integrated. Figure 2-2 illustrates each part method using bowling.

Both the whole and part methods of practice offer distinct advantages. The part method of practice is of greatest value when a skill is very complex and involves separate, independently performed parts. For example, a gymnastics floor exercise routine is suited to the part method of practice because each individual trick can be practiced independently. Also, using this method, the gymnast can devote more practice time to particularly difficult tricks in the routine without practicing the easier ones, thus making practice more efficient. However, the successful gymnastics routine is more than a series of

Part-Whole	Progressive Part	Repetitive Part
• Approach • Push Away • Pendulum Swing • Delivery • Approach + Push Away + Pendulum Swing + Delivery	• Approach • Push Away • Approach + Push Away • Pendulum Swing • Approach + Push Away + Pendulum Swing • Delivery • Approach + Push Away + Pendulum Swing + Delivery	• Approach • Approach + Push Away • Approach + Push Away + Pendulum Swing • Approach + Push Away + Pendulum Swing + Delivery

Figure 2-2 **Illustration of part practice techniques using bowling**

well-executed individual movements. The transitions between individual elements must be executed smoothly so that the entire performance flows as a coherent unit. An inherent timing or rhythmic structure among certain components characterizes most serial activities of reasonably long duration. The coach must be careful to identify the components within the routine that go together and have the athletes practice them as a unit so as not to disrupt the essential timing.

The undue adherence to the part method can also result in the development of a series of well-learned components that are disconnected and are performed in a disjointed and segmented fashion when combined into a whole. Learning a skill through the part method therefore requires both learning the individual parts and connecting them into a cohesive unit. By demonstrating the whole skill before breaking it down for part practice and explaining how the parts are associated, coaches can facilitate the athletes' understanding of how the parts fit into the whole.

The decision to practice a motor skill as a whole or by parts should be based on the nature of the skill *and* the nature of the learner. Christina and Corcos (1988) provide several excellent suggestions for how to do this. In general, the whole method is favored if (a) the skill is not too complicated and can be understood in a meaningful way; (b) the skill is not too dangerous and can be practiced with a reasonable degree of success (many gymnastics and diving routines, certain wrestling maneuvers, and pole vaulting, for example, because of the potential for injury, lend themselves to part practice); (c) the athlete is capable, highly motivated, and has an extensive background in various sports; and (d) the athletes' attention span is long enough to deal with the whole. Skills with components that are highly interdependent also are best served by whole practice.

There also are times when parts of an activity should be practiced separately. For example, when one particular skill or phase of the overall activity is causing difficulty, such as a tennis player having problems tossing the ball accurately and consistently, concentration and practice on this particular component are appropriate for a time. This allows additional practice where it is most needed. However, too much part practice on an isolated component can cause it to become disconnected from the surrounding components. The coach should seek to integrate the troublesome part back into the whole skill as quickly as possible.

Teaching Several Skills: Blocked versus Random Practice

In most sports, athletes are challenged to learn a variety of different skills. Swimmers, for example, must learn four competitive strokes, along with starts and turns. Gymnasts must learn many routines on several pieces of equipment. Tennis players must learn forehand and backhand ground strokes, several different serves, net play, and appropriate strategies. Golfers are charged with learning to hit many different clubs over a variety of distances and often through various obstacles. Novice athletes have to learn the many skills of their sport before the first competition. Experienced athletes have to practice these many skills in order to maintain peak performance.

Considering the large number of skills most sports comprise and the often-restricted practice time available, coaches are forced to teach more than one skill in a week; often, several skills must be taught in a single practice session. How can a coach sequence the practice of several tasks during the practice period to maximize learning?

Suppose that an age group swim team practices four times a week for an hour per session. The coach would like to devote 2 weeks to teaching the four competitive strokes: butterfly, backstroke, breast-stroke, and freestyle. A commonsense approach to scheduling would be to practice the butterfly for two sessions, then the backstroke for two sessions, and so on until all four strokes are completed. This schedule of practice is called **blocked practice,** where all the trials of a given task are completed before moving on to the next task. Note that the order in which the strokes are practiced could be arbitrary as long as practice on one stroke is completed before beginning practice on the next stroke. Intuitively, blocked practice seems to make sense because it allows the swimmers to concentrate on one stroke at a time without worrying about interference from the other strokes.

An alternative approach to scheduling would be to practice all four strokes within each practice period but to do so in a random order so that the swimmers never practice the same stroke on two consecutive trials. This is called a **random practice** schedule. It is important to note that, at the end of the two-week period, both practice schedules would have provided the same amount of practice on each of the four strokes.

Which of these practice schedules might produce more efficient learning in our swimmers? At first glance, the obvious answer would be blocked practice as it would appear that random practice

would present a more difficult environment for the athlete because of the constant switching between tasks. Indeed, if we plotted the swimmers' performance of the four strokes over the two-week learning period, we would probably find better performance under blocked practice. However, a sizable body of research seems to contradict this intuitive view about practice. The results of many laboratory-based experiments indicate that blocked practice produces better acquisition performance than random practice, but poorer long-term learning, as measured by delayed retention and **transfer,** the application of the practiced skill in a new situation (e.g., Li & Wright, 2000; Shea & Morgan, 1979). Studies using more real-world sport skills, such as learning different badminton serves (Goode & Magill, 1986; Wrisberg & Liu, 1991), forehand and backhand ground strokes in tennis (Hebert, Landin & Solmon, 1996), the golf putt and pitch shot (Porter, Landin, Hebert & Baum, 2007) and different snowboarding skills (Smith, 2002) lend additional support to this notion. This phenomenon is known as the **contextual interference** effect, based on the early work of Battig (1966). (For reviews on contextual interference see Barreiros, Figueiredo, & Godinho, 2007; Brady, 2008.)

Essentially, contextual interference proposes that making the practice environment more difficult for the learner, as with random practice, leads to better learning, even though performance during acquisition is depressed. This is certainly a counterintuitive idea. Attempts to explain why random practice is more effective than blocked practice for learning suggest two possible mechanisms. First, when several tasks are present in the athletes' working memory at the same time, they have to use more elaborate processing strategies to keep the tasks distinct. The more effortful processing produces better memory representations for the tasks (Shea & Zimny, 1983, 1988). Second, when athletes practice a task on Trial 1 but do not repeat that task until several trials later, there may be some forgetting of the "solution" to the task. Consequently, the athletes are forced to go through more solution generations with random practice, which ultimately leads to better retrieval (Lee & Magill, 1983).

Practice Strategy	Time	Session 1	Session 2	Session 3	Session 4	Session 5	Session 6	Session 7	Session 8
Blocked Practice	40 min	FLY	FLY	BK	BK	BR	BR	FR	FR
Repeated Blocked Practice	5 min 5 min 5 min 5 min } ×2	FLY BK BR FR	FLY BK BR FR	FLY BK BR FR	FLY BK BR FR	FLY BK BR FR	FLY BK BR FR	FLY BK BR FR	FLY BK BR FR
Random Practice	40 min	FLY BK BR FR BR FR BK FLY BR FR FLY BK Etc.	FLY BR FR BK BR FR BR FLY BK BR FLY FR Etc.	BK BR FR BK FR FLY BR FR BK BR FR FLY Etc.	FR BR FLY BK BR FLY BR BR BK FLY BR Etc.	BK BR FR BR FR FLY FR FR BK BR FR FLY Etc.	FLY BK FR BK BR FR BR BK BK BR FLY FR Etc.	FR BR FLY BK BR FLY FR BK FR BK FLY BR Etc.	FLY BK BR FR BR FR BK FLY BR FR FLY BK Etc.

Figure 2-3 Three practice variations for practicing swimming strokes
(FLY = butterfly; BK = backstroke; BR = breaststroke; FR = freestyle)

Although the research on contextual interference discussed thus far implies that a random practice schedule would optimize learning, one additional factor should be considered. Evidence exists indicating that during the initial stage of skill acquisition, when the learner is getting the idea of the movement, blocked practice conditions may be more beneficial than random practice (e.g., Landin & Hebert, 1997). However, once the basic movement pattern is acquired, the amount of contextual interference must be increased. Aside from doing so through random practice, Landin and Hebert (1997) propose the use of a third approach to scheduling, **repeated blocked practice,** which may combine the advantages of both blocked and random practice. Using the swimming example, rather than practicing the butterfly for two sessions followed by the backstroke for two sessions and so on until all four strokes are completed (blocked practice), or practicing all four strokes within each practice period where the same stroke is never practiced consecutively (random practice), repeated blocked practice would be organized such that several successive trials of each stroke are performed with the rotation repeated throughout the practice period. Figure 2-3 shows sample practice variations for all three strategies.

Although Keller, Li, Weiss, and Relyea (2006) found support for repeated blocked practice in pistol shooting skills, more field-based research in a variety of sports is needed before we can be truly confident about the learning benefits of both repeated blocked and random practice. Nevertheless, the available research should encourage coaches to at least think about some of their deeply rooted traditional practice methods.

Teaching Several Variations of a Skill: Variable Practice

In the preceding discussion, the coach's goal was to teach several *different* tasks. There also are times, however, when only a single task is to be learned during a practice session, such as shooting a jump shot, kicking a field goal, or fielding a ground ball. How should the coach structure practice for these situations to maximize learning?

Consider the task of fielding a ground ball and throwing to first base. This task essentially involves perceiving a stimulus (the ground ball), moving the body in front of the ball, fielding it, and making an accurate throw. Coach A believes the best way to learn this task would be to practice under **constant** conditions. She will give her shortstop 100 ground balls to field, but each one will be thrown by a pitching machine, have constant velocity, come to the same spot on the field, and have exactly the same bounce and roll characteristics. Coach A feels that this type of practice will allow her shortstop to master the fundamentals of fielding and to "groove" her response.

Coach B adopts a **variable** practice approach. She also will give her shortstop 100 balls to field, but each one will be hit by a batter, possess different bounce and roll characteristics, and go to different spots on the field, forcing the player to move to multiple locations and adapt to the ever-changing demands presented. Coach B reasons that in the real game no two ground balls are exactly alike, so variability of practice would be more likely to produce the specific skills needed by a shortstop. This type of drill more realistically simulates actual game conditions. It is also possible that in an actual game a shortstop will have to field a ball that is slightly different from any of the 100 variations experienced during practice.

The variable practice approach adopted by Coach B has been shown to result in better learning than the constant conditions offered by Coach A's practice (e.g., Douvis, 2005; Shoenfelt, Snyder, Maue, McDowell, & Woolard, 2002). Coach B's shortstop would be more likely to experience success when faced with a "novel" fielding situation than Coach A's shortstop because of all the practice with similar versions of the task. What is actually being learned through variable practice is more than simply the specific actions practiced. The shortstop develops a general capability to produce fielding responses, a capability that enhances generalizability, allowing athletes to transfer their learning to actions not specifically experienced in practice. According to schema theory (Schmidt, 1975), variable practice allows

the learner to discover relationships among environment conditions (her location on the field, speed and bounce characteristics of the ball, distance from first base); what she "told" her muscles to produce (how fast to move, where to put her glove, how hard to throw); and the outcomes that these movements produced (missed/caught the ball, threw too far or too short). Through variable practice, the athlete's understanding of these relationships becomes stronger, and she develops a schema or rule that relates the initial environment conditions, such as distance of the throw, to the force and trajectory requirements that must be selected to produce a correct throw. When the shortstop is called on to execute a "new" fielding response, one that she has never experienced before, her variable practice experiences allow her to better estimate the response specifications needed by her motor program to produce the new response. The athlete who has experienced only one version of the task, through constant practice, may be able to execute that version very well but will be limited in developing a repertoire of responses that may be needed in the criterion activity.

Before we leave the topic of variable practice, a word of caution may be in order. As discussed with blocked and random practice, the skill level of the athlete should be considered prior to deciding whether to employ constant or variable practice. When athletes have no prior experience in an activity, then it may be advantageous to begin with constant practice at one version of the task, shooting a jump shot from one spot on the court, for example, before introducing variable practice. Initial constant practice will allow the pure beginner to master the basics of the skill and pass through the cognitive phase of learning. Once this is accomplished, however, variable practice should be introduced to develop the schemas needed in the actual sport.

Improving Performance

Critical to an athlete's skill development is the design and implementation of a variety of intervention strategies for error correction. Effective error correction is, however, dependent on the coach's ability to accurately analyze the skill and the context in which it is performed. Proficiency in skill analysis cannot be underrated. Failure to identify the underlying cause of an error has clear implications regarding the potential success of the corresponding intervention strategy.

Error Identification and Diagnosis

Skill analysis begins with a systematic observation whereby the athlete's technique is compared with correct technique (see Knudson, 2013 and Hall, 2012 for more details on conducting a systematic observation). The key here is to focus on the basic movement pattern rather than on small idiosyncrasies in individual style. In other words, is the athlete's technique fundamentally sound?

Next, the coach must determine the cause of the error(s) observed. Errors in performance are not always related to technique. However, since we can see only the output of a learner's performance, there is a tendency to focus on only those technical aspects of the skill that can be seen and the underlying processes that led to the performance can be overlooked (Coker, 2013). Errors can be a function of technique, physiological deficiencies, inaccurate or delayed decision making, drill design, or psychological factors (see Figure 2-4).

To illustrate, fatigue, incorrectly anticipating a teammate's location, or a technique error could all be viable causes of an off-target pass in soccer. Similarly, in baseball, consistently fouling off to the right could be the result of misidentifying the pitch, a delay in its identification, slow bat speed due to the use of a long, swooping swing, or the misdirection of attentional focus as is the case when an athlete is thinking about past failures against the pitcher rather than adopting the needed narrow-external focus (see Chapter 15) to locate critical cues about the pitch. Because the appropriate intervention strategy will be different for each possibility, correctly identifying the true cause of the error is critical to the performance enhancement process. In addition, before assuming that the error observed is the fault of the performer, coaches should ensure that the drill or activity selected matches the target goal and that equipment and tasks are developmentally appropriate. For example, the technique used by youngsters when shooting a basketball often resembles that of a shot-putting motion. While the intent of the practice may be proper technique development, the goal of the performer is to get the ball in the basket. If the youngster is not strong enough to successfully propel the ball using proper form, he or she will likely adopt a technique that will allow for the generation of more force (similar to a shot-put motion), in order to achieve the goal of getting the ball in the basket. The appropriate intervention in this case is not to attempt to correct the technical flaws viewed but to instead lower the basket and/or use a smaller ball. By making the activity more developmentally appropriate, a new movement pattern will be adopted resulting in improved technique.

Once errors and their cause have been identified, the next step is to select which error to correct. With beginners especially, several performance errors are probably occurring simultaneously. If the coach tried to give feedback about every error observed, the athlete would likely be overloaded with too much information, resulting in very little correction on the next trial. Consequently, only one error should

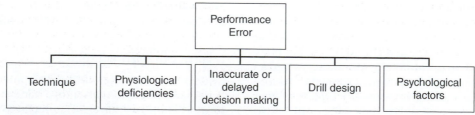

Figure 2-4 Possible sources of performance errors

be addressed at a time. Given multiple errors, where does one begin? The coach should try to identify the error that is most fundamental or critical. This error will often be associated with the skill's fundamental movement pattern, or the key technical components that influence the final outcome. Very often, one error is the cause of other errors, and if the critical error can be corrected, others may be eliminated. Another approach is to identify the critical error that occurs earliest in the sequence. For example, in diving, if the approach on the board is incorrect, the takeoff, the dive itself, and the entry will likely be adversely affected. By correcting the faulty approach, the errors that emerged later in the sequence as a consequence are likely to be eliminated. Finally, when multiple errors seem unrelated, a good strategy is to select the one that is easiest to learn and leads to the greatest improvement. This strategy is advantageous in that it will motivate the athlete to continue to put forth the effort needed to learn the skill.

Intervention Strategies

Once an error has been identified and its source determined, the role of the coach shifts to the provision of feedback and/or the manipulation of task or practice variables to improve performance.

Feedback

The provision of performance related feedback is considered essential for motor skill acquisition as it assists in guiding the learner in modifying subsequent movement attempts. More specifically, it can reinforce a behavior, provide information about the correctness of a performance attempt, explain why an error occurred, prescribe how to fix an error and motivate athletes to continue working toward their goals (see Figure 2-5). However, practitioners should not make the assumption that simply providing feedback will lead to positive change. Feedback acts as a constraint that shapes a learner's efforts to achieve the task goal. Because the learner will attempt to achieve what was prescribed, feedback can either hinder or facilitate skill development depending on its

frequency, timing, amount, precision, and the learner's task-related experiences (Magill, 2013).

Because of its guidance quality, many people intuitively think that the more feedback given, the greater the gains in learning and performance. This, however, is not the case. While athletes do need a higher frequency of feedback initially to develop an understanding of the movement being learned, those who are refining their skills should actually receive less. When feedback is given too often, athletes become accustomed to receiving it. As a result, rather than evaluating response-produced sensory information, they will simply wait for the coach to tell them what they did and how to fix it. This results in passive learners whose dependency on their coach not only impedes skill development but can also have detrimental effects on performance when feedback is withdrawn as it often is during competition (e.g., Butki & Hoffman, 2003).

Several methods for reducing feedback frequency have been found effective for skill development. In the *faded feedback* approach, coaches give feedback more often early in the learning process, then gradually reduce the rate as athletes' skill proficiency increases (Winstein & Schmidt, 1990). In *bandwidth feedback,* the coach identifies an acceptable error tolerance, or "bandwidth," and provides feedback only when the athlete's performance falls outside this range (e.g., Smith, Taylor & Withers, 1997; Chambers & Vickers, 2006). For example, a bandwidth for putting performance in golf could be a two-foot radius around the hole with mid-length putts; if the putt stops anywhere outside of this range, the athlete would be provided with feedback, perhaps related to swing ratio. The advantage of this method is that it is based on the athlete's actual performance rather than some arbitrary, fixed schedule. Finally, *learner-regulated feedback,* where augmented feedback is provided to the athlete only when he or she requests it, is an alternative strategy that has also been shown to be effective (e.g., Chen, Kaufman, & Chung, 2001; Chiviacowsky & Wulf, 2002, 2005). Because athletes control when augmented feedback is given, feedback frequency is individualized. Moreover, the athlete is thought to benefit by becoming actively engaged in the learning process.

To further promote active learning, coaches should not only give their athletes the opportunity to attend to and process response-produced sensory information before offering corrections (Anderson, Magill, Sekiya, & Ryan, 2005) but also encourage them to assess their performance before telling them what was observed (Chen, 2001). Prompt them to do so by asking whether or not they achieved their movement goal and then ask more specific follow-up questions. This *questioning* approach promotes reflective thinking and facilitates the athletes' development of the necessary problem-solving skills to determine their own errors and the corresponding adjustments needed for their correction (Chambers and Vickers, 2006).

Since feedback plays a major role in how a learner will modify subsequent movement attempts, coaches must also choose their words carefully when conveying information. In some instances, a movement pattern that may not be ideal for the individual may be imposed and adopted as a result of the correction(s) prescribed (Williams, & Hodges, 2005). Good feedback encourages learners to explore a variety of movement solutions allowing for the discovery

of the optimal pattern suited for that particular learner (Williams, 2003). Good feedback also focuses on one correction at a time, is positive, short, and simple, and matches the learner's developmental level. The common practice of providing movement-related feedback should also be reconsidered. Porter, Wu and Partridge (2010) reported that 84.6 percent of elite track and field coaches gave feedback related to specific body and limb movements. This form of feedback prompts athletes to adopt an *internal focus* of attention, which mounting evidence disputes. Instead, superior learning and performance has been found when athletes are prompted to focus on the effects their actions have on the environment (*external focus;* see Wulf, 2007 for a review). In other words, rather than telling a sprinter to increase the turnover of their leg action to increase speed (internal focus), the athlete could alternatively be given the external focus of minimizing ground contact (Porter, Wu & Partridge, 2010). The latter prescription is less likely to disrupt the natural flow of the movement and allows for the discovery of how to achieve the movement goal enhancing learning and performance.

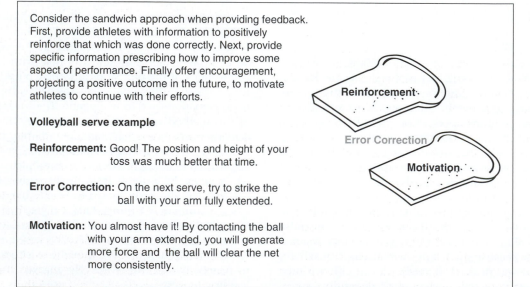

Consider the sandwich approach when providing feedback. First, provide athletes with information to positively reinforce that which was done correctly. Next, provide specific information prescribing how to improve some aspect of performance. Finally offer encouragement, projecting a positive outcome in the future, to motivate athletes to continue with their efforts.

Volleyball serve example

Reinforcement: Good! The position and height of your toss was much better that time.

Error Correction: On the next serve, try to strike the ball with your arm fully extended.

Motivation: You almost have it! By contacting the ball with your arm extended, you will generate more force and the ball will clear the net more consistently.

Reinforcement

Error Correction

Motivation

Figure 2-5 **The sandwich approach for providing feedback**

Table 2-2 **Examples of Task and Practice Variables that can be Manipulated to Facilitate the Emergence of Improved Technique and/or tactics**

Rules	Equipment	Task Criteria	Situational Factors	Playing Area
• Size of playing area • Movement skills used to play the game • Number of players • Scoring system • Number of contacts	• Size • Weight • Length • Grip diameter • Texture	• Distance • Speed • Accuracy • Force • Size of goal or target	• Relative positioning of players • Number of attackers vs. defenders • Terrain, layout, and/or conditions of a course • Ball distribution	• Size • Shape • Position of goals/shooting areas

From *Motor Learning and Control for Practitioners*, 3e, by Cheryl A. Coker. Copyright © 2013 by Holcomb Hathaway Publishers. Used with permission.

Manipulating Task and/or Practice Variables

While there is a tendency to rely on the provision of feedback for error correction, coaches can also influence change by manipulating task and/or practice variables. By imposing rule modifications, changing equipment characteristics, altering playing area dimensions, manipulating situational factors during performance and altering task criteria, practitioners can create action possibilities that allow for the emergence of improved techniques and/or tactics by capitalizing on the process of guided discovery (Williams, 2003). For example, a no contact rule could be established forcing defensive players to learn positioning and funneling strategies (Turner, 2005). Soccer skills can be improved by playing Futsal. The smaller pitch demands rapid decision making as players are constantly under pressure from the opposition and playing area boundaries. Also, the smaller low-bounce ball of Futsal promotes the development of greater ball control. In lacrosse, defenders can be strategically positioned at different distances between the shooter and the target to allow for the exploration of different shooting strategies (manipulating situational factors). Finally, improved skill performance can be achieved by manipulating task criteria as demonstrated by Chow, Davids, Button and Koh (2008), whose participants learned the soccer chip shot through practice kicking a ball over a height barrier to targets at varying distances in the absence

of any instruction regarding technique. See Table 2-2 for other examples of task and practice variables that can be manipulated to facilitate the emergence of improved technique and/or tactics.

Case Study

What follows is a case study with corresponding questions designed to test your ability to integrate the motor learning concepts from this chapter. Read through the situation presented. Assess the characteristics of the learner, the task(s), and the performance context, then determine what you would do to design a more effective learning experience. Compare your completed answers to the sample responses provided for Situation #1. If your answers fall short, review them to assure that they are as thorough and thoughtful as the sample response to Situation #1.

1. The varsity basketball coach at your high school is taking a leave of absence in the middle of the season and you have been hired as the interim coach. To assist with the transition, you observe the coach's practices the week before his departure. You note that the players appear to have good fundamentals and can execute the coach's drills without much challenge. For example, to work on shooting the athletes dribbled the ball to six positions around the key taking 15 shots at each location before moving to the next one.

The shooting percentage during this drill was impressive. The players' performance in the game later that week however, was much different. They seemed flustered, were hesitant when deciding whether to shoot, pass or drive to the basket, and missed many of their shots.

Question

Based on the information provided in the above situation, describe how you will design practice to improve game performance.

2. The coach is getting frustrated that his players can't execute their offense the way they did in practice. He calls a time-out to give his team the following feedback:

What is going on out there? We practiced moving around the court to get into position to receive the ball all week! You need to cut to the basket, come off screens aggressively, and move around! Now get back out there and make their defense work. If you can't figure it out, I'll put someone else in who can!

Questions

a. Rewrite the above feedback statement to increase its effectiveness. Explain why your rewrite is more effective.

b. Design a drill to improve the players' proficiency at finding an open space on offense.

Situation #1 Sample Response

Learner

Given that the athletes are on the varsity basketball team, it can be assumed that they are in the associative stage of learning for the skills of shooting, dribbling, and passing.

Task

With the exception of the free throw, the skills used in the game of basketball are classified as open skills. Accordingly, practice should promote diversification as the athlete needs to be able to quickly adapt to the demands of the performance situation. In other words, practice should be game-like so that the athlete becomes better at anticipating changes in the performance context.

Performance Context

For shooting, the performance context variations that will influence how the athlete must execute the skill include the distance and angle from the basket, taking the shot off a dribble or pass, the type of pass that precedes the shot, the position and actions of the defensive players, and the position and actions of teammates.

Designing Practice

The shooting drill described above where players dribbled the ball to six positions around the key taking 15 shots at each location before moving to the next one is an example of blocked practice, a strategy more appropriate for beginners who are trying to get the idea of the movement. Because these athletes are in the associative stage of learning and the task of shooting during a game is an open skill, drill design should promote diversification and increased levels of contextual interference. This is accomplished through a combination of variable and random practice. In other words, multiple skills and skill variations (as determined through the assessment of the performance context) should be practiced in a repeated blocked or random order. While this can be accomplished in numerous ways, the following is an example of how the shooting drill described in the scenario could be redesigned:

To improve players' decision making regarding whether to shoot, pass, or drive to the basket, they must be taught what critical cues to look for, where to look for them, and be provided with a variety of practice experience where they have to identify and respond to those cues. For example, if there are two defenders in the lane, driving to the basket will be ineffective. However, when a defender is guarding too closely, an opportunity to drive to the basket presents itself. In addition, the defender is vulnerable on the side of

A player dribbles to 1 and executes a shot. Then he runs to 2 where he receives a bounce pass and shoots. He follows his shot, gets the rebound and dribbles to 3 where a defender will challenge him and he has the option to shoot or drive to the basket. At 4 another defender awaits. The player receives a chest pass and has to decide whether to penetrate the lane or pass to a player standing under the basket. If he penetrated the lane, he rebounds and dribbles to 5. If he decided to pass, the receiver passes the ball back to him at 5 where he executes an undefended jump shot, follows his shot, rebounds then dribbles to 6 and shoots over a defender.

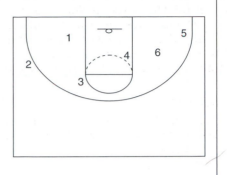

Figure 2-6 **Sample redesign of case study shooting drill**

his forward foot, which typically corresponds to the arm held in the highest position. Rather than cue players to look at their opponents' feet, direct their visual attention to the torso area allowing them to both read the defender's arm position and see the floor.

Summary

This chapter has focused on one of the most important roles of a coach, that of a teacher of motor skills. The motor learning process is incredibly complex. Coaches should strive to develop a working knowledge of that process because it is foundational to the structuring of optimal practice experiences and the design of effective intervention strategies for skill acquisition and performance enhancement.

Study Questions

1. Define the term *motor learning* and explain why learning must remain an inference based on performance.
2. Briefly describe Fitts and Posner's three phases of motor skill learning.
3. How is proprioception, or "feel," important in motor performance?
4. What are the effects of asking highly skilled performers to consciously attend to their movements?
5. Explain why the coach's role as motivator is so important during the autonomous phase of learning.

6. Describe how a coach should proceed to change a highly skilled athlete's well-learned technique.

7. What general guidelines should a coach consider in deciding to use the whole method versus the part method of practice?

8. How could one use blocked practice to teach several skills? Random practice? Which would be more effective and why?

9. Give an example of how a coach could use variable practice to teach several variations of a skill.

10. What changes should take place in the frequency of feedback given as a learner progresses from the cognitive to the associative stage of learning? Fully explain the reasons for these changes and provide one example of a method that can be used to accomplish this.

11. What variables can be manipulated to prompt the emergence of improved techniques and/or tactics by capitalizing on the process of guided discovery?

References

Anderson, D. I., Magill, R. A., Sekiya, H., & Ryan, G. (2005). Support for an explanation of the guidance effect in motor skill learning. *Journal of Motor Behavior, 37,* 231–238.

Barreiros, J., Figueiredo, T., & Godinho, M. (2007). The contextual interference effect in applied settings. *European Physical Education Review, 12,* 195–208.

Battig, W. F. (1966). Facilitation and interference. In E. A. Bilodeau (Ed.), *Acquisition of skill* (pp. 215–244). New York: Academic Press.

Brady, F. (2008). The contextual interference effect in sport skills. *Perceptual and Motor Skills, 106,* 461–472.

Butki, B. D., & Hoffman, S. J. (2003). Effects of reducing frequency of intrinsic knowledge of results on the learning of a motor skill. *Perceptual and Motor Skills, 97,* 569–580.

Chambers, K. L., & Vickers, J. N. (2006) The effect of bandwidth feedback and questioning on competitive swim performance. *The Sport Psychologist, 20,* 184–197.

Chen, D. D. (2001). Trends in augmented research and tips for the practitioner. *Journal of Physical Education, Recreation, and Dance, 72*(1), 32–36.

Chen, D. D., Kaufman, D., & Chung, M. W. (2001). Emergent patterns of feedback strategies in performing a closed motor skill. *Perceptual and Motor Skills, 93,* 197–204.

Chiviacowsky, S., & Wulf, G. (2002). Self-controlled feedback: Does it enhance learning because performers get feedback when they need it? *Research Quarterly for Exercise and Sport, 73,* 408–415.

Chiviacowsky, S., & Wulf, G. (2005). Self-controlled feedback is effective if it is based on the learner's performance. *Research Quarterly for Exercise and Sport, 76,* 42–48.

Christina, R. W., & Corcos, D. M. (1988). *Coaches' guide to teaching sport skills.* Champaign, IL: Human Kinetics.

Coker, C. A. (2013). *Motor learning and control for practitioners.* Scottsdale, AZ: Holcomb Hathaway Publishers.

Coker, C. A. (2006). To break it down or not break it down: That is the question. *Teaching Elementary Physical Education, 17,* 27–28.

Chow, J. Y., Davids, K. W., Button, C. & Koh, M. (2008). Coordination changes in a discrete multi-articular action as a function of practice. *Acta Psychologica, 127*(1), 163.

Douvis, S. (2005). Variable practice in learning the forehand drive in tennis. *Perceptual and Motor Skills, 101,* 531–545.

Ericsson, K. A. (2003). Development of elite performance and deliberate practice: An update from the perspective of the expert performance approach. In J. L. Starkes & K. A. Ericsson (Eds.), *Expert performance in sports: Advances in research on sport expertise* (pp. 49–83). Champaign, IL: Human Kinetics.

Ericsson, K. A., Krampe, R. T., & Tesch-Römer, C. (1993). The role of deliberate practice in the acquisition of expert performance. *Psychological Review, 100,* 363–406.

Fitts, P. M., & Posner, M. I. (1967). *Human performance.* Pacific Grove, CA: Brooks/Cole.

Gentile, A. M. (2000). Skill acquisition: Action, movement, and the neuromotor processes. In J. H. Carr, R. B. Shepard, J. Gordon, A. M. Gentile, & J. M. Hind (Eds.), *Movement science: Foundations for physical therapy in rehabilitation* (pp. 111–187). Rockville, MD: Aspen.

Goode, S., & Magill, R. A. (1986). Contextual interference effects in learning three badminton serves. *Research Quarterly for Exercise and Sport, 57,* 308–314.

Hall, S. J. (2012). *Basic biomechanics.* New York: McGraw-Hill.

Hebert, E. P., Landin, D., & Solmon, M. A. (1996). Practice schedule effects on the performance and learning of low- and high-skilled students: An applied study. *Research Quarterly for Exercise and Sport, 67,* 52–58.

Janelle, C. M., Champenoy, J. D., Coombes, S. A. & Mousseau, M. B. (2003). Mechanisms of attentional cueing during observational learning to facilitate motor skill acquisition. *Journal of Sports Sciences, 21,* 825–838.

Keller, G. J., Li, Y., Weiss, L. W. & Relyea, G. E. (2006). Contextual interference effect on acquisition and retention of pistol shooting skills. *Perceptual and Motor Skills, 103,* 241–252.

Knudson D. V. (2013). *Qualitative diagnosis of human movement: Improving performance in sport and exercise.* Champaign, IL: Human Kinetics.

Landin, D., & Hebert, E. P. (1997). A comparison of three practice schedules along the contextual interference continuum. *Research Quarterly for Exercise and Sport, 68,* 357–361.

Lee, T. D., & Magill, R. A. (1983). The locus of contextual interference in motor-skill acquisition. *Journal of Experimental Psychology: Learning, Memory, and Cognition, 9,* 730–746.

Li, Y., & Wright, D. L. (2000). An assessment of the attention demands of random and blocked practice. *Quarterly Journal of Experimental Psychology, 53A,* 591–606.

Magill, R. A. (2004). Motor learning and control: Concepts and applications. *Motor learning: Concepts and applications.* St. Louis, MO: McGraw-Hill.

Magill, R. A. (2013). *Motor learning and control: Concepts and applications.* St. Louis, MO: McGraw-Hill.

Magill, R. A. (1998). Knowledge is more than we talk about: Implicit learning in motor skill acquisition. *Research Quarterly for Exercise and Sport, 69,* 104–110.

Nagano, T., Kato, T., & Fukuda, T. (2004). Visual search strategies of soccer players in one-on-one defense situations on the field. *Perceptual and Motor Skills, 99,* 968–974.

Raab, M., Masters, R. S. W., & Maxwell, J. P. (2005). Improving the 'how' and 'what' decisions of elite table tennis players. *Human Movement Science, 24,* 326–344.

Passos, P., Araujo, D., Davids, K. W., & Shuttleworth, R. (2010) Manipulating task constraints to improve tactical knowledge and collective decision-making in rugby union. In I. Renshaw, K. W. Davids & G.J.P Savelsbergh (Eds.), *Motor Learning in Practice: A Constraints-Led Approach,* pp. 120–130. London: Routledge (Taylor & Francis Group).

Porter, J. M., Landin, D., Hebert, E. P., & Baum, B. (2007). The effects of three levels of contextual interference on performance outcomes and movement patterns in golf skills. *International Journal of Sports Science & Coaching, 2*(3), 243–255.

Porter, J. M., Wu, W. F. W., & Partridge, J. (2010). Focus of attention and verbal instructions: Strategies of elite track and field coaches and athletes. *Sport Science Review, 19,* 199–211.

Schmidt, R. A. (1975). A schema theory of discrete motor skill learning. *Psychological Review, 82,* 225–260.

Shea, J. B., & Morgan, R. L. (1979). Contextual interference effects on the acquisition, retention, and transfer of a motor skill. *Journal of Experimental Psychology: Human Learning and Memory, 5,* 179–187.

Shea, J. B., & Zimny, S. T. (1983). Context effects in memory and learning movement information. In R. A. Magill (Ed.), *Memory and control of action* (pp. 345–366). Amsterdam: North-Holland.

Shea, J. B., & Zimny, S. T. (1988). Knowledge incorporation in motor representation. In O. G. Meijer & K. Roth (Eds.), *Complex movement behaviour: "The" motor-action controversy* (pp. 289–314). Amsterdam: Elsevier Science Publishers B. V.

Shoenfelt, E. L., Snyder, L. A., Maue, A. E., McDowell, C. P., & Woolard, C. D. (2002). Comparison of constant and variable practice conditions on free throw shooting. *Perceptual and Motor Skills, 94,* 1113–1123.

Smith, P. J. K. (2002). Applying contextual interference to snowboarding skills. *Perceptual and Motor Skills, 95,* 999–1005.

Smith, P. J. K., Taylor, S. J., & Withers, K. (1997). Applying bandwidth feedback scheduling to a golf shot. *Research Quarterly for Exercise and Sport, 68,* 215–221.

Turner, A. P. 2005. Teaching and learning games at the secondary level. In L. L. Griffin and J. L. Butler (Eds.), *Teaching games for understanding: Theory, research and practice,* 71–90. Champaign, IL: Human Kinetics.

Vickers, J. N. (2007). *Perception, cognition and decision training: The quiet eye in action.* Champaign, IL: Human Kinetics.

Williams, A. M. (2003). Learning football skills effectively: Challenging tradition. *Insight: The FA Coaches Association Journal, 6*(2), 37–39.

Williams, A. M. & Hodges, N. J. (2005). Practice, instruction and skill acquisition: Challenging tradition. *Journal of Sport Sciences, 23*(6), 637–650.

Williams, A. M., Jannelle, C. M., and Davids, K. (2004). Constraints on the search for visual information in sport. *International Journal of Sport and Exercise Psychology, 2*(3), 301–318.

Winstein, C. J., & Schmidt, R. A. (1990). Reduced frequency of knowledge of results enhances motor skill learning. *Journal of Experimental Psychology: Learning, Memory, and Cognition, 16,* 677–691.

Wrisberg, C. A., & Liu, Z. (1991). The effect of contextual variety on the practice, retention, and transfer of an applied motor skill. *Research Quarterly for Exercise and Sport, 62,* 406–412

Wulf, G. (2007a). *Attention and skill learning.* Champaign, IL: Human Kinetics.

Wulf, G. (2007). Attentional focus and motor learning: a review of 10 years of research. *E-Journal Bewegung und Training,* 1–11.

A Positive Approach to Coaching Effectiveness and Performance Enhancement

Ronald E. Smith, *University of Washington*

Profound responsibilities come with teaching and coaching. You can do so much good–or harm. It's why I believe that next to parenting, teaching and coaching are the two most important professions in the world.

—Hall of Fame basketball coach John Wooden

You've got to be careful if you don't know where you're going cause you might not get there.

—Yogi Berra, Hall of Fame baseball player

Much of human interaction consists of attempts to influence the behavior of other people. Influence attempts occur constantly in virtually every life setting. Sometimes the attempts are directed at influencing attitudes, motives, values, or emotions. At other times social interactions or task performance are the targets of influence attempts.

Sport is a setting where all of these targets of influence—thoughts, emotions, motivational factors, and behaviors—are relevant. Influence attempts occur constantly as athletes interact with teammates, opponents, officials, and their coaches. In the discussion to follow I will focus on influence attempts directed by coaches to their athletes and provide a conceptual framework to which other topics in this book, such as motivational processes (Chapter 4), goal setting

(Chapter 11), and intervention programs directed toward coaches (Chapter 18) may be related. My focus will be primarily on enhancing sport performance, although, as you'll see, this goal is intimately related to the psychosocial climate created by interactions among coaches and athletes. Although emphasis is on improving coaching effectiveness, the principles discussed can be applied by sport psychologists in their work and to such diverse situations as parenting skills.

Coaches try to influence their players in many important ways. One of their most important goals is to create a good learning situation where athletes can acquire the technical skills needed to succeed as individuals and as a team. Another priority for most coaches is to create a social environment where the participants can experience positive interactions with one another. This is certainly a key factor in building team cohesion, in making athletes more receptive to technical instruction, and in fostering a supportive environment where athletes can develop teamwork, dedication, "mental toughness," and other valued traits. Indeed, virtually everything coaches do can be viewed as attempts to increase certain desired behaviors and to decrease undesirable behaviors.

The "psychology of coaching" is essentially a set of strategies designed to increase a coach's ability to influence the behavior of others more effectively. It is often said that stripped of its jargon and complexities, psychology is basically the application of common sense. I believe the basic principles of learning discussed in this chapter—positive (as opposed to aversive) control, reinforcement, and performance feedback—make good sense. But more important, they have been shown in many scientific studies to be among the most effective ways to increase motivation, morale, enjoyment of the athletic situation, and performance.

Operant Conditioning: The ABCs of Behavior Control

To understand what motivates people and controls their behavior, we must take into account the relations between people and their environment, and this is the focus of research on **operant conditioning** (Martin & Pear, 2007).

The operant analysis of behavior involves the study of relations between three kinds of events: **antecedents** (A), or environmental stimuli; behaviors (B) in which the person engages; and consequences (C) that follow the behaviors and either strengthen or weaken them. The relations that exist among these "if, then" elements are called **contingencies.** The ABCs of contingencies can be expressed in the following way:

IF antecedent stimuli (A) are present

AND behavior (B) is enacted,

THEN a particular consequence (C) will occur.

Two aspects of these relations are of interest. The first is the relation between antecedents and behaviors (A and B); the second is the contingency between behavior and its consequences (B and C).

Antecedents: Stimulus Control of Behavior

Through experience we learn which behaviors have which consequences under which conditions. Antecedents that signal the likely consequences of particular behaviors in given situations are known as **discriminative stimuli.** These signals help guide our behavior so that it is "appropriate" and will most likely lead to positive consequences. Much skill learning in sports involves learning to "read" the environment and respond appropriately. Thus, a basketball player learns how to set up the offense when the opponent switches from one defense to another. The same player also may learn that it is not a good idea to crack jokes in the presence of the coach after a tough loss. When antecedents are influential in governing a behavior, that behavior is said to be under **stimulus control.**

With experience in sports, many behaviors come under stimulus control, and we react automatically and mindlessly to changing stimulus conditions. The same thing occurs in the realm of social behaviors.

Response Consequences

The key feature in operant conditioning is what happens after a response is made. In general, consequences always involve either the presentation, the nonoccurrence, or the removal of a positive or an unpleasant or aversive stimulus. For example, in the coach–athlete interaction a positive stimulus may be a word of praise or a smile, and an aversive stimulus may be critical comments by the coach.

Figure 3-1 shows five basic response consequences that result from the presentation or removal of positive or aversive stimuli in response to a given behavior. Presentation of a positive (rewarding) stimulus is called **positive reinforcement,** and it increases the likelihood

	Present	**Remove**
Positive Stimuli	Positive reinforcement *(strengthens behavior)*	Extinction *(weakens behavior)* Response cost punishment *(weakens behavior)*
Aversive Stimuli	Aversive punishment *(suppresses/weakens behavior)*	Negative reinforcement *(strengthens behavior)*

Figure 3-1 Five basic response consequences created by the presentation or removal of positive or negative stimuli and their effects on behavior

that the behavior will occur in the future under the same conditions. **Negative reinforcement** involves *removal or avoidance* of aversive stimuli, the effect being a strengthening of the behavior that results in successful escape or avoidance. For example, an athlete may drop out of a sport program to escape an abusive coach, or a gymnast who has been injured may avoid performing a particular routine because of anxiety concerning possible reinjury. In the latter case the avoidance response may become stronger over time because each time it occurs it is negatively reinforced by anxiety reduction.

Removal of a positive stimulus that has in the past followed the behavior results in **extinction,** reducing the likelihood of the behavior. Extinction of operant behaviors occurs when reinforcement stops. Thus, if an athlete stops getting attention for inappropriate comments, that behavior is likely to decrease. When previously reinforced behaviors no longer "pay off," we are likely to abandon them and replace them with more successful ones.

Other consequences involve either presentation or removal of unpleasant, aversive stimuli, as the two forms of punishment illustrate. **Aversive punishment** entails the *presentation* of aversive stimuli, with the effect of suppressing the behavior. Thus, a coach who harshly criticizes an athlete for being late for practice will probably find a marked reduction in tardiness in the future. Another form of punishment, known as **response cost,** involves *removal of something*

positive, as when an athlete is benched after performing poorly. Here is another example of response cost punishment:

> *The legendary baseball umpire Bill Klem once called a batter out on a close third strike. The enraged batter flung his bat high into the air and whirled around to argue the call. Klem whipped off his mask, fixed the batter with a steely gaze, and said, "If that bat comes down, it'll cost you 100 bucks."* (Smith, 1993, p. 280)

The term *negative reinforcement* is sometimes confused with punishment, but the two are clearly different. Punishment reduces the likelihood of a behavior, whereas negative reinforcement, like positive reinforcement, strengthens the behavior.

Positive and Aversive Approaches to Influencing Behavior

As our cursory examination of response consequences and their influence on behavior suggests, two basic approaches can influence the behavior of others. Psychologists refer to these as **positive control** (use of positive reinforcement) and **aversive control (use of punishment).** Both forms of control are based on the fact that behavior is strongly influenced by the consequences it produces. Positive and aversive control, in turn, underlie the *positive approach* and the *negative approach* to coaching (see Chapter 18).

The positive approach is designed to strengthen desired behaviors by motivating players to perform them and by reinforcing the behaviors when they occur. The negative approach involves attempts to eliminate unwanted behaviors through punishment and criticism. The motivating factor in this approach is fear. Observational studies of coaches indicate that most coaches use a combination of positive and aversive control (Smith, Shoda, Cumming, & Smoll, 2009).

In our society, aversive control through punishment is perhaps the most widespread means of controlling behavior. Our system of laws is backed up by threats of punishment. Similarly, fear of failure is one means of promoting school achievement, social development, and other desired behaviors. The reason punishment is the glue that holds so much of our society's fabric together is that, for the most part, it seems to work. It is the fastest way to bring behavior under control. In sports it finds one mode of expression in the negative approach to coaching.

Frequently in sport we hear the statement, "The team that makes the fewest mistakes will win"—and, indeed, this is usually the case. Many coaches, therefore, develop coaching tactics oriented toward eliminating mistakes. The most natural approach is to use aversive control. To get rid of mistakes, we simply punish and criticize athletes who make them. The assumption is that if we make players fearful enough of making mistakes they are more likely to perform well.

Negative Side Effects of Punishment

When you punish your people for making a mistake or falling short of a goal, you create an environment of extreme caution, even fearfulness. In sports it's similar to playing "not to lose"—a formula that often brings on defeat.

John Wooden

There is clear evidence that punishment and criticism can decrease unwanted behaviors. Unfortunately, the evidence is equally compelling that punishment has certain undesirable side effects that can actually interfere with what a coach is trying to accomplish. First, punishment works by arousing fear. If used excessively, punishment promotes the development of fear of failure, and this is undoubtedly the least desirable form of athletic motivation. If it becomes the predominant motive for athletic performance, it not only decreases enjoyment of the activity but also increases the likelihood of failure. The athlete with a high fear of failure is motivated not by a positive desire to achieve and enjoy "the thrill of victory" but by a dread of "the agony of defeat." Athletic competition is transformed from a challenge into a threat. Because high anxiety disrupts motor performance and interferes with thinking, the high fear of failure athlete is prone to "choke" under pressure because he or she concentrates more on the feared consequences of mistakes than on what needs to be done in a positive sense. Research has shown that athletes having high fear of failure not only perform more poorly in competition but also are at greater risk for injury, enjoy the sport experience less, and are more likely to drop out (Smith, Smoll, & Passer, 2002). The research literature also shows that the quickest and most effective way to develop fear of failure is by punishing people when they fail. Thus, coaches who create fear of failure through the use of punishment may, ironically, increase the likelihood that their athletes will make the very mistakes they are trying to prevent and may make athletes afraid to take risks of any kind.

Punishment has other potential side effects that most coaches wish to avoid. A predominance of aversive control makes for an unpleasant teaching situation. It arouses resentment and hostility, which may be masked by the power differential that exists between coach and athlete. It may produce a kind of cohesion among players based on their mutual hatred for the coach, but most coaches would prefer other bases for team cohesion. It is even possible that players may consciously or subconsciously act in ways that sabotage what the coach is trying to accomplish. Moreover, coaches occupy a role that athletes admire, and they should not overlook their importance as role models. The abusive coach is certainly not exhibiting the kind of behavior that will contribute to the personal growth of athletes who emulate the coach.

Does this mean coaches should avoid all criticism and punishment of their athletes? Not at all. Sometimes these behaviors are necessary for instructional or disciplinary purposes, but they should be used sparingly and with a full appreciation for their potential negative side effects. The negative approach should never be the primary approach to athletes. This is particularly the case where child athletes are concerned, but it also applies at higher competitive levels, including professional sports.

Although abusive coaches may enjoy success and may even be admired by some of their players, they run the risk of losing other players who could contribute to the team's success and who could profit personally from an athletic experience. Those who succeed through the use of aversive control usually do so because (a) they are also able to communicate caring for their players as people, so athletes don't take the abuse personally; (b) they have very talented athletes; (c) they recruit thick-skinned athletes who are less affected by aversive feedback; or (d) they are such skilled teachers and strategists that these abilities overshadow their negative approach. In other words, such coaches win in spite of, not because of, the negative approach they espouse.

The second form of punishment, response cost, involves depriving people of something they value. This form of punishment has two distinct advantages over aversive punishment. First, even though response cost may arouse temporary frustration or anger, it does not create the kind of fear that aversive punishment does. It is therefore less likely to cause avoidance of the punisher or the punishing situation, and it may actually increase the attractiveness of the withdrawn reinforcer (which can then be used to reinforce desired alternative behaviors). Second, the punisher is not modeling abusive aggression, so there is less opportunity for learning aggression through imitation. For these reasons, the response cost procedure is a preferred alternative to aversive punishment. In using such punishment, it is useful to verbalize the contingency in a matter-of-fact fashion, without expressing anger, for example, "I don't like to do this, but because you were late for practice, it automatically means you get less playing time during our next game."

The Positive Alternative

Fortunately, there is an alternative to the negative approach. As a means of influencing behavior, it can accomplish everything aversive control does and much more—without the harmful side effects. The positive approach is aimed at strengthening desired behaviors through the use of encouragement, positive reinforcement, and sound technical instruction carried out within a supportive atmosphere. From this point of view the best way to eliminate mistakes is not to try to stamp them out with punishment but to strengthen the correct or desired behaviors. The motivational force at work here is a positive desire to achieve rather than a negative fear of failure. Mistakes are seen not as totally negative occurrences but as, in the words of John Wooden, "stepping stones to achievement that provide the information needed to improve performance." The positive approach, through its emphasis on improving rather than on "not screwing up," fosters a more positive learning environment and tends to promote more positive relationships among coaches and athletes. Research has clearly shown that athletes like positive coaches better, enjoy their athletic experience more and report higher team cohesion when playing for them, and perform at a higher level when positive control techniques are used (Smith & Smoll, 2011). Even negative control procedures work more effectively if they occur within a context of positive interactions.

The cornerstone of the positive approach is the skillful use of positive reinforcement to increase motivation and to strengthen desired behaviors. Another highly effective technique is the use of performance feedback. Let's discuss these specific techniques.

Positive Reinforcement: Getting Good Things to Happen

As noted earlier, positive reinforcement is any consequence that increases the likelihood of a behavior that it follows. Reinforcement can take many possible forms: verbal compliments, smiles or other nonverbal behaviors that convey approval, increased privileges, awards, and so on.

The effective use of reinforcement to strengthen behavior requires that a coach (a) find a reinforcer that works for a particular athlete, (b) make the occurrence of reinforcement dependent on performance of the desired behavior, and (c) make sure the athlete understands why the reinforcement is being given. The relations between behaviors and their consequences are termed **reinforcement contingencies.**

Choosing Effective Reinforcers

You can observe a lot by watching.

—*Yogi Berra*

Choosing a reinforcer is not usually difficult, but in some instances the coach's ingenuity and sensitivity to the needs of individual athletes may be tested. Potential reinforcers include social behaviors such as verbal praise, smiles, nonverbal signs such as applause, or physical contact such as a pat on the back. They also include the opportunity to engage in certain activities (such as extra batting practice) or to play with a particular piece of equipment.

Social reinforcers are most frequently employed in athletics, but even here the coach must decide what is most likely to be effective with each athlete. One athlete might find praise given in the presence of others highly reinforcing, whereas another might find it embarrassing. The best way for a coach to find an effective reinforcer is to get to know each athlete's likes and dislikes. If at all possible, it is a good idea to use a variety of reinforcers and vary what one says and does so that the coach does not begin to sound like a broken record. In the final analysis the acid test of one's choice of reinforcer is whether it affects behavior in the desired manner.

The effectiveness of verbal reinforcement can be increased by combining it with a specific description of the desirable behavior the athlete just performed. For example, a coach might say, "Way to go, Bob. Your head stayed right down on the ball on that swing." In this way the power of the reinforcement is combined with an instructional reminder of what the athlete should do. This also cues the athlete to what the coach wants him to concentrate on.

Selecting and Reinforcing Target Behaviors

Systematic use of reinforcement forces coaches to be specific in their own minds about exactly which behaviors they want to reinforce in a given athlete at a particular time. Obviously, they will not want to reinforce everything an athlete does correctly, lest the power of the reinforcer be diluted. The most effective use of "reward power" is to strengthen skills an athlete is just beginning to master. In many instances complex skills can be broken down into their component subskills, and coaches can concentrate on one subskill at a time until it is mastered. For example, a football coach might choose to concentrate entirely on the pattern run by a pass receiver, with no concern about whether or not the pass is completed. This is where a coach's knowledge of the sport and of the mastery levels of individual athletes is crucial. Athletes can enjoy lots of support and reinforcement long before they have completely mastered the entire skill if coaches are attentive to their instructional needs and progress.

Shaping

Through the use of an operant approach called shaping, gradual but dramatic performance improvements can be accomplished as the desired behaviors are reinforced under increasingly stringent requirements. To use shaping effectively, start with what the athlete is currently capable of doing, and then gradually require a more skillful level of performance before reinforcement is given. It is important that the shift in demands be realistic and that the steps be small enough so that the athlete can master them and be reinforced. For example, a youth softball coach may at first praise novice infielders whenever they stop a ball (with any part of their anatomy). As proficiency increases, however, she may require that the players field the ball in the correct position, and later that they field the ball cleanly in the correct position and make an accurate throw. Used correctly, shaping is one of the most powerful of all the positive control techniques. Case Study 1 illustrates the use of positive reinforcement to shape football performance.

Case Study 1

Using Positive Reinforcement and Shaping to Improve Football Performance

The systematic use of positive reinforcement and shaping to improve the performance of a youth football team's offensive backfield was described by Judi Komaki and Fred Barnett (1977). The coach selected three different offensive plays, each of which was broken down into five stages judged to be crucial to the execution of the play and was presented to the players accordingly. For example, one of the plays included the following stages: (1) quarterback-center exchange; (2) quarterback spin and pitch; (3) right halfback and fullback lead blocking; (4) left halfback route; and (5) quarterback block. Breaking down the play in this manner allowed the coach to respond to the elements that were run correctly, give specific feedback to the players about their execution of each of the five stages, and gradually shape their learning of the entire play.

During the first phase of the experiment, data were carefully collected on how often the stages of each play were executed correctly. Then the coach began to systematically apply reinforcement procedures to Play A. Each time the play was run in practice, the coach checked off which of the elements had been successfully executed and praised the players for the stages that were run successfully. Reinforcement was not applied when Plays B and C were run. After a period of time, the reinforcement procedure was shifted to Play B only, and later to Play C only. Applying the technique to only one play at a time permitted a determination of the specific effects of reinforcement on the performance of each of them.

A comparison of the percentage of stages executed correctly before and after introduction of the reinforcement procedure indicated that performance increased for all three plays, but only after reinforcement was introduced. The level of performance for Play A improved from 61.7 to 81.5 percent when reinforcement was applied, but execution of B and C did not improve until reinforcement was also applied to them. When this occurred, execution of play B improved from 54.4 to 82 percent, and execution of Play C improved from 65.5 to 79.8 percent. Clearly, the systematic use of reinforcement led to a substantial improvement in performance. Other studies have shown similar performance improvement in gymnastics, swimming, baseball, golf, and tennis (see Smith, Smoll, & Christensen, 1996 for a review).

Schedules and Timing of Reinforcement

One of the most frequently asked questions is how often and how consistently reinforcement should be given. Fortunately, a great deal of research has been done concerning the effects of so-called **schedules of reinforcement** on behavior change. Reinforcement schedules refer to the pattern and frequency with which reinforcement is administered. Although there are many different kinds of schedules, the most important distinction is between *continuous* and *partial* schedules. On a continuous schedule, every correct response is reinforced. On partial schedules, some proportion of correct responses are reinforced and some are not.

During the initial stages of training, reinforcement is best given on a continuous schedule. Frequent reinforcement not only helps strengthen the desired response but also provides the athlete with frequent feedback about

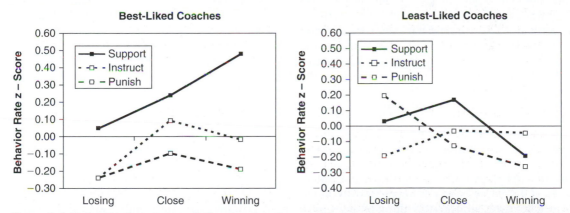

how well he or she is doing. Once the behavior is learned, however, reinforcement should be shifted to a partial schedule. Research has shown that behaviors reinforced on partial schedules persist much longer in the absence of reinforcement than do those that have been reinforced only on a continuous schedule (Skinner, 1969). For example, people will put a great many coins into slot machines, which operate on partial schedules. In contrast, they are unlikely to persist long in putting coins into soft drink machines that do not deliver because these machines are supposed to operate on a continuous schedule. Thus, the key principle in using schedules is to start with continuous reinforcement until the behavior is established, then to shift gradually to partial reinforcement to maintain a high level of motivation and performance (Martin & Pear, 2007).

When reinforcement (and punishment) have their strongest effects is another consideration. During a large-scale observational study of coaching behaviors in youth baseball coaches, we coded coaching behaviors and the score of the game at the end of each half-inning, enabling us to determine how individual coaches behaved when their teams were winning, losing, or tied or with a one-run differential (Smith et al., 2009). Coaches exhibited consistent but individualized situation-behavior patterns that we termed

behavioral signatures. We then examined behavioral signatures in relation to postseason ratings of how much the athletes liked their coaches and found clear differences between best-liked and least-liked coaches. Rate of supportive behaviors delivered while the team was winning correlated highly with liking, whereas supportive behaviors given while losing bore no relation to liking for the coach. The opposite occurred for punitive behaviors, which were strongly and negatively related to liking when delivered in losing situations, but were only weakly related when given during winning situations. The impact of instructive behaviors was not affected by the score at the time it occurred. These relations became clear when the behavioral signature profiles of the best-liked (left side of Figure 3-2) and least-liked coaches were compared.

These findings may be understood in terms of *mood congruence*, which is known to enhance emotional processing and memory. The impact of positive supportive behaviors in an emotionally pleasant winning situation may be better encoded and remembered. Conversely, negatively toned punitive behaviors that occur during losing situations while the athletes are feeling bad may be encoded more deeply and affect how the athletes felt about their coach during the season. Such encoding could well influence postseason attitudes toward the coach.

Figure 3-2 Behavioral signature (behavior-situation profiles) for best-liked and least-liked coaches
Reprinted from Smith, R. E., Shoda, Y., Cumming, S. P., & Smoll, F. L. (2009). Behavioral signatures at the ballpark: Intraindividual consistency of adults' situation-behavior patterns and their interpersonal consequences. *Journal of Research in Personality, 43*, 187–195.

The timing of reinforcement is another important consideration. Other things being equal, the sooner after a response that reinforcement occurs, the stronger are its effects on behavior. Thus, whenever possible, try to reinforce a desired behavior as soon as it occurs. If this is not possible, try to find an opportunity to praise the athlete later on.

Reinforcing Effort and Other Desirable Behaviors

To this point, I have discussed the use of reinforcement to strengthen skills. It is important to realize, however, that reinforcement can be used to strengthen other desirable behaviors as well. For example, the positive approach can be used to reduce the likelihood of disciplinary problems by reinforcing compliance with team rules. There is no reason why a coach should not recognize and reinforce exemplary conduct on the part of particular athletes or the team as a whole. One of the most effective ways of avoiding disciplinary problems is by strengthening the opposite (desired) behaviors through reinforcement (Smith & Smoll, 2012).

Similarly, instances of teamwork and of athletes' support and encouragement of one another should be acknowledged and reinforced from time to time. Doing so not only strengthens these desirable behaviors but also creates an atmosphere in which the coach is actually serving as a positive model by supporting them. Research has shown that the best predictor of liking for the coach and desire to play for him or her in the future is not the won-lost record of the team but how consistently the coach applies the positive approach and avoids the use of punishment (Smith & Smoll, 1991).

One of the most important points of all has been saved until last. It's easy to praise an athlete who has just made a great play. It is less natural to reinforce an athlete who tried but failed. A good principle is to reinforce effort as much as results. After all, the only thing athletes have complete control over is the amount of effort they make; they have only limited control over the outcome of their efforts. Coaches have a right to demand total effort, and this is perhaps the most important thing of all for them to reinforce. If athletes have had good technical instruction, are free from self-defeating fear of failure, and are making maximum effort (all of which should be promoted by the use of the positive approach), then performance and winning will take care of themselves within the limits of the athletes' ability. John Wooden, the legendary "Wizard of Westwood," placed great emphasis on this concept:

> You cannot find a player who ever played for me at UCLA that can tell you he ever heard me mention "winning" a basketball game. He might say I inferred a little here and there, but I never mentioned winning. Yet the last thing that I told my players, just prior to tipoff, before we would go on the floor was, "When the game is over, I want your head up—and I know of only one way for your head to be up—and that's for you to know that you did your best. . . . This means to do the best YOU can do. That's the best; no one can do more. . . . You made that effort. (personal communication, 1975)

Reinforcement and Intrinsic Motivation

Motivation theorists make an important distinction between **intrinsic motivation** and **extrinsic motivation** (see Chapter 4). When people are motivated to perform an activity for its own sake, for "the love of the game," they are said to be **intrinsically motivated.** When they perform the activity only to obtain some external reward, they are **extrinsically motivated.**

Can positive reinforcements like trophies and money undermine intrinsic motivation? Under some circumstances, yes. If external rewards are suddenly introduced for performance of a behavior that is intrinsically rewarding, a person may come to attribute his or her performance to the extrinsic reward and cease performing the behavior if the external reward is withdrawn.

Most of us would like athletes to be intrinsically motivated to participate in athletics. Is it possible that the positive approach, with its emphasis on reinforcement from the coach, could undermine their love of the game for its own sake?

It now appears that if extrinsic reinforcement is given to acknowledge a specific level of performance, it is unlikely to undermine intrinsic motivation (Deci, Koestner, & Ryan, 1999). Rather, it provides important information to an athlete that she has met a standard of excellence and thereby provides a basis for positive self-reinforcement by the athlete. Positive internal self-evaluations can strengthen behavior and also maintain and even increase intrinsic motivation (Cervone, 1992). Thus, it is a good idea for coaches to instill self-pride in their athletes with statements like "Great job! You ought to feel proud of yourself for that effort." There is considerable evidence that standards for self-reinforcement are often adopted from other people, and a coach can be an influential source of standards of excellence that athletes can internalize, particularly if the coach has developed a strong positive relationship with them.

Positive Reinforcement and the Mastery Motivational Climate

Positive reinforcement can be applied to virtually any behavior. For example, we could choose to reinforce effort, persistence, and improvement, or we could give reinforcement only when an athlete is outperforming others, both teammates and opponents. The positive approach described earlier has emphasized reinforcement for effort, improvement, and meeting internal standards of performance. This approach is designed to foster a ***mastery (task)-oriented motivational climate,*** in which athletes will feel successful and competent when they have learned something new, experienced skill improvement, mastered the task at hand, or given their best effort. Importantly, even if athletes perceive themselves as possessing lower ability than others, they can still feel competent and successful if focused on mastery-oriented achievement goals (see Chapter 4).

By contrast, when young athletes are in a state of *ego involvement,* their definitions of personal success and demonstrated competence are *other-referenced.* The goal here is to show that one is superior to relevant others or to avoid appearing inferior to others. When coaches make reinforcement contingent on outperforming others or winning, punish unsuccessful performance, and fail to attend to effort or to developing personal goals for improvement, they can easily create an ***ego-oriented motivational climate.***

Research has shown that the motivational climate created by teachers and coaches has strong effects on achievement goals, standards of success, and behavior. Children are more likely to invest in learning, develop intrinsic motivation, and adopt adaptive achievement strategies in mastery climates in which the emphasis is on learning, personal improvement, and developing new skills rather than on interpersonal evaluation and social comparison with others. By contrast, maladaptive achievement strategies, fear of failure, and motivational problems tend to occur in ego-involving motivational climates, in which mistakes are punished, children with greater ability receive more encouragement and rewards, and social comparison is emphasized (Ames, 1992; McArdle & Duda, 2002; see Chapter 4). As John Wooden and other progressive coaches have recognized, focusing on effort, preparation, and dedication to personal improvement pays dividends not only in performance but also in the development of healthy attitudes and values concerning sport participation. Especially noteworthy is the fact that athletes report greater enjoyment of their sport experience when coaches create a mastery motivational climate. One study found that coaches creating a mastery environment was 10 times more important than the team's won-lost record in accounting for how much young athletes liked their coach (Cumming, Smoll, Smith, & Grossbard, 2007). Knowing what to reinforce is a key to creating such a climate.

Other research has shown that training coaches in how to create a mastery climate has notable positive effects on young athletes. In response to a decreased emphasis on winning, such athletes exhibited significant decreases in performance anxiety over the course of the season, whereas athletes' trait anxiety increased in a control condition whose coaches did not receive the mastery approach to coaching intervention (Smith, Smoll, & Cumming, 2007; see Chapter 17 for details). Athletes also showed salutary changes in their achievement goals, defining success in terms of personal improvement, enjoying teammates, and having fun, rather than winning or besting others (Smoll, Smith, & Cumming, 2007).

Performance Feedback: Providing Information Needed to Improve Performance

Approval is a greater motivator than disapproval, but we have to disapprove on occasion when we correct. It's necessary. I make corrections only after I have proved to the individual that I highly value him. If they know we care for them, our correction won't be seen as judgmental. I also try to never make it personal.

—John Wooden

Positive reinforcement serves not only as a reward for desirable behavior but also as a form of performance feedback (see Chapter 2 for more details on feedback). In other words, providing knowledge of results communicates the message that performance has met or exceeded the coach's standards. When it is possible to measure desired and undesired behaviors objectively, the coach can utilize the highly effective tool of performance feedback to increase motivation and performance.

Performance feedback is a prominent feature of what many successful coaches do. For example, psychologists Ronald Gallimore and Roland Tharp (2004) charted all of John Wooden's behaviors during 15 practice sessions. They found that 75 percent of Wooden's comments to his players contained instructional feedback. Most of his comments were specific statements of what to do and how the players were or were not doing it. Indeed, Wooden was five times more likely to inform than to merely praise or reprimand. Wooden once remarked, *"I believe correcting is the positive approach. I believe in the positive approach. Always have."*

Informational and Motivational Benefits of Feedback

If a pitcher throws one good pitch during the whole morning, you have something to work on. Let him know it. That will give him all the incentive he needs. He too sees that he can do a certain thing. He may not know exactly how he did it. He has to find that out from his own study.

—The late Branch Rickey, legendary baseball executive

Objective feedback is effective in improving performance for a variety of reasons. For one thing, feedback can correct misconceptions. Athletes, like other people, often have distorted perceptions of their own behavior. Objective evidence in the form of statistics or numbers can help correct such misconceptions and may motivate corrective action. For example, it can be a sobering experience for a basketball player who fancies himself a great ball handler to learn that he has more turnovers than assists.

Feedback also creates internal consequences by stimulating athletes to experience positive (or negative) feelings about themselves, depending on how well they performed in relation to their standards of performance. An athlete who is dissatisfied with his or her level of performance may not only be motivated to improve, but will also experience feelings of self-satisfaction that function as positive reinforcement when subsequent feedback indicates improvement. Such self-administered reinforcement can be even more important than external reinforcement from the coach in bringing about improved performance (Cervone, 1992). Promoting self-motivation in athletes also reduces the need for coaches to reinforce or punish. When feedback is public, as in posting statistics, the actual or anticipated reactions of others to one's performance level can serve as an additional motivator of increased effort and performance. Improvement is also likely to result in reinforcement from teammates.

A final motivational function of objective feedback is in relation to formal goal-setting programs. Because goal setting is discussed in detail in Chapter 11, I will simply point out that successful goal-setting programs provide clear feedback that informs workers as to their performance in relation to the goal (Locke & Latham, 1990). Without such feedback, goal setting does not improve performance, and without clear and specific goals that are either assigned by others or set internally, performance feedback has little effect on performance. For example, in a study by Albert Bandura and Daniel Cervone (1983) participants engaged in a strenuous aerobic task on an arm-powered exercise bicycle. Four experimental conditions were created by the presence/absence of challenging assigned goals and the presence/absence of performance feedback. Over the three performance periods, those who had both assigned goals and feedback improved their level of performance 59 percent. In contrast, those who had only goals without feedback or received only feedback improved from 20 to 25 percent, no more than the group that received neither goals nor feedback. The presence of both challenging goals and performance feedback provided a powerful motivational boost to task performance.

Performance feedback can also result in increases in self-efficacy, the belief that one is capable of successful behavior (Cervone, 1992). In one study, participants performed an athletic task, in this case, the hurdles. Performance feedback contributed to subsequent self-efficacy, choice of more difficult hurdles, and improved performance (Escarti & Guzman, 1999).

Instructional Benefits of Feedback

Feedback has not only motivational but also instructional effects (see Chapter 2, this volume). Objective performance feedback provides information about (a) the specific behaviors that should be performed, (b) the levels of proficiency that should be achieved in each of the skills, and (c) the athlete's current level of proficiency in these activities. This instructional function of feedback can be especially valuable when execution of a given skill is broken down into its stages or components, as was done in the football study described earlier. When the skill is a highly complex one, such as hitting a baseball,

verbal or video feedback on how frequently a hitter executes each of the essentials (keeping the bat in the correct position, shifting one's weight correctly, striding with the hips closed, keeping one's head down during the swing, and so on) can be very valuable in pinpointing areas of strength and weakness so that attention can be directed toward correcting mistakes. The information provided by subsequent objective feedback allows both coach and athlete to monitor progress in a more useful fashion than by depending on a more global measure of proficiency, such as batting average.

The foregoing discussion suggests a number of principles for giving effective feedback to athletes. Feedback should be contingent on what the athlete has just done, and it should be framed so that it can help the athlete continue to improve. The athlete is provided with feedback both on correct aspects of performance and on errors that were made. However, the athlete should then be told or shown very specifically how to correct the error, emphasizing the good things that will happen when the correction is made. This is an excellent way to combine corrective instruction with encouragement and reinforcement and turn a communication that could be construed as negative into something positive and supportive.

Implementing a Performance Measurement and Feedback System

As in the application of positive reinforcement, a successful feedback program requires that coaches identify specific and measurable behaviors or consequences—something that can be counted. The performance measures can be fairly global (e.g., number of rebounds per minute) or more specific and dealing with subskills (e.g., percentage of rebound plays in which the opponent is boxed out).

In many instances, coaches can choose between measuring a desired behavior or its undesirable counterpart. In line with the positive approach to coaching, I strongly recommend choosing the correct behavior for feedback rather than the mistake (or, at the very least, presenting

Case Study 2

Using Instruction and Feedback to Improve Pitching Performance

In the world of professional baseball, organizations spend millions of dollars to develop talent for the major leagues. The key to organizational success is successful instruction. An example of the successful use of feedback-enhanced instruction is seen in the following case.

The athlete was a pitcher in his first year of minor league baseball. He had an excellent fast-ball, but it was clear that he needed another pitch to compete successfully at an elite level. He had a rudimentary curve ball over which he had limited command. The pitching instructor planned a systematic program of instruction, an important component of which was throwing his curve ball at an apparatus known as "the string zone." The apparatus was set up at home plate in front of the catcher. The heavy strings, arranged in a rectangular shape, framed the strike zone and could be slid up, down, or sideways to create different target areas. Following instruction on how to hold and release the ball and some warm-up pitches, the pitcher would throw a series of 25–30 pitches at the string target under the watchful eye of the instructor. A record was kept of the percentage of pitches that passed through the strike zone at each pitching session. Thus, the pitcher received intrinsic feedback from his muscular and visual senses, extrinsic feedback from the instructor, and graphical feedback on the percentage of strikes thrown at each test session. On days when the pitcher appeared in games, the percentage of curve balls regarded as strikes by viewing the video recording from center field was also charted.

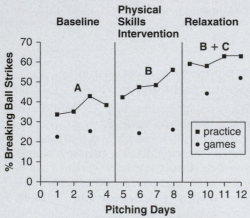

Figure 3-3 **Percentage of curve ball strikes thrown by the pitcher in test sessions and games prior to instruction and feedback, during instruction, and following relaxation training combined with instruction.**

Figure 3-3 shows the data collected on the test and game days. At baseline (Phase A, before the intervention), the pitcher showed limited ability to hit the target. Once formal instruction began (Phase B), he showed steady improvement in practice sessions, but not in games. He attributed this to anxiety experienced during games, so at that point, a second component, relaxation training (see Chapter 12), was introduced as technical instruction continued (Phase B + C). Increased command over his arousal level as he learned to relax during games (see Chapters 12 and 13) helped reduce the practice–game discrepancy in accuracy. Though not shown in this figure, the expert instruction resulted not only in greater accuracy, but also in a much sharper break on his curve ball over time. By his second year in the minor leagues, his curve ball rivaled his fastball in its effectiveness. The pitcher went on to a success-ful major league career.

both). This puts a coach in the position of reinforcing improvement rather than punishing or criticizing mistakes. It also focuses players' attention on what they should do rather than on what they should *not* do. Case Study 2 illustrates the use of positive performance feedback combined with expert instruction.

Finally, it is important to note that performance feedback measures can be derived not only for individual players but also for subgroups or even for the team as a whole. Such measures can help to promote team cohesion by emphasizing the importance of teamwork and by providing a specific measure of group performance.

Positive reinforcement and performance feedback techniques can be applied to sports in many ways. Given the success they have enjoyed in a wide variety of performance settings, these strategies have the potential to increase coaching effectiveness at all competitive levels, from children's programs to the demanding and exacting realm of elite and professional sports. Table 3-1 presents some practical guidelines based on the positive approach emphasized in this chapter.

Table 3-1 Getting Positive Things to Happen: Some Practical Guidelines

Administering positive reinforcement

1. Be liberal with reinforcement, particularly in the early stages of learning.
2. Have realistic expectations and consistently reinforce compliance with your standards.
3. Try to reinforce desired behaviors as soon as they occur.
4. Reinforce effort and perseverance, not just results.
5. Pair reinforcement with a statement of what the athlete did correctly, e.g., "Way to go, you blocked out really well."
6. Verbally reinforce compliance with team rules to help prevent disruptive behavior.
7. Help athletes set positive, individualized, behavioral performance goals. Use written or statistical performance feedback to track improvement and stimulate self-reinforcement processes in athletes.

Reacting to mistakes

1. Regard mistakes as learning opportunities.
2. Ask the athlete what should have been done instead to reinforce the performance principle.
3. If the athlete knows how to correct the mistake, give encouragement. If not, demonstrate.
4. The "positive sandwich" is an excellent way to combine instruction with encouragement and reinforcement. First, find something the athlete did right and reinforce it (e.g., "You did a good job of getting to that fly ball."). Then tell the athlete how to correct the mistake, emphasizing the good things that will happen as a result (e.g., "Now, if you catch the ball with both hands, you'll hang onto it and make that play."). Finally, end with an encouraging statement (e.g., "Keep working on this and you're going to be a good fielder.").
5. Restrict criticism to behaviors that are in the athlete's control, such as lack of effort.
6. Avoid aversive punishment as much as possible. It builds fear of failure, the athlete's worst enemy. Response cost is a more desirable alternative if punishment is used.

Adapted with permission from Smith, R. E., & Smoll, F. L. (2012). *Sport psychology for youth coaches: Developing champions in sports and life.* New York: Rowman & Littlefield Publishers.

Summary

In this chapter I have focused on some of the advantages of a positive approach to coaching that uses reinforcement (a) to strengthen desired behaviors and (b) to promote the development of a positive motivation for success rather than fear of failure. Objective performance feedback on specific aspects of performance is a highly successful motivational and instructional technique. Both systematic reinforcement and objective feedback require that the coach identify specific behaviors that are important to individual and team success. This is in itself a highly desirable practice because it focuses both coach and player attention on exactly what needs to be mastered and executed. It also promotes goal setting based on specific behaviors rather than on more general goals that are difficult to measure. Systematic use of positive reinforcement and objective feedback has yielded impressive results in many performance settings, including sports, and their utilization is appropriate at all competitive levels of athletics.

Study Questions

1. In what ways can coaching be viewed as attempts to influence behavior?

2. What are the ABCs of behavior control within an operant conditioning analysis of behavior?

3. Define the four basic consequences created by the presentation or removal of positive or aversive stimuli, and explain their effects on behavior.

4. Differentiate between negative reinforcement and punishment.

5. Define positive reinforcement and contrast it with punishment in terms of its effects on behavior and the motivational factors that underlie its effectiveness.

6. What are the direct effects and undesirable side effects of punishment? Distinguish between aversive punishment and response cost. How can we explain the fact that highly punitive coaches are sometimes very successful in eliciting high levels of athlete performance?

7. What are reinforcement contingencies, and how are they applied in shaping?

8. Summarize the schedules of reinforcement described in the text, as well as their effects on performance.

9. What is the importance of reinforcing effort rather than focusing entirely on outcome?

10. How can the positive approach be used to reduce disciplinary problems?

11. Differentiate between intrinsic and extrinsic motivation. Under what conditions can intrinsic motivation be undermined by positive reinforcement, and what can be done to reduce this danger?

12. How would you use positive reinforcement to create (a) a task-oriented motivational climate and (b) an ego-oriented motivational climate?

13. What are the effects of performance feedback on task performance, and what are the mechanisms whereby feedback is assumed to motivate behavior? What is the instructional value of feedback?

14. What are some of the key principles in implementing a performance feedback program? How are these related to the positive approach to coaching?

References

Ames, C. (1992). Achievement goals and adaptive motivational patterns: The role of the environment. In G. C. Roberts (Ed.), *Motivation in sport and exercise* (pp. 161–176). Champaign, IL: Human Kinetics.

Bandura, A., & Cervone, D. (1983). Self-evaluative and self-efficacy mechanisms governing the motivational effects of goal systems. *Journal of Personality and Social Psychology, 45,* 1017–1028.

Cervone, D. (1992). The role of self-referent cognitions in goal setting, motivation, and performance. In M. Rabinowitz (Ed.), *Applied cognition* (pp. 79–96). New York: Ablex.

Cumming, S. P., Smoll, F. L., Smith, R. E., & Grossbard, J. R. (2007). Is winning everything? The relative contributions of motivational climate and won-lost percentage in youth sports. *Journal of Applied Sport Psychology, 19,* 322–336.

Deci, E. L., Koestner, R., & Ryan, R. M. (1999). A meta-analytic review of experiments examining the effects of extrinsic rewards on intrinsic motivation. *Psychological Bulletin, 125,* 627–668.

Escarti, A., & Guzman, J. F. (1999). Effects of feedback on self-efficacy, performance, and choice on an athletic task. *Journal of Applied Sport Psychology, 11,* 83–96.

Gallimore, R., & Tharp, R. (2004). What a coach can teach a teacher, 1975–2004: Reflections and reanalysis of John Wooden's teaching practices. *The Sport Psychologist, 18,* 119–137.

Komaki, J., & Barnett, F. T. (1977). A behavioral approach to coaching football: Improving the play execution of an offensive backfield on a youth football team. *Journal of Applied Behavior Analysis, 10,* 657–664.

Locke, E. A., & Latham, G. P. (1990). *A theory of goal setting and task performance.* Englewood Cliffs, NJ: Prentice Hall.

Martin, G., & Pear, J. (2007). *Behavior modification: What it is and how to do it* (7th ed.). Englewood Cliffs, NJ: Prentice Hall.

McArdle, S., & Duda, J. K. (2002). Implications of the motivational climate in youth sports. In F. L. Smoll & R. E. Smith (Eds.), *Children and youth in sport: A biosocial perspective* (2nd ed.). Dubuque, IA: Kendall/Hunt.

Skinner, B. F. (1969). *Contingencies of reinforcement: A theoretical analysis.* New York: Appleton-Century-Crofts.

Smith, R. E. (1993). *Psychology.* Minneapolis, MN: West.

Smith, R. E., & Smoll, F. L. (1991). Behavioral research and intervention in youth sports. *Behavior Therapy, 22,* 329–344.

Smith, R. E., & Smoll, F. L. (2011). Cognitive-behavioral coach training: A translational approach to theory, research, and intervention. In J. K. Luiselli & D. D. Reed (Eds.), *Behavioral sport psychology: Evidence-based approaches to performance enhancement* (pp. 227–248). New York: Springer. doi 10.1007/978-1-4614-0070-7_14

Smith, R. E., & Smoll, F. L. (2012). *Sport psychology for youth coaches: Developing champions in sports and life*. New York: Rowman & Littlefield Publishers.

Smith, R. E., Shoda, Y., Cumming, S. P., & Smoll, F. L. (2009). Behavioral signatures at the ballpark: Intraindividual consistency of adults' situation-behavior patterns and their interpersonal consequences. *Journal of Research in Personality, 43,* 187–195.

Smith, R. E., Smoll, F. L., & Christensen, D. S. (1996). Behavioral assessment and interventions in youth sports. *Behavior Modification, 20,* 3–44.

Smith, R. E., Smoll, F. L., & Cumming, S. P. (2007). Effects of a motivational climate intervention for coaches on children's sport performance anxiety. *Journal of Sport & Exercise Psychology, 29,* 39–59.

Smith, R. E., Smoll, F. L., & Passer, M. W. (2002). Sport performance anxiety in young athletes. In F. L. Smoll & R. E. Smith (Eds.), *Children and youth in sport: A biosocial perspective* (2nd ed.). Dubuque, IA: Kendall/Hunt.

Smoll, F. L., Smith, R. E., & Cumming, S. P. (2007). Effects of a psychoeducational intervention for coaches on changes in child athletes' achievement goal orientations. *Journal of Clinical Sport Psychology, 1,* 23–46.

The Motivational Climate, Athlete Motivation, and Implications for the Quality of Sport Engagement

Joan L. Duda, *The University of Birmingham, UK*
Darren C. Treasure, *Competitive Advantage International, USA*

"I'm proud of the way I've dealt with setbacks. It's hard when you feel down and you think, 'Why is the world doing this to me?' But you have to pick yourself up again. That's what makes you a better athlete."

Jessica Ennis—London 2012 Olympics Heptathlon Champion

"You can't put a limit on anything. The more you dream, the farther you get."

Michael Phelps—American swimmer and the most decorated Olympian of all time, with a total of 22 medals.

"People don't understand that when I grew up, I was never the most talented. I was never the biggest. I was never the fastest. I certainly was never the strongest. The only thing I had was my work ethic, and that's been what has gotten me this far."

Tiger Woods—Winner of 14 Major Golf Championships and a total of 104 professional golf tournaments.

Jessica Ennis, Michael Phelps, and Tiger Woods speak to the very essence of why understanding motivation is of such interest to coaches, parents, sport psychologists, and athletes alike. Motivation is the foundation of sport performance and achievement. Without it, even the most talented athlete is unlikely to reach his or her full potential. Motivation also is pertinent to how the athlete experiences and responds to sport. Whether or not sport contributes positively or negatively to athletes' welfare is linked to motivation-related factors. In spite of its significance in the athletic milieu, however, motivation is one of the most misunderstood psychological constructs among sport participants and practitioners.

What is motivation, and how does an athlete or his or her coach optimize it? Some think that whether an athlete is high or low in motivation is somehow inherent in the athlete's personality— a relatively unchangeable characteristic of the person. Others believe coaches "motivate" athletes, perhaps in their pre-game "pep talks" or in the techniques they use in practice to foster their athletes' focus and intensity. There is, perhaps, some truth in each of these perspectives. However, sport motivation is more complex and multifaceted than either of them.

Contemporary research shows motivation to be dependent both on some malleable, psychological tendencies of the athletes themselves *and* on aspects of the social environments in which they develop, train, and compete. In particular, variations in motivation are held to be a function of the diverse ways in which athletes *interpret* their sport-related experiences. These different ways of interpreting sport stem from individual dispositional differences between athletes and situational dynamics.

How do we decide if an athlete is motivated? Is good or poor performance the best or only indicator? In general, researchers suggest that motivation is inferred from variability in **behavioral patterns.** For example, John, a club tennis player, seeks out opponents who really challenge his game. Whether practicing or competing, John tries his hardest to get to every shot and to hit it well, even when down love–40 in a game or behind 1–5 in a set. John maximizes the tennis talent that he has. When an athlete such as John tries hard, seeks out challenge, persists in the face of adversity, and performs up to his ability level on a reasonably consistent basis, we typically conclude that this person is highly motivated. In contrast, if John were to hold back in training or a match and not give his best effort, prefer to play opponents or work on drills that are too easy or way beyond his capabilities, regularly experience performance impairment or fail to live up to his potential, and contemplate dropping out or actually quitting tennis, we infer that motivational problems abound.

A number of factors need to be considered before we can determine the degree to and way in which the participant is motivated. It is important to take into account how much motivation the individual has (i.e., the *quantity* of motivation) as well as the *quality* of that motivation (Duda, 2001, 2005). Typically, the quantity

of motivation is reflected in how "into" her or his sport the athlete is at the present time and how well she or he is currently performing. However, it is important to keep in mind that there are different reasons why an athlete may be "motivated" in the short term. There may be high quantity of motivation at the moment, but what about the quality of that motivation?

The quality of motivation is inferred by the athlete's sustained and positive as well as healthy engagement in the sport. This includes both the athlete's accomplishments and development over time as well as the degree of enjoyment and psychological and physical benefits associated with sport involvement. Variability in the quantity and quality of sport motivation are intricately linked with how athletes *think* before, during, and after their engagement in sport.

What thoughts appear critical to variations in motivation? Researchers (e.g., Ryan & Deci, 2002) have shown that individuals feel and act more motivated when they think they have the competence to meet the demands of the task at hand and believe they have some control, or autonomy, in regard to their participation. The assumption that perceptions of ability and autonomy are critical to motivational patterns is fundamental to a number of popular contemporary theories of motivated behavior. Two of those theoretical frameworks, which have provided a foundation for research and practice on sport motivation, will be reviewed here. These are the achievement goal frameworks, and self-determination theory.

Achievement Goals: The Importance of How We Judge Our Competence

"The principle is competing against yourself. It's about self-improvement, about being better than you were the day before."

Steve Young, MVP Super Bowl XXIX.

"For me, losing a tennis match isn't failure, it's research."

Billie Jean King—Former number 1 women's professional tennis player; winner of 39 Grand Slam titles, including 12 singles, 16 women's doubles, and 11 mixed doubles titles.

The larger psychology literature as well as anecdotal experience point to the relevance of feelings of competence to achievement striving in sport and other life domains. Our contemporary understanding of sport motivation recognizes, however, that adaptive versus problematic motivational patterns are not merely a function of whether an athlete has high or low perceptions of his or her ability. Rather, we also need to consider the criteria that athletes use to decide whether they are able or not. That is, how does the athlete define demonstrated competence and what are the implications for how this athlete experiences and responds to sport?

To answer such questions, one area of work that we need to address is grounded in achievement goal frameworks. These frameworks assume that perceptions of **competence** (how able we think we are) as well as differences in **goal perspectives,** or the ways in which individuals judge their competence and perceive success, are the critical antecedents to quantity and particularly the quality of our motivation (Duda, 2001).

Fundamental to achievement goal models is that there are, at least, two central achievement goal perspectives (task and ego) that govern the way athletes think about achievement and guide subsequent decision making and action (Nicholls, 1989). According to Nicholls (1989), task and ego goal states entail distinct ways of processing an activity and can fluctuate throughout the course of an event. When **task involved,** an athlete's main purposes are to gain skill or knowledge, to exhibit effort, to perform at one's best, and to experience personal improvement. This athlete is focused on what he or she is doing and is thinking primarily about how to accomplish the task. If such purposes are achieved, the individual feels competent and successful. When **ego involved,** athletes are preoccupied with the adequacy of their ability and the demonstration of superior competence compared to others. Perceptions of competence and subjective achievement, in this case, entail social comparisons with others. High ability is demonstrated for the ego-involved athlete when his or her performance is perceived to exceed that of others or to be equivalent with less effort exerted. The athlete's focus is on whether he or she is good

enough (if confidence is low) and how to prove (rather than improve) his or her high level of competence (if confidence is high).

When task involvement is manifested, it is assumed that the athlete will think, act, and feel in a motivated manner regardless of her or his level of perceived ability. A task-involved athlete is expected to possess high *quality* motivation. Ego involvement, too, can correspond to positive achievement patterns (e.g., high performance or persistence) and high *quantity* of motivation, as long as the athlete is quite certain that her or his ability is high. When an athlete is ego involved and thinks the possibility of demonstrating superior competence is "slim to none," the achievement-related cognitions, emotions, and behaviors displayed are far less than optimal. That is, the *quantity* and, in particular, the *quality* of motivation is diminished.

Achievement goal theory states that an individual's goal perspective state—task or ego involvement—is the result of both individual differences and situational factors. With respect to the former, an athlete's proneness for task and ego involvement is assumed to be captured by his or her dispositional task and ego goal orientations. We will first discuss the nature and implications of these goal orientations in the athletic domain.

Significance of Goal Orientations

Achievement goal orientations are not bipolar opposites (Nicholls, 1989). Rather, they are independent dimensions. As a result, an athlete can be high ego/low task, high task/low ego, high task/high ego, or low task/low ego. From both a theoretical and an applied perspective, it is important to consider athletes' degree of proneness for both task and ego goals to get a more complete view of their motivational processes.

Findings from studies involving male and female athletes from a variety of competitive levels and age groups show that an adaptive achievement profile is one of high task and high ego orientation (Duda, 2001). But why might this be the case? Some researchers have suggested that a high task orientation might, to some degree, insulate highly ego-oriented individuals from the negative consequences of low perceived ability when they are performing poorly and, thus, be motivationally advantageous in the long run (Nicholls, 1989). Athletes who are high in both task and ego orientation have multiple sources for feeling successful and competent. They have the flexibility of focusing on either task or ego goals at different times in their training or competitions to enhance their motivation *quantity* (Duda, 2001). We should note that there are some questions regarding whether a high-task/high-ego orientation profile is most adaptive when the focus is on indexes of the *quality* of motivation (Duda, 2001). For example, research examining the subjective well-being and moral functioning of athletes suggests that high-task/high-ego participants can be similar to their low-task/high-ego counterparts in expressing maladaptive views about and exhibiting negative responses to sport (Reinboth & Duda, 2004).

In general, a significant body of research has revealed that task and ego goal orientations are associated with qualitatively different behavioral, cognitive, and affective patterns in sport that are likely to have an impact not only on short-term performance but also on the quantity and quality of long-term participation. Researchers have found a task orientation to be related to positive motivational outcomes—for example, the belief that effort is a cause of success, the use of problem-solving and adaptive learning strategies, enjoyment, satisfaction, and intrinsic interest (Duda, 2001, 2005; Roberts, Treasure, & Kavussanu, 1997). Previous work has also revealed a task orientation to be associated with the belief that one's level of physical ability is changeable or malleable (Sarrazin, Biddle, Famose, Cury, Fox, & Durand, 1996). This is very important in the context of sport, because elite level performers usually reach their potential only after years of training. If an athlete believed this commitment to training was not going to lead to increases in ability (i.e., given that she or he holds the view that sport ability is "fixed"), it is unlikely that the athlete would be optimally motivated to train over time.

In contrast, an ego orientation has been found to be associated with boredom, the belief that deception is a cause of success, and reported anxiety (Duda, 2001; Roberts et al., 1997). Ego orientation also has been found to be related to the belief that ability is an important determinant of success and the idea that sport competence is stable and a "gift" (Sarrazin et al., 1996). Such a belief system may lead an athlete who is questioning his or her ability not to be as motivated or committed to long-term training. These individuals believe that ultimately "You've either got it or you haven't," and the possession of "it" is deemed a prerequisite to sport achievement.

Achievement goal models state that individuals in a state of ego involvement who have high perceptions of perceived ability are likely to respond in a fashion similar to competitors who are task involved, regardless of whether their perceived competence is high or low. This has led a number of leading sport psychology researchers to contend that a high ego orientation may not be detrimental to performance. Indeed, it has been argued that it is hard to see how an individual could succeed, particularly at the elite level, without having a strong ego orientation. The assumption here is that elite athletes are primarily motivated by winning and outperforming others.

Although we would agree that it is likely that all elite level athletes perceive success in an ego-involving fashion at certain times, we would caution those who want to *promote* ego orientation. Indeed, high levels of ego orientation may not be motivating at the elite level of sport as even these athletes sometimes doubt their ability (e.g., due to injury, during a performance slump). At such times, a predominant ego orientation coupled especially with moderate or low task orientation puts individuals at jeopardy for feeling incompetent because their focus is primarily on their performance compared to others (Duda, 2001; Nicholls, 1989). Because of the social comparative nature of sport and the high demands placed on competitors, both in training and competition, athletes (particularly those who are elite) are involved in an activity that is designed to challenge the adequacy of their perceived ability on a day-to-day basis.

Pertinent to any debate of the advantages or disadvantages of an ego orientation in sport are contemporary extensions of achievement goal models (e.g., Elliot, 1999; Elliot & McGregor, 2001). That is, recently some researchers have called for a reconsideration of dichotomous task/ego approaches to achievement goals and have instead advocated consideration of approach and avoidance aspects of an ego goal focus. An athlete would be considered ego-approach oriented when he or she is preoccupied with demonstrating superior ability compared to others. In contrast, an athlete emphasizing an ego-avoidance goal would be most concerned about not revealing his or her inferiority. For this athlete, the most important thing is to avoid showing that he or she does not possess adequate levels of ability. Central to this elaboration of the two-goal model of achievement goals (Nicholls, 1989) is the assumption that an ego approach goal orientation would positively relate to achievement striving, whereas an ego avoidance goal emphasis would be coupled with negative motivational outcomes.

Drawing from the existent research and similar to the findings of studies based on the dichotomous goal models, results regarding the presumed positive implications of ego-approach goals in sport-related settings have been equivocal (Adie, Duda, & Ntoumanis, 2008a; Nien & Duda, 2008). Our understanding of the nature, antecedents, and consequences of ego-avoidance goals, especially in contrast to an ego-approach goal perspective, is still in its infancy (Duda, 2005). An ego-avoidance perspective on sport achievement has been linked to greater fear of failure, stronger beliefs that sport ability is fixed or unchangeable, perceptions of an ego-involving climate, heightened anxiety, lower intrinsic motivation, and greater amotivation (Nien & Duda, 2008; Papaioannou, Zourbanos, Krommidas, & Ampatzoglou, 2012).

Regardless of skill level, or whether their ego goal focus is approach or avoidance oriented, those who are particularly concerned about how they are doing compared to others (ego-involved athletes) are likely to become prime candidates for questioning their competence. This might be a regular occurrence for those of us who are less talented but could strike *any* athlete at *any*

time. It is important at this point to remember that we are discussing *perceived* ability here, not *actual* ability. Although actual ability may not be altered during a game of tennis or a round of golf, athletes' perceptions of ability can and do change, often in a relatively short period of time, and are seldom stable over a long period of time. Indeed, recent lab-based research by Nien and Duda (2006) found that (in contrast to those focused on a task goal), the performance and affective responses of study participants who emphasized ego-approach goals were no different than what was observed for participants geared toward ego-avoidance goals following competitive losses in cycling races. Whether approach or avoidance-oriented, centering on ego goals translated into negative processes and outcomes when coupled with failure to demonstrate superiority. Such findings are not surprising when one considers that sport studies to date have found a strong positive correlation between ego approach and ego avoidance goal emphases (e.g., Nien & Duda, 2008). Moreover, aligned with theoretical expectations (Elliot, 1999), both ego-approach and ego-avoidance goals have been found to be tied to fear of failure in the sport domain (Nien & Duda, 2008).

How can ego involvement set the stage for performance impairment? Nicholls (1989) has suggested that the negative relationship between ego involvement and performance is instigated by the expectation an individual holds about looking incompetent. This expectation of looking low in ability can result in a decrease in performance in a number of ways. First, in an attempt to protect one's perceptions of competence, it may cause an athlete to select sport tasks that are too easy or too difficult. Although choosing to engage in less challenging tasks prevents the unhappy prospect of making errors and appearing to be less able, it simultaneously hinders an individual from developing a variety of sport skills to the maximum. Likewise, selecting tasks that are much too hard provides the athlete with a ready-made justification for the unsuccessful outcome as he or she is able to state, "I failed, but so did everyone else." This strategy, however, will be costly for the athlete in terms of maintaining or enhancing his or her skill development over time.

Second, the expectation of looking incompetent can result in a lack of trying when failure is looming and when it looks like one will appear less able compared to others. For example, athletes who back off at the end of a race because the outcome is already determined (i.e., they won't be the winner) and coast to the finish line or athletes who begin to engage in inappropriate achievement strategies or unsportspersonlike behavior when it looks like they will not be the best on that day are unlikely to ever reach their full potential.

Finally, if the expectation of demonstrating low ability becomes chronic, it may lead to regular and high levels of anxiety and, eventually, a devaluing of, and loss of interest in, the activity. If this chain of events occurs, it is likely that these athletes may find themselves in a state of amotivation (Vallerand, 2001). At the very least, if such high ego, approach-oriented athletes stay in sport, we might expect them to become strongly ego avoidance goal-oriented over time (Duda, 2005).

Elliot and McGregor (2001) also have distinguished between the approach and avoidance facets of task (or mastery-based) goals. This distinction has led to what is termed the 2 × 2 achievement goal framework. A task (or mastery) approach goal entails a focus on the development of personal competence and realization of task mastery. A task (or mastery) avoidance goal, on the other hand, centers on the avoidance of demonstrating self-referenced incompetence. To date, sport studies grounded in the 2 × 2 achievement goal model have pointed to the same advantages of a task approach goal as has been revealed in the multitude of studies based on dichotomous achievement goal frameworks (Duda, 2001, 2005; Dweck, 1999; Nicholls, 1989). Task approach goals have been found to correspond positively to perceptions of a task-involving climate, intrinsic motivation, perceived competence, self-esteem, life satisfaction, and the belief that sport competence is an

attribute that can be enhanced through training (e.g., Castillo, Duda, Alvarez, Merce, & Balaguer, 2011). Consistent with the predictions emanating from the 2 × 2 achievement goal model (Elliot & McGregor, 2001), task avoidance goals have been linked to negative processes and outcomes such as amotivation, self-handicapping, fear of failure, and anxiety (Nien & Duda, 2008). In a longitudinal study of young male soccer players, Adie, Duda, and Ntoumanis (2010) found task approach goals to positively predict and task avoidance to negatively correspond to changes in athletes' reported well-being over two competitive seasons. In contrast, players endorsing task approach goals at the beginning of the season exhibited less burnout when the season concluded.

Significance of the Sport Context

A key variable in determining the motivation of athletes is situational and relates to the salience of task- and ego-involving cues in the achievement context. The focus here is on how the *perceived* structure of the environment, often referred to as the **motivational climate** (Ames, 1992; Duda & Balaguer, 2007), can make it more or less likely that a particular goal state is manifested in training or competition. This perception of the motivational climate affects the achievement patterns of individuals through their view of what goals are reinforced in that setting (Treasure, 2001). In essence, perceptions of the goal perspectives emphasized in these social environments are assumed to be predictive of variability in motivational processes.

Sport research has shown that a perceived task-involving setting is characterized by the athletes' view that the coach does reinforce high effort, cooperation among team members, as well as learning and improvement, and the perception that everyone on the team (regardless of ability level) contributes to the team's achievements (Newton, Duda, & Zin, 1999). A perceived ego-involving team climate, in contrast, is marked by athletes perceiving that the coach punishes their mistakes, fosters rivalry among team members, and gives much of his or her attention to the most talented athletes on the team.

Research has shown a perceived task-involving climate to be associated with more adaptive motivational and affective patterns than perceptions of a performance or ego-involving climate in sport (Duda & Balaguer, 2007). For example, perceptions of task-involving coach-created environments have corresponded to greater enjoyment, more adaptive coping strategies, perceived competence, greater team cohesion and more positive peer relationships, and higher levels of moral functioning. Studies also have shown perceptions of a task-involving climate to be negatively related to claimed self-handicapping behavior in elite level sport (e.g., Kuczka & Treasure, 2005). **Self-handicapping** is evident when athletes who might be concerned about not performing well "set the stage" to provide an excuse or "scapegoat" to explain their poor subsequent performance. In so doing, failure could be attributed to the "handicap" rather than any inadequacy in personal ability. Such a strategy also allows athletes to save face in front of others.

In contrast, perceptions of an ego-involving motivational climate have been linked to greater anxiety and performance-related worry, dropping out of sport, greater peer conflict, greater self-handicapping, and lower levels of moral functioning (Duda & Balaguer, 2007). Other work has found perceptions of an ego-involving climate to positively predict indexes of physical ill-being among athletes (e.g., reported physical exhaustion and symptoms; Reinboth & Duda, 2004). Moreover, the degree to which the sport environment is deemed ego-involving appears to have implications for athletes' level of self-esteem and the degree to which their self-worth is tied to athletic performance (Reinboth & Duda, 2004). When athletes train and compete in a highly ego-involving motivational climate and have some doubts about their sport competence, they also are more likely to question their worth as a person overall. When a highly ego-involving atmosphere is deemed to be operating on a team, athletes also perceive their coach to provide less social support and positive feedback and be more punishment oriented (Duda & Balaguer, 2007).

Consideration of situational criteria from within achievement goal theories would not be complete, particularly in the context of youth sport, without taking into account the influence peers (Vazou, Ntoumanis, & Duda, 2007) and parents (White, 1996) have in the development of children's and adolescents' achievement motivation. The majority of the work on the motivational climates created by such significant others in the sport setting has concentrated on parental influences. This research points to the benefits of task-involving parents and the negative implications of an ego-involving parental climate (Duda, 2001).

Implications for Practice

The existent research establishing links between task and ego goals (whether dispositional or situational in nature or approach or avoidance centered) and various motivational patterns has contributed to our understanding of motivational processes in sport. But how do we enhance motivation based on the research grounded in achievement goal frameworks? According to theoretical predictions and existing empirical findings, high ego/low task athletes are the most susceptible to motivational difficulties. The evidence suggests that a sport psychology consultant should try to enhance the dispositional task goal orientation for these athletes, perhaps by introducing task involving, process or performance centered goal setting (see Chapter 11; Roberts & Kristiansen, 2012), and/or self-regulation techniques (e.g., Duda, Cumming, & Balaguer, 2005; see Chapter 12). We should consider implementing strategies that encourage athletes to focus on gains in skill or knowledge, monitoring effort levels, and self-referenced criteria for success. It may be very difficult in the ego-involving milieu of sport to reduce an athlete's ego orientation, and it is likely that many athletes and coaches will be unwilling to moderate what they believe is a vital ingredient in developing motivation in sport—namely, focusing on winning and being superior. A high ego orientation is not necessarily detrimental to achievement striving (at least from a quantity of motivation perspective; Duda, 2001), but it is especially problematic when coupled with low task orientation and low perceived competence, and/or grounded in a fear of looking incompetent. All in all, techniques designed to increase task orientation are likely to be more readily accepted by practitioners in the sport world and probably will be a more effective strategy for an applied sport psychologist to pursue.

Focusing on the individual to enhance the quality of motivation by affecting his or her dispositional goal orientations may seem a viable option, but practically speaking this strategy may be most suitable for an elite athlete who has access to a sport psychologist on a regular basis. Concentrating on individual change in dispositional tendencies may not be the most efficient and feasible alternative for a team or, especially, in the youth sport setting where the goal should be the development of *all* players rather than the performance of a select few. However, in a relatively short period of time, a coach may be able to structure a context in such a way as to influence athletes' recognition that they participate in a more task-involving motivational climate. In so doing, the coach can have a positive impact on the quality of athletes' sport participation.

In addition to coaches, particularly youth coaches, interventions designed to enhance motivation should target the attitudes and behaviors of Moms and Dads and other significant people in the athletes' lives. By making certain types of goals and performance feedback salient, a parent can influence young athletes' views about themselves, perceptions of the sport activity per se, and the criteria they use to evaluate success and failure. For example, when a young sport participant returns from a weekly tennis game and a parent asks, "Did you win?" the athlete receives a rather clear message as to what the parent considers most important. This

message may counter or compromise the efforts of a coach or sport psychologist to enhance task involvement. We would suggest, therefore, that any intervention designed to promote task involvement in sport recognize the role parents and other significant adults (e.g., league officials) and peers (Vazou et al., 2007) may play in determining a young athlete's views on how to define sport success and the manner in which he or she tends to judge demonstrated competence.

To enhance motivation, coaches, parents and sport psychologists should critically evaluate what they do and how they do it in terms of task and ego goals. For example, how do you define sport success for your players or children? Is it in terms of development and effort, or winning and losing? As a coach, do you design practice sessions that optimally challenge your players, or do you repeat well-learned skills that may delay or stifle development even though they increase the probability of winning today or right now? How do you evaluate performance? What behaviors do you consider desirable? Do you congratulate players and your children when they win and outperform others or when they try hard and improve? How do you react when the team, your athlete, or your child loses? If you feel that you coach, parent, or consult in a task-involving manner, then you are probably fostering the quality of athletes' motivation and promoting adaptive beliefs and positive achievement strategies. If your style of coaching, parenting, or consulting is ego-involving, you may be setting up more mature athletes or children, even those who are currently the most successful, for motivational difficulties in the future.

To assist the coach, parent, or sport psychologist in modifying the motivation-related atmosphere being created for athletes, Table 4-1 lists some suggestions on how to develop a task-involving motivational climate (Duda & Balaguer, 2007; Treasure, 2001). These suggestions have been organized around the task, authority, recognition, grouping, evaluation, and timing (TARGET) situational structures Epstein (1989) has argued make up the "basic building blocks" of the achievement environment.

Table 4-1 Description of TARGET Structures and Strategies That Enhance Task Involvement

TARGET Structure	Strategies
Task. What athletes are asked to learn and what tasks they are given to complete (e.g., training activities, structure of practice conditions).	Provide the athlete with a variety of moderately demanding tasks that emphasize individual challenge and active involvement.
	Assist athletes in goal setting.
	Create a developmentally appropriate training environment by individualizing the demands of the tasks set.
Authority. The kind and frequency of participation in the decision-making process (e.g., athlete involvement in decisions concerning training, the setting and enforcing of rules).	Encourage participation by your athletes in the decision-making process.
	Develop opportunities for leadership roles.
	Get athletes to take responsibility for their own sport development by teaching self-management and self-monitoring skills.
Recognition. Procedures and practices used to motivate and recognize athletes for their progress and achievement (e.g., reasons for recognition, distribution of rewards, and opportunities for rewards).	Use private meetings between coach and athlete to focus on individual progress.
	Recognize individual progress, effort, and improvement.
	Ensure equal opportunities for rewards to all.
Grouping. How athletes are brought together or kept apart in training and competition (e.g., the way in-groups are created during practice).	Use flexible and mixed ability grouping arrangements.
	Provide multiple grouping arrangements (i.e., individual, small group, and large group activities).
	Emphasize cooperative solutions to training problems set.
Evaluation. Standards set for athletes' learning and performance and the procedures for monitoring and judging attainment of these standards.	Develop evaluation criteria based on effort, improvement, persistence, and progress toward individual goals.
	Involve athletes in self-evaluation.
	Make evaluation meaningful. Be consistent.
Timing. Appropriateness of the time demands placed on learning and performance (e.g., pace of learning and development, management of time and training schedule).	Training programs should recognize that athletes, even at the elite level, do not train, learn, or develop at the same rate.
	Provide sufficient time before moving on to the next stage in skill development.
	Spend equal time with all athletes.
	Assist athletes in establishing training and competition schedules.

Doing It for the Joy: The Determinants of Intrinsic Motivation and Self-Determination

"Money is not a motivating factor. Money doesn't thrill me or make me play better because there are benefits to being wealthy. I'm just happy with a ball at my feet. My motivation comes from playing the game I love. If I wasn't paid to be a professional footballer I would willingly play for nothing."

Lionel Messi—Four-time winner of FIFA's world football player of the year award.

Sport is an achievement activity. Therefore, knowing how competent athletes perceive themselves and being aware of the criteria by which these athletes define their competence is relevant to their motivation in sport. Also relevant to motivational patterns are the reasons *why* athletes decide to participate in their selected sport activity. The reasons for sport engagement can range from autonomous reasons (i.e., one participates because of a "love of the game" and/or because he/she personally values the benefits of participation) to more controlling reasons (i.e., one participates to obtain extrinsic rewards outside the activity itself and/or because he or she feels compelled to engage in sport).

Self-determination theory (SDT; Ryan & Deci, 2002) has become a very popular approach to understanding motivation and behavior in sport. Fundamentally, SDT distinguishes between behaviors that individuals perform freely or autonomously and those that they pursue for more or less extrinsic or controlled reasons. The theory examines why an individual acts (i.e., the level that their motivation is more or less self-determined), how various types of motivation lead to different outcomes, and what social conditions support or undermine optimal functioning and well-being via the satisfaction of basic psychological needs.

There are different types of autonomous and controlled motivation, and according to Deci and Ryan (2002) they vary along a self-determination continuum (Figure 4-1). We will start by describing the least self-determined types of motivation

and move toward a portrayal of more autonomous motivational regulations (Vallerand, 2001). First are those athletes characterized by **amotivation.** These athletes have no sense of personal control with respect to their sport engagement, and there are no extrinsic (or intrinsic) reasons for doing the activity. Amotivated athletes are no longer sure of why they are playing their sport.

Next on the continuum come three forms of extrinsic motivation, with the least autonomous being **external regulation.** In this case, behavior is performed to satisfy an external demand or stems from the external rewards an athlete expects to secure. For example, an athlete might say "I'm going to practice today but only because my scholarship depends on it." With the second form of extrinsic motivation, **introjected regulation,** athletes participate because they feel they *have* to play sport. Such motivation is still extrinsic in nature; it only replaces the external source of control with an internalized contingency. For example, "I'm going to practice today because I can't deal with the guilt I will feel if I miss." With the third type of extrinsic motivation, **identified regulation,** behavior is undertaken out of free choice but as a means to an end (and in terms of some personally endorsed value and benefit). For example, an athlete who has high identified motivation and wants to improve his fitness level chooses not to miss any sessions during off-season conditioning and preseason training. The athlete engages in this regular fitness training out of personal choice, even though the activity is very demanding and can be unpleasant.

At the opposite end of the self-determination continuum is the classic state of **intrinsic motivation,** in which an athlete participates in an activity for its own sake and because he or she personally chooses to do so. It is highly autonomous and represents the quintessential state of self-determination (Ryan & Deci, 2002).

Interviews with elite Australian track and field athletes (Mallett & Hanrahan, 2004) offer support for Deci and Ryan's (1985) multidimensional conceptualization of extrinsic motivation. Mallett and Hanrahan found that in addition to excitement, enjoyment, a love for competing

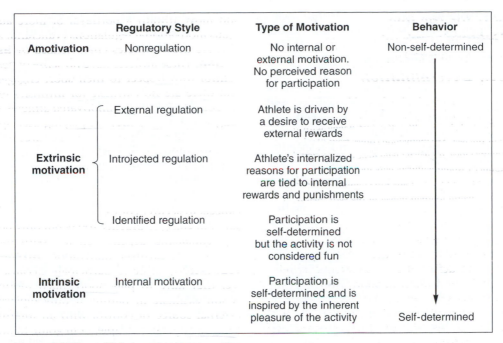

Regulatory Style	Type of Motivation	Behavior

Amotivation   Nonregulation — No internal or external motivation. No perceived reason for participation — Non-self-determined

Extrinsic motivation
- External regulation — Athlete is driven by a desire to receive external rewards
- Introjected regulation — Athlete's internalized reasons for participation are tied to internal rewards and punishments
- Identified regulation — Participation is self-determined but the activity is not considered fun

Intrinsic motivation   Internal motivation — Participation is self-determined and is inspired by the inherent pleasure of the activity — Self-determined

Figure 4-1 The self-determination continuum
Source: Deci & Ryan, 1985, 1992. With kind permission of Springer Science and Business Media.

at the highest level, and a sense of relatedness with fellow athletes, less self-determined motives for participation emerged. Specifically, these elite level athletes identified money and social recognition as motives while others spoke to the job aspect of the sport. The data showed, however, that the athletes had successfully managed to internalize and integrate the more self-determined extrinsic motivation regulations into their personal values as elite level performers. This is an important finding as motivation-related differences between athletes who engage in sport for more or less self-determined reasons are likely to be great.

A fundamental tenet of self-determination theory is that autonomous motivation is *quality* motivation. Individuals engaged in an activity by choice and intrinsic reasons will experience better consequences than those whose participation is less autonomous. Research has found a positive relationship between autonomous motivation and higher levels of task perseverance and

psychological well-being and found it to be negatively related to feelings of stress, anxiety, and self-criticism in sport (e.g., Gagné, Ryan, & Bargmann, 2003; Krane, Greenleaf, & Snow, 1997). Consistent with this line of inquiry, recent studies have suggested that SDT may provide a useful framework to understand burnout in sport. In a sample of elite level swimmers, Lemyre, Treasure, and Roberts (2006) found that over the course of a competitive swimming season, susceptibility to burnout was more likely to occur when an athlete's reasons for participating shift to a more extrinsic motivation regulation. Aligned with the findings of Lemyre and colleagues, a study by Cresswell and Eklund (2005) on burnout among top amateur rugby union players showed intrinsic motivation to be negatively associated, amotivation positively associated, and extrinsic regulation not related to reported burnout.

According to SDT, whether or not an athlete has more or less self-determined reasons for engaging in sport is dependent on his or her degree of basic need satisfaction. More specifically, Deci and Ryan (2002; Ryan & Deci, 2002) propose that all of us, athletes and nonathletes alike, need to feel **competent** (i.e., feel sufficiently efficacious to interact effectively with the environment), **autonomous** (i.e., perceive we are acting according to our own volition and have options and choices), and **connected** with others (i.e., view relationships with important individuals as being supportive and respectful) within our various life domains. When the sport environment meets these three basic needs, we expect to witness greater self-determination, investment, and well-being in the athletic setting (Adie, Duda, & Ntoumanis, 2008b, 2012; Alvarez, Balaguer, Castillo, & Duda, 2009; Reinboth, Duda, & Ntoumanis, 2004) and reduced indicators of athlete ill-being (Adie, Duda, & Ntoumanis, 2008b; Reinboth, Duda, & Ntoumanis, 2004).

Understanding the social contexts that facilitate athletes' motivation, performance, and well-being via the satisfaction of these needs is an important line of inquiry. To this end, research in youth (e.g., Reinboth et al., 2004) and amateur as well as elite sport (e.g., Adie, Duda, & Ntoumanis, 2008b, 2012; Balaguer, Castillo, & Duda, 2008; Reinboth & Duda, 2006; Treasure, Lemyre, Kuczka, & Standage, 2007) has shown that perceptions of autonomy support (and the degree of involvement or social support offered) from the coach positively predict the satisfaction of the participants' needs for competence, relatedness, and autonomy. Coaches who are autonomy supportive solicit their athletes' input, offer meaningful choices, provide a rationale for their requests, and downplay the presence of or potential motivating impact of extrinsic rewards. Socially supportive coaches are there to help when needed and indicate they care and respect their athletes (even if they are not performing well!).

More recently, SDT-based research in the sport domain has considered the implications of autonomy supportive *and* controlling coach behaviors on need satisfaction as well as the *thwarting* of athletes' basic needs for competence, autonomy and relatedness (Bartholomew, Ntoumanis, & Thogersen-Ntoumani, 2011). Highly controlling coaches tend to intimidate their athletes, run their team in an autocratic fashion, and use extrinsic rewards to control the behavior of the players on their team. When athletes' needs are thwarted by a coach, there is an active attempt to have athletes feel incompetent, "like a pawn on a chessboard" and disconnected from the coach (and potentially their own teammates). In their research on young male soccer players across a competitive season, Balaguer and colleagues found changes in coaches' autonomy–supportive behaviors to correspond to the athletes feeling greater need satisfaction and reporting less need thwarting over time. When the players felt more competent, autonomous, and related over the season they also experienced greater vitality (i.e., feelings of energy) and reported fewer burnout symptoms. On the other hand, changes in the players' perceptions of a controlling coach-created environment corresponded to players reporting greater need thwarting across the season. Need thwarting was positively associated with increases in player burnout.

Galen Rupp, Olympic Silver Medalist Nike Oregon Project

"Running is my profession and I take it very seriously. It is how I make my living and support my family. However, money has never been the reason for running a race and I firmly believe that you have to love what you do first. The love of the sport and the love of competition is the reason why I run."

At the 2012 London Summer Olympics, Galen Rupp became the first American male to medal in the 10,000 meters since 1964, finishing only behind training partner and Nike Oregon Project teammate Great Britain's Mo Farah. Both Rupp and Farah are coached by Alberto Salazar and are part of an elite

need thwarting?

distance running group based at Nike's World Headquarters in Portland, Oregon. Rupp's own words speak to the self-determined nature of his motivation for engagement in running and echoes research conducted by Mallett and Hanrahan (2004) that has examined motivation types in elite level sport. Similar to Mallett and Hanrahan's findings with elite male and female Australian track and field athletes, Rupp's participation motives emphasize excitement, enjoyment, and a love for competing at the highest level. Financial considerations are also a factor in determining why he participates in professional running but they are clearly not a primary motivation factor.

One of the authors of this chapter (Treasure) has been fortunate to work with Rupp since he was a 19-year-old sophomore at the University of Oregon. By then, Galen had been training and competing at an elite level for over 4 years. He received an athletic scholarship to attend and compete for the university. Consistent with Cognitive Evaluation Theory (Deci & Ryan, 1980), Galen always viewed the scholarship he received as affirmation of his ability and the choices he had made during high school and throughout his time at Oregon. It is really important to understand that like many sports, the lifestyle of an elite level distance runner is far from glamorous. During the hardest training phase of the year, Galen will run upwards of 120 miles in a week, lift weights two or three times per week, and attend to his daily ongoing physical therapy needs. During the intense training period, Galen's days are dominated with three primary activities, namely running, eating, and sleeping. His year is split into two macro-training blocks with a peaking period at the end of each

block. Following each peak he takes two weeks off before starting the next macro cycle. The challenges both physically and mentally are staggering and would be very difficult to overcome over a long period of time if an athlete was participating primarily or solely for extrinsic reasons.

Working with Galen readily reveals how he evaluates and brings into congruence the behaviors and demands of an elite level distance runner with his own values and needs. He is very self-aware and understands what he needs to do to be successful in his chosen profession. In addition to his own more self-determined motivation, Galen trains and competes in an environment that is more likely to be adaptive, based on the fundamental tenets of self-determination and achievement goal theories.

Recognizing that motivation is the foundation of athletic development and performance, the Oregon Project coaches and support staff purposefully and proactively work at establishing a need-supportive environment (Ryan & Deci, 2000) that is more task involving (Nicholls, 1989). Specifically, we strive to create a training environment in which each athlete's psychological needs are satisfied and perceptions of competence are self-referenced. The coaches provide constructive, detailed, and positive feedback and are always striving to optimize the training demands to facilitate each athlete's perceptions of ability (Deci & Moller, 2005). Although evaluation in any sport is inherently socially comparative, each Oregon Project athlete has an individual performance plan that is self-referenced and based on his/her individual advancement. Each athlete is an active participant in determining training goals and establishing a year-long race plan helping to ensure an internal *perceived locus of control and the belief that individuals are the origin of his or her own behavior. Given the arduous nature of the lifestyle and training demands of Oregon Project athletes, the coaches spend considerable time in providing a meaningful rationale for what each athlete is to do on a daily basis (Ericsson, 2006).*

In addition to facilitating the basic needs of competence and autonomy each athlete's need for relatedness is purposefully addressed. Indeed, the quality of relationships among the athletes, coaches, and support staff has been widely acknowledged as a critical factor in the success of the Oregon Project. The dedication of time and attention ensures that each athlete has a true understanding and perception that the staff cares about them not just as competitors but also as individuals. Beyond the daily interactions both on and off the track, the ongoing evaluation process that is central to the Oregon Project system (e.g., regular performance reviews, training/race evaluations) is specifically designed to afford the opportunity for any dissatisfaction and/or objections to be shared by the athletes and thus ensure that each athlete's voice is heard and respected (Reeve, 2009).

Intrinsic Motivation in the Often Extrinsic World of Sport

At all competitive levels, some athletes play sport for intrinsic reasons. The sources of that intrinsic interest may vary. It may be the continuous learning that sport affords, the possibility of personal accomplishment and mastery, or the opportunity to experience pleasant sensations whether they be sensory or aesthetic (Vallerand, 2001). All in all, intrinsically motivated athletes find sport pleasurable in and of itself and

are maximally motivated both quantitatively and qualitatively. Indeed, we would argue that it is most unlikely that athletes, even multimillionaires, would be able to sustain high levels of motivation and commitment throughout their careers if they did not have high levels of intrinsic motivation for engaging in their sport, particularly during periods of adversity, duress, and poor performance.

From youth sport onward, competitive athletics is dominated by extrinsic reinforcements. One can win medals and trophies. Fame and fortune may be the consequences of sport involvement for some. Talented college athletes in the United States may be rewarded with scholarships. Athletes at the professional level are paid for their sport achievements. An interesting question, therefore, is, What is the effect of extrinsic rewards on intrinsic motivation? The answer to this question is, "It depends." Athletes who are intrinsically motivated and receive extrinsic rewards are not necessarily more motivated. Indeed, research has indicated that extrinsic rewards can diminish intrinsic interest (Deci & Ryan, 1985). Rewards, however, also can foster intrinsic motivation. What seems to be critical in sport is to consider how extrinsic reinforcements are interpreted by individual athletes. That is, what do these rewards mean to the athlete?

Extrinsic rewards have a *controlling* aspect. The use of extrinsic reinforcements by coaches and parents can provide athletes with a sense of "who is pulling the strings" in terms of their sport involvement. Rewards are detrimental to intrinsic motivation when they take away from athletes' sense of self-determination. Consider how a coach might refer to an intercollegiate athlete's scholarship and the resulting impact on that athlete's intrinsic interest in the sport. Perhaps, during the recruitment process, the coach repeatedly used the scholarship to coax the athlete to come play for his or her team. In this case the athlete's decision to play for this coach might be more likely to be perceived as contingent on this external reward rather than being self-determined. When that athlete performs poorly, if the coach says, "How can you play like that? We're paying you to perform!", the athlete might think of his or her participation as more like work and less like an inherently enjoyable activity, which may lead to motivational difficulties.

It is important to keep in mind that sometimes rewards inform us about our level of competence and worth. When receiving the reward is contingent on personally controllable aspects of performance and an athlete obtains the reward, this should increase his or her perceived ability while not undermining self-determination. As a result, it should foster intrinsic motivation. The social environment that surrounds athletes (which is created by coaches, parents, sport psychologists, peers, the media, and fans) has a huge impact on the meaning of extrinsic rewards. Whether extrinsic reinforcements are likely to be viewed as controlling or informational regarding one's ability is a function of characteristics of these environments. In sport situations that allow athletes little autonomy, the rewards are more likely to be interpreted in a controlling manner.

Implications for Practice

> "Yes, we're disciplined with what we do. But that's not enough. Relationships with people are what it's all about. You have to make players realize you care about them. And they have to care about each other and be interested in each other. Then they start to feel a responsibility toward each other. Then they want to do for each other."
>
> Greg Popovich, Head Coach San Antonio Spurs—Popovich is the longest tenured coach in the NBA. He has won four NBA championships as the head coach of the Spurs.

The literature on intrinsic motivation and self-determination in sport provides another rationale for cultivating perceived competence as well as perceived personal control and feelings of connection among sport participants. In essence, this research indicates that perceived adequate ability, feelings of autonomy, and feeling that one is cared for and respected in the sport setting are the fuel that fire athletes' intrinsic motivation. Caution in the use (and especially the overuse) of extrinsic reinforcements in athletic settings is required. Extrinsic rewards must be salient to the athletes to have any influence, positive or negative, and should be used sparingly so that athletes are less likely to construct a behavior–reward contingency (i.e., "If I do this, I will get that"). This can promote an external locus of control in the athlete's sport involvement. The goals cooperatively set among coach, sport psychologist, and athlete (see Chapter 12) should be performance rather than primarily outcome based, more task involving (Roberts & Kristiansen, 2012) and intrinsic in nature (Deci & Ryan, 2002). They also should be realistic, that is, optimally challenging with the exertion of effort. Achieving these goals will enhance perceptions of competence and are more within the athlete's personal control than goals tied to competitive outcomes.

Finally, coaches and other significant people in athletes' lives can foster their self-determination (Reinboth et al., 2004) in other ways. We have already discussed the motivational significance of a task- versus ego-involving sport environment. Drawing from the SDT literature, it is important to try to make the athletic environment as autonomy supportive as possible. Considering the athletes' perspective and allowing them to make choices in training and competition events should cultivate a greater sense of personal autonomy. SDT and related research also points to the relevance of socially supportive sport environments (Reinboth et al., 2004). Socially supportive coaches are there to assist athletes when they need help and convey that they care about their athletes as people rather than only as sport performers. Committed and compatible coach–athlete relationships (Olympiou, Jowett, & Duda, 2008) and the fostering of positive social exchanges between and cooperation among team members should also lead to an enhanced sense of relatedness and social support.

Summary

Research and the wisdom gleaned from practice suggest motivation is a key ingredient in athletes' success, and we need to recognize that the quantity *and* quality of athletes' motivation is inferred from a constellation of behaviors, emotions, and cognitive variables—not from competitive sport performance alone. Athletes are more likely to exhibit an adaptive form of motivation when they perceive they have the necessary capabilities to match the psychological and physical challenges of the sport in question, have a sense of personal autonomy, and feel connected to others in regard to their sport involvement. Motivation deficits appear when an athlete doesn't think he or she "has what it takes," perceives him or herself to be like "a pawn on a chessboard," and/or feels disenfranchised from or not respected by relevant others in the sport setting. In other words, understanding variations in sport motivation implies that we pay attention to athletes' thoughts regarding issues of competence, personal control, and connectedness to others.

When sport participants feel competent and in charge of their own destiny, their motivation to participate is more likely to be more internalized. When athletes play sport for the love of the game and other self-determined reasons, they do not need external rewards to encourage or legitimize their involvement. As a consequence, coaches, sport psychologists, and other significant social agents in athletes' lives need to be careful when considering the use of extrinsic reinforcements as a means to increase motivation so that they do not diminish intrinsic interest. External reward contingencies can lead to self-determination if they inform athletes about their gains in competence, are not employed in overabundance, and are provided in an autonomy–supportive manner. Otherwise, they may cause more harm than good.

Research on achievement goals has indicated that how athletes judge their competence level is also critical to motivational processes and outcomes. A focus on task involvement in the athletic setting has several advantages, including that the source of subjective success is more within the athlete's direct influence and is less likely to result in feelings of incompetence. Defining sport competence in terms of self-referenced effort or task mastery criteria repeatedly stokes the motivation fire.

An emphasis on ego involvement can advance an athlete's desire to excel too, but it can also have its motivational costs. First, a strong ego focus, whether approach or avoidance oriented, leads athletes to perceive opponents and teammates as primarily reference points for feeling more or less competent, rather than cohorts with whom we learn, collaborate to improve individually and collectively, or cooperate in competition. Thus, an emphasis on ego goals can jeopardize an athlete's sense of connectedness in the sport environment.

Second, when aiming to reach ego-centered goals, the criteria for success (showing superiority or avoiding the demonstration of inferiority) are less within the athlete's control, which endangers her or his sense of autonomy. Finally, no matter the degree of athletic prowess or the competitive level of the athlete, emphasizing ego goals can prove detrimental if that individual's confidence starts to waiver and she or he possesses a weak task orientation. In this instance, the athlete desperately wants to be the best, fears he or she will not be, and has no other meaningful way of redefining her or his goals and sense of competence to feel good about the performance. Because the world of sport is competitive, challenging, and conducive to competence questioning, coaches, parents, and sport psychologists should encourage task involvement in an attempt to optimize sport motivation.

Study Questions

1. What are the behavioral characteristics that reflect whether an athlete's motivation is high or low?

2. What is the difference between the quantity and quality of motivation among athletes?

3. How do task- and ego-involved athletes differ in the way they judge their competence and perceive success in sport?

4. What are the distinctions between and consequences of being more ego-approach or ego-avoidance goal oriented?

5. Define and give an example of a task (or mastery) approach and task avoidance goal focus.

6. Illustrate how being primarily oriented to ego goals can set the stage for performance impairment and motivational difficulties.

7. What do we mean when we say that an athlete is intrinsically motivated in contrast to extrinsically motivated?

8. Describe the process by which external rewards can influence the intrinsic motivation of athletes.

9. What are ways in which we can make a sport environment more autonomy supportive and less controlling?

References

Adie, J., Duda, J. L., & Ntoumanis, N. (2008a). Achievement goals, competition appraisals and the psychological and emotional welfare of sport participants. *Journal of Sport and Exercise Psychology, 30,* 302–322.

Adie, J., Duda, J. L., & Ntoumanis, N. (2008b). Autonomy support, basic need satisfaction and optimal functioning in adult male and female sport participants: A test of basic needs theory. *Motivation and Emotion, 32,* 189–199.

Adie, J. W., Duda, J. L., & Ntoumanis, N. (2010). Achievement goals, competition appraisals and the well- and ill-being of elite youth soccer players over two competitive seasons. *Journal of Sport and Exercise Psychology, 32,* 555–579.

Adie, J. W., Duda, J. L., & Ntoumanis, N. (2012). Perceived coach-autonomy support, basic need satisfaction and the well- and ill-being of elite youth soccer players: A longitudinal investigation. *Psychology of Sport and Exercise, 13,* 51–59.

Alvarez, M. S., Balaguer, I., Castillo, I., & Duda, J. L. (2009). Coach autonomy support and quality of sport engagement in young soccer players. *The Spanish Journal of Psychology, 12,* 138–148.

Alvarez, M. S., Balaguer, I., Castillo, I., & Duda, J. L. (2012). The coach-created motivational climate, young athletes' well-being, and intentions to continue participation. *Journal of Clinical Sport Psychology, 6,* 166–179.

Ames, C. (1992). Achievement goals, motivational climate, and motivational processes. In G. C. Roberts (Ed.), *Motivation in sport and exercise* (pp. 161–176). Champaign, IL: Human Kinetics.

Balaguer, I., Castillo, I., & Duda, J. L. (2008). Apoyo a la autonomia satisfacción de las necesidades, motivation, y bienestar en deportistas de competición: Un analysis de la teoria de la autodeterminación (Autonomy support, needs satisfaction, motivation and well-being in competitive athletes: A test of Self-Determination Theory). *Revista de Psicología del Deporte, 17,* 123–139.

Balaguer, I., González, L., Fabra, P., Castillo, I., Mercé, J., & Duda, J. L. (2012). Coaches' interpersonal style, basic psychological needs and the well- and ill-being of young soccer players: A longitudinal analysis. *Journal of Sports Sciences, 30(15),* 1–11.

Bartholomew, K. J., Ntoumanis, N., & Thogersen-Ntoumani, C. (2011). Self-determination theory and the darker side of athletic experience: The role of interpersonal control and need thwarting. *Sport and Exercise Psychology Review, 7,* 23–27.

Castillo, I., Duda, J. L., Alvarez, M. S., Merce, J., & Balaguer, I. (2011). Motivational climate, approach-avoidance achievement goals and well-being in young soccer players. *Revista De Psicologia Del Deporte, 20,* 149–164.

Cresswell, S. L., & Eklund, R. C. (2005). Motivation and burnout among top amateur rugby players. *Medicine and Science in Sports and Exercise, 37,* 469–477.

Deci, E. L., & Moller, A. C. (2005). The concept of competence: A starting place for understanding intrinsic motivation and self-determined extrinsic motivation. In A. J. Elliott & C. S. Dweck (Eds.), *Handbook of competence and motivation* (pp. 579–597). New York: Guildford Press.

Deci, E. L., & Ryan, R. M. (1980). The empirical exploration of intrinsic motivation processes. In L. Berkowitz (Ed.), *Advances in experimental social psychology* (pp. 39–80). New York, Academic Press.

Deci, E. L., & Ryan, R. M. (1985). *Intrinsic motivation and self-determination in human behavior.* New York: Plenum.

Deci, E. L., & Ryan, R. M. (2002). (Eds.). *Handbook of self-determination research.* Rochester, NY: University of Rochester Press.

Duda, J. L. (2001). Goal perspective research in sport: Pushing the boundaries and clarifying some misunderstandings. In G. C. Roberts (Ed.), *Advances in motivation in sport and exercise* (pp. 129–182). Champaign, IL: Human Kinetics.

Duda, J. L. (2005). Motivation in sport: The relevance of competence and achievement goals. In A. J. Elliot & C. S. Dweck (Eds.), *Handbook of competence and motivation* (pp. 318–335). New York: Guildford Publications.

Duda, J. L., & Balaguer, I. (2007). The coach-created motivational climate. In S. Jowett & D. Lavalee (Eds.), *Social psychology of sport* (pp. 117–130). Champaign, IL: Human Kinetics.

Duda, J. L., Cumming, J., & Balaguer, I. (2005). Enhancing athletes' self regulation, task involvement, and self-determination via psychological skills training. In D. Hackfort, J. Duda, & R. Lider (Eds.), *Handbook of applied sport psychology research* (pp. 159–181). Morgantown, WV: Fitness Information Technology.

Dweck, C. S. (1999). *Self-theories and goals: Their role in motivation, personality, and development.* Philadelphia, PA: Taylor & Francis.

Elliot, A. J. (1999). Approach and avoidance motivation and achievement goals. *Educational Psychologist, 34,* 169–189.

Elliot, A. J., & McGregor, H. A. (2001). A 2 × 2 achievement goal framework. *Journal of Personality and Social Psychology, 80,* 501–519.

Epstein, J. (1989). Family structures and student motivation: A developmental perspective. In C. Ames & R. Ames (Eds.), *Research on motivation in education: Vol. 3* (pp. 259–295). New York: Academic Press.

Ericsson, K. A. (2006). The influence of experience and deliberate practice on the development of superior expert performance. In K. A. Ericsson, N. Charness, P. Feltovich, & R. R. Hoffman (Eds.), *Cambridge handbook of expertise and expert performance* (pp. 685–706). Cambridge, UK: Cambridge University Press.

Gagne, M., Ryan, R. M., & Bargmann, K. (2003). Autonomy support and need satisfaction in the motivation and well-being of gymnasts. *Journal of Applied Sport Psychology, 15,* 372–390.

Isoard-Gautheur, S., Guillet-Descas, E., & Duda, J. L. (2013). How to achieve in elite training centers without burning out? An achievement goal theory perspective. *Psychology of Sport and Exercise, 14,* 72–83.

Krane, V., Greenleaf, C. A., & Snow, J. (1997). Reaching for gold and the practice of glory: A motivational case study of an elite gymnast. *The Sport Psychologist, 11,* 53–71.

Kuczka, K., & Treasure, D. C. (2005). Self-handicapping in competitive sport: Influence of the motivational climate, self-efficacy and perceived importance. *Psychology of Sport and Exercise, 6,* 539–550.

Lemyre, P. N., Treasure, D. C., & Roberts, G. C. (2006). Influence of variability of motivation and affect on elite athlete burnout susceptibility. *Journal of Sport and Exercise Psychology, 28,* 32–48.

Maddux, J. E. (1995). Self-efficacy theory: An introduction. In J. E. Maddux (Ed.), *Self-efficacy, adaptation, and adjustment* (pp. 3–33). New York: Plenum.

Mallett, C. J., & Hanrahan, S. J. (2004). Elite athletes: Why does the "fire" burn so brightly? *Psychology of Sport and Exercise, 5,* 183–200.

Newton, M. L., Duda, J. L., & Yin, Z. (2000). Examination of the psychometric properties of the perceived motivational climate in sport questionnaire-2 in a sample of female athletes. *Journal of Sports Sciences, 18,* 275–290.

Nicholls, J. (1989). *The competitive ethos and democratic education.* Cambridge, MA: Harvard University Press.

Olympiou, A., Jowett, S., & Duda, J. L. (2008). The psychological interface between the coach-created motivational climate and the coach-athlete relationship in team sports. *The Sport Psychologist, 22,* 423–438.

Nien, C. L., & Duda, J. L. (2006). The effect of situationally-emphasised achievement goals and win/loss on engagement in a cycle ergometer task. Presented at Annual Conference of the British Association of Sport and Exercise Sciences, Wolverhampton, UK. ISSN 0264-0414 print/ISSN1466-447X online.

Nien, C., & Duda, J. L. (2008). Antecedents and consequences of approach and avoidance achievement goals: A test of gender invariance. *Psychology of Sport and Exercise, 9*, 352–372.

Nien, C., & Duda, J. L. (in press). Construct validity of multiple achievement goals: A multitrait-multimethod approach. *International Journal of Sport and Exercise Psychology.*

Olympiou, A., Jowett, S., & Duda, J. L. (2008). The psychological interface between the coach-created motivational climate and the coach-athlete relationship in team sports. *The Sport Psychologist, 22*, 423–439.

Papaioannou, A., Zourbanos, N., Krommidas, C., & Ampatzoglou, G. (2012). The place of achievement goals in the social context of sport: A comparison of Nicholls' and Elliot's models. In G. C. Roberts & D. C. Treasure (Eds.), *Advances in Motivation in Sport and Exercise* (pp. 59–90). Champaign, IL, Human Kinetics.

Reeve, J. (2009). Why teachers adopt a controlling motivating style toward students and how they can become more autonomy supportive. *Educational Psychologist, 44*, 159–175.

Reinboth, M., & Duda, J. L. (2004). Relationship of the perceived motivational climate and perceptions of ability to psychological and physical well-being in team sports. *The Sport Psychologist, 18*, 237–251.

Reinboth, M., & Duda, J. L. (2006). Perceived motivational climate, need satisfaction and indices of well-being in team sports: A longitudinal perspective. *Psychology of Sport and Exercise, 7*, 269–286.

Reinboth, M., Duda, J. L., & Ntoumanis, N. (2004). Dimensions of coaching behavior, need satisfaction, and the psychological and physical welfare of young athletes. *Motivation and Emotion, 28*, 297–313.

Roberts, G. C., & Kristiansen, E. (2012). Goal setting to enhance motivation in sport. In G. C. Roberts & D. C. Treasure (Eds.) *Advances in Motivation in Sport and Exercise* (pp. 207-227). Champaign, IL, Human Kinetics.

Roberts, G. C., Treasure, D. C., & Kavussanu, M. (1997). Motivation in physical activity contexts: An achievement goal perspective. In M. L. Maehr & P. R. Pintrich (Eds.), *Advances in motivation and achievement. Vol. 10* (pp. 413–447). Greenwich, CT: JAI Press.

Ryan, R. M., & Deci, E. L. (2000). Self-determination theory and the facilitation of intrinsic motivation, social development, and well-being. *American Psychologist, 55*, 68–78.

Ryan, R. M., & Deci, E. L. (2002). An overview of self-determination theory: An organismic-dialectical perspective. In E. L. Deci & R. M. Ryan (Eds.), *Handbook of self-determination research* (pp. 3–33). Rochester, NY: University of Rochester Press.

Ryan, R. M., & Deci, E. L. (2007). Active human nature: Self-determination theory and the promotion and maintenance of sport, exercise and health. In M. S. Haggar and N. L. D. Chatzisarantis (Eds.) *Intrinsic motivation and self-determination in exercise and sport,* (pp. 1–20). Champaign, IL: Human Kinetics.

Sarrazin, P., Biddle, S. J. H., Famose, J. P., Cury, F., Fox, K. R., & Durand, M. (1996). Goal orientations and conceptions of sport ability in children: A social cognitive approach. *British Journal of Social Psychology, 35*, 399–414.

Treasure, D. C. (2001). Enhancing young people's motivation in physical activity. In G. C. Roberts (Ed.), *Advances in motivation in sport and exercise* (pp. 79–100). Champaign, IL: Human Kinetics.

Treasure, D. C., Lemyre, P. N., Kuczka, K. K., & Standage, M. (2007). Motivation in elite level sport: A self-determination perspective. In M. S. Haggar and N. L. D. Chatzisarantis (Eds.) *Intrinsic motivation and self-determination in exercise and sport,* (pp. 153–166). Champaign, IL: Human Kinetics.

Vallerand, R. (2001). A hierarchical model of intrinsic and extrinsic motivation in sport and exercise. In G. C. Roberts (Ed.), *Advances in motivation in sport and exercise* (pp. 263–320). Champaign, IL: Human Kinetics.

Vazou, S., Ntoumanis, N., & Duda, J. L. (2007). Perceptions of peer motivational climate in youth sport: Measurement development and implications for practice. In S. Jowett & D. Lavalee (Eds.), *Social psychology of sport* (pp. 145–156). Champaign, IL: Human Kinetics.

White, S. A. (1996). Goal orientation and perceptions of the motivational climate initiated by parents. *Pediatric Exercise Science, 8,* 122–129.

The Self-Fulfilling Prophecy Theory: When Coaches' Expectations Become Reality

Thelma Sternberg Horn, *Miami University*
Curt L. Lox, *Southern Illinois University*
Francisco Labrador, *Wittenberg University*

I couldn't believe it! This kid came to the first day of Little League draft tryouts with bright purple and spiked hair! Me and all of the other coaches . . . none of us wanted him on our team. But, in the last round of draft picks, I got stuck with him. The funny thing is that by the end of the season, he turned out to be our team's Most Valuable Player! Once you got past the purple hair, the kid was a real solid baseball player.

—*Coach of a Little League Baseball Team*

In 1968 Rosenthal and Jacobson published the results of an experiment they had conducted with teachers and students in 18 elementary school classrooms. This research study, which was appropriately titled "Pygmalion in the Classroom," had been designed to determine whether the academic progress of students could actually be affected by their teachers' expectations or beliefs concerning their intellectual abilities. To investigate this issue, Rosenthal and Jacobson informed the sample of teachers that certain children in each of their classes had been identified, via scores on a standardized test of academic ability, as latent achievers or "late bloomers" who could be expected to show big gains in academic achievement over the coming school year.

In actuality, the identified children had been selected at random from the total group, and there was no reason to expect that they would show any greater academic progress than their classmates. At the end of the school year, however, many of the targeted children, especially those in the lower elementary grades, had made greater gains intellectually than had children who were not so identified. Rosenthal and Jacobson (1968) concluded that the false information given to the teachers had led them to hold higher expectations for the targeted children and then to act in ways that would stimulate better performance from those students. Thus, the authors were suggesting that the teachers' expectations served as self-fulfilling prophecies by initiating a series of events that ultimately caused the expectations to be fulfilled.

The publication of this study stimulated an impressive amount of research during the next several decades on the topic of expectancy effects, primarily as they might occur in the academic classroom but also in physical education classrooms or in competitive sport contexts (e.g., Horn, 1984; Martinek, 1988; Papaioannou, 1995; Rejeski, Darracott, & Hutslar, 1979; Sinclair & Vealey, 1989; Solomon, Golden, Ciapponi, & Martin, 1998; Solomon, Trouilloud, Sarrazin, Bressoux, & Bois, 2006). Several excellent reviews of the educationally based research studies have been compiled (e.g., Good & Brophy, 2000; Jussim & Harber, 2005), and the results indicate that teachers' expectations certainly do have the potential to affect the academic progress of individual students. However, these writers also caution that the overall effects of teacher expectations appear to be relatively small, with effect sizes ranging from .1 to .3. Furthermore, there does appear to be considerable variability between teachers (and, by extension, coaches) in the degree to which their expectations can and do affect their own behavior as well as the learning and performance of their student-athletes. Specifically, researchers (e.g., Jussim, Eccles, & Madon, 1996; Kuklinski & Weinstein, 2001; Trouilloud et al., 2006) have found that under some conditions the impact of teachers' expectations on student learning and performance is much more powerful than the average effect size would suggest. Thus, although many teachers and coaches are not Pygmalion-prone (i.e., they do not allow their expectations to affect the performance or the achievement of their students and athletes), there certainly does appear to be a subset of teachers and coaches who exhibit expectancy biases in educational and sport settings.

Such variation among teachers and coaches implies that those who are aware of and understand the self-fulfilling prophecy phenomenon can avoid becoming Pygmalion-type coaches or teachers. Therefore, it is the purpose of this chapter to present coaches with information concerning the expectation–performance process. In the following pages, we will examine how coaches' expectations or judgments of their athletes can influence the athletes' performance and behavior, how such expectancy effects can be particularly negative for selected athletes, and how coaches can individualize their interactions with athletes to avoid behaving in expectancy-biased ways and thus facilitate the performance of all athletes.

The Expectation–Performance Process

According to the self-fulfilling prophecy theory, the expectations coaches form about the ability of individual athletes can serve as prophecies that dictate or determine the level of achievement each athlete will ultimately reach. Several researchers who have studied the self-fulfilling prophecy phenomenon in educational contexts (e.g., Brophy, 1983; Jussim, 1986) have proposed a sequence of steps to explain how the expectation–performance connection is accomplished. These models or sequences of events can be adapted to describe how the self-fulfilling prophecy phenomenon can also occur in sport settings.

Step 1: The coach develops an expectation for each athlete that predicts the level of performance and type of behavior that athlete will exhibit over the course of the year.

Step 2: The coach's expectations influence his or her treatment of individual athletes. That is, the coach's behavior toward each athlete differs according to the coach's belief concerning the athlete's competence.

Step 3: The way in which the coach treats each athlete affects the athlete's performance and rate of learning. In addition, differential communication tells each athlete how competent the coach thinks he or she is. This information affects the athlete's self-concept, achievement motivation, and level of aspiration.

Step 4:   The athlete's behavior and performance conform to the coach's expectations. This behavioral conformity reinforces the coach's original expectation, and the process continues.

We will now examine each of these steps in detail.

Step 1: Coaches Form Expectations

At the beginning of an athletic season most coaches form expectations for each athlete on their teams. These expectations are really initial judgments or assessments regarding the physical competence or sport potential of each athlete and are based on certain pieces of information available to the coach. In particular, the research indicates that coaches most often use three types, or categories, of information.

The first category contains what we can label as **person cues** and includes such informational items as the individual's socioeconomic status, racial or ethnic group, family background, gender, physical attractiveness, body size, physique, and style of dress. The exclusive use of any or all of these person cues to form judgments about an athlete's physical competence would certainly lead to inaccurate and very stereotypic expectations as will be discussed later in this chapter. Fortunately, not all coaches form their expectations based solely on person cues. Rather, many coaches also rely on **behaviorally based information.** This can include performance-related information such as the athlete's scores on certain physical skills tests, the athlete's past performance achievements (e.g., previous season statistics), as well as other teachers' or coaches' comments concerning the athlete's performance and behavior. Coaches also base initial impressions of athletes on observation of their behavior in practice or tryout situations (e.g., observation of the player's work ethic, response to criticism, interaction with teammates).

A third and more recently identified category of information that coaches can and do use includes **psychological characteristics.** Solomon and her colleagues (e.g., Becker & Solomon, 2005; Solomon, 2010; Solomon & Rhea, 2008) have conducted a series of studies showing that coaches' preseason expectations for their athletes' sport potential are based, at least in part, on their (coaches') estimates of athletes' psychological abilities (e.g., perceptions of the athletes' coachability, role acceptance, self-discipline, maturity). To enhance efforts by researchers and practitioners to examine the bases of coaches' expectations, Solomon (2008) recently developed the Solomon Expectancy Sources Scale (SESS) that provides a quantitative measure of the primary criteria that individual coaches use to assess their athletes' ability in the sport domain.

Although the initial expectations formed by most coaches quite probably are based on information from a variety of sources, individual coaches likely differ in regard to the weight they assign to each source. That is, some coaches may particularly value the comments of other coaches in evaluating an athlete during recruitment or at the beginning of the season, whereas other coaches may place greater emphasis on the player's physical attributes (e.g., speed, size, strength, body build). Therefore, two coaches could form very different sets of expectations for the same athlete on the basis of what sources of information each valued most.

Exercise 1

Assume that you have just been appointed to be the new varsity coach for a high school soccer team. Because you are new to the school, you know very little about the players who will try out for your team. However, your assistant coach has been in the program for several years and knows all the players. Team tryout days arrive, and you realize that you will have to make some difficult cuts. How much will you rely on your own observation of the players' performance and behavior during tryouts rather than on the feedback provided by your assistant coach based on her or his years of work with these players?

It obviously follows, then, that a coach's initial judgment of an athlete may be either accurate or inaccurate depending on the sources of information used. Accurate assessments of a player's competence generally pose no problem as they usually do not adversely affect the player's subsequent performance. However, inaccurate expectations (i.e., expectations that are either too high or too low) that are *also* inflexible can be very disruptive for athletes and can interfere with their optimal athletic progress. Consider, for example, the coach who misjudges a particular athlete at the beginning of the season and falsely believes that individual to be less competent than he or she really is. If the coach's expectation or judgment is flexible (i.e., changes when the athlete demonstrates better performance than expected), then the initial false expectation does not cause a problem. In contrast, a coach who is very inflexible and resistant to modifying her or his initial beliefs may well "see" only what she or he expects to see from that player. Solomon and her colleagues (e.g., Solomon & Kosmitzki, 1996; Solomon, Golden et al., 1998) have referred to this characteristic of coaches as "perceptual flexibility" or, by extension, "perceptual inflexibility." Coaches who develop expectations of players at the beginning of the season that are not flexible or fluid tend to perceive individual athletes' performance and behavior from a very rigid perspective. That is, these coaches will perceive in their athletes' performance and behavior exactly what they expect to see. This type of situation is illustrated in Example 1 where the coach's initial expectations or judgments concerning the relative athletic ability of both Samantha and Betty are formed on the basis of the previous season's performance. These initial expectations, which may *no longer* be accurate, cause the coach to *perceive* the two athletes' performance differently. Such differential perceptions, in turn, affect the way the coach reacts or responds to that player. This type of situation leads to the second step in the sequence of events composing the self-fulfilling prophecy phenomenon.

Step 2: Coaches' Expectations Affect Their Behavior

To determine if coaches' expectancies affect their behavior, researchers have conducted studies to address the crucial question, "Do coaches treat athletes they believe have high ability (i.e., high-expectancy individuals) differently from athletes they believe have low ability (i.e., low-expectancy individuals)?" Generally this question has been examined by observing and recording the type, frequency, and quality of instructional behavior coaches exhibit toward individual athletes. The overall conclusion from this research (e.g., Becker & Wrisberg, 2008; Horn, 1984; Rejeski et al., 1979; Sinclair & Vealey, 1989; Solomon & Kosmitzki, 1996; Solomon, DiMarco, Ohlson, & Reece, 1998; Solomon, Golden et al., 1998; Solomon, Striegel et al., 1996) indicates that *some* coaches do indeed show differential instructional behaviors to these two groups of athletes. Applying the results of this research to any specific athletic setting, we could expect the Pygmalion-type coach to show differential behavior to high- and low-expectancy athletes in regard to (a) the frequency and quality of interactions the coach has with the individual athletes, (b) the quantity and

---

Example 1

Tryouts have just gotten under way for the Bayside Rollers, a highly competitive roller derby team. Among the potential team members are "Slammin Samantha," a returning player who was the team's leading jammer in the previous season and "Black-Eye Betty," who rode the bench on last year's team. The athletes are warming up by skating around the track at progressively higher speeds. At Turn 2 of the rink, Black-Eye Betty skids out and falls. The coach, who has developed the expectancy that Betty is not a talented athlete, sees this incident as proof of her lack of innate coordination. Thus, he responds by turning to his assistant coach and saying, "Clearly, she's no better than last year!" If, however, it had been Slammin Samantha who had skidded out, the coach, who perceives Samantha to be an excellent skater, might assume that the track was dusty and/or wet in that area. Based on this perception, the coach orders that all skaters stop until the rink manager can come over to sweep or mop up that part of the track.

quality of instruction given to each athlete, and (c) the frequency and type of performance feedback given to each athlete.

In the first behavioral category, **frequency and quality of coach–athlete interactions,** a Pygmalion-prone coach typically initiates less interpersonal contact (either of a social or a skill-related nature) with athletes she believes to be less skilled. As a result, the coach spends more time with athletes who are highly skilled (see Example 2). In addition, the quality of coach–athlete interactions also may differ, with high-expectancy players being shown more warmth and positive affect (e.g., smiling, head nodding) than their low-expectancy teammates.

Perhaps of greater consequence is the differential treatment that high- and low-expectancy players may receive in the **quantity and quality of instruction.** If a coach firmly believes certain players on his team do not have the requisite athletic competencies to be successful (i.e., the low-expectancy players), that coach may, first of all, reduce the amount of material or skills those players are expected to learn, thus establishing a lower standard of performance for them. Second, the coach may allow the low-expectancy players less time in practice drills. As

a result, these athletes may spend relatively more practice time in non-skill-related activities such as shagging balls, waiting in line, and keeping score. Finally, the coach may be less persistent in helping low-expectancy athletes learn a difficult skill (see Example 3).

In addition to differences in the quality of instruction, researchers also have found differences in the **type and frequency of feedback** that coaches give to high- and low-expectancy players. One of the primary ways coaches respond differently to individual athletes is in their use of praise and criticism. In regard to praise, the expectancy-based research studies (e.g., Horn, 1984; Martinek, 1988; Rejeski et al., 1979; Solomon, DiMarco et al., 1998; Solomon, Striegel et al., 1996) generally have suggested that Pygmalion-prone coaches do one of two things. First, they may give high-expectancy students and athletes more reinforcement and praise after a successful performance than they do low-expectancy individuals. Alternatively, Pygmalion-prone coaches may actually give proportionately more reinforcement to the low-expectancy students and athletes. Unfortunately, however, this higher frequency of reinforcement or praise given by coaches and teachers to these low-expectancy individuals may actually be qualitatively suspect because the reinforcement is often given inappropriately (i.e., given for a mediocre performance or for success at a very easy task) (see Example 4).

Example 2

Ashton and Kari, who are teammates on their school's varsity basketball team, stay after practice to play a game of one-on-one. Their coach comes over to watch. When Ashton (a high-expectancy athlete) executes a successful fake and drive, the coach responds with approval but also stops the game to provide Ashton with further instruction (i.e., what she should do in a similar situation if the weak side defender moves across the key). Later when Kari (a low-expectancy player) executes the same successful fake and drive, the coach responds with approval only ("Good move, Kari") but then goes on to show Ashton how she should have prevented or defended against such an offensive move.

Example 3

During a practice scrimmage, Ashton (the high-expectancy player in Example 2) is having problems running a particularly difficult offensive pattern. The coach stops the team drill and spends 3 or 4 minutes helping Ashton learn the pattern. When Kari (the low-expectancy athlete) later evidences the same difficulty, the coach removes her from the scrimmage team by saying to another player, "Joci, come here and take Kari's place. Let's see if you can run this play."

Example 4

During the course of a varsity volleyball match, a hitter approaches the net for a spike. Seeing her opponents put up a single block, she reaches out to "tip" the ball around the block. No point is scored, but the ball is kept in play. The athlete, who is a high-expectancy player, is told by her coach, "OK, Keisha, at least you kept the ball in play. But next time you go up against a single block, hit the ball. Your spike is good enough to get it through that block." If, however, a low-expectancy player executes the same play, the Pygmalion-type coach might respond with approval only: "Great work, Kara, you kept the ball away from the block. That was smart."

Example 5

Jared and Charlie have both joined an age-group swimming team. Although both swimmers begin the season at the same level of performance, their coach has very high expectations for Jared's improvement and ultimate success because of his "natural" physical attributes. The coach does not have the same high expectations for Charlie. At the first meet of the season, both swimmers take fifth place in their respective events. The coach responds to Jared's performance by telling him that he can considerably reduce his time if he improves his technique on the turns. The coach concludes with the comment, "We'll work on those turns all next week so you'll be ready for the next meet." In contrast, the coach responds to Charlie's fifth- place performance by saying, "Good job, Charlie. Hang in there."

Observation of teachers' and coaches' feedback also has revealed differences in the amount of corrective or technical instruction given. In the sport setting, this may be especially evident in the feedback coaches provide their athletes following a performance. As illustrated in Example 5, high-expectancy performers receive informational and corrective feedback that tells them how to improve their performance. In contrast, low-expectancy performers receive a positive communication from the coach but no accompanying technical information to tell them what they can do to improve their performance. These differences in feedback responses may well be due to the different expectations the coach holds for the various athletes. For example, because the coach fully expects Jared's performance to improve, he is more apt to provide Jared with technical information to help him achieve skill success. However, the low expectations the coach holds for Charlie lead the coach to believe that corrective instruction may be fruitless and certainly not useful for Charlie.

Finally, coaches may also differ in the type of attribution they use to explain the cause of the high- and low-expectancy athletes' successful or unsuccessful performances. Although this aspect of performance feedback has received

very little research attention, we certainly might speculate that a coach's beliefs concerning the competence or incompetence of selected players on his or her team would induce that coach to verbalize different attributions for the athletes' performance outcome. For instance, the coach in Example 6 holds different perceptions or expectations concerning the physical competence of Jonathan (a high-expectancy player) and P.J. (a low-expectancy player). These expectations lead the coach to attribute these players' performance to different causes. When P.J. reaches first base safely, the coach immediately, and in this case verbally, attributes that success to the opposing team's error (i.e., a lucky break for P.J.). In comparison, the coach verbally attributes the same performance by Jonathan to Jonathan's ability (i.e., his batting prowess and speed). Similarly, the coach's response to these athletes' performance errors may also be affected by the coach's judgment of each player's ability. In Example 7 the coach attributes Jonathan's lack of success in stealing a base to poor positioning and thus suggests that the performance can be corrected. The coach attributes a similar failure by P.J. to P.J.'s lack of ability (i.e., his lack of speed).

Example 6

During a baseball game, P.J. (a low-expectancy athlete) hits a pitched ball sharply toward the left side of the infield. The shortstop makes a nice backhanded move for the ball and fields it. Although he then slightly mishandles it, he does throw it hard to first for a close play, with the runner (P.J.) being called safe. The coach comments, "What a break, P.J.! We were lucky he [the shortstop] bobbled it, or you would have been out." However, in a similar situation with Jonathan (a high-expectancy player) as the batter/runner, the coach responds to the same performance by exclaiming, "Way to hit the hole, Jonathan, and great speed! You beat the throw again!"

As the previous examples illustrate, coaches may indeed treat their high- and low-expectancy athletes differently. However, we need to exercise caution in regard to these observed differential coaching behaviors. That is, we must not jump to the conclusion that it is essential for coaches to treat all athletes on their teams in exactly the same way. Because athletes differ in their skills as well as in their personalities, coaches are well advised to individualize their instructional

Example 7

Later in the game described in Example 6, Jonathan (the high-expectancy player) attempts to steal second without the coach's giving a steal sign. Jonathan is easily thrown out. As he reaches the dugout, the coach tells him, "Good try, Jonathan. That would have been a good pitch to steal on, but you didn't have a big enough lead to go. Next time, you should . . . ." When P.J. (the low-expectancy player) attempts the same performance, the coach angrily responds, "What are you doing out there? I didn't tell you to go . . . you're too slow to steal second, especially on that catcher."

behavior to accommodate the uniquenesses of each athlete. Therefore, it is important at this point to emphasize that observable differences in a coach's behavior toward individual athletes on his or her team do not automatically imply that the coach is acting in a biased manner. If the differences in the coach's behavior are designed to and actually do facilitate the performance and achievement of *each* athlete, then such differential coaching behavior is appropriate. However, if the differential treatment an athlete or a group of athletes *consistently* receives from their coach in practices and games limits the athletes' ability or opportunity to learn, then such differential coaching behavior is dysfunctional, and the coach's expectations may be serving as self-fulfilling prophecies.

Step 3: Coaches' Behavior Affects Athletes' Performance and Behavior

The third step in the sequence of events in the self-fulfilling prophecy phenomenon occurs when a coach's expectancy-biased treatment of an individual athlete affects that athlete's performance and psychological growth. It is easy to understand how the biased behavior described in the preceding section is likely to maximize the athletic progress of high-expectancy athletes while limiting the achievements of their low-expectancy teammates. Players who are *consistently* given less effective and less intensive instruction or who are allowed less active time in practice drills will not show the same degree of skill improvement as their teammates who are given optimal learning opportunities (see Chapter 2 for more in-depth information on organizing and designing effective practice sessions). In Examples 2 and 3, Ashton and Kari obviously are not being given the same quality of instruction. If this instructional behavior is typical of the treatment these athletes receive from their coach over the season, we might well anticipate that after a certain period of time Ashton's basketball skills will be considerably better than Kari's. Their coach will attribute these skill differences to what she believes to be innate differences in the athletes' physical talents. Given the observed variation in the coach's instructional behavior toward these two athletes, it is equally likely that the coach's original expectation or judgment concerning each athlete's sport potential actually *determined,* rather than just *predicted,* the level of achievement that Ashton and Kari reached. The coach's expectations, then, served as self-fulfilling prophecies by setting in motion a series of events (i.e., consistent differences in the quality of instruction) that ultimately caused the original expectations to be fulfilled.

In addition to the negative effects that a coach's biased instructional behavior has on an athlete's rate of learning and level of achievement, such behavior can also affect the athlete's psychological growth. Recent research in sport psychology has demonstrated that the type of instructional behaviors a coach exhibits in games and in practices is correlated with, and can actually cause, changes in athletes' self-concept, perceived competence, intrinsic motivation, and level of competitive trait anxiety over a season (see Chapters 3 and 17 as well as scholarly reviews by Carpentier & Mageau, 2013; Erickson & Gilbert, 2013; Gould & Wright, 2012; and Horn, 2008). This association between coaches' behavior and changes in athletes' self-perceptions, intrinsic motivation, and anxiety is quite consistent with several developmental, cognitive, and social psychological theories (e.g., Bandura, 1997; Eccles, 2005; Harter, 1999; Ryan & Deci, 2000; Weiner, 2007) that suggest that the evaluation or feedback adults provide is an important source of information that children and adolescents use to determine how competent or incompetent they are.

In the athletic setting, then, the type of feedback coaches give to individual athletes may affect the athletes' self-perceptions (e.g., their self-confidence, self-efficacy, and anxiety) by communicating to the athletes how competent or skilled the coach thinks they are. In Example 4, Keisha and Kara have demonstrated the same level of performance, but each receives a different response from the coach. This differential feedback may be communicating to these athletes what standard of performance each is expected to achieve. Kara, who is clearly

reinforced for that level of performance, may be receiving information telling her that she is at the maximum level she is capable of achieving. Keisha, however, is led to believe her performance, although acceptable, can and should be improved because she has the requisite skills to perform at a higher level.

Correspondingly, in Example 5, the coach responds to Jared's fifth-place performance with corrective feedback, thus overtly telling him that his performance can be improved with effort and covertly supplying him with the perception that he is capable of a higher level of skill. In contrast, although the coach gives Charlie a positive and encouraging response for a similar level of performance, the coach does not provide Charlie with the additional information to tell him that he can improve his performance and that he is capable of achieving at a higher level. Thus, the coach has indirectly communicated his expectations or judgments concerning each athlete's level of ability.

Similarly, there is reason to believe that the differential feedback received by high- and low-expectancy athletes would also affect these athletes' levels of anxiety in sport contexts. Specifically, researchers (e.g., Smith, Smoll, & Barnett, 1995) have found that athletes who receive higher frequencies of technically instructive and corrective feedback, delivered by coaches in a positive and encouraging way, may have fewer problems with performance anxiety in sport contexts than do athletes who receive punishment-oriented or no corrective feedback. Thus, the differential type of feedback that high- and low-expectancy athletes receive from their coaches may determine the degree of anxiety they will experience in performance situations.

Finally, as noted in the previous section, coaches also may affect their athletes' self-perceptions by the attributions they make for their athletes' performance. When a coach attributes an athlete's successful performance to the athlete's innate ability (e.g., Example 6), the athlete develops a high expectancy for future success and a positive attitude toward the sport activity. In contrast, when a coach attributes successful performance to luck, the attribution does not encourage an athlete to believe that he can attain the same performance in the future and provides the athlete with no information concerning personal competence. Similarly, a coach who attributes an athlete's skill error to lack of effort, lack of practice, or some other athlete-controlled factor will do more to facilitate future motivation, decrease feelings of helplessness, and encourage a positive attitude than attributing the athlete's failure to lack of ability. In Example 7, Jonathan's performance failure is attributed by his coach to incorrect skill execution (a controllable and correctable error), whereas P.J.'s failure is attributed to his lack of speed (a less controllable and less correctable cause). The differential messages carried via these coaching communications may affect each athlete's future performance and motivation.

Step 4: The Athlete's Performance Conforms to the Coach's Expectations

The final step in the chain of events in the self-fulfilling prophecy phenomenon occurs when the athlete's performance and behavior conform to the coach's original expectation. This behavioral conformity is, in itself, a very important component in the chain of events because it reinforces for the coach that his or her initial judgment of the athlete was accurate. This confirms for the Pygmalion-prone coach that he or she is a very astute judge of sport potential and can recognize true athletic talent at the beginning of the season.

As a final point in regard to the self-fulfilling prophecy process, it is important to recognize that not all athletes allow their coach's behavior or expectations to affect their performance or psychological responses (see discussion by Horn, 2008 on this topic). Specifically, there are some athletes who are resistant to the Pygmalion process. If these athletes do receive biased feedback from their coach, they are able to discount that information and use other informational sources (e.g., feedback from peers, parents, or other adults) to form their perceptions of how competent or skilled they are. Research from the educational psychology literature (e.g., Madon, Jussim,

& Eccles, 1997) has suggested that high-achieving students in academic classrooms are almost completely invulnerable to negative teacher perceptions/expectations, whereas their lower-achieving classmates are very susceptible to their teachers' expectations. Assuming that such interindividual variability also occurs in the athletic setting, then there are some athletes (perhaps the higher-achieving ones) who will be resistant to their coaches' expectations. Thus, even if a coach shows biased treatment of such an athlete, the self-fulfilling prophecy process will short-circuit.

Sport Applications

The research and theory detailed in the previous pages describe the processes by which coaches' expectations and behavior can affect the performance and psychological growth of individual athletes on their team. Some of this information is based on research that has been conducted in the academic classroom and that is then applied to the sport domain. Although these two instructional contexts certainly have many similarities, some factors make each domain unique. This section discusses three expectancy-related issues that are particularly relevant to the sport context.

Maturation, Maturational Rates, and the Sport Expectancy Process

A contextual factor that may be particularly important in the physical activity domain relates to the idea that children vary considerably in the rate at which they grow and mature. Children who mature early will reach full physical maturation 2 to 3 years earlier than children who mature at a more average rate. Furthermore, children who mature late will not reach full physical maturation until 2 or 3 years later than their average maturing peers and 4 to 5 years later than the early maturing child. As a result, within any given chronological age group (e.g., within a team of 12-year olds), there will likely be considerable variation in children's physical status. Such differences in maturational rates may not only affect children's and adolescents' performance and behavior but may also cause coaches to hold differential expectancies for individual athletes.

On a seventh-grade basketball team, for example, all boys may be between 12 and 13 years old chronologically, but they may differ in terms of their biological and physical status. The early maturing 12-year-old boy may be at a stage of physical development comparable to that of the average 14- or 15-year-old boy. In contrast, a late maturing 12-year-old may be at a stage of development comparable to that of a 9- or 10-year-old boy. Given such obvious differences in rate of maturation, the early maturer's physical and motor abilities are likely to be superior to those of the late maturer. It is important to know, however, that the late maturing boy's disadvantage is only temporary—he will eventually catch up to and may even surpass his early maturing peers in physical size and athletic performance. Unfortunately, however, because the late maturing boy in many youth sport programs is falsely diagnosed by unwitting coaches to be a low-expectancy athlete (i.e., a child who is not now and never will be physically competent), that child may not receive optimal instruction, adequate playing time, or effective performance feedback and may even, in fact, be cut from the program. Thus, even though the late maturing boy could develop into a proficient athlete, he may be inhibited from doing so because of expectancy-biased coaching behaviors. Therefore, we should consider late maturing boys to be at an especially high risk for negative expectancy effects.

A more complicated pattern of expectancy bias may occur for girls in sport. Although early maturing girls may have the same advantages as early maturing boys during the childhood years (before the age of 12), the reverse may be true after this age. That is, early maturing girls could begin experiencing the effects of a negative expectancy bias on the part of their coaches around or after the time that these girls reach puberty. This could occur because some of the physical changes that girls experience as they reach puberty (e.g., breast development, menarche, increase in hip width) are typically not perceived in Westernized societies as conducive to sport proficiency. Thus, some coaches may perceive or believe that these physical changes, which occur at an earlier age for the early maturing girls, will be detrimental to their sport proficiency and performance. In addition, gender-biased coaches may believe girls who are becoming more "womanly" in appearance may no longer be interested in sport, because such gender-biased individuals still perceive participation in sport as antithetical to femininity. Thus, early maturing girls (i.e., girls who reach puberty earlier than their female peers) may suddenly be seen by gender-biased coaches as less physically competent and less interested in sport participation.

This argument is consistent with the biosocial hypothesis developed by Malina (1994, 2002) to explain the correlational relationship that links girls' participation in intensive sport training with a delay in age of menarche. As Malina suggests, coaches may use a linear body build (narrow hips, flat chest, relatively low body fat), which is more typical of a late rather than an early maturing girl, to select athletes into particular sport programs such as gymnastics, dance, track, volleyball, swimming, and diving. Thus, early maturing girls who no longer exhibit a linear build may either be cut from sport programs once they reach puberty or be socialized out of sport (i.e., be encouraged to turn to more feminine activities). It is the early maturing girl, then, who may be at especially high risk for negative expectancy effects once she reaches (early) puberty.

An issue related to maturational variability is the phenomenon known as the Relative Age Effect (RAE) (see recent reviews of this research by Dixon, Horton, & Weir, 2011 and Hancock, Adler, & Cote, 2013). The body of work in this area indicates that in some sports, children who are born in the later months of their chronological age group year (i.e., those who are the youngest) may be more apt to be cut from competitive youth sport teams and/or receive less instruction or support from coaches. As noted by Hancock et al. in their recent analysis of this research, the RAE may be, in part, a reflection of the self-fulfilling prophecy phenomenon.

Another concern relating to maturation and expectancy effects in the sport setting centers around the concept of **developmental vulnerability.** Specifically, research in the educational setting (e.g., Rudolph, Lambert, Clark, & Kurlakowsky, 2001) has indicated that children and adolescents may be more susceptible to socioenvironmental factors at particular times in their educational careers. These particularly vulnerable times appear to be at important transition points (e.g., from kindergarten to first grade and from elementary to middle or junior high school). The increased vulnerability of children and adolescents to experience academic or psychological problems at these time points is likely because of the uncertainty, unfamiliarity, or novelty that are characteristic of a new achievement situation as well as the increased demands that are placed on them in the new (higher level) achievement context (see arguments on this point by Eccles, Wigfield, & Schiefele, 1998 and Jussim & Harber, 2005). Applying this concept to expectancy effects in the sport setting, we might hypothesize that individual children may be more susceptible to their coaches' expectancy-biased behavior when such children make transitions from the recreational to the more select or competitive level (i.e., from sport programs in which everyone makes the team to programs where tryouts are held and only select players make the team). Similarly, transitions from middle school or junior high programs to high school sport programs, and, eventually, from junior varsity to varsity programs, may result in greater susceptibility of children/adolescents to their coaches' expectancy-biased behavior.

Exercise 2

You have just been appointed director of an age-group youth sport program for a particular sport. This program provides nonschool competitive sport opportunities for children from ages 8 to 16 years. The previous director of this program had used an ability tracking system. That is, at each age level, children had been assigned, based on a tryout system, into one of three ability-differential teams: (a) a high-level competitive, travel-oriented team comprised of the best athletes at that age level; (b) a moderate-level competitive team that competed at the local or regional level; and (c) a low-level competitive team that was open to all those who tried out and that was primarily instructional in nature. Will you continue this practice of ability tracking children/adolescents at each age group? What are the arguments for and against such a practice? Should your decision on this issue be different for different age groups?

Sport Stereotypes and the Expectancy Process

Another expectancy issue concerns selected stereotypes that are related to the performance and behavior of individuals in sport situations. Two particularly pervasive stereotypes in the sport setting are those concerning ethnicity and gender (see also Chapter 19 in this volume). In regard to race, it is commonly believed that African-American individuals are "naturally" gifted in particular sports and physical activities (e.g., basketball, sprinting events). Although this may initially appear to be a positive stereotype, it has certain negative ramifications for those African-American children who are not "as good as they are supposed to be." Coaches may perceive an African-American child who, for example, does not score *higher* than his Euro-American (White) peers on a series of sport skills tests as either lazy or "untalented." Such perceptions may be reflected in the fact that African-American athletes in some programs must either make the starting lineup or be cut from the team (i.e., they will not make the team unless they are significantly more talented than the other athletes). Thus, African-American children may be held to a higher standard of performance in these sports because of the stereotypes concerning their physical prowess.

Another aspect of racially biased stereotypes involves perceptions concerning athletes' mental capabilities. Specifically, although African-American athletes are perceived to be very competent in regard to physical capabilities (e.g., speed, reaction time, strength), Euro-American athletes are perceived to be better in regard to mental capabilities (i.e., they are believed to be better decision makers and leaders). Pygmalion-prone coaches who subscribe to such ethnic stereotypes will act in ways that reflect these biased beliefs. Thus, African-American athletes may not be considered for sport leadership or decision-making positions (e.g., football quarterback, basketball point guard, volleyball setter, baseball catcher). Even if they are given the opportunity to practice or play at such positions, their "mistakes" will be perceived as evidence of their innate inability to perform well in these roles rather than as an indicator that they may need more instruction or practice to acquire the necessary skills.

The situations described in the previous paragraphs illustrate only *some* of the race-related stereotypes that abound in the sport context. There are certainly many more (see Brooks & Althouse, 2013). The examples given in the previous paragraphs show that expectations based on race are not accurate and certainly can inhibit the progress of individual athletes or groups of athletes. Support for this idea is evident in the educational psychology literature where researchers (e.g., Jussim et al., 1996) have found that teacher expectations or teacher stereotypes have greater effects on the academic achievement of African-American students and students from lower socioeconomic backgrounds than they do on children who are not from these backgrounds.

A number of gender-related stereotypes also are evident in the sport and physical activity setting (see summaries of this literature by Chalabaev, Sarrazin, Fontayne, Boiche, & Clement-Guillotin, 2013; Messner, 2002). These stereotypes often are based on perceptions that males and females differ in selected physical (e.g., height, body composition, limb length) and/or psychological traits (e.g., competitiveness, aggressiveness) that are relevant to performance outcomes in different types of physical activity. These gender-related stereotypes generally portray girls, as a whole, to be less proficient in sports/activities that require strength, speed, or power while boys, as a whole,

may be perceived to be less competent in other types of activities (e.g., dance, gymnastics, synchronized swimming). Coaches who hold such gender-stereotyped beliefs may certainly interact with their male and female athletes in very expectancy-biased ways. Thus, girls in some coeducational youth sport programs (e.g., baseball, basketball) may be more apt to be treated as low-expectancy athletes. That is, their coaches may give them less instruction in practice and less playing time in games. When they do play in games, they may be relegated to positions where they are inactive for large amounts of time (see observational studies by Clark & Paechter, 2007; Hasbrook & Harris, 1999; Landers & Fine, 1996; and Messner, 2000 for interesting detail regarding gendered behavior in children's physical activity contexts). Even on all-girl teams, a coach's stereotyped belief that girls are not and cannot be physically competent may cause her or him to establish lower standards of performance for them and to give greater amounts of inappropriate praise (i.e., to accept and praise mediocre performance accomplishments). Such expectancy-biased behavior may be particularly negative during the childhood years because girls may then be less apt to develop the necessary fundamental motor and sport skills that will serve as an inhibitor of sport performance in the postpubertal years. Thus, as several researchers and writers have suggested, any differences that are observed in the physical performance capabilities of postpubertal males and females may be primarily due to inadequate instruction, participation, and training during the childhood years rather than to actual physiological or biological differences between males and females (Smoll & Schutz, 1990; Thomas & French, 1985). Furthermore, even if there are postpubertal gender differences in strength, speed, power, flexibility, and balance, this does not necessarily mean that all girls are less strong or less fast than all boys or that all females are more flexible than all males. Thus, coaches who develop expectations concerning the physical competencies of children and adolescents based solely or primarily on gender ignore the reality that there is as much (or more) variation within each gender as there is between genders. Thus, coaches' expectations should be based to a greater extent on character-istics specific to each individual child rather than on the racial group or biological gender to which that child belongs.

Stereotyping at the Collegiate Level

Athletes at the college level may face their own unique brand of stereotyping. Specifically, recent research articles (e.g., Feltz, Schneider, Hwang, & Skogsberg, 2013; Simons, Bosworth, Fujita, & Jensen, 2007) have documented the continuing presence of the "dumb-jock" stereotype that por-trays athletes as intellectually inferior to their classmates. Such stereotyped attitudes toward collegiate athletes have been reported to be held by professors, teaching assistants, classmates, and other university personnel (see quotes con-tained in Example 8). Although this dumb-jock stereotype appears to be somewhat generic in its application to all college athletes, the research studies to date indicate that other contextual factors such as race, ethnicity, gender, and sport type interact to place some athletes (e.g., espe-cially minority male athletes from high revenue sports) at particularly high risk.

Stereotype threat theory (Steele, 1997; Steele & Aronson, 1995) and critical race theory (Agyemang & DeLorme, 2010; Ladson-Billings & Tate, 1995) have been used to demonstrate that negative stereotypes can undermine aca-demic performance as well as motor and sport performance via a number of physiological, neuromuscular, psychological, and cognitive mechanisms (see, for example, Beilock, Jellison, Rydell, McConnell, & Carr, 2006; Chalabaev et al., 2013; Schmader, Johns, & Forbes, 2008; Stone & McWhinnie, 2008).

Interestingly, a recent study by Feltz and her colleagues (Feltz et al., 2013) has indicated that college athletes who perceived that their coach exhibited a positive regard for their aca-demic ability were less susceptible to stereotyped threat perceptions. Thus again, coaches, even at the collegiate level, may be a key factor in either enhancing or undermining the potentially nega-tive effects of the dumb-jock stereotype that ath-letes may face in the academic classroom.

Example 8

Lived experiences reported by NCAA Division I athletes who were participants in a study conducted by Simons et al. (2007) that focused on the **athlete stigma** *in higher education.*

> *White male water polo athlete: "If a professor knows you are an athlete, you are assumed to be stupid until you can prove otherwise" (p. 251).*
>
> *African-American female basketball player: "Professor asked the student athletes to stand on the first day of class and said, "These are the peo-ple who will probably drop this class" (p. 251).*
>
> *White male swimmer: In a big class (400 people). Before test professor said, "It's an easy test. Even athletes can pass." (p. 251).*
>
> *White male rugby player: "Student (classmate) says her diploma loses some value when they let basketball players in" (p. 262).*

Coaches' Personal Characteristics, Their Leadership Styles, and the Sport Expectancy Process

As noted earlier in this chapter, the research conducted to date suggests that not all coaches are expectancy biased. Given this variability in coaches' tendency to be Pygmalion prone, it would seem to be of interest to determine what types of coaches are most apt to fall into this cat-egory. That is, what characteristics distinguish those coaches who act in expectancy-biased ways from coaches who do not do so?

Many characteristics of coaches could be investigated as possible correlates or predictors of expectancy-biased behavior. Based on the research concerning stereotypes related to gender and sexual orientation in sport settings (e.g., Kauer & Krane, 2006; Krane, 2001; and Messner, 2002), it might be hypothesized that coaches of male athletes who hold strong gender-stereotyped and sexually prejudiced beliefs would act very posi-tively toward the players on their team who "fit" the masculine stereotype (i.e., those who have broad shoulders, high muscle mass, and who act in aggressive ways) while acting less positively toward the players who do not fit this masculine stereotype (i.e., players who have a more linear body shape and lower amounts of muscle mass, and who do not exhibit aggressive behaviors). Similarly, gender-biased and sexually prejudiced coaches of female athletes might act more positively to the athletes on their team who conform to the "feminine" ideal (i.e., female athletes who have longer hair, have boyfriends, wear makeup off the court) than to those athletes who do not conform to this image.

Exercise 3

As a college coach, your philosophy is that you want to be as fair as possible to all athletes on your team and to provide all of them with equal opportunities. How do you balance this coaching philosophy of equity for all with the pressure you feel from the university and the fans to train and play only the best athletes so that you can win games? Would your answer to this question be different if you were a high school varsity coach? A high school junior varsity coach? A junior high school coach?

A more recent concept that certainly may be related to coaches' perceptions of control concerns their implicit theories regarding individuals' traits or abilities. This concept was introduced by Carol Dweck and her colleagues (e.g., Dweck & Molden, 2007; Levy, Stroessner, & Dweck, 1998) to describe two types of individuals. **Entity theorists** are those individuals who believe that people's traits and abilities are fixed. In contrast, **incremental theorists** are those individuals who believe that traits and abilities are malleable (i.e., that abilities can be changed or improved over time or with effort). In a series of experiments, Dweck and her colleagues have shown that entity theorists, as compared to incremental theorists, (a) made more extreme judgments about others' traits and abilities based on a small sample of their behavior; (b) believed

more strongly that individuals would show a high degree of consistency in their behavior over time; (c) showed a lesser tendency to adjust their initial trait judgments of another person even when exposed to information that was contrary to their initial trait judgment of that individual; and (d) more strongly agreed with societal stereotypes regarding particular ethnic and occupational groups. Assuming that coaches also can be identified or categorized as either entity or incremental theorists, it would follow that coaches who adhere to an **entity perspective** (i.e., that an athlete's traits and abilities are fixed) should be more apt to be Pygmalion prone whereas coaches who adhere to an **incremental perspective** (i.e., that an athlete's traits and abilities are malleable) should be less at risk for developing and exhibiting Pygmalion-prone behaviors.

From a somewhat different perspective, we could also look at the research on coaches' leadership styles (see Chapter 6 as well as scholarly reviews by Chelladurai, 2007; Horn, 2008, and Mageau & Vallerand, 2003) to identify possible predictors of Pygmalion-prone behaviors. For example, coaches who adopt a more autonomy-supportive interpersonal style (Mageau & Vallerand, 2003) can be described as those who try to help their athletes take responsibility for their own learning, performance, and behavior. Thus, such coaches provide athletes with opportunities for choice (within limits), engage athletes in the decision-making process, and give them informationally based feedback that focuses on controllable aspects of their performance. In contrast, coaches who exhibit a controlling interpersonal style use more external methods to direct and control their athletes' performance and behavior. Thus, they threaten athletes with punishment, use guilt-inducing methods of behavioral control, and allow athletes little or no involvement in any decision-making processes. Given such contrasting interpersonal styles, it would seem reasonable to hypothesize that coaches who adopt a more controlling leadership style would be more apt to act in expectancy-biased ways than would coaches who adopt a more autonomy-supportive style.

From a related perspective, we can contrast coaches who create a more **mastery-oriented** team climate with coaches who create a more **performance-oriented** team climate. Based on the literature in this area (e.g., Braithwaite, Spray, & Warburton, 2011; Duda & Balaguer, 2007), coaches who create a performance-oriented climate can be described as those who place heavy emphasis in practices and games on performance outcomes (e.g., winning or losing). Such coaches also create a team environment that encourages between-player rivalries (e.g., coaches try to motivate athletes to outperform each other) and focuses attention on a limited number of players (e.g., only the "stars" get attention from the coach). In addition, in this type of team climate, player mistakes are perceived as extremely negative and deserving of punishment. In contrast, coaches who create a mastery-oriented team climate place greatest emphasis in practices on the development of individual players' skills

(e.g., reinforcement and rewards given to all individuals who work hard and who show improvement in skills). Such coaches also view player mistakes as part of the learning process and distribute their time and attention to all players on the team and not just the stars. Again, based on behavioral differences between these two contrasting leadership styles, we could hypothesize that performance-oriented coaches would be more apt to exhibit expectancy-biased behaviors than would mastery-oriented coaches (see corresponding research on this hypothesized link by Papaioannou, 1995 in the physical education context).

As the comments in this section indicate, certain coaching characteristics, attitudes, beliefs, and leadership styles may be more conducive than others to the occurrence of expectancy effects in the sport setting. A summary of these personal factors is provided in Table 5-1. Coaches who adopt, assume, or exemplify the

Table 5-1 Characteristics, Attitudes, Beliefs, and Behaviors of Pygmalion-Prone and Non-Pygmalion-Prone Coaches

	Pygmalion-Prone Coach	Non-Pygmalion-Prone Coach
Beliefs about Athletic Ability	"Good athletes are just born that way."	"Athletic ability is something that can be developed through practice and good training."
Beliefs about Coaching Success	"I can be a successful coach if I recruit or get good athletes." "If my team does not have a successful season, it's because I did not have good athletes, or because my athletes did not do what they could or should have done to be successful. I don't have to change any of my strategies or behaviors next season. I just need to get better athletes or more cooperative athletes."	"I can be a successful coach if I work hard to design and conduct good practices and institute the right game strategies and tactics." "If my team does not have a successful season, I will consider the possibility that I could or should have done something differently. I will likely change some of my strategies, behaviors, and tactics next season in an effort to improve my coaching effectiveness."
Stereotypic Beliefs	The Pygmalion-prone coach holds stereotypic beliefs regarding gender, race/ethnicity, country of origin, and socioeconomic status. These stereotypic beliefs affect or determine the coach's attitude toward, and behaviors with, individual athletes.	The non-Pygmalion-prone coach does not subscribe to stereotypic beliefs regarding gender, race/ethnicity, country of origin, or socioeconomic status. The coach's behaviors toward and with athletes are individualized.

(continued)

	Pygmalion-Prone Coach	Non-Pygmalion-Prone Coach
Preseason Expectations	This coach tends to form preseason expectations for individual athletes based on "person" cues (e.g., race/ethnicity, gender, body size, and appearance).	This coach forms preseason expectations for individual athletes based primarily on performance-related information sources (i.e., how athletes perform in drills, scrimmages, and other performance contexts).
Perceptual Flexibility	This coach's preseason expectations are rigid and fixed. Thus, coach sees in each athlete's performance and behavior in practices and games exactly what he or she expected to see.	This coach's preseason expectations are fluid and flexible. Thus, expectations for individual athletes may change as the athlete's performance and behavior in practices and games provide new information for the coach to use in evaluating that athlete.
Leadership Style	This coach exhibits an autocratic or controlling leadership style. Source of power lies within the coach. Athletes are not consulted about any team decisions, rules, strategies, or practices. Coach is central source of authority, and he or she conveys the attitude that "it's my way or the highway."	This coach exhibits a democratic or autonomous leadership style. Although coach is clearly the team leader, he or she regularly consults with athletes regarding team decisions, team rules, strategies, practices, etc. Coach encourages athletes to take personal responsibility for their own behaviors, motivation levels, training, etc.
Team Climate	This coach creates a climate in practices and games that is performance-oriented or ego-involving. In this climate, player mistakes are punished; better players receive more attention, encouragement, and rewards; and intrateam rivalry is encouraged.	This coach creates a team climate in practices and games that is mastery-oriented or task-involving. In this climate, each team member is perceived to be a valuable contributor, emphasis is placed on individual effort and skill improvement, and mistakes are viewed as opportunities to learn and improve.

characteristics, beliefs, attitudes, and behaviors descriptive of the Pygmalion-prone coach may certainly be at risk for undermining the performance and behavior of individual athletes on their team.

Exercise 4

As a head coach, you know there are a number of ways to select team captains. You can let members of your team vote on who they want to be their captain(s). You can pick the captain(s) yourself with no input from your athletes. Or, you can use a combination of these methods. Using information from this chapter about coaches' leadership styles, describe how the autonomy-supportive and controlling coaches might differ in their approach to the selection of team captains. Also, discuss the positive and negative effects of the different ways to select team captains.

Behavioral Recommendations for Coaches

The information on how coaches' expectations and behavior can affect the performance and psychological growth of individual athletes on their team can and should be used to promote positive coach–athlete interactions. Therefore, the following recommendations can help coaches and prospective coaches evaluate and perhaps modify their own behavior in the athletic setting.

1. *Coaches should determine what sources of information they use to form preseason or early season expectations for each athlete.* Performance-based information sources are generally more reliable and accurate predictors or indicators of an individual's physical competence than are person cues such as the athlete's gender, ethnic background, socioeconomic status, or physical appearance.

2. *Coaches should realize that their initial assessments of an athlete's competence may be inaccurate and thus need to be revised continually as the season progresses.* As the research literature in the motor learning area suggests, individuals do not always learn or progress at the same rate (see Chapter 2). Some individuals may show rapid progress early in the season but then slow down or even plateau toward the middle and end of the season. Other athletes may start slowly but then evidence a rapid increase in performance during the latter part of the season. Obviously, then, expectations based on initial assessments of an athlete's capabilities may soon become inaccurate. Thus, coaches should maintain a certain degree of flexibility with regard to their expectations or judgments concerning individual athletes' abilities.

3. During practices, *coaches should keep a running count of the amount of time each athlete spends in non-skill-related activities (e.g., shagging balls, waiting in line, sitting out of a scrimmage or drill).* Certainly it is advisable for coaches to ask a friend or another coach to observe their practices and record the amount of time a starter (usually a high-expectancy athlete) and a nonstarter (usually a low-expectancy athlete) spend in practice drills.

4. *Coaches should design instructional activities or drills that provide all athletes with an opportunity to improve their skills.* In planning practice activities, the Pygmalion-type coach typically uses skill drills that are most appropriate for the highly skilled players. When the less skilled athletes cannot keep up, the coach then gives up on these athletes because he or she believes their failure is inevitable because of low skill abilities. The more effective coach, upon finding that his or her less skilled players cannot master the skill, will implement instructional activities designed to help them ultimately achieve success (e.g., break the skill down into component parts, employ performance aids, or ask the athlete to stay a few minutes extra after practice for more intensive work). See Chapter 2 for more information on the design and organization of practice activities.

5. As a general rule, *coaches should respond to skill errors with corrective instruction* that tells each athlete what she or he can do to improve the skill performance. Also, praise and criticism should be given contingent to or consistent with the level of performance that was exhibited. For further information on the quality of coaches' feedback, the interested reader should see a recent article by Carpentier and Mageau (2013) as well as Chapters 3 and 17.

6. *Coaches should emphasize skill improvement as a means of evaluating and reinforcing individual athletes* rather than using absolute performance scores or levels of skill achievement. To the degree that a coach conveys the attitude that *all* athletes can *improve* their skill performance, no matter what their present level, then positive expectations can be communicated to each athlete.

7. *Coaches should interact frequently with all athletes on their team to solicit information concerning athletes' perceptions, opinions, and attitudes regarding team rules*

and practice organization. Such individual coach–athlete interactions should allow each athlete to feel like a valued member of the team no matter what his or her level of skill is.

8. *Coaches should try to create a mastery-oriented climate in team practices.* Such a climate is most conducive to the development of skill in all players and to the maintenance of a team-oriented attitude.

Summary

Coaches' preseason judgments of individual athletes can serve as self-fulfilling prophecies by initiating a series of events that cause the coaches' initial expectations to become reality. This self-fulfilling prophecy phenomenon can be most detrimental when a coach forms an initial expectation that is inaccurate and underestimates an athlete's true ability. The coach's biased judgment of the athlete's sport potential, in turn, causes the coach to provide that player with less frequent and less effective instruction. Not only does such biased coaching behavior ultimately interfere with the athlete's opportunity to learn, but it also has a negative effect on his or her motivation and self-confidence. When the athlete subsequently exhibits an inability to perform well and a lack of motivation in practice situations, the coach's original but false judgment of incompetence is fulfilled.

Fortunately, the research that has been conducted in academic classrooms as well as in physical activity settings shows that all coaches are not Pygmalion prone. That is, some coaches do not allow their preseason judgments of individual athletes to affect the quality of their interaction with those players. It seems likely that coaches who are made aware of the effects that their expectations may have on athletes and who are trained to monitor their own instructional behavior may become more effective in working with individual athletes. The results of this research demonstrate that it is important that researchers and coaches more closely examine coaching behavior as one of the major factors that affect the performance and psychological growth of young athletes. See Chapter 17 for more recommendations regarding effective coaching behavior and for a Coach Self-Report Form that can be used by practicing coaches to evaluate their own behavior.

Study Questions

1. Identify and briefly describe the four steps in the expectation–performance process.

2. What sources of information might coaches use to form initial expectations for individual athletes on their team?

3. A coach's initial expectations for an individual athlete can vary along two dimensions (accuracy and flexibility). Briefly describe the consequences of the four possible combinations.

4. Do all coaches show expectancy-biased behavior? Explain what is meant by the term *Pygmalion-prone* coach.

5. Explain what the term *late-maturing child* means, and then explain why late-maturing boys may be at an especially high risk for negative expectancy effects.

6. Explain why early-maturing girls may be at greater risk for negative expectancy effects once they reach puberty.

7. Describe the stereotypes in the sport setting associated with ethnicity. Explain how such stereotypes may affect selected groups of athletes.

8. Define the terms *entity theorist* and *incremental theorist.* Explain why coaches who adhere to an entity theorist perspective of athletic ability might be more apt to be Pygmalion prone in their interactions with individual athletes.

9. Explain how a mastery-oriented team climate differs from a performance-oriented one.

Applied Experiences

1. **Observation Study:** Assign students in groups of two or three to attend and observe a practice session for a team in their local community (e.g., high school, youth sport, college, recreation). Each student should bring along a timing device (e.g., stopwatch, phone, iPad), and each one should identify one athlete to observe (ideally including a starter/regular player and a non-starter/substitute). Each observer should then record the number of minutes out of that practice that her/his athlete is mentally and/or physically active (e.g., participating in skill drills, scrimmages, listening to, or observing, coach demonstrations/lectures) as compared to the number of minutes that the athlete is non-active (e.g., sitting out of drills/scrimmages, shagging balls, setting up equipment, keeping score). Observers should also take notes regarding the type of feedback given by the coach to their particular athlete. After the observation is completed, students within groups should write a report documenting their findings. The report should be based on the expectancy-biased information presented in this chapter. NOTE: This assignment could also be revised to incorporate ideas obtained from Chapter 2 in this volume that focus on effective practice organization and design and/or from Chapter 17 that focus on behavioral interventions with coaches.

2. **Preparation of Scenarios:** Students within the class should be divided into eight small groups. Each group should be assigned one of the eight examples that were provided throughout this chapter. Then, students within groups will identify a sport of their choice and prepare a scenario (or multiple scenarios) that illustrate(s) the same expectancy-biased concept as that portrayed in their assigned example. At the end of the class, students should act out for their classmates the sport-specific scenario they prepared with appropriate discussion regarding the implications of the expectancy-biased behavior that they portrayed.

3. **Interview Project:** Each student (or group of students) should interview 2 to 3 coaches with the intent of identifying the criteria that these coaches use to evaluate their athletes during tryouts. Students might develop their interview questions based on the studies that Solomon and her colleagues conducted on the topic of the origins of coach expectancies (see Solomon, 2008, 2010; Solomon & Rhea, 2008).

References

Agyemang, K. J. A., & DeLorme, J (2010). Examining the dearth of Black head coaches at the NCAA football bowl subdivision level: A critical race theory and social dominance theory analysis. *Journal of Issues in Intercollegiate Athletics, 3,* 35–52.

Bandura, A. (1997). *Self-efficacy: The exercise of control.* New York: Freeman.

Becker, A. J., & Solomon, G. B. (2005). Expectancy information and coaching effectiveness in intercollegiate basketball. *The Sport Psychologist, 19,* 251–266.

Becker, A. J., & Wrisberg, C. A. (2008). Effective coaching in action: Observations of legendary collegiate basketball coach Pat Summitt. *The Sport Psychologist, 22,* 197–211.

Beilock, S. L., Jellison, W. A., Rydell, R. J., McConnell, A. R., & Carr, T. H. (2006). On the causal mechanisms of stereotype threat: Can skills that don't rely heavily on working memory still be threatened? *Personality and Social Psychology Bulletin, 32,* 1059–1071.

Braithwaite, R., Spray, C. M., & Warburton, V. E. (2011). Motivational climate interventions in physical education: A meta-analysis. *Psychology of Sport and Exercise, 12,* 628–638.

Brooks, D., & Althouse, R. (Eds.). (2013). *Racism in college athletics: The African-American athlete's experience* (3rd ed.). Morgantown, WV: Fitness Information Technology.

Brophy, J. (1983). Research on the self-fulfilling prophecy and teacher expectations. *Journal of Educational Psychology, 75,* 631–661.

Carpentier, J., & Mageau, G. A. (2013). When change-oriented feedback enhances motivation, well-being and performance: A look at autonomy-supportive feedback in sport. *Psychology of Sport and Exercise, 14,* 432–435.

Chalabaev, A., Sarrazin, P., Fontayne, P., Boiche, J., & Clement-Guillotin, C. (2013). The influence of sex stereotypes and gender roles on participation and performance in sport and exercise: Review and future directions. *Psychology of Sport and Exercise, 14,* 136-144.

Chelladurai, P. (2007). Leadership in sports. In G. Tenenbaum & R. C. Eklund (Eds.), *Handbook of sport psychology* (3rd ed.) (pp. 113–135). New York: John Wiley.

Clark, S., & Paechter, C. (2007). "Why can't girls play football?": Gender dynamics and the playground. *Sport, Education, and Society, 12,* 261–276.

Dixon, J., Horton, S., & Weir, P. (2011). Relative age effects: Implications for leadership development. *International Journal of Sport and Society, 2,* 1–15.

Duda, J. L., & Balaguer, I. (2007). Coach-created motivational climate. In S. Jowett & D. Lavalee (Eds.), *Social psychology in sport* (pp. 117–130). Champaign, IL: Human Kinetics.

Dweck, C. S. & Molden, D. C. (2007). Self-theories: Their impact on competence motivation and acquisition. In A. J. Elliot & C. S. Dweck (Eds.), *Handbook of competence and motivation* (pp. 122–140). NY: Guilford.

Eccles, J. S. (2005). Subjective task value and the Eccles et al. model of achievement-related choices. In A. J. Elliott & C. S. Dweck (Eds.), *Handbook of competence and motivation* (pp. 105–121). New York: Guilford Press.

Eccles, J. S., Wigfield, A., & Schiefele, U. (1998). Motivation to succeed. In W. Damon (Series Ed.) & N. Eisenberg (Vol. Ed.), *Handbook of child psychology: Vol 3. Social, emotional and personality development* (5th ed., pp. 1017–1094). New York: John Wiley & Sons.

Erickson, K., & Gilbert, W. (2013). Coach-athlete interactions in children's sport. In J. Cote & R. Lidor (Eds.), *Conditions of children's talent development in sport* (pp. 139–156). Morgantown, WV: Fitness Information Technology.

Feltz, D. L., Hwang, S., Schneider, R., & Skogsberg, N. J. (2013). Predictors of collegiate student-athletes' susceptibility to stereotype threat. *Journal of College Student Development, 54,* 184–201.

Good, T. L., & Brophy, J. E. (2000). *Looking in classrooms* (8th ed.). New York: Longman.

Gould, D., & Wright, E. M. (2012). The psychology of coaching. In S. Murphy (Ed.), *The Oxford Handbook of Sport and Performance Psychology* (pp. 343–363). NY: Oxford University Press.

Hancock, D. J., Adler, A. L., & Cote, J. (2013). A proposed model to explain Relative Age Effect in sport. *European Journal of Sport Science,* 1–8.

Harter, S. (1999). *The construction of the self: A developmental perspective.* New York: Guilford Press.

Hasbrook, C. A., & Harris, O. (1999). Wrestling with gender: Physicality and masculinities among inner-city first and second grades. *Men and Masculinities, 1,* 302–318.

Horn, T. S. (1984). Expectancy effects in the interscholastic athletic setting: Methodological considerations. *Journal of Sport Psychology, 6,* 60–76.

Horn, T. S. (2008). Coaching effectiveness in the sport domain. In T. S. Horn (Ed.), *Advances in sport psychology* (3rd ed.) (pp. 237–267). Champaign, IL: Human Kinetics.

Jussim, L. (1986). Self-fulfilling prophecies: A theoretical and integrative review. *Psychological Review, 93,* 429–445.

Jussim, L., Eccles, J., & Madon, S. (1996). Social perception, social stereotypes, and teacher expectations: Accuracy and the quest for the powerful self-fulfilling prophecy. In M. P. Zanna (Ed.), *Advances in experimental social psychology, Vol. 28* (pp. 281–388). San Diego, CA: Academic Press.

Jussim, L., & Harber, D. (2005). Teacher expectations and self-fulfilling prophecies: Knowns, unknowns, resolved and unresolved controversies. *Personality and Social Psychology Review, 9,* 131–155.

Kauer, K. J., & Krane, V. (2006). "Scary dykes" and "feminine queens": Stereotypes and female collegiate athletes. *Women in Sport and Physical Activity Journal, 15,* 42–55.

Krane, V. (2001). "We can be athletic and feminine," but do we want to? Challenges to femininity and heterosexuality in women's sport. *Quest, 53,* 115–133..

Kuklinski, M. R., & Weinstein, R. S. (2001). Classroom and developmental differences in a path model of teacher expectancy effects. *Child Development, 72,* 1554–1578.

Ladson-Billings, G., & Tate, W. F. (1995). Toward a critical race theory of education. *Teachers College Record, 97,* 47–69.

Landers, M. A., & Fine, G. A. (1996). Learning life's lessons in tee ball: The reinforcement of gender and status in kindergarten sport. *Sociology of Sport Journal, 13,* 87–93.

Levy, S. R., Stroessner, S. J., & Dweck, C. S. (1998). Stereotype formation and endorsement: The role of implicit theories. *Journal of Personality and Social Psychology, 74,* 1421–1436.

Madon, S., Jussim, L., & Eccles, J. (1997). In search of the powerful self-fulfilling prophecy. *Journal of Personality and Social Psychology, 72,* 791–809.

Mageau, G., & Vallerand, R. J. (2003). The coach–athlete relationship: A motivational model. *Journal of Sports Sciences, 21,* 883–904.

Malina, R. M. (1994). Physical growth and biological maturation of young athletes. In J. O. Holloszy (Ed.), *Exercise and sport science reviews, Vol. 22* (pp. 388–433). Baltimore, MD: Williams & Wilkins.

Malina, R. M. (2002). The young athlete: Biological growth and maturation in a biocultural context. In F. L. Smoll & R. E. Smith (Eds.), *Children and youth in sport: A biopsychosocial perspective* (2nd ed.) (pp. 261–292). Dubuque, IA: Kendall/Hunt.

Martinek, T. (1988). Confirmation of a teacher expectancy model: Student perceptions and causal attributions of teaching behaviors. *Research Quarterly for Exercise and Sport, 59,* 118–126.

Messner, M. A. (2000). Barbie girls versus sea monsters: Children constructing gender. *Gender and Society, 14,* 765–784.

Messner, M. A. (2002). *Taking the field: Women, men and sports.* Minneapolis: University of Minnesota Press.

Papaioannou, A. (1995). Differential perceptual and motivational patterns when different goals are adopted. *Journal of Sport and Exercise Psychology, 17,* 18–34.

Rejeski, W., Darracott, C., & Hutslar, S. (1979). Pygmalion in youth sports: A field study. *Journal of Sport Psychology, 1,* 311–319.

Rosenthal, R., & Jacobson, L. (1968). *Pygmalion in the classroom: Teacher expectations and pupils' intellectual development.* New York: Holt, Rinehart & Winston.

Rudolph, K. D., Lambert, S. F., Clark, A. G., & Kurlakowsky, K. D. (2001). Negotiating the transition to middle school: The role of self-regulatory processes. *Child Development, 72,* 929–946.

Ryan, R. M., & Deci, E. L. (2000). Self-determination theory and the facilitation of intrinsic motivation, social development, and well-being. *American Psychologist, 55,* 68–78.

Schmader, T., Johns, M., & Forbes, C. (2008). An integrated process model of stereotype threat effects on performance. *Psychological Review, 115,* 336–356.

Simons, H. D., Bosworth, C., Fujita, S., & Jensen, M. (2007). The athlete stigma in higher education. *College Student Journal, 41,* 251-273.

Sinclair, D. A., & Vealey, R. S. (1989). Effects of coaches' expectations and feedback on the self-perceptions of athletes. *Journal of Sport Behavior, 12,* 77–91.

Smith, R. E., Smoll, F. L., & Barnett, N. P. (1995). Reduction of children's sport anxiety through social support and stress-reduction training for coaches. *Journal of Applied Developmental Psychology, 16,* 125–142.

Smoll, F. L., & Schutz, R. W. (1990). Quantifying gender differences in physical performance: A developmental perspective. *Developmental Psychology, 26*, 360–369.

Solomon, G. B. (2008). The assessment of athletic ability in intercollegiate sport: Instrument construction and validation. *International Journal of Sports Science and Coaching, 3*, 513–525.

Solomon, G. B. (2010). The assessment of athletic ability at the junior college level. *International Journal of Sports Sciences and Coaching, 5*, 37–46.

Solomon, G. B., DiMarco, A. M., Ohlson, C. J., & Reece, S. D. (1998). Expectations and coaching experience: Is more better? *Journal of Sport Behavior, 21*, 444–455.

Solomon, G. B., Golden, A. J., Ciapponi, T. M., & Martin, A. D. (1998). Coach expectations and differential feedback: Perceptual flexibility revised. *Journal of Sport Behavior, 21*, 298–310.

Solomon, G. B., & Kosmitzki, C. (1996). Perceptual flexibility and differential feedback among intercollegiate basketball coaches. *Journal of Sport Behavior, 19*, 163–176.

Solomon, G. B., & Rhea, D. J. (2008). Sources of expectancy information among college coaches: A qualitative test of expectancy theory. *International Journal of Sports Science and Coaching, 3*, 251–268.

Solomon, G. B., Striegel, D. A., Eliot, J. F., Heon, S. N., Maas, J. L., & Wayda, V. K. (1996). The self-fulfilling prophecy in college basketball: Implications for effective coaching. *Journal of Applied Sport Psychology, 8*, 44–59.

Steele, C. M. (1997). A threat in the air. How stereotypes shape intellectual identity and performance. *American Psychologist, 52*, 613–629.

Steele, C. M., & Aronson, J. (1995). Stereotype threat and the intellectual test performance of African-Americans. *Journal of Personality and Social Psychology, 69*, 797–784.

Stone, J., & McWhinnie, C. (2007). Evidence that blatant versus subtle stereotype threat cues impact performance through dual processes. *Journal of Experimental Social Psychology, 44*, 445–452.

Thomas, J. R., & French, K. E. (1985). Gender differences across age in motor performance: A meta-analysis. *Psychological Bulletin, 98*, 260–282.

Trouilloud, D., Sarrazin, P., Bressoux, P., & Bois, J (2006). Relation between teachers' early expectations and students' later perceived competence in physical education classes: Autonomy-supportive climate as a moderator. *Journal of Educational Psychology, 98*, 75–86.

Weiner, B. (2007). Motivation from an attribution perspective and the social psychology of perceived competence. In A. J. Elliot & C. S. Dweck (Eds.), *Handbook of competence and motivation* (pp. 73–84). NY: Guilford.

Leadership in Sports: The Critical Importance of Coach and Athlete Leadership

Julia D. Sterrett, *Lehigh University*
Jeff Janssen, *Janssen Sports Leadership Center*

"Talent is important. But the single most important ingredient after you get the talent is internal leadership."

—Coach Mike Krzyzewski, Duke University Men's Basketball

Why is it that some teams consistently perform up to their full potential while others, even with strong talent, fail to live up to expectations? How do some teams develop and sustain a championship level program year after year, even though athletes come and go on a regular basis? How do some teams build and maintain a winning culture where people not only survive, but also thrive individually and collectively?

While many factors determine a team's success, few are as influential as the all-encompassing power of strong and credible leadership. Many people automatically assume that as the primary leader of a team, the coach is the common denominator among strong programs. While the coach's leadership is absolutely critical to success, the best leaders know their effectiveness ultimately is determined not by manipulating a large number of followers, but by empowering others. Top programs and coaches consistently invest time and energy in the development of a leadership culture within their teams. In fact, because of the rich learning laboratory inherent in sport and the ample opportunities to apply core leadership concepts in practical and tangible ways, many coaches, parents, leagues, and organizations, including an increasing number of institutions of higher education, are capitalizing on the opportunity to intentionally develop leadership skills in student-athletes.

Inspired by compelling curiosities, anchored in leadership theory and research, and written from a practitioner's perspective, this chapter focuses on three important questions: *Why is leadership important?, What really is leadership?, and, How can core leadership concepts and strategies be applied in sport to develop and enhance personal, interpersonal and team effectiveness?* For the sake of clarifying expectations (a leadership practice that is extremely valuable in working with coaches, athletes and teams), please note that this chapter does not intend to neatly define leadership. Instead, it acknowledges that leadership is a powerful, complex, and heuristic process involving the psychology, sociology and spirit of people in social situations. Accordingly, the goal of this chapter is to facilitate a leadership journey, exposing the reader to a range of perspectives and offering some practical strategies which may enhance the leadership development of coaches, athletes, and teams.

Simon Sinek (2010) shares a simple but powerful idea about using inside-out communication to inspire effective leadership and change, illustrated in a "Golden Circle" that depicts three circles nested within each other. The outermost circle represent "what," with "how" in the middle circle and "why" in the innermost circle.

Sinek explains that anyone can tell you *what* they do, and most can tell you *how* they do it (and people and organizations typically introduce themselves in that order, from the outside in), but those who have experienced noteworthy success through transformation (including the Wright Brothers, Martin Luther King, Jr., and Steve Jobs at Apple) begin by sharing *why* they do what they do.

Exercise 1

*Take a moment to apply the golden circle to your own work: begin by asking yourself **why** you do what you do, followed by **how** you do it, and finish by defining **what** it is that you do. Write down your answers. Bonus Experiment: Ask three others to answer the same questions: why, how, and what? Are there themes among the strongest leaders in your life or organization?*

Aside from its relevance as a strategy for developing strong cultures of leadership within sports teams (which we will directly address later in this chapter), Sinek's message that "People don't buy *what* you do, they buy *why* you do it" compels us to begin this chapter by answering the question, *Why is leadership in sport so important?*

We would be hard-pressed to find anyone who doesn't believe now more than ever that strong leadership is needed to support the fast-paced and dynamically changing environments in which our sport organizations and teams are attempting to flourish. As sport scandals "go viral" and are played out very publicly (e.g., the widespread viewing of the video showing the abusive tirade of Rutgers' men's basketball coach) there is a growing "trust gap" between leaders and their people (Maak & Pless, 2009; Pless, Maak & Waldman, 2012). We need different and effective educational approaches to overcome this trust gap. We must intentionally develop quality leaders in our emerging generations who will make strong decisions, balancing the needs of athletes and the pressure to deliver results.

Today's teams need the objective realism of great managers and the vision and passion of great leaders in order to achieve team goals (Bolman & Deal, 2008). Many top coaches and sport leadership experts would agree that leadership is a differentiating element of a championship experience. Former North Carolina athletics director, Dick Baddour, asked his coaches what they needed to become one of the top athletic departments in the nation; the resounding answer from his coaches was effective leadership from the student-athletes (Baddour, 1994). Said legendary North Carolina women's soccer coach Anson Dorrance, "The final piece in a championship team is leadership. The most attractive type of leadership to me is the student-athlete who is a coach on the field. I want a driving verbal force who won't let standards slip. That's how teams with ordinary talent can win championships" (Dorrance, 1994).

For decades, researchers and practitioners have been searching for traits, behaviors and strategies that prove that leadership "works." The reality is that leadership is difficult to measure, perhaps because it seems to be invisible when it is done well (processes and people function smoothly and seamlessly), and we are most acutely aware of its value in its absence or in times of transition and change. Even though research has not delivered consistent facts proving that leadership is *the* key to a team's success, a number of studies have correlated contemporary and multifaceted leadership approaches to enhanced interpersonal relationships, trust, morale, and satisfaction, which can all facilitate greater collective efficacy, teamwork, and improved performance over time (Callow et al., 2009; Loughead & Hardy, 2005). Zacharatos, Barling, and Kelloway (2000) found that peer transformational leadership behaviors were positively related to athlete satisfaction and effort, team cohesion, and collective efficacy. Peer leaders who frequently inspire, motivate, enhance creativity, solve problems, and use contingent rewards are associated with teammates who experience great joy and satisfaction playing the sport, are motivated to pursue challenging tasks with great effort, and are interested in learning skills (Glenn, 2003; Price & Weiss, 2011).

Clearly, leadership development is and will continue to be a critical element in the stability and forward progression of our individuals, teams, organizations, institutions, and corporations. The good news is that we believe leadership can be taught, learned, practiced and improved upon by anyone who cares deeply about facilitating positive change within a team- which leads us to the next critical question: *How is leadership (and leadership in sports) developed?*

"Few would deny that leadership is of great practical significance in the effective functioning of social groups. Yet, the sheer number of personal and situational factors that must be taken into account, as well as the complexity of cognitive processes and social interactions that occur within the leadership setting, pose formidable challenges for researchers. Because of the diversity of leadership situations, the most fruitful approach may be to delimit the focus of research and theory construction to more specific and well-defined settings in which variables of

interest can be more readily specific and measured" (Smoll & Smith, 1989, p. 1523).

As indicated by Smoll and Smith's quote above, the good news for researchers is that sport provides an excellent environment in which to study leadership. The great news for coaches and athletes is that sport can be one of the best vehicles for developing individual leadership while enhancing a team's chances for desired success. As sport psychologists and coaches well know, participation in athletics provides numerous psychological, social, and developmental opportunities, including learning to perform under pressure, dealing with adversity, developing self-confidence and decision-making strategies, and learning communication skills, which are all skills often associated with effective leadership (Chen, Snyder & Magner, 2010).

While it is true that sport provides an environment rich in opportunities to experiment with leadership awareness and skills, we simply cannot leave to chance the leadership learning of our coaches and athletes. Debunking the myth that leaders are born and not made, enhanced leadership capacity is linked to formal training programs (Dugan, 2006), where the synthesis of core concepts and skills result from discussion and reflection upon situations, behaviors, and the evolving leadership needs of a team. Formal leadership training complements the daily, informal development efforts by coaches at practice, and thus is most effective when integrated as a part of team culture and routines rather than being scheduled as an added obligation (in addition to strength/conditioning, tactical/technical skill development, mental training, community service, team building, etc.). Investment by athletes and coaches is most sincere when formal leadership programming is reinforced as a key element of program planning, and when the developmental efforts are shared by key constituents (coaches, athletes, support staff, parents).

Ultimately, sport experiences and formal training can be only as influential as participants are disciplined. Leadership effectiveness can be enhanced through a conscious commitment to learning about, experimenting with, and assessing strategies and behaviors. As former Princeton University men's basketball coach Pete Carril (1997) said, "Great philosophers of education have said there are two things important in learning. Both begin with a definition of the words *to know.* One is learning facts, data-information. The other is knowing how to behave intelligently. That is what discipline means: *behaving wisely*" (p. 21). The objective nature of sport reinforces the practice of behaviors that produce winning results, providing extra incentive for teams to invest time and energy in refining their understanding and applications of the behaviors that become leadership. Studies highlighting proven strategies for personal, interpersonal, and team leadership development are explored with further detail in the latter part of this chapter.

Having established the compelling reasons for cultivating effective leaders and having acknowledged the incredible opportunity sport provides to do so, we must examine the elusive question about what we are attempting to develop: *what is leadership?*

The Evolution of Leadership Theory

Leadership is a complex phenomenon which has existed since the earliest human civilizations; in every group of people there is at least one person who mobilizes others toward the achievement of a vision. Over the past half-century, researchers have explored key elements of leadership effectiveness, sparking an evolution of thought manifested in thousands of published definitions and numerous theories and models. To the extent that they can be chronologically ordered (many scholars have revisited philosophies of leadership throughout the years), the table below (Table 6-1), adapted from John Storey,

Table 6-1 Evolution of Major Leadership Theories

Theory	Focus	Key Texts
Trait Theories	Innate qualities; great "man" theories	Hendry, 1972, 1974; Sage, 1975; Gardner, J., 1990; Zacarro, 2007
Behavioral Theories	Task and relationship related; style theories (autocratic vs. democratic)	Feltz, Chase, Moritz & Sullivan, 1999; Loughead & Hardy, 2005
Situational Theories	Demands, organization, and characteristics of people in specific situations	Yukl, 2009; Chelladurai,1978; Thompson & Vecchio, 2009
Exchange and Path Goal Models	Relationship between leader/follower; series of trades	Graen and Uhl-Bien, 1995; House, 1971; House, 1996
Charismatic, Visionary and Transformational Leadership Theories	Inspiration/motivation	Burns, 1978; Bass, 1985; Kouzes and Posner, 1997
Leadership in Learning Organizations	Creative and collective process; distributed leadership	Senge, 1990
Spiritual/Authentic Leadership	Post-charismatic and post-transformational leadership	Khurana, 2002a, 2002b; Maccoby, 2000; Fullan, 2001a, 2001b; Boyatzis and McKee, 2005; Tamkin et al., 2010

depicts the evolution of major leadership theories (2011, p. 17).

Unlike the earlier perspectives outlined in table above, during the 1980s, the scope of leadership expanded to entire organizations instead of just individuals and small groups and attention shifted to the ideas of transformational, charismatic, visionary, and inspirational leadership (e.g., Charbonneau, Barling & Kelloway, 2001; Zacharatos, Barling & Kelloway, 2000). These conceptualizations of leadership include much more integrated and relationship-based approaches (e.g., Hogg et. al., 2005), focusing on group roles and processes, collaboration, and shared goals (Dugan, 2010). Outlined below are a few of these integrated approaches to leadership whose key elements are directly applicable to sport.

Bass's (1985) **Transformational Leadership Theory** describes a course of action where both leaders and participants engage in a mutual, ongoing process of raising one another to higher levels of motivation, moral reasoning, and self-consciousness. By appealing to social and community values, transformational leadership encourages collaboration and interdependence, including the follower as an essential element of leadership (teamwork in sport). Within this theory, every participant has the potential to lead, and leadership is not based on position or title, but rather on the development of individual potential and performance to promote positive action toward the achievement of team goals. The four primary components of Transformational Leadership include:

- *Idealized Influence:* Leaders behave in ways that allow them to serve as role models and that result in admiration, respect, and trust from participants. In sport, coaches and team captains earn the respect of team members through leadership by example and modeling team standards (e.g., team captains must pass team fitness tests to maintain credibility).

- *Inspirational Motivation:* Leaders motivate and inspire those around them through purpose and challenge. Enthusiasm and optimism are displayed as participants are engaged in helping leaders create an exciting and attractive future. Great coaches and captains learn

about what motivates and frustrates their team members and identify meaningful roles that put athletes in positions to succeed. Recognition of small wins accumulates and contributes to overall team morale (e.g., using a sticker system to publicly acknowledge great performance, effort or character when athletes meet or exceed team standards).

- *Intellectual Stimulation:* Leaders and participants' efforts are more creative and innovative as a result of questioning assumptions, reframing problems, and encouraging creativity in one another. Each person's knowledge and abilities are enhanced through this process. Buy-in by athletes is greatly enhanced when team members are involved in pre-season team development sessions including goalsetting, brainstorming action steps, and systems of accountability. Follow-through on the suggestions of athletes goes a long way in building trust and engendering ownership of team ideals among team members. Encouraging athletes to continue learning about leadership is also a great way to spark creativity and intellectual stimulation (e.g., small groups of athletes assume responsibility for educating team members about a different leadership topic monthly, presenting what they have observed and learned and making suggestions for team improvement).

- *Individualized Consideration:* Leaders grow future leaders by paying attention to each individual participant's needs for achievement and growth. They serve as a supporter, mentor, and coach for participants, thereby increasing those individuals' potential for growth and development. Vocal leadership by coaches or captains cannot only address the masses; one-on-one dialogue, feedback, and attentiveness are incredibly important in developing team members who are committed to team goals above personal pursuits (e.g.: Coaches find time for individual meetings at the beginning, middle, and end of their seasons to check in with team members about expectations, perceptions, and progress).

Supporting the application of the transformational leadership theory in sport, Price and Weiss (2013) linked coach and peer transformational leadership behaviors to positive individual and team outcomes including enhanced individual and collective efficacy. These discoveries are consistent with previous studies' findings that transformational leadership behaviors were associated with followers' empowerment, self-confidence, effort and team unity, cooperation, and confidence (Bass & Riggio, 2006; Zacharatos et al., 2000). Furthermore, a study examining an athletics department in the Football Championship Subdivision demonstrated that the transformational leadership style of the athletics director, in addition to an organizational culture prioritizing relationships, strong communication, and employee participation in the change process, contributed positively to navigating change with little resistance from employees (Welty Peachey, Bruening, & Burton, 2011).

Emotionally intelligent leadership is another more recent approach which is predicated upon enhanced understanding of self and others for maximized performance (Chan & Mallet, 2011; Meyer & Fletcher, 2007). **Emotional Intelligence,** made popular by Daniel Goleman (1998), expanded upon Gardner's (1983) concepts of intrapersonal (the ability to know one's own emotions) and interpersonal (the ability to understand others' emotions and intentions) intelligences. Goleman introduced the five components of emotional intelligence as self-awareness (the ability to recognize and understand one's own moods, emotions, and drives as well as their effects on others), self-regulation (the ability to control impulses and think before acting), motivation (passion to pursue goals with energy and persistence), empathy (the ability to understand and react to the emotions of others), and social skills (the abilities to find common ground and build relationships with others).

It is clear that each of these elements of emotional intelligence also is necessary in sport: composure is a critical element of peak performance, and sustainable leadership in the face of adversity requires mature self-awareness and regulation. Most of sport's greatest leaders are self-motivated and demonstrate uncommon commitment, inspiring others through their behavior or performance (this is the same idea as idealized influence in transformational leadership). Team leaders with the greatest impact also employ empathy and social skills necessary to sustain significant relationships with and generate meaningful action from team members.

Chelladurai and Saleh (1980) created the **Multidimensional Model of Leadership** (MML), and identified team member satisfaction and performance as the two outcomes for leadership behaviors which are influenced by situational, leader, and member characteristics. According to this model, coaches and athlete leaders must balance the demands of the situation and the required behaviors with the individual preferences of team members to take the most appropriate action that will lead to peak performance and satisfaction. This model is aligned with the core tenants of emotionally intelligent leadership, suggesting that coach and athlete leaders must constantly be aware of themselves (mental states, biases, behavioral and style tendencies), others' preferences (related to motivation, communication, action, etc.) and the current situation (dynamic and changing in sport) in order to lead most effectively.

There is no doubt that self-awareness is a critical component of contemporary leadership (Avolio & Gardner, 2005; Komives, Lucas, & McMahon 1998, Komives & Posner, 2007). This assumption has given rise to the idea that the most effective leadership involves the expression of, and operation from, one's truest self. **Authentic Leadership** (Avolio & Luthans, 2006; Gardner et al., 2005; George 2007; Kernis, 2003; Luthans & Avolio, 2003) involves the integrity of leading from one's true core (predicated upon self-awareness, self-acceptance, authentic actions), as well as genuine relationships between leaders and followers, characterized by "(a) transparency, openness, and trust, (b) guidance toward worthy objectives, and (c) an emphasis on follower development" (Gardner et al., 2005, p. 345). As stated previously, coaches and team leaders earn respect and trust by being honest and genuine with teammates. Athletes or coaches who attempt to lead for the sake of approval, popularity, or selfish motives will quickly fail in the face of urgency and adversity.

The diversity and evolution of perspectives within the discipline of leadership and the simultaneous need for increased effectiveness have only intensified the level of intrigue among dynamic audiences of managers, coaches, students, athletes, parents, and researchers alike. While leadership is far more complex than any singular approach, enduring themes of leadership inherent in the aforementioned theories and evident in sport are summarized below in a comparative listing of what leadership "is" and "is not."

Leadership Is . . .
- process-oriented;

- awareness and skills that can be taught, learned, practiced, and improved upon by anyone;

- using multiple lenses to interpret people and situations in order to influence behavior and manage relationships;

- layered: Effectiveness and sustainability require awareness, learning, action, growth, and influence on personal, interpersonal and community levels;

- strengthened by diversity

- enhanced by specific goals and clearly defined collective achievement.

Leadership Is Not . . .
- a quick fix; it takes a consistent commitment to see tangible results and changed behavior;

- the appointment of a title or position, event, or result;

- limited to individuals who possess specific qualities or characteristics or behave in certain ways;

- exclusive, narrow-minded or stereotypical;

- mManagement;

- lLinear or hierarchical

Practical Applications of Leadership in Sport

Effective leadership in sport involves the interplay of many of the defining elements of the traditional and contemporary philosophies described above. Of great importance, especially in the domain of competition where urgency is inherent, is the understanding that athletics leadership development is a process. For optimal effectiveness, it takes time, thoughtfulness, practice, coaching, feedback, and a community of support. Perhaps equally significant is the recognition that leadership has the power to catalyze positive individual growth and unleash the potential of team performance. In short, developing leadership in coaches, athletes, and teams is worth the investment.

Coach leadership development. Coaches are highly influential in the quality and success of an athlete's experience (Kenow & Williams, 1999). Perhaps even more challenging than fostering satisfaction and growth in individual student-athletes is the responsibility of a coach to produce extraordinary results with ordinary people (Kouzes & Posner, 2008). Extraordinary results may be defined differently depending on the level of competition, philosophy of the coach, and desired outcomes of the program or organization, but across the board, a coach's essential leadership role is to influence and facilitate individual and collective peak performance in pursuit of a shared goal (Yukl, 2012). Many coaches exceed their basic responsibilities by assuming, either intentionally or unintentionally, the roles of life skills educator, holistic developer, and mentor.

Accordingly, it is critical for coaches to recognize that contemporary leadership models, predicated upon relationships, inclusion, and trust, appeal to the modern-day athlete more so than traditional, dictatorial, and hierarchical approaches (Rieke, Hammermeister, & Chase, 2008). Business leadership and management guru Peter Drucker recognized this when he declared, "The leader of the past was a person who knew how to tell. The leader of the future will be a person who knows how to ask" (Gold-smith & Morgan, 2008, p.6).

Recent studies aiming to identify optimal leadership behaviors in sport find that elements of the transformational leadership theory and emotionally intelligent leadership are suited to enhance the leadership effectiveness of a coach at any level (Price & Weiss, 2013; Rieke, Hammermeister & Chase, 2008; Yukl, 2012). These behaviors include:

1. **Lead Yourself First:** Model composure (see Chapter 3), ethical decision making, congruence between values and actions, and a commitment to serving the team
   - List desirable and appropriate core values and identify key behaviors through which they can be modeled to athletes
   - Identify standards of operation which will not be compromised under any circumstance (team rules, disciplinary procedures, etc.)
   - Utilize a self-monitoring form to estimate the percentage of instances whereby technical instructionand encouragement and/or praise of good performance and effort are employed in a practice or competition (see Chapter 17)

2. **Provide a Roadmap:** Motivate athletes to work hard toward a compelling vision of what is possible
   - Engage athletes in a discussion in which they describe an ideal team culture
   - Identify tangible goals and specify concrete action steps (see Chapter 11)
   - Engage your athletes in imagery exercises, envisioning the execution of defined action steps and goals (see Chapter 13)
   - Provide examples and stories of athletes and teams who have experienced similar success to that which is desired
   - Infuse practice with drills publicly rewarding competitiveness and effort

3. **Connect:** Develop positive and authentic rapport with athletes
   - Demonstrate genuine care and concern about areas outside of athletics (ask about their day, school, families, etc.)
   - Discuss core beliefs and values
   - Learn more about each other's personalities
   - Actively listen; summarize conversations and verify that the athlete's perspective was accurately heard (see Chapter 8)
   - Communicate clearly and concisely and request reiteration by the athlete to ensure coach perspective was accurately heard (see Chapter 8)

4. **Empower:** Help your athletes develop the skills and confidence they need to fulfill realistic responsibilities and roles
   - Work with athletes to build their confidence (see Chapter 14)
   - Help athletes to identify realistic process goals (see Chapter 11)
   - Regularly solicit feedback from athletes and incorporate suggestions where appropriate
   - Provide leadership responsibilities to athletes in a variety of settings and affirm a job well done

5. **Cultivate:** Reinforce behavior and provide constructive feedback after desirable and undesirable performances and effort
   - Employ the Positive Sandwich Technique—find something to commend about the play, followed by specific technical instruction to correct the mistake; end with note of encouragement (Smoll & Smith, 1989)
   - Learn how to help athletes reduce anxiety (see Chapter 13)
     ○ Identify signs of high cognitive anxiety in athletes
     ○ Employ simple relaxation techniques

The presence of the relationship-oriented behaviors described above does not eliminate the need for task-oriented behaviors in coaching. In fact, it is the balance of behaviors that are task-oriented (planning, clarifying, monitoring, problem solving), relations-oriented (supporting, developing, recognizing, empowering), change-oriented (envisioning change, encouraging innovation and facilitating collective learning), and external (networking, monitoring, and representing) that will most effectively influence the performance of a team (Joshi, Pandey & Han, 2009; Marrone, 2010; Yukl, 2012;). Leadership and management are different and equally important. A team without an effective leader lacks enthusiasm and purpose. A team without an effective manager may be derailed by reality (Bolman & Deal, 2008).

This multifaceted approach to leadership may seem difficult or even counterintuitive for coaches who are intensely competitive, focused, and results-oriented; however, studies show that athletes who play for coaches employing strategies consistent with those outlined above not only report greater satisfaction with their experience, but they also perform better (Loughead & Hardy, 2005; Price & Weiss, 2013). Olympic athletes met or exceeded performance expectations when they had healthy relationships with their coaches predicated upon trust, effective communication, and a detailed plan to perform well during competition (Gould et al., 1999). Recent studies by Price and Weiss (2011, 2013) linked coaches who exhibit transformational leadership behaviors with athletes' levels of enjoyment, confidence in their abilities, and perceived preparedness for future team success.

Jeff Janssen and Greg Dale (2002) have developed a leadership model and training program for coaches called *The Seven Secrets of Successful Coaches*. Their central idea is that effective coaches develop and maintain credibility with their athletes as their primary method of leadership influence. Credible coaches seek leadership influence through collaborative coaching methods of respect, trust, and communication. To earn credibility with their athletes, Janssen and Dale posit that credible coaches are: (a) character-based, (b) competent, (c) committed,

(d) caring, (e) confidence-Builders, (f) communicators, and (g) consistent. Through their training, coaches not only are exposed to the model but also have an opportunity to self-assess their strengths and areas for improvement as well as receive helpful feedback from their athletes on each of the components.

When it comes to leadership effectiveness, perception is reality: "Leader effectiveness resides in both the behaviors of the leader and the eyes of the beholder" (Smoll & Smith, 1989, p. 1544). However, research also shows that coaches' perceptions of their own behaviors differ drastically from their actual behaviors, and from those perceived by athletes (Kenow & Williams, 1999). As such, coaches must be willing to monitor their own behavior and honestly self-evaluate, as well as seek behavioral feedback from others with genuine openness to making important changes. As Hogg and colleagues (2005) support, in both individual and team sport settings athlete satisfaction and performance may be enhanced through increasing the coaches' awareness and monitoring of the exchanges between coaches and athletes.

Building on these findings, Kenow and Williams (1992, 1999) developed the Coaching Behavior Questionnaire (CBQ), which measures athletes' perceptions and reactions to five categories of coaching behavior:

1. Cognitive/Attentional Effects of Coach's Behavior

2. Supportiveness

3. Emotional Control and Composure

4. Communication

5. Somatic Effects of Coaches' Behavior

Interestingly, Kenow and Williams found that athletes with low self-confidence perceived less supportiveness and composure from their coach. Athletes with high anxiety perceived that their coach's behavior during a game made them more tense, negatively influencing attention and performance, while athletes who were compatible with their coach (able to find common ground through shared goals, personalities or beliefs) evaluated their coaches' behaviors more favorably. Coaches can utilize the CBQ to evaluate the effectiveness of their efforts in helping athletes to perform better through optimal mental states and focus.

Studies by Jowett and colleagues (Jowett & Cockerill, 2002, Jowett & Ntoumanis, 2003) also highlight the role of the coach-athlete relationship in the athlete's physical and psychosocial development. Key factors in a sustainable and effective relationship include closeness (feeling cared for, liked and valued, and mutually trusting), shared perspectives (common goals, values, beliefs developed through open communication), shared knowledge (self-disclosure and regular information exchange), and shared understanding (appropriate reaction to each other's' needs, aspirations, and problems).

The key to achieving positive long-term changes in their own and others' behaviors lies in the commitment to leadership development by the coach. Leadership is a contact sport: follow-up and follow-through are universally respected elements of leadership (Goldsmith & Morgan, 2004). Athletes assume that if a coach does not follow up or respond to feedback, he does not care. Leaders who regularly ask for input are perceived as stronger leaders.

Athlete Leadership Development

"Having great leadership is a big key to success. It's really the leaders' team, because they are the ones whom the rest of the players, especially the freshmen, look up to when setting the standards. Our team will go as far as our leaders are willing to take us."

—Mike Candrea, Head Coach,
University of Arizona Softball

"The quality of your team leaders can make or break your season."

—Kay Yow, Former Head Coach,
North Carolina State Women's Basketball

Intelligent coaches know that while they are ultimately responsible for the satisfaction and performance of their teams, the most direct strategy for success is to develop the leadership of their athletes (Price & Weiss, 2011). In fact, coaches become more powerful when they share and expand their power or influence through others. Scholars have defined an athlete leader as "an individual occupying either a formal or an informal leadership role within a team who influences team members toward the achievement of a common goal" (Bucci, Bloom, Loughead, & Carron, 2012, p. 243). Student-athlete leadership development mirrors that of a coach, though coaches also play a key role in facilitating the evolution of the athlete. Five practical stages of athlete leadership development include determining and selecting athlete leaders, developing a partnership, educating athletes about leadership, providing opportunities for application, and giving regular feedback and engaging athletes in reflection.

Determining/Selecting athlete leaders. Athlete leaders may be formally named as a captain or they may emerge informally based on their credibility and influence among peers (Bucci et al., 2012). Supporting the idea of multiple athletes leading a team, are the findings of Loughead and Hardy (2005). Two-thirds of the athletes they surveyed perceived that both captains and teammates served as peer leaders (identifying approximately one-fourth of their teammates as leaders on their team). Interestingly, interviews conducted by Bucci et al. (2012) indicated that some coaches rely on a leadership group. One coach shared, "I like for each player to be a leader within his [or her] strength" (p. 252).

Evidently, the variety in number, type, and selection methods of team leaders indicate that there is not necessarily a right way to formally identify athlete leaders. Methods of selecting athlete leaders (some options are listed below) vary by team according to the coach's preference, team need, and qualified nominees in a given year. Some captain selection policies are even influenced by the athletics department. For example, in honor of a longstanding tradition at Yale University, each team may formally recognize only a single team captain. To determine the best method for their teams, coaches should discuss their captain selection process with other coaches, as well as their own athletes, to ensure maximum buy-in and potential for positive influence by subsequently elected leaders. Strongly encouraged is an objective team dialogue where leader-criteria (characteristics, skills, behaviors) are identified collectively, followed by open nominations based on that criteria. This process, of course, requires maturity from team members, but the results can be incredibly empowering and educational for an entire team.

Exercise 2

Potential Options for Determining Formal Team Leaders (Janssen, 2004, p. xxi,):

   List the pros/cons of each method. Discuss with other coaches for additional insights.

1. *Coach chooses captains*

2. *Players vote for captains*

3. *Athletes nominate/coach makes final decision*

4. *Seniors automatically named captains*

5. *Create a team council*

6. *No official captains named*

7. *Other?*

Developing a partnership. As we learned from the previous section on coach leadership development, the quality of the coach-athlete relationship not only influences athletic and personal development, it also can leverage or limit athlete leadership effectiveness (Kenow & Williams 1999; Philippe & Seiler, 2006). Trusting relationships, which are the key to a strong leadership partnership between the athlete and coach, are fostered through open communication. Coaches interviewed by Bucci et al. (2012) all mentioned the value of meeting regularly with their team leaders; athlete leaders are more likely to fully embrace the responsibilities and risks of peer leadership when they know the

coach believes in them. For more information on developing efficacy and motivation of athletes, see Chapter 4. Coaches should also be intentional about defining leadership and clarifying associated behavioral expectations with their athlete leaders at the beginning of each season. Common language helps both coaches and athletes to articulate thoughts more clearly, make strong decisions, provide honest feedback, and evaluate efforts consistently.

Exercise 3 (For athlete leaders and coaches to complete/discuss)

• *What are realistic coach expectations of an athlete- leader?*

• *What are realistic leader expectations of a coach?*

• *How do we define leadership on our team? What are we, the leadership team, trying to accomplish?*

Strengthening the case for a leadership partnership between coaches and athlete leaders is the fact that athletes look to their teammates for transformational leadership behaviors that contribute to team unity and cooperation, but rely on coaches for positively influencing individual outcomes (including inspiration, motivation, confidence, and goal attainment) as well as overall team efficacy (Price & Weiss, 2013). Athletes who saw their teams as cohesive, efficient, goal-achieving, and confident about future team success also identified transformational leadership behaviors in coaches *and* peers. It is paramount that coaches and team leaders understand their potential collective influence on positive team outcomes and individual development of team members. Besides serving as role models whose actions will likely be emulated by athletes on the team, peer leaders and coaches "have the potential to be powerful motivators and inspirational leaders who can influence athletes' psychological responses and team outcomes" (Price & Weiss, 2013, p. 277).

Educating athletes about leadership. Before athletes can be expected to lead, they need to develop the awareness and skills to execute their responsibilities. Comprehensive athlete leadership education involves three developmentally incremental stages: leadership of self, leadership of others, and development of a championship team culture. Jeff Janssen's **Team Captains Leadership Model** (2004) (Figure 6-1), is an example of a strong framework for student-athlete leadership education addressing each of these stages. Focusing on the two types of leadership that are clearly evident in sport, leadership by example, or the ability to lead oneself, and vocal leadership, this model and associated modular training helps athletes to connect each core concept to skills that can be practiced within a team setting.

The "four C's" comprising the inside square serve as the four keys and foundation to effective leadership by example (these four qualities also represent the "idealized influence" and "inspirational motivation" elements of the transformational leadership theory, which are linked to enhanced levels' confidence about future team performance by teammates). Once an athlete consistently displays high levels of commitment, confidence, composure and character, he or she has likely earned the respect and credibility among coaches and teammates to lead vocally by encouraging teammates and by enforcing team standards.

In studies examining the ideal characteristics and roles of athlete leaders and their potential impact on teams (e.g., Dupuis, Bloom & Loughead, 2006; Moran & Weiss, 2006; Price & Weiss, 2011), five main themes consistently emerge as keys to effective peer leadership: demeanor, performance, relationships, character, and cultivation of future leaders.

An individual's demeanor can be defined as outwardly recognizable manners and behaviors, especially those directed toward others. Coaches and teammates can often pinpoint specific attributes of successful team leaders. For example, an effective team leader may be said to possess a consistently strong work ethic, a certain kind of toughness, undaunted composure, or an especially

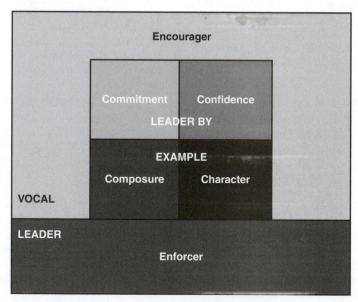

Figure 6-1 The team captains leadership model

positive attitude. With careful and deliberate effort, coaches and sport psychologists can develop each of these attributes in their athletes. Successful coaches often pay close attention to the demeanor of their athletes, and they spend a large amount of their time and energy on developing and sustaining what they see as the right demeanor for their teams. The most successful coaches know that while they can dictate the amount of drills and exercises a team does, they cannot simply give their athletes a genuinely strong work ethic, make them tougher or more composed by command, or force them to be more positive. Instead, they create the conditions in which their athletes' natural, intrinsic motivations flourish.

As an example, consider a coach who wants a particular athlete to demonstrate his or her toughness by playing through the pain of a minor injury. An effective strategy might be to ask the athlete to identify the most inspiring instances of athletes playing through injuries of equal or greater severity. The athlete learns, actively adjusts his or her own self-expectations accordingly and, ideally, competes with a fuller effort and conviction. Inspirational anecdotes can be extremely powerful because they expand the realm of possibility within an athlete's mind.

> "Workers get the most out of themselves; when a body has limited talent, it has to muster all its resources of character to overcome this shortcoming. If you think you are working hard, you can work harder. If you think you are doing enough, there is more that you can do. No one really ever exhausts his [or her] full potential. Winning takes character and intelligence. It is the most important thing you can do because it's a reaffirmation of your character."
>
> —Pete Carril, former Princeton University Basketball Coach

Performance is another key to effective peer leadership. Athlete leaders must be able to demonstrate a high level of skill, consistently execute their performance roles within a team's plan or according to a coach's instructions, and demonstrate an advanced knowledge of their sport. For many coaches, creating successful performance is their central task. The best way to ensure peak performance is through informed strategy, focused repetition in practice, physical conditioning, and pre-performance mental preparation techniques, such as visualization. Successful coaches and athletes know their own strengths and weaknesses, strategically match their own strengths and weaknesses with those of their opponents, practice the execution of those strategies, and mentally prepare themselves at the time of competition.

Demeanor and performance are easily identifiable as elements of effective athlete leadership, but they are not totally sufficient because they do not necessarily influence others. Athlete leaders must be able to build and sustain strong relationships, consistently exhibit sound moral character, and cultivate future leaders. Athlete leaders can build strong relationships by communicating openly and honestly with their teammates and coaches, serving as an extension of and liaison to their coaching staff, practicing the ability to give feedback constructively and receive feedback maturely, and conveying genuine concern not only for winning, but also for the overall well-being of the individual members of the team. Ultimately, relationships among teammates and coaches either encourage or inhibit success. The group dynamics within a team are either conducive to peak performance or an obstruction to it. Athletes and coaches who develop strong relationships with each other invariably make each other better because they are willing to work harder for one another, openly challenge one another, and make sacrifices for one another in pursuit of common goals.

Perhaps one of the most difficult elements of athlete leadership is navigating the fine line between friendship and teammate expectations. Often, a peer leader must confront teammates who may not be complying with team rules or standards, but may fail to do so effectively for fear of losing a friend. To help athlete leaders separate the two, coaches or sport psychologists can remind athletes that if they have earned genuine trust and credibility from their friends, the only issue to be concerned with is the strategy used to deliver the communication. Many relationship problems, when closely examined, turn out to in fact be communication problems.

A widely used and preferred method of conflict resolution within teams is the D.E.S.C. method, wherein an individual:

1. *Describes or defines* an undesired behavior,
2. *Expresses* why the behavior is problematic,
3. *Specifies* possible solutions and alternatives, and
4. Identifies the *consequences* that will ensue if the behavior is not altered.

The D.E.S.C. method is an effective tool for athlete leaders to use when dealing with their peers because it separates individuals from their behaviors and makes clear that the behavior is what is being challenged, not the individual his or her self.

> *"I realize over the years that individuals who sincerely care about others, who are generous in every sense of the word, and who pay attention to their teammates are often the best leaders because they do not have any enemies on the team. These players are also able to be hard on their teammates, as well as discuss both the positive and negative realities without their teammates holding a grudge"* (anonymous interviewed coach from Bucci et al., 2011).

Athlete leaders who consistently exhibit sound moral character command the respect of their coaches and teammates, thus fortifying their relationships and giving weight to their communications. Athlete leaders who do the right thing on and off the field, modeling team values, and who act selflessly and maturely, are often those who embody the kind character that is trusted and admired by other team members. Recent generations of athletes have grown up in a highly subjective, postmodern world, a world in which traditional notions of morality and character have lost nearly all objective meaning. As a result, coaches and sport psychologists must spend time collaborating with athlete leaders on the identification of common core values and common understanding of ethically acceptable behaviors. In a world where common ethics seem to be steadily disintegrating and disappearing, it is becoming increasingly apparent that athletics

provide not only a much needed opportunity, but also an ideal venue for character development. Highly effective teams unite around common values and create their own moral codes.

On such teams, the most successful athlete leaders are often the individuals who best exemplify the collective ethos. As a result, those individuals greatly influence other teammates to uphold team values and become future leaders. The best athlete leaders are those who hold teammates accountable to team standards, efficiently mobilize their teammates to act, inspire, and motivate their teammates, and develop leadership in younger team members by appropriately delegating responsibilities. After identifying and developing initial generations of athlete leaders, coaches and sport psychologists should pay careful attention to which athlete leaders most effectively cultivate future leaders in accordance with the ongoing evolution of the team's values and goals.

Providing opportunities for application. In addition to cultivating the aforementioned characteristics, awareness, and skills, athletes need opportunities to practice leading. Athlete leaders must be challenged and supported to think independently by being given opportunities to make their own decisions. An anonymous coach in an interview study shared this sentiment: "If I want to control everything, I am not developing anything" (Bucci et al., 2011, p. 252). Coaches must empower players by giving them leadership responsibilities such as:

- Running the warm-up in practice or running an entire off-season practice
- Organizing pre-practice and/or post-practice huddles, or responsibility for calling refocusing time-outs during practice
- Managing team logistics (rides to practice, meal decisions, hotel room assignments during travel, etc.)
- Facilitating appropriate team-building activities
- Making difficult decisions about keeping troubled or uncommitted team members on the roster

Giving Regular Feedback and Engaging Athletes in Reflection.   To reap the benefits that effective team leaders can provide, coaches must continue to offer guidance and direction, especially after providing leaders the opportunity to practice their skills. After analyzing the situation together, coaches must help athletes to evaluate what worked, what didn't, and why. As we gleaned from the authentic leadership theory, effective leadership of self by coaches and athletes is a prerequisite for influencing others and leading a team. Leading oneself is about knowing and trusting oneself while continuing to learn and grow. In referencing a leader's ability to think on the fly and make confident decisions, Bolman and Deal (2008) suggest, "the quality of your judgment depends on the information you have at hand, your mental maps, and how well you have learned to use them. . . . There is no shortcut to developing this kind of expertise. It takes effort, time, practice, and feedback. Some of the effort has to go into learning frames and the ideas behind them. Equally important is putting the ideas to use. Experience, one often hears, is the best teacher, but that is only true if you reflect on it and extract its lessons" (Bolman & Deal, 2008, p. 12).

An example of this approach comes from Lehigh University, where student-athletes and coaches have the opportunity to engage in comprehensive leadership training. Recognizing that reason, reflection, and application build self-awareness and lead to improvement, the educational leadership programs teach athletes to think critically and independently by utilizing case studies, real-time team scenarios, regular discussions, and evaluation tools. Athletes are actively engaged in the leadership process and regularly reflect on their efforts, effectiveness, and progress toward team goals. For example, coaches can have an emerging team leader develop a written plan for team success, including tangible goals and values, which the coach reviews with the athlete. The athlete can then be encouraged to communicate these goals and values to teammates. In order to promote selfless thought and action to uphold team core values and goals, facilitators regularly ask athletes to practice swapping roles with each other and identifying the ways their personal actions affect others. For example, the star basketball player gets injured and is out for the remainder of the season. He imagines what impact the media's focus on his injury may have on his team. As a result, he politely requests that media respect his decision not to do a press conference, because he doesn't want any attention taken away from his teammates who are still competing hard for a championship. An example of a student who values regular reflection in order to learn, unlearn, and re-learn for maximum effectiveness is a senior captain who, after receiving all positive feedback from her teammates about her leadership, thanks her peers for the confidence, but asks for constructive suggestions about how to improve, noting that she is unable to serve the team in a greater capacity without working on her shortcomings.

To provide structure in the reflection process, Janssen (2004) has developed a template for leaders called the *Captain's Weekly Monitoring Sheet* (included as an exercise below). In addition to reflecting on the previous week's successes and lessons by considering the specific situations they confronted, the actions they took or failed to take, and the response by teammates, captains and team leaders are encouraged to discuss the sheet with coaches on a weekly basis. This regular meeting not only provides the leadership team with an opportunity to continually monitor the team's chemistry, commitment, confidence, and culture, it also provides the coach with a productive forum to provide feedback to the leaders on how they are doing.

Exercise 4 Captain's weekly monitoring sheet

Date:

Self-Leadership

How would I rate myself as a leader this past week on a 1 (terrible) to 10 (great) scale?
Commitment, Confidence, Composure, Character, Encourager, Enforcer
What went well? (highlights)

What didn't go so well? (concerns)
What might I do differently next time? (lessons)

Team Leadership

What is the mood of our team right now?
distracted 1 2 3 4 5 6 7 8 9 10 *focused*
scared 1 2 3 4 5 6 7 8 9 10 *confident*
passive 1 2 3 4 5 6 7 8 9 10 *aggressive*
conflicted 1 2 3 4 5 6 7 8 9 10 *unified*
fatigued 1 2 3 4 5 6 7 8 9 10 *fresh*
apathetic 1 2 3 4 5 6 7 8 9 10 *motivated*
frustrated 1 2 3 4 5 6 7 8 9 10 *having fun*

Who is struggling right now - how might I reach out to her or him?
Is there anything I need to prepare for/guard against this coming week?
Observations/Comments:

The Team Captain's Leadership Manual
© Janssen Peak Performance • www. jeffjanssen.com • 1-888-721-TEAM

Team Leadership Development

"At Lehigh, our competitive goal is to win championships. Having a talented team is obviously important to the success of any program, but championships are not won by talent alone. Championships are won by teams who have the ability to distinguish themselves by achieving at a higher standard than anyone else. Strong team leadership results in a culture that is committed to continually raising the bar and doing whatever it takes to reach it."

—*Sue Troyan, Head Coach,*
Lehigh University Women's Basketball

As sport psychologists, coaches, and leadership trainers of athletic teams understand, building and sustaining a culture of leadership is not possible through the isolated efforts of a few standout athlete leaders. Sustaining peak performance requires a collective commitment to developing leadership that is tightly aligned with team objectives (Goldsmith & Morgan, 2004). Former director of General Electric's Crotonville and current Michigan Business School professor Noel Tichy writes in *The Cycle of Leadership,*

A well-designed leadership pipeline, discipline, and commitment are absolutely essential in order for an organization to assure that it will have the leaders it needs, when and where it needs them. Without a deliberate and formal pipeline structure, leadership development is only random. Some leaders will emerge, but their emergence will not be predictable, there will not be nearly enough of them, nor will they have the diversity and level of skills of those who have been systematically taught and tracked (2002, p.170).

Preparing future leaders and creating a strong culture of team leadership requires enhanced coordination and communication within and across the team (Eccles & Tran, 2012).

In a generation where values and virtues seem to be determined by an individual's immediate needs (Elmore, 2010), the opportunity to voice diverse perspectives is the norm. Further, levels of urgency, competitiveness, and expected results in sport are ever intensifying, so it can be challenging to establish common ground among teammates and coaches. Lou Holtz, former Notre Dame and South Carolina head football coach, observed that "the difference between athletes now and 25 years ago is that today everybody wants to talk about his/her rights and privileges, whereas 25 years ago people talked about their obligations and responsibilities." Nevertheless, melding individual strengths, weaknesses, desired roles, and individual goals into one cohesive unit is absolutely critical to the effective functioning of a team. The following exercise outlines a practical team leadership development process (which can be facilitated creatively through an experiential learning tool like a ropes course or simply through a series of focused discussions).

Exercise 5 (For teams to complete collectively)

1. ***Define leadership.*** *What individual leadership responsibilities does each team member have? What do we expect of our team captains and coaches?*

2. ***Identify a vision.*** *What would our team look like, feel like, and sound like in its ideal form?*

3. *Determine team core values. Identify guiding principles that serve as guardrails for team member actions (what are we unwilling to compromise under any circumstance?).*

4. *Identify concrete team goals. What are we collectively working toward in this segment of our season (short term), this year overall (medium term, and in the future (longer term)?*

5. *Outline behavioral expectations. List the tangible, observable, and repeatable actions that support or negate progress toward the team goals and the upholding of team core values.*

6. *Discuss Accountability. How will we recognize team members who behave according to our plan? How will we discourage destructive behaviors through systems of accountability?*

A great example of an outcome of the leadership development process described in Exercise 5 is the team commitment contract in Figure 6-2, compiled by a collegiate men's wrestling team. Facilitated by team leaders (this served as an excellent opportunity for practicing leadership), this process encouraged each team member to engage with the larger team goal in a meaningful way, recognizing his personal responsibility and willingness to be held accountable by teammates.

Janssen (1999) identifies seven elements of championship team building for high school and university teams (common coal, commitment, complementary coles, communication, constructive conflict, cohesion, credible leadership) that can be incorporated into team leadership development sessions. A corresponding evaluation can be found online (http://www.janssensportsleadership.com/resources/free-championship-team-building-evaluation/)

LEHIGH WRESTLING

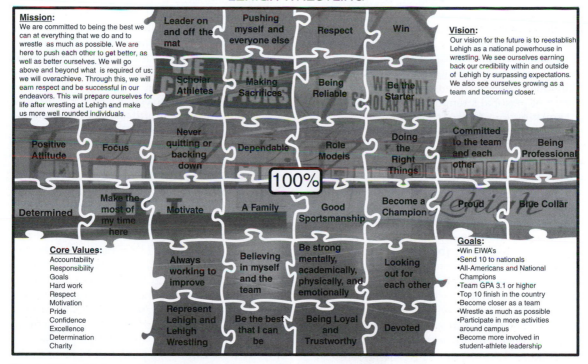

Figure 6-2 **Lehigh wrestling covenant**

and serves as a useful tool to compare and discuss perceptions of team members, peer leaders, and coaches.

Just as individual athlete or coach leadership development begins with an inward focus on the willingness and ability to lead oneself, effective team leadership development must begin with an internal identification of a shared purpose and mission. Team goal-setting sessions, where team members collectively and clearly define desired process, performance, and outcome goals, have been found to have the greatest impact on performance (see Chapter 11 for more information about goal setting). Consistent with the process orientation of leadership development, the longer the duration of the team development and team building processes, the greater its effectiveness (Paradis & Martin, 2012).

Once common ground has been established by involving everyone in the identification of desired team outcomes, each team member must affirm his or her commitment level. It is helpful for an athlete to honestly consider the reasons he or she is willing and able to be committed to team goals, and perhaps even to share these reasons with teammates and coaches. Making time for this conversation is empowering for the individual and helps to create team trust by clarifying intentions. Also helpful in solidifying an individual athlete's commitment level is the discovery of personal strengths and greatest potential contributions toward the team goal.

Acknowledging the importance of and then working to develop complementary roles often is challenging for teams comprised of many talented individuals; however, this element of development is vital to effective team leadership. Paradis and Martin found that "coach-athlete interviews"—"a process whereby (a) coaches write down their beliefs relating to each athlete's role on the team and (b) athletes write down their perceptions of their respective roles, followed by a discussion" (2012, p. 163), is a great way to manage role expectations. Additionally, having teammates provide anonymous feedback to their peers can assist with role clarity. They may write "In order for us to be successful, Player X must do this . . ." (p. 163). A follow-up

meeting among team members can further enhance team cohesion and understanding of its members by reviewing responses and personal reactions to the shared perceptions. A third strategy to improve role identity and acceptance is to have the entire team collectively list every role that would be necessary for the team to be successful, followed by individual presentation of the role he/she currently plays and/or wishes to play in the future. This method also helps unsung heroes to be recognized publicly for their efforts (Paradis & Martin, 2012). Emphasis on role acceptance (willingness to fulfill the duty for the good of the team) over satisfaction (playing one's ideal role) can contribute to a team-first mentality where role players are valued. It can also be helpful for the coach to establish a team-wide understanding that roles are not set in stone and can evolve over the course of the season (Carron & Eys, 2012).

Clarifying a shared goal, conversing about and defining commitment, and identifying important complementary roles help teams establish a solid foundation by promoting habits of honest and consistent communication. Hopefully, these proactive steps in building team leadership will help teams navigate conflict as it inevitably arises. Great teams with solid leadership learn how to utilize adversity as a springboard for greater cohesion and team performance. The best way to help teams learn how to navigate conflict constructively is by providing athletes opportunities to give and receive honest feedback from each other, regularly. This habit encourages team members to approach conflict assertively and respectfully, rather than shying away from it or exacerbating the problem further. Former head women's basketball coach at the University of Tennessee, Pat Summitt has engrained the value of this kind of behavior in her program: "The entire aim of our policies at Tennessee is to get our players to discipline each other. We have evolved a system in which I don't have to do a whole lot of punishing, penalizing, or pushing them. Our upperclassmen become the disciplinarians of our team instead of me." Constructive conflict management is really about maturity in managing relationships and communication relative to team goals.

Knowing how to navigate conflict appropriately certainly helps in sustaining effective relationships, but it is also important to continue learning about those with whom you interact regularly. Recent studies have identified the need for positive team dynamics and improved social interactions (to foster mutual trust within team members), as well as the value of team building in the enhanced performance and functioning of groups (Martin, Carron & Burke, 2009; Weinberg & Gould, 1999). In a meta-analysis of 17 studies, team-building experiences in sport have been found to have a small to moderate positive effect on task and social cohesion, clarity, acceptance, and satisfaction of roles and performance and athlete satisfaction and self-confidence (Paradis & Martin, 2012). Despite being the most regular and effective strategy for developing enhanced group functioning, coaches have indicated that team-building techniques are challenging to implement effectively (Yukelson, 1997). Part of this perception may come from a lack of comfort or confidence in strategies and process. Involving coaches and athletes in the planning process can enhance buy-in and ownership (Carron & Spink, 1993). For more information on effective team building, and group cohesion, see Chapter 7.

Summary

Aligned with the frameworks of transformational and emotionally intelligent leadership, leadership development in sport happens on individual (coach and team leader), small group (several peer leaders and partnerships with coaches), and team levels, perhaps simultaneously. Great leaders in sport possess keen awareness of self, others, and context and demonstrate the capacities to manage themselves, positively influence others, and intentionally develop a culture of leadership within a program. It is difficult to catalyze positive change when only certain members of an organization are invested or involved. As such, leadership development must be approached as an inclusive process whereby key constituents and all members are involved at appropriate levels. The key to changing behavior is "learning to learn" from those around us, and then modifying our behavior on the basis of their suggestions and in the context of a larger team goal.

Leadership is perhaps best understood as both a science and an art: "Artistry is neither exact nor precise; the artist interprets the experience, expressing it in forms that can be felt, understood and appreciated" (Bolman & Deal, 2008, p. ix). Leadership is as much about emotional intelligence as it is about analysis and strategy. Leadership is a life-long process requiring a commitment to learning and self-improvement in pursuit of individual and team outcomes. A leader, who thinks she or he knows it all, knows nothing. As Coach John Wooden prophetically said, "It's what you learn after you know it all that counts."

Study Questions

1. Why are integrated approaches to leadership development applicable in sport?
2. How are early leadership approaches different from more modern approaches?
3. Why is it important for coaches and athletes to partner in executing team leadership?

4. How could you partner with coaches, student-athletes, or a sport psychologist to strengthen the leadership within a team? Provide a specific example.

5. What is the transformational leadership theory? List the four key tenants.

6. What are the keys to effective self-leadership?

7. What are key elements of leading others effectively?

References

Ancona, D. G., & Caldwell, D. F. (1992). Bridging the boundary: External activity and performance in organizational teams. *Administrative Science Quarterly, 37,* 634–665.

Avolio, B. J., & Gardner, W. L. (2005). Authentic leadership development: Getting to the root of positive forms of leadership. *Leadership Quarterly, 16,* 315–338.

Avolio, B. J., & Luthans, F. (2006). *The high impact leader: Moments that matter in authentic leadership development.* New York: McGraw-Hill.

Baddour, R. (1994). Personal interview with J. Janssen.

Bass, B. (1990). From transactional to transformational leadership: Learning to share the vision. *Organizational Dynamics, 18*(3), 19–31.

Bass, B. M., & Riggio, R. E. (2006). *Transformational leadership* (2nd ed.). Mahwah, NJ: Erlbaum.

Bolman, L. G., & Deal, T. E. (2008). *Reframing organizations: artistry, choice, and leadership* (4th ed.). San Francisco: Jossey-Bass.

Bucci, J., Bloom, G., Loughead, T. M., & Caron, J. G. (2012). Ice hockey coaches' perceptions of athlete leadership. *Journal of Applied Sport Psychology, 24,* 243–259.

Callow, N., Smith, M. J., Hardy, L., Arthur, C. A., & Hardy, J. (2009). Measurement of transformational leadership and its relationship with team cohesion and performance level. *Journal of Applied Sport Psychology, 21,* 395–412.

Carril, P., & White, D. (1997). *The smart take from the strong: the basketball philosophy of Pete Carril.* New York: Simon & Schuster.

Carron, A. V., & Eyes, M. A. (2012). *Group dynamics in sport* (4th ed.), Morgantown, WV: Fitness Information Technology.

Carron, A. V., & Spink, K. S. (1993). Team building in an exercise setting. *The Sport Psychologist, 7,* 8–18.

Chan, J. T., & Mallett, C. J. (2011). The value of emotional intelligence for high performance coaching. *International Journal of Sports Science & Coaching, 6*(3), 315–328.

Charbonneau, D., Barling, J., & Kelloway, E. K. (2001). Transformational leadership and sports performance: The mediating role of intrinsic motivation. *Journal of Applied Social Psychology, 31,* 1521–1534.

Chelladurai, P., & Saleh, S. (1980). Dimensions of leader behaviors in sports: Development of a leadership scale. *Journal of Sport Psychology, 2,* 34–45.

Chen, S., Snyder, S., & Magner, M. (2010). The effects of sport participation on student-athletes' and non-athlete students' social life and identity. *Journal of Issues in Intercollegiate Athletics, 3,* 176–193.

Dorrance, A. (1994). Carolina Leadership Academy. [Pamphlet]. North Carolina. n.p.

Dugan, J. P. (2006). Involvement and leadership: A descriptive analysis of socially responsible leadership. *Journal of College Student Development, 47,* 335–343.

Dupuis, M., Bloom, G. A., & Loughead, T. M. (2006). Team captains' perceptions of athlete leadership. *Journal of Sport Behavior, 29,* 60–78.

Eccles, D. W., & Tran, K. B. (2012). Getting them on the same page: Strategies for enhancing coordination and communication in sports teams. *Journal of Sport Psychology in Action, 3,* 30–40.

Elmore, T. (2010). *Generation iY: Our last chance to save their future.* Atlanta, GA: Poet Gardener Publishing.

Gardner, H. (1983). *Frames of mind: the theory of multiple intelligences.* New York: Basic Books.

Gardner, W. L., Avolio, B. J., Luthans, F., May, D. R., & Walumba, F. O. (2005). "Can you see the real me?" A self-based model of authentic leader and follower development. *Leadership Quarterly, 16,* 343–372.

George, B., (with) Simms, P. (2007). *True north: Discover your authentic leadership.* San Francisco, CA: Jossey-Bass.

Glenn, S. D. (2003). *Filling the leadership void: The impact of peer and coach leaders on team dynamics and performance.* Unpublished doctoral dissertation, Moscow, ID: University of Idaho.

Goldsmith, M., & Morgan, H. (2004). Leadership is a contact sport. *Strategy+ Business, 36,* 70–79.

Goleman, D. (1998). What makes a leader? *Harvard Business Review, 76,* 93–102.

Gould, D., Guinan, D., Greenleaf, C., Medbery, R., & Peterson, K. (1999). Factors affecting Olympic performance: Perceptions of athletes and coaches from more and less successful teams. *The sport psychologist, 13,* 371–394.

Hogg, M. A., Martin, R., Epitropaki, O., Mankad, A., Svensson, A., & Weeden, K. (2005). Effective leadership in salient groups: Revisiting leader–member exchange theory from the perspective of social identity theory of leadership. *Personality and Social Psychology Bulletin, 31, 7,* 991–10041.

Janssen, J. (1999). *Championship team building: what every coach needs to know to build a motivated, committed & cohesive team.* Tucson, AZ: Winning the Mental Game.

Janssen, J. (2004). *The team captain's leadership manual: the complete guide to developing team leaders whom coaches respect and teammates trust.* Cary, NC: Winning the Mental Game.

Janssen, J., & Dale, G. A. (2002). *The seven secrets of successful coaches: how to unlock and unleash your team's full potential.* Cary, NC: Winning The Mental Game.

Joshi, A., Pandey, J., & Han, G. H. (2009). Bracketing team boundary spanning: An examination of task-based, team-level, and contextual antecedents. *Journal of Organizational Behavior, 30,* 731–759.

Jowett S., Cockerill I. (2002). Incompatibility in the coach - athlete relationship. In: Cockerill I, ed. *Solutions in Sport Psychology.* London: Thompson Learning.

Jowett, S., & Ntoumanis, N. (2003). The Coach—Athlete Relationship Questionnaire (CART – Q): Development and initial validation. *Scandinavian Journal of Medicine & Science in Sports, 14,* 245–257.

Kenow, L. J., & Williams, J. M. (1992). Relationship between anxiety, self-confidence, and evaluation of coaching behaviors. *The Sport Psychologist, 6,* 344–357.

Kenow, L., & Williams, J. (1999). Coach–athlete compatibility and athlete's perception of coaching behaviors. *Journal of Sport Behavior, 22,* 251–259.

Kernis, M. H. (2003). Toward a conceptualization of optimal self-esteem. *Psychological Inquiry, 14,* 1–26.

Komives, S. R., Lucas, N., & McMahon, T. R. (2007). *Exploring leadership: For college students who want to make a difference* (2nd ed.). San Francisco: Jossey-Bass.

Kouzes, J. M., & Posner, B. Z. (2008).*The student leadership challenge: five practices for exemplary leaders*. San Francisco: Jossey-Bass.

Loughead, T. M., & Hardy, J. (2005). An examination of coach and peer leader behaviors in sport. *Psychology of Sport and Exercise, 6,* 303–312.

Loughead, T. M., Hardy, J., & Eys, M. A. (2006). The nature of athlete leadership. *Journal of Sport Behavior, 29,* 142–158.

Luthans, F. & Avolio, B. J. (2003). Authentic leadership: A positive developmental approach. In K. S. Cameron, J. E. Dutton, & R. E. Quinn, (Eds.), *Positive organizational scholarship* (pp. 241–261). San Francisco, CA: Barrett-Koehler.

Maak, T., & Pless, N. M. (2006). Responsible Leadership in a stakeholder society—A relational perspective. *Journal of Business Ethics, 66,* 99–115.

Marrone, J. A. (2010). Team boundary spanning: A multilevel review of past research and proposal for the future. *Journal of Management, 36,* 911–940.

Martin, L. J., Carron, A. V., & Burke, S. M. (2009). Team building interventions in sport: A meta-analysis. *Sport and Exercise Psychology Review, 5,* 3–18.

Meyer, B. B., & Fletcher, T. B. (2007). Emotional intelligence: A theoretical overview and implications for research and professional practice in sport psychology. *Journal of Applied Sport Psychology, 19,* 1–15.

Moran, M. M., & Weiss, M. R. (2006). Peer leadership in sport: Links with friendship, peer acceptance, psychological characteristics and athletic ability. *Journal of Applied Sport Psychology, 18,* 97–113.

Paradis, K. F., & Martin, L. J. (2012). Team Building in Sport: Linking Theory and Research to Practical Application. *Journal of Sport Psychology in Action, 3,* 159–170.

Peachey, J. W., Bruening, J., & Burton, L. (2011). Transformational leadership of change: success through valuing relationships in a Football Championship Subdivision athletic department. *Journal of Contemporary Athletics, 5,* 127–152.

Philippe, R. A., & Seiler, R. (2006). Closeness, co-orientation and complementarity in coach-athlete relationships: What male swimmers say about their male coaches. *Psychology of Sport and Exercise, 7,* 159–171.

Pless, N. M., Maak, T., & Waldman, D. A. (2012). Different approaches toward doing the right thing: Mapping the responsibility orientations of leaders. *Academy of Management, 26*(4), 51–65.

Price, M. S., & Weiss, M. R. (2013). Relationships among coach leadership, peer leadership, and adolescent athletes' psychosocial and team outcomes: a test of transformational leadership theory. *Journal of Applied Sport Psychology, 25,* 265–279.

Price, M. S., & Weiss, M. R. (2011). Peer leadership in sport: Relationships among personal characteristics, leader behaviors and team outcomes. *Journal of Applied Sport Psychology, 23,* 49–64.

Rieke, M., Hammermeister, J., & Chase, M. (2008). Servant leadership in sport: A new paradigm for effective coach behavior. *International Journal of Sport Science & Coaching, 3,* 227–240.

Sinek, S. (2010, May). Simon Sinek: How great leaders inspire action [Video file]. Retrieved from http://www.ted.com/talks/simon_sinek_how_great_leaders_inspire_action.html.

Smoll, F. L., & Smith R. E. (1989). Leadership behaviors in sport: A theoretical model and research paradigm. *Journal of Applied Social Psychology, 19,* 1522–1551.

Storey, J. (2011). *Leadership in organizations current issues and key trends* (2nd ed.). New York, NY: Routledge.

Tichy, N. M., & Cardwell, N. (2002). *The cycle of leadership: How great leaders teach their companies to win.* New York, NY: HarperBusiness.

Weinberg, R. S., & Gould, D. (1999). *Foundations of sport and exercise psychology* (3rd ed.). Champaign, IL: Human Kinetics.

Yukelson, D. (1997). Principles of effective team building interventions in sport. A direct services approach at Penn State. *Journal of Applied Sport Psychology, 9,* 73–96.

Yukl, G. (2012). Effective leadership behaviors: What we know and what questions need more attention? *Academy of Management Perspectives, 26*(4), 66–85.

Zacharatos, A., Barling, J., & Kelloway, E. K. (2000). Development and effects of transformational leadership in adolescents. *Leadership Quarterly, 11,* 211–226.

The Sport Team as an Effective Group

Mark A. Eys, *Wilfrid Laurier University*
Shauna M. Burke, *Western University*
Paul Dennis, *High Performance Coach, York University*
Blair Evans, *Wilfrid Laurier University*

I can tell you one thing, and this is the great thing about this team: no matter how many good players we've got, the team spirit is unbelievable. We are like a family and every time we come here, we are not even thinking about who is going to play the game. It's all about whoever is on the pitch just giving everything.

—Belgian fullback (defender) Vincent Kompany following a 2014 FIFA World Cup qualifying soccer match against Scotland ("Kompany", 2012).

Membership and involvement in groups is a fundamental characteristic of our society. We band together in a large number and variety of groups for social reasons or to carry out more effectively some job or task. Thus, each of us interacts daily with numerous other people in group settings—in the family, at work, in social situations, on sport teams. The result is a reciprocal exchange of influence; we exert an influence on other people in groups and, in turn, those groups and their members have an influence on us. The following two examples illustrate just how powerful this influence can be.

In February 2013, the Coronado T-Birds, an El Paso (Texas) high school basketball team, substituted Mitchell Marcus into the final two minutes of their last regular season game. What was special about this substitution is that Marcus was a student with developmental disabilities whose passion for basketball landed him the general manager position of the team and the respect and comradeship of the other players. During these last few moments of the season, Marcus' teammates continually passed him the ball with the hope of having him score a basket; to no avail. However, with the other team in possession of the ball out of bounds, in the last seconds of the game, an opposing player purposefully passed the ball to Marcus, who promptly scored two points. As Rush (2013) relays, "The crowd went into a frenzy, and Marcus was carried off the court like a conquering hero. His mother said she could cry about this moment forever. It was his first high school game and his last." The example is powerful and moving; it also illustrates the importance of team members' support and chemistry. The second illustration, however, shows another side of group influence.

In November 2011, Robert Champion was the victim of a hazing ritual as a member of the Florida A&M University band. Hazing is a process of humiliating new group members and represents an extreme of initiation rites. In Champion's case, one activity involved walking through a dark bus while being physically abused by other members of the team. Rafferty (2013) describes the tragic outcome of this event: "After he pushed his way through the beat-down and made it to the end of the bus, Champion complained of feeling sick. Shortly afterwards he collapsed and died [of] 'hemorrhagic shock caused by blunt-force trauma,' according to his autopsy."

These anecdotes show the dramatic influence groups can have on their members. In the first example the influence was a positive one, whereas in the hazing case the influence was negative and destructive. The fundamental question is how groups can come to exert such influence on individual members and their behaviors. From a coaching perspective, insight into this issue could produce possible prescriptions for the development of a positive, productive sport group—an effective, cohesive team. In this chapter, both the nature of groups and group cohesion are discussed, and some suggestions for the development of effective groups in sport settings are offered.

The Nature of Sport Groups

Definition

As Carron and Eys (2012) noted, "every group is like all other groups, like some other groups, and like no other group" (p. 12). What this means, of course, is that every group not only contains characteristics that are common to every other group but it also possesses characteristics that are unique to itself. The uniqueness or diversity among groups has led group dynamics theoreticians to advance a variety of definitions in an attempt to portray what a group is. With

regard to sport groups, Carron and Eys defined a team as:

> a collection of two or more individuals who possess a common identity, have common goals and objectives, share a common fate, exhibit structured patterns of interaction and modes of communication, hold common perceptions about group structure, are personally and instrumentally interdependent, reciprocate interpersonal attraction, and consider themselves to be a group. (p. 14)

To understand how this definition applies within sport teams, explanations for each of the key characteristics are provided in Table 7-1.

Many of the characteristics of a group summarized by Carron and Eys (2012) underpin a concept termed "groupness" (Spink, Wilson, & Priebe, 2010). Although groupness is likely present *to some degree* on all sport teams, each group will vary in the amount that is evident. For example, interactive team sports such as soccer or hockey generally necessitate teamwork among members during competition—a feature that is less evident in sequential team sports (e.g., baseball) and typically absent among members of teams in individual sports like running or golf (Evans, Eys, & Bruner, 2012). Hence, these sports differ in the degree to which they require group processes—this is important to consider when (a) predicting how group members will interact and (b) developing efforts to improve the group environment.

Nonetheless, groups in each of these settings rely on one another in several ways (e.g., sharing a collective group goal) and, as such, team members are likely to have a powerful influence on one another. Thus, coaches or leaders of all types of sport teams must develop a strong sense of "we" to encourage positive group outcomes. Hand-in-hand with developing a sense of "we" is the development of cohesiveness.

Group Cohesion

Definition

Groups are dynamic, not static. They exhibit life and vitality, interaction, and activity. Their vitality may be reflected in many ways—some

Table 7-1 **Characteristics that are Used to Describe a Sport Group**

Characteristic	Description	Sport example
Common identity and/ or self categorization	Members collectively view themselves as group members	High school basketball team wearing team coats around school and referring to the group as "we"
Common goals or objectives	Implicit or explicit long- and short-term goals that relate to all members	Cheerleading squad that has goals regarding performance during the season outlining what they expect to achieve
Common fate	Success or failure is shared by team members to some extent	A national ski-jumping team whose existence depends on receiving funding from the national governing body
Structured pattern of interaction and communication	Verbal and nonverbal communication and interaction styles that are specific to the group	A football team with highly refined verbal and nonverbal communication to convey plays
Group structure	Developing common beliefs and behaviors involving roles, status, and norms	Swim team with structured expectations for behavior (e.g., being at the pool before 6 A.M.) and with established leadership roles
Personal and task interdependence	Members rely on one another to perform, to achieve goals, and to develop relationships	An ice hockey team whose members rely on one another to work together on the ice, to host social events, to get to practice, etc.
Interpersonal attraction	Friendships and closeness typically develop among teammates	A rock-climbing squad whose members become friends and spend time together away from the gym

positive, others negative. For example, at times the group and its members may be in harmony; at other times, conflict and tension may predominate. Sometimes communication may be excellent between leaders and members, but at other times, it may be nonexistent. Also, commitment to the group's goals and purposes may vary over time. All of these variations represent different behavioral manifestations of an underlying, fundamental group property that is referred to as "cohesiveness." Carron, Brawley, and Widmeyer (1998) proposed that **cohesion** is "a dynamic process which is reflected in the tendency for a group to stick together and remain united in the pursuit of its instrumental objectives and/or for the satisfaction of member affective needs" (p. 213).

Cohesion has many dimensions or aspects—it is perceived in multiple ways by different groups and their members. As one major differentiation, perceptions about the degree of unity within the group are assumed to be manifested in two principal ways: in relation to the group's **task** and in terms of the **social** aspects of the unit. This task versus social cohesion distinction appears to be important for all age groups (e.g., Carron, Widmeyer, & Brawley, 1985; Eys, Loughead, Bray, & Carron, 2009; Martin, Carron, Eys, & Loughead, 2012). With respect to adult sport groups, a finer distinction was proposed (Carron et al., 1985) in that these perceptions of the group are organized and integrated by individual members into two additional categories (see Figure 7-1). **Group integration** represents each individual's perceptions about the closeness, similarity, and bonding within the group as a total unit, set, or collection (i.e., it consists

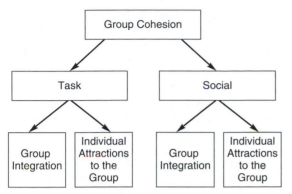

Figure 7-1 **A conceptual model for group cohesiveness**
Source: Brawley, Carron, & Widmeyer, 1987;
Carron, Widmeyer, & Brawley, 1985;
Widmeyer, Brawley, & Carron, 1985.

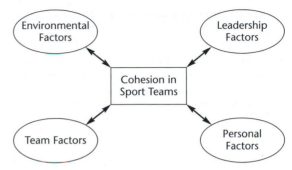

Figure 7-2 **A general framework for examining the correlates of cohesion in sport teams**
Source: Reprinted by permission from Carron & Eys, 2012.

of "we" and/or "us" evaluations). **Individual attractions to the group** represent each individual's personal attractions to the group and, more specifically, what personal motivations act to retain an individual in the group (i.e., consists of "I" and/or "me" evaluations). As Figure 7-1 shows, cohesion within sport groups is considered to have four facets: individual attractions to the group–task, individual attractions to the group–social, group integration–task, and group integration–social. However, it should be noted that qualitative and quantitative studies with youth and children suggest that their perceptions of cohesion appear to be less defined, and that assessing the broader dimensions of task and social cohesion is sufficient to gain an understanding of their group environment.

The Correlates of Cohesiveness

Because cohesiveness is multidimensional, it is associated with a wide variety of correlates or factors. Carron and Eys (2012) provided a framework to discuss the main correlates of cohesion in sport teams. Figure 7-2 shows the four general categories: *environmental factors, personal factors, leadership factors,* and *team factors.* In the following sections, some of the main correlates within each general category are discussed.

Environmental Factors

Perhaps the most easily identifiable correlates of cohesion are environmental factors—those factors that are demonstrated by the setting in which group members interact (e.g., physical characteristics of the environment). Most notably, individuals who are in close **proximity** (i.e., who are physically close to each other) have a greater tendency to bond together. Being in close contact provides the opportunity for interaction and communication, which may hasten group development. To provide this opportunity, team members should be placed into situations that make interaction inevitable. Some situations in sport that ensure physical proximity among group members include having a team locker room, encouraging team members to take classes with one another, or scheduling games that require the team to travel and/or stay with one another.

The team's **size** also is associated with the development of cohesiveness. Widmeyer, Brawley, and Carron (1990) demonstrated that there is an inverted-U relationship between social cohesion and team size in intramural basketball teams. That is, moderate-sized groups showed the greatest cohesiveness, and larger and smaller groups exhibited the least. Interestingly, the results of this study also showed that task cohesiveness decreased with increasing group size.

Widmeyer and colleagues felt that this decrease could be attributed to the fact that it is more difficult to obtain consensus and task commitment in larger groups. Although these studies are limited to a basketball setting, it is clear that the number of athletes, coaches, and staff members have an influence on team cohesiveness.

Personal Factors

Personal factors that are associated with cohesion include the characteristics, beliefs, or behaviors of group members. An important personal factor associated with the development of both task and social cohesion in sport teams is **satisfaction.** Satisfaction is derived from many sources, such as whether or not a team provides opportunities to feel valued and competent, as well as whether an individual feels socially related to his or her teammates (Reimer & Chelladurai, 1998). Satisfaction also results from the recognition from others and, as such, the coach-athlete relationship is a key contributor. Ultimately, satisfied athletes are likely to have a positive influence on team functioning and, conversely, athletes who experience high cohesiveness will likely feel more satisfied (Widmeyer & Williams, 1991).

Competitive state anxiety is another personal factor that is related to cohesion. Athletes who perceive their teams to be higher in task cohesion experience less cognitive anxiety and are more likely to view their symptoms of both cognitive (e.g., worry) and somatic (e.g., sweaty palms) anxiety as beneficial and necessary for peak performance (Eys, Hardy, Carron, & Beauchamp, 2003). In describing the relationship between cohesion and anxiety, Wolf, Sadler, Eys, and Kleinert (2012) proposed that athletes feel like they have more resources at their disposal, and feel less pressure, when they are members of cohesive teams. Thus, cohesive settings should lead to more facilitative perceptions of anxiety because athletes perceive the sport situation as a challenge (i.e., "this is an exciting situation that I can cope with") as opposed to a threat (i.e., "this is an impossible situation and I am hopeless"). Chapter 12 contains more information about competitive anxiety.

Another personal factor related to cohesion is the degree to which athletes engage in **social loafing**—the tendency for individuals to decrease the amount of effort they expend when completing a group task compared to the amount of effort expended when alone. There are several reasons why individuals reduce their effort in a group. One primary reason is that it is easy for an individual to get "lost in a crowd" and, thus, reduce his or her effort because others can't identify how much or how little individual effort is exerted. However, McKnight, Williams, and Widmeyer (1991) found that members of swimming relay teams who reported high levels of task cohesion were less likely to be social loafers.

Leadership Factors

The interrelationships among the coach, the athlete, cohesiveness, and performance are complex. In a mutiny, for example, cohesion is high, the leader–subordinate relationship is poor (and the leader is excluded from the group), and performance from an organizational perspective is poor. One example of the complex interrelationship among coach, athlete, cohesiveness, and performance comes from a study by Widmeyer and Williams (1991). They had golf coaches rate the importance they attached to task cohesion and to social cohesion, and the number of techniques they used to foster cohesiveness. These measures were not related to their athletes' perceptions of the amount of team cohesiveness. In short, coaches did not appear to play a crucial role in the development of group cohesion.

However, the coach's *decision style* can have an influence on the level of cohesiveness within the team. When people have ownership over a decision, they tend to support that decision more strongly. Team members engage in behaviors more persistently, with greater intensity, and for a longer duration when they have had an opportunity to participate in decision making. As Westre and Weiss (1991) found, when high school coaches were viewed as engaging in more democratic behaviors, their players perceived the team to have higher cohesion. Furthermore, recent literature in sport psychology highlights the importance of transformational leadership (see Chapter 6), which describes at least four influential behaviors (Bass & Riggio, 2006) including idealized influence (e.g., setting positive examples and adhering to group values), inspirational motivation (e.g., clearly conveying the shared vision for the group), intellectual stimulation (e.g., encouraging followers to be involved in problem solving), and individualized consideration (e.g., paying attention to the needs of each group member). Generally speaking, transformational leadership behaviors have been demonstrated to have a positive association with athletes' perceptions of team cohesion (Price & Weiss, 2013; Smith, Arthur, Hardy, Callow, & Williams, 2013).

Team Factors

When a set of individuals is brought together with the intention of performing as a group, cohesion can be influenced by a number of structural characteristics that emerge as the group develops (e.g., roles and norms), processes that take place among group members (e.g., group goals, communication), and group performance outcomes that occur throughout the duration of its existence. The emergence of these factors is inevitable and essential if the set of individuals is to become a more cohesive group.

Roles. A **role** is a set of behaviors that is expected from the occupants of specific positions within the group. Thus, when we think of the "role of a coach," a number of expectations for behavior come to mind: instruct athletes; set up the team's offensive and defensive alignments; communicate with parents, media, and the general public; organize practices; and so on.

Within every group there are two general categories of roles: formal and informal (Mabry & Barnes, 1980). As the term suggests, **formal roles** are explicitly set out by the group or organization. Coach, team captain, and manager are examples of explicit leadership roles within a team. Spiker and setter in volleyball; forward, guard, and center in basketball; and scrum-half

and prop in rugby are examples of explicit performance roles. The sport team as an organization requires specific individuals to carry out each of these roles. Thus, individuals are trained or recruited for these roles, and specific expectations are held for their behavior. **Informal roles** evolve as a result of the interactions that take place among group members but are not specifically prescribed. Some examples of the informal roles that often emerge on a sport team are leader (vocal or "lead by example" leaders), task booster (spark plug), enforcer, mentor, social convener, cancer, distracter, team player, star player, and comedian (Cope, Eys, Beauchamp, Schinke, & Bosselut, 2011). Informal roles can have a positive (e.g., mentor) or negative (e.g., distracter) influence on the team. For example, Cope, Eys, Schinke, and Bosselut (2010) interviewed coaches regarding their perceptions of individuals occupying the "cancer" or "bad apple" role. They noted several consequences of dealing with this type of individual including increased distractions to the group, negativity spreading among members, clique formations, performance decrements, member attrition, and decreased cohesion.

A variety of elements associated with athletes' roles determine how effectively they can be performed. One element is the degree to which athletes understand, or do not understand, what constitutes their role. **Role ambiguity** refers to the lack of clear consistent information regarding one's role (Kahn, Wolfe, Quinn, Snoek, & Rosenthal, 1964). Beauchamp, Bray, Eys, and Carron (2002) noted that it is important for athletes to understand four aspects of their role: (a) the scope of their responsibilities or generally what their role entails, (b) the behaviors that are necessary to successfully fulfill their role responsibilities, (c) how their role performance will be evaluated, and (d) what the consequences are should they not successfully fulfill their role responsibilities. In general, previous research has shown that athletes who understand their roles better are more satisfied (Eys, Carron, Bray, & Beauchamp, 2003), experience less anxiety (Beauchamp, Bray, Eys, & Carron, 2003), and are likely to view their teams as more cohesive (Bosselut, McLaren, Eys, &

Heuzé, 2012). A National Hockey League coach once observed that the worst thing that could happen to a team was to have its "enforcer" score a few goals in successive games. The enforcer would then begin to see himself as (and prefer the role of) goal scorer, to the detriment of the team as a whole. In sum, the roles that individuals are expected to perform should be clearly spelled out.

A second element of role involvement related to group cohesiveness is the degree to which athletes accept their role responsibilities (Benson, Eys, Surya, Dawson, & Schneider, 2013). An athlete may be more inclined to accept his or her role responsibilities within a group that is united and on the same page with respect to their collective goal. Role acceptance also is enhanced when the coach minimizes the status differences among roles. Thus, the success of the total team and the importance of all roles for team success should continually be emphasized. When all group members perceive that their responsibilities are important and make a contribution to the common good, they more willingly accept and carry them out.

Finally, other elements of role involvement that are important to the group environment and are likely contributors to the cohesiveness of sport teams are briefly defined in Table 7-2. The applied practitioner or coach should be conscious of these role elements when working with sport teams.

Norms.   The presence of **norms** also is associated with increased cohesiveness (Gammage, Carron, & Estabrooks, 2001). A norm is a standard for behavior that is expected of members of the group. It may be task irrelevant or task relevant; in either case, a norm reflects the group's consensus about behaviors that are considered acceptable. The athletes' treatment of team managers (Gammage et al., 2001) or trainers is one example of a task-irrelevant norm. On one team the manager might be regarded and treated as little more than an unpaid servant; on another team he or she might be considered a member of the coaching staff. In both cases new team members quickly become aware of the standard of behavior considered acceptable in their interactions with the manager and begin to act accordingly.

In a sport setting, Munroe, Estabrooks, Dennis, and Carron (1999) asked athletes to identify the types of norms that exist within their teams. They found that important, and sometimes similar, norms existed in four different contexts: *competition, practice, off-season,* and *socially.* That teammates put forth maximum effort and support each other were the most relevant in competition and practice. Off-season norms included continuing training and development as well as maintaining contact with other group members. Finally, in *social* situations, group members were expected to attend social events (e.g., parties) and have respect for each other.

Table 7-2 Important Role Elements for Sport Teams

Element	Definition
Role ambiguity	A lack of clear consistent information regarding one's role (Kahn et al. 1964)
Role acceptance	The willingness of the athlete to execute his/her role responsibilities (Benson et al., 2013)
Role efficacy	Athletes' beliefs about their capabilities to carry out role responsibilities (Bray, Brawley, & Carron, 2002)
Role conflict	Athletes' perceptions about the incongruent expectations of others (Kahn et al., 1964)
Role overload	Athletes having too many role expectations and/or being unable to prioritize them appropriately
Role satisfaction	How happy athletes are with their given role(s) on the team
Role performance	Athletes' behaviors pertaining to role responsibilities

The relationship between the presence of group norms and the degree of group cohesiveness is circular. The development of norms contributes to the development of cohesiveness. With increased group cohesiveness there is also greater conformity to group standards for behavior and performance. A recently formed group has minimal influence over its members. But as the group develops and becomes more cohesive, adherence to norms for behavior increases. Failure to conform can lead to sanctions or punishment. For example, the group can control the amount of interaction it permits members, their degree of involvement in decision making, and their accessibility to task and social rewards. Controlling the opportunity to interact and to influence the group is probably the most powerful sanction the group possesses. As a group increases in cohesiveness, its members place increasing value on social approval and the opportunities to interact with other group members. Therefore, they show an increasing tendency to adhere to the group norms and to give in to the group influence—even if that influence is negative.

An important aspect of group norms is their *stability*. An arbitrary norm can persist for four or five generations after the original members have been removed from the group (Jacobs & Campbell, 1961). Thus, if a sport team develops negative norms, such as abusive behavior toward officials or other team members, a laissez-faire attitude toward training, or a reliance on individual versus team goals, those norms could persist over a number of seasons unless steps are taken to eliminate them.

Thus, establishing positive group norms is extremely important in sport teams, particularly if an inappropriate norm is in place. One technique that has been used successfully is to enlist the formal and informal leaders of the group as active agents. If athlete leaders (in addition to the coach) accept and adhere to specific standards, other group members soon follow. In some instances the athlete leaders may be resistant to change. This poses a problem because on sport teams the formal and informal leaders are usually the most highly skilled. If this is the case, the coach must decide how important

the new standard is to the long-term success of the organization. In the event that the new standard is considered to be very important, the coach may have to release the resistant team members.

Group processes. Another important team factor that influences the development of team cohesion is the interactive processes that occur among the members. One process is the establishment of *group goals and rewards*. In most group activities, including track and field, swimming, baseball, and even basketball, hockey, and soccer, there is an opportunity for the gifted individual competitor to obtain special recognition and rewards. This is inevitable. However, to ensure that a concept of unity develops, the coach must emphasize the group's goals and objectives as well as the rewards that will accrue to the group if these are achieved. Individual goals and rewards should be downplayed.

Communication is another group process associated with increased group cohesiveness. As the level of communication relating to task and social issues increases, cohesiveness is enhanced. And as the group becomes more cohesive, communication also increases. Group members are more open with one another, and they volunteer more, talk more, and listen better. In short, the exchange of task information and social pleasantries increases with cohesiveness.

Performance outcome. As has been the case with so many other factors, the relationship between cohesion and performance outcome is a circular one. More specifically, cohesiveness contributes to performance success, and performance success increases cohesiveness. Carron, Colman, Wheeler, and Stevens (2002) conducted a meta-analysis to examine the cohesion–performance relationship, from which a number of issues arose. First, *both* task and social cohesion were positively related to performance and the relationships were cyclical (as mentioned earlier). That is, the strength of the cohesion to performance relationship was as strong as the performance to cohesion relationship. Second, there was no significant difference between the strengths of the task cohesion–performance relationship (i.e., effect size = .61) and the social cohesion–performance relationship (i.e., effect size = .70) although the latter was slightly greater. Finally, these relationships (a) existed equally for teams that were task interdependent (e.g., volleyball) and those more individual in nature (e.g., track and field), (b) were present across the spectrum of skill and competitive levels, and (c) were found to be stronger in female teams. Overall, performance success is an important team factor for developing cohesion. Consequently, if possible, a coach should try to avoid an excessively difficult schedule early in a season.

Team Building

What makes the U.S. [cross country ski] team so successful is that every single member is committed to being a team player. . . . That kind of team chemistry doesn't happen overnight, and it doesn't happen without conscious thought.

—Jessie Diggins, World Champion Cross Country Skier, discussing the United States Women's ski team's success during the 2012–13 season (Diggins, 2013, para. 5).

The importance of developing an effective sport group environment is recognized even among athletes whose performances are almost exclusively individual. As such, coaches and sport psychology specialists invariably seek ways to build an effective team by using the process of **team building**—defined by Carron and Eys (2012) as "team enhancement or team improvement for both task and social purposes" (p. 368). Team building uses strategies to help members work together more effectively and provides meaningful experiences that ultimately lead to a greater sense of unity.

Team building can either be directly applied by sport psychology specialists (e.g., a specialist conducting a goal setting seminar with athletes and coaches) or indirectly applied, where coaches and sport psychology specialists develop an intervention together and then the intervention is applied by the coach. Sport team building interventions are often indirect to permit the coach to be the primary arbitrator of the group environment.

Carron and Spink (1993) Team Building Approach

Although team building promotes a number of individual and group outcomes (e.g., self-confidence, communication, role understanding, trust), cohesion is typically at the core of any team building program (Bruner, Eys, Beauchamp, & Côté, 2012; Martin, Carron, & Burke, 2009). Notably, cohesion is a primary focus of the team building approach developed by Carron, Spink, and Prapavessis (Carron & Spink, 1993; Prapavessis, Carron, & Spink, 1996; Spink & Carron, 1993), which is the most commonly adopted approach in sport research (Bruner et al., 2012). The following paragraphs describe how it is used within sport.

The Spink and Carron approach involves an indirect intervention process comprised of an *introductory stage*, a *conceptual stage*, a *practical stage*, and an *intervention stage*. The initial three stages occur during coach–sport psychology specialist interactions as the coach learns about group dynamics and prepares strategies that will be used to develop cohesion within his or her team (Carron & Spink, 1993). In the introductory stage, the sport psychology specialist teaches the coach about group dynamics and the general benefits of group cohesion (e.g., the relationship between perceptions of cohesiveness and enhanced team dynamics can be discussed). This understanding is further established during the conceptual stage; here the sport psychology specialist teaches the coach about the various components of the team building protocol and helps the coach identify key areas to focus efforts on (e.g., the specific needs of the group).

During the practical stage, coaches engage in an interactive brainstorming session with the sport psychology specialist and/or other coaching staff to generate strategies to use for team building in their group. Active involvement of the coach(es) is valuable for three reasons:

(a) Coaches differ in personality and preferences, so a strategy that might be effectively implemented by one coach might not be by another.

(b) Given that groups differ, an intervention strategy that is effective with one group might be ineffective with another. Coaches are the individuals most familiar with their groups and will have a sense for the most appropriate strategies.

(c) Coaches have control over the protocol, which leads to increased coach investment and commitment to team building.

Although coaches are largely responsible for this brainstorming process, it is helpful to provide examples of strategies that can be used.

Table 7-3 contains examples of these team building strategies that are applied to sport.

The team building protocol is finally introduced and maintained by coaches during the intervention stage. The intervention stage may last throughout the entire season, as coaches continually use team building strategies and evaluate the process and suitability of strategies.

Additional Team Building Approaches

Team building approaches are rarely designed to suit all situations, and many team building intervention alternatives are available in addition

Table 7-3 Examples of Team Building Strategies for Coaches to Enhance Group Cohesiveness

Factor	Example Strategies
Distinctiveness	• Provide the team with unique identifiers (e.g., shirts, logos, mottos, etc.). • Emphasize any unique traditions and/or history associated with the team.
Individual roles	• Create a team structure in which there is a clear differentiation in team positions/roles. • Ensure that all members understand how their role(s) can contribute to team success. • Establish mentorship opportunities between veterans and rookies.
Group norms	• Establish standards of conduct across all team-related settings (competition, school, etc.). • Use input from team members to form norms. • Show individual team members how group standards can contribute to more effective team performance and a greater sense of team unity. • Reward team members who adhere to the group's standards and sanction those who do not.
Individual sacrifices	• Encourage important team members to make sacrifices (e.g., ask a veteran athlete to sit out to give a novice athlete more playing time). • Members contribute to fund raising or other community-related activities (e.g., assisting in the maintenance of a trail used for training).
Interaction and communication	• Provide opportunities for athlete input. • Create an environment that fosters mutual trust and respect so that athletes feel comfortable communicating. • Have all players identify (on paper) why they want their fellow players on the team, then create a summary sheet for each player. • Establish an online group or forum on social networking websites.

Adapted from: Bull, Albinson, & Shambrook, 1996; Bruner & Spink, 2011; Carron, & Spink, 1993; Munroe, Terry, & Carron, 2002; Prapavessis, Carron, & Spink, 1996; Yukelson, 1984; Zander, 1982.

to the Carron and Spink approach. Although many of these cannot be fully described within the confines of this chapter, it is important to consider approaches that may be used to suit the needs of distinct groups.

One example of an approach that is typically used to increase mutual understanding and cohesion late in the season (e.g., during playoffs) with well-established groups is the Personal-Disclosure Mutual-Sharing intervention (PDMS; Dunn & Holt, 2004). During PDMS, sport psychology specialists assign team members with "homework" by asking the team to prepare a written passage that answers a personal question about their sport involvement (e.g., "why do you compete in this sport?" or "what are you willing to sacrifice for your team?"). Once all members have prepared their passage, the specialist leads a team meeting where members read their passage aloud. These group sessions can be very powerful and often last several hours. PDMS demands a high level of responsibility to ensure that the statements remain confidential and should be used only when members are comfortable enough to reflect on personal experiences as a group.

Another example that may be useful in facilitating team building is the Mastery Approach to Coaching (MAC; Smoll & Smith, 2008), which is ideal for youth sport settings. The MAC is a coach training system based on principles described by Ronald Smith and Frank Smoll (see Chapter 17). The use of the MAC protocol for team building is based on the expectation that positive and task-oriented coaching behaviors will enable positive group environments. McLaren (2013) recently conducted an intervention study to compare soccer players' perceptions of coaches who participated in a MAC training session early on in the season with coaches who did not experience the training. He found that athletes who belonged to teams with coaches who attended a MAC training session reported increased group cohesion, providing evidence for the usefulness of MAC training for youth sport team building.

Finally, sport psychology specialists may be well advised to include athletes as active contributors to team building strategies, particularly experienced athletes who may prefer ownership over the process. The applied example found in the below box highlights a protocol the Toronto Maple Leafs (of the National Hockey League) used to develop "team values" that enlisted and depended on the opinions of all team members. The inclusion of selected high-status members of the team (i.e., captains, co-captains) in implementing this team building strategy was considered particularly critical for its delivery.

Developing team values

The Toronto Maple Leafs hockey team, a member of the National Hockey League, has engaged in several values-based team building exercises. Values are beliefs that influence behavior and serve as guidelines to evaluate behavior (Crace & Hardy, 1997). A modified version of the Crace and Hardy intervention model was introduced to the Toronto Maple Leafs at the beginning of the 2005–2006 season. Although the model recommends that the players and coaches be introduced to the principles behind team building interventions, it was felt that professional hockey players already had a clear understanding of what constitutes a functional team environment.

Thus, the session began with players divided into four groups of six, each table with a group leader who was one of the team's captains. The Player Development coach asked the leaders to discuss in their groups the important beliefs that would help guide their behavior and motivation for the upcoming season. After a 20-minute discussion, the group leaders reported three or four of their groups' most important beliefs. A general discussion ensued and the players collectively rank-ordered the beliefs. Following are the results:

Team Values Summary, 2005–2006 Season

1. *Team Toughness: Mentally and physically, never quit. Stick up for one another.*

2. *Team Speed: We must all take short shifts so we can wear down our opponents by the third period. We'll be able to win the close games if we can do this.*

3. *Team Defense: We can score, but in the past we've hung the goalies "out-to-dry." We need a commitment to play solid defense.*

4. *Work Ethic: On and off the ice strive toward your goal. Push yourself to be better.*

5. *Accountability: Being truthful and up front to your teammates. Don't make excuses. It has to be 24 players held accountable by each other and the coaches.*

6. *Respect: Respect must be earned. Respect each other's roles and what different players bring to the table, for example, goal scoring, checking, penalty killing.*

7. *Positive Attitude: We need to be more positive. No complaining about line combinations, defense partner and so on.*

8. *Loyalty: Don't cheat yourself or your teammates from your best effort. If you play 5 minutes or 20 minutes, work hard whenever you get the chance.*

9. *Leadership: There are 24 leaders in this dressing room, no passengers.*

10. *Commitment: Make the commitment to team concepts, systems, and off-ice conditioning.*

The 10 beliefs the players presented to the coaching staff were transformed into a plaque, and each player took ownership by signing his name to it. The plaque was mounted in the dressing room as a reminder of what the group valued as a team. Throughout the season, head coach Pat Quinn often referred to one of the values as a theme to begin his team meetings in preparation for an upcoming game. In addition, if the team was underachieving, he would target one of the belief statements. For example, if there was a lackluster effort after a period, the coach would refer to "loyalty," which the players had defined as not cheating themselves or their teammates from giving their best effort. The coach implied that they were letting each other down and not adhering to their own values. Such tactics would help motivate the players into giving a more concerted effort to achieve their goals.

Summary

Like all groups, sport teams are dynamic. As such, they are subject to change, to growth, to modification, and to improvement. The coach is probably in the best position to influence change in a positive direction. To do this efficiently and effectively, it is beneficial to draw on the wealth of research information that has been developed over a number of years in management science, social psychology, sociology, physical education, and kinesiology. Given the influence that groups have on their members, knowledge of group structure, group dynamics, and group cohesiveness is essential for coaches. This understanding will provide an excellent base from which to weld athletes into a more effective team.

Study Questions

1. Briefly describe the six characteristics of sport groups.

2. Define cohesiveness. What are the four specific facets of cohesion?

3. List the four factors that contribute to cohesiveness and give one specific example of each.

4. Discuss the relationship of team size to group cohesiveness.

5. Describe the environmental, personal, and leadership factors that contribute to the development of cohesiveness.

6. Four team factors related to cohesion are roles, norms, group processes, and performance outcome. Distinguish among each of these factors and describe how the factors might be manipulated or modified to enhance team cohesion.

7. Give at least one example (using a sport of your choice) of a strategy that a coach or sport psychologist could employ to enhance group cohesiveness using each of the following factors: (a) distinctiveness, (b) individual positions, (c) group norms, (d) individual sacrifices, and (e) interaction and communication.

References

Bass, B. M., & Riggio, R. E. (2006). *Transformational leadership* (2nd ed.). Mahwah, NJ: Lawrence Erlbaum.

Beauchamp, M. R., Bray, S. R., Eys, M. A., & Carron, A. V. (2002). Role ambiguity, role efficacy, and role performance: Multidimensional and mediational relationships within interdependent sport teams. *Group Dynamics: Theory, Research, and Practice, 6,* 229–242.

Beauchamp, M. R., Bray, S. R., Eys, M. A., & Carron, A. V. (2003). The effect of role ambiguity on competitive state anxiety. *Journal of Sport and Exercise Psychology, 25,* 77–92.

Benson, A., Eys, M. A., Surya, M., Dawson, K., & Schneider, M. (2013). Athletes' perceptions of role acceptance in interdependent sport teams. *The Sport Psychologist, 27,* 269–280.

Bosselut, G., McLaren, C. D., Eys, M. A., & Heuzé, J. (2012). Reciprocity of the relationship between role ambiguity and group cohesion in youth interdependent sport. *Psychology of Sport and Exercise, 13,* 341–348.

Brawley, L. R., Carron, A. V., & Widmeyer, W. N. (1987). Assessing the cohesion of teams: Validity of the Group Environment Questionnaire. *Journal of Sport Psychology, 9,* 275–294.

Bray, S. R., Brawley, L. R., & Carron, A. V. (2002). Efficacy for interdependent role functions: Evidence from the sport domain. *Small Group Research, 33,* 644–666.

Bruner, M. W., Eys, M. A., Beauchamp, M. R., & Côté, J. (2013). Examining the origins of team building in sport: A citation network and genealogical approach. *Group Dynamics: Theory, Research, and Practice, 17,* 30–42.

Bruner, M. W., & Spink, K. S. (2011). Effects of team building on exercise adherence and group task satisfaction in a youth activity setting. *Group Dynamics: Theory, Research, and Practice, 15,* 161–172.

Bull, S. J., Albinson, J. G., & Shambrook, C. J. (1996). *The mental game plan: Getting psyched for sport.* Eastborne, UK: Sports Dynamics.

Carron, A. V., Brawley, L. R., & Widmeyer, W. N. (1998). The measurement of cohesiveness in sport groups. In J. L. Duda (Ed.), *Advancements in sport and exercise psychology measurement* (pp. 213–226). Morgantown, WV: Fitness Information Technology.

Carron, A. V., Colman, M. M., Wheeler, J., & Stevens, D. (2002). Cohesion and performance in sport: A meta-analysis. *Journal of Sport and Exercise Psychology, 24,* 168–188.

Carron, A. V., & Eys, M. A. (2012). *Group dynamics in sport* (4th ed.). Morgantown, WV: Fitness Information Technology.

Carron, A. V., & Spink, K. S. (1993). Team building in an exercise setting. *The Sport Psychologist, 7,* 8–18.

Carron, A. V., Widmeyer, L. R., & Brawley, L. R. (1985). The development of an instrument to assess cohesion in sport teams: The Group Environment Questionnaire. *Journal of Sport Psychology, 7,* 244–266.

Cope, C. J., Eys, M. A., Beauchamp, M. R., Schinke, R. J., & Bosselut, G. (2011). Informal roles on sport teams. *International Journal of Sport and Exercise Psychology, 9,* 19–30.

Cope, C. J., Eys, M. A., Schinke, R. J., & Bosselut, G. (2010). Coaches' perspectives of a negative informal role: The "Cancer" within sport teams. *Journal of Applied Sport Psychology, 22,* 420–436.

Diggins, J. (2013, May). [Web log post]. *Why this team works so well.* Retrieved from http://jessiediggins.com/

Dunn, J. G. H., & Holt, N. L. (2004). A qualitative investigation of a personal-disclosure mutual sharing team building activity. *The Sport Psychologist, 18,* 363–380.

Evans, M. B., Eys, M. A., & Bruner, M. W. (2012). See the "we" in "me" sports : The need to consider individual sport team environments. *Canadian Psychology, 53,* 301–308.

Eys, M. A., Carron, A. V., Bray, S. R., & Beauchamp, M. R. (2003). Role ambiguity and athlete satisfaction. *Journal of Sports Sciences, 21,* 391–401.

Eys, M. A., Hardy, J., Carron, A. V., & Beauchamp, M. R. (2003). The relationship between task cohesion and competitive state anxiety. *Journal of Sport and Exercise Psychology, 25,* 66–76.

Eys, M. A., Loughead, T. M., Bray, S. R., & Carron, A. V. (2009). Development of a cohesion questionnaire for youth: The Youth Sport Environment Questionnaire. *Journal of Sport and Exercise Psychology, 31,* 390–408.

Gammage, K. L., Carron, A. V., & Estabrooks, P. A. (2001). Team cohesion and individual productivity: The influence of the norm for productivity and the identifiability of individual effort. *Small Group Research, 32,* 3–18.

Jacobs, R. C., & Campbell, D. T. (1961). The perpetuation of an arbitrary tradition through several generations of a laboratory microculture. *Journal of Abnormal and Social Psychology, 62,* 649–658.

Kahn, R. L., Wolfe, D. M., Quinn, R. P., Snoek, J. D., & Rosenthal, R. A. (1964). *Occupational stress: Studies in role conflict and ambiguity.* New York: Wiley.

Kompany: Belgium's team spirit is unbelievable. (2012, October). *Fifa.com*. Retrieved from http://www.fifa.com/worldcup/preliminaries/news/newsid=1787336/index.html.

Mabry, E. A., & Barnes, R. E. (1980). *The dynamics of small group communication*. Englewood Cliffs, NJ: Prentice Hall.

Martin, L. J., Carron, A. V., & Burke, S. M. (2009). Team building interventions in sport: A meta-analysis. *Sport and Exercise Psychology Review, 5,* 3–18.

Martin, L. J., Carron, A. V., Eys, M. A., & Loughead, T. (2012). Development of a cohesion questionnaire for children's sport teams. *Group Dynamics: Theory, Research, and Practice, 16,* 68–79.

McKnight, P., Williams, J. M., & Widmeyer, W. N. (1991, October). *The effects of cohesion and identifiability on reducing the likelihood of social loafing*. Presented at the Association for the Advancement of Applied Sport Psychology Annual Conference, Savannah, GA.

McLaren, C. (2013). *Coach-initiated motivational climate: The effect on group cohesion and intentions to return following an intervention program* (Unpublished master's thesis). Wilfrid Laurier University, Waterloo, Ontario, Canada.

Munroe, K., Estabrooks, P., Dennis, P., & Carron, A. V. (1999). A phenomenological analysis of group norms in sport teams. *The Sport Psychologist, 13,* 171–182.

Munroe, K., Terry, P., & Carron, A. (2002). Cohesion and teamwork. In B. Hale & D. Collins (Eds.), *Rugby tough* (pp. 137–153). Champaign, IL: Human Kinetics.

Price, M. S., & Weiss, M. R. (2013). Relationships among coach leadership, peer leadership, and adolescent athletes' psychosocial and team outcomes: A test of transformational leadership theory. *Journal of Applied Sport Psychology, 25,* 265–279.

Prapavessis, H., Carron, A. V., & Spink, K. S. (1996). Team building in sport. *International Journal of Sport Psychology, 27,* 269–285.

Rafferty, A. (2013, March). Former Florida A&M band members face stiffer charges for hazing death. *NBCNews.com*. Retrieved from http://usnews.nbcnews.com/_news/2013/03/04/17184496-former-florida-am-band-members-face-stiffer-charges-for-hazing-death?lite

Riemer, H. A. & Chelladurai, P. (1998). Development of the Athlete Satisfaction Questionnaire (ASQ). *Journal of Sport and Exercise Psychology, 20,* 127–156.

Rush, C. (2013, February). Mitchell Marcus sinks one basket and lifts crowd's hearts. *The Toronto Star*. Retrieved from http://www.thestar.com/sports/2013/02/27/mitchell_marcus_sinks_one_basket_and_lifts_crowds_hearts.html

Smith, M. J., Arthur, C. A., Hardy, J., Callow, N., & Williams, D. (2013). Transformational leadership and task cohesion in sport: The mediating role of intrateam communication. *Psychology of Sport and Exercise, 14,* 249–257.

Smoll, F. L., & Smith, R. E. (2008). *Coaches who never lose: Making sure athletes win, no matter what the score*. (3rd. Ed.). Palo Alto, CA: Warde.

Spink, K. S., & Carron, A. V. (1993). The effects of team building on the adherence patterns of female exercise participants. *Journal of Sport and Exercise Psychology, 15,* 39–49.

Spink, K. S., Wilson, K. S., & Priebe, C. S. (2010). Groupness and adherence in structured exercise settings. *Group Dynamics: Theory, Research, and Practice, 14,* 163–173.

Westre, K. R., & Weiss, M. R. (1991). The relationship between perceived coaching behaviors and group cohesion in high school football teams. *The Sport Psychologist, 5,* 41–54.

Widmeyer, W. N., Brawley, L. R., & Carron, A. V. (1985). *The measurement of cohesion in sport teams: The Group Environment Questionnaire.* London, ON: Sports Dynamics.

Widmeyer, W. N., Brawley, L. R., & Carron, A. V. (1990). The effects of group size in sport. *Journal of Exercise and Sport Psychology, 12,* 177–190.

Widmeyer, W. N., & Williams, J. M. (1991). Predicting cohesion in a coacting sport. *Small Group Research, 22,* 548–570.

Wolf, S. A., Sadler, P., Eys, M. A., & Kleinert, J. (2012). Team cohesion predicts athletes' precompetitive appraisals: Is this a link between cohesion and emotion. *Journal of Sport and Exercise Psychology, 34,* S304–305.

Yukelson, D. P. (1984). Group motivation in sport teams. In J. M. Silva & R. S. Weinberg (Eds.), *Psychological foundations of sport.* Champaign, IL: Human Kinetics.

Zander, A. (1982). *Making groups effective.* San Francisco: Jossey-Bass.

CHAPTER 8

Communicating Effectively

David P. Yukelson, *The Pennsylvania State University*

> *I wish my coach was a little clearer with me. I wish I knew where I stood with her. I wish she believed in me more. Right now, I feel like I'm working really hard but nothing ever seems to be good enough. Anytime I go into my coach's office to talk, things get turned around and I'm always on the defensive. I wish the communication between us was better and more open.*
>
> —*Penn State University Student-Athlete*

In my work with intercollegiate student-athletes, I often am asked to address the topic of communication, particularly as it pertains to group cohesion, team dynamics, and interpersonal relationships. Effective communication is critical to the success of any team or organization and its members. The ability to express one's thoughts, feelings, and needs effectively and reciprocally to be able to understand the thoughts, feelings, ideas, and needs of others, is central to good communication.

One day following a workshop on communication and team building, a football player came up to me and remarked that, to him, communication is what teamwork and group chemistry are all about. From a group perspective, it is tied to oneness of thought, synchronization of roles, and everyone being on the same page. He elaborated by saying, "If I can walk up to the line of scrimmage and know that the offensive tackle next to me is thinking the same thing I

am, has internalized what needs to be done on this particular play, transmits to me a nonverbal signal indicating it's time to take care of business, then I know with great confidence, we are going to execute the upcoming play with precise timing, intensity, and cohesiveness." His remarks reminded me that there is much more to communication than meets the ear. From a global perspective, communication goes beyond talking and listening; rather, it's about connecting with people in a meaningful way.

Although coaches, athletes, and sport psychologists talk about the importance of effective communication in team success, surprisingly very little has been written about the subject, particularly as it pertains to sport. Hence, the purpose of this chapter is to explore what effective communication is as it relates to sport, identify barriers to effective communication, and develop strategies for improving communication processes within athletic environments.

Communication Defined

The philosopher and social theorist John Dewey notes the word "communication" shares the same etiology or root as the word "community," and is the result of people feeling engaged in shared projects and meaningful social interactions (Stuhr, 1997). At the core of this statement is the notion of engaged communication processes and connecting with people in a meaningful way. When an individual feels engaged in conversation, it connotes a feeling the other person is listening and genuinely cares about what is being said. The quote at the beginning of the chapter points to the importance of engagement and the athlete's desire to connect with her coach on a meaningful level.

Communication is a multidimensional process that involves sending, receiving (encoding), and interpreting (decoding) messages through a variety of sensory modalities (Crocker, 1990; Harris & Harris, 1984). These messages can be verbal (as in written or spoken communication) or nonverbal (facial expressions, body language, body positioning) and can be distinguished in terms of content and emotion. The way a message is expressed will influence how the message is received and interpreted. Likewise, communication does not exist in a vacuum; rather, content and context interact to produce meaning in every communication episode (Clampitt, 2005).

From a social psychological perspective, both person and situation variables influence this dynamic process. An individual's personality, upbringing, values, beliefs, personal mannerisms, and style of communicating interact with a variety of situation-specific circumstances to influence the way messages are transmitted and received. Contextual factors come into play such as your relationship with the other person (e.g., history you share, perceived level of trust, power and control issues), the environment you find yourself in (e.g., office, practice field, public or private setting), and the cultural context from which communication is to take place (e.g., learned rules and behaviors that are supposed to be followed). Although there are individual differences in the way people respond, understanding the dynamics that surround these contexts can attenuate misunderstanding and influence individuals' interpersonal effectiveness (Beebe, Beebe, & Redmond, 1996; Clampitt, 2005).

Other factors such as stress, perceptual filtering, and psychological expectancies can all influence the way messages are expressed, received, and interpreted (Henschen & Miner, 1989; Vealey, 2005). In the process of interpreting verbal and nonverbal messages, information may be lost or distorted. Sometimes we think we hear a person say one thing when, in fact, he or she said something different. We then act on the basis of what we think the person said. Many communication problems are rooted in this kind of misunderstanding.

The following example provides an illustration of how a compliment can be misinterpreted due to stress, selective filtering, or emotional mood states. During a practice, an athlete misses an offensive rebound, yet the coach compliments him for demonstrating good positioning, footwork, and intensity. Stressed over a variety of things going on in his life (e.g., two midterms, limited playing time recently, breaking up with his partner), the athlete processes the compliment as an insult. For reasons not apparent to the coach, tension builds and tempers fly. Angry over the turn of events, the coach verbally denounces the athlete's reaction as stupid, mumbles to himself, "I can't control how he took it," and benches the athlete. Consequently, a wall is formed, communication blocked, and the intent of the message is never received.

Likewise, during the course of a long competitive season, coaches also are susceptible to heightened job stress, multiple demands, and emotional mood swings (Dale & Weinberg, 1990; Smith, 1986), which in turn can have an adverse effect on their communication. I recall a situation midway through the course of a season; a coach was not happy with the way her team was playing. The pressure to win, coupled with increased travel demands and injuries to key personnel, resulted in the coach being extremely stressed. Frustrated and impatient toward the end of practice, the coach chastised a young, inexperienced first year player for making a mistake. The coach's comments were so demeaning, her tone of voice so penetrating and hurtful, her nonverbal body language so piercing that the athlete shut down and tuned out anything positive that was said thereafter. The whole situation was unfortunate because the athlete, talented yet low in self-confidence, began to fear failure, was scared to make a mistake, and never quite recovered for the rest of the season.

Practically speaking, it has been my experience that many interpersonal problems in teams result from individuals' lack of understanding of each other's needs and feelings. As Orlick (2008) astutely notes, "It is difficult to be responsive to another's needs or feelings when you do not know what they are" (p. 283). Consequently, an important goal of interpersonal communication is to learn how to simply express oneself so the other person is in a position to better understand. This entails active listening and engaged mutual sharing, both from a verbal and nonverbal perspective.

These examples show how communication is an attitude that goes beyond the content of what is said. How one sends the message is just as important as what is said, especially when one is stressed. Consequently, coaches and athletes must make certain the message conveyed is the message received. Tone of voice, facial expression, body posture/spatial distance, and eye contact are some of the nonverbal cues that influence communication. As a general rule, become aware of how you come across to others, and make sure you say what you mean and mean what you say.

Communication in Sport

With regard to sport, so much of what goes on in athletics revolves around communication. Research in this area predominantly has looked at leadership and communication styles as they relate to variables such as motivation, individual and team expectations, coaching effectiveness,

reinforcement and constructive feedback, team cohesion, and conflict resolution skills (Connelly & Rotella, 1991; Horn, 1985, 2008; Jowett & Chaundry, 2004; Martens, 1987, 2004). Although styles of communication vary from coach to coach, it is important to communicate in a manner consistent with one's own personality and coaching philosophy (Wooten, 1992). Similarly, Martens (1987) notes that clear, honest, and direct communication with no hidden agenda is what coaches should strive for in developing successful coach–athlete relationships. In addition, empathy, consistency, approachability, and responsiveness to individual differences have also been shown to be critical elements for effective communication in sport settings (Lorimer, 2013; Yukelson, 1997).

As noted earlier, communication is a dynamic process that involves mutual sharing which implies reciprocal participation (e.g., two parties sharing thoughts, feelings, ideas, or information about a particular subject). Likewise, to truly understand or comprehend another individual's perspective, people need to be adept at the art of listening. In essence, mutual sharing leads to mutual understanding (through sharing, the other person is in a better position to truly understand). In the context of a team, if a group is to function effectively, its members must communicate openly and honestly with one another about the efficiency of group functioning and the quality of interpersonal relationships (Yukelson, 1997). Effective communication is apparent when team members listen to one another and attempt to build on each other's strengths and contributions (Sullivan, 1993; Yukelson, 1997).

For coaches, the foundation for effective communication skills is having credibility in the eyes of their athletes, and having developed trust and respectful relationships (Orlick, 2008; Yukelson, 1984). Credibility is reflected in the athletes' attitudes about the trustworthiness of what you say and do (Martens, Christina, Harvey, & Sharkey, 1981; Vealey, 2005). Trust is linked to the concepts of honesty, integrity, authenticity, and respect. Lack of honesty and betrayal of trust can lead to many interpersonal problems within a team including feelings of tension, anger, hostility, resentment, divisions, and jealousy. It is very difficult to regain someone's trust once it is broken.

Athletes seem to be motivated most by coaches for whom they have a lot of respect (Lynch, 2001). Respect often is not communicated directly in words; rather, it is demonstrated through actions, sincerity, genuineness, and social influence (Egan, 1994). Athletes will lose respect for their coaches if they feel betrayed, manipulated, and deceived, or perceive their coach is not listening. To illustrate the point, I remember a situation where a coach "heard through the grapevine" that a particular athlete violated a long-standing team rule. The coach, who liked to be in control of everything, failed to garner all the facts. She solicited information from other teammates as to what had happened, but never talked directly to the person in question. As a consequence, the athletes felt betrayed and angry, respect for the coach was shattered, and interpersonal relations among the athletes became strained. A good rule is to solicit all the facts before passing judgment, and treat people exactly the way you want to be treated. Putting yourself in the shoes of others and seeing things from their perspective (i.e., empathy) helps to build credibility, trust, and mutual respect.

Coaches who are good communicators have credibility with their athletes. They establish open lines of communication; they are honest, fair, authentic, sincere, and consistent. They accept individuals for who they are, and genuinely care about them as people outside of athletics. This values-based perspective is consistent with applied research by Janssen and Dale (2002), who found credible coaches to be character-based, competent, committed, caring, consistent, confidence builders, and good communicators.

From a tactical standpoint, coaches who are good communicators explain, clarify, and individualize instruction to meet the athlete's needs and personality. They observe performance analytically and are able to help athletes improve performance by providing clear and constructive behavioral feedback in a nonthreatening manner (Smith, 1986; Martin & Hrycaiko, 1983). The following discussion between a coach and a fencer between competitive bouts highlights the point: "Kathy, you are too anxious on the strip. You are telegraphing messages to your opponent as to what your intentions are. Relax, see things develop, trust your decisions and actions, and when you see the window of opportunity open up, go for it!" The importance of giving constructive tactical feedback in relation to training methods and goals an individual or team is striving to accomplish cannot be overstated.

Athletes react in various ways to how coaches communicate with them. They know the characteristics they like and dislike in coaches. From a developmental perspective, research in the area of youth sports indicates young athletes like coaches who are knowledgeable and instructive, supportive and encouraging, enthusiastic and motivated, reliable, fair, and consistent (Martens, 2004; Martens et al., 1981; Smith, Smith, & Smoll, 1983). In contrast, young athletes dislike coaches who are judgmental, manipulative, capricious, inconsistent, or constantly negative. Personally, I believe the same principles hold true for older athletes. My observation has been that intercollegiate athletes respond best to coaches who are open, honest, sincere, approachable, and caring. Most athletes do not mind being yelled at as long as they know the coach cares. One of our coaches at Penn State notes "I have a tendency to raise the decibel level in my voice because I am trying to get their attention, but that does not mean I don't understand or that I don't care. You want players to feel comfortable around you, but at the same time, realize you are the authority figure." He goes on to say, "A coach can gain trust with their athletes by being honest, consistent, and approachable. I try to get my athletes to respect me by attempting to be fair in my decisions and truthful when giving assessment and advice." Again, from a philosophical perspective, this example points to the importance of engaging athletes in the communication processes, creating an atmosphere that reflects a "community" of caring. Athletes work hard to achieve their goals and want to feel a sense of connection with their coach on a genuine and meaningful level. They expect to be treated with dignity and respect, and should give the same back in return. Similarly, athletes (and people in general) want to know their role is valued and contributions appreciated.

Communication and Groups

One of the most gratifying experiences a coach or athlete can have is to be a member of a team that gets along well and works together efficiently in a cohesive, harmonious, task-oriented manner (Orlick, 2008; Yukelson, 1984). Communication lies at the heart of group process. If a group is to function effectively, members must be able to communicate easily and efficiently with one another (Shaw, 1981). Because communication directly affects group solidarity, collective efficacy, and team performance (Zaccaro, Blair, Peterson, & Zazanis, 1995), I spend a great deal of time talking with teams about group process, team dynamics, and methods for improving harmonious team relations. Team building comes from a shared vision of what the group is striving to achieve and is tied to commitment, individual and mutual accountability, collaboration, communication, and teamwork (Yukelson, 1997). A shared vision that has meaning and purpose creates synergistic empowerment. Likewise, in successful teams, coaches and athletes talk openly and honestly about interpersonal and task-related issues that affect them directly, and everyone works together to develop a positive group atmosphere/team culture conducive for team success (Collins, 2001; Goleman, Boyatzis, & McKee, 2002; Pain & Harwood, 2009).

Unfortunately, not every group functions cohesively. Many interpersonal problems on teams stem from poor communication. Interpersonal conflict is often the result of misunderstanding or miscommunication of feelings. Henschen and Miner (1989) have identified five types of misunderstandings that often surface within groups: (1) a difference of opinion resolvable by common sense, (2) a clash of personalities in the group, (3) a conflict of task or social roles among group members, (4) a struggle for power between one or more individuals, and (5) a breakdown of communication between

the leader and the group or among members of the group itself. Misunderstandings are also the result of inaccessibility to relevant information (not being privy to certain sources of information); inattentiveness (failing to listen, not paying attention, being distracted); lack of assertiveness (failure to speak up); or misperceiving someone's motives, intentions, or behavior (inference mind reading). Similarly, people are often afraid to express how they truly feel for fear of being ridiculed or rejected for saying what is truly on their minds (Holt, Knight, & Zukiwski, 2012; Orlick, 1986).

Several teams I have worked with have had their fair share of interpersonal communication problems and conflict. Problems have ranged from interpersonal jealousies within the team to power struggles, control issues, perceived injustices, and coach–athlete as well as athlete–athlete inequities. Learning how to express oneself in a constructive manner and communicate effectively is an important initial step in preventing and solving problems. It has been stated that the more open you can be with each other, the better your chances are of getting along and achieving both individual and team goals (Orlick, 1986). Thus, it is important for coaches and athletes to learn how to express their thoughts and feelings about various issues that affect them directly. Team building requires a group climate of trust, mutual respect, openness, and genuine support in which airing problems and matters of concern is not just appropriate but encouraged (Orlick, 2008; Yukelson, 1997).

Team Communication Dynamics

As already mentioned, many communication problems on teams are the result of misunderstanding or miscommunication between the coach and the team or among athletes themselves. Over the course of a season, there are a variety of contextual factors that can influence the way relevant information is disseminated or received (e.g., emotional disappointment following a tough loss, inconsistency during practices or games, diminished playing time, interpersonal cliques, or other perceived barriers that make someone apprehensive about communicating). Harris and Harris (1984) offer an interesting framework to examine communication processes in athletic teams. The framework consists of three different communication configurations: coach–team, coach–athlete, and athlete–athlete interactions.

Coach–team communications. From a coach–team perspective, group synergy and team chemistry are of vital importance. According to DePree (1989), group synergy comes from leaders (in this case coaches) sharing a vision of what could be if everyone puts his or her skills and resources together to achieve team goals and objectives. Individual and mutual accountability, passion and belief, and a genuine commitment to a common team goal are needed. Athletes unite behind common goals, so it is important to get athletes to think in terms of the philosophy, operating procedures, and values that govern the team (Yukelson, 1984). Similarly, homogenous attitudes and expectations (e.g., unity of purpose) as well as shared ideals and covenants to live by are required (Riley, 1993; Walsh, 1998). In terms of shared ideals, it is important to obtain *consensus and commitment* from the team regarding team goals, operating procedures, rules of engagement, and normative behaviors including appropriate methods for achieving them (Carron & Hausenblas, 1998; Goleman et al., 2002; Holt & Dunn, 2006; Kouzes & Posner, 1995; Pain & Harwood, 2009; Yukelson, 1997). To this end, the coach should solicit input from team members regarding their perceptions of what needs to be done for everyone to come together and be an effective team. Everyone on the team must be on the same page, working together with a collective desire to be successful. To achieve these ends, a coach may find the following communication principles useful: impart, inspire, monitor, clarify, and reinforce.

- *Impart* relevant information regarding team rules, expectations, operating procedures, and goals the group is striving to achieve. Clarify the team's mission and purpose, outline strategies and action plans to reach team goals and objectives, involve staff and athletes in decisions that affect them directly.

- *Inspire* everyone to reach for their best. Communicate with a sense of inspired enthusiasm the effort and focus required to reach team goals. Be honest, direct, clear, and empowering. Instill a sense of pride, passion, belief, and team spirit. Strive to make everyone on the team feel valued and significant.

- *Monitor the progress team is making.* Set up a constructive goal-setting program with short-term process goals and action plans leading to long-term visionary objectives (e.g., performance goal boards are often very helpful). Monitor, evaluate, and adjust goals as needed. Give athletes feedback on how they are doing in relation to individual and team goals. Challenge everyone involved to improve and become better. (See Chapter 11 for more information about goal setting.)

- *Clarify* how things are going. Talk openly about the commitment that is required to achieve team goals and what needs to be done to keep things on task. Challenge everyone to take responsibility for their own actions and to work hard with passionate determination, meaningful effort, and sustained focus.

- *Reinforce* behavior that you want repeated. Catch people doing things right; provide lots of informational and emotional support, encouragement, and positive reinforcement; discipline athletes according to your coaching philosophy and team mission statement; and correct errors in a positive way.

Coach–athlete communications. As for coach–athlete lines of communication, coaches should build a psychological and social environment conducive to goal achievement and team success. They should take the time to get to know their athletes as unique individuals and find out their strengths, talents, interests, and needs. The principles of transformational leadership (see Chapter 6) and reciprocal influence are applicable here in the context of athletes and coaches working together to clarify goals, expectations, and need fulfillment (Goleman et al., 2002; Martens, 1987; Yukelson, 1993). Coaches should be open, honest, and up-front with athletes about various decisions that affect them directly. Likewise, as already noted, athletes need feedback as to where they stand and how they are progressing in relation to individual and team goals. Research indicates that *evaluative feedback* is an important part of communication and the goal-setting process (see Chapter 11 and Locke & Latham, 1990). Unfortunately, some coaches are not very good at giving feedback in a positive and supportive manner (Orlick, 2008). Similarly, some athletes have difficulty internalizing feedback for what it is and, as a consequence, take feedback personally as opposed to constructively. Developing strategies to improve coach–athlete communication processes can rectify many misunderstandings and hurt feelings.

In terms of coaching for accountability, four-time national coach of the year Russ Rose has a unique way of providing feedback with his athletes on the Penn State Women's Volleyball Team, something he refers to as "The One Minute Drill." At various times during the season, Coach Rose will pull aside a player individually in the gym for a one-minute meeting and point out "this is what I think you are doing well, this is what I think you need to work on, and here is where I see you making the best contribution to the team during the next training cycle. Do you have any questions?" The One Minute Drill provides open, honest, and direct feedback in a forthright manner. It clarifies expectations, alleviates uncertainty, and lets the athlete know exactly where she stands. The volleyball players may not like what the coach has to say, but afterward they know what is expected and what they have to work on to improve (Yukelson & Rose, 2014). Likewise, recognizing the importance of composure, emotional self-control, and body language on team performance, Penn State women's soccer coach Erica Walsh and her staff periodically will splice together video snippets of the team demonstrating poor body language in game situations and point out the destructive impact it can have on team energy

and team synergy during competitive contests. Although Coach Walsh is a master tactician and a very positive coach, the example highlights the importance of a coach using feedback creatively to get her message across about the significance of nonverbal communication and its influence on concentration, role responsibilities, and team composure. She puts the ownership and responsibility on the team to make appropriate in-game adjustments and holds them accountable for maintaining high standards of performance effectiveness throughout the year.

Positive coach–athlete relationships are so important at all levels. In addition to providing tangible feedback about performance accomplishments, many athletes will seek out their coach to talk about things outside of sport that affect their lives and self-esteem. In intercollegiate settings, this might include concerns about various transition and adjustment issues, academic and time management problems, and ways to navigate interpersonal relationships. Thus, a coach often is asked to take on many mentoring roles (e.g., counselor, confidant, teacher, friend, role model, and sometimes substitute parent). For these reasons, it is important that lines of communication be open between athlete and coach, and that a trusting relationship be established.

As for breakdowns in coach–athlete communications, many athletes are not confident approaching a coach if they do not feel valued, included, or respected. Although it is common for coaches to have a so-called open-door policy, many athletes find it difficult to walk through the door if they feel the coach is not going to listen to their concerns with genuine interest, fear retaliation for opening up, or perceive there to be hidden agendas. Connelly and Rotella (1991) note that some athletes go so far as to "fake honesty"—tell coaches what they think coaches want to hear so the athletes don't have to deal with the situation at hand.

Situations often arise during the course of a season that can exasperate coach–athlete communication problems (e.g., general frustration associated with not performing well, decreased playing time, personality clashes, stress, fatigue, and injury to name just a few). In situations like these, athletes often perceive the coach as being insensitive, unappreciative, unapproachable, or uninterested. As a consequence, it is not unusual for an athlete to feel apprehensive about approaching the coach. Rather than clam up, athletes need to learn how to express themselves in an assertive manner. A practical technique I have found to be useful is to have athletes write on a cue card three main points they would like to express to the coach. We then role-play and simulate potential scenarios. Athletes visualize themselves communicating their message in a confident and successful manner. This type of preparation helps to build confidence and desensitize athletes to situations they perceive to be stressful.

Proactively, coaches should also consider developing an individualized communication plan with their athletes for interacting effectively at the competition site (Orlick, 2008). Because athletes prepare and respond differently in competitive environments, it is suggested coaches assess ahead of time their athletes' needs and preferences and respond accordingly. Prior to competition, some athletes like to be left alone; others appreciate a word of encouragement or a task-oriented cue that reminds them to concentrate and bring their best focus forward. The same holds true for post-competition feedback. Some athletes are very emotional after competition and don't want to be disturbed; others want feedback immediately. Thus, a coach–athlete communication plan for competition helps to alleviate stress and possible misunderstandings that may arise.

In summary, communication is a two-way street; hence, both the coach and the athlete have a responsibility to make it work. In the sport psychology literature, there are several practical cognitive–behavioral interpersonal techniques that can be used to facilitate improved coach–athlete relations (e.g., Janssen & Dale, 2002; Jowett & Poczwardowski, 2007; Orlick, 2008; Martens, 2004; Vealey, 2005). Following is a summary of tips for improving coach–athlete communications. If these suggestions don't work, it might be appropriate for a sport psychologist to intervene.

- To communicate successfully, you must understand that each person with whom you communicate has had different experiences and perhaps even different cultural upbringing from you. Hence, recognize individual differences in the way people respond. Do not assume that you (the communicator) and the other person(s) (the receiver) will interpret the information in the same manner.

- Use a style of communication that is comfortable for you. Whether you are laid back, animated, relaxed, vocal, or somewhere in between, communicate in a manner that is consistent with your personality and coaching philosophy.

- Characteristics of effective communication include being open, honest, direct, sincere, and consistent. Sarcasm, ridicule, and degrading or demeaning comments are poor communication techniques and should be discouraged.

- Convey rationales as to why athletes should or should not do certain behaviors.

- Never underestimate the power of positive social influence techniques. Focus on being positive and consistent. Be generous with praise, encouragement, and positive reinforcement. Catch people doing things correctly. The skillful use of positive reinforcement can increase motivation and strengthen a person's confidence and self-esteem (see Chapters 2 and 3).

- Reduce uncertainty; clarify expectations and be supportive. As a coach, you play a vital role in helping athletes feel worthy and important. Strive to create a supportive atmosphere in which athletes feel their efforts and contributions to the team are valued and appreciated.

- Work to improve nonverbal communication skills. Remember the axiom: "Your actions speak louder than words."

- Work on developing empathy skills. Put yourself in the other's shoes. Listen attentively to feelings and concerns. Collaborate to find appropriate solutions.

- Evaluate and monitor group process. Set aside time with the team to discuss openly how things are going (e.g., what is working, what is not, what you need more or less of from coaches, teammates, trainers, sport psychologist, support staff). This is an excellent way to open communication channels and show athletes you care about their feelings and opinions.

- Recognize the impact stress and losing can have on emotions, both from a coach and athlete perspective. When stress builds and coaches and athletes lose control of their emotions, frustration may distort or override the content of what gets heard.

- If you have an open-door policy, show athletes (and your assistants) that you are sincere about using it!

Athlete–athlete communications. As for intra-team athlete communication, it is important that teammates establish and maintain harmonious working relationships with each other. Ideally, they should have each other's back and show genuine support for each other both on and off the athletic field. In reflection, some of the most cohesive teams I have ever been associated with had a special relationship off the field (i.e., a "bonding together feeling") that propelled them to be successful as a team during competitions.

Athletes can be a great source of social support for one another; they often spend a lot of time together and share common experiences that are unique to their own peer subculture. In order for teams to get to know one another better, I often employ team-building activities at the beginning of the year that promote personal disclosure through mutual sharing. As an example, I might have a team go around a circle discussing individual and team assets and strengths, or have them do a time line exercise depicting life events that significantly influenced them as a person or team. For instance, in basketball, I had each member of the team reflect on 3-5 critical events that have shaped their life as a person or basketball player. On a horizontal axis depicting their life span (one to current age), positive influential experiences are marked above the line (e.g., instrumental coach at age 14), negative experiences below the line (e.g., overcoming adversity). In front of the team, each player discloses why the events listed were unique and instrumental to her or him. This interpersonal team building exercise is a great activity for learning unique things about each other and developing team camaraderie. Likewise, drawing on my business consulting experiences, I have found the Johari Window (Luft, 1970) to be a useful heuristic communication exercise and feedback tool in helping athletes discover their own interpersonal strengths and weaknesses, and how they come across to others. Athletes are asked to choose five adjectives from a list of 56 that best describe their own personality. Teammates are asked to rate each athlete on the same list of adjectives with responses mapped onto a 4-window grid; open area known to self and others, hidden area not known to others but known to self, blind spot known to others but not known to self, and unknown quadrant not known to self or others. Through self-disclosure and feedback, the idea is to make the open area known to self and others as large as possible, which in turn builds greater interpersonal trust among participants. The benefits of using personal disclosure/mutual sharing team-building activities have been well documented in the literature (e.g., Dunn & Holt, 2004; Gould et al.,1999; Holt & Dunn, 2006; Pain & Harwood, 2009; Yukelson, Sullivan, Morett, & Dorenkott, 2003; Yukelson, 1997). In summary, I believe these team-building activities are excellent at promoting inclusion and team cohesion, lending depth to better understanding teammates, interpersonal relationships, group processes, and team culture.

Along these lines, athletic teams are very much like families. Some degree of tension, frustration, and conflict is inevitable. At the intercollegiate level, several teams I have worked with have had their fair share of interpersonal communication problems and conflict. Problems have ranged from roommate problems (e.g., incompatibility, intolerance, general needs not being met), to interpersonal jealousies within the team, to coach–athlete inequities, to freshmen adjustment and other transition issues. Typically, the underlying issues revolve around misunderstanding, insensitivity, distrust, betrayal, and athletes feeling, in general, like they are not being heard or listened to.

Likewise, in a multicultural athletic environment some degree of conflict or misunderstanding often occurs. When teammates come from different racial, ethnic, religious, or socioeconomic backgrounds, dissimilarities due to deeply rooted cultural systems can lead to intercultural misunderstandings (Schinke & Hanrahan, 2009). Because values, beliefs, relational roles, and attitudes in one culture are often different from those held in another, athletes need to learn to be tolerant, accepting, respecting, and understanding (Parham, 1996). See Chapter 18 to learn more about becoming culturally competent.

Learning how to communicate effectively is an important first step in developing satisfying interpersonal team relationships. Recognizing that it is difficult to be responsive to someone else's thoughts, feelings, and needs when you don't know what they are, here are some suggestions derived from Orlick (1986, 2008) and from my personal experiences to help improve interpersonal communication processes within a team:

- Make sure everyone is pulling in the same direction (team comes first). Recognize that the more open you can be with each other, the better your chances are of getting along and achieving your goals.

- Discuss strategies for improving team harmony, including ways to support and help each other both on and off the athletic field.

- Listen to others; they will listen to you! Put yourself in the shoes of others; try to understand the other person's perspective.

- Learn how to give and receive feedback or criticism constructively. Listen to the *intent* of what is being said; avoid taking things personally.

- Learn how to tolerate each other better. Accept team members for who they are, including their flaws, personality quirks,

idiosyncrasies, and funny little habits that make them unique.

- Avoid backstabbing and gossiping about teammates. Interpersonal cliques and petty jealousies will destroy team morale quickly.

- Keep confrontations private, deal with the person directly.

- Recognize not all conflicts can be resolved, but most can be managed better if both parties communicate.

Active Listening and Empathy

Whether you are a sport psychologist, coach, athlete, or friend, listening is an essential interpersonal skill to develop. Many of us have heard the axiom "listen to others, they will listen to you." It seems so simple, almost intuitive, but it has been my experience counseling coaches and athletes the last 30 years that most communication problems in interpersonal relationships stem from lack of listening.

Rosenfeld and Wilder (1990) have identified three levels of listening, each representing a different degree of listening effectiveness. **Active listening** is the preferred mode of listening in which the listener is attuned, connected, and engaged, demonstrating a caring attitude and desire to truly understand what the other person has to say (Pietsch, 1974). The second level of listening, **superficial** or **inattentive listening,** occurs when listeners tune out quickly once they think they have enough information to decipher what the speaker's intent is. Although listeners at this level may grasp the basic meaning of the message, they often fail to comprehend the emotional feeling or underlying concepts of what is being communicated. Level three listening could be characterized as **arrogant listening.** Here, listeners seem to be more interested in what they have to say as opposed to what the other person is saying. These individuals often wait for pauses in the conversation so they can jump in and hear themselves speak.

By far the most useful tool for improving communication is active listening (Martens, 1987). When people talk about themselves, they do so in terms of experiences (things that happen to them), behaviors (what they do or fail to do), and emotional affect (the feelings that accompany these experiences and behaviors). Elements of good listening skills include attending physically and psychologically to the person you are communicating with (e.g., adopt a posture that indicates active involvement), listening to become more aware of what it is the person is really trying to say (both verbally and nonverbally), paraphrasing or clarifying to ensure your understanding is correct, and some form of summarizing statement to pull everything together in a respectful empathetic way (Egan, 1994). Along these lines, the acronym SOLER outlined by Egan (1994) has proven to be a very useful nonverbal technique facilitating the attending process: *Square* and face the client (adopt a posture that indicates involvement); espouse an *Open* posture to communicate openness and availability to the client; *Lean* toward your client (this connotes you are interested in what the client has to say); maintain good *Eye* contact (this deepens your level of engagement); *Relax* body position (being natural puts people at ease).

Reflective listening is one of the most powerful methods of demonstrating to the person you are working with that you are actively listening and striving to understand. It has been said that reflective listening is to verbal communication as video feedback is to physical skill instruction (Henschen & Miner, 1989). The skills of questioning, clarifying, encouraging, paraphrasing, reflecting, empathetic understanding, and summarizing make up the basic listening sequence. The following reflective listening techniques (Egan, 1994) may facilitate better communication between athlete and sport psychologist (or coach):

- *Questioning.* Use open-ended questions and statements that encourage the athlete to continue speaking. ("How are you feeling about the injury?" "Tell me more about what happened.") As a general rule, avoid initial "why" questions. This may put the person you are talking with on the defensive. Wait until he or she has reached an appropriate comfort level.

- *Clarifying.* Make clear to the other person what has been heard. Clarifying does not mean "I agree with your opinion," but rather, it lets the speaker know someone cares enough to truly listen. Some good lead-ins include "What I hear you saying is . . ."; "I am not sure I quite understand, but it sounds as though you are angry with the coach because she benched you. Is that it?"

- *Encouraging.* Use a variety of verbal and nonverbal statements or mannerisms to prompt athletes to keep talking. These include head nods, gestures, a phrase such as "uh-huh," or the simple repetition of key words the athlete has uttered.

- *Paraphrasing.* Checks whether the responder understands the message. Similar to reflective listening, paraphrasing involves using one's own words, in concise comments, to feed back to the athlete the essence of what has just been said.

- *Reflecting.* Let the person know you hear the content and feelings of what is being said. ("You're sad because . . ."; "You feel confident of your ability to play at this level but worry about getting in.")

- *Empathetic Understanding.* Use empathic statements to keep the person you are dealing with focused on the task at hand. ("It must be hard for you to sit and watch teammates practice while you are recovering from arthroscopic knee surgery. Stay committed to your rehab, you will be back at practice soon enough stronger than ever.")

- *Summarizing.* Pull together all the main ideas and feelings of what has been said. ("It sounds as if you have mixed feelings about the situation. On one hand, you have more time for yourself, but you're also concerned about getting your starting job back.")

The skills of attending and listening are not always sufficient in and of themselves to provide quality relationships with people. Of primary interest is the concept of **empathy.** Empathy is a special kind of mindfulness and understanding. In essence, it means putting yourself in the shoes of the other person, trying to understand and feel what the other person is experiencing from his or her own perspective. Empathy is not the same thing as sympathy. Rather, it is an acquired skill that reflects an overall attitude of genuine concern, caring, and interest (Egan, 1994). Empathetic listeners reflect what they hear by restating ideas heard in their own words and by asking good probing questions (Rosenfeld & Wilder, 1990). Through active and reflective listening, a coach will be in a better position to accurately infer the psychological state of an athlete, and thus be more responsive to athletes' changing needs, something researchers refer to as empathetic accuracy (Lorimer, 2013; Lorimer & Jowett, 2009). The following example gives two responses, one low and one high in empathy:

Athlete describes presenting problem: I really get mad when my coach criticizes me without letting me explain anything. I get angry not because he criticizes me, but because he does it in such a degrading way.

Sport psychologist (low empathy): "You don't like being criticized."

Sport psychologist (high empathy): "You get really mad when he criticizes you and his insulting manner makes you feel personally attacked."

It is important to remember not all problems can be resolved and not all people want help. Listen to what the athlete is asking for, and respond accordingly. Perhaps the following guidelines will help you be a more effective listener:

- *Focus* on the person who is talking. Be attentive, nonjudgmental, and supportive.
- Be attuned to *body language* and listen for both *content* and *feelings*.
- Show *empathetic understanding* by paraphrasing and summarizing main points.
- Set *goals* and develop concrete *action plans* based on what it is the individual is striving to achieve. Introduce role-playing scenarios

and coping rehearsal techniques to help the individual feel prepared and confident to take immediate action.

Assertiveness Training: The Need for Expression

At times athletes need to stand up for their rights and be able to express themselves in a forthright yet respectful manner. **Assertiveness** refers to the honest and straightforward expression of a person's thoughts and feelings in a socially appropriate way that does not violate or infringe on the rights of others (Connelly & Rotella, 1991; Lazarus, 1973).

Assertiveness is a learned social skill that takes time and practice to be perfected. Learning to assert oneself in a respectful and considerate manner comes easy for some yet is difficult for others. Reasons people have difficulty include lack of confidence (i.e., it takes courage to be assertive), vulnerability (i.e., risk of making oneself known has potential negative consequences), interpersonal concerns (e.g., being hesitant to speak up for fear of hurting someone's feelings), and lack of awareness (i.e., failure to learn how to be assertive) (Connelly, 1988; Connelly & Rotella, 1991; Egan, 1994; Holt, Camilla, & Zukiwski, 2012). As an example, some first-year players may be afraid to speak up in team meetings for fear of looking bad in the eyes of others, or be intimidated or hesitant to ask for help. Sociocultural upbringing and other socialization factors may also affect one's decision to be assertive (Schinke, Yukelson, Bartolacci, Battochio, & Johnstone, 2011). For example, it may be awkward or perceived as disrespectful for a newcomer of Asian or Latin American descent to feel comfortable speaking up, particularly to an authority figure.

The following *DESC* formula proposed by Greenberg (1990) is a good example of how people can express themselves more assertively:

1. *Describe* the situation as you see it, paint a verbal picture of the other person's behavior or the situation to which you are reacting: "What I see happening is this . . ."; "When my play is criticized, I feel. . . ."

2. *Express* your feelings regarding the other person's behavior or the situation you have just described: "When you do this, it makes me feel like . . ."; "I get angry and frustrated when you talk behind my back."

3. *Specify* what changes you would like to see take place: "I would prefer you give me feedback in a more constructive, less degrading manner"; "I would appreciate it if you did not talk behind my back."

4. *Consequences* to expect: "If you don't get off my case, I will ask coach to meet with us to straighten this situation out."

In terms of resolving team conflicts, Vealey (2005) offers an innovative communication strategy called the "Four Olves": invOLVE, resOLVE, absOLVE, and evOLVE. Making the group the target of change, begin by having the team talk about what constitutes an effective team culture and the commitment required from each member to make it work; as problems or conflict arise during the season, have them collaborate and come up with collective solutions for problems discussed and hold each other accountable and responsible for their actions. Once the issue is resolved, move on free of any lingering repercussions (e.g., do not make them feel they are in the doghouse once things are resolved), and finally, always find positive lessons, use each episode as an opportunity to learn and grow into a smarter, more experienced cohesive unit. Vealey goes on to note most people do not enjoy confrontations, but by communicating honestly and directly in a respectful manner, good things will occur.

The Sport Psychologist as a Skilled Helper

Throughout the chapter I have talked about the importance of coaches and athletes developing good listening and communication skills. Likewise, sport psychologists must develop good interpersonal communication skills to work effectively with coaches, athletes, and teams. For sport psychologists to do a good job, they must be able to develop rapport, listen attentively, speak the appropriate sport language, and earn the trust of both the coach and athlete and other support personnel.

In my own day-to-day interactions I find myself working with a variety of people within the intercollegiate athletics hierarchy: student-athletes, coaches, parents, athletic administrators, academic counselors and support personnel, sports medicine doctors and athletics trainers, strength trainers, and alumni. These people have a wealth of information and experience to draw upon. They all have their own personality and comfort level from which they work and communicate. There are certain protocols to follow, appropriate chains of command to work through, and written and unwritten rules and policies that can't be violated. But it is impossible to implement a thorough and effective applied sport psychology program if one is unable to gain the trust and support of key personnel at all levels of the athletics organization. This can be accomplished by establishing open lines of communication, listening, gathering facts, being visible and accessible, and observing as much as possible about the dynamics surrounding the team. Gaining entry and building trust is an interpersonal process that takes time and patience.

The same communication principles presented for coaches and athletes apply to sport psychologists. With regard to individual consultations, the sport psychologist must be a skilled interviewer, adept at listening, good at probing, able to fit in with the team culture, and skilled at individualizing interventions based on the people's needs and concerns (Yukelson, 1997; 2012). Drawing from counseling theory, (Danish, D'Augelli, & Ginsberg, 1984; Egan, 1994; Lorimer & Jowett, 2009), general communication skills sport psychologists need to be effective include:

- genuineness (responding with honesty, sincerity, authenticity, and integrity),
- openness (accepting others nonjudgmentally as they are, even if you don't agree with them),

- warmth (helping people feel at ease when expressing intimate thoughts and feelings),
- empathetic (accepting, genuine concern and understanding, active listening skills),
- creative and skillful (good at generating alternative ways of looking at problems), and
- trustworthiness (consistent, respectful, able to maintain confidences).

Summary

Communication is a multifaceted process that involves the transmission or exchange of thoughts, ideas, feelings, or information through verbal and nonverbal channels. Effective communication involves mutual sharing and mutual understanding. Its foundation is based on trust and mutual respect. Open lines of communication can help alleviate many problems that arise within sport environments. An important aspect of communication that has been highlighted is the need to be honest, sincere, direct, and consistent. Because messages transmitted are not always received and interpreted the same way, coaches, athletes, and sport psychologists must strive to be consistent in their verbal and nonverbal communications. Often when incongruent messages are transmitted, the receiver can become confused as to the true meaning of the message, thus leaving the door open for miscommunication and misunderstanding.

   Although much of this chapter has focused on coach–athlete communications, many principles discussed carry over to the applied sport psychologist working in an athletics environment. The communication skills we teach coaches and athletes are the same skills we use as effective consultants. Gaining entry, building rapport, developing trust, and individualizing a mental skills training program based on the needs and desires of coaches and athletes all require good listening and communication skills.

Study Questions

1. Why is communication an important tool for a coach and sport psychologist to possess?

2. What factors interfere with effective communication processes in sport?

3. Give some behavioral examples of verbal and nonverbal communication in sport.

4. As a sport psychologist, what are some things you would do to improve coach–athlete communications?

5. As a coach or sport psychologist, what would you do to intervene if interpersonal conflict arose among team members that resulted in disruption of group cohesion and team harmony?

6. The volleyball team at Nike University has a tendency to clam up when the going gets tough (i.e., communication breaks down; the team loses its intensity, enthusiasm, and focus in critical situations and fails to make appropriate adjustments to things that are going on during competition). How would you intervene as either a sport psychologist or coach to deal with this situation?

7. Why are active listening and empathy such important skills for a sport psychologist to develop in working with coaches and athletes?

8. What are some things you could do to become a better listener?

References

Beebe, S. A., Beebe, S. J., & Redmond, M. V. (1996). *Interpersonal communication: Relating to others*. Boston: Allyn and Bacon.

Carron, A. V., & Hausenblas, H. A. (1998). *Group dynamics in sport* (2nd ed.). Morgantown, WV: Fitness Information Technology.

Clampitt, P. G. (2005). *Communicating for managerial effectiveness* (3rd ed.). Thousand Oaks, CA: Sage Publications.

Collins, J. (2001). Level 5 leadership: The triumph of humility and fierce resolve. *Harvard Business Review*, January 2001, 65–76.

Connelly, D., & Rotella, R. J. (1991). The social psychology of assertive communication: Issues in teaching assertiveness skills to athletes. *The Sport Psychologist, 5*, 73–87.

Crocker, P. (1990). Facial and verbal congruency: Effects on perceived verbal and emotional feedback. *Canadian Journal of Sport Science, 15*, 17–22.

Dale, J., & Weinberg, R. (1990). Burnout in sport: A review and critique. *Journal of Applied Sport Psychology, 2*, 67–83.

Danish, S., D'Augelli, A. R., & Ginsberg, M. (1984). Life development intervention: Promotion of mental health through the development of competence. In S. Brown & R. Lent (Eds.), *Handbook of counseling psychology* (pp. 520–544). New York: John Wiley.

DePree, M. (1989). *Leadership is an art*. New York: Doubleday.

Dunn, J. G. H., & Holt, N. L. (2004). A qualitative investigation of a personal-disclosure mutual-sharing team building activity. *The Sport Psychologist, 18*, 363–380.

Egan, G. (1994). *The skilled helper: A problem management approach to helping* (5th ed.). Pacific Grove, CA: Brooks/Cole.

Goleman, D., Boyatzis, R., & McKee, A. (2002). Primal leadership: Realizing the power of emotional intelligence. Boston, MA: Harvard Business School Press.

Gould, D., Greenleaf, C. A., Guinan, D., Medbery, R., Strickland, M., Lauer, L., & Chung, Y. (1999). Effective and ineffective coaching lessons learned from Atlanta. *Olympic Coach, 9*(1), 2–6.

Greenberg, J. S. (1990). *Coping with stress: A practical guide*. Dubuque, IA: William C. Brown.

Hardy, C. J., & Crace, R. K. (1997). Foundations of team building: Introduction to the team building primer. *Journal of Applied Sport Psychology, 30*, 411–431.

Harris, D. V., & Harris, B. L. (1984). *Sports psychology: Mental skills for physical people*. Champaign, IL: Leisure Press.

Henschen, K., & Miner, J. (1989). *Team principles for coaches*. Ogden, UT: Educational Sport Services.

Holt, N. L., & Dunn, J. G. (2006). Guidelines for delivering personal-disclosure mutual-sharing team building interventions. *The Sport Psychologist, 20*, 348–367.

Holt, N. L, Knight, C. J., & Zukiwski, P. (2012). Female athletes' perceptions of teammate conflict in sport: Implications for sport psychology consultants. *The Sport Psychologist, 26,* 135–154.

Horn, T. S. (1985). Coaches' feedback and changes in children's perceptions of their physical competence. *Journal of Educational Psychology, 77,* 174–186.

Horn, T. S. (2008). Coaching effectiveness in the sport domain. In T. S. Horn (Ed.), *Advances in Sport Psychology,* 3rd ed., (pp. 239–267). Champaign, IL: Human Kinetics.

Janssen, J., & Dale, G. (2002). *The seven secrets of successful coaches: How to unlock and unleash your team's full potential.* Cary, NC: Winning the Mental Game.

Jowett, S., & Chaundry, V. (2004). An investigation into the impact of coach leadership and coach–athlete relationship on group cohesion. *Group Dynamics: Theory, Research, and Practice, 8,* 302–311.

Jowett, S., & Poczwardowski, A. (2007). Understanding the coach–athlete relationship. In S. Jowett, & D. Lavallee (Eds.), *Social psychology in sport* (pp. 3–14). Champaign, IL: Human Kinetics.

Kouzes, J. J., & Posner, B. Z. (1995). *The leadership challenge: How to keep getting extraordinary things done in organizations* (2nd ed.). San Francisco: Jossey-Bass.

Lazarus, A. A. (1973). On assertive behavior: A brief note. *Behavior Therapy, 4,* 697–699.

Locke, E. A., & Latham, G. P. (1990). *A theory of goal setting and task performance.* Englewood Cliffs, NJ: Prentice Hall.

Lorimer, R. (2013). The development of empathetic accuracy in sport coaches. *Journal of Sport Psychology in Action, 4,* 26–33.

Lorimer, R., & Jowett, S. (2009). Empathetic accuracy, meta-perspective, and satisfaction in the coach–athlete relationship. *Journal of Applied Sport Psychology, 21,* 201–212.

Luft, J. (1970). *Group processes: An Introduction to group dynamics* (2nd ed.). Palo Alto, CA: National Press Books.

Lynch, J. (2001). *Creative coaching.* Champaign, IL: Human Kinetics Publishers.

Martens, R. (1987). *Coaches guide to sport psychology.* Champaign, IL: Human Kinetics.

Martens, R. (2004). *Successful coaching* (3rd ed.). Champaign, IL: Human Kinetics.

Martens, R., Christina, R. W., Harvey, J. S., & Sharkey, B. J. (1981). *Coaching young athletes.* Champaign, IL: Human Kinetics.

Martin, G., & Hrycaiko, D. (1983). Effective behavioral coaching: What's it all about? *Journal of Sport Psychology, 5,* 8–20.

Orlick, T. (1986). *Psyching for sport.* Champaign, IL: Human Kinetics.

Orlick, T. (2008). *In pursuit of excellence* (4th ed.). Champaign, IL: Human Kinetics.

Pain, M., & Harwood, C. (2009). Team building through mutual sharing and open discussion of team functioning. *The Sport Psychologist, 27,* 523–542.

Pietsch, W. V. (1974). *Human being: How to have a creative relationship instead of a power struggle.* New York: New American Library.

Riley, P. (1993). *The winner within.* New York: Putnam.

Rosenfeld, L., & Wilder, L. (1990). Communication fundamentals: Active listening. *Sport Psychology Training Bulletin, 1*(5), 1–8.

Schinke, R. & Hanrahan, S. (Eds.) (2009). *Cultural sport psychology: From theory to practice.* Champaign, IL: Human Kinetics.

Schinke, R., Yukelson, D., Bartolacci, G., Battochio, R., & Johnstone, K. (2011). The challenges encountered by immigrated elite athletes. *Journal of Sport Psychology in Action, 2,* 1–11.

Shaw, M. E. (1981). *Group dynamics: The psychology of small group behavior* (3rd ed.). New York: McGraw-Hill.

Smith, R. E. (1986). Toward a cognitive-affective model of athletic burnout. *The Journal of Sport Psychology, 8,* 36–50.

Smith, N. J., Smith, R. E., & Smoll, F. L. (1983). *Kidsports: A survival guide for parents.* Reading, MA: Addison-Wesley.

Stuhr, J. (1997). *Genealogical pragmatism: Philosophy, experience, and community.* Albany: State University of New York.

Sullivan, P. A. (1993). Communication skills training for interactive sports. *The Sport Psychologist, 7,* 79–91.

Vealey, R. S. (2005). *Coaching for the inner edge.* Morgantown, WV: Fitness Information Technology.

Walsh, B. (1998). *Finding the winning edge.* Champaign, IL: Sports Publishing Inc.

Weinberg, R., & Gould, D. (2011). *Foundations of Sport and Exercise Psychology* (5th edition), Champaign, IL: Human Kinetics.

Wooten, M. (1992). *Coaching basketball effectively.* Champaign, IL: Human Kinetics.

Yukelson, D. (1984). Group motivation in sport teams. In J. Silva & R. Weinberg (Eds.), *Psychological foundations in sport* (pp. 229–240). Champaign, IL: Human Kinetics.

Yukelson, D. (1997). Principles of effective team building interventions in sport: A direct service approach at Penn State University. *Journal of Applied Sport Psychology, 9,* 73–96.

Yukelson, D. (2012). Expert approaches to sport psychology. In M. Aoyagi & A. Poczwardowski (Eds.), *Expert approaches to sport psychology: Applied theories of performance excellence* (pp. 255–272). Morgantown, WV: Fitness Information Technology.

Yukelson, D., & Rose, R (2014). *The psychology of ongoing excellence: An NCAA coach's perspective on winning consecutive multiple national championships. Journal of Sport Psychology in Action,* (5), in press.

Yukelson, D., Sullivan, B. A., Morett, C., & Dorenkott, B. (2003). *Coaches' perspectives on applying sport psychology into their coaching.* Invited symposium presented at the annual meeting of the Association for the Advancement of Applied Sport Psychology, Philadelphia, PA.

Zaccaro, S. J., Blair, V., Peterson, C., & Zazanis, M. (1995). Collective efficacy. In J. Maddox (Ed.), *Self-efficacy, adaptation, and adjustment* (pp. 305–328). New York: Plenum Press.

Mental Training for Performance Enhancement

Psychological Characteristics of Peak Performance

Vikki Krane, *Bowling Green State University*
Jean M. Williams, *University of Arizona*

Trying to articulate the zone is not easy because it's such an indescribable feeling. That moment doesn't happen often, and when it does happen, you feel like you're playing out of your head! You aren't feeling any tension or any pressure and physically your strokes are just flowing, every ball you hit is going in. Emotionally you're really calm. There's no strain involved. It's a euphoric feeling. The feeling that whatever you touch turns to gold. Whatever you do, whatever decision you make on the court, whatever stroke or shot you try, you know it's going to work.

—Chris Evert, Tennis Champion

Peak performances are those magic moments when an athlete puts it all together—both physically and mentally. The performance is exceptional, seemingly transcending ordinary levels of play. Privette defined **peak performance** as "an episode of superior functioning" (1983, p. 1361). Competitively, these performances often result in a personal best. They are the ultimate high, the thrilling moment that athletes and coaches work for in their pursuit of excellence. Unfortunately, they also are relatively rare and, according to many athletes, nonvoluntary. But are they truly nonvoluntary? Can athletes be trained so that peak performances occur more frequently? If not to produce a peak performance, can athletes be trained so they consistently play closer to their optimal level? To answer these questions, it is first necessary to know if there are any

common characteristics that identify peak performances. If so, is this ideal state similar from one athlete to another or one sport to another? More important, if common qualities are identified, can they be learned and developed?

It is safe to assume that peak performance is a consequence of both physical and mental factors. Mind and body cannot be separated. A precondition to peak performance is a certain level of physical conditioning and mastery of the necessary physical skills. Obviously, the higher the level of physical skill and conditioning, the more potential control the athlete has over his or her performance. Yet one must realize that peak performance is relative to each athlete's present level of ability. Peak performances are most likely to occur when athletes' skills match the demand or challenge of the situation (Csikszentmihalyi,

1990). Absolute skill level is not important; rather, it is important that the athlete has the skills to match the expected level of play. Thus, concern for enhancing peak performance is as relevant to coaches and sport psychologists who work with less skilled and youth sport athletes as it is to coaches and sport psychologists who work with professional or elite amateur athletes.

Overview of Peak Performance

The focus of this chapter is the mental side of peak performance and how the mind interacts with the body in ultimately producing performance. Most athletes and coaches will acknowledge that at least 40 to 90 percent of success in sports is due to mental factors. The higher the skill level, the more important the mental aspects become. In fact, on the elite competitive level, it is not uncommon to hear that the winner invariably comes down to who is the strongest athlete—mentally—on a given day!

If the mental side of performance is so important to success, then perhaps an ideal internal psychological climate exists during peak performance. Before discussing the research supporting this premise, we must offer a caution. Do not think that the field of sport psychology has found all the answers. There is, however, a growing foundation for understanding the mental side of performance. As we identify an optimal psychological state for peak performance, we also provide a foundation for developing a mental skills training program. In fact, research now exists showing that psychological skills training can improve performance. This chapter and the following chapters in this section reflect the latest state of knowledge and the current thinking and practices of those involved in mental training for peak performance.

Psychological Characteristics During Peak Experiences in Sport

In early research in this area, athletes were interviewed and asked to describe their greatest moment in sport (Ravizza, 1977) and how they felt when they were playing at their best or doing something extraordinarily well (Garfield & Bennett, 1984; Loehr, 1984). These feelings were summed up as "being in the cocoon" (feeling completely detached from the external environment and any potential distractions) (Garfield & Bennett, 1984) and "like playing possessed, yet in complete control" (Loehr, 1984, p. 67). Across these early studies, the athletes gave surprisingly similar accounts. Common psychological characteristics associated with peak performances included

- Loss of fear—no fear of failure
- Total immersion in the activity
- Narrow focus of attention on the present
- Feeling in complete control
- Time/space disorientation (usually slowed down)
- Feeling that performance was automatic and effortless
- Control over emotion, thoughts, and arousal
- Highly self-confident
- Physically and mentally relaxed
- Highly energized

Exercise 1

Think back to a time when you had a best ever performance. Make a list of what you were feeling and thinking, and how your body felt. Then think back to a time when you performed very poorly. Write down what you were feeling and thinking, and how your body felt at that time. Compare the two lists and develop a profile of the characteristics of your ideal mindset for performance.

Privette and Bundrick (1997) further identified what they called the "peak performance dyad," which encompassed full focus on the activity and "self in process." They described it this way: "focusing fully on the relevant task of the game, whether narrowly on the placement of the ball or broadly over the entire field, while simultaneously being acutely aware of self as the doer, underlay peak performance" (p. 331). They concluded that peak performances are personally meaningful, rewarding, and fulfilling. Not surprisingly, athletes frequently associate this state with fun or enjoyment (e.g., Partington, Partington, & Olivier, 2009).

Flow and Peak Performance

Often associated with peak performance is the psychological construct *flow,* defined as "the state in which people are so involved in an activity that nothing else seems to matter" (Csikszentmihalyi, 1990, p. 4). Csikszentmihalyi (1985) considers flow the basis of intrinsically motivated experiences or self-rewarding activity. This was supported by Schuler and Brunner (2008) who found that runners' flow during a marathon was associated with motivation for future training. Flow is not analogous to peak performance. One may be in flow and not necessarily be having a peak performance; however, when an athlete experiences peak performance, she or he appears to be in a flow state.

Jackson (1996) distinguished between flow and peak performance, suggesting that flow may be a precursor to, or the psychological process underlying, peak performance and it has been found to be positively related to performance (e.g., Lindsay, Maynard, & Thomas, 2005). Nine dimensions of flow have been described (Csikszentmihalyi, 1990; Jackson, 2000). When athletes are in flow, they experience the following:

- The challenge of the situation matches the skills of the athlete, and these challenges and skills are at a personal high level.
- Awareness and action merge, the athlete "ceases to be aware of herself as separate from her action" (Jackson, 2000, p. 142).
- Goals are clear.
- Unambiguous feedback indicates that what is being done is correct.

- Total and complete concentration on the task at hand occurs.
- There is a paradox of control, or the sense of being in complete control without actively attempting to be in control (also described as effortless and without fear of failure).
- Loss of self-consciousness whereby one is aware of performing but is not concerned with self-evaluation.
- Time seems to speed up or slow down.
- The experience is autotelic—the activity is enjoyable and participation becomes its own reward.

Interviews with a wide range of athletes (e.g., Jackson 1996; Partington, Partington, & Olivier, 2009; Sugiyama & Inomata, 2005) revealed psychological states that coincided with these characteristics of flow, which are very similar to those reported to accompany peak performances. Researchers also have examined the factors perceived by athletes to disrupt or facilitate flow. In a review of flow studies, Swann, Keegan, Piggott, and Crust (2012) summarized the factors that facilitated the likelihood of achieving flow as: having an appropriate focus, optimal mental and physical preparation, optimal motivation, optimal arousal, positive thoughts, positive emotions, confidence, positive feedback, good team play and interaction, and optimal environmental and situational conditions. The factors that prevented flow were the exact opposite (e.g., having an inappropriate focus, lack of motivation, or negative thoughts).

Studies employing flow questionnaires have found that athletes who experience flow, compared to those who do not, have higher pre-event self-confidence (Catley & Duda, 1997), higher perceived ability, a task goal orientation, and lower anxiety (Jackson, Kimiecik, Ford, & Marsh, 1998). Jackson et al. (1998) concluded that high perceptions of one's athletic abilities appear to be crucial to the experience of flow. As they stated, "athletes who believe in their capabilities are probably more likely to experience a balance between challenge and skills, even when the challenge of a specific sport competition is relatively high" (p. 373).

Exercise 2

Think of a time when you were in flow in sport. Remember what it was like to feel that way. Now also pay attention to the circumstances surrounding that performance: what were your goals and expectations going into the event; how were your coaches and teammates acting; did you notice the fans, the weather, the playing conditions? Compare this experience to a time when you were not able to focus and could not mentally get into the game. How do your experiences compare with those described in this chapter?

When considering the characteristics of flow and the factors that facilitate or disrupt it, it seems that using psychological skills may enhance the likelihood of experiencing flow. Several intervention studies have examined this. A series of studies employing a hypnosis intervention (which consisted of relaxation, imagery, hypnotic induction and regression, and use of a trigger) showed greater intensity of flow experiences and improved performances after learning the skills (Lindsay et al., 2005; Pates & Maynard, 2000; Pates, Oliver, & Maynard, 2001). Similarly, teaching athletes imagery (Nicholls et al., 2005), having them listen to asynchronous music (Pates, Karageorghis, Fryer, & Maynard, 2003), or combing imagery and asynchronous music (Pain, Harwood, & Anderson, 2011) also were related to increased flow experiences and improved performances.

Currently, some researchers are examining the concept of mindfulness as it relates to flow. "Mindfulness is defined as the nonjudgmental focus of one's attention on the experience that occurs in the present moment" (Bernier, Thienot, Codron, & Fournier, 2009, p. 320). Mindfulness approaches encourage acceptance of, and participation with, unwanted thoughts (Bernier et al., 2009). Athletes are taught to "accept their cognitions, emotions, and sensations and to commit themselves to action, rather than fighting against negative thoughts and unpleasant emotions" (Bernier et al., 2009, p. 330). With roots in Eastern meditational practice, mindfulness is a form of present-moment awareness and has been linked to flow and peak performance. More specifically, research has found that mindfulness is associated with task relevant attention, loss of self-consciousness, and a sense of control, which also are characteristics of flow (Gardner & Moore, 2004; Kee & Wang, 2008). Further, Kee and Wang (2008) found high mindfulness in university student athletes was positively related to the likelihood of experiencing flow and use of mental skills. Initial intervention studies support that mindfulness training (which can include meditation and breathing exercises with an emphasis on awareness of body sensations, thoughts, and emotions) is associated with increased flow and improved performance (Bernier et al., 2009; Kaufman, Glass, & Arnkoff, 2009).

These findings suggest that athletes can learn prerequisite skills that may enhance the likeliness of experiencing flow. Athletes who learn to be confident, focus their attention on the task at hand, control their anxiety, and have appropriate and challenging goals may experience flow and peak performance more often.

The Individualized Zone of Optimal Functioning

Another approach to examining psychological states during successful athletic performance focuses on performance-related emotions (Hanin, 2000a). The Individualized Zone of Optimal Functioning (IZOF) model (Hanin, 2000b) attempts to identify emotional patterns associated with individual athletes' successful performances. Optimal performance states, which are unique to individual athletes, can include both positive and negative emotions. This model includes four groups of emotional states: positive performance-enhancing, positive performance-impairing, negative performance-enhancing, and negative performance-impairing. For example, elite Finnish athletes described feeling energetic as a positive performance-enhancing emotion, whereas easygoing was considered a positive emotion that was performance-impairing (Hanin, 2000c). Tense and dissatisfied were described as negative performance-enhancing emotions, whereas feeling tired was considered negative and performance-impairing. To identify individuals' IZOFs, athletes complete an assessment identifying emotions related to their successful and unsuccessful performances. Different athletes may include different emotions in their profiles (e.g., Robazza, Bortoli, & Hanin, 2006). This assessment results in identifying a range of optimal and dysfunctional emotions, and an IZOF iceberg profile emerges. As Figure 9-1 shows,

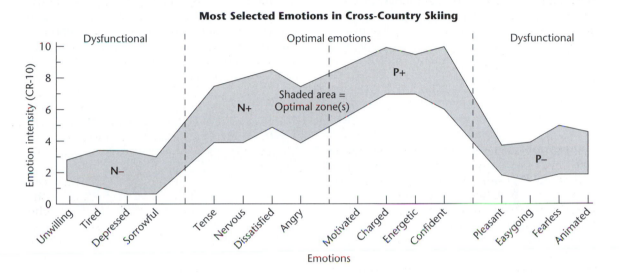

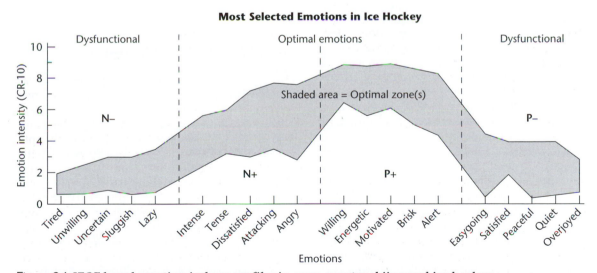

Figure 9-1 IZOF-based-emotion iceberg profiles in cross-country skiing and ice hockey
Source: Reprinted from Hanin, Y. L. (2000c). Successful and poor performance and emotions. In Y. L. Hanin (Ed.), *Emotions in sport* (p. 185). Champaign, IL: Human Kinetics.

both positive and negative emotions considered performance-enhancing comprise the optimal zone, and performance-impairing emotions comprise the dysfunctional zones.

Athletes whose emotional states are within their IZOF are more successful than athletes with emotional profiles out of their IZOFs (Hanin, 2000c). For example, Pellizzari, Bertollo, and Robazza (2011) found that gymnasts' emotions within their optimal zones were associated with good performances whereas poor performances were associated with emotions in dysfunctional zones. Also, more elite athletes had a higher intensity of facilitating positive emotions than less elite athletes (Robazza & Bortoli, 2003). Similarly, upon recall of best and worst performances by elite figure skaters and gymnasts, high intensity of optimal-pleasant emotions was related to best performances whereas high intensity of dysfunctional emotions was associated with poor performance (Robazza et al., 2006).

This research supports the conclusion that performance-enhancing and performance-impairing IZOFs can be identified for individual athletes. Interestingly, these patterns of optimal and dysfunctional emotions differed not only across athletes, but also across contexts. Elite Finnish cross-country skiers identified different IZOFs for races, intensive training, and technical training (Hanin & Syrja, 1997). Teaching athletes to maintain their emotional state within their performance-enhancing zones may increase the likelihood of peak performance or assist athletes to perform more consistently.

Hanin extended the IZOF approach to include the "metaphor self-generation method" in which athletes develop a personally meaningful, symbolic image "that allows for understanding something unknown (or difficult to describe)" (Hanin & Stambulova, 2002, p. 397). Individual metaphor profiles revealed that when considering their best performances, athletes' metaphors were action-oriented and symbolized strength, power, and skill (e.g., "a tiger ready to pounce," "a well-working pipeline"). Not surprisingly, when considering worst performances, athletes generated converse images reflecting weakness and lack of readiness (e.g.,

"an empty bottle," "a cow on the ice," "a sinking boat"). Notably, it was not unusual for athletes to describe negative images and unpleasant feelings pre-event, even when describing best-ever performance. However, these negative feelings and images changed to productive feelings and images during the event. Additionally, Ruiz and Hanin (2004) found these symbolic images remained relatively stable over a five-month period, yet they also evolved and reflected new experiences. Ruiz and Hanin concluded that metaphors can both increase awareness of competitive emotions and be used to change dysfunctional images and beliefs.

Exercise 3

Develop a metaphor that represents your athletic ability. Pick one skill and think about the movements and what they feel like. Then consider what symbolizes those movements. The image needs to make sense only to you. It can be an animal, something in nature, a machine, or anything else that feels right. It should remind you of what it feels like to perform really well.

Psychological Attributes and Skills of Successful and Less Successful Athletes

Although it is interesting to understand the psychological characteristics associated with peak performances, it may be considered even more important to know how athletes achieve these psychological states. Hence, a substantial amount of research has examined the psychological skills that successful athletes use, often by comparing more and less successful athletes with the goal of learning why some individuals outperform others.

Researchers have developed a variety of scales that measure psychological skills used by athletes. The earliest questionnaire, developed by Mahoney and Avener (1977), assessed confidence, concentration, anxiety, self-talk, and imagery. Using this scale, or modifications of it, studies revealed consistent results across samples: The more successful athletes had high self-confidence and few self-doubts, used imagery more often, and controlled their anxiety better than the less successful athletes (e.g., Gould, Weiss, & Weinberg, 1981; Highlen & Bennett, 1983). Subsequently developed questionnaires focused on assessing the use of psychological skills. These scales included the Psychological Skills Inventory for Sport (PSIS; Mahoney, Gabriel, Perkins, 1987), the Test of Performance Strategies (TOPS; Thomas, Murphy, & Hardy, 1999), and the Ottawa Mental Skill Assessment Tool (Durand-Bush, Salmela, & Green-Demers, 2001). Generally, these scales assessed athletes' use of goal setting, relaxation, activation, imagery, self-talk, attentional control, negative thinking, emotional control, and automaticity. While each of these questionnaires measures slightly different aspects of mental preparation and psychological skill use, findings from studies using them are remarkably similar. It seems that regardless of how it is measured, elite and successful athletes consistently report using the following psychological skills, which likely contribute to their high-level performances (e.g., Durand-Bush et al., 2001; Hayslip, Petrie, Macintire, & Jones, 2010; Taylor, Gould, & Rolo, 2008):

- Imagery
- Attentional focusing
- Maintaining concentration
- Controlling anxiety and activation
- Positive self-talk
- Goal setting

Employing a different methodological approach, qualitative researchers examining peak performance have interviewed athletes to obtain a more detailed description of the athletes' perceptions and experiences than can be expressed through questionnaires. The explosion of qualitative research with Olympic and other elite athletes has greatly expanded our understanding of psychological attributes associated with peak performances. These studies have provided comprehensive assessment of Olympic athletes (e.g., Legg, Mackie, & Park, 2005; Gould, Dieffenbach, & Moffett, 2002; Orlick & Partington, 1988), U.S. Olympic teams (e.g., Gould, Guinan, Greenleaf, Medbury, & Peterson, 1999), and professional athletes (McCaffrey & Orlick, 1989). Across these studies, a consistent pattern emerged of what Orlick and Partington (1988) called "mental links to excellence." These athletes described

- Total commitment
- Clearly defined goals
- High confidence
- A positive attitude
- Control of arousal levels and a facilitative interpretation of anxiety
- Daily imagery practice
- Well-developed concentration and focusing skills
- Well-honed practice and competition plans
- Distraction control strategies
- Postcompetition evaluation and continual refinement of their mental approach
- Emphasis on quality rather than quantity of practice
- Use of competition simulation

Adding to the previous findings, Fletcher and Sarkar (2011) interviewed Olympic gold medalists about their resilience. Their findings revealed the champions were conscientious, innovative, open to new experiences, emotionally stable, and optimistic. These findings are consistent with Gould, Dieffenbach, and Moffett's (2002) interviews with Olympic champions. In addition, Gould et al. found that the gold medalists had high levels of dispositional hope (i.e., a sense of control in setting and achieving goals), high productive perfectionism (i.e., personal standards), and low unproductive perfectionism (i.e., concerns about mistakes, parental criticism and expectations, doubts).

The champion athletes in both studies possessed what Gould and colleagues called "sport intelligence," which included analyzing skills and performances, being innovative, making good decisions, being proactive, and taking responsibility for their actions.

In contrast to the preceding mental links to excellence, these qualitative researchers typically found that poor performances or failure to meet one's goals was associated with feeling listless, over- or underarousal, lacking concentration, irrelevant or negative thoughts, and worrying about losing (e.g., Eklund, 1994). Perhaps one of the most salient differences between more and less successful performances is the extent to which athletes adhere to their mental preparation plans and precompetition routines and how well practiced and internalized their coping strategies were. Overall, successful athletes have highly developed techniques for coping with distractions, which act as "automatized buffers" that reduce the impact of negative unforeseen events or allow them to interpret these occurrences positively. Coping strategies often included using positive thinking; a narrow, specific focus of attention; and changing their environment (e.g., avoiding potential irritants, moving away from others) (e.g., Gould, Eklund, & Jackson, 1993; Gould & Maynard, 2010). The less successful athletes departed from their normal routines, abandoned competitive plans when under pressure, lost competitive focus, and did not rigorously adhere to their mental preparation plans.

Edwards and colleagues' (Edwards, Kingston, Hardy, & Gould, 2002) qualitative study also sheds light on the mental links to poor performance. They interviewed eight elite male athletes about a "catastrophic performance." A drop in confidence was the most evident characteristic of these performances, followed by increases in cognitive anxiety, inferring their incapacitating effect on performance. These athletes also recalled feeling a loss of control as performance deteriorated and eventually resignation and withdrawal of effort.

Across all these quantitative and qualitative studies, there appear to be some commonalities

in the psychological characteristics of more successful athletes. For successful athletes, the most consistent finding is that they are highly confident. They also tended to be "psyched up" rather than "psyched out" by demanding competitive situations, such as the Olympics or World Championships. These athletes had numerous other commonalities and they used a wide array of psychological skills. Overall, the psychological characteristics associated with successful elite athletic performance include the following:

- High self-confidence
- Total commitment
- A strong performance focus
- The ability to cope well with stress and distractions
- Good attention-focusing and refocusing skills
- Ability to rebound from mistakes
- An optimistic, positive attitude
- High personal standards
- Well-developed precompetition and competitive plans
- The ability to control emotions and remain appropriately activated
- A view of anxiety as beneficial
- Use of performance goals
- Use of imagery

Another interesting theme that has emerged from studies with elite performers links peak performance with being creative, engaging in self-reflection, developing perspective, and having balance in one's life (Fletcher & Sarkar, 2011; Gould, Dieffenback, & Moffett, 2002). Comparable to Gould, Dieffenback, and Moffett's (2002) notion of sport intelligence, optimal performance appears to be related to training smart. Developing talent, according to Csikszentmihalyi et al. (1993), involves viewing difficult situations as challenging and enjoying the hardships inherent in perfecting skills. Being creative and reflective may allow athletes to view challenges more like a puzzle to complete rather than as a difficult situation. As Csikszentmihalyi et al. (1993) found with talented teenagers, creativity is associated with flow experiences, and flow is an enjoyable state. In all, enjoyment is one of the primary determinants of developing talent (Csikszentmihalyi et al., 1993). Part of enjoying sport excellence and being mentally tough is having balance in one's life. This theme suggests that a broader view of psychological influences on peak performance may be appropriate.

A Profile of Mental Toughness

It seems that throughout this chapter we have been discussing what may be termed *mental toughness*. When discussing what it takes to be successful in sport, athletes often express that to have consistently strong athletic performances, they need to be mentally tough. Although athletes, coaches, and sport psychologists commonly use this term, mental toughness can be described in many different ways. Jones, Hanton, and Connaughton (2002, 2007) developed a description of mental toughness based on interviews with elite athletes (competitors from the Olympic and Commonwealth Games), "super-elite" athletes (Olympic and world champions), and coaches and sport psychologists who worked with super-elite athletes. Based on these studies, Jones et al. (2007) proposed a mental toughness framework that contains two subcomponents: belief and focus. Mental toughness is composed of an unshakable belief that one can achieve her or his goals regardless of obstacles or setbacks. Through focus, mentally tough athletes prioritize their long-term sport goal over all other life goals, yet they also possess the ability to switch off this focus to maintain balance in their lives, which then contributes to their success.

Further, the super-elites expressed the importance of long-term goal setting, controlling the environment, and pushing oneself to the limit in training. During competitions, mentally tough athletes:

- Have an "unshakable belief" (they know they can do anything they set their minds to do).

- Stay focused.

- Regulate performance (increase effort as necessary).

- Cope well with pressure.

- Are aware of, and control, their thoughts and feelings.

- Control the environment (i.e., are not affected by things out of their control).

Postcompetition, these athletes are able to cope with both failure and success. They learn from their failures and use them to motivate themselves toward future success. Balancing competitive demands with other life priorities is another essential aspect of being mentally tough.

More recent studies have focused on how mental toughness is fostered. Connaughton, Hanton, and Jones (2010) re-interviewed the super-elites, focusing on the development and maintenance of mental toughness. As they summarized, mental toughness development programs "should initially concentrate on skill mastery, enjoyment, competitiveness, a disciplined and structured training regimen, and finally, building a belief of superiority" (p. 191). Also important was having international competitive experiences, reflective practice, and strong social support in and out of sport. These findings have been complimented by other research in which coaches provided their perceptions of mental toughness. Experienced swim coaches (Driska, Kamphoff, & Armentrout, 2012) identified two additional components of mental toughness: coachability, and "retaining psychological control on poor training days" (p. 202). Coaches also believed that they could play an important role in helping athletes develop mental toughness through hard physical practice, fostering climates that promoted mental toughness, building confidence, and encouraging mental skill development (Driska et al., 2012; Weinberg, Butt, & Culp, 2011).

Exercise 4

Reflect on a recent performance during an athletic competition. Identify the skills you did well. What can you do to try to improve further upon these skills? Now identify two to three mistakes that you made. What would you do differently or what can you do in practice to avoid making that mistake again? Consider these as lessons learned and make a plan to improve future performances. Name three things you can do to become more mentally tough.

Bull, Shambrook, James, and Brooks (2005) have developed a framework of mental toughness that seems to integrate Hanin's metaphor concept with athletes' perceptions of mental toughness. Their four-level pyramid of mental toughness reflects a developmental approach to elite athlete performance (see Figure 9-2). At the base of the pyramid, the environment provides the foundation for developing mental toughness, which is illustrated with an image of

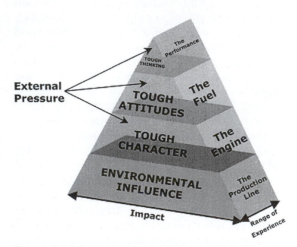

Figure 9-2 The mental toughness pyramid
Source: In Bull, S. J, Shambrook, C. J., James, W., & Brooks, J. E. (2005). Towards an understanding of mental toughness in elite English cricketers. *Journal of Applied Sport Psychology, 17,* 209–227.

a production line. Then athletes' tough character (i.e., fairly stable personality attributes such as independence, resilient confidence, competitiveness) is akin to the engine which is fueled by athletes' tough attitudes (i.e., belief in preparation, "never say die," and "go the extra mile" mindsets), ultimately resulting in tough thinking leading to the performance.

Team, Coach, Family, and Organizational Influences on Peak Performance

To this point, we have emphasized factors within athletes that help or hinder peak performance. Another consideration is the effect that other people may have on high-level athletic performance, such as teammates, coaches, family members, and administrators. For example, Olympic athletes believed that team cohesion was an important contributor to their success (Gould, Greenleaf, Chung, & Guinan, 2002). In particular, having a positive team leader and strong team chemistry were considered helpful while lacking trust and confidence in one's teammates interfered with optimal performance. Athletes on Olympic teams that achieved their team goals also described having positive social support from friends and family (Gould et al., 1999). Conversely, members of less successful teams noted poor team cohesion and a lack of trust among team members. See Chapter 7 for a more complete discussion of cohesion and its role in performance.

Coaches also can be quite influential on athletes. Ideally, coaches help athletes learn the psychological, physical, and tactical skills needed to be successful. However, coaches may unintentionally interfere with success. U.S. Olympic athletes identified that coaches with strong commitment and those who implemented a clear performance plan assisted successful performances (Gould, Greenleaf, Chung, & Guinan, 2002; Gould, Guinan, Greenleaf, & Chung, 2002). Conversely, the following coach attributes hindered team success:

- Inability to deal with crises
- Unrealistic expectations
- Overcoaching and excessive interactions with team members
- Inability to make decisive and fair decisions
- Inability to "keep it simple"

Coaches and athletes who were on teams that did not meet their Olympic expectations also believed that negative attitudes toward the coach and poor coach–athlete communications were at least partially to blame (Gould, Guinan, et al., 2002).

Research also highlights the critical role that parents and family members played in elite athletes' support network (Gould, Dieffenbach, & Moffett, 2002; Gould & Maynard, 2009; Gucciardi, Gordon, Dimmock, & Mallett, 2009). Families provided social and emotional support and encouragement, guided athletes through good and bad experiences, and promoted autonomy. Additionally, family members voiced their belief in the athlete's ability to succeed, and encouraged a "can-do attitude."

Another issue affecting athletes' ability to perform optimally is organizational stress, or concerns that arise because of the management of teams. Interviews with British Olympic and elite (i.e., international competitors) athletes revealed that they experienced concerns related to finances, travel, accommodations, team selection, coaching styles, and team atmosphere (Fletcher & Hanton, 2003; Woodman & Hardy, 2001). Some athletes overtly claimed that when faced with interpersonal or financial difficulties, they had less than ideal performances (Woodman & Hardy, 2001). In their review of Olympic preparation, Gould and Maynard (2009) identified the following social and situational factors that can influence athlete performance: team confidence, team cohesion and harmony, team residency program (i.e., spending dedicated time training together), support of friends and family, good coach–athlete relationships, media training, having experienced support personnel, and having plans for coping with travel concerns

and equipment problems. In all, it seems that team and environmental factors affect the likelihood of peak performance.

Conclusion: What It Takes to "Make It"

There seems to be a fairly strong consensus that to become a successful elite athlete takes commitment, dedication, mental toughness, and the ability to pursue a dream in a rational manner. When asked, coaches, scouts, and athletes state the importance of psychological states and mental skill use. Top coaches and scouts in the National Hockey League used words such as desire, determination, attitude, heart, and self-motivation when asked what determines who does and does not make it at the professional level (Orlick, 2007). Olympic coaches felt that to be successful, athletes needed confidence, social support, and cohesive teams as well as to be able to maintain their composure, be prepared to cope with distractions, and have a sound competitive plan (Gould, Guinan, et al., 1999; Gould, Guinan, et al., 2002).

Similarly, that mental preparation is important for success was a consistent theme across studies of Olympic athletes (see Gould & Maynard, 2009). The Canadian Olympians in Orlick and Partington's (1988) study believed that through psychological skills training they improved their performance level and learned to perform more consistently at their best. Many of the Olympic athletes interviewed by Orlick and Partington stated that they could have obtained their best performances much sooner had they strengthened their mental skills earlier in their athletic careers. As U.S. Olympic athletes who met or exceeded their goals pointed out, mental preparation was essential (Gould et al., 1999), whereas athletes on less successful teams felt that they did not spend enough time on mental preparation. All of these attributes may be developed or enhanced by using psychological skills. Gould, Guinan, et al. (2002) concluded that, according to Olympic coaches, "the role of psychological variables was perceived as especially salient and reinforces the need for psychological skills training" (p. 248).

Coaches of developmental and elite youth programs also consistently express the importance of mental skills training (e.g., Grobbelaar, 2007; Mills, Butt, Maynard, & Harwood, 2012). For example, expert coaches of British elite youth soccer (football) players considered the following skills as particularly essential to the success of their athletes: confidence, optimistic attitude, coping with setbacks, coping with pressure, focus, self-awareness, coachability, and sport intelligence (Mills et al., 2012). These beliefs are consistent with U.S. university team coaches who also acknowledged the importance of athletes' psychological skills (Weinberg et al., 2011).

At this point, a word of caution is needed regarding the interpretation of the research summarized in this chapter. All of the studies presented were either descriptive or correlational. What this means is that they generated descriptions of successful athletic experiences or identified relationships between psychological skills and peak performances. Based on this type of research, we cannot make any conclusions about cause-and-effect relationships—we cannot say certain mental states cause peak performances; we can note only that they are related. When considering the question, "Are the psychological differences between successful and less successful athletes critical to performance differences?" there seems to be a lot of evidence suggesting that psychological characteristics are associated with peak performances. Still, we do not know if athletes first learned the psychological skills necessary to achieve an ideal mental state or if they developed these characteristics by being consistently successful (that is, being successful leads to being confident of continued success) (Heyman, 1982). It also is plausible that athletes with certain psychological strengths are drawn to elite-level sport. We may never know what causes an ideal mental state. However, given the weight of the evidence presented, it seems safe to assume that (a) elite athletes have consistent psychological profiles when they compete at elite levels, (b) they use psychological skills in pursuit of their athletic goals, and (c) these skills can be learned.

Summary

This chapter began with the questions "Is there an ideal body–mind state associated with peak performance?" and "If so, is this ideal state similar from one athlete to another or one sport to another?" Across a wide range of sources, a certain psychological profile appears to be linked with successful athletic performance. Although there are individual variations, in most cases this general profile is depicted by the characteristics listed in Table 9-1. This ideal performance state does not just happen. Top-level athletes have learned to create and maintain this state voluntarily so that their talents and physical skills thrive. Additionally, successful athletes have strong support networks that include their families, friends, teammates, and coaches. Having high team cohesion, good communication and relationships with coaches, and minimal organizational stress are associated with elite performances. Problems with travel and accommodations, concerns about team selection, financial problems, and other administrative issues also may negatively affect athletes.

The commonalities in mental states and psychological skill use have led researchers and practitioners to conclude that the right psychological climate helps mobilize mental and physical reactions that are essential to performing at one's best. Psychological skills are learned through knowledge and practice, just as physical skills and competitive strategies are learned.

Table 9-1 **Mental Links to Peak Performance**

Psychological Profile of Successful Elite Athletes	Mental Skills associated with Peak Performances
• High self-confidence and expectations of success • Self-regulation of arousal (energized yet relaxed) • Feeling in control • Total concentration • Keen focus on the present task • Viewing difficult situations as exciting and challenging • Productive perfectionism (i.e., have high standards, yet flexibility to learn from mistakes) • Positive attitude and thoughts about performance • Strong determination and commitment	• Setting goals • Imagery • Developing competition plans • Practicing coping skills so they become automatic • Employing competitive simulation • Thought control strategies • Arousal management techniques • Attention control • Developing refocusing skills and plans

Some gifted athletes may perfect these mental states on their own, but most need to be taught specific training techniques. The remaining chapters in this section of the book provide techniques for creating and maintaining desirable mental and physiological states. Just as improving physical skills, strategies, and conditioning increases the likelihood of peak performance, learning to control psychological readiness and the ideal mental climate for peak performance also enhances performance.

Study Questions

1. Define peak performance.
2. Summarize the psychological states typically associated with peak performances.
3. Define *flow* and describe its dimensions.
4. What are factors that will enhance and hinder flow experiences?
5. What is the IZOF model and how does it relate to peak performance?
6. Describe several metaphors you associate with successful and less successful performances.
7. What are the primary psychological characteristics that distinguish between more and less successful athletic performances?
8. Summarize the major psychological characteristics of elite athletes.
9. What are the primary psychological skills that elite athletes use? What is the association between these skills and peak performance?
10. Describe mental toughness and its relationship to performance.
11. Describe how athletes' relationships with their teammates may influence optimal performance.

12. What are things that coaches may do that will interfere with peak performance?

13. What is organizational stress and how might it influence athletes' performances?

14. If you were a coach or administrator, how would you minimize the problems faced by Olympic athletes who did not achieve their goals?

References

Bernier, M., Thienot, E., Codron, R., & Fournier, J. (2009). Mindfulness and acceptance approaches in sport performance. *Journal of Clinical Sports Psychology, 4,* 320–333.

Bull, S. J., Shambrook, C. J., James, W., & Brooks, J. E. (2005). Towards an understanding of mental toughness in elite English cricketers. *Journal of Applied Sport Psychology, 17,* 209–227.

Catley, D., & Duda, J. L. (1997). Psychological antecedents of the frequency and intensity of flow in golfers. *International Journal of Sport Psychology, 28,* 309–322.

Connaughton, D., Hanton, S., & Jones, G. (2010). The development and maintenance of mental toughness in the world's best performers. *The Sport Psychologist, 24,* 168–193.

Csikszentmihalyi, M. (1985). Emergent motivation and the evolution of the self. In D. Kleiber & M. Maehr (Eds.), *Advances in motivation and achievement,* Vol. 4 (pp. 93–119). Greenwich, CT: JAI.

Csikszentmihalyi, M. (1990). *Flow: The psychology of optimal experience.* New York: Harper & Row.

Csikszentmihalyi, M., Rathunde, K., & Whalen, S. (1993). *Talented teenagers: The roots of success and failure.* New York: Cambridge University Press.

Driska, A. P., Kamphoff, C., & Armentrout, S. (2012). Elite swimming coaches' perceptions of mental toughness. *The Sport Psychologist, 26,* 186–206.

Durand-Bush, N., Salmela, J. H., & Green-Demers, I. (2001). The Ottawa Mental Skills Assessment Tool (OMSAT-3). *The Sport Psychologist, 15,* 1–19.

Edwards, T., Kingston, K., Hardy, L., & Gould, D. (2002). A qualitative analysis of catastrophic performances and the associated thoughts, feelings, and emotions. *The Sport Psychologist, 16,* 1–19.

Eklund, R. C. (1994). A season-long investigation of competitive cognition in collegiate wrestlers. *Research Quarterly for Exercise and Sport, 65,* 169–183.

Fletcher, D., & Hanton, S. (2003). Sources of organizational stress in elite sports performers. *The Sport Psychologist, 17,* 175–195.

Fletcher, D., & Sarkar, M. (2012). A grounded theory of psychological resilience in Olympic champions. *Psychology of Sport & Exercise, 13,* 669–678.

Gardner, F. L., & Moore, Z. E. (2004). A mindfulness-acceptance-commitment-based approach to athletic performance enhancement: Theoretical considerations. *Behavior Therapy, 35,* 707–723.

Garfield, C. A., & Bennett, H. Z. (1984). *Peak performance: Mental training techniques of the world's greatest athletes.* Los Angeles: Tarcher.

Gould, D., Dieffenbach, K., & Moffett, A. (2002). Psychological characteristics and their development in Olympic champions. *Journal of Applied Sport Psychology, 14,* 172–204.

Gould, D., Eklund, R. C., & Jackson, S. A. (1993). Coping strategies used by U.S. Olympic wrestlers. *Research Quarterly For Exercise and Sport, 64,* 83–93.

Gould, D., Greenleaf, C., Chung, Y., & Guinan, D. (2002). A survey of U.S. Atlanta and Nagano Olympians: Variables perceived to influence performance. *Research Quarterly for Exercise and Sport, 73,* 175–186.

Gould, D., Guinan, D., Greenleaf, C., & Chung, Y. (2002). A survey of U.S. Olympic coaches: Variables perceived to have influenced athlete performances and coach effectiveness. *The Sport Psychologist, 16,* 229–250.

Gould, D., Guinan, D., Greenleaf, C., Medbery, R., & Peterson, K. (1999). Factors affecting Olympic performance: Perceptions of athletes and coaches from more and less successful teams. *The Sport Psychologist, 13,* 371–394.

Gould, D., & Maynard, I. (2009). Psychological preparation for the Olympic Games. *Journal of Sports Sciences, 27,* 1393–1408.

Gould, D., Weiss, M., & Weinberg, R. (1981). Psychological characteristics of successful and nonsuccessful Big Ten wrestlers. *Journal of Sport Psychology, 3,* 69–81.

Grobbelaar, H. W. (2007). A survey of South African provincial netball coaches' opinions, abilities and limitations regarding mental skills training. *South African Journal for Research in Sport, Physical Education & Recreation, 29*(2), 27–39.

Hanin, Y. L. (2000a). *Emotions in sport.* Champaign, IL: Human Kinetics.

Hanin, Y. L. (2000b). Individual zones of optimal functioning (IZOF) model: Emotion–performance relationships in sport. In Y. L. Hanin (Ed.), *Emotions in sport* (pp. 65–89). Champaign, IL: Human Kinetics.

Hanin, Y. L. (2000c). Successful and poor performance and emotions. In Y. L. Hanin (Ed.), *Emotions in sport* (pp. 157–187). Champaign, IL: Human Kinetics.

Hanin, Y. L., & Stambulova, N. B. (2002). Metaphoric description of performance states: An application of the IZOF model. *The Sport Psychologist, 16,* 396–415.

Hanin, Y. L., & Syrja, P. (1997). Optimal emotions in elite cross-country skiers. In E. Muller, H. Schwameder, E. Kornexl, & C. Raschner (Eds.), *Science and skiing* (pp. 408–419). London: SPON.

Hayslip, B., Petrie, T. A., MacIntire, M. M., & Jones, G. M. (2010). The influences of skill level, anxiety, and psychological skills use on amateur golfers' performances. *Journal of Applied Sport Psychology, 22,* 123–133.

Heyman, S. R. (1982). Comparisons of successful and unsuccessful competitors: A reconsideration of methodological questions and data. *Journal of Sport Psychology, 4,* 295–300.

Highlen, P. S., & Bennett, B. B. (1983). Elite divers and wrestlers: A comparison between open-and closed-skill athletes. *Journal of Sport Psychology, 5,* 390–409.

Jackson, S. A. (1996). Toward a conceptual understanding of the flow experience in elite athletes. *Research Quarterly for Exercise and Sport, 67,* 76–90.

Jackson, S. A. (2000). Joy, fun, and flow state in sport. In Y. L. Hanin (Ed.), *Emotions in sport* (pp. 135–156). Champaign, IL: Human Kinetics.

Jackson, S. A., Kimiecik, J. C., Ford, S. K., & Marsh, H. W. (1998). Psychological correlates of flow in sport. *Journal of Sport & Exercise Psychology, 20,* 358–378.

Jones, G., Hanton, S., & Connaughton, D. (2002). What is this thing called mental toughness? An investigation of elite sport performers. *Journal of Applied Sport Psychology, 14,* 205–218.

Jones, G., Hanton, S., & Connaughton, D. (2007). A framework of mental toughness in the world's best performers. *The Sport Psychologist, 2,* 243–264.

Kaufman, K. A., Glass, C. R., & Arnkoff, D. B. (2009). Evaluation of mindful sport performance enhancement (MSPE): A new approach to promote flow in athletes. *Journal of Clinical Sport Psychology,* 334–356.

Kee, Y., & Wang, C. K. (2008). Relationships between mindfulness, flow dispositions and mental skills adoption: A cluster analytic approach. *Psychology of Sport and Exercise, 9,* 393–411.

Legg, S. J., Mackie, H. W., & Park, N. (2005). Characteristics of twelve New Zealand champion Olympic class sailors. *New Zealand Journal of Sports Medicine, 33,* 58–60.

Lindsay, P., Maynard, I., & Thomas, O. (2005). Effects of hypnosis on flow states and cycling performance. *The Sport Psychologist, 19,* 164–177.

Loehr, J. E. (1984, March). How to overcome stress and play at your peak all the time. *Tennis,* 66–76.

Mahoney, M. J., & Avener, M. (1977). Psychology of the elite athlete: An exploratory study. *Cognitive Therapy and Research 1,* 135–142.

Mahoney, M. J., Gabriel, T. J., & Perkins, T. S. (1987). Psychological skills and exceptional athletic performance. *The Sport Psychologist, 1,* 181–199.

McCaffrey, N., & Orlick, T. (1989). Mental factors related to excellence among top professional golfers. *International Journal of Sport Psychology, 20,* 256–278.

Mills, A., Butt, J., Maynard, I., & Harwood, C. (2012). Identifying factors perceived to influence the development of elite youth football academy players. *Journal of Sports Sciences, 30,* 1593–1604.

Nicholls, A., Polman, R., & Holt, N. (2005). The effects of individualized imagery interventions on golf performance and flow states. *Athletic Insight, 7,* 43–64.

Orlick, T. (2007). *In pursuit of excellence* (4th ed.). Champaign, IL: Human Kinetics.

Orlick, T., & Partington, J. (1988). Mental links to excellence. *The Sport Psychologist, 2,* 105–130.

Pain, M., Harwood, C., & Anderson, R. (2011). Pre-competition imagery and music: The impact on flow and performance in competitive soccer. *The Sport Psychologist, 25,* 212–232.

Partington, S., Partington, E., & Olivier, S. (2009). The dark side of flow: A qualitative study of dependence in big wave surfing. *The Sport Psychologist, 23,* 170–185.

Pates, J., Cummings, A., & Maynard, I. (2002). The effects of hypnosis on flow states and three-point shooting performance in basketball layers. *The Sport Psychologist, 16,* 34–47.

Pates, J., Karageorghis, C. I., Fryer, R., & Maynard, I. (2003). Effects of asynchronous music on flow states and shooting performance among netball players. *Psychology of Sport and Exercise, 4*, 415–427.

Pates, J., & Maynard, I. (2000). Effects of hypnosis on flow states and golf performance. *Perceptual and Motor Skills, 91*, 1057–1075.

Pates, J., Oliver, R., & Maynard, I. (2001). The effects of hypnosis on flow states and golf-putting performance. *Journal of Applied Sport Psychology, 13*, 341–354.

Pellizzari, M., Bertollo, M., & Robazza, C. (2011). Pre- and post-performance emotions in gymnastics competitions. *International Journal of Sport Psychology, 42*, 278–302.

Privette, G. (1983). Peak experience, peak performance, and flow: A comparative analysis of positive human experiences. *Journal of Personality and Social Psychology, 45*, 1361–1368.

Privette, G., & Bundrick, C. M. (1997). Psychological processes of peak, average, and failing performance in sport. *International Journal of Sport Psychology, 28*, 323–334.

Ravizza, K. (1977). Peak experiences in sport. *Journal of Humanistic Psychology, 17*, 35–40.

Robazza, C., & Bortoli, L. (2003). Intensity, idiosyncratic content and functional impact of performance-related emotions in athletes. *Journal of Sport Sciences, 21*, 171–189.

Robazza, C., Bortoli, L., & Hanin, Y. (2006). Perceived effects of emotion intensity on athletic performance: A contingency-based individualized approach. *Research Quarterly for Exercise & Sport, 77*, 372–385.

Ruiz, M. C., & Hanin, Y. L. (2004). Metaphoric description and individualized emotion profiling of performance states in top karate athletes. *Journal of Applied Sport Psychology, 16*, 258–273.

Schüler, J., & Brunner, S. (2009). The rewarding effect of flow experience on performance in a marathon race. *Psychology of Sport and Exercise, 10*, 168–174.

Sugiyama, T., & Inomata, K. (2005). Qualitative examination of flow experience among top Japanese athletes. *Perceptual and Motor Skills, 100*, 969–982.

Swann, C., Keegan, R. J., Piggott, D., & Crust, L. (2012). A systematic review of the experience, occurrence, and controllability of flow states in elite sport. *Psychology of Sport & Exercise, 13*, 807–819.

Taylor, M. K., Gould, D., & Rolo, C. (2008). Performance strategies of U.S. Olympians in practice and competition. *High Ability Studies, 19*, 15–32.

Thomas, P. R., Murphy, S. M., & Hardy, L. (1999). Test of performance strategies: Development and preliminary validation of a comprehensive measure of athletes' psychological skills. *Journal of Sports Sciences, 17*, 697–711.

Weinberg, R., Butt, J., & Culp, B. (2011). Coaches' views of mental toughness and how it is built. *International Journal of Sport & Exercise Psychology, 9*(2), 156–172.

Woodman, T., & Hardy, L. (2001). A case study of organizational stress in elite sport. *Journal of Applied Sport Psychology, 13*, 207–238.

CHAPTER

10

Increasing Awareness for Sport Performance

Kenneth Ravizza, *California State University at Fullerton*
Angela Fifer, *United States Military Academy*

The end of the soccer game results in a critical penalty kick. Both teams have played hard and well and now it comes down to one player shooting the shot that will determine the outcome. All too often, the coach's instruction is "Just relax" or "Concentrate," and frequently this results in even more perceived pressure by the athlete, because now the coach knows she is not relaxed or focused.

The underlying basis of psychological interventions for performance enhancement involves teaching athletes the importance of the recognition, or awareness, of the need to do something to gain control. Athletes will not be aware of the need to gain control unless they first identify their own ideal performance state (see Chapter 9) and can contrast that state with the present one. Thus, **awareness** is the first step to gaining control of any pressure situation. The athlete must "check in" and determine if his or her arousal level, emotional state, thought processes, and focus are where they need to be and, if not, adjust them to give the best opportunity for success. For example, the athlete must be aware of an arousal level that is too low or too high and adjust it as needed to reach the optimal arousal

level for performance. Then the athlete must attend to the appropriate focal points that will fine-tune or lock in his or her concentration. For example, a softball player will get only two or three great pitches to hit in a game. The player must be fully focused on each pitch so that when the right pitch comes she is ready to make solid contact.

Lack of awareness in athletes is almost always the result of excessive concern with achieving the end result. For example, the baseball player in the pressure situation focuses on the end result of getting a hit. Awareness and control are part of the process of skill execution—specifically, execution in the present moment. The anxiety lies in the end result. Thus, the field-goal kicker in football must focus on the key components of kicking such as wind, ground conditions, the opponents' alignment, getting proper distance, and his target. At this point the athlete is totally focused on the task at hand and is ready to react spontaneously to the situation with controlled intensity. This type of appropriate focus of attention is essential to maximize performance.

The athlete's challenge is to focus on basic skills even when his or her physiology may increase significantly. The situation can be seen as speeded up or out-of-the-usual perspective because of the perceived threat. This chapter does not suggest a multitude of performance changes; instead, it suggests that athletes be encouraged to become aware of their own ideal performance state and *routine behaviors* they are already using to achieve this state. The athlete performs many of the techniques we talk about in sport psychology instinctively. Awareness of these instinctive routines provides athletes with something to focus on to regain control and empowers them to take responsibility for their physical and mental games. Sport psychology consultants have contributed to enhancing performance by providing a structure or consistent framework for the various mental skills athletes have often developed and practiced haphazardly.

The purpose of this chapter is to discuss the importance of awareness in reaching peak performance in sport. A model of performance resilience, The R's, will be discussed to give athletes a process and vocabulary to assess how their performance is going and to have a plan to adjust if needed. Awareness, an essential step in self-regulation, will be discussed in relation to skill development and the management of performance stress and other psychological factors. The final section will discuss specific methods athletes can use to develop heightened awareness.

The Importance of Awareness in Athletics

Peak performance is about compensating and adjusting. While the flow state is often desired, we find athletes to be in the "zone" only 10–20 percent of the time. So why are athletes so concerned with feeling just right and surprised when they are not? Lou Pinella, a veteran professional baseball manager, claimed, "A player must learn to feel comfortable being uncomfortable." "So what, deal with it!" is what we tell athletes. But this is only after they have practiced dealing with adversity in practice and recognizing that they have "something to go to" (mental skills)

to get them refocused. As athletes work on this ability to deal with adversity in practice, it only increases their confidence to know they do not have to feel great to perform well.

A helpful structure for athletes to develop is a seven-step process called "The R's" (Statler & Tilman, 2010; Tilman, Ravizza, & Statler, 2011). This structure clarifies for athletes the fact that there is a relationship between the various things they do to maximize performance, particularly during times of adversity. When they can begin to understand that they have control over their own reactions, attitudes, and behaviors no matter what the situation presents, they begin to take responsibility for their performance, which is the first step in truly becoming aware. Figure 10-1 is a visual of the R's cycle and will be referred to throughout the chapter.

The R's provide a framework for athletes and coaches to establish control and take responsibility for performance. Using the R's as a framework (see Figure 10-1), athletes can work through any situation by choosing to focus on the right things. At the center of the figure is **Responsibility,** where athletes start by taking accountability for their actions. Responsibility is central to the process because the athlete

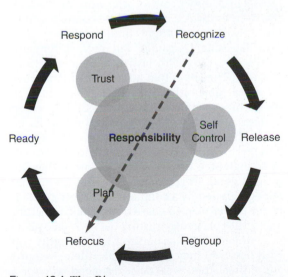

Figure 10-1 The R's

must understand that distractions and mistakes are inevitable, but by being proactive and controlling oneself, performance control can also be achieved. Self-control encompasses the next three R's, where it is up to the athlete to get their body and mind back under control. It begins with **Recognize** the internal and external factors that affect performance, e.g., the stressors and distractions; **Release** anything disrupting optimal performance using a purposeful physical or mental mechanism to "let it go"; and then **Regroup** by adjusting composure and regaining a centered balance.

Once an athlete is in the present moment, he or she can check back in on their plan by **Refocusing** and possibly adjusting the plan to the situation. The refocus should be positive, process-oriented, and couched in the present moment (3 P's), thus giving the athlete task-relevant cues on which to focus. Being **Ready** is a commitment during which the athlete takes a centered breath and focuses on the plan. Athletes may need a physical signal from themselves to know they are all set, for example, stepping into a ready position.

Finally, athletes can trust in their training, the plan, and themselves and just **Respond.** Hopefully athletes are now focused, present, and feeling back under control after working through the steps of the R's. If everything comes together perfectly, athletes might find themselves in a flow-like state (A game), but more often athletes are battling with less than their best (B or C game). The key is that athletes trust what they have that day, rather than trying extra hard to make things perfect. The R's are a tool by which athletes take control of the situation and let go of the things outside of their control. The R's can be a continuous cycle the athlete moves through or a single step he or she checks into if they are feeling good. For example, a distance runner may get passed by a competitor but recognizes it is not in her plan to chase down the competitor and settles back into trusting her own race plan.

Athletes must recognize their strengths and weaknesses so they can maximize their strengths and correct their weaknesses. A good way for a player to develop more awareness in this area is to have players write a scouting report on themselves. What is the opponent saying about them? Also, have them write about what they would like the opponent to say about them. Julie Wilhout, Loyola Marymount's women's basketball coach, uses this technique to help the players increase their awareness of where they need to direct their attention. Another practical way to remind players to have a mission for practice is to have them establish a routine. For example, when you put on your shoes, set two goals for today's practice or game, and when you take your shoes off, evaluate how you did. The reality is that each day we either take a step toward our goal, remain the same, or take a step back. Always remember, failure can be a step forward if you learn from it.

Awareness as It Relates to Skill Development

Athletes must learn the difference between merely performing skills and experiencing skills. For example, try this exercise. Raise your right arm over your head five times—one . . . two . . . three . . . four . . . five—and halt. Now deeply inhale as you slowly raise your right arm over your head. Breathe slowly and steadily as you feel the movement, experience the muscles involved, feel the gentle stretch through the different muscles, feel that extension all through the arm, and now slowly let the arm down.

The difference between just going through the motions and really experiencing the skills hinges on the awareness involved. Feldenkrais (1972), a movement specialist, offers the following analogy:

> A man without awareness is like a carriage whose passengers are the desires, with the muscles for horses, while the carriage itself is the skeleton. Awareness is the sleeping coachman. As long as the coachman remains asleep the carriage will be dragged aimlessly here and there. Each passenger seeks a different destination and the horses pull different ways. But when the coachman is wide awake and holds the reins the horses will pull and bring every passenger to his proper destination (p. 54).

Like the coachman, athletes must gain control of muscles, emotions, and thoughts and integrate them into a smooth performance. When athletes are aware and focused on the sport experience, they exert more control over the situation. They recognize sooner when their balance is off, when too much tension is present in certain muscle groups, or when thoughts have become self-defeating. Aware athletes are more attuned to subtle fluctuations in the flow of the contest and can adjust that much sooner. Aware athletes can conserve vital energy by exerting no more than the needed intensity.

Learning the Basics

Awareness requires that athletes totally focus their attention on the task. This ability must be developed in practice. Coaches want their athletes to be intense and totally involved in practice because this aids in creating quality practice time. Many coaches also realize the importance of mental training for performance, but the challenge is to find time for it. For this reason, it is important to incorporate awareness training with the physical skills that are already being performed in practice. For example, coaches and sport psychology consultants should encourage athletes to develop concentration as they stretch before practice by feeling the stretch and breathing into it.

With the U.S. Olympic women's field hockey team, we established a set warm-up procedure to aid the athletes in mentally and physically preparing for practice. The players began by stretching, then hit the ball back and forth to work out any kinks, and finally executed focused hitting. Focused hitting involves hitting the ball to exact locations—for example, to the receiver's right, middle, and left. This sequence is followed for 5 minutes. These are basic field hockey skills, but there is a difference when they are done with awareness. If the player's attention is on other aspects of the day, such as a party coming up or an argument with a friend, consistency in the focused hitting drill will be impossible. This type of drill has two major advantages for the coach. First, visible objective performance demonstrates whether or not the athlete is concentrating. More important, awareness training is incorporated into the practice of basic skills. This sophisticated approach to basic skills allows coaches to make the most of practice time by integrating mental or awareness skills training with basic fundamentals.

During one practice, the Cal State Fullerton baseball team engaged in a focused bat and catch drill for 90 minutes because they had not been hitting exact locations consistently. This emphasis on basics was crucial because the players realized the coach was serious about executing the basics. The difference between performing the basics and focusing on the basics lies in the players' awareness. Athletes must learn to concentrate when the pressure is on, and the focal points for concentration become the task-relevant cues. Augie Garrido, former Cal State Fullerton baseball coach, gave the following example:

> We are really working on having the players clear their minds. Yesterday one player was given a bunt signal and he proceeded to pop out. His next time at the plate he was in a bunting situation and tried to bunt but missed. So I called him over and said, "You've tried two times and failed, and you are about to fail again because you still have the other two times on your mind. Give yourself the best chance to be successful by seeing the ball and bunting the ball. You can do that. Stay right with the ingredients of bunting. You've done it a hundred times, but you have to get the other times off your mind. The player proceeded to lay down a perfect bunt (1982).

When athletes practice physical skills and mental skills together, their confidence increases because they are ready and experienced in the subtle skill of concentration.

The All-or-None Syndrome

Awareness develops in the process of participating in sport, and this is where athletes experience self-control. Gymnasts learning new skills cannot expect to master them immediately; they must work through a series of progressions. Often, in the midst of this process, gymnasts feel they have *either* hit the move *or* missed. If they hit it, they are delighted, but if they miss, frustration begins to set in. The challenge is to maintain motivation throughout the hours of practice and frustration.

At Cal State Fullerton, we have established gradations of execution for the gymnasts to evaluate their skill development. For example, even if a move is "missed," certain aspects of the movement were probably successful, and it is important that they be identified. Similarly, in baseball a pitcher is told that he needs to raise his arm on a fastball release. The number 5 is given for the ideal release distance, and a 1 is given for a side-arm release. After each pitch the player is asked to assign a numerical value from 1 to 5 to the arm location. It is essential that the athlete reflect on the position of his arm because this requires awareness. The coach can then give an evaluation from 1 to 5. This aids the athlete in beginning to adjust his awareness to what the proper position feels like (based on a principle from Gallwey, 2010). The use of film or real-time video can greatly enhance the performance feedback.

When athletes gain more awareness, they can make more accurate adjustments in their performance. This ability to refine the subtle intricacies of performance is a critical skill as athletes reach for maximum performance. In addition to improving self-control, the athletes experience a feeling of growing success. Even though the outcome is not perfect, players develop a more positive attitude about the skill and will keep their motivation level where it needs to be. Within the R's model, this player would move directly from recognize to refocus, where they check in, get ready, and just play.

Playing the Edge of Peak Performance

To reach their full sport potential, athletes in every sport must learn to play the performance edge. For example, they must learn to control that delicate balance between power and grace. This type of control necessitates that athletes be aware. They must monitor their performance to recognize when it is at its peak. In athletic training, athletes frequently push too hard or do not push hard enough. At such times the athletes

need to relate to their movement experience with the precision of a surgeon so that they can make needed adjustments. For example, runners constantly monitor their body for subtle messages so that they can make adjustments to reach that edge of peak performance.

One awareness technique I use with runners is the blindfold run. A blindfolded runner and a partner run a specified distance together, with the partner providing physical support and removing any dangers. The blindfold alters the runner's perspective, as the runner is now totally focused on the present moment. The new perspective suspends the athlete's usual thoughts and distractions, and about 5 minutes into the run, the athlete experiences running in a more aware fashion.

Coaches and sport psychology consultants are encouraged to discuss with their athletes this idea of playing the edge so that each athlete can begin to understand and identify where that edge is for him or her. Figure 10-2 and the chapter appendix suggest ways of keeping records of the mental aspects of performance.

Awareness in Managing Performance Stress

To move consistently toward peak performance, each athlete must know and be aware of his or her own experience of optimal performance. Athletes must learn to control the excitement of the sport situation so their energy can be channeled into the performance, or to reorganize when the arousal level is too low and activate it as needed. To gain this control, athletes must learn how competitive stress affects individual performance (see Chapter 12). The first step goes back to the R's and **recognizing** one's arousal level and then to either **release** if something is not going well or **refocus** if everything is on track. The athlete must recognize which situations or stressors tend to negatively affect his or her performance. Knowledge of stressful areas allows for the development of a strategy to prepare and cope effectively with them. For example, playing in front of a crowd or in the presence of scouts is stressful; thus, the athlete can mentally prepare to deal with the situation

PERFORMANCE FEEDBACK SHEET

Name _____

Opponent _____

1. What were your stressors for today's game?

2. How did you experience the stress (thoughts, actions, body)?

3. How was your level of arousal for today's game? What were your feelings at these various points?

   a. Bus ride to game: _____
   b. Warm-up on field, court, etc.: _____
   c. Just before the game: _____
   d. During the game: _____

   0 ———— 5 ———— 10
   Too Low   Perfect   Too High

4. What techniques did you use to manage the stress and how effective were you in controlling it?

5. How was your self-talk? (Describe.)

6. What did you learn from today's game that will help you in your next game?

7. What mental training techniques were most effective for you?

8. Briefly describe one play or segment of the game that you enjoyed.

9. How would you rate your play? _____

10. Briefly describe how you felt about today's game.

    0 ———— 5 ———— 10
    Terrible   OK   Great

11. Anything you want to say?

Figure 10-2 Sample performance feedback sheet

to avoid surprise. The athlete has time to get support from teammates and the coaching staff and also to develop his or her own strategy such as making a fist and releasing it, throwing some grass down, or wiping your hand down your leg.

Once the athlete understands the stressors, the next step is to be aware of the way that stress is experienced since the manifestations of stress vary greatly among individuals. For example, "As the pressure mounts, my shoulders and neck tighten, my thoughts jump around, and I tend to get jittery." Changes in breathing are another bodily cue that often signals too much stress. Athletes should be trained to become sensitive to how their breathing responds to stress. For example, do they start to breathe more rapidly and shallowly? Do they hold their breath? Do they have difficulty breathing? These manifestations of stress may be perceived as problems, but they can be used as signals to provide feedback to the athlete as to whether the arousal level is appropriate. The athlete gains this personal knowledge by reflecting on previous performances and essentially using sport experiences like a biofeedback machine. Release the physical tension by taking a deep breath, tensing and releasing various muscles, or shrugging one's shoulders.

To help athletes understand the concept of self-monitoring as a way to increase awareness, the coach or sport psychologist can use the analogy of a traffic signal light (Ravizza & Hanson, 1994; Tilman, Ravizza, & Statler, 2011). Sport performance is similar to driving a car. Most of the time that we are driving, we are not thinking about the mechanics or technical aspects of driving. When we come to a signal light, we must be aware of the light, or check in; if it is green, we continue. Similarly, when athletes are playing well, there is no need to think about it, but they must check in for that split second. When we are driving and the light is yellow, we have to observe the intersection in more detail to determine whether it is safe to continue as well as check our rearview mirror for a police officer. When the light is red, we must stop.

Using this analogy, the athlete must be aware of his or her signal lights and recognize the impact they have on his or her arousal level, self-talk, breathing patterns, and ability to focus. Thus, if the athlete can be aware of when he or she is shifting from a green light to a yellow light, and it is recognized early, it can be turned around more easily. When the signal light is not recognized until it is red, it is much more difficult to get it turned around. The signal light analogy can be an incredibly useful tool to:

• Indicate the way an athlete experiences the situation

• Monitor potential stressors

• Aid in the development of a contingency plan to cope effectively with stressors

• Build confidence in ability to handle adverse situations

• Provide a vocabulary for coaches, athletes, and sport psychology consultants to discuss situational awareness

• Allow athletes to "check-in" during practice and performances and make necessary adjustments

Figure 10-3 is an illustration of the signal light that includes examples for a softball player to help her recognize what her green, yellow, and red lights are.

Working through the softball player example, when she lets it happen and just thinks, "see ball, hit ball," she is in the green light. After a strikeout, however, she may be headed to a yellow light. If she carries her mistake into the field for defense and yells at a teammate for missing a tough fly ball, she is rapidly approaching a red light.

The athlete's consistent focus on his or her thoughts and feelings and use of appropriate interventions allows his or her to maintain an optimal performance state despite distractions and adversity. Interventions may include relaxation and activation techniques, concentration methods, thought control, and use of imagery (see Chapters 12–15 for specific techniques). There are also situations when the athlete must recognize that it is time just to flow with the experience and let it happen (Ravizza, 1984; Ravizza & Osborne, 1991).

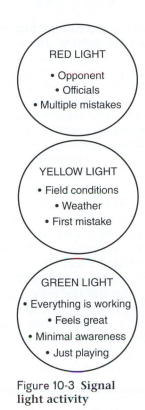

RED LIGHT
- Opponent
- Officials
- Multiple mistakes

YELLOW LIGHT
- Field conditions
- Weather
- First mistake

GREEN LIGHT
- Everything is working
- Feels great
- Minimal awareness
- Just playing

Figure 10-3 **Signal light activity**

Techniques for Developing Awareness

Many techniques are available to increase awareness. Athletes can utilize the R's as a process to both develop awareness and improve their performance. For example, a basketball player can work through the R's after missing his first free throw shot by taking responsibility for his being out of control. The athlete should recognize he is upset with missing the shot, release it by bouncing the ball, and then regroup by taking a centered breath. He refocuses on his plan (elbow up and follow through), steps into his stance, and trusts his shot. Swoosh, he hits the next shot.

Another valuable technique is keeping a sport journal. The sport journal provides a structured method to reflect on sport performances and to capitalize on the wealth of experiential knowledge gained from the performance. The journal guidelines in the appendix ask questions about stressors, manifestations of stress, and feelings associated with performance, concentration, and skill execution. After teams play a game, they can discuss what the members have learned so that, with the coach, they can establish new goals or modify earlier ones. Similarly, feedback sheets, as discussed earlier (see Figure 10-2), allow athletes to process the subjective information gained and bring closure to the performance so they can begin to focus on the next performance. This is particularly helpful in tournament play when the athletes have to perform many times during a short period, because it is critical to bring closure, or let go of one performance before beginning another.

With the athlete's permission, coaches and sport psychology consultants can read these journals and feedback sheets, using the information as a foundation for better understanding the athlete and what behavior or intervention might best facilitate performance and personal growth. Athletes often perceive writing feelings in a journal or on a feedback sheet as less threatening than verbal discussions. Such writing often forges an understanding that promotes discussion.

Some coaches and sport psychologists have helped athletes glean information regarding ideal psychological states for peak performance by having them fill out psychological questionnaires just before beginning performance. Ideally, this should be done prior to a number of competitions, enabling a comparison between performance and scores on the questionnaires. The intention is to find what psychological state(s) typically occurred when athletes performed at their best. The Competitive State Anxiety Inventory-2 (CSAI-2) (Martens, Vealey, & Burton, 1990) is one example of an appropriate questionnaire for this purpose. The CSAI-2 assesses the athlete's current cognitive anxiety, somatic anxiety, and self-confidence. We know from the research discussed in Chapter 11 that each of these psychological states may be relevant to performance. See some of the questionnaires discussed in other chapters for additional examples of potentially appropriate instruments. It should be noted that not all sport psychology consultants find these questionnaires useful. It is critical that the consultant discuss the results with the athletes to determine whether the information obtained is accurate for that athlete.

Athletes who are adept at imagery can use that skill to gain awareness of their ideal performance state. This technique is particularly effective if the athletes are in the off-season or in a situation where actual competition is not possible. Imagery is used to relive previous excellent performance, with particular attention given to identifying what feelings, arousal level, thoughts, muscle tension, attentional focus, and so forth might have occurred. There also may be merit in imaging previous bad performances in order to contrast their psychological state with what appears to be a more optimal state. Monitoring relevant physiological systems, such as heart rate, is another tool for gaining awareness regarding ideal performance states. Monitoring should be done before a number of critical competitions, and then compared with subsequent performance to determine an athlete's optimal level of arousal.

Group discussion is another method that coaches and sport psychology consultants can use to increase athlete awareness. Coaches should provide their athletes with an opportunity to discuss a performance by encouraging but not requiring them to do so. Sport psychology consultants should do the same thing after practicing certain mental training techniques. Coaches and sport psychology consultants can also foster this form of communication through one-on-one discussions. Coaches and sport psychology practitioners should share their perspective or expertise, but also encourage the athletes to talk about the experience by asking questions about arousal and confidence levels, stressors, and manifestations. Every team is capable of this type of teambuilding interaction, but such dialogue is frequently difficult to facilitate at first. As the athletes become much more aware of the needs of their teammates, team cohesion and a mental game vocabulary will be more likely to result. In turn, athletes gain new insights into their own sport performances. For example, if teammates understand that one athlete responds to stress by withdrawing to mentally prepare for performance, they will not think there is something wrong with the athlete who is quiet.

A good time to begin group discussions is after a positive experience because the feelings are nonthreatening. For example, after a great practice, the coach can ask the athletes to discuss what made the practice so good. How was it different from a nonproductive practice session?

In regard to specific methods of increasing awareness, it is important that practitioners do what they are comfortable with. However, it is strongly suggested that coaches and sport psychology consultants slowly integrate the various methods discussed in this chapter.

Summary

Developing awareness is a critical element of peak performance because it provides athletes with the experiential knowledge to gain control of the performance. Awareness is the first step in raising self-control in sport participation. Initially, athletes need to become aware of their ideal performance state. Next, athletes need to recognize when they are no longer at that ideal state. As athletes develop awareness skills, they will recognize earlier when they are not focused or aroused appropriately. This early recognition aids athletes in gaining control and refocusing on the present task. Athletes with a range of interventions can use them to get their mental-emotional and physical states to more nearly approximate what they have found leads to peak performance. The R's process, journal keeping, performance feedback sheets, assessing precompetitive performance states through psychological questionnaires and physiological monitoring, using imagery to relive past performances, and group discussions are all effective techniques for developing awareness. Depending on the athlete's preferences and the circumstances, certain techniques may be more effective than others at any given moment.

Study Questions

1. Why is it important that athletes be aware of their ideal performance state?
2. What is the difference between merely performing skills and experiencing skills?
3. Why is it important to incorporate awareness training with the physical skills that are already being performed in practice?
4. Give an example of focused practice.
5. Describe how the all-or-none syndrome can be overcome.
6. What is meant by playing on the edge? What techniques can help an athlete become aware of this skill?
7. How can a sport journal and performance feedback sheets be used to increase awareness? Describe what might be included in a journal and feedback sheets.
8. How can psychological questionnaires and physiological monitoring be used to increase awareness of ideal performance states?
9. When might imagery and group discussion be used to increase awareness?
10. What are the R's? How does awareness fit into the model?

References

Feldenkrais, M. (1972). *Awareness through movement.* New York: Harper & Row.

Gallwey, T. (2010). *The inner game of tennis.* New York: Random House.

Garrido, A. (1982, December 7). Interview with author. Fullerton, CA.

Martens, R., Vealey, R. S., & Burton, D. (1990). *Competitive anxiety in sport.* Champaign, IL: Human Kinetics.

Raiport, G. (1988). *Red gold: Peak performance techniques of the Russian and East German Olympic victors.* Los Angeles: Tarcher.

Ravizza, K. (1984). Qualities of the peak experience in sport. In J. Silva & R. Weinberg (Eds.), *Psychological foundations for sport.* Champaign, IL: Human Kinetics.

Ravizza, K., & Hanson, T. (1994). *Heads-up baseball: Playing the game one pitch at a time.* Indianapolis: Masters Press.

Ravizza, K., & Osborne, T. (1991). Nebraska's 3R's: One play-at-a-time preperformance routine for collegiate football. *The Sport Psychologist, 5,* 256–265.

Statler, T., & Tilman, T. (2010, August). Compensate and adjust: A model for mental resiliency. *Techniques for Track and Field and Cross Country,* 28–30.

Tilman, T., Ravizza, K., & Statler, T. (2011, January-April). Clear your mind to clear the way: Managing the moment. *Engineer,* 46–49.

Guidelines for Keeping a Sport Journal

The sport journal is a tool to help you further develop your mental skills for sport performance. The first step in gaining self-control is to develop an awareness of your sport performance so that you can recognize when you are pulled out of the most appropriate mental state for you. The journal provides you with an opportunity to record the different intervention strategies that you experiment with to regain control. The long-range goal is to develop various techniques that you can implement in stressful situations to perform to your utmost ability.

If you choose, the journal also can be a place to record your feelings and the personal knowledge that you are gaining about yourself, the game, your teammates, and any other factors. This is one of the few times in your life that you will ever direct so much energy toward one specific goal. There is a lot to learn from your pursuit of excellence. This journal will give you something to reflect on after your high-level participation is completed.

The journal also can serve as a place where you can express your feelings in writing and drawings. It is beneficial to get these feelings out in some way so that they don't build up and contribute to unproductive tension. The use of colored pens is often helpful to express yourself. You do not have to make an entry every day, but date the entries you do make. The journal is an informal record of your thoughts and experiences as you train for high-level performance.

If you choose to have someone read your journal, please feel free to delete any parts that you think are too personal to share. The intention of someone who is reviewing your writing should be to guide you and make *suggestions* that may facilitate your self-exploration in reaching your goals.

I would suggest that you try this technique, but it is not for everyone. If you decide not to use it, that is your choice. If you try the technique, assess the following areas with the accompanying questions/descriptors:

1. *Peak Performance.* What does it feel like when you play or practice at your best? Describe some of your most enjoyable experiences playing your sport. What have you learned from these moments when you are fully functioning?

2. *Stressors.* Outside the sport: write down your thoughts about various events outside your sport that are distracting to you—for example, parents, boy/girlfriends, peers, job hassles, financial issues, community (hometown expectations). On the field: do the same for distractions on the field, such as importance of contest, location, and spectators.

3. *Coaching Staff.* What do you need from your coaches? What can you give them in order to reach your goals? What can you do to make your relationship with your coaches more productive?

4. *Teammates.* What do you want from your teammates? What can you give them? How do you relate and work with your teammates? Write about your relationship

with other teammates. Any unfinished business?

5. *Confidence*. At this time how confident are you in regard to achieving your goals? What can you do differently to feel more confident? What can you ask of yourself, coach, or teammates?

6. *Manifestations of Your Stress*. How do you experience high levels of anxiety in performance? Assess your thoughts and physiological and behavioral reactions. What did you do to intervene and keep in balance?

7. *Awareness and Concentration*. What changes do you observe in your performance when you are aware? What concentration methods are you experimenting with? What are your focal points for various skills?

8. *Relaxation Training*. How are your relaxation skills developing? Are there any parts of your body that are more difficult than others to relax? What method is best for you? How are you able to relate this to your play? How quickly can you relax?

9. *Thought Control*. How is your self-talk affecting your performance? Write out some of your negative self-talk and make it positive.

10. *Centering/Concentration Skills*. What are you doing to concentrate appropriately before the contest and during the contest? What has been successful? Unsuccessful? Describe your preperformance routine.

11. *Imagery*. How are your imagery skills developing? Do you see a TV screen–type image or is it more of a feeling image? At what point do you notice lapses in concentration? How clear are your images? Can you control the speed and tempo of the image?

12. *Controlling Your Arousal Level*. What are you doing to control your arousal level? What are you doing to increase arousal and intensity? What are you experimenting with to reduce arousal levels? What is working for you and what is not working?

13. *Pressure Situations*. How are you handling pressure situations? What are you doing differently? What are you doing to learn to cope more effectively?

14. *Quality Practice Time*. What do you do to mentally prepare for practice? How do you keep your personal difficulties from affecting your play? What are you doing to take charge? What works for you and what hasn't worked?

15. *Anything You Want to Address.*

Goal Setting for Peak Performance

Daniel Gould, *Michigan State University*

Without goals you are like a ship without a rudder—heading in no particular direction.
—Roy Williams, head basketball coach at the University of North Carolina

Goal setting is one of the most used techniques in applied sport psychology. It has been shown to influence the performance of athletes of varied age and ability levels and also been linked to positive changes in important psychological states such as anxiety, confidence, and motivation. It is clearly a technique that coaches and sport psychologists should employ regularly.

Unfortunately, goal setting is not always employed effectively. Coaches and athletes may falsely assume, for example, that because athletes set goals on their own these goals will automatically facilitate performance. This is seldom the case. Many athletes set inappropriate goals or do not set goals in a systematic fashion while coaches and sport psychologists often forget to initiate the follow-up and evaluation procedures that are necessary if goal setting is to be effective. To use goal setting effectively, coaches and sport psychologists must understand the goal-setting process and the many factors that can affect it.

This chapter has a fourfold purpose: (1) to examine psychological and sport psychological research and theory on goal setting, (2) to discuss fundamental goal-setting guidelines, (3) to present a system for effectively initiating goal-setting procedures, and (4) to identify and offer solutions for common problems that arise when setting goals. Each of these will be discussed.

Goal-Setting Research and Theory

Before examining the research on goal setting and theoretical explanations for the relationships between goal setting and performance, we must first define goals and distinguish between various types of goals.

Defining Goals

Locke and Latham (2002) have generated the most widely accepted definition for the term *goal*. For these investigators, a **goal** is an "objective or aim of action" defined as attaining "a specific standard of proficiency on a task, usually within a specified time limit" (p. 705). From a practical perspective, then, goals focus on achieving some standard, whether it is increasing one's batting average by 10 percentage points, lowering one's time in the 800 meters, or losing 5 pounds. This definition also implies that such performance standards will be achieved within some specified unit of time, such as by the end of the season, within two weeks, or by the end of practice.

Martens (1987) and Burton (1983, 1984, 1989) have made distinctions between **outcome goals,** which represent standards of performance that focus on the results of a contest between opponents or teams (e.g., beating someone), and **performance goals,** which focus on improvements relative to one's own past performance, (e.g., improving one's time in the mile). Hardy, Jones, and Gould (1996) extended the outcome-performance goal distinction to include **process goals,** which specify the procedures in which the athlete will engage during performance (e.g., a skier focusing on keeping his hands in front of him during a downhill run, a tennis player on keeping her feet moving when fatigued). These distinctions are important because evidence suggests that certain types of goals are more useful in changing behavior than other types of goals.

Finally, Weinberg and Gould (2011, p. 355) have defined group goals as attaining ". . . specific standards of group (not individual) proficiency, usually within a specified time." Typical group goals include having the volleyball team win the regional tournament, a football team reduce the number of offside penalties called by 20 percent over the first half of the season, or having a golf team reduce the average number of putts taken per round. Research reveals that it is important to set both individual and team goals as group goals have powerful influences on performance (Widmeyer & DuCharme, 1997). In fact, some have suggested that group goals have more powerful effects than individual goals (Burke, Shapcott, Carron, Bradshaw, & Estabrooks, 2010).

Goal-Effectiveness Research

Extensive psychological research has been conducted on the topic of goal setting (see Locke, Shaw, Saari, & Latham, 1981; Locke & Latham, 1990, 2002; Tubbs, 1991, for extensive reviews). Typically, this research has involved a comparison of the performance of individuals who set goals or certain types of goals (e.g., specific-explicit goals) with the performance of individuals who are simply told to do their best or are given no goals. Studies sometimes manipulate other factors, such as individual characteristics (e.g., race, educational level, personality) or situational variables (e.g., the presence or absence of feedback).

Psychological research on goal setting is impressive in that it has been conducted in a variety of laboratory and field settings and has used a wide variety of tasks, ranging from truck loading to brainstorming sessions; it has employed diverse samples, including elementary school children, uneducated laborers, managers, and scientists. In addition, a clear pattern of results has emerged with ready implications for sport psychologists and coaches alike.

The most important result generated from this line of research is that goal setting clearly and consistently facilitates performance. In their excellent and comprehensive review of well over a hundred studies on goal setting, for example, Locke and colleagues (1981) concluded that "the beneficial effect of goal setting on task performance is one of the most robust and replicable findings in the psychological literature. Ninety percent of the studies showed positive or partially positive effects. Furthermore, these effects are found just as reliable in the field setting as in the laboratory" (p. 145). Thus, a review of the psychological research clearly shows that goal setting is a powerful technique for enhancing performance.

Given the abundance of research on goal setting and the consistent pattern of results found in the psychological literature, it is not surprising that sport psychology researchers have been studying goal setting for over three decades. Botterill (1977) conducted one of the earliest studies when he had youth ice hockey players perform an exercise endurance task under various combinations of goal difficulty, goal explicitness specificity, and goal type (group, individual, or experimenter-set) conditions. Consistent with the psychological literature, the results revealed that goal setting facilitated performance. Similarly, difficult goals were more effective in enhancing performance than easy goals, and explicit goals were more effective than general "do your best" goals. Finally, research concluded that explicit, difficult, and group-set goals were most effective in enhancing endurance task performance.

Intense interest in sport psychological goal-setting research was spurred by a 1985 *Journal of Sport Psychology* review article written by noted goal-setting researchers Locke and Latham, which suggested that goal-setting research principles found in the general psychological literature were applicable to the sport context. This has led to a series of sport psychology studies testing Locke and Latham's proposition in the sport environment (see Burton, Naylor, & Holliday, 2002, and Burton & Weiss, 2008, for excellent reviews of these studies) and some healthy dialogue on how to study the process by which goal setting functions in sport (see Locke, 1991; Locke, 1994; Weinberg & Weigand, 1996).

More recent sport psychology goal-setting research investigations have examined such issues as whether specific goals are more effective than general "do your best" goals, the effectiveness of long-term versus short-term goals, and the relationship between goal difficulty and task performance, how different types of goals influence performance, and the effectiveness of goal setting interventions. Results of these studies have shown that goal setting works well in sport, but not as well as in other settings such as business (Burton et al., 2002, Burton & Weiss, 2008). Robert Weinberg, one of the leading sport psychology researchers in the area, has indicated that research efforts are characterized by a number of methodological problems such as spontaneous goal setting by control group participants, competition between comparison group participants, and the failure to control levels of participant motivation and commitment (Weinberg, 1994). Burton et al. (2002) also noted task complexity, the failure to use appropriate goal implementation strategies, and the fact that athletes often operate closer to their performance potential as

issues that arise in sport goal-setting research. Goal setting, then, is more complex to apply in sport than it might appear on the surface.

While goal-setting research in sport has not been easy or simple, it has clearly shown that goal setting can and does influence performance in sport settings. In fact, in a meta-analytic or statistical review of 36 independent sport and exercise goal-setting studies conducted by Kyllo and Landers (1995), it was concluded that goal setting was a successful technique for improving performance. Similarly, in the most recent review of goal setting in sport Burton and Weiss (2008) found that 70 of 88 studies (80 percent) showed moderate to strong effects.

Many of these studies were field based. For example, Anderson, Crowell, Doman, and Howard (1988) examined goal setting along with publicly posted performance and praise on "checking" in a collegiate ice hockey team. The results showed that this behavioral intervention increased checking behavior over a baseline and that the goal-setting component was associated with improved performance. It was concluded not only that goal setting was associated with improved performance but also that performance feedback moderates these effects.

In another study, Swain and Jones (1995) examined goal setting in four university basketball players over a series of games. Using a single-subject baseline design, results revealed goal setting had positive consequences on three out of four identified behaviors. Hence, goal setting was found to be effective in changing desired behaviors.

In a very well-designed multiple baseline study using four female speed skaters, Wanlin et al. (1997) had participants take part in a goal-setting package. This package involved developing an overall mission (general subjective goal), a long-term goal, subgoals and practice goals, self-talk, and goal visualization. It was taught to each skater, and performance was compared prior to and after the goal-setting package was used. Results revealed that the goal-setting package was effective in influencing the skaters to work harder and show fewer off-task behaviors. Race times also improved. Hence, goal setting was effective in facilitating desirable behaviors and performance in the skaters and decreasing undesirable behaviors.

Finally, recent studies fall in line with these results. For example, Vidic and Burton (2010) found that an 8-week goal setting program involving long, intermediate, and short-term goals enhanced the confidence, motivation, and performance of female collegiate tennis players. O'Brien, Mellalieu, and Hanton (2009) found that a 10-week goal-setting program facilitated targeted performance measures, self-confidence, and facilitative interpretations of anxiety in boxers, although results were more consistent with elite versus non-elite participants.

Taken together, these field studies support the earlier findings of Burton (1983, 1989). They also reinforce a main contention of this chapter; that is, goal setting will only be effective when a systematic approach is adopted and a knowledgeable professional customizes the goal-setting process to his or her particular setting and athletes.

In summary, although not unequivocal, the results of the psychological and sport psychology research literature provide strong support for using goal-setting procedures to facilitate athletic performance. Moreover, these findings are further strengthened by the fact that they have been demonstrated in studies using varied tasks and largely different populations in both laboratory and field settings. A survey of leading sport psychology consultants working with U.S. Olympic athletes has also shown that goal setting is the most often used psychological intervention in both individual athlete–coach and group consultations (Gould, Tammen, Murphy, & May, 1989). Data from Orlick and Partington's (1988) extensive study of Olympic athletes supports the survey results from the sport psychologists. The athletes reported daily goal setting as a part of their training program.

Examining Athletes' and Coaches' Uses of Goal Setting

Burton, Weinberg, and their colleagues (Burton, Gillham, Weinberg, Yukelson, & Weigand, 2013;

Burton, Weinberg, Yukelson, & Weigand, 1998; Weinberg, Burton, Yukelson, & Weigand, 1993, 2000; Weinberg, Butt, Knight, & Perritt, 2001) have spearheaded a line of research examining the goal-setting practices actually employed by athletes and coaches. For example, Burton et al. (1998) studied 321 male and 249 female collegiate athletes representing 18 sports who were surveyed regarding their goal-setting practices. Findings revealed that most of the athletes set goals but rated them as only moderately effective, preferred moderate to very difficult goals, and more often reported problems with setting goals that were too hard versus easy.

Most interesting was the researchers' comparison between more and less effective goal setters, which found that more effective goal setters used all types of goals and implemented productive goal-setting strategies more frequently than did their less effective counterparts. Based on these results, it was concluded that coaches and athletes underutilize goal setting and need further goal-setting education. In particular, more emphasis must be placed on teaching athletes about process-oriented performance goals, the relationship between long- and short-term goals, skill and fitness goals, and implementing goals in practice and competition.

Other studies in this line of research showed that Olympic athletes all set some type of goals (Weinberg et al., 2000). Interviews with collegiate coaches from a variety of sports also showed that they used individual, team, practice, and competition goals (Weinberg et al., 2001), although there was some divergence in how systematic the coaches were in their use of goal setting.

Summarizing much of this research, Weinberg (2010) indicates that coaches and athletes set both short- and long-term goals; it is important to set goals in practice and competitions; many athletes fail to implement action plans for achieving their goals; coaches and athletes do not consistently write down their goals; and barriers to goal setting include a perceived lack of time, stress, fatigue, social relationships, injury, and a lack of confidence.

Theoretical Explanations for the Relationship between Goal Setting and Performance

The old adage that there is nothing more practical than a good theory is an appropriate way to view the goal-setting process. It is important to know that goal setting influences performance, but it is equally important for coaches and sport psychologists to understand how and why goal setting is effective, especially when problems occur in goal setting and these individuals must assess the situation and make adjustments.

Several explanations have been proposed to describe how goals influence performance. More specifically, in their **mechanistic theory,** Locke and Latham (2002) contend that goals influence performance in four ways. First, goals direct the performer's attention and action to important aspects of the task. For example, by setting goals a basketball player will focus attention and subsequent action on improving specific skills such as blocking out under the boards or decreasing turnovers as opposed to becoming a better ball player in general. Second, goals help the performer mobilize effort. For example, by setting a series of practice goals, a swimmer will exhibit greater practice effort in attempting to achieve these objectives. Third, goals not only increase immediate effort but also help prolong effort or increase persistence. As a case in point, the boredom of a long season is offset and persistence is increased when a wrestler sets a number of short-term goals throughout the year. Finally, research has shown that performers often develop and employ new learning strategies through the process of setting goals. Golfers, for instance, may learn new methods of putting in an effort to achieve putting goals that they have set in conjunction with their coach or sport psychologist.

Locke and associates' subsequent writings (Locke & Latham, 1990; 2002) suggest that a number of factors mediate the goal setting-performance relationship. These include factors such as importance, self-efficacy, feedback, and task complexity. In essence, Locke has argued against a simple relationship between goals and behavior indicating that a number of factors combine to influence effective goal setting.

In contrast, Burton's **cognitive theory** (1983) focuses solely on how goal setting influences performance in athletic environments. Athletes' goals are linked to their levels of anxiety, motivation, and confidence. That is, when athletes focus solely on outcome or winning goals, unrealistic future expectations often result; such expectations can lead to lower levels of confidence, increased cognitive anxiety, decreased effort, and poor performance. Unlike outcome goals, performance goals are both in the athlete's control and flexible. Moreover, when properly employed, performance goals assist the athlete in forming realistic expectations. This, in turn, results in optimal levels of confidence, cognitive anxiety, and motivation, and, ultimately, in enhanced performance.

Burton and his colleagues (Burton & Naylor, 2002; Burton & Weiss, 2008) further developed his theoretical view of goal setting. The most interesting aspect of this update was the contention that an athlete's goal motivational orientation interacts with perceived ability to produce one of three goal styles: a performance orientation where the athlete defines success based on learning and self-improvement and has high perceived ability (although the perceived ability is not judged to be critical to this one orientation); a success orientation where the athlete defines success on social comparison and winning and has high perceived ability; and a failure orientation where the athlete defines success on social comparison and winning but has low perceived ability. They predict that goal setting should best increase performance for the performance-oriented athlete, moderately increase performance for the success-oriented athlete, and slightly decrease performance for the failure-oriented athlete. Moreover, recent evidence collected with prospective Olympic athletes supports these predictions (Burton et al., 2013). Goal setting, then, interacts with a variety of personal and situational factors and these motivational factors must be taken into consideration in any goal-setting program. The implication is that the goal setting will work differently depending on one's goal-setting style.

When setting goals, then, coaches and sport psychologists should make every effort to become aware of the mechanisms causing performance changes to occur. Simply stated, theorists indicate that performance changes occur because of the influence of goals on such psychological attributes as anxiety, confidence, satisfaction, and motivation; directing attention to important aspects of the skill being performed; mobilizing effort; increasing persistence; and fostering the development of new learning strategies.

Life Skills Goal-Setting Programs

Goals can also be used to enhance personal development. For example, sport psychologist Steve Danish and his colleagues have used goal setting as a cornerstone of programs designed to enhance life skills, particularly in at-risk populations (Danish, Nellen, & Owens, 1996; Danish, Petitpas, & Hale, 1995; Papacharisi, Goudas, Danish, & Theodorakis, 2005). In particular, these scholars have initiated intervention programs that are designed to promote health-enhancing behaviors (such as learning how to learn, staying healthy) and decrease health-compromising behaviors (e.g., drug and alcohol use) in participants, particularly at-risk youth. Because of the importance of sport in the lives of many youth, these programs focus on identifying and learning life skills like goal setting, and then transferring the valuable life skills learned in the sport environment to other more general life situations. Organizers focus on effectively setting and achieving sport goals by helping athletes clarify their training and competition objectives. Efforts are then made to "teach for transfer" by helping participants apply their new goal-setting skills to other life contexts. An example of the steps followed in such a program is given in Danish et al. (1996):

> (a) the identification of positive life goals, (b) the importance of focusing on the process (not the outcome) of goal attainment, (c) the use of a general problem solving model, (d) the identification of health-comprising behaviors that can impede goal attainment, (e) the identification of health-promoting behaviors that can facilitate goal attainment, (f) the importance of seeking

and creating social support, and (g) ways to transfer these skills from one life situation to another. (p. 215)

Finally, these steps are implemented in a series of 10 one-hour workshops.

Additional research on the efficacy of programs to develop life skills based on goal setting is needed, but initial reports are encouraging (e.g., Papacharisis et al., 2005). Moreover, these programs clearly demonstrate the importance of looking beyond goal setting as simply an athletic performance enhancement technique to looking at it as a general skill that can positively influence all aspects of one's life. The programs also emphasize the need to teach for transfer and not assume that just because a person can effectively set goals in sport he or she will automatically use goal setting in other life contexts.

Goal-Setting Guidelines

The research clearly shows that goal setting facilitates performance. It is misleading to think, however, that all types of goals are equally effective in enhancing athletic performance. Research reviews conducted by Burton et al. (2002), Burton and Weiss (2008), Locke and Latham (1990), Weinberg (1994), and Kyllo and Landers (1995) indicate that this is not the case. Their work has produced specific guidelines concerning the most effective types of goals to use. Similarly, sport psychologists (Bell, 1983; Botterill, 1983; Carron, 1984; Gould, 1983; Harris & Harris, 1984; Orlick, 1990; Weinberg, 2010) who had had extensive experience in employing goal-setting techniques with athletes have been able to derive a number of useful guidelines for those interested in utilizing such techniques, the most important of which are summarized here.

Set Specific Goals in Measurable and Behavioral Terms

Explicit, specific, and numerical goals are more effective in facilitating behavior change than general "do your best" goals or no goals at all. The research has convincingly shown that "when people are asked to do their best, they do not do so" (Locke & Latham, 2002, p. 706). Therefore, it is of the utmost importance that in the athletic environment goals be expressed in terms of specific measurable behaviors. Goals such as doing one's best, becoming better, and increasing one's strength are least effective. More effective goals include being able to high jump 6 feet 5 inches by the end of the season or increasing one's maximum lift on the bench press to 240 pounds. If athletes are to show performance improvements, specific measurable goals must be set!

Set Moderately Difficult but Realistic Goals

Locke and his associates (1981) have found a direct relationship between goal difficulty and task performance. That is, the more difficult the goal, the better the performance. It must be remembered, however, that this relationship is true only when the difficulty of the goal does not exceed the performer's ability. Unrealistic goals that exceed the ability of an athlete only lead to failure and frustration. In fact, in their meta-analysis, Kyllo and Landers (1995) found that moderately difficult (as opposed to extremely difficult) goals lead to the best performance. Thus, it is recommended that goals be set so that they are difficult enough to challenge athletes but realistic enough to be achieved (McClements, 1982).

Set Short-Range as well as Long-Range Goals

When asked to describe their goals, most athletes identify long-range objectives such as winning a particular championship, breaking a record, or making a particular team. However, a number of sport psychologists (Bell, 1983; Carron, 1984; Gould, 1983; Harris & Harris, 1984) have emphasized the need to set more immediate short-range goals. The superiority of combining short- and long-term goals as compared to focusing only on long-term goals was also demonstrated in the Kyllo and Landers (1995) meta-analysis. Research also has revealed that both short- and long-range goals are needed to maintain motivation and

performance (Weinberg, Butt & Knight, 2001). Short-range goals are important because they allow athletes to see immediate improvements in performance and in so doing enhance motivation. They have been found to be especially important with complex tasks (Locke & Latham, 2002). Additionally, without short-range goals, athletes often lose sight of their long-range goals and the progression of skills needed to obtain them.

An effective way to understand the relationship between short- and long-range goals is to visualize a staircase (see Figure 11-1). The top stair represents an athlete's long-range goal or objective and the lowest stair her or his present ability. The remaining steps represent a progression of short-term goals of increasing difficulty that lead from the bottom to the top of the stairs. In essence, the performer climbs the staircase of athletic achievement by taking a step at a time, accomplishing a series of interrelated short-range goals.

Set Process and Performance Goals as well as Outcome Goals

Many societies place tremendous emphasis on the outcome of athletic events. Because of this, most athletes are socialized to set only outcome goals (e.g., winning, beating a particular opponent). However, outcome goals have been shown to be less effective than performance goals (Burton, 1984, 1989; Burton et al., 2002).

Theorists suggest that focusing on outcome goals has several inherent weaknesses (Burton, 1984, 1989; Martens, 1987; Burton & Weiss, 2008). First, athletes have, at best, only partial control over outcome goals. For example, a cross-country competitor can set a personal best but fail to achieve the outcome goal of winning because he or she came in second. Despite her or his superior effort, this runner could not control the behavior of the other competitors.

A second important weakness of outcome goals is that athletes who employ them usually become less flexible in their goal-adjustment practices. For example, an athlete who sets an outcome goal of winning every game but loses the initial contest will often reject goal setting

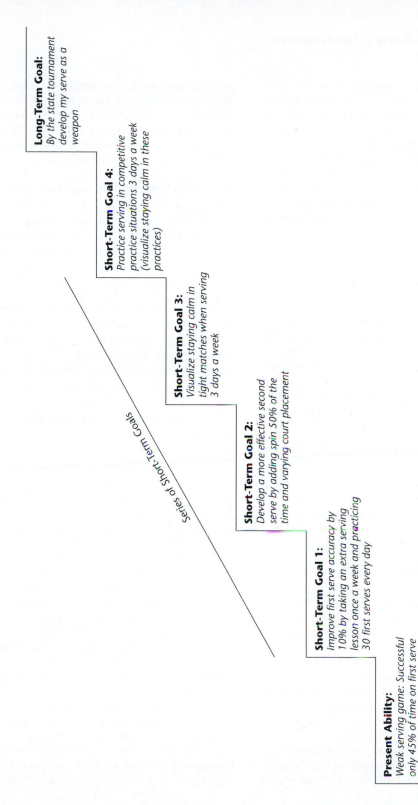

Present Ability:
Weak serving game: Successful only 45% of time on first serve and no variation on second serve

Short-Term Goal 1:
Improve first serve accuracy by 10% by taking an extra serving lesson once a week and practicing 30 first serves every day

Short-Term Goal 2:
Develop a more effective second serve by adding spin 50% of the time and varying court placement

Short-Term Goal 3:
Visualize staying calm in tight matches when serving 3 days a week

Short-Term Goal 4:
Practice serving in competitive practice situations 3 days a week (visualize staying calm in these practices)

Long-Term Goal:
By the state tournament develop my serve as a weapon

Series of Short-Term Goals

Figure 11-1 Goal Staircase: A series of short-term goals leads to long-term goals for improved tennis serve

altogether. However, an athlete who sets an individual performance goal such as decreasing her or his 100-meter breaststroke time by $^5/10$ of a second and fails to achieve this goal is more likely to reset the goal to $^1/10$ of a second.

Finally, process goals (e.g., watch the ball longer by focusing on the pitcher's release, get back on defense) orient the athlete to focus on task-relevant strategies and procedures that need to be executed to have a good performance. Focusing on outcome goals can distract athletes, as they tend to worry about the event outcome and do not attend to task-relevant strategies (Hardy et al., 1996).

Although focusing on outcome goals, especially at the time of competition, has weaknesses, this does not mean outcome goals have no benefits. They can facilitate short-term motivation by helping athletes set long-term priorities and may be especially useful away from competition when athletes may lack the motivation to practice. Athletes with high levels of confidence may also be less affected by the negative side effects of outcome goals (Hardy et al., 1996). It is clear, however, that at or near competitions it is best to emphasize process and performance goals and that focusing exclusively on outcome goals is ineffective.

Research by Filby, Maynard, and Graydon (1999) has also provided support for the idea of setting performance and process, as well as outcome goals. Moreover, looking across all goals, Burton et al. (2002) reported that 9 out of 10 studies supported the notion of using a combination of process, performance, and outcome goals. Finally, recent evidence reveals that setting holistic process goals like "push" or "smooth" were effective in allowing skilled but anxious athletes to perform their best in high stress situations (Mullen & Hardy, 2010).

In summary, by emphasizing personal performance and process goals in an environment where outcome goals predominate, coaches create greater opportunities for meeting the success needs of all athletes. Those highly gifted competitors who easily exceed the performances of their opponents learn to compete against themselves and, in turn, reach new performance heights. Similarly, the less skilled athletes on the team are no longer doomed to failure; they learn to judge success and failure in terms of their own performance, not solely on the basis of peer comparisons. Finally, focusing on process goals directs the athlete's attention away from outcome and puts it on task-relevant cues.

Set Goals for Practice and Competition

When implementing a goal-setting program, people frequently make the mistake of setting only goals that relate to competition. This does not imply that setting competitive performance goals is inappropriate; rather, it suggests that *practice* goals should not be forgotten (Bell, 1983). In fact, Orlick and Partington (1988) found that one characteristic of highly successful Olympians was their practice of setting clear daily practice goals.

Common practice goals may include focusing 100 percent, making five sincere positive statements to teammates, running to and from all drills, and achieving various performance standards. These are typically not the most frequently cited goals of athletes, but they take on special significance when one considers the amount of time athletes spend in practice as opposed to competition. Moreover, most athletes report that it is easier to get "up" and motivated for a game or match, whereas additional motivation is often needed for daily practices.

Set Positive Goals as Opposed to Negative Goals

Goals can be stated in either positive terms (e.g., increase the percentage of good first serves in tennis) or negative terms (e.g., don't drop the ball). Although it is sometimes necessary for athletes to set goals in negative terms, it has been suggested that, whenever possible, goals should be stated positively (Bell, 1983). That is, identify behaviors to be exhibited as opposed to behaviors that should not be exhibited. Instead of having goal tenders in ice hockey strive to decrease the number of unblocked shots, have them set goals of increasing the number of saves they can make. This positive goal-setting procedure helps athletes focus on success instead of failure.

Identify Target Dates for Attaining Goals

Not only should goals describe the behavior of focus in specific measurable terms, but they should also identify target dates for goal accomplishment. Target dates help motivate athletes by reminding them of the urgency of accomplishing their objectives in realistic lengths of time.

Identify Goal-Achievement Strategies

All too often goals are properly set but never accomplished because athletes fail to identify goal-achievement strategies. That is, the athlete fails to understand the difference between setting goals and developing and initiating effective goal-achievement strategies. In fact, it has been reported that athletes who use multiple goal-setting strategies have the best performance (Weinberg, Butt, & Knight, 2001). An important ingredient for any effective goal-setting program, then, is identification of multiple ways of achieving goals. For example, a wrestler needing to lose 10 pounds prior to the start of the season should identify an achievement strategy of cutting out a midafternoon snack and running an additional 2 miles a day.

Record Goals Once They Have Been Identified

Coaches and athletes are not consistent in writing down their goals (Weinberg, 2002). It is easy for athletes to focus attention on their goals soon after those goals have been set. Over the course of a long season, however, goals are sometimes forgotten. Therefore, it is useful for athletes to record their goals in written form and place them where they will be seen (e.g., in their lockers). In fact, in the previously mentioned speed skating study, Wanlin et al. 1997 concluded that using a log book was a particularly important component of a successful goal-setting package. Additionally, Harris and Harris (1984) recommend that athletes keep notebooks recording goals, goal-achievement strategies, and goal progress on a daily or weekly basis. Finally, Botterill (1983) suggests that the coach develop a contract stating all goals and goal-achievement strategies

for each athlete. Each athlete then signs her or his contract, and the coach keeps the contracts on file. Later the coach can use the contracts to remind the athletes of their goals.

Provide for Goal Evaluation

Based on their review of the research, Locke and his associates (1981) concluded that evaluative feedback is absolutely necessary if goals are to enhance performance. Therefore, athletes must receive feedback about how present performance is related to both short- and long-range goals. In many cases feedback in the form of performance statistics such as batting average, assists, goals scored, or steals made is readily available. Other goals, however, require that coaches make special efforts to provide evaluative feedback. For instance, a coach helping an athlete control his or her temper on the field may have a manager record the number of times the player loses his or her temper in practice. Similarly, a softball coach helping outfielders attain their goal of efficiently backing up one another may have an observer record the number of times players move into or fail to move into correct positions after the ball is hit. In Chapter 16, the authors suggest that sport psychologists might help athletes become more aware of negative thoughts by having them put a box of paper clips in a pocket, then transfer one paper clip at a time to another pocket for each negative thought during practice.

Provide Support for Goals

A goal-setting program will not succeed unless those individuals who are paramount in the athlete's life support it. This typically includes the coach, the athlete's family, and teammates. Recent research with British youth soccer players, however, indicates that this does not always occur (Holt, Kinchin, & Clarke, 2012). Therefore, efforts must be made to educate these individuals about the types of goals the athlete sets and the importance of their support in encouraging progress toward the goals. For instance, if an athlete sets performance goals as opposed to outcome goals but significant others in the athlete's life stress only the outcome of the game or match, it is unlikely that performance goals will change behavior. Simply stated, significant others must understand the goal-setting process and support it!

Set Group Goals

Although the bulk of sport psychologists' attention has focused on individual athlete goals, Widmeyer and Ducharme (1997) emphasized the need to set group goals. A particularly important point these authors make is that understanding group goals involves more than knowing individual athletes' goals. The group task must be clearly specified along with the process for achieving group goals. When setting group goals, long-term team objectives should be identified, clear sequences of short- and long-term goals specified, team goal progress assessed, progress toward group goals rewarded, and team confidence fostered in group goals. All team members should have input into the team goal-setting process.

Dawson, Bray, and Widmeyer (2002) also have shown that when setting group goals, the process involves more than setting collective goals. In contrast, they found evidence for four types of goals on any team: (1) an individual member's goals for self (e.g., be the leading scorer on the team); (2) an individual's goal for the team (e.g., qualify for postseason play by finishing in the top half of the league); (3) the group's goals (e.g., win the league title); and (4) the group's goal for the individual member (e.g., lead the team in assists). They also showed that individual goals and expectations might differ from those generated by the collective. For example, one athlete might see his role as the point scorer on the team while the team sees him as an assist leader. Therefore, it is of the utmost importance that coaches and team leaders discuss and integrate individual goals with team goals. Role clarification and definition are critical if effective team performance is to result (see Chapter 7).

A Goal-Setting System for Coaches

Goal-setting research and guidelines provide coaches with the information necessary for implementing goal-setting techniques with athletes. To be successful in implementing goal-setting procedures, however, coaches must develop and employ a goal-setting system. Botterill (1983) has outlined the essentials of such a system in detail. Of the many elements Botterill discusses, three are paramount and can be incorporated into a three-phase, goal-setting system: (1) the planning phase, (2) the meeting phase, and (3) the follow-up/evaluation phase.

The Planning Phase

Coaches will be ineffective if they attempt to set goals without first spending considerable time planning them. Before discussing goals with athletes, for instance, coaches must identify individual and team needs. These needs may focus on any number of areas such as player fitness, individual skills, team skills, playing time, good sport behavior, and enjoyment.

Following this needs analysis, coaches must identify potential team and individual goals. Most coaches can identify a large number of potential goals for their athletes, so it is important for them to consider how likely it is that their athletes will agree to and accomplish the goals. In doing so, coaches should consider the athletes' long-range goals, individual potential, commitment, and opportunity for practice. Finally, coaches must begin to consider possible strategies that they can use to help athletes achieve their goals. For example, a segment of each practice could be devoted to the accomplishment of identified goals, or extra practices could be held.

The Meeting Phase

Once coaches have considered individual athlete and team needs, they should schedule goal-setting meetings. The first of these meetings should include the entire team. At the first meeting, coaches should convey basic goal-setting information (e.g., the value of setting goals, areas in which to set goals, types of goals to set, the importance of performance and process goals) and ask the athletes to think about their general objectives for participation, as well as specific team and individual goals. Coaches must then give the athletes time to reflect on their reasons for participation and to formulate potential goals.

A few days after the initial meeting, a second meeting should be held for the purpose of discussing some of the athletes' goals. It is especially important to examine goals in respect to their importance, specificity, and realistic nature. It is also desirable to examine possible strategies for achieving these goals.

In most cases it will be impossible to set specific goals for each athlete during these initial group meetings. Therefore, coaches must also hold a number of meetings with individual athletes and small subgroup meetings (e.g., forwards, centers, and guards in basketball). In these meetings individual goals should be recorded, specific strategies for achieving these goals identified, and goal evaluation procedures determined. Before and after practice are often the most effective times for holding such meetings.

The Follow-Up/Evaluation Phase

As previously stated, goal setting will not be effective unless evaluative feedback is provided to athletes. Moreover, recent research shows that public postings and oral feedback are critical for goal success. Unfortunately, because of the hectic nature of the season, this is often forgotten. It is therefore a good idea to schedule goal evaluation meetings throughout the season. At these meetings, subgroups of athletes should discuss their goals and progress made toward achieving them and reevaluate unrealistic goals or goals that cannot be achieved because of injury or sickness.

Finally, to facilitate goal follow-up and evaluation, coaches should develop systematic ways of providing feedback. Figure 11-2 contains such a system for the sport of basketball. Prior to the season, the coach prints goal-achievement cards that athletes complete during the preseason or seasonal meetings. These cards contain places for the athletes to rate their present skills, identify specific goals, describe goal achievement strategies, and develop goal evaluation schedules. In addition, performance evaluation cards are printed (see Figure 11-2) and used to evaluate performance on a percentage scale

(0 percent = poor; 100 percent = excellent). The evaluation cards are completed after various competitions and, when combined with other available statistics, serve as feedback for weekly goal follow-up meetings. Although written in the vernacular of the coach, this goal-setting system can also be used by sport psychologists as they work with athletes on goal setting. The suggestions are equally appropriate for goals in the physical and mental skills domains, but they may need to be somewhat modified for sport psychologists working with an individual rather than the entire team.

Common Problems in Setting Goals

Goal setting is not a difficult psychological skill to use. However, it would be a misconception to think that problems do not arise when setting goals. Some of the more frequently encountered problems are outlined below.

Setting Too Many Goals Too Soon

A natural mistake that occurs when one first implements a goal-setting system is to set too many goals too soon. For example, it is not uncommon for coaches and athletes to set 5 or 10 specific goals. This usually has negative results. The athletes have so many individual goals that they cannot properly monitor goal progress, or if they do monitor progress, they find the record keeping overwhelming and lose interest. A more effective approach is to prioritize goals and focus on accomplishing the one or two most important ones. When these goals are achieved, the athletes then focus on the next most important prioritized goals. As the athletes become more experienced in goal setting, they also learn to handle greater numbers of goals more efficiently.

Failing to Recognize Individual Differences

Not all athletes will be excited about setting goals, and some may even have a negative attitude. Coaches and sport psychologists must expect this and not overreact. *Forcing* athletes to set goals is ineffective, for individual commitment is needed.

Goal Achievement Card—Basketball

Name _B. Jones_   Date _9-27-13_

Position _Forward_   Years Experience _2_

Skill–Activity	Strong	Average	Needs improvement	Specific goal	Strategy	Target date
Shooting				To correctly execute 8 out of 10 jump shots from the 8' to 10' range	Shoot 4 sets of 10 jump shots before practice every day	Oct. 27
lay-ups	✓					
jump shots			✓			
free throws		✓				
Ball handling		✓				
Rebounding	✓					

Performance Evaluation Card—Basketball

Name _B. Jones_   Date _12-4-13_

Position _Forward_   Game _3_

Skill–Activity	Available statistics/Coach performance rating (0–100%)	Comments
Overall offensive play	80%	
Overall defensive play	94%	
Shooting	70%	Jump shot release ball at peak of jump
lay-ups	2 for 2	
jump shots	2 for 6	
free throws	3 for 4	
Ball handling	90%	
turnovers	1	
Rebounding	90%	

Figure 11-2 Sample goal-achievement and performance evaluation cards for the sport of basketball

Rather, expose all the athletes to goal setting, and then work with those who show interest. Over time, their success will convince other less committed athletes to begin setting goals.

The importance of recognizing individual differences when setting goals with athletes was demonstrated in an investigation by Lambert, Moore, and Dixon (1999). They found that the most effective type of goal setting depended on the participant's locus of control. Specifically, female gymnasts characterized by an internal locus of control (those who felt they could control what happened to them) spent more time on task when they set their own goals. In contrast, external locus of control gymnasts (those who felt they had little control over what happened to them) responded better to coach-set goals. Hence, goal-setting effectiveness was dependent on the gymnast's personality.

As mentioned earlier in this chapter the theorizing and research of Burton and his colleagues shows that performance-oriented athletes respond better to goal setting than failure-oriented athletes. Yet failure-oriented athletes, who judge success by comparing themselves to others and have low perceived ability, could profit greatly from setting performance and process goals that when achieved will help enhance their confidence. So special coaching efforts are needed to get failure-oriented individuals to focus on performance and process, as opposed to outcome goals.

Setting Goals That Are Too General

Throughout this chapter, the emphasis has been on the need for setting specific, measurable goals. Unfortunately, this does not always occur. Inexperienced goal setters will often set goals that are too general. Improving one's first serve in tennis, executing a better Yamashita vault in gymnastics, and lessening the frequency of negative thoughts are too vague. These goals are more effectively stated as increasing the number of good first serves from 50 to 55 percent in tennis, improving the Yamashita vault by sticking the landing 8 out of 10 times, and reducing negative thoughts to five or less during each practice session. When stating goals, always ask, "How can we make this goal measurable and specific?"

Failing to Modify Unrealistic Goals

In his extensive 5-month study of goal setting, Burton (1989) found that competitive collegiate swimmers had problems readjusting goals once they were set. Although the swimmers had little difficulty raising their goals once they were achieved, a number of athletes failed to lower goals that became unrealistic because of illness or injury. Coaches must recognize this problem and continually emphasize the appropriateness of lowering goals when necessary.

Failing to Set Process and Performance Goals

The work of Martens (1987), Burton (1984, 1989), and Filby et al. (1999) has demonstrated the value of setting performance and process goals as opposed to outcome goals. For too many athletes, however, winning or outcome goals are the only worthy goals. This is psychologically destructive and illogical but occurs because of the tremendous emphasis Americans place on winning. Coaches must be aware of this problem and continually emphasize the attainment of performance and process goals. For instance, coaches must continually remind athletes that great performances will typically lead to the best possible outcomes. Finally, coaches must realize that changing their athletes' perception of the importance of outcome versus performance and process goals may take a long-term effort.

Understanding the Time Commitment Needed to Implement a Goal-Setting Program

It is not uncommon for a coach to become interested in goal setting and to begin to implement a goal-setting program with her or his athletes during the preseason or early season. However, as the season progresses, less and less time is spent on goal setting. By the end of the season the goal-setting program is all but forgotten.

Like other psychological skills, goal setting takes time to implement. It must be recognized that a good deal of commitment on the part of the coach is needed. When planning your goal-setting program, think about the busiest time of your team's season and how much time is available to commit to goal setting. It is much better to devote 20 minutes a week to goal setting throughout the season and follow through on that plan than to say you will devote 20 minutes a day to goal setting and not follow through on it. Similarly, time spent in preseason planning and organization (e.g., mass-producing goal-achievement cards and goal-evaluation forms) makes the goal-setting process much more efficient and realistic to implement.

Finally, consider program efficiency when organizing your program. One collegiate basketball coach, for example, simply had her athletes write down a practice goal on index cards for the next day's practice. The coaching staff then evaluated and provided feedback relative to these practice goals during each postpractice cool-down period. This was a time-efficient yet effective program that was easy to implement for the entire season.

Setting Only Technique-Related Goals

It is very easy to focus all of one's attention on technique-related goals (e.g., shooting statistics, faster running times). However, as previously mentioned, athletes may want to use goal setting in a number of other areas. For example, a high school volleyball coach who was having trouble with his team's cohesion found it useful to have several key players set goals of giving sincere positive feedback to teammates at least five times per practice; the team manager recorded the number of positive remarks made. Similarly, an injured runner set specific goals for the number of times per week she would practice imagery. Finally, a

football coach whose team seemed unenthusiastic and burned out at the end of a long season had considerable success asking the players to identify what elements of football were most fun for them (e.g., lineman throwing and catching the football) and then setting team goals to incorporate specified amounts of fun activities in every practice.

As I discussed earlier, a coach may also adopt a life skills approach by helping an athlete who has learned to set goals in the sport domain (e.g., to improve free throw shooting percentage by shooting 20 extra shots a day) to transfer this goal-setting ability to other life contexts (e.g., improve his or her math grades by setting a goal of studying 30 additional minutes a day).

Failing to Create a Supportive Goal-Setting Atmosphere

To reiterate, coaches and sport psychologists cannot set goals for their athletes or force them to participate in the goal-setting process. The athletes must be self-motivated and committed to the program. For this reason, the goal-setting leader needs to create a supportive goal-setting atmosphere, and in creating such an atmosphere, communication style is critical. Coaches and sport psychologists must act as facilitators of goal-setting discussions, not as dictators (Botterill, 1983). They must share limitations with athletes and identify unrealistic goals, while simultaneously avoiding pessimistic remarks and putdowns. In essence, the leader must adopt a positive communication style that includes good listening skills, a sincere orientation, and a positive approach (see Chapter 8).

Summary

This chapter has provided strong empirical and experiential support for the utility of using goal setting in helping athletes attain personal growth and peak performance. Goals are effective because they influence psychological states such as self-confidence, direct attention to important aspects of the task, mobilize effort, increase persistence, and foster the development of new learning strategies. Guidelines for effective goal setting include setting behaviorally measurable goals, difficult yet realistic goals, short-range as well as long-range goals, performance and process goals as well as outcome goals, practice and competition goals, and positive as opposed to negative goals. Equally important are identifying target dates for attaining goals, identifying goal-achievement strategies, recording goals once they have been identified, providing goal evaluation procedures, providing for goal support, and setting group goals. Lastly, common problems that arise when setting goals include setting too many goals too soon, failing to recognize individual differences, setting goals that are too general, failing to modify unrealistic goals, failing to set process and performance goals, not understanding the time and commitment needed to implement a goal-setting program, setting only technique-related goals, and failing to create a supportive goal-setting atmosphere. These problems can be easily avoided or controlled if they are recognized at the onset of the goal-setting process.

Like other psychological skills, goal setting is not a magic formula that guarantees success. Goal setting is a tool, a very effective tool, that when combined with hard work and discipline can help coaches, athletes, and sport psychologists reap the fruits of personal athletic growth and peak performance. It is highly recommended, then, that coaches and sport psychologists at all levels of competition engage in goal setting with their athletes.

Study Questions

1. Define what a goal is and differentiate between the following types of goals: (a) specific objective, (b) outcome, (c) performance, (d) process, and (e) group goals.

2. Briefly describe Locke and colleagues' (1981) mechanistic and Burton's and his colleagues cognitive explanations for the relationship between goal setting and performance.

3. Describe what is meant by saying life skill goal-setting programs teach for goal-setting transfer.

4. Think of your own sport and physical activity involvement and identify two goals you have set in the past. Evaluate your two goals relative to the 12 goal-setting guidelines presented in this chapter.

5. Describe the three phases of a goal-setting system for coaches and sport psychologists.

6. Indicate why failing to set performance and process goals is a common problem when setting goals with athletes.

7. Is it easier to adjust goals upward or downward? Explain.

8. Give an example of goal setting that is not technique related.

9. Four types of group goals have been set: individual group members' goals for themselves, the group's goals for individual members, the group's goals for the group, and individual members' goals for the group. Imagine that you are a member of a basketball team and provide an example of each type of goal. For your team to be effective, how best should these goals be related?

10. How can a coach create a supportive goal-setting atmosphere?

References

Anderson, D. C., Crowell, D. R., Doman, M., & Howard, G. S. (1988). Performance posting, goal setting, and activity-contingent praise as applied to a university hockey team, *Journal of Applied Psychology, 73,* 87–95.

Bell, K. F. (1983). *Championship thinking: The athlete's guide to winning performance in all sports.* Englewood Cliffs, NJ: Prentice Hall.

Botterill, C. (1977, September). *Goal setting and performance on an endurance task.* Paper presented at the Canadian Psychomotor Learning and Sport Psychology Conference, Banff, Alberta.

Botterill, C. (1983). Goal setting for athletes with examples from hockey. In G. L. Martin & D. Hrycaiko (Eds.), *Behavior modification and coaching: Principles, procedures, and research* (pp. 67–85). Springfield, IL: Thomas.

Burke, S. M., Shapcott, K. M., Carron, A. V., Bradshaw, M. H., & Easterbrook, P. A. (2010). *International Journal of Sport and Exercise Psychology: Group goal setting and group performance in a physical activity context,* 8, 245–261.

Burton, D. (1983). *Evaluation of goal setting training on selected cognitions and performance of collegiate swimmers.* Unpublished doctoral dissertation, University of Illinois, Urbana.

Burton, D. (1984, February). Goal setting: A secret to success. *Swimming World,* 25–29.

Burton, D. (1989). Winning isn't everything: Examining the impact of performance goals on collegiate swimmers' cognitions and performance. *The Sport Psychologist, 3,* 105–132.

Burton, D., Gillham, A., Weinberg, R., Yukelson, D., & Weigand, D. (2013). *Journal of Sport Behavior,* 36, 23–44.

Burton, D., & Naylor, S. (2002). The Jekyll/Hyde nature of goals: Revisiting and updating goal-setting in sport. In T. S. Horn (Ed.), *Advances in sport psychology* (2nd ed.) (pp. 459–499). Champaign, IL: Human Kinetics.

Burton, D., Naylor, S., & Holliday, B. (2002). Goal setting in sport. In R. N. Singer, H. A. Hausenblas, & C. M. Janelle (Eds.), *Handbook of sport psychology* (2nd ed.) (pp. 497–528). New York: John Wiley & Sons.

Burton, D., Weinberg, R., Yukelson, D., & Weigand, D. (1998). The goal effectiveness paradox in sport: Examining the goal practices of collegiate athletes. *The Sport Psychologist, 12,* 404–418.

Burton, D., & Weiss, C. (2008). The fundamental goal concept: The path to process and performance success. In T. Horn (ed.). *Advances in sport psychology* (3rd ed.) (pp. 339–375). Champaign, IL: Human Kinetics.

Carron, A. V. (1984). *Motivation: Implications for coaching and teaching.* London, ON: Sports Dynamics.

Danish, S. J., Nellen, V. C., & Owens, S. S. (1996). Teaching life skills through sport: Community-based programs for adolescents. In J. K. Van Raalte & B. W. Brewer (Eds.), *Exploring sport and exercise psychology* (pp. 205–225). Washington, DC: American Psychological Association.

Danish, S. J., Petitpas, A., & Hale, B. (1995). Psychological interventions: A life development model. In S. Murphy (Ed.), *Clinical sport psychology* (pp. 19–38). Champaign, IL: Human Kinetics.

Dawson, K. A., Bray, S. R., & Widmeyer, W. N. (2002). Goal setting by intercollegiate sport teams and athletes. *Avante, 8*(2), 14–23.

Filby, W. C. D., Maynard, I. W., & Graydon, J. K. (1999). The effect of multiple-goal strategies on performance outcomes in training and competing. *Journal of Applied Sport Psychology, 11,* 230–246.

Gould, D. (1983). Developing psychological skills in young athletes. In N. L. Wood (Ed.), *Coaching science update.* Ottawa, ON: Coaching Association of Canada.

Gould, D., Tammen, V., Murphy, S., & May, J. (1989). An examination of U. S. Olympic sport psychology consultants and the services they provide. *The Sport Psychologist, 3,* 300–312.

Hardy, L., Jones, G., & Gould, D. (1996). *Understanding psychological preparation for sport: Theory and practice of elite performers.* Chichester, UK: Wiley.

Harris, D. V., & Harris, B. L. (1984). *The athlete's guide to sports psychology: Mental skills for physical people.* New York: Leisure Press.

Holt, J. E., Kinchin, G., & Clarke, G. (2012). Effects of peer-assessed feedback, goal setting and a group contingency on performance and learning by 10 to-12-year-old academy soccer players. *Physical Education & Sport Pedagogy,* 17(3), 231–250.

Kingston, K., & Hardy, L. (1997). Effects of different types of goals on processes that support performance. *The Sport Psychologist, 11,* 277–289.

Kyllo, L. B., & Landers, D. M. (1995). Goal setting in sport and exercise: A research synthesis to resolve the controversy. *Journal of Sport and Exercise Psychology, 17,* 117–137.

Lambert, S. M., Moore, D. W., & Dixon, R. S. (1999). Gymnasts in training: The differential effects of self- and coach-set goals as a function of locus of control. *Journal of Applied Sport Psychology, 11,* 72–82.

Locke, E. A. (1991). Problems with goal-setting research in sports—and their solution. *Journal of Sport & Exercise Psychology, 8,* 311–316.

Locke, E. A. (1994). Comments on Weinberg and Weigand. *Journal of Sport & Exercise Psychology, 16,* 212–215.

Locke, E. A., & Latham, G. P. (1985). The application of goal setting to sports. *Journal of Sport Psychology, 7,* 205–222.

Locke, E. A., & Latham, G. P. (1990). *A theory of goal setting and task performance.* Englewood Cliffs, NJ: Prentice Hall.

Locke, E. A., & Latham, G. P. (2002). Building a practically useful theory of goal setting and task motivation: A 35-year odyssey. *American Psychologist, 57*(9), 705–717.

Locke, E. A., Shaw, K. N., Saari, L. M., & Latham, G. P. (1981). Goal setting and task performance. *Psychological Bulletin, 90,* 125–152.

Martens, R. (1987). *Coaches guide to sport psychology.* Champaign, IL: Human Kinetics.

McClements, J. (1982). Goal setting and planning for mental preparations. In L. Wankel & R. B. Wilberg (Eds.), Psychology of sport and motor behavior: Research and practice. *Proceedings of the Annual Conference of the Canadian Society for Psychomotor Learning and Sport Psychology* (pp. 165–172). Edmonton: University of Alberta.

Maitland, A., Gervis, N. (2010). Goal-setting in youth football. Are coaches missing an opportunity? *Physical Education & Sport Pedagogy,* 15(4), 323–343.

Mullen, R., & Hardy, L. (2010). Conscious processing and the process goal paradox. *Journal of Sport & Exercise Psychology, 32,* 275–297.

Orlick, T. (1990). *In pursuit of excellence* (2nd ed.). Champaign, IL: Human Kinetics.

Orlick, T., & Partington, J. (1988). Mental links to excellence. *The Sport Psychologist, 2,* 105–130.

Papacharisis, V. P., Goudas, M., Danish, S. J., & Theodorakis, Y. (2005). The effectiveness of teaching a life skills program in a sport context. *Journal of Applied Sport Psychology, 17*(3), 247–254.

Swain, A. B. J., & Jones, G. (1995). Goal attainment scaling: Effects of goal setting interventions on selected subcomponents on basketball performance. *Research Quarterly for Exercise & Sport, 66,* 51–63.

Tubbs, M. E. (1991). Goal setting: A meta-analytic examination of the empirical evidence. *Journal of Applied Psychology, 71,* 474–483.

Vidic, Z., & Burton, D. (2010). The roadmap: Examining the impact of a systematic goal-setting program for collegiate women's tennis. *The Sport Psychologist, 24*(4), 427–447.

Weinberg, R. S. (1994). Goal setting and performance in sport and exercise settings: A synthesis and critique. *Medicine & Science in Sport & Exercise, 26,* 469–477.

Weinberg, R. (2002). Goal setting in sport and exercise. In J. Van Raalte & B. Brewer (eds.). Exploring sport and exercise psychology. (2nd ed) (pp. 25–48), Washington, DC: American Psychological Association Press.

Weinberg, R. (2010). Making goals effective: A primer for coaches. *Journal of Sport Psychology in Action,* 1(2), 57–65.

Weinberg, R. S., Burton, D., Yukelson, D., & Weigand, D. (1993). Goal setting in competitive sport: An exploratory investigation of practices of collegiate athletes. *The Sport Psychologist, 7,* 275–289.

Weinberg, R., Burton, D., Yukelson, D., & Weigand, D. (2000). Perceived goal setting practices of Olympic athletes: An exploratory investigation. *The Sport Psychologist, 14,* 279–295.

Weinberg, R., Butt, J., & Knight, B. (2001). High school coaches' perceptions of the process of goal setting. *The Sport Psychologist, 15,* 20–47.

Weinberg, R., Butt, J., Knight, B., & Perritt, N. (2001). Collegiate coaches' perceptions of their goal-setting practices: A qualitative investigation. *Journal of Applied Sport Psychology, 13,* 374–398.

Weinberg, R. S., & Gould, D. (2011). *Foundations of sport and exercise psychology* (5th edition). Champaign, IL: Human Kinetics.

Weinberg, R. S., & Weigand, D. (1996). Let the discussions continue: A reaction to Locke's comments on Weinberg and Weigand. *Journal of Sport & Exercise Psychology, 18,* 89–93.

Widmeyer, W. N., & Ducharme, K. (1997). Team building through team goal setting. *Journal of Applied Sport Psychology, 9,* 61–72.

Wanlin, C. M., Hrycaiko, D. W., Martin, G. L., & Mahon, M. (1997). The effects of a goal-setting package on the performance of speed skaters. *Journal of Applied Sport Psychology, 9*(2), 212–228.

Understanding and Managing Stress in Sport

Sheldon Hanton, *Cardiff Metropolitan University, UK*
Stephen Mellalieu, *Swansea University, UK*
Jean M. Williams, *University of Arizona, Emeritus*

"Nerves can be brilliant because they get your adrenalin going and it means you care and want to do well. There's a fine line, though. Getting too nervous can ruin a race and that's happened to me. . . . After Beijing the 800m took a bit of a dip and it became this challenge. I just got so nervous and so worked up that I literally dived in and I completely stiffened up. I'd never experienced it before. The whole way through the race I didn't feel myself and it was that moment where I learnt I had to relax. I realized there was no point in harming myself, getting that nervous, and that I had to just chill out and enjoy the experience."

—Rebecca Adlington, 2012, Double Olympic, World, European and Commonwealth Swimming Champion.

The potential for high levels of stress in elite sport and the challenges associated with the environments that surround the modern day athlete are widely acknowledged. Indeed, an integral element of an athlete's preparation program will include some form of stress management with the goal to achieve an optimal mental and physical state ready to perform, together with an armory of strategies ready to cope with any challenges that may present themselves during competition.

This chapter aims to describe sports psychologists' contemporary understanding of stress, outline the various ways in which stress manifests itself in sport, and the process through which stress is proposed to influence performance. The remainder of the chapter then provides an overview of the major skills and strategies that sport psychologists and coaches can utilize to help athletes successfully manage stress.

Cognitive-Behavioral Stress Management in Sport Psychology

Contemporary approaches to understanding stressful encounters experienced by athletes in and around the environment in which they compete frequently adopt a cognitive-behavioral focus, that is, one that seeks to change cognitions and thought patterns to influence behavior (i.e., performance). The most popular cognitive approach used in sport psychology is Lazarus' (1991) cognitive motivational relational theory (CMRT). CMRT describes the experience of stress as an ongoing evaluation or appraisal by an athlete of the demands faced in relation to themselves and their surrounding environment (i.e., the relationship between the individual and the environment). An athlete's view of a potentially stressful situation, known as a stress appraisal, will usually focus on whether threat, harm/loss, or challenge is to be experienced. The athlete will evaluate that situation (termed a primary appraisal) to determine if the demands faced are likely to be stressful, and subsequently whether the athlete views that they possess the necessary physical and mental resources to deal with the stress and the likely outcomes that will ensue (secondary or further appraisal of the situation). Threat is experienced when resources are perceived as insufficient to meet the demands of the situation and that threat elevates the more the individual perceives dire consequences for failure to meet the demands.

Central to CMRT is the concept of "transaction" and the specific relational-meaning interpreted by the athlete operating in a particular sporting environment. Transaction refers to the dynamic relationship that exists between the demands of the environment an individual faces and the resources they possess to deal with it (see Example 1). Relational meaning describes the meaning a person interprets from their relationship with this environment. Based on these views and the resultant physical changes that occur in the body due to the stress process the individual will then attempt to manage the situation accordingly. Under the cognitive-behavioral approach to stress management athletes are taught to utilize cognitive, affective, and behavioral strategies to cope with the specific internal or external demands faced in sport.

Consider a professional tennis player competing in a match at a major championship in front of a large audience against a highly ranked opponent whom they have never beaten. The athlete may initially evaluate the demands faced (major championship, high ranked opponent, large audience) as threatening and out of their control (primary appraisal of the situation), become anxious and, consequently, suffer performance decrements in the match. In the break between games, the player reflects again on their emotional state (further appraisal of the situation), identifies the cause of their symptoms, and subsequently addresses how to cope with the situation and their emotions. During the next game, the athlete may now think and behave (i.e., perform) more effectively as a result of this continued ongoing process of further appraisal.

Causes of and Responses to Stress

Before deciding on appropriate stress management strategies to recommend to athletes it is important to understand what factors may cause stress in sport (i.e., the demands faced) and how athletes typically respond to the stress experienced.

Causes of Stress

The intense physical and psychological demands (also known as stressors) athletes face when competing in sport come from a range of sources relating to competition, organization, and personal factors that exist within their environment (see Fletcher, Hanton, & Mellalieu, 2006).

- Competitive stressors are the demands primarily and directly associated with competitive performance (e.g., the level of physical preparation attained; the standard of the opponent; the internal and external pressures and expectations to perform).

- Organization stressors are the demands associated primarily and directly with the sports organization (e.g., the performer's role in the sport organization; sport relationships and interpersonal demands).

- Personal stressors are the demands associated primarily and directly with the personal life of the individual(s) (e.g., lifestyle issues, financial demands, the relationships with family or significant others).

Responses to Stress

In addition to understanding the demands athletes face it is also important to recognize the mental and physical symptoms that these demands produce.

Arousal and activation.   **Arousal** refers to a generalized physiological and psychological activation of the person with neural excitation varying on a continuum from deep sleep to extreme excitement. It serves an energizing function and thus reflects the intensity level of motivation and is nondirective. Whether the arousal starts with a thought or an external stimulus, the result is autonomic nervous system responses such as increased heart and respiration rates, butterflies in the stomach, muscle tension, and sweating. **Activation** is used synonymously with the term arousal, and it also refers to the overall physical and mental state that is required by an athlete **to be ready to perform** a respective task or activity (Hardy, Jones, & Gould, 1996; p. 118).

If increases in an athlete's levels of arousal or overall activation state come from experiencing high stress when competing in sport, or preparing to compete, one of the products of this process, physical tension, in particular can have immediate and powerful effects on an athlete. For example, when a muscle tenses up due to worry and anxiety, or trying too hard, it contracts or is shortened. This is due to the voluntary muscles in humans being arranged in pairs. When a muscle tightens because of perceived stress, its opposite sets up a counter tension to hold the segment of the body in place. The resulting double pull can build up formidable heights of tension over much of the body, yet most people will not identify it. This double pull explains why a person can be scared stiff and rigid with anger or unable to move because of fright. It also explains

why an athlete shoots air balls, misses a short putt, passes with too much force, or over hits a tennis ball. The principle of the double pull, sometimes referred to as **bracing,** has great significance for the athlete. When excessive muscular tension occurs, it interferes with execution of the skill because it prevents appropriately coordinating movement (see Exercise 1). Proper form in any movement involves using just the right amount of tension at any given time in the relevant muscles. Athletes can learn the right amount of contraction, that is, to expend only those energies necessary to execute the skill. This is called **differential relaxation.**

Exercise 1 Illustrates how excessive tension disrupts speed and coordination

Rest your dominant forearm and hand palm down on a desk or tabletop. Tense all the muscles in the hand and fingers and then try to alternately tap the index and middle fingers back and forth as quickly as possible. Relax all the muscles in the forearm and hand and repeat the exercise.

Competitive anxiety.   The typical emotion associated with the experience of **stress** in sport is competitive anxiety. Competitive anxiety is a situation-specific negative (unpleasant) emotional response to one's view of competitive stressors, and the general involvement in competition, as threats (Martens, Vealey, & Burton, 1990). The competitive anxiety response may include symptoms such as worry, together with a heightened perception of one's physiological state or level of arousal. These two distinct responses represent the mental (cognitive) and perceived physical (somatic) components of anxiety.

Cognitive anxiety responses represent the thoughts experienced in stressful situations and include worries, negative expectations, and apprehensions about performance (i.e., mental responses to stressors). Somatic responses represent an athlete's perceptions of their physiological arousal state in stressful environments (i.e., perceived physical response to stressors). Somatic anxiety symptoms include factors such as muscular tension, butterflies in the stomach, increased heart rate, dry mouth, cold and clammy hands, and perspiration.

Differences exist in how competitive anxiety is experienced in relation to the individual (personal) and the environment in which they compete (situational). These factors include the athlete's gender, skill level, and type of sport performed (see Mellalieu, Hanton, & Fletcher, 2006 for a review). For example, female athletes' cognitive anxiety experiences are predicted by their perceptions of readiness to perform and the importance of doing well. In contrast, males' cognitive anxiety responses are predicted by perceptions of their opponents' ability in relation to themselves and their perceived likelihood of winning (Jones, Swain, & Cale, 1991).

Although competitive stressors might lead athletes to experience some type of anxiety response, the potential effect is not inherently negative. For example, one athlete might perceive a racing heart as a positive "psyched-up" feeling while another appraises the same anxiety symptom as negative nervousness. Hanton and Jones (1999) identified a large body of research that has consistently identified that certain athletes have the ability, or have learned over time, the skills that enable them to interpret their negative anxiety symptoms as necessary and beneficial toward performance (see Example 2) whereas others see such symptoms as detrimental. The expression of getting one's butterflies to "fly in formation" illustrates having positive interpretation skills.

"I discovered the symptoms helped me psych up for races. If you knew the nerves were there the adrenaline would flow and make me perform better . . . concentrate harder. They (the symptoms) would make me concentrate on the race . . . help me prepare to swim fast . . . to get off the blocks quickly, get in the pool and swim fast."

(Quote from an Olympic Swimmer describing how they interpreted their symptoms as positive and the subsequent effects on their concentration efforts and performance, cited in Hanton & Jones, 1999, p. 10.)

The preceding distinctions highlight the importance of examining not just the athletes' anxiety symptoms and their intensity, but also whether they interpret their anxiety responses as having a facilitative or debilitative effect on their performance. In essence, interpretation of the direction of the anxiety effect represents a further appraisal of the initial symptoms experienced. In line with the cognitive-behavioral approach to stress management, the key message for sport psychologists is to understand that how athletes evaluate and appraise the symptoms they experience will influence subsequent efforts and strategies toward maintaining optimal performance states.

Studies have also found some important individual attributes that are related to having a positive interpretation of anxiety symptoms. For example, athletes who view competitive anxiety symptoms as having a beneficial effect on performance demonstrate better overall performance standards, are higher in skill level, feel more in control, exhibit higher levels of self-confidence, demonstrate a more resilient personality, and are more experienced and highly competitive when compared to those who interpret anxiety symptoms as more negative toward performance (see Wagstaff, Neil, Mellalieu, & Hanton, 2011 for a review).

Given this association with better performance and desirable personal qualities, applied researchers have sought to identify and explore the factors that enable athletes to achieve a positive interpretation of their competitive anxiety symptoms. This research has been undertaken with the explicit aim of informing the structure and content of possible stress management programs and has helped construct the interventions used within the restructuring approach described later in the chapter. Further, athletes with a positive interpretation of their anxiety consistently suggest the application of strategies that help them appraise their symptoms in a positive way are most valuable to their performance preparation. The important psychological strategies involved in this approach are self-regulatory skills that provide a sense of perceived control over oneself and one's environment enabling maintenance of high self-confidence to protect against negative anxiety interpretation.

Measurement of Stress-Related Symptoms

Prior to practitioners providing any form of intervention, an accurate assessment of the experiences of the stress process, and its consequences, should be undertaken. Here, sport psychologists typically adopt a combined approach to assess the demands (i.e., stressors) perceived and the context in which these demands occur, how mentally and physically anxious an athlete may be (the level or intensity of anxiety symptoms), associated physiological responses (i.e., arousal level), and whether the athlete views the symptoms experienced as having a beneficial or detrimental influence on performance (directional interpretation of symptom effects). This assessment often uses a combination of validated psychometric questionnaires alongside interviewing procedures with the athlete in question and sometimes their coaches or support staff.

Questionnaires assess athletes' typical and situation-specific anxiety responses to competition (i.e., their trait and state anxiety respectively). **Trait anxiety** is a general predisposition to respond across many situations with high levels of anxiety because of typically appraising situations as threatening (i.e., individuals rate how they generally feel). **State anxiety** is more specific (i.e., rate how they feel "right now"); it varies from moment-to-moment and fluctuates proportionately to the perceived threat of a situation (Spielberger, 1966). Individuals high in trait anxiety are expected to respond with elevated state anxiety. A common trait anxiety measure is the Sport Anxiety Scale-2 (SAS-2; Smith, Smoll, Cumming, & Grossbard, 2006). It has a somatic scale and two cognitive scales (worry, concentration disruption). The revised Competitive State Anxiety Inventory-2 (CSAI-2; Cox, Martens, & Russell, 2003) assesses the intensity of state cognitive and somatic anxiety symptoms as well as self-confidence. In addition, modified CSAI-2 scales exist (e.g., Jones & Swain, 1992) that add subscales to assess directional interpretation of anxiety symptoms.

One note of caution regarding these psychometric scales is that their use in applied settings is often intrusive due to their format, length, and time to complete (see Krane, 1994). Brief self-report measures are an alternative that allows examination of anxiety symptoms experienced closer to and, in certain non-continuous sports, during competition. These include scales such as the Anxiety Rating Scale (ARS-2; Cox, Robb, & Russell, 1999), Mental Readiness Form (MRF; Krane, 1994), and Immediate Anxiety Measurement Scale (IAMS; Thomas, Hanton, & Jones, 2002). All adopt a brief and simple response format. For example, the MRF has three 1–11 point scales with anchors of "calm-worried," "relaxed-tense" and "confident-scared," respectively, for assessment of "My thoughts are," "My body feels" and "I am feeling."

An additional consideration when using anxiety questionnaires is that not all individuals are willing to give open and honest responses. Particularly problematic are athletes with a repressive coping style. Repressors represent individuals who "avoid disturbing cognitions in an attempt to minimize distress and negative emotions . . . [and] typically deny having elevated levels of anxiety even though their behavior and physiological symptoms suggest otherwise" (Williams & Krane, 1992; p. 136). Thus, a repressor would report low anxiety levels when they are, in fact, quite high; making questionable any determination of the anxiety-performance relationship and its intervention implications.

For all athletes, and particularly so for probable repressors, sport psychologists should seek a comprehensive range of assessment strategies to fully diagnose stress experiences in addition to psychometric assessment. For example, sport psychologists may ask athletes to record their stress-related symptoms in some form of diary or logbook (would not work for repressors) and may observe and record the athlete's behavior in-vivo. Here, the use of digital video technology and match analysis techniques can facilitate objective observation and assessment of player behavior during training and competition and form the basis of a post-event evaluation interview.

Data from measurement of physiological arousal such as heart rate, blood pressure, muscle tension (electromyography), and sweating (skin conductance) would be helpful, and particularly so with repressors. If the equipment and monetary resources are available, brain wave data and the measurement of epinephrine, norepinephrine, and corticosteroids (all released into the bloodstream during stress) could be undertaken. One limitation with physiological assessment of the stress response is the notion of response stereotypy (Lacey, 1967). Specifically, in the same stressful situation, one athlete might display an increase in blood pressure, and another might show an elevated heart rate. Consequently, an athlete's most relevant physiological response to stressful encounters needs to be identified to enable the most meaningful collection of information.

Following this comprehensive assessment of the stress experiences of an athlete in and around competition, and the subsequent behavioral/performance outcomes that ensue, sport psychologists collate and analyze the information. This information then underpins the selection of a relevant treatment framework for the athlete.

Explaining the Relationship of Stress to Performance

Before recommending the implementation of appropriate stress management interventions, a final consideration is to understand the various approaches that sport psychologists have adopted to describe and explain the effects of stress, and related constructs, upon performance and how these have influenced the development of intervention strategies. These stress-performance explanations are grouped around three themes: early arousal-based approaches, contemporary anxiety theories, and mechanistic explanations.

Early Arousal-Based Approaches

Sport psychologists initially referred to the arousal-based concepts of drive theory and the inverted-U hypothesis to describe the stress or arousal–performance relationship (see Woodman & Hardy, 2001, for a review). According to drive theory (Spence & Spence, 1966), increases in drive or arousal are associated with linear increases in performance providing that the task is well learned, that is, the dominant response of the athlete is the correct one. Drive theory is no longer used because neither research nor anecdotal evidence supports its premise.

Alternatively, the inverted-U hypothesis (Yerkes & Dodson, 1908) describes the relationship between arousal and performance through an inverted-U function. Increases in arousal from drowsiness to alertness result in progressive performance gains up to an optimal level of arousal, beyond which increases in arousal result in progressive performance decrements (see Figure 12-1).

The characteristics of the task and the performer determine the optimal level of arousal. Tasks that are complex, that are high in decisional demands, or that require fine motor skills for precision and steadiness benefit from lower levels of arousal for optimal performance whereas simple tasks, gross motor skills, and strength and speed tasks benefit from higher levels of arousal. For example, the desirable mental and physical state to demonstrate readiness to perform as a target rifle shooter is very different from the state of readiness needed to perform well as a weight lifter—composure, accuracy, and calmness are key factors within the fine muscular control event of target shooting, whereas strength, power, and assertiveness are key determinants of performance within the gross muscular activity of weight lifting. In terms of individual difference factors, athletes with higher skill levels, more experience in the competitive setting, good stress-coping skills, lower trait anxiety, or an extroverted personality can handle higher arousal levels without performance deficits in contrast to those with the opposite profile (see Figure 12-2).

With the inverted-U approach, the challenge is for the athlete to determine what level of arousal (usually a range) typically leads to best performance on a given task and to then try to reproduce this arousal state more consistently from one competition to the next, thus the need to know

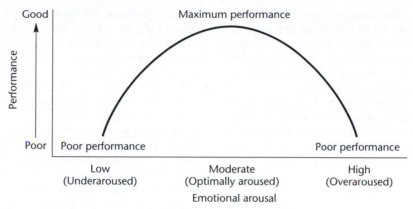

Figure 12-1 **The inverted-U relationship between arousal and performance**

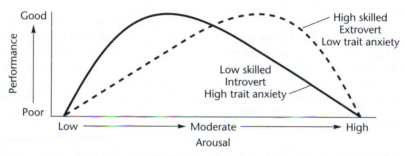

Figure 12-2 **Individual difference factors and optimal levels of arousal**

how to raise or reduce levels of arousal accordingly (see Exercise 2). Although the inverted-U hypothesis provides some useful information for determining arousal level and interventions, it is too simplistic and has too many limitations (e.g., fails to consider cognitive anxiety and its interaction with arousal) to be used solely in explaining the stress–performance relationship or for prescribing stress management strategies.

Exercise 2 Estimating optimal arousal levels for given tasks

Select 6-8 different sport skills (avoid global activities such as basketball or tennis) and rank their optimal arousal level (use 1–5 scale with 1 = low) by

analyzing factors such as number of muscle actions to execute and amount of coordination, fine versus gross motor, precision and steadiness versus strength and speed, and decision characteristics (number of, alternatives, speed to make).

Contemporary Anxiety Theories

In an attempt to more accurately describe the stress and performance relationship, sport psychologists have developed theories and models from investigations grounded within actual experiences of competing in sport.

Zone of optimal functioning. The first, the zone of optimal functioning (ZOF) hypothesis

(Hanin, 1980, 1986) is seen as a practical tool for helping an athlete establish his or her individual optimal levels of pre-performance anxiety, within which performance levels are proposed to be greatest. If, however, anxiety levels are outside of the optimal zone, performance will not occur at maximum levels. This idiographic method has received some support in the sport psychology literature that has adopted a multidimensional perspective on anxiety and does offer practical significance as an applied tool that is intuitively appealing to athletes regarding the notion of "getting in the zone" and reducing or raising symptoms accordingly. However, the ZOF hypothesis has been criticized for its lack of explanation as to why individual levels of cognitive and somatic anxiety may be optimal or detrimental for performance (see Woodman & Hardy, 2001). More contemporary approaches have also sought to apply the ZOF approach across wider emotional experiences in and around competition using an individualized zone of optimal functioning (IZOF; Hanin, 2000) perspective, which appears to have broader appeal as concept and applied technique. See Chapter 9 for a more detailed discussion of this approach.

Multidimensional anxiety theory. This theory (MAT, Martens et al., 1990) makes distinctions between competitive state cognitive and somatic anxiety on the premise that they have different antecedents and relationships to performance. Somatic anxiety is predicted to display an inverted-U relationship with performance and cognitive anxiety a negative linear relationship (i.e., as cognitive anxiety increases, performance progressively deteriorates). Thus, like the IZOF approach, MAT suggests that an appropriate level of somatic anxiety can have positive performance effects, but not so for cognitive anxiety. These symptoms should always be reduced. MAT also considers self-confidence and its relationship with performance. Although self-confidence is not a component of competitive anxiety, it is proposed to exhibit a positive linear association with performance (i.e., parallel increases in self-confidence and performance occur). MAT has received only

partial support in the sport psychology literature, potentially due to the fact it does not consider the beneficial effects of cognitive anxiety on performance and, according to Woodman and Hardy (2001), because it fails to consider the interactive effects of the competitive anxiety subcomponents upon performance.

Cusp catastrophe model. To overcome some of the existing limitations with MAT, the cusp catastrophe model of anxiety and performance (Hardy, 1990) describes the interactive effects of cognitive anxiety and physiological arousal (as opposed to somatic anxiety) on performance (Figure 12-3). Specifically, cognitive anxiety determines whether the effect of physiological arousal on performance will be smooth and small, large and catastrophic, or somewhere in between the two extremes (Woodman & Hardy, 2001).

In contrast to MAT, therefore, the catastrophe model suggests that elevations in cognitive anxiety can have positive performance consequences dependent upon the levels of physiological arousal. For example, when cognitive anxiety levels are low, variations in physiological arousal

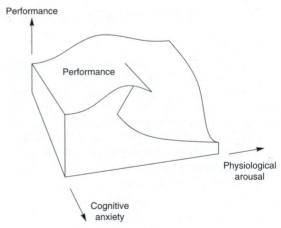

Figure 12-3　**Cusp catastrophe model of anxiety and performance (Hardy, 1990), describing the interactive effects of cognitive anxiety and physiological arousal on performance**

will lead to small performance effects character-ized by an inverted-U type relationship. Under high cognitive anxiety conditions, increasing physiological arousal will, up to a threshold, lead to positive effects on performance. However, continued increases in physiological arousal beyond this threshold are proposed to result in a "catastrophic" drop in performance.

While support for the initial cusp catastro-phe model has been mixed, subsequent adap-tations to include additional factors on the anxiety–performance relationship have proved more fruitful. Hardy and colleagues (1990; Hardy & Parfitt, 1991) have proposed five-dimensional, higher-order butterfly catastrophe models that include additional factors such as self-confidence and the difficulty of the task demands (see also Hardy, Beattie, & Woodman, 2007). For example, increased self-confidence allows athletes to toler-ate higher levels of physiological arousal when mentally anxious before suffering a decrement in performance (Hardy, Woodman, & Carrington, 2004). The implications for practitioners from the higher order butterfly catastrophe model highlight the importance of having suitable strat-egies and skills to be able to enhance or main-tain (protect) levels of self-confidence in order to enable successful stress management.

Mechanistic Explanations

Although the cusp catastrophe model gives a clear explanation for the relationship between stress and performance, it provides insight only into what may occur. In reality, the model and the theories discussed so far do not fully explain the mechanisms by which stress and its associ-ated response, competitive anxiety, influence performance. A number of approaches are dis-cussed here which attempt to explain the stress and performance relationship and the implica-tions for sport psychology practice.

Processing efficiency theory.   The first of these approaches, Eysenck and Calvo's (1992) process-ing efficiency theory (PET), has been used by Hardy and associates (Hardy et al., 2007; Hardy & Parfitt, 1991) to explain the debilitating and facilitating effects of cognitive anxiety on per-formance described by catastrophe models. PET suggests that when a person is anxious, a pro-portion of their attentional capacity for the task is filled by task-irrelevant cognitive worry, effec-tively reducing their working memory capacity, impairing cognitive processing efficiency and, potentially, performance. It is also worth noting that cognitive anxiety or worry may also signal the importance of the task to the individual and lead to an increased investment in the task. For example, many athletes suggest being "nervous" means the race or match is important and leads them to focus more intently and try harder with regards to subsequent preparation for/execution of performance.

Attentional control theory.   An extension to PET is that of attentional control theory (ACT, Eysenck, Derakshan, Santos, & Calvo, 2007), which explains how anxiety affects attention and perfor-mance. Specifically, anxiety impairs the efficiency of attention because it causes a shift in attention to threat-related stimuli rather than toward task and goal relevant information, thereby negatively affecting performance. The inability to exercise attentional control may, however, be compen-sated for by inhibition and shifting functions that stop the effect of the threat-related stimuli and shift attentional resources to task demands. Therefore, while anxiety influences efficiency (the relationship between effective task performance and the use of attentional resources) it does not influence effectiveness (outcome in terms of per-formance accuracy).

Support for both PET and ACT has been estab-lished in sport (e.g., Hardy et al., 2007; Nieuwen-huys, Pijpers, Oudejans, & Bakker, 2008; Wilson, Smith, Chattington, Ford, & Marple-Horvat, 2006; Wilson, Wood, & Vine, 2009) with both theo-ries assuming there is a fundamental distinction between performance effectiveness (quality of per-formance) and processing efficiency (the relation-ship between performance effectiveness and use of processing resources), and that anxiety impairs processing efficiency more than performance effectiveness. The implication for sport psychologists here is that the experience of high levels of cognitive anxiety are not inherently negative and that it can serve to motivate athletes to increase effort to prevent their anxiety from impairing performance, but at the expense of using a greater amount of their available concentration (attentional) resources.

Conscious processing hypothesis. A final theory of attentional processes is the conscious processing hypothesis (Masters, 1992, CPH). CPH attempts to explain the mechanisms underlying anxiety-induced performance decrements. Here, a high-anxious performer starts to use excessive thinking (reinvestment), which leads to the execution of skills with an inward attention that in turn can lead to a failure to execute the skill successfully (Masters & Maxwell, 2008; Weiss, 2011), a process that is commonly referred to as "paralysis by analysis." That is, skills that are normally undertaken with little or no thought become disrupted due to the skilled athlete trying to "consciously" control the movement. In doing so, the athlete is adopting a mode of control based on explicit or declarative knowledge (i.e., factual knowledge) that is associated with early stages of learning of a skill (Gucciardi & Dimmock, 2008). The implication for sports psychologists is that attempts to solely focus on encouraging athletes to exert conscious control over previously automated skills will cause performance impairments whereby anxiety may induce regression from implicit/automatic control to explicit/verbal control.

The attentional-based mechanistic explanations for the anxiety performance relationship are most closely related to the concept of "choking" in sport. Indeed, choking is a term that is frequently cited in the media to label unexpected or sudden failures in athletic performance due to anxiety when performing under high-pressure situations. Extremely high arousal and anxiety symptoms and the feeling that the harder one tries the worse one's performance characterize choking.

Generally, researchers agree that choking is the product of misguided attention control combined with elevated arousal and anxiety. Specifically, it is caused by concern with excessive self-consciousness and the mechanics of skill execution. Chapter 16 presents a detailed consideration of choking and specific choking prevention techniques.

Implications for Stress Management Interventions

As discussed in the preceding sections, many different explanations have been forwarded in an attempt to describe or explain the effect of the typical symptoms associated with stress (i.e., competitive anxiety and arousal) upon performance. These explanations have implications for potential interventions, with the result that interventions have typically been grouped into one of three approaches adopted by sport psychology practitioners. The first perspective is that when elevated arousal and competitive anxiety has a detrimental effect on performance, it requires a **reduction** approach to reduce the symptoms associated with stress. The second perspective is based on the principle that high levels of anxiety and arousal associated with an athlete's stress experience need not be detrimental, but may be interpreted in a positive way that actually benefits sport performance. Under these conditions anxiety is viewed as a signal that indicates the presence of threat and stimulates action including heightened attention, planning, motivation, and effort toward managing the demands placed upon them (i.e., the coping processes). This notion is fundamental to the **restructuring** approach to stress management in which athletes are taught to restructure interpretations of symptoms from a negative to a positive viewpoint (i.e., debilitative to facilitative). The third and final perspective describes circumstances whereby athletes possess an insufficient activation state in relation to their sporting task or activity (i.e., under arousal). Here, sport psychologists may consider increasing arousal levels to perform an **energizing** function to enhance performance.

The preceding approaches, which are the ones typically used in the management of the experiences of stress in sport, fall under an "emotion-focused" coping umbrella. Emotion-focused coping reflects coping efforts to regulate the emotional and associated responses (e.g., anxiety and arousal) that emanate from the problem causing the stress (i.e., the stressors). We describe many such interventions later in the chapter. Although used less often, another effective strategy for managing stress is that of problem-focused coping. It involves efforts to prevent or manage the stressful demands the individual experiences. Teaching individuals a range of both emotion- and problem-focused strategies would best prepare them to cope with stress and subsequently produce effective behavior and performance.

Stress Management Skills and Strategies: Preventative Approaches

Problem-focused or preventative strategies to manage competition stress involve efforts that deal with the stressor causing the symptoms as a way to bring relief. Problem-focused strategies aim to possibly **remove** or more likely reduce the stressor by targeting the causes of stress in practical ways that tackle the issue, consequently directly reducing the stress and providing a long-term solution to stress management. They work, however, only when the athlete is able to exert some control over eradicating the stressor. When not possible, emotion-focused coping strategies are more appropriate treatments. Examples of problem-focused strategies appropriate for sport include advice seeking, information gathering, planning, problem solving, and proactive behavior.

Advice-seeking. This is a process of seeking support from an individual, group of individuals, or organization in an attempt to cope with a stressor. Social support helps to provide relief from stress, increase perception of control over events, and reduce susceptibility to illness (Holt & Hoar, 2006). Having good social support means being involved in social relationships,

feeling connected with other people, and feeling understood and cared for. Social support provides individuals with tangible assistance, information, and emotional support. Tangible and informational support offer specific information and direction to an athlete to thrive in a competitive setting while caring and emotional support provides a valuable sense of being understood and appreciated. In sport, this may take the form of athletes asking a coach, support staff or management personnel, fellow athlete, friends or family for advice with regard to how to manage the competition stress they are experiencing. Athletes can be encouraged to engage in social support activities (sharing problems) with others and generally seek to build up their support networks. For example, a young professional soccer player struggling to perform in their first season may be encouraged to seek an "elder" on the team who can empathize and share personal experiences of the challenges faced in being a rookie athlete. While everyone needs social support, athletes in individual sports in particular may lack the large social support resources typically found in team sports. This may leave them vulnerable to stress when the pressure mounts, meaning it is especially important to ensure they have suitable support networks.

Information gathering. Here athletes actively seek information regarding a stressor they are faced with in order to empower themselves with the knowledge to determine how best to cope. In sport, a common competition stressor is concerns around one's opposition or opponent. Problem-focused information gathering in this respect would involve athletes undertaking an analysis of their future or past opposition. By gathering information and familiarizing himself with an opponent's tactics and strategies the athlete becomes more informed, in control of his performance, and able to perceive (appraise) the opposition as less of a threat than before the information was available. Similar problem-focused approaches can be adopted to deal with other competition and organization stressors such as practicing at a novel or difficult venue in advance of competition or holding pre-competition training camps in order to familiarize athletes and teams with their new environment.

Planning. Planning is the process of thinking about the activities required to achieve a desired goal on some scale. Depending upon the activities, a plan can be long, intermediate, or short range. Planning is synonymous with goal setting and helps facilitate goal achievement and growth both in personal and performance terms. In sport a common example of planning to prevent or manage stress is a pre-competition plan. Pre-competition plans are essentially global competition preparation strategies. They typically are comprised of a sequence of process-orientated goals (Hardy et al., 1996) that provide a simple way to help focus on priority sources of information and key aspects of performance; and in this case preparation for performance—whether technical or emotional. In order to develop a competition plan, athletes should first perform a retrospective analysis of what they did and what they felt prior to their best and worst performances. The athlete is then helped to use these profiles to construct a pre-competition plan (see Figure 12-4). The plan should specify what the athlete should do: the day before the event; when preparing to leave for the competition; arrival at the competition site; during the warm up and the countdown to performing; and during the event itself.

It is important to make the plan specific to the athlete in question, using the time scales or significant moments/critical incidents that they see as meaningful in achieving optimal preparation in their lead up to competition. Further sensitivity to the athlete's idiosyncrasies can be developed by considering the relevant or desired cognitions (thoughts), emotions (feelings), and behaviors (performances) experienced across these significant moments. Once constructed, pre-competition plans can be tested out, revised, and modified as desired. Visual reminders can be kept as hard copies (in kit bags or on changing room/accommodation walls or lockers) or in electronic format (mobile devices, tablets) to provide forms of reinforcement.

	Night Before	Competition Day	Travel & Arrival At Venue	Pre-Race Warm-Up	On The Track
	24 Hr To Start	3 Hr To Start	2 Hr To Start	45 Min To Start	10 Min To Start
Doing	Watch TV Pack Kit Bag Stretch & Nutrition	Keep Busy Watch TV	Listen to IPod Get Used to the Facilities Walk Around Track	Race Drills Personal Warm-Up	Quiet 5 minutes Breathing Routine
Thinking	Relax	Keep Mind Occupied with Nonathletics Things	Begin Thinking Through Each Part of My Race (Start/Middle/End)	Getting Feet on Track Getting Sharp	Visualize/Think About My Race Think Positive
Feeling	Relaxed	Calm	Confident	Sharp Big & Powerful	Confident & Big

Figure 12-4 **Example of a pre-competition plan for a track and field athlete**

Problem solving. Problem solving refers to the athlete sitting down to think about possible solutions to a problem with which they are confronted (i.e., experiencing competition stress). Consider an athlete who has become anxious about his or her ability to sink free throws during the crucial moments of the game. A problem-solving strategy would be to think about a course of action to cope with the potential stressor, such as working out a new practice regime or speaking to the coach or sport psychologist about a technical element of their pre-shot routine. Problem solving would not be the act of going to the coach or engaging in the practice itself, but rather the thought process involved in arriving at a solution to the problem. To facilitate problem solving, athletes can be encouraged to:

- Identify the problem—an athlete can't manage their stress unless they know what's causing it.

- Break the problem down into specific parts—describe all elements. Who and what are involved? Where and when does it happen? How do they react?

- List all the possible solutions, decide what they want out of the situation, and think about ways to solve problem. Ask these questions: Can they change the stressful situation? Can they avoid it? Can they change how they respond?

- Explore the consequences of each solution—look at the pros and cons for each option. How does it make them feel? What affect will it have on the other people involved? What are the short-term and long-term consequences? Do the benefits outweigh the costs? Choose the solution that promises the best outcome.

- Set the course—write down the plan, discuss/revise it with a trusted coach, support staff member, or fellow team member.

- Go for it and take some time to reflect in detail on what helped and what didn't.

Proactive behavior. This is the engagement of forms of coping in advance to prevent or mute the influence of events that are potential future stressors. Proactive behaviors comprise the building up of a reserve of personal coping resources, recognizing potential stressors, initially appraising the stressors, and preliminary coping efforts seeking and using feedback about the success of one's efforts. Athletes who are proactive take responsibility for their training and performance rather than looking for causes in other circumstances or people. They seek to develop all areas of their performance through learning new skills and knowledge in relation to their physical (new strength and conditioning regimes), technical, and tactical (keeping up to date with new styles of play, rule, or law changes), emotional (seeking new social support networks), and holistic resources (managing and organizing non-sport demands). Proactivity is distinct from action taking in that the latter refers to taking actions in the present to cope with a problem whereas proactive behavior refers to the future, taking actions to prevent future negative outcome.

Stress Management Skills and Strategies: Reduction Approaches

Interventions that seek to **reduce** physiological arousal and the intensity of competition anxiety symptoms can be classified broadly into **muscle-to-mind** and **mind-to-muscle** approaches. Muscle-to-mind techniques focus on the bodily aspects and include breathing exercises and progressive relaxation (PR). Mind-to-muscle strategies focus on efferent nerve control, or the stimulation from the brain to the muscles, and include meditation, visualization, and autogenic training. Reviews of research findings clearly indicate the effectiveness of these relaxation techniques in enhancing sport performance (see the meta-analysis by Meyers, Whelan, & Murphy, 1996).

Overall, treatments attempt to target or **match** the dominant anxiety symptoms experienced in stressful situations (Davidson & Schwartz, 1976), as greater reduction in muscular problems follows muscular interventions and symptoms that primarily involve cognitive processes tend to respond particularly well to cognitive therapies or mind-to-muscle strategies. When anxiety problems manifest themselves equally cognitively and somatically, the most effective intervention integrates physical and cognitive techniques. Fortunately, interventions for one aspect of anxiety often impact the other, that is, reducing somatic symptoms can have a similar reducing effect on cognitive symptoms just as interventions aimed at reducing cognitive symptoms can have a corollary effect on somatic symptoms. Also note that reduction techniques are less likely to be needed when the activation demands for a given sport skill are high, as discussed earlier, compared to when activation demands are low. In fact, using them may have a detrimental effect on performance if it lowers activation below the levels appropriate for the optimal execution of the task and for the given individual.

Normally, techniques such as thought stopping, positive thought control, and cognitive restructuring would also be presented as alternative techniques for reducing cognitive symptoms, and these techniques are covered in Chapter 14. The relaxation skills in this chapter are described as a series of logical and progressive steps. To help athletes acquire the skills in question, sport psychologists regularly adopt a common learning framework that follows phases:

• The athlete learns the skill fundamentals in a comfortable position while in a quiet, warm stress-free environment, working closely with the practitioner.

• Increasing independence from the practitioner, the athlete becomes more self-directed and begins to apply the skill in non-threatening situations.

• The athlete is instructed to use, and also test the efficacy of the skill, in a non-sporting stressful environment.

• The final stage of learning and acquiring the skill involves the athlete being able to apply the skills across a range of increasingly demanding sporting situations: practice, warm-up, and competitive events.

Coaches and teachers often shout "relax" to an athlete or learner whose performance is suffering because of being too tense, for example, a beginning swimmer going into the deep end for the first time or a skilled athlete becoming frustrated because performance is not up to expectations. Although the instruction to relax is certainly appropriate, more often than not these performers are clueless as to how to relax, particularly when in an uptight state. To learn to avoid too much tension, athletes need to be taught to recognize unwanted tension and to relax or release it. The tension sensation comes from the contraction of skeletal muscle fibers. Relaxation comes from no more than stopping the contraction, thus releasing the tension from the contracted muscle. Total relaxation means letting go and doing absolutely nothing with the muscles so that no messages are traveling either to or from the brain.

Why would an athlete want to be completely relaxed, that is, to experience what **zero-activation** level feels like? The answer is that in learning to train the muscles to relax totally, athletes develop a much greater sensitivity to their bodily feelings and responses and what causes their reactions. This awareness increases their sensitivity to tension levels and their ability to regulate different levels of tension to match the demands of the performance situation. In addition, once trained in deep relaxation, athletes can use this skill to remove localized tension that contributes to headaches or lower back pain or pain surrounding injuries. Complete relaxation can also facilitate recovery from fatigue and it can promote the onset of sleep and reduce other insomnia problems that plague many athletes prior to competition. The progressive relaxation exercise in Appendix A is an excellent one for learning total relaxation, but meditation, visualization, and autogenic training also work for some athletes.

Finally, the ability to relax completely provides the foundation for learning the skill of **momentary relaxation,** which can be done quickly and does not achieve as deep a relaxation state as complete relaxation. Examples of momentary exercises are the briefer ones such as those found in the breathing section and the quick muscle relaxation exercises. Momentary relaxation skills are extremely important for athletes because they can be used to reduce over activation at any point during practices and competition. When the nerves are carrying worry messages instead of the stimuli for smooth, coordinated, integrated efforts, performance suffers. Momentary relaxation lowers arousal and, particularly important, removes excessive muscular tension and, hopefully, worry and anxiety stimuli. The momentary respite also allows the athlete to return to a point of controlled balance. Every aspect of performance is enhanced: coordination, attentional focus, awareness, confidence, precision, speed, and so on.

Momentary relaxation can be used just before and during warm-up. In fact, stretching in preparation for competition is a good time to utilize the strategies of momentary relaxation and to focus on the upcoming performance. The more uptight the athlete is prior to performance, the longer the session of momentary relaxation should be. After the competition, this type of relaxation can be used to return to a controlled, balanced state that enables focusing on other aspects of the athlete's life. During the competition, depending on the specific sport, brief periods or lapses in play allow for momentary relaxation as needed, but athletes must first learn to become aware of excessive tension. Doing a quick momentary relaxation exercise can also facilitate concentration and imagery practice because it eliminates or reduces thoughts and stimulation that interfere with the needed single-minded focus.

Breathing exercises. Breathing properly is relaxing and facilitates performance by, for example, increasing the amount of oxygen in the blood and carrying more energy to the muscles. Athletes who experience stress during a high-pressure performance situation find their breathing is usually affected in one of two ways—they either hold their breath or breathe rapidly and shallowly from the upper chest. Both of these adjustments create even more tension and impairment of performance.

Exercise 3 Increasing awareness of ineffective breathing

Raise your shoulders way up and notice what happens to your breathing. This posture forces your breathing to move into just the upper chest and to become rapid and shallow.

Learning to take a deep, slow, complete breath from the belly will usually trigger a relaxation response. This breath is the basis for a variety of breathing exercises (see Mason, 1980, for further details and for the exercises from which some of the below are adapted).

Complete breath. Proper breathing comes from the **diaphragm,** the thin muscle separating the lung and abdominal cavities. With a complete breath, the diaphragm pulls down, causing the belly to expand and a vacuum to occur in the lungs, filling the lungs up from the bottom. To facilitate learning what this feels like, athletes should forcefully empty all the air from their lungs and notice what happens on the next inhalation. When practicing a complete breath, athletes should imagine that their lungs are divided into three levels and that inhalation occurs in three steps. First, they fill the lower section of the lungs with air by relaxing the belly and letting it gently swell out as they deeply inhale from the diaphragm. Next, they fill the middle portion of the lungs by expanding the chest cavity and raising the rib cage. Finally, they bring the breath (air) all the way to the top of the lungs by raising the collarbones and widening the shoulder blades. All three inhalation stages progress continuously and smoothly. Once athletes are comfortable with this sequential inhalation, they should emphasize taking a long, slow, deep inhalation through the nose, inhaling as much air as possible.

During the exhalation, the emphasis is on feeling as if the air drains out of the bottom of the lungs. First empty the top of the lungs, then the rib-cage area, and finally the lower part of the lungs. To force out the last bit of air from the lungs, pull the belly in even further. The exhalation should be long, slow, and complete and result in all tension leaving the body as the air is fully exhaled. Direct athletes to focus on feeling the stillness and calm at the moment directly after fully exhaling, as this is the quietest or calmest time of the breath. If athletes can feel this quietness, they are learning how to relax. Whenever athletes get too tense, they should try to recreate this moment of peace and calm by momentarily practicing this exercise.

Exercise 4 Confirming diaphragmatic breathing

Put one hand on your abdomen and the other on your upper chest. If you are taking a deep, complete breath from the diaphragm, the hand on your abdomen will move out with the inhalation and in with the exhalation, while the hand on the chest remains relatively still.

After learning the procedure, athletes should take at least 30 to 40 deep breaths each day. Associating deep breathing with events that naturally occur during the day, such as texting, downloading e-mail, or waiting for class to begin, will facilitate practice. A good time to use this breathing exercise is whenever athletes need momentary relaxation, such as before a free throw shot, tennis serve, or golf putt.

Sighing with exhalation. Instruct athletes as follows: "Exhale completely through the mouth, making an audible sigh. Then close the mouth and inhale quietly through the nose to a count of 4. Then hold your breath for a count of 7, feeling the tension building in the throat and chest. Exhale audibly through the mouth to the count of 8 as you let go of the tension in the rib cage." Repeat the cycle until the desired level of relaxation is achieved.

Rhythmic breathing. Athletes inhale to a count of 4, hold their breath for a count of 4, exhale to a count of 4, and pause for a count of 4

before repeating the sequence. They can alter the rhythm of their breathing by changing the count.

1:2 ratio. The athletes take a deep, full breath and then exhale fully and completely. Have them breathe again, only this time to a count of 4 on the inhalation and a count of 8 on the exhalation. If athletes run out of breath before reaching 8, suggest that next time they take a deeper breath and exhale more slowly. Emphasize awareness of a full inhalation and exhalation. With more practice and deepened relaxation on the part of the athletes, the athlete may need to change the count to 5:10 or 6:12. This exercise creates a very powerful relaxation response if done properly.

5-to-1 count. Instruct the athlete as follows: "Say to yourself and visualize the number 5 as you take a deep, full, slow breath. Exhale fully and completely. Mentally count and visualize the number 4 with your next inhalation. During the exhalation, say to yourself, 'I am more relaxed now than I was at number 5.' Do not rush the thought. Inhale while mentally counting and visualizing the number 3. With the exhalation, say to yourself, 'I am more relaxed now than I was at number 4.' Allow yourself to feel the deepening relaxation. Continue until you reach number 1. As you approach number 1, you should feel totally calm and relaxed." The complete exercise takes 1 to 2 minutes. If done properly, it should lead to more relaxation than practicing a single complete breath. The athlete can use this exercise before or during practices and competition, depending on how much time is available and how much relaxation is needed.

Concentration breathing. This is a good exercise for athletes to practice when they are having problems with distracting thoughts. Have athletes concentrate on focusing their attention on their breathing rhythm. If their mind wanders to some other thought between inhaling and exhaling, they should redirect attention back to their next breath, letting the intruding thought disappear. The next step is to think of becoming more relaxed with each exhalation as they continue to focus on the rhythm of their breathing.

Progressive relaxation. Initially developed by Jacobson (1930) under the assumption that an anxious mind cannot exist within a relaxed body, progressive relaxation (PR) consists of a series of exercises that involve contracting a specific muscle group, holding the contraction for 5–7 seconds, and then relaxing. The exercises progress from one muscle group to another. The contraction phase teaches awareness and sensitivity to what muscular tension feels like. The letting go, or relaxation phase, teaches an awareness of what absence of tension feels like and that it can voluntarily be induced by passively releasing the tension in a muscle. Thus, in the learning process, the athlete simply identifies a localized state of tension, relaxes it away, and then contrasts the tension sensations with the ensuing relaxation that comes from the elimination of tension. By practicing this internal sensory observation, the athlete can become quite proficient at recognizing unwanted tension sensations wherever they may occur and can then easily release the tension rapidly in practically any stressful situation.

Initial practice requires 25-30 minutes and should be done daily. The coach or sport psychologist should take athletes through the initial session, then provide a handout or audio track containing instructions for progressing through the muscle groups (see Appendix A for a PR script and guidance for using it). Once the skill is acquired, shorter practice sessions will achieve a state of complete relaxation and variations can occur, both for achieving complete and momentary relaxation.

Differential PR. Use the script in Appendix A, but after the all-out contraction and relaxation generate half as much tension and relax and then just enough tension to identify and let it go. Thus, differential active PR consists of studying and releasing tension of ever-decreasing intensity. Throughout the exercise, stress having tension only in the muscle group being contracted and only at the predetermined level of intensity. Practice of this exercise enables athletes to better accomplish the differential relaxation required during practice and competition, as well as throughout the day, because they become more sensitive to the slightest unwanted tension in different muscle groups and more confident in their ability to control the level of tension.

Abbreviated active PR. Once skilled at achieving a constant and desirable state of total relaxation, athletes can use a shorter procedure to achieve deep muscle relaxation by combining some of the muscle groups. Tense each group for 5 to 10 seconds and then relax for 30 to 40 seconds. See the following example:

> "Make a tight fist with both hands, tighten the biceps and forearms, hold. . . and relax. . . ."

> "Tense all of the facial and neck muscles. . . . Relax . . . ."

> "Raise the shoulders while making the stomach hard and tightening the buttocks. HOLD. . . . Relax and let go. . . ."

> "Tighten the muscles of both legs and feet by straightening your legs and pointing your toes. HOLD. . . . Relax and let go of all the tension. . . ."

Passive PR. Once athletes have learned the skill of active, deep muscle relaxation, they can relax the muscles without first tensing them. Many people find this passive form of relaxation more effective and pleasant than the active form. With passive PR, the participant merely lets go whatever level of muscular tension is in the muscle group. There is a slow progression from one part of the body to another as the participant relaxes each body part more deeply by letting go of any remaining tension. The same sequence of complete or abbreviated body parts can be used for passive PR as for active PR.

Progress through the specific body parts with directions such as the following: "Turn your attention to your dominant hand. Just tune in to how this hand feels. Become aware of any tension that might be in it and let go of the tension—even more and more. Let go of all the muscles in your dominant hand. Allow it gradually to become looser and heavier. Think about letting go further. Now go to your nondominant hand. Think of your nondominant hand getting looser, heavier, just letting go of the muscles in your nondominant hand. Let go further, more deeply, and now feel the relaxation coming into your left and right forearms. Feel your forearms getting looser and heavier. Enjoy the relaxation that is now coming into your forearms . . ."

Momentary muscle relaxation exercises. These exercises take 10–30 seconds and are best used during performance, such as just before serving, shooting a free throw, batting, or even while running, particularly middle or long distances. Also use them during daily life whenever you start to get uptight. **Quick body scan:** Quickly scan the body from head to toe (or toe to head), stop only at muscle groups where the tension level is too high, and release the tension and continue the scan down (or up) the body. **Neck and shoulder check:** It is very common to carry excessive tension in the neck and shoulders when worried or anxious so scan these muscles periodically for any undue signs of tension and, if you feel it, tense and relax or release it passively. Releasing excessive tension in these two areas tends to spread relaxation to the rest of the body; it may also have a calming effect on the mind. *Sport muscle check:* This momentary exercise is identical to the preceding but substitute whatever muscle group is most appropriate for the sport skill. Fox example, batters could squeeze their bat and golfers their club followed by relaxing to the appropriate level.

Meditation. Regular meditation helps one achieve a state of deep relaxation and facilitates concentration by disciplining the mind. Four basic components are common to most forms of meditation: a quiet environment, a comfortable position, a mental device, and a passive attitude. A mental device, such as a mantra or fixed gazing at an object, quiets the mind by providing a nonarousing and nonstimulating focus of attention. A mantra is a nonstimulating, meaningless rhythmic sound of one or two syllables that a person regularly repeats while meditating.

It is critical that athletes do not worry about how well they are performing the technique or "try hard" because this disrupts effective meditation. Emphasize a "let it happen" attitude; this passive attitude is perhaps the most important element in learning to meditate. If distracting thoughts or mind wandering occur the athlete should redirect attention to the mental device, focusing on this cue and letting all other thoughts move on through consciousness with a passive attitude, making no attempt to attend to them.

The **relaxation response** developed by Herbert Benson (1975) is a generalized version of Eastern transcendental meditation, but without reference to mysticism and unusual postures. For a mental device, athletes use a word such as **calm** or a word/sound of their choosing and adopt the following instructions:

1. Sit in a comfortable position in a quiet place and close eyes.

2. Deeply relax all muscles, beginning at the top of head and progressing to feet (feet to head if preferred) and keep them relaxed.

3. Concentrate on breathing as they breathe easily and naturally through the nose. With each breath out, say the word *calm* or some other word or nonsense sound silently to oneself.

4. When finished, sit quietly for several minutes, at first with eyes closed and later with eyes open. Do not stand for a few minutes.

The athlete does the preceding for 5 minutes initially and, with practice, builds to 15–20 minutes, trying to remain passive by letting the relaxation happen and not worry about the time or whether the strategy is working. The technique is practiced 1-2 times daily, but not within one hour after any meal as the digestive processes can interfere with elicitation of the relaxation response.

Visualization. Visualizing being in a place conducive to relaxation is another technique for eliciting relaxation. For example, an athlete might visualize lying on a beach feeling the warm sand and sun on the body while listening to the continuous rhythm of breaking waves and smelling the salt air. Other images might be sitting in the midst of a beautiful mountain scene or lying in a grassy valley by a gentle, gurgling stream. Whatever image provides the athlete with a sense of calm and relaxation is the one he or she should use.

Autogenic training. Autogenic training consists of a series of exercises designed to produce two physical sensations typically associated with relaxation— warmth and heaviness (see Linden, 1993). Essentially a technique of auto-hypnosis or self-hypnosis it focuses attention on the sensations one is trying to produce. As in meditation, it is important to let the feeling happen in a passive manner. There are six stages in the training and the athlete must learn each stage before progressing to the next stage (see Appendix B for a full description). The progression can be modified to suit athletes' learning rates as well as the training program and length of season of the sport. Several months of 10–40 minutes of daily practice, spread across one to six sessions, are required to become proficient to experience heaviness and warmth in the limbs and produce the sensation of a relaxed, calm heartbeat and respiratory rate accompanied by warmth in the abdomen and coolness in the forehead. Once athletes have reached that level of training and can attain a relaxed state, they can use imagery to increase the depth of relaxation.

Autogenic training with visualization. After athletes have mastered the six stages of autogenic training and can induce the desired state in a few minutes and sustain it, they are ready to move to the next phase of training, which combines autogenic exercises with visualization. The progression goes from first doing the autogenic exercise to then visualizing the desired feeling or objective. For example, athletes might build confidence by imaging some peak performance when everything went just right or they might program success by imaging the proper execution of a skill or strategy for an upcoming competition. The visualization applications are without limit, but the athlete must first have skill at imagery (see Chapter 13).

Despite the time required to become proficient in autogenic training, many athletes find it a satisfactory means of training for relaxation and imagery. The approach is particularly appealing to those athletes who respond to autosuggestion.

Multimodal stress management techniques. As alternatives to the stress management reduction techniques outlined above, more complex multimodal frameworks have been proposed and successfully tested, including stress inoculation training (Meichenbaum, 1985) and stress management training (Smith & Rohsenow, 1987). The rationale behind these approaches is that rather than "match" the intervention to the prominent anxiety response, interventions should be designed to treat both cognitive and somatic anxiety simultaneously because of their shared overlap; so any attempt to reduce one of the anxiety components is likely to "cross-over" and influence the other.

Stress inoculation training. This approach combines the skills of imagery, self-talk, and relaxation to develop a coping skills program. Imagery is initially used to rehearse exposure to increasingly "stair-step" stressful encounters and then paired with relaxation at each step to induce a relaxed state while maintaining the image before progressing to imaging a slightly more stressful situation. The athlete is then exposed to challenging but manageable stressful environments where these coping skills are tested in real life. The intensity of the demands is steadily increased so that coping skills are built up to effectively deal with the most stressful situation the athlete may encounter, thereby "inoculating" the athlete to the effects of the stressors.

Stress management training. This approach adheres to similar underlying principles of stress inoculation training, however, the distinguishing factor is the focus on coping with emotional and affective responses to the stressor(s):

1. Imagery rehearsal; athlete asked to focus on emotional and affective responses to demand(s) being visualized.

2. Rehearsal phase; practitioner encourages strong and intense emotional response through use of verbal propositions.

3. Athlete instructed to "turn off" intense emotional and affective response by implementing coping responses in form of relaxation and self-instruction skills.

4. Skills transferred from imagined rehearsal scenarios to real-life settings of a steadily increasing stressful nature.

Stress Management Skills and Strategies: Restructuring Approaches

The key distinction of restructuring interventions over those that solely seek to reduce arousal and anxiety is the presence of an appraisal process whereby athletes gain control over their anxiety by restructuring, that is, interpreting their anxiety symptoms (both mental and physical) as beneficial (or positive) for optimal performance. The restructuring approach advocates combining various techniques into an integrated framework: imagery to first recreate anxious thoughts and feelings; self-talk (cognitive restructuring and rationalization) to challenge these experiences; goal setting to provide control over the situation; and imagery to emphasize control over emotions and depict successful performance in the stressful situation.

Recreating symptoms.   Athletes first use imagery to recreate symptoms associated with anxious thoughts and feelings related to competition. For example, the athlete is asked to identify stressful situations where the images have been experienced, and then recall experiences of these symptoms, possibly with the aid of video footage or a diary/competition log (imagery scripts and audio tracks can also be used to aid with creation of symptoms). The athlete is encouraged to include as much information as possible in order to recreate a vivid image. The information gleaned is then used to create a series of images depicting the symptoms associated with the stressful situations.

Rationalizing and restructuring symptoms.   Once athletes can recreate anxious thoughts and feelings, they are taught to rationalize and restructure symptoms via the use of self-talk and rational-emotive behavioral therapy (REBT). These skills are based on the notion that athletes experience and appraise situations that lead to beliefs that are either rational (i.e., positive interpretation of anxiety symptoms) or irrational (i.e., negative interpretation of anxiety symptoms). Rational beliefs lead to functional (beneficial) consequences for performance, whereas irrational beliefs lead to dysfunctional (harmful) consequences. Self-talk and REBT are used to question the interpretation of the negative symptoms experienced and turn them around to form a positive interpretation, thereby creating beliefs that lead to functional consequences for performance.

Traditionally, three progressive stages are used that focus on **identifying, disputing,** and then **replacing** negative interpretations of anxiety symptoms: First, athletes' record/describe the negative mental and physical anxiety symptoms they experience, then they **identify** the symptoms are indeed irrational and will have a negative impact upon preparation and performance. This is achieved through guided questioning in relation to the symptoms experienced: "Is my appraisal based on fact?" "Does my appraisal help me achieve my sporting goals?" and "Does my appraisal help me to feel positive about my upcoming sport performance?" If athletes answer "no" to these questions, then they are asked to challenge this initial appraisal and provide examples of how these interpretations can be **disputed.** Here, practitioners educate the athlete to dispute this irrational appraisal and **replace** it with a rationalized or restructured thought process, thereby creating a positive anxiety interpretation for performance. Continuing the example, athletes would be educated to change the appraisal of their symptoms by questioning whether the symptoms reported are always detrimental to performance. Athletes would be asked to replace these thoughts with ones suggesting that the worries experienced highlight the personal importance of the event and create an importance that equates to increased effort and a more focused and concentrated state.

Finally, athletes are educated to consider that the physical symptoms experienced actually indicate a level of physical preparedness for the task and a readiness to perform optimally. Initially, application of these skills can be challenging, and it is advised athletes progress through the stages with a high degree of conscious thought and reliance on a trained sport psychologist. Tapes, diaries, and scripts are often used to assist and educate the performer during this process to help create individualized restructuring programs. However, as athletes practice the skill and engage in ongoing dialogue with the practitioner, the application of the skill becomes a more automatic process.

Confidence management. Following rationalization and restructuring of symptoms, imagery can be employed as a confidence management strategy to allow individuals to image themselves successfully managing the emotions that accompany participating in competitive sport (e.g., completing a pre-shot routine under stressful conditions). The content of such images fall broadly into two categories: mastery of performance-related plans (e.g., tactical plans/strategies being executed correctly) and specific skills related to the athlete's role (e.g., successful shooting skills such as a penalty kick in soccer). Initially, athletes develop a series of imagery scripts and audio tracks to use to perfect their imagery skills. For example, if the core of the imagery routine that athletes require is a focus on images depicting mastery of certain skills within their sport under stressful conditions, athlete are asked to: (a) record the key skills for their role in their sport, for example, shooting skills as a goal attack in netball; (b) recount recent good performances of these skills, possibly making use of video; and (c) include as much information as possible to recreate a vivid image. The athlete is then asked to use this information to develop a series of imagery routines to create images depicting mastery of skills while

experiencing the symptoms associated with the stressful situation. The information athletes input to this process, and the use of their knowledge base of the sport, are key features in creating individualized imagery routines that have relevance to the individual. After gaining competence at recreating images in non-threatening situations away from the competitive arena, use of the skill is incorporated into progressively increasing stressful environments within the athlete's sport to gain full control over the skill in intense, pressurized competitive settings.

Goal setting. A further strategy to assist athletes to gain control over themselves, the situation, and the symptoms they experience is effective goal setting. When greater control occurs, an individual is more likely to interpret anxiety symptoms as facilitating performance. Encourage athletes to set performance or process goals rather than outcome goals (see Chapter 11) because they fall within the realm of what the athlete can control. Nevertheless, the strong motivational properties of outcome goals cannot be ignored even though unrealistic outcome goals can actually create anxiety. Therefore, athletes should set all three types of goals, but place a greater degree of importance on performance and process goals as the competitive event becomes more imminent.

The effectiveness of restructuring is well documented, but there are caveats for its use such as when athletes are performing skills that typically require low activation levels and their arousal level and perceived anxiety symptoms are extremely high. For example, if you need to sink a putt or shoot a free throw, but you are breathing rapidly, have rigid muscles, and are so worried about failure that thoughts cannot be focused, it is best to take a reductionist approach rather than trying to convince yourself that such anxiety symptoms are okay because they can facilitate performance.

Case Studies

Examples of the reduction and restructuring stress management strategies sport psychologists may utilize to treat anxiety symptoms experienced as a consequence of competition stress follow.

Case Study 1

Todd

The athlete. *Todd is a 25-year-old professional golfer who has been competing in his event for 3 years.*

   Reason for referral. *Todd contacted the sport psychologist as he felt he was struggling to deal with potentially negative and distracting thoughts when preparing to play his shot. In addition, he also reported high levels of physical tension in his arms and shoulders prior to swinging the golf club. He indicated he was feeling anxious prior to his competitions, he felt his performances were below average, and he did not remember thinking or feeling a similar way when he had performed at his best.*

   Background. *Todd was asked to complete a series of validated questionnaires to assess the levels of anxiety symptoms he was experiencing and to keep a diary of any thoughts and feelings experienced directly before competing in important events. Video footage was also collected of Todd's pre-shot routine and his general body language during the rounds. The sport psychologist also sat down in a one-to-one consultation with Todd and discussed these issues. These assessments determined that Todd had high levels of cognitive and somatic anxiety both prior to performance and between shots on the golf course.*

   Professional assessment. *As relatively low levels of both mental and physical symptoms are required to achieve an optimal readiness to perform in golf, the sport psychologist recommended an intervention program that followed the reductionist treatment approach. As Todd reported his level of negative thoughts (i.e., cognitive anxiety) and negative feelings (i.e., somatic anxiety) were inhibiting his performance, and the evaluation indicated both of these responses were high, the intervention targeted reduction of arousal and both physical and mental anxiety symptoms.*

   Intervention. *A progressive muscle relaxation program was provided to treat his physical arousal and anxieties, and a transcendental meditation program was given to help manage the mental anxieties experienced. Due to Todd reporting his symptoms as distracting both prior to and during competition (i.e., between shots), both programs were designed as full progressive techniques in order for Todd to be able to use them before competing and between shots on the golf course.*

   Outcome. *Following the successful learning and application of the physical and mental relaxation programs recommended by the sport psychologist (a process taking approximately 12 weeks), Todd reported he could now control his physical symptoms effectively during the round. However, while he felt the transcendental meditation program was having a degree of success at reducing his mental anxieties, he still had problems. The sport psychologist subsequently recommended the adoption of a calming imagery technique. Following a further 6 weeks of training and practicing this additional skill, Todd reported that he felt comfortable and able to regulate cognitive anxiety levels experienced before and during his shots on the course.*

Case Study 2

Elizabeth

The athlete. *Elizabeth is a 36-year-old bobsled athlete who competed in her event for 12 years and represented her country at numerous World Championships and two Olympic Games. Although achieving the qualification time for the Olympic Games at her recent national trials, she felt that her performance and time in this event failed to satisfy the expectations of herself, her teammates, and her coach.*

   Reason for consultancy. *Elizabeth had indicated to her national team's sport psychologist that prior to the recent Olympic trials and, indeed, during the warm-up events to the trials, she was having problems dealing with distracting negative thoughts and high levels of muscle tension when in the waiting room at the top of the mountain preparing to race. Elizabeth suggested that she was conscious of these mental and physical symptoms prior to the race, and felt they were having a negative impact on her pre-race preparation. While these symptoms had been present throughout her career, Elizabeth now felt she was unable to control their impact on herself and her performance.*

   Professional assessment. *Elizabeth was asked to complete a series of validated questionnaires assessing the level of pre-race anxiety symptoms and whether she viewed experiencing these symptoms had a positive or negative impact on her upcoming performance. A one-on-one interview between the sport psychologist and Elizabeth further explored Elizabeth's understanding of her anxiety responses. Following this consultation it was established that Elizabeth's pre-race anxiety levels were high and that she viewed these symptoms as having a detrimental effect on performance. As bobsled is an explosive event that requires the production of a high degree of force over a short distance at the start (Elizabeth was the brake woman in her team and responsible for maximizing the velocity of the sled), the optimal activation state for readiness to perform is a relatively high level of controlled physical and mental symptoms. Consequently, the sport psychologist recommended an intervention program that adhered to the principles of the restructuring approach. If the sport psychologist had prescribed techniques that sought only to reduce the symptoms Elizabeth experienced, it likely would have led to a detrimental effect upon performance because Elizabeth may have become too mentally and physically relaxed for the activation demands of the bobsled start.*

   Intervention program. *An intervention program based upon restructuring the interpretation (negative to positive) of both mental and physical anxiety was provided to Elizabeth. The emphasis was for Elizabeth to restructure her anxiety interpretations to allow her to view her mental symptoms as indicators of the importance of the event and her physical ones as indicators of her physical readiness to perform. The sport psychologist also provided confidence maintenance techniques (i.e., mental imagery and goal setting). Over time, Elizabeth was taken through the restructuring program outlined in this chapter.*

   Outcome. *After undertaking the intervention program for a 12-week period, the treatment resulted in a reinterpretation of Elizabeth's anxiety from negative to positive without reducing the level of anxiety symptoms experienced (suggesting that Elizabeth had obtained a suitable state of activation prior to competition). In addition, Elizabeth indicated after the intervention that her physical and mental symptoms now signified to her the importance of the event, the amount of effort she was prepared to invest toward it, and how the symptoms could actually improve her performance.*

Stress Management Skills and Strategies: Energizing Approaches

As discussed earlier, sometimes performance suffers not because athletes are experiencing the debilitating effects of stress, but because they lack a sufficient stimulus to create the optimum mental and physical activation state for performance. This problem is more likely to occur when the activation demands are higher due to the task characteristics of the sport (see the inverted-U section). Other common times are during tedious practices and when athletes are fatigued, discouraged, or approaching burnout. Athletes need to learn how to recognize signs and symptoms of low energy and activation. As an example, a track athlete should be sensitive to and then energize dead legs during a race or a weightlifter may want to put all available energy into the legs and arms to attain a particular lift.

When athletes are not sufficiently activated, there are a variety of effective techniques for energizing or increasing arousal and activation. Meta-analysis has documented their effectiveness at enhancing performance (Meyers et al., 1996). Many of these techniques come from simply reversing the focus of the interventions outlined in the reduction approach so that they become energizing rather than calming.

Breathing exercises. For example, consider a breathing exercise whereby the athlete is instructed to consciously deepen and increase their breathing rate and imagine that with each inhalation they are increasing energy levels to reach an optimum activation state. If the athlete is also fatigued, add imagining breathing fatigue out with each exhalation. This breathing technique can be combined with self-talk cues such as "energy in" on the inhalation and "fatigue out" on the exhalation.

Energizing imagery. Hundreds of **images** can be conjured up for generating energy. For example, images of trains moving slowly, gaining momentum and speed; images of heavy machinery where working parts move rapidly; images of natural forces such as powerful waves and winds and images of animals sprinting and moving rapidly. Instruct the athlete to develop a supply of energizing images that work for them in various situations encountered in their particular sport. Then establish a plan ahead of time for their use, such as lapses in action or, if appropriate, during actual performance (e.g., running). Then practice them on a regular basis. Energizing imagery is particularly effective when fatigue is beginning to set in, when discouraged by a series of points that have been lost, or when a sudden burst of energy is needed to finish play.

Energizing verbal cues. In the midst of a performance, verbal cues can be effective energizers. Words such as "explode," "charge," "psych up," and "power" help facilitate the process of energizing. Raiport (1988), a former Russian sport psychologist, described a technique that combined **energizing words, images, and breathing** that was used by Eastern European sport psychologists to help athletes self-induce greater activation. The breathing pattern is one of exhaling on the first part of the phrases and inhaling on the italicized part. For example, take the phrase "I am breathing *deeper, inhaling energy.*" The most meaningful part of the phrase (in italics) is combined with the inhalation, which naturally facilitates energy physiologically. Repeat this pattern until achieving the desired activation. Raiport recommended other phrases such as "Strength is *flowing into my body*," "I am *vigorous and alert*," and "My muscles are *quivering with energy.*" Whatever the phrase, imagine creating that sensation when saying it.

Transferring energy. Performers can be taught to transfer energy from other sources. Take activation and arousal that result from anger, frustration, or some other emotion that tends to interfere with performance, and convert it into positive energy to accomplish performance goals. Use the environment as a source for transferring energy, such as drawing energy from the spectators or even from the opponent, both when it appears the opponents have the momentum and when they have clearly lost it.

Disassociate from fatigue. Another way to deal with under activation caused by fatigue is to focus attention away from it. Most athletes do the opposite, thereby increasing fatigue the more they tune into it. Instead suggest that they apply their concentration skills and focusing ability on what is happening or about to happen within the performance setting rather than on how they are feeling. Long distance runners also use dis-association strategies, that is, they think about something completely unrelated to running.

Exercise 5 Applying what you have learned

Design an optimal intervention for each particular scenario described below.

1. *David, an American football quarterback, goes to a sport psychologist because the demands of professional football have him so stressed that he is having difficulty sleeping. During games, he is so tense that his throws are often erratic and he can't find his secondary receivers. He reports that it seems like he's "looking at the field through a roll of toilet paper." What interventions might a coach or sport psychology consultant implement to help David? Indicate how to sequence them and describe how they might be practiced.*

2. *Jeff, a sport psychologist, finds that his relaxation training with Doug, a promising ice hockey forward, to help manage pre-game mental worries and physical anxieties is leading to Doug feeling "flat" and "cold" on the ice. Explain why Jeff's intervention with Doug is not working and describe an alternative strategy that might help him manage his pre-game symptoms more effectively.*

3. *Sue, a high school coach, finds that her team usually competes up to its potential. She is frustrated, however, with their play during practice. She feels that the team's development is not what it could be because the players often lack intensity and focus. What might the coach do to try and correct this problem?*

Summary

The experience of stress in sport is a phenomenon widely acknowledged as having a significant impact upon athletic performance, often with detrimental repercussions. Stress management strategies can be taught to athletes using a cognitive-behavioral framework that considers the demands athletes face, how they appraise these demands, the subsequent mental and physical symptoms that arise (including arousal levels and activation state), and how these symptoms are viewed as affecting performance. Central to this approach is the need to understand the relational-meaning (appraisals) athletes ascribe to their changing stress experiences over time (transactions). In an effort to successfully cope with stress in sport, athletes can adopt problem-focused strategies that aim to prevent or manage the amount of stress experienced and emotion-focused techniques that seek to reduce symptoms, restructure their meaning, or raise arousal levels to achieve suitable activation states.

Study Questions

1. Explain Lazarus' (1991) cognitive motivational relational theory (CMRT) and its role in the stress process.

2. Discuss the role of appraisal in how an athlete experiences and manages the stress associated with competing in sport.

3. Give examples of the potential demands athletes may encounter when competing in sport.

4. Summarize the typical responses athletes report associated with stress in sport.

5. Consider how negative emotions such as anxiety that occur as a consequence of the stress process can actually have beneficial effects for performance.

6. Identify three different methods sport psychologists can use to measure athletes' experiences of stress.

7. Briefly summarize and discuss the merits of the five different approaches that have been offered to describe the relationship between stress and performance in sport.

8. Name and outline the principles of the three "contemporary" mechanistic explanations for the stress and performance relationship.

9. Compare and contrast the concepts underlying an emotion- versus problem-focused coping strategy to managing stress in sport.

10. Provide examples of three problem-focused coping stress management strategies athletes may use in sport.

11. Compare the three emotion-focused coping approaches to dealing with the symptoms associated with demands of competing in sport.

12. Summarize the two main strategies that sport psychologists recommend to "reduce" the intensity of symptoms experienced when associated with competing in sport and describe the interventions within each strategy.

13. Describe a typical "restructuring" stress management intervention with an athlete.

14. Provide five examples of energizing techniques a sport psychologist might recommend to athletes to enhance their activation state.

References

Benson, H. (1975). *The relaxation response.* New York: Avon Books.

Bernstein, D. A., & Carlson, C. R. (1993). Progressive relaxation: Abbreviated methods. In P. M. Lehrer & R. L. Woolfolk (Eds.), *Principles and practice of stress management* (2nd edition) (pp. 53–87). New York: The Guilford Press.

Cox, R. H., Martens, M. P., & Russell, W. D. (2003). Measuring anxiety in athletics: The revised Competitive State Anxiety Inventory-2. *Journal of Sport and Exercise Psychology, 25,* 519–533.

Cox, R. H., Robb, M., & Russell, W. D. (1999). Order of scale administration and concurrent validity of the Anxiety Rating Scale. *Perceptual and Motor Skills, 88,* 271–272.

Davidson, R. J., & Schwartz, G. E. (1976). The psychobiology of relaxation and related stress: A multiprocess theory. In D. I. Mostofsky (Ed.), *Behavioral control and modification of physiological activity* (pp. 399–442). Englewood Cliffs, NJ: Prentice Hall.

Eysenck, M. W., & Calvo, M. G. (1992). Anxiety and performance: The processing efficiency theory. *Cognition and Emotion, 6,* 409–434.

Eysenck, M. W., Derakshan, N., Santos, R., & Calvo, M. G. (2007). Anxiety and cognitive performance: Attentional control theory. *Emotion, 7,* 336–353.

Fletcher, D., Hanton, S., & Mellalieu, S. D. (2006). An organizational stress review: Conceptual and theoretical issues in competitive sport. In S. Hanton & S. D. Mellalieu (Eds.), *Literature reviews in sport psychology* (pp. 321–373). Hauppauge, NY: Nova Science.

Gucciardi, D. F., & Dimmock, J. A. (2008). Choking under pressure in sensorimotor skills: Conscious processing or depleted attentional resources? *Psychology of Sport and Exercise, 9,* 45–59.

Hanin, Y. L. (1980). A cognitive model of anxiety in sports. In W. F. Straub (Ed.), *Sport psychology: An analysis of athlete behavior* (pp. 236–249). Ithica, NY: Movement Publications.

Hanin, Y. L. (1986). State-trait anxiety research on sports in the USSR. In C. D. Spielberger & R. Diaz-Guerrero (Eds.), *Cross-cultural anxiety* (Vol. 3, pp. 45–64). Washington, DC: Hemisphere.

Hanin, Y. L. (Ed.). (2000). *Emotions in sport.* Champaign, IL: Human Kinetics.

Hanton, S., & Jones, G. (1995). Antecedents of multidimensional state anxiety in elite competitive swimmers. *International Journal of Sport Psychology, 26,* 512–523.

Hanton, S., & Jones, G. (1999). The acquisition and development of cognitive skills and strategies. I: Making the butterflies fly in formation. *The Sport Psychologist, 13,* 1–21.

Hardy, L. (1990). A catastrophe model of anxiety and performance. In J. G. Jones & L. Hardy (Eds.), *Stress and performance in sport* (pp. 81–106). Chichester, UK: Wiley.

Hardy, L., Beattie, S., & Woodman, T. (2007). Anxiety-induced performance catastrophes: Investigating effort required as an asymmetry factor. *British Journal of Psychology, 98,* 15–31.

Hardy, L., Jones, G., & Gould, D. (1996). *Understanding psychological preparation for sport: Theory and practice of elite performers.* Chichester, England: Wiley.

Hardy, L., & Parfitt, G. (1991). A catastrophe model of anxiety and performance. *British Journal of Psychology, 82,* 163–178.

Hardy, L., Woodman, T., & Carrington, S. (2004). Is self-confidence a bias factor in higher-order catastrophe models? An exploratory analysis. *Journal of Sport and Exercise Psychology, 26,* 359–368.

Holt, N. L., & Hoar, S. D. (2006). The multidimensional construct of social support. In S. Hanton & S. D. Mellalieu (Eds.), *Literature reviews in sport psychology* (pp. 199–225). Hauppauge, NY: Nova Science.

Jacobson, E. (1930). *Progressive relaxation.* Chicago: University of Chicago Press.

Jones, G., & Swain, A. B. J. (1992). Intensity and direction dimensions of competitive state anxiety and relationships with competitiveness. *Perceptual and Motor Skills, 74,* 467–472.

Jones, G., Swain, A. B. J., & Cale, A. (1991). Gender differences in precompetition temporal patterning and antecedents of anxiety and self-confidence. *Journal of Sport and Exercise Psychology, 13,* 1–15.

Krane, V. (1994). The mental readiness form as a measure of competitive state anxiety. *The Sport Psychologist, 8,* 189–202.

Lacey, J. (1967). Somatic response patterning and stress: Some revisions of activation theory. In M. Appley & R. Trumbell (Eds.), *Psychological stress: Issues in research* (pp. 14–42). New York: Appleton-Century-Crofts.

Lazarus, R. (1991). *Emotion and adaptation.* New York: Oxford University Press.

Linden, W. (1993). The autogenic training method of J. H. Schultz. In P. M. Lehrer & R. L. Woolfolk (Eds.), *Principles and practice of stress management* (2nd Edition, pp. 205–229). New York: The Guilford Press.

Mason, L. J. (1980). *Guide to stress reduction.* Culver City, CA: Peace Press.

Martens, R., Vealey, R. S., & Burton, D. (1990). *Competitive anxiety in sport.* Champaign, IL: Human Kinetics.

Masters, R. S. W. (1992). Knowledge, knerves, and know-how: The role of explicit versus implicit knowledge in the breakdown of a complex motor skill under pressure. *British Journal of Psychology, 83,* 343–358.

Masters, R. S. W., & Maxwell, J. P. (2008). The theory of reinvestment. *International Review of Sport and Exercise Psychology, 1,* 160–183.

Meichenbaum, D. (1985). *Stress inoculation training.* New York: Pergamon.

Mellalieu, S. D., Hanton, S., & Fletcher, D. (2006). A competitive anxiety review: Recent directions in sport psychology research. In S. Hanton & S. D. Mellalieu (Eds.), *Literature reviews in sport psychology* (pp. 1–45). Hauppage, NY: Nova Science.

Mesagno, C., & Mullane-Grant, T. (2010). A comparison of different pre-performance routines as possible choking interventions. *Journal of Applied Sport Psychology, 22,* 343–360.

Meyers, A. W., Whelan, J. P., & Murphy, S. M. (1996). Cognitive behavioral strategies in athletic performance enhancement. In M. Hersen, R. M. Eisler, & P. M. Miller (Eds.), *Progress in behavioral modification,* Vol. 30 (pp. 137–164). Pacific Grove, CA: Brooks/Cole.

Nieuwenhuys, A., Pijpers, J. R., Oudejans, R. R. D., & Bakker, F. C. (2008). The influence of anxiety on visual attention in climbing. *Journal of Sport and Exercise Psychology, 30,* 171–185.

Raiport, G. (1988). *Red gold peak performance techniques of the Russian and East German Olympic victors.* Los Angeles: Tarcher.

Smith, R. E., & Rohesenow, D. J. (1987). Cognitive-affective stress management training: A treatment and resource manual. *Social and Behavioral Sciences Documents, 17,* 2.

Smith, R. E., Smoll, F. L., Cumming, S. P., & Grossbard, J. R. (2006). Measurement of multidimensional sport performance anxiety in children and adults: The Sport Anxiety Scale-2. *Journal of Sport and Exercise Psychology, 28,* 479–501.

Spence J. T., & Spence, K. W. (1966). The motivational components of manifest anxiety: Drive and drive stimuli. In C. D. Spielberger (Ed.), *Anxiety and behavior* (pp. 291–326). New York: Academic Press.

Thomas, O., Hanton, S., & Jones, G. (2002). An alternative approach to short-form self-report assessment of competitive anxiety. *International Journal of Sport Psychology, 33,* 325–336.

Thomas, O., Mellalieu, S. D., & Hanton, S. (2009). Stress management in sport: A critical review and synthesis. In. S. D. Mellalieu & S. Hanton (Eds.), *Advances in applied sport psychology: A review* (pp. 124–161). London: Routledge.

Wagstaff, C., Neil, R, Mellalieu, S. D., & Hanton, S. (2011). Key movements in directional research in competitive anxiety. In J. Thatcher, M. Jones, & D. Lavallee (Eds.), *Coping and emotion in sport* (2nd Edition, pp. 44–75). London: Routledge.

Weiss, S. M. (2011). The effects of reinvestment of conscious processing on switching focus of attention. *Research Quarterly for Exercise and Sport, 82,* 28–36.

Williams, J. M., & Krane, V. (1992). Coping styles and self-reported measures on state anxiety and self-confidence. *Journal of Applied Sport Psychology, 4,* 134–143.

Wilson, M., Smith, N. C., Chattington, M., Ford, M., & Marple-Horvat, D. E. (2006). The role of effort in moderating the anxiety-performance relationship: Testing the prediction of processing efficiency theory in simulated rally driving. *Journal of Sports Sciences, 24,* 1223–1233.

Wilson, M. R., Vine, S. J., Wood, G. (2009). The influence of anxiety on visual attentional control in basketball free throw shooting. *Journal of Sport & Exercise Psychology, 31,* 152–168.

Woodman, T., & Hardy, L. (2001). Stress and anxiety. In R. Singer, H. A. Hausenblas, & C. M. Janelle (Eds.), *Handbook of research on sport psychology* (pp. 290–318). New York: Wiley.

Yerkes, R. M., & Dodson, J. D. (1908). Feeling and thinking: Preferences need no inferences. *American Psychologist, 35,* 151–175.

Active Progressive Muscle Relaxation Script and Guidance for Using It

General instructions: Practice PR either sitting or lying down. The latter is usually more conducive to relaxation, but athletes should sit up if they tend to fall asleep. The lying down position is on the back with the head, neck, and trunk in a straight line. The legs should be straight and 6–12 inches apart with the heels inward and the toes pointing outward. Rest the arms comfortably at the sides with the hands a little way from the thighs, palms up, and fingers comfortably bent. Put a small pillow (rolled up sweats are a good substitute) under either the knees or neck (not both) for additional comfort. If using a sitting position the athletes should sit upright, hips against the backrest, with the arms and legs uncrossed and the feet flat on the floor. The hands rest comfortably on the thighs (palms down). Throughout the exercise emphasize the importance of following instructions passively. This is particularly essential during the relaxation phase. Just let the relaxation happen—don't force it. Relaxation requires no effort—just let go of the muscle contraction. Any effort to relax causes tension. Read the following script beginning in a normal, conversational tone but, over the course of the session, your voice should progressively and subtly become smoother, quieter, and more monotonous while giving the relaxation phase instructions and, in contrast, should increase slightly in volume and speed during the tension phase:

"Sit or lie down in a comfortable position and try to put yourself in a relaxed state. (Note: Close your eyes and take a long, slow, deep breath through your nose, inhaling as much air as you can. Then exhale slowly and completely, feeling the tension leaving your body as you exhale. Take another deep breath and let the day's tensions and problems drain out of you with the exhalation. [Pause.] Relax as much as possible and listen to what I say. Remember not to strain to relax. Just let it happen. During the session, try not to move any more than necessary to stay comfortable. Particularly, try not to move muscles that have already been relaxed.

"As we progress through each of 12 muscle groups, you will first tense the muscle group for approximately 5 to 7 seconds and then relax for 20–30 seconds. Do not start the tensing until I say 'NOW.' Continue to tense until I say 'OKAY' or 'RELAX,' at which time immediately let go of all the tension.

"Begin with tensing the muscles in the dominant hand and lower arm by making a tight fist and bending your hand back at the wrist NOW. Feel the tension in the hand and up into the lower arm. . . . Okay, relax by simply letting go of the tension. Notice the difference between tension and relaxation [pause 20 to 30 seconds]. . . . Make another fist NOW [pause 5 to 7 seconds]. Okay, relax. Just let the relaxation happen by stopping the contraction; don't put out any effort [pause 25 to 30 seconds].

"Next tense the muscles of the dominant upper arm by pushing your elbow down against the floor or back of the chair. Tense NOW. Feel the tension in the biceps without involving the muscles in the lower arm and hand. . . . Okay, release the tension all at once, not gradually. Just let it happen. Let it all go. . . . Tense NOW. . . . Okay, release it. Contrast the difference between tension and letting go into relaxation. Relaxation is no more than the absence of tension.

"With your nondominant hand, make a tight fist and bend your wrist back NOW. Feel the tension in your hand and lower arm, but keep the upper arm relaxed. . . . Okay, relax by simply draining all of the tension out. . . . NOW tense again. . . . Okay, relax and feel the difference between the tension and relaxation. . . . NOW push the elbow down or back to tighten the nondominant upper arm. . . . Okay, relax. . . . NOW tense the upper arm again. Note the discomfort. . . . RELAX. Let all the tension dissolve away. . . . Enjoy the feelings of relaxation. . . . Notice the sensations you have in the muscles of both arms and hands. . . . Perhaps there is a sort of flow of relaxation—perhaps a feeling of warmth and even heaviness in these muscles. Notice and enjoy this feeling of relaxation.

"Turn your attention to the muscles in your face. Tense the muscles in your forehead by raising your eyebrows NOW. Feel the tension in your forehead and scalp. (Pause for only 3- to 5-second contractions with these smaller muscle groups.) Okay, relax and smooth it out. . . . Enjoy the spreading sensation of relaxation. . . . NOW frown again. . . . RELAX. Allow your forehead to become smooth again. . . . Your forehead should feel smooth as glass. . . .

"Next squint your eyes very tightly and at the same time pucker your lips and clinch your teeth, but not so tightly that it hurts. Tense NOW. Feel the tension. . . . Okay, relax. . . . Let the tension dissolve away. . . . NOW tense again. . . . Okay, let all the tension go. . . . Your lips may part slightly as your cheeks and jaw relax.

"Next tense the muscles of the neck and shoulders by raising your shoulders upward as high as you can while pulling your neck down into your shoulders. Tense NOW. . . . feel the discomfort. . . . RELAX. Drop your shoulders back down and feel the relaxation spreading through your neck, throat, and shoulders. . . . Let go more and more. . . . Tense NOW by raising your

shoulders and sinking your neck. . . . Okay, relax. Let go more and more. Enjoy the deepening sensation of relaxation. . . . Remember relaxation is simply the absence of tension.

"Next tighten your abdomen as though you expect a punch while simultaneously squeezing the buttocks together. Tense NOW. You should feel a good deal of tightness and tension in the stomach and buttocks. . . . RELAX, release the tension, let it all drain out. Just let it happen. . . . NOW tense again. . . . Okay, relax. Feel the spreading sensation of relaxation. Let go more and more. . . .

"Turn your attention to your legs. Tighten the muscles in your thighs by simultaneously contracting all the muscles of your thighs. Tense NOW. Try to localize the tension only to your thighs. . . . Note the sensation. Okay, relax. Contrast the tension and relaxation sensations. Remember relaxation is merely the absence of tension; it takes no effort except merely releasing the tension. . . . NOW tighten the thighs again. . . . Okay, release the tension—just passively let it drain out. Enjoy the feeling of relaxation. . . .

"Next flex your ankle as though you are trying to touch your toes to your shin. Tense NOW. You should be feeling tension all through your calf, ankle, and foot. Contrast this tension with when you tensed the thigh. Okay, relax. Simply release the tension; let go of any remaining tension. . . . NOW tense again. . . . Okay, slowly release all the tension. . . .

"Next straighten your legs and point your toes downward. Tense NOW. Note the discomfort. . . . Okay, relax. Feel the spreading sensation of relaxation as you relax deeper and deeper. . . . NOW straighten your legs. . . . RELAX. Release all the tension. Let go more and more. . . .

"Relax all the muscles of your body—let them all go limp. You should be breathing slowly and deeply. Let all last traces of tension drain out of your body. You may notice a sensation of warmth and heaviness throughout your body, as though you are sinking deeper and deeper into the chair or floor. Or you may feel as though you are as light as air, as though you are floating on a cloud. Whatever feelings you have, go with them. . . . Enjoy the sensation of relaxation. . . . Relax deeper and deeper. . . . Scan your body for any places that might still feel tension. Wherever you feel tension, do an additional tense and relax.

"Before opening your eyes, take several deep breaths and feel the energy and alertness flowing back into your body. Stretch your arms and legs if you wish. Open your eyes when you are ready."

Take several minutes to discuss athletes' reactions to this PR exercise. Get them to identify what it felt like and how successful they thought they were at relaxing. For those who had difficulty relaxing, stress again the importance of the absence of effort, of being passive and just letting it happen. Also remind them of the need to practice regularly. Just like any physical skill, PR takes practice. See if any of the athletes became aware of places in their body where they tend to hold tension. The goal is to spot this tension and release it before it leads to headaches and backaches, or performance problems.

Six stages in the training of autogenic responses

Throughout all the stages, emphasize letting the feeling happen in a very passive manner. In the first stage, the athlete focuses attention on the dominant arm while silently saying: (1) "My right (left) arm is heavy" (repeat phrase six times); (2) "I am calm" (or, "I am at peace") (optional and said only once and then alternated with the first step until completing three to six cycles of these two steps). The athlete then cancels out the effect by bending their arm, taking a deep breath, and opening their eyes. The canceling out should always occur with each part of the heaviness stage, and the following stages, in order to ultimately maximize the effect. The preceding is practiced two or three sessions a day (it takes only 1 or 2 minutes each time) until the heaviness starts to spread to the opposite arm. When this occurs, replace "my right arm" with "my left arm" and, once effective, "my arms." Once the heaviness starts to generalize to the legs, replace "my arms" with "my legs are heavy" and, once effective, "my arms and legs are heavy." Ultimately, the entire body starts to feel heavy. If the mind wanders, emphasize passively redirecting attention back to the task at hand. Some athletes may be able to produce a sense of heaviness immediately; others may take 1 or 2 weeks of three or more times of practice daily to accomplish the sensation.

Once the heaviness experience has been well trained and can be induced rapidly and reliably, add the second stage, which is "warmth" and may take longer to achieve. Instructions follow the same general content and format as the first stage except "heavy" is replaced with "warmth." Before practicing the warmth phrases, however, the athlete begins by repeating the final suggestion for the preceding stage:

1. "My arms and legs are heavy" (repeat six times).

2. "I am calm" (or "at peace"; say only once).

3. "My right (left) arm is warm" (and so forth, as done in stage one).

If athletes are having difficulty feeling the appropriate sensation, facilitate learning by having them first physically experience the sensation. For example, if trying to achieve heaviness in the right arm, put a pillow over the arm and, if need be, a book or two on top of the pillow. For the warmth sensation, immerse hands in hot water or put a heating pad or hot water bottle over the hands while they initially do the exercise.

Regulation of the heartbeat is the third stage and consists of the autosuggestion, "My heartbeat is regular and calm." The athlete may need to be sensitized to their own heart activity by putting their hand over their heart when initially doing the exercise. Again, follow the progressive procedure described previously; only this time begin with the phrase, "My arms and legs are heavy. My arms and legs are warm." Follow the same additive protocol for the fourth, fifth, and sixth stages, which consist of the following:

Stage 4: Breathing rate "My breathing rate is slow, calm, and relaxed: It breathes me."

Stage 5: Warmth in the solar plexus "My solar plexus is warm" (hand placed on upper abdominal area); or say, "Sun rays are streaming quiet and warm."

Stage 6: Coolness of the forehead "My forehead is cool."

Once the athlete has learned all the stages, the entire sequence can be practiced as follows:

"My arms and legs are heavy" six times; "I am calm" once.

"My arms and legs are warm" six times; "I am calm" once.

"My heartbeat is regular and calm" six times; "calm" once.

"It breathes me" six times; "calm" once.

"My solar plexus is warm" six times; "calm" once.

"My forehead is cool" six times; "calm" once.

CHAPTER

13

Understanding and Using Imagery in Sport

Robin S. Vealey, *Miami University*
Samuel T. Forlenza, *Michigan State University*

"Nothing is impossible. With so many people saying it couldn't be done, all it takes is imagination, and that's something I learned and something that helped me."

—Michael Phelps, most decorated Olympian of all time with 22 medals, 18 gold.

Eight months before the Vancouver Games, Lindsey Vonn skis the Olympic downhill in her mind. She is in a subterranean workout room . . . in Salzburg, Austria, balanced with each foot on a nylon slack line suspended three feet off the pebbled orange rubber floor. She is crouched in an aerodynamic tuck, her hands thrust out in front of her chin. [Her trainer] speaks gently into her right ear: *You're on the downhill course at Whistler. . . .* Vonn closes her eyes and begins shifting her weight rhythmically from one foot to the other as if executing high-speed turns on a Canadian mountainside more than 5,000 miles away.

She exhales and inhales forcefully, mimicking the aerobic demands of high-speed racing, alternately gliding and turning. Close your eyes with her and you can almost hear the chattering of snow beneath skis. After nearly a minute—shorter than the Olympic downhill but a long time on wobbly strips of thick cloth—she relaxes her body and jumps to the floor . . . aglow from three hours of training on a warm summer morning. "I love that exercise," says Vonn. "Once I visualize a course, I never forget

it. So I get on those lines and go through exactly the run that I want to have. I control my emotions and just make it routine" (Layden, 2010).

Lindsey Vonn took advantage of her most powerful weapon—her mind—in her preparation for the 2010 Winter Olympic Games. Along with her talent and physical preparation, her use of imagery as part of a systematic mental training regimen enabled her to win not only the 2010 Olympic downhill, but also four World Cup overall championships. Not all of us are world-class athletes like Vonn, but all of us can enhance our personal performances through the systematic use of imagery. Our goal in this chapter is to help you understand imagery as a basic mental training tool, and to provide you with some practical ideas about how to use imagery in sport training.

What Is Imagery?

Imagery is using one's senses to re-create or create an experience in the mind. Research indicates that when individuals engage in vivid imagery, their brains interpret these images as identical to the actual stimulus situation (Jeannerod, 1994). This is what makes imagery so powerful! An Alpine skier can imagine herself skiing a downhill run, and her brain will interpret her images and fire the muscles in her legs as if she actually was skiing the course (Suinn, 1980). The power of imagery allows athletes to practice sport skills, strategies, and mental skills without physically being in the training or competitive environment.

Imagery as Re-creating or Creating

Through imagery we are able to re-create as well as to create experiences in our mind. Athletes spend a lot of time re-creating their performances in their minds. We all can remember the nights after competition when we went over and over our performances in our heads. Athletes often get stuck in this type of imagery by focusing on their mistakes and failures, and they replay these miscues without any type of planned strategy for dealing with them. The key for athletes is to learn to use imagery in a productive and controlled manner to learn from performance mistakes and to program their minds and bodies to respond optimally.

Example

Professional baseball player Todd Helton has a video iPod loaded with clips of each of the 1,509 hits he stroked in his eight major league seasons. Helton states: "It's good to watch right before a game. I can see how each [pitcher] pitched me the last time . . . and I can see my good swings, so I'll have a good feeling going in. I use it on the plane, on the bus, sitting at my locker" (Reiter, 2006, p. 36). Helton has a career .334 batting average, so several of his teammates have followed his lead and set up their own personal iPod hitting videos.

We can also use imagery to create new experiences in our minds. Although imagery is essentially a product of memory, our brain is able to put the pieces of the internal picture together in different ways. As designers of their own imagery programs, athletes can build images from whatever pieces of memory they choose. You Tube has shown clips of NHL hockey player Mike Cammalleri sitting on the bench prior to a game using imagery to create perfect shifts in his mind. He has his stick in his hands, and moves it as he scans the empty ice and visualizes the movements, passes, and shots he will make in the upcoming game.

Football quarterbacks may use imagery in this way to create offensive game plans based on the defensive tactics of upcoming opponents. By viewing films of the opponent's defense, a quarterback can create an offensive game plan and visualize the successful execution of this strategy without having previously played against that particular opponent. Athletes should use imagery to prepare mentally for hostile crowds on the road or difficult travel conditions by creating effective responses to questions such as, "What will it be like?" and "How will you respond?"

Imagery as a Polysensory Experience

The second key to understanding imagery is realizing that imagery is a **polysensory** experience that should involve all relevant senses, from visual to auditory, olfactory, gustatory, tactile, and kinesthetic. Auditory refers to sound, such as hearing the crack of the bat in baseball or the sweet sound of a perfect golf drive. Olfactory refers to smell, such as a swimmer smelling chlorine in the pool. Tactile is the sensation of touch, such as feeling the grip of a golf club or the textured leather of a basketball. Gustatory refers to the sense of taste, such as tasting salty sweat in your mouth. **Kinesthetic** sense is the feel or sensation of the body as it moves in different positions. The kinesthetic sense would be important for a gymnast using imagery to practice a balance beam routine or a diver using imagery to feel the rotations before reaching for the water. The more vivid the image, the more effective it is. Let's use the example of a wide receiver in football to stress the importance of using different senses. The receiver uses his visual sense to read the defense and focus on the ball before catching it. He uses his auditory sense to listen to the snap count barked by the quarterback. He uses his tactile and kinesthetic senses to run his pattern, jump in the air, catch a hard thrown ball, and land with both feet touching in bounds. He might also smell freshly mown grass and the sweat of his opponent's jersey when he is tackled. He may even taste the saltiness of his own sweat. All senses should be utilized when practicing imagery to create vivid images of sport experiences.

In addition to the senses just discussed, the emotions associated with various sport experiences are also an important part of imagery. In using imagery to help control anxiety, anger, or pain, athletes must be able to re-create these emotions in their minds. For example, athletes could re-create their thoughts and feelings experienced during competition to understand how and why anxiety hurt their performance. In using imagery to re-create past outstanding performances, athletes should feel the emotions associated with those experiences such as elation, satisfaction, pride, and self-esteem.

Imagery as a Mental Training Tool

Athletes must use imagery in a systematic manner for it to qualify as mental training. Dreaming or random imagery is not systematic, and there is no evidence that these forms of imagery enhance athletes' performance. This doesn't mean that athletes have to spend numerous hours a day engaged in imagery for it to help their performance. However, they must use it in some sort of continuing, organized manner, even if in small doses, to have the desired effect on performance. This is similar to physical training, in which random, occasional physical practice won't do much to increase an athlete's skills. However, systematic, repetitive physical (and mental) practice clearly pays off in performance improvement in any sport.

Athletes must learn to control their imagery to use it effectively as a mental training tool.

Controllability is the ability of athletes to imagine exactly what they intend to imagine, and also the ability to manipulate aspects of the images that they wish to change. Dreams are for the most part uncontrollable—we simply experience them during sleep. Imagery, by contrast, must be controllable so that athletes can manipulate images in productive ways to program themselves for optimal performance. As we all remember as athletes, often our images become uncontrollable, such as when we "choke" under pressure or experience dreaded performance slumps. Thus, coaches and sport psychology consultants must help athletes gain control of their images so that imagery can be used effectively in mental training. In addition to controllability, the other key to using imagery effectively in mental training is vividness. **Vividness** refers to how clearly athletes can see an image and how detailed the image appears to them. Vividness involves such features as whether the image is in color, how many senses are being used, and the emotion or physical sensations experienced when engaging in imagery.

Overall, imagery as a mental training tool involves the systematic practice and use of engaging in vivid and controllable polysensory images to enhance performance. When athletes first begin using imagery, it is typical to lack vividness and especially controllability of images. However, systematic practice has been shown to be very effective in increasing imagery ability (Williams, Cooley, & Cumming, 2013). It is important to encourage athletes if they are not skilled in their initial attempts at imagery. Let them know that imagery is a skill that takes time to train, but it is a learnable skill that they can improve with practice. This is true even with world-class athletes, as the following example shows:

> It took me a long time to control my images and perfect my imagery, maybe a year, doing it every day. At first I couldn't see myself, I always saw everyone else, or I would see my dives wrong all the time. I would get an image of hurting myself, or tripping on the board, or I would "see" something done really bad. As I continued to work at it, I got to the point where I could see myself doing a perfect dive and the crowd yelling at

the Olympics. But it took me a long time. . . . I started to see myself on the board doing my perfect dive. But some days I couldn't see it, or it was a bad dive in my head. I worked at it so much it got to the point that I could do all my dives easily. Sometimes I would even be in the middle of a conversation with someone and I would think of one of my dives and "see" it.
—Olympic gold medalist, springboard diving (Orlick & Partington, 1988, p. 114)

Internal and External Imagery Perspectives

When you spontaneously engage in imagery, do you see yourself as if you're watching videotape or do you see yourself from behind your own eyes? This question differentiates between an external and an internal imagery perspective. Athletes who use an **external imagery perspective** see the image from outside their bodies as if they are viewing themselves with a video camera from either behind, in front, or either side. When athletes use an **internal imagery perspective,** they see the image from inside their bodies the way their eyes normally see. Consider the imagery perspectives used by three different female gymnasts (Post & Wrisberg, 2012, p. 113).

> "I would see the skill as if I was actually like, doing the routine per se . . . where I would look if I was doing the skill."

> "There are times where I would visualize things from like . . . a coaching standpoint, like watching from the side and seeing the vault as a whole."

> "I can see the whole thing like watching it on a video. I can watch myself from the side, the back, from the top . . . basically whatever I want."

Research has demonstrated that imagery can be effective using both internal (Wright & Smith, 2009) and external (Hardy & Callow, 1999) perspectives, with more experienced performers benefiting from switching between the two (Smith, Collins, & Hale, 1998). However, there is evidence that kinesthetic imagery can only be experienced using an internal perspective (e.g., Smith, Wright, Allsopp, & Westhead, 2007). In addition, athletes with a preference for one type of imagery perspective may have greater imagery

ability with that perspective because it is used more often (Callow & Roberts, 2010).

Overall, athletes should be encouraged to practice both perspectives to be competent and comfortable with each. One way to develop athletes' imagery ability is to have them actually perform the skill (e.g., serve a volleyball, noting all the sensations) and then immediately close their eyes and try to replay the serve using an internal perspective (as if from inside their body). Repeat until the athlete can discern little difference between actual and imaged performance. Do this physical-mental practice routine again, only this time with an external imagery perspective (as if seen on videotape). Once athletes are more skilled in imagery, they may prefer to keep their eyes open and may discover a preference for using one perspective more than another.

Does Imagery Work to Enhance Athletes' Performance?

As Figure 13-1 shows, research evidence supporting the effectiveness of imagery as a mental training tool is divided into three areas. First, imagery has been shown to enhance sport performance and learning. Second, imagery has been shown to enhance thoughts and emotions in athletes that are critical to athletes' performance. And, third, research shows that successful athletes use imagery more extensively and systematically than less successful athletes.

Enhancing Sport Performance and Learning

Of primary interest to coaches and athletes is the effectiveness of imagery in enhancing athletes' performance. The research in this area is divided into three sections: mental practice of skill over time, preparatory imagery for competition, and imagery as part of multimodal mental training programs (see Figure 13-1).

Mental practice research. Using imagery to perform a specific sport skill repetitively in the mind is called **mental practice.** Typically,

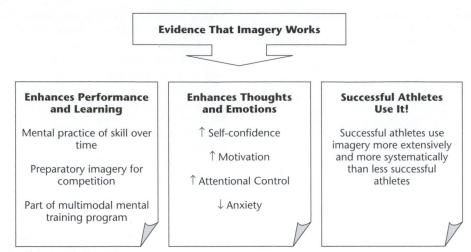

Figure 13-1 **Summary of research support for the effectiveness of imagery**

mental practice occurs across a period of time in an intermittent learning style similar to a distributed physical practice schedule. A plethora of research has been conducted in this area, and comprehensive reviews have concluded that mental practice enhances performance and is better than no practice at all (e.g., Martin, Moritz, & Hall, 1999). Improvement across a wide range of sport skills has been documented through mental practice.

Nothing takes the place of deliberate, repetitive physical practice in refining sport skills! However, mental practice is better than no practice, and it complements physical practice. For example, athletes can engage in physical practice for only finite periods of time, because of fatigue and attentional overload. Mental practice allows athletes to refine their sport skills without having to physically engage in the activity. A Canadian Olympic gold medalist in the bobsled emphasizes this point:

> In bobsledding, you can only do two or three runs per day. I would have liked to do 20 of them but I couldn't. The physical demands were too high. . . . So I did a lot of imagery instead and it was a real learning process. . . . Each track filled up a videotape in my head. (Durand-Bush & Salmela, 2002)

Preparatory imagery. Research also has shown that using imagery immediately before performance can help athletes perform better. Often, imagery is used just prior to performing to "psych up," calm down, or focus on relevant aspects of the task. Consider how Larry Bird, three-time NBA champion and Hall of Famer, used imagery during the playing of the national anthem just prior to games:

> People have noticed that during the national anthem at home games I am always looking up to the Boston Garden ceiling. . . . The thing I look at up there are our championship flags. I focus on the three championships my teams have won and I always look at them in order. I start at 1981, move to 1984 and shift over to 1986. I try to capture how I felt when we won each one and play the championship through my mind. It doesn't take very long to zip through that. (Bird, 1989)

Imagery as a preparatory strategy used prior to performance has improved performance on strength tasks (Tynes & McFatter, 1987), muscular endurance tasks (Gould, Weinberg, & Jackson, 1980; Lee, 1990), and golf putting (Murphy & Woolfolk, 1987; Woolfolk, Parrish, & Murphy, 1985). Imagery also has been shown to be an effective part of athletes' preperformance routines, which involve a planned sequence of thoughts and behaviors that lead to automatic performance execution (Lidor & Singer, 2003).

Multimodal mental training interventions. The effects of imagery on performance and learning also have been examined within multimodal mental training interventions that are implemented with athletes over a period of time. For example, a mental training program consisting of imagery, relaxation, and self-talk training was implemented with soccer players during the season to improve three soccer-specific skills (Thelwell, Greenlees, & Weston, 2006). Multiple mental training intervention studies across many types of sports have shown that performance may be enhanced using a multimodal intervention approach, including imagery.

Multimodal mental training intervention for a tennis player

Christy was a 14-year-old tennis player ranked in the top 25 of her age group nationally. She came to a mental trainer to improve two key aspects of her performance. First, she had a poor net game and was fearful of coming to the net for volleys. Second, she tended to "choke" on her second serve, worrying about double-faulting. Thus, her mental training goals were to overcome her fear of the net game and to develop a focused and confident mental routine to allow her to execute a successful "kick" second serve.

Christy began working on her net game by physically practicing net volleys on shots that began very easy and progressed to harder. She verbalized the cue word seams *out loud that made her focus her attention on the seams of the ball coming toward her and also occupied her mind to prevent negative thinking or worry. Before and after training, she mentally*

practiced net volleys in various situations, using her cue word to create the correct visual picture. Using imagery, she mentally practiced various net tactics for different competitive situations. A performance goal was set for her to hit at least one winner per game from the net. In training, she did not win the game or end the drill until she accomplished this goal. Her net performance improved over the course of the 25-week intervention so that she won, on average, 4 points per match from the net.

To deal with her double-fault problem, Christy developed a preservice routine using relaxation, self-talk, and imagery. The routine started with bouncing the ball four times and catching it. Then she took a relaxation breath, during which she imagined air passing through her body and dissipating any tension in it. She used the cue word smooth *to program a relaxed, smoothly executed serve. She then used the kinesthetic image of her racquet making contact with the ball for a perfect kick serve and a visual image of the ball "kicking" successfully within her opponent's service box. This routine was developed and practiced in parts, and was completed and refined over three months of practice. Christy was able to gain fluidity and smoothness in her second serve, and to significantly decrease her double-fault percentage as the result of the mental training (modified from Mamassis & Doganis, 2004).*

Enhancing Competition-Related Thoughts and Emotions

In addition to helping athletes perform better, research findings indicate that imagery enhances the competition-related thoughts and emotions of athletes. This is important because a basic objective of sport psychology is to help athletes think better—to enable them to manage their thoughts and emotions effectively to create a productive competitive focus. Imagery can enhance self-confidence (Callow, Hardy, & Hall 2001; Mamassis & Doganis, 2004); motivation (Beauchamp et al., 1996; Martin & Hall, 1995), and attentional control (Calmels, Berthoumieux, & d'Arripe-Longueville, 2004). It also can change athletes' perceptions of anxiety from harmful and negative to facilitative and challenging (Cumming, Olphin, & Law, 2007; Mamassis & Doganis, 2004; Page, Sime, & Nordell, 1999) and can help decrease or control precompetitive anxiety when combined with other mental training methods such as relaxation and stress inoculation training (Kerr & Leith, 1993; Ryska, 1998). In addition, imagery can affect the self-confidence of coaches (Short, Smiley, & Ross-Stewart, 2005).

A highly successful Olympic pistol shooter states:

> As for success imagery, I would imagine to myself, "How would a champion act? How would a champion feel? How would she perform on the line?" This helped me find out about myself, what worked and didn't work for me. . . . That helped me believe that I would be the Olympic champion. (Orlick & Partington, 1988, p. 113)

Professional golfer Bob Ford, admired by peers for his ability to clear his mind for competition, describes his unique imagery practice of imagining himself on an elevator as he walks to the first tee at a tournament. When he gets to the first tee, the doors open and he envisions being on a "whole new floor." Ford explains this image allows him to leave all problems and extraneous thoughts behind on another "floor," and enables him to focus in on the "competition floor." These examples demonstrate how athletes can use imagery to identify and create the kind of thoughts, feelings, and focus that maximize chances for competitive success.

Incidence of Imagery Use

Successful elite athletes use imagery more extensively and systematically, and they have better imagery skill than less accomplished athletes (Calmels, d'Arripe-Longueville, Fournier, & Soulard, 2003; Gregg & Hall, 2006). Of 235 Canadian Olympic athletes who participated in the 1984 Olympic Games, 99 percent reported using imagery (Orlick & Partington, 1988). During training they engaged in preplanned systematic imagery at least once a day, 4 days per week, for about 12 minutes each time. At the Olympic site, some reported engaging in imagery for 2 to 3 hours in preparation for their events. In addition, mental training (including imagery) to develop systematic competitive routines and plans was a critical factor in the successful performance of athletes at the 1996 Olympic Games (Gould, Guinan, Greenleaf, Medbery, & Peterson, 1999). Coaches attending a mental skills training workshop reported using imagery with their athletes more than any other mental training technique and that it was their most useful mental technique (Hall & Rodgers, 1989).

Experiential Evidence That Imagery Works

Perhaps it would be helpful to learn firsthand from athletes themselves about how imagery works for them. Several athletes who have at one time been the best in the world at their sport advocate the use of imagery, including Michael Phelps and Lindsey Vonn. Chris Evert, the great tennis champion, admitted that she practiced imagery before important matches by painstakingly visualizing opponents' specific styles of play and then visualizing her successful responses to these opponents. Phil Mickelson, one of the top golfers in the world, states, "When I see a shot, I see in my mind's eye a 'window' I want the ball to pass through at the apex of its flight."

Colleen Hacker, sport psychology consultant for the U.S. women's soccer team that won the 1996 and 2004 Olympic Games and the 1999 World Cup, created individualized audio and video imagery tapes for the players prior to these competitions as well as every other major world event. The tapes are full of confidence-building trigger words, phrases, and images, all set to each player's favorite songs. The tapes became a powerful source of team chemistry when the players ended up watching them as a group. Kristine Lilly, who made a key header save in the World Cup final against China, stated: "The tapes give me that little extra confidence, remind me about who I am and what I can give. I'm inspired watching my teammates' tapes. And I'm reminded of what they do well, so I'll never second-guess them" (Lieber, 1999, p. 2c).

The following excerpt from an interview with a Canadian Olympic diver attests to this athlete's extreme commitment to and belief in imagery (Orlick & Partington, 1988):

> I did my dives in my head all the time. At night, before going to sleep, I always did my dives. Ten dives. I started with a front dive, the first one that I had to do at the Olympics, and I did everything as if I was actually there. I saw myself on the board with the same bathing suit. Everything was the same. . . . If the dive was wrong, I went back and started over again. It takes a good hour to do perfect imagery of all my dives, but for me it was better than a workout. Sometimes I would take the weekend off and do imagery five times a day.

Similarly, observe the commitment to imagery by Alex Baumann, Olympic double gold medalist in swimming:

> The best way I have learned to prepare mentally for competition is to visualize the race in my mind. . . . In my imagery I concentrate on attaining the splits I have set out to do. About 15 minutes before the race I visualize the race in my mind. I think about my own race and nothing else. I try to get those splits in my mind, and after that I am ready to go. My visualization has been refined more and more over the years. That is what really got me the world record and Olympic medals. (Orlick, 1998, p. 70)

How Does Imagery Enhance Athletes' Performance?

Many theoretical explanations for how imagery facilitates performance have been advanced in the literature (Morris, Spittle, & Watt, 2005), and it is beyond the scope of this chapter to review all of them. Three of the most contemporary and practical theoretical explanations for how imagery enhances performance are presented here.

Bioinformational Explanation

Bioinformational theory (Lang, 1977, 1979) assumes that a mental image is an organized set of propositions, or characteristics, stored in the brain's long-term memory. When individuals engage in imagery, they activate **stimulus characteristics** that describe the content of the image for them and **response characteristics** that describe what their responses are to the stimuli in that situation. For example, imagining shooting a basketball free throw in the final seconds of a close game would involve the stimulus characteristics of the feel of the ball in the hand, the sight of the basket, and the sound of the crowd. The response characteristics for this image might include muscular tension in the shooting arm, increased perspiration, feelings of anxiety, and the joyous sight of the ball swishing through the net. According to bioinformational theory, for imagery to facilitate sport performance, response characteristics must be activated so they can be modified, improved, and strengthened. Imagery enhances performance by repeatedly accessing response characteristics for a particular stimulus situation and modifying these responses to represent perfect control and execution of a skill.

Research has shown that response-oriented imagery results in greater physiological reactivity than stimulus-oriented imagery (Bakker, Boschker, & Chung, 1996; Cumming et al., 2007) and also that images of situations with which athletes have personal experience create greater physiological reactivity than less familiar images (Hecker & Kaczor, 1988). Moreover, athlete performance has been improved to a greater degree through imagery that included both stimulus and response characteristics, as opposed to imagery that just included stimulus characteristics (Smith & Collins, 2004; Smith, Holmes, Whitemore, Collins, & Devenport, 2001). Interestingly, response-oriented imagery has been shown to create more "priming" responses in the brain as measured by electroencephalographic (EEG) activity when compared to stimulus-oriented imagery (Smith & Collins, 2004).

An important implication from this is that coaches, athletes, and sport psychologists involved in imagery training should include many response characteristics when using imagery. Specifically, images should contain not only the conditions of the situation (swimming in a pool, water is rough, championship meet) but also the athlete's *behavioral* responses (swimming strongly, right on pace), *psychological* responses (feeling confident, focusing on the race), and *physiological* responses (feeling energized) to the situation. By including these positive responses, the image will be more vivid and should result in psychophysiological changes in the body and thus improved performance. (Note the positive responses to an upcoming competition described in the sample imagery script provided in Appendix A.) Also, it is important to encourage use of kinesthetic imagery to emphasize feeling the physical sensations of performing a specific skill, which will further strengthen effective response characteristics.

Functional Equivalence Explanation

In this second theoretical explanation, imagery causes the brain to activate the same areas and processes as when the movement being imaged is actually executed. This approach has been referred to as the functional equivalence explanation for the effects of imagery on performance (Holmes & Collins, 2001; Jeannerod, 1994). Using one's imagination to simulate a movement recruits the same parts and sequences in the brain as the actual physical execution of the movement. The term **functional equivalence** means that imagery has a similar functional outcome as the actual movement.

Research has shown that more functionally equivalent imagery had a greater positive effect on both youth and adult sport performance than imagery that was less functionally equivalent (Smith, Wright, Allsopp, & Westhead, 2007). Imagery is more functionally equivalent when it

- Includes important senses and feelings associated with competition.
- Is practiced in a posture similar to one's performance posture, wearing performance clothes, holding performance implements,

and in a similar environment to the performance environment.
- Is timed at the same pace as the actual timing of the skill.
- Is internal in perspective.

An interesting study found that golfers who practiced imagery by watching a video or listening to an audiotape of themselves putting successfully performed better than golfers who practiced imagery using a written script (Smith & Holmes, 2004). This finding supports the functional equivalence idea, in that the videotape and audiotape conditions stimulated the golfers' brains in more functionally equivalent ways (e.g., seeing or hearing the putt struck and falling into the cup in real time, having visual and auditory cues) than doing imagery from a written script.

Mental Readiness Explanation

The mental readiness explanation of how imagery works is not a theory but an intuitive description of the role of imagery in helping athletes to optimize arousal, attention, and confidence. Athletes commonly use imagery to psych up or calm down to meet the energy demands of a particular sport, as well as to visualize aspects of the upcoming competition to sharpen the focus they need to be successful. For example, a wrestler may use imagery before a match to psych himself up to a high energy level and to focus his attention on the specific strategies and moves he needs to use against a particular opponent.

Research has shown that imagery is effective in optimizing arousal, attention, and confidence in athletes (Calmels et al., 2004; Cumming et al., 2007; Hale & Whitehouse, 1998). A national level gymnast explains that imagery "helped her to think more clearly and 'not get all worked up,'" and an elite canoeist described imagery as helping her "feel 'switched on' and able to keep 'away from everybody'" (White & Hardy, 1998). A youth athlete stated that "Imagery helps you, like 'you can do it'" (Cumming et al., 2007), which is a great statement of self-confidence!

Can Imagery Hurt Athletes' Performance?

Often, coaches and athletes ask if imagery can ever hurt their performance. It's a good question, and yes, imagery *can* hurt athletes' performance *if* they focus on the *wrong* images at the *wrong* times. When individuals used negative imagery by imaging performing unsuccessful putts, their golf putting accuracy declined (Short et al., 2002; Woolfolk, Parrish, & Murphy, 1985). This research indicates that imagery can hurt athletes' performance if they systematically imagine bad performance. This doesn't mean that athletes should not use imagery, as the point of imagery training is to enable athletes to control their previously uncontrollable images. Athletes are going to experience images whether they engage in mental training or not, so it seems productive to enable them to become more skillful in their use of imagery to avoid the debilitating effects of negative imagery. The point is for athletes to create a mental blueprint for perfect responses, NOT to create a mental blueprint for disastrous responses! Consider how Ken Dryden, then a 23-year-old rookie goalie for the Montreal Canadiens, created the wrong mental blueprint the night before he was to face the Boston Bruins in Game 7 of the quarterfinals at hostile Boston Garden:

> [I turned on the television in my hotel, and] the only thing I could find was *The Bruins Week in Review*. All they kept showing was the Bruins' scoring goal after goal. "Esposito scores! Orr scores! Esposito scores again!" I was already nervous, and I turned downright depressed. I went to bed and dreamed about those goals. (McCallum, 2004, p. 56)

Additional research has shown that constant attempts to suppress negative thoughts and images from conscious awareness can increase the probability that these negative thoughts and images will influence performance (Beilock, Afremow, Rabe, & Carr, 2001). In this study, individuals in a golf putting task were told, "Be careful to try not to image hitting the ball short of the target. Don't image undershooting the target!" When individuals were told what not to image, they performed poorly, even when they attempted to suppress these negative images. From a practical perspective, this indicates that athletes should avoid programing themselves to not do something, or constantly focus on negative images and attempt to suppress them. Likewise, coaches should refrain from "negative coaching," or giving verbal feedback such as "Don't pop up!" or "Stay away from the out-of-bounds on the left." These well-meaning, yet negative, coaching comments often create mental blueprints in athletes' heads of the exact performance the coach is suggesting that they not do.

So there is a grain of truth in the popular notion that "thinking too much" can hurt an athlete's performance. The key is to think productively and to simplify one's thinking to the point of automatic performance. This may be difficult during a performance slump, when one's controllability of images slips a bit and negative images pop up during competition. However, the goal of systematic imagery training is to develop more and more skill in controlling one's thoughts and images.

How Do You Set Up an Imagery Training Program?

Setting up the imagery program has four phases. First, sell the athletes on the use of imagery. Second, evaluate the imagery skill of the athletes so they understand their imagery abilities and areas that need improvement. Third, have athletes practice developing basic imagery skills. Fourth, implement a systematic program of imagery practice and then monitor it.

Introduce Imagery to Athletes

Imagery works for athletes only if they believe in it. While convincing athletes that imagery can indeed help them perform better, you should avoid unnecessary hype or unrealistic claims. Make sure they understand that imagery will not guarantee success. It is simply a mental training technique that has been shown to enhance sport performance.

An approach that we have found useful in introducing imagery to athletes is the analogy of building a machine. When athletes continuously practice a sport skill over and over, they are in essence attempting to build a machine. Divers attempt to fine-tune their body to make their muscles react flawlessly in a dive. Shot putters work hours refining their technique in order to uncoil their body in maximum thrust. Coaches and athletes spend a great deal of time using drill and repetition attempting to build a flawless, automatic machine. Why not use imagery to help? Make the point that building a machine for optimal sport performance requires mental training as well as physical training.

The introduction of imagery can take place in an informal group setting if you are working with a team. We recommend that you spend no more than 20 minutes summarizing some important points about imagery. An introduction to imagery might include the following steps.

Hook 'em. Grab athletes' attention right away: You could (a) discuss the concept of building a machine, (b) ask them if they use imagery and have them describe how they use it, and (c) explain how several famous, successful athletes use imagery. Be creative! Also, it is critical that you are enthusiastic and model your confidence and strong belief in the power of imagery.

Define and give evidence. Briefly explain what imagery is by using a definition such as "practicing in your head" or "building your mental blueprint." Without bogging them down with scientific research, provide some brief evidence that imagery does work to enhance performance. It is helpful to use testimonials from famous coaches and athletes who believe in imagery.

Explain how it works. Provide a simple and brief explanation for how imagery works to enhance performance. The amount of detail you get into here depends on the level of the athletes. We usually explain that imagery creates a mental blueprint of a particular skill and that by using imagery they are ingraining or strengthening

that mental blueprint to make their skills automatic or to build a machine. Athletes are always intrigued when they learn that innervation of their brains during imagery is similar to when they are performing the skill. To emphasize the way imagery works, you may want to take your athletes through one or both of the following exercises so they can immediately experience the power of imagery.

String and bolt. Give each athlete a string approximately 14 to 16 inches long threaded through a heavy bolt (a neck chain and heavy ring also will work). Stabilizing the elbow, ideally on a table top, have each athlete lightly hold the two ends of the string between the thumb and forefinger with the weight suspended directly below. Focusing on the weight, each athlete in his or her mind's eye should imagine the weight moving right and left like the pendulum of a clock. Once most athletes have at least some movement right and left, have them change the image so the weight swings directly away from and then toward the chest. Again, once successful, change the image so the weight moves in a clockwise circle and finally in a counterclockwise circle. In discussing this exercise, you will find most athletes are impressed at how imagining the movement ultimately translates to the actual physical movement of the pendulum. Once completed, you can explain to the athletes that the subtle muscle innervation in the arm and hand created by the imagery is responsible for the movement of the pendulum.

Arm as iron bar. Pair each athlete with a partner of similar height and strength. While directly facing each other, one partner extends his dominant arm straight out, palm up, so the back of the wrist is resting on the partner's opposite shoulder. The other partner cups both of his hands above the bend in the partner's elbow. The person whose arm is extended then maximally tightens all the muscles in the arm, trying to make it as strong as possible. Then the partner tests for strength by pushing down at the elbow with both hands, trying to see how much strength it takes to bend the arm. Then switch roles. Afterward, resume the initial position with the original partner. This time, to create strength, the partner is to close everything out of his mind and imagine that the arm is a thick steel bar. Not only is the arm a hard, steel bar, but it extends out through the opposite wall. Once the partner has created the image of an unbendable, strong steel bar, he indicates such by raising a finger on the opposite hand. This signals the partner to again test for strength. Again, switch roles. In follow-up discussion you will find that most athletes will be amazed at how much stronger their arm was using the iron bar image.

Give specifics about how imagery will be used.   At this point let the athletes know exactly how they will incorporate imagery into their training. For example, a basketball team could start by using mental practice for free throws and imagery to mentally rehearse specific team plays. It is a mistake to try to do too much too soon. However, it is important for athletes to quickly see how imagery can be applied to meet their practical needs.

Help Athletes Evaluate Their Imagery Ability

After sparking athletes' interest in imagery, the next step is to help them evaluate their imagery abilities. One method of evaluation is to take the athletes through some of the Basic Training imagery exercises provided in this chapter. By discussing their images with them, you could determine whether certain areas need to be strengthened. Another way to evaluate imagery ability is to administer the Sport Imagery Evaluation (see Appendix B), which measures athletes' abilities to experience different senses, emotions, and perspectives during imagery. There are other inventories designed to measure imagery ability, but this evaluation seems to be most useful to the coach/practitioner.

For best results, direct athletes through the exercises in the evaluation (it takes approximately 15 minutes). Encourage athletes to answer honestly on the basis of their imagery ability. Afterward, discuss the results informally with athletes to better understand their unique imagery abilities and to target areas that can be improved through practice.

Basic Training

Basic Training is similar to a preseason physical conditioning program. By developing a foundation of strength and endurance, athletes are better equipped to fine-tune their physical skills when the season begins. By strengthening their imagery "muscles" in Basic Training, athletes are more likely to benefit from the use of imagery during the season.

Basic Training includes three types of imagery exercises. First, athletes need to develop *vivid* images. Like using a fine-tuning control on a television, increasing the vividness of images sharpens the details of the image. Second, athletes must be able to *control* their images. Controllability exercises involve learning to manipulate images by will. Third, athletes need to enhance their ability to engage in *self-awareness*. It is a skill to use imagery to become more aware of underlying thoughts and feelings that often influence our performance without our realizing it.

It is helpful for athletes to gain proficiency in all three types of imagery exercises. The example exercises purposely use vague descriptors to encourage you to develop your own imagery exercises that are tailored specifically for you or your athletes. It is also helpful to develop additional exercises in areas in which athletes are having trouble.

Vividness

Exercise 1

Place yourself in a familiar place where you usually perform your sport (gym, pool, rink, field, track, etc.). It is empty except for you. Stand in the middle of this place and look all around. Notice the quiet emptiness. Pick out as many details as you can. What does it smell like? What are the colors, shapes, and forms that you see? Now imagine yourself in the same setting, but this time there are many spectators there. Imagine yourself getting ready to perform. Try to experience this image from inside your body. See the spectators, your teammates, your coach, and the opponents. Try to hear the sounds of the noisy crowd, your teammates' chatter, your coach yelling encouragement, and the particular sounds of your sport (e.g., ball swishing through the net, volleyball spike hitting the floor). Re-create the feelings of nervous anticipation and excitement that you have before competing. How do you feel?

Exercise 2

Choose a piece of equipment in your sport such as a ball, pole, racket, or club. Focus on this object. Try to imagine the fine details of the object. Turn it over in your hands and examine every part of the object. Feel its outline and texture. Now imagine yourself performing with the object. First, focus on seeing yourself very clearly performing this activity. Visualize yourself repeating the skill over and over. See yourself performing from behind your own eyes. Then step outside of your body and see yourself perform as if you were watching yourself on film. Now, step back in your body and continue performing. Next, try to hear the sounds that accompany this particular movement. Listen carefully to all the sounds that are being made as you perform this skill. Now, put the sight and the sound together. Try to get a clear picture of yourself performing the skill and also hear all the sounds involved.

Exercise 3

Pick a very simple skill in your sport. Perform the skill over and over in your mind and imagine every feeling and movement in your muscles as you perform that skill. Try to feel this image as if you were inside your own body. Concentrate on how

the different parts of your body feel as you stretch and contract the various muscles associated with the skill. Think about building a machine as you perform the skill flawlessly over and over again and concentrate on the feeling of the movement.

Now try to combine all of your senses, but particularly those of feeling, seeing, and hearing yourself perform the skill over and over. Do not concentrate too hard on any one sense. Instead, try to imagine the total experience using all of your senses.

Once athletes have mastered these exercises, you might consider follow-up variations to imagine more complex skills, grouping skills together, or placing the skill in the context of competition (such as reacting to certain defenses, executing strategy, etc.).

Controllability

Exercise 1

Choose a simple sport skill and begin practicing it. Now imagine yourself performing this skill either with a teammate or against an opponent. Imagine yourself executing successful strategies in relation to the movements of your teammate or opponent.

Exercise 2

Choose a sport skill that you have trouble performing. Begin practicing the skill over and over. See and feel yourself doing this from inside your body. If you make a mistake or perform the skill incorrectly, stop the image and repeat it, attempting to perform perfectly every time. Re-create past experiences in which you have not performed the skill well. Take careful notice of what you are doing wrong. Now imagine yourself performing the skill correctly. Focus on how your body feels as you go through different positions in performing the skill correctly. Build a perfect machine!

Self-Awareness

Exercise 1

Think back and choose a past performance in which you performed very well. Using all your senses, re-create that situation in your mind. See yourself as you were succeeding, hear the sounds involved, feel your body as you performed the movements, and reexperience the positive emotions. Try to pick out the characteristics that made you perform so well (e.g., intense concentration, feelings of confidence, optimal arousal). After identifying these characteristics, try to determine why they were present in this situation. Think about the things you did in preparation for this particular event. What are some things that may have caused this great performance?

Repeat this exercise, imagining a situation in which you performed very poorly. Make sure you are very relaxed before practicing this image, as your mind will subconsciously resist your imagery attempts to re-create unpleasant thoughts, images, and feelings. Attempt to become more self-aware of how you reacted to different stimuli (e.g., coaches, opponents, officials, fear of failure, needing approval from others) and how these thoughts and feelings may have interfered with your performance.

Exercise 2

Think back to a sport situation in which you experienced a great deal of anxiety. Re-create that situation in your head, seeing and hearing yourself. Especially re-create the feeling of anxiety. Try to feel the physical responses of your body to the emotion and also try to recall the thoughts going through your mind that may have caused the anxiety. Now attempt to let go of the anxiety and relax your body. Breathe slowly and deeply and focus on your body as you exhale. Imagine all of the tension being pulled into your lungs and exhaled from your body. Continue breathing slowly and exhaling tension until you are deeply relaxed. Now repeat this exercise imagining a situation in which you experienced a great deal of anger, and then relax yourself using the breathing and exhalation technique.

Exercise 3

The purpose of this exercise is to help you become more aware of things that happen during competition that bother you when you perform. Think about the times when your performance suddenly went from good to bad. Re-create several of these experiences in your mind. Try to pinpoint the specific factors that negatively influenced your performance (e.g., officials, teammates, opponents' remarks, opponent started to play much better). After becoming aware of these factors that negatively affected your performance, take several minutes to re-create the situations, develop appropriate strategies to deal with the negative factors, and imagine the situations again; but this time imagine yourself using your strategies to keep the negative factors from interfering with your performance. Reinforce yourself by feeling proud and confident that you were able to control the negative factors and perform well.

Implement a Systematic Program

Athletes are now ready to begin a *systematic* program of imagery. Imagery practice must be systematic to be effective, so always follow the KISS principle (keep it simple and systematic)! The first concern is to build the imagery program into the athletes' routine. The imagery program must *not* be something extra but should instead be an integral part of training and practice.

Another key is to fit the needs of the athlete. The imagery program need not be long and complex. In fact, when first starting it is a good idea to keep it concise and simple. Initially, choose a sport skill or strategy that is easy to control, such as when the environment is stable rather than reactive. For example, in basketball you could start with free throw shooting and in racket sports with the serve. As your athletes become more proficient at and accepting of the program, you can increase its complexity.

Imagery Cookbook for Coaches and Practitioners

It is impossible to design an imagery program appropriate for all sports. For that reason, we have designed this section like a cookbook, which itemizes the necessary ingredients of an imagery program. The ingredients listed include ways to use imagery, times in which imagery may be practiced, and strategies to enhance imagery practice. It is up to you to choose which ingredients are most relevant for the needs of your athletes.

Ways to Use Imagery

Athletes can use imagery in a number of ways to enhance sport performance. These include

- Learning and practicing sport skills.
- Correcting mistakes.
- Learning and practicing performance strategies.
- Preparing a mental focus for competition.
- Automating preperformance routines.
- Building and enhancing mental skills.
- Aiding in the recovery from injuries.

Learning and practicing sport skills. One of the best places for athletes to start using imagery is mental practice, or the repetitive practice of a sport skill in their minds. They should choose one or two skills in their sport, and mentally practice these skills. Urge athletes to mentally practice on their own, but they will be more inclined to do so if mental practice is incorporated as part of their regular training. Coaches can implement a volleyball serving drill in which athletes serve 10 balls and mentally practice each serve prior to physically performing it. This also could be applied to shooting free throws, executing wrestling moves, serving in tennis, sprinting over a set of hurdles, or hitting a baseball. Mental practice is also useful to aid beginners in learning sport skills by helping them to develop a "mental blueprint for perfect responses."

Athletes can strengthen or build their mental blueprints for perfect responses by using verbal triggers and symbolic images. **Verbal triggers** are words or phrases that help athletes focus on key aspects in an image to make their mental blueprint for performance correct. Triggers are used to program the proper image. Coaches use triggers all the time in teaching skills or as points of emphasis they want athletes to think about when performing. Softball players are told to "throw their hands" and focus on a "quick bat." Volleyball serving is taught by having athletes focus on the "bow and arrow" technique. Basketball players are taught to "plant" their inside foot and "square up" for perfect jump shot form. Cross-country skiers think "quick" for their uphill technique to trigger the quick, short kick technique needed on hills. A famous golfer kept the word *oooom-PAH* written on her driver to program the image of an easy slow backswing and a strong and vigorous downswing.

Symbolic images are mental symbols or models for desired components of performance. Archers can envision a string extending from the center of the target that pulls their arrows directly into the bull's-eye. Sprinters may imagine the explosive energy in their legs as coiled springs that will catapult them from the starting blocks. U.S. biathletes have used the symbolic image *Rock of Gibraltar* to program the steady body state they need to shoot effectively. Golfers can imagine turning their body inside a barrel to ensure proper body rotation on the swing and can imagine their arms as a pendulum swinging from the shoulders for the proper putting stroke. A gymnast may visualize her back against a cold, steel wall to perfect the image and movement of a perfectly straight body during a floor exercise routine.

As you read earlier in the chapter, imagery can only hurt performance if athletes imagine the wrong responses. Triggers and symbolic images help athletes lock in the proper responses so that the imagery is "programmed" in the right way. Mental practice using triggers and symbolic images may be helpful for athletes who are mired in a slump or who are having technique problems. They should imagine themselves performing perfectly and attempt to analyze how their present technique is different from their perfect performance. It may be helpful for athletes to view videotapes of themselves performing well and then internalize that performance by using kinesthetic imagery. Coaches should help athletes identify the triggers and symbolic images that really lock in those perfect responses within a sound performance mental blueprint.

Correcting mistakes.   A very simple use of imagery for athletes is in correcting mistakes. Athletes receive constant feedback and corrections from coaches and imagery is a great tool that athletes can use to gain the most benefit from these corrections. Athletes should listen to their coaches' feedback or correction and then see it and feel it as they incorporate the information from the coach into their image and execution of the skill.

Coaches should teach and expect athletes to use imagery each time they receive feedback by requesting them to imagine the desired correction in performance; coaches should ask each time: Can you see it? Can you feel it? Using imagery to correct mistakes is also helpful when watching videotape of performances. When athletes and coaches identify flaws or mistakes in athletes' performance when watching video, athletes should be cued immediately to imagine the correction by seeing it and feeling it. Coaches also can help athletes build in triggers or symbolic images to help athletes lock in the mental blueprint for perfect responses.

Coaches can help athletes "calibrate" their images by observing athletes perform and then comparing their observations with what the athletes perceive is occurring in their performance (Simons, 2000). Simons describes how a high jumper attempts to recall the image of her jump immediately after each attempt. She describes her image of her jump to her coach, who then describes her observations of the jump. In this way, the coach is calibrating the athlete's image of the jump to ensure that the athlete's perception and image of what she is doing is indeed correct in form.

Learning and practicing performance strategies. Imagery is very useful in helping athletes learn and practice performance strategies, such as tactics, systems of play, and decision making. For example, football quarterbacks can mentally rehearse various plays in relation to specific defenses, even imagining reacting to blitzes and changing defensive formations to audible and completing the appropriate offensive counter to this defense. When introducing a new basketball offense or out-of-bounds play, coaches can direct athletes to walk through the new pattern and then immediately follow this physical practice by imagining their movements through the patterns. Then, before competition, coaches can lead athletes in mentally rehearsing these previously learned offensive and defensive strategies and plays. Similarly, skiers may ski over a particular course in their mind to prepare for an upcoming downhill race. Softball outfielders may use imagery to practice throws from the outfield based on various situations that may arise in a game. Tennis players can mentally rehearse their planned strategy against a particular opponent.

Preparing a mental focus for competition.   Imagery can be used by athletes to create and practice in their heads the strong, unshakable mental focus needed for specific competitions. Coaches should help athletes answer two questions: "What will it be like?" "How will I respond?" "What will it be like?" refers to the external factors of competition, or the physical and social environment. For each competitive situation that athletes face, they should vividly imagine what it will be like in terms of the facilities, crowd, potential distracters, officials, weather, and so on.

The second question, "How will I respond?" is by far the most important question for athletes.

Athletes should plan to respond, not react. Responding requires mental skill and toughness to manage one's thoughts and emotions and performance when faced with obstacles, surprises, and disappointments. Reacting doesn't take any skill at all—it is typically a raw emission of emotion (anger, anxiety, fear) in which athletes allow the competitive environment to control them and make them reactive. Imagery is the tool athletes can use to practice over and over in their heads the ways in which they will respond to any type of competitive pressure they might face, and even those that they can't anticipate. Athletes should program the answers to the two questions into a short imagery routine that they practice over and over in their heads in the days and weeks leading up to a particular competition. Imagery used in this way is an attempt to help athletes gain "experience" in responding to competitive challenges. The idea is to create a sense of expectancy, so that athletes expect certain obstacles and pressures, even the unexpected. If they have been mentally trained to expect the unexpected and to respond productively to the unexpected, they will be less likely to react emotionally in ways that will hurt their performances.

Coaches should attempt to simulate competitive conditions at times in practice so that athletes can practice their mental focus plan for competition. The best coaches are masters at simulation who can create all types of situations that athletes might face in competition. These "dress rehearsals" might include wearing uniforms, using clocks and officials, and simulating environmental conditions such as noise, distractions, heat, cold, and pressure. Peter Vidmar, collegiate national champion gymnast and Olympic gold medalist, describes how he and his teammates would simulate competition during practice:

> The team did really weird things to prepare for [the Olympics]. In practice, we would turn off the radio so it was silent in the gym. We would go through the dialogues, like this next routine is the Olympic Games and it's the team finals. It's the last event, and we were neck-and-neck with the Chinese. It was only make-believe when we

did it, but what if we really were neck-and-neck with the Chinese during the Games and this routine was our only chance to beat them and win the gold? We'd set the whole thing up, and my heart would be pounding and I would be imagining I was in Pauley Pavilion at the Olympic Games with all the pressure and people watching. I would get really nervous, take those few deep breaths and imagine I was there at the meet and [Coach] was the head judge. Tim [Daggett] would be Mr. Loudspeaker. "Okay. Next up for the USA," he would say, "Mr. Peter Vidmar." We were dead serious when we were doing this.

> During the Olympics, a funny thing happened. It was the last event and the USA just happened to be on the high bar and . . . I just happened to be the last up. We just happened to be neck-and-neck with the Chinese. It's the same scenario we had gone through every day for the last six months and here we were actually living it. [Coach] said, "Okay, Pete. Let's go do it just like in the gym." So I imagined I was in the UCLA gym. Consciously, I knew I was at the Olympics, but I was able to put myself in the frame of mind that I was back at the gym. I was even able to geographically orient that bar to the gym as if there was a pit over there and the wall there, etc. I did my routine and landed successfully. . . . We won the gold. (Ravizza, 1993, pp. 94–95)

Automating preperformance routines. A **preperformance routine** is a preplanned, systematic sequence of thoughts and behaviors in which an athlete engages prior to performing a specific skill. Athletes typically use preperformance routines prior to executing specific sport skills, such as a golf shot, basketball free throw, gymnastics vault, volleyball or tennis serve, field goal kick in football, start in swimming, or any of the jumping and throwing events in track and field. Research has supported preperformance routines as facilitative to athletes' performances (Lidor & Singer, 2003).

Often, imagery is included in athletes' preperformance routines (e.g., seeing the ball float softly over the front of the rim into the basket). Imagery also should be used to systematically practice preperformance routines to make them more automatic. Then, during the pressure of competition, these routines are used to lock athletes into "autopilot," where their best performances occur.

Building and enhancing mental skills. Imagery, as a mental training tool, can be used to build and enhance all types of mental skills important to an athlete's performance.

Self-confidence. Athletes can nurture a self-image of competence and success by re-creating past successful performances and the positive feelings associated with these successes. An imagery exercise called Ideal Self-Image (ISI) is useful to work on confidence. To practice the ISI exercise, athletes should imagine themselves displaying the skills and qualities that they would most like to have, such as more assertive communication skills, a confident posture after performance errors, or the ability to manage emotions during competition. Then, they should compare their ISI with their current self-image. This should enable them to understand specific behaviors and thoughts that they can actively engage in to begin to move toward their ISI. The ISI exercise should be used continuously to understand differences between their real and ideal selves. Imagery then can be used to practice new behaviors and ways of responding that move athletes toward their ISI.

Energy management. Athletes who need to increase their energy (arousal) to psych up for competition can imagine playing intensely and assertively in front of a roaring crowd. Athletes who need to decrease their energy or arousal before competition can mentally recall their preparation and good performances in practice and previous competitions and then visualize themselves handling the pressure and performing successfully in the upcoming competition.

An imagery exercise called the Energy Room can help athletes regulate arousal from different competitive demands. The Energy Room image involves athletes walking down a dark tunnel to a door that leads them into a room that is very comfortable and pleasing. (You can create whatever type of room you wish.) Imagine the room is sealed and special air is piped in that creates the type of energy that is needed for this specific athlete in his or her event. The athletes feel themselves become more energized or relaxed with each inhalation and feel increasing focus,

intensity, or relaxation. The breathing continues until the athletes feel appropriately energized and walk back through the tunnel feeling relaxed, focused, intense, centered, or confident. Whatever variation is used in this image, the main objective is for athletes to have an imaginary place that they can go to create optimal energy and use any mental strategies they want to employ. The room should become comfortable and familiar so it is an easy place for athletes to go in their minds to manage and control their physical and mental arousal levels.

Stress management. Energy management is usually needed just before or during competition. Imagery may also be helpful to reduce stress that occurs because of an overload of life demands (e.g., job pressure, exams, deadlines). Coaches and athletes both should have two or three relaxing images that they can use when they need to reduce stress and help them to relax and unwind. These images might be of a favorite place or a warm beach. An example stress reduction imagery script is provided in the following box.

Sample imagery script for relaxation/ stress reduction

1. *Get into a comfortable position and close your eyes. Take several deep, cleansing breaths to relax and center yourself. Take a moment to scan your muscles. If you feel tension anywhere, gently remind yourself to "let it go." Continue to scan the muscles of your body. Wherever you feel any tension, allow yourself to consciously "let it go." As you do this, repeat the words "let it go" to yourself.*

2. *I would like you to visualize a very thick rope that is tied into a big knot. See the knot in your mind's eye. Notice the tightly intertwined pieces of the rope that are stretched taut against each other. Now visualize the knot slowly loosening,*

slowly loosening—a little bit of slack at a time until it is slack, limp, and completely uncoiled.

3. Now visualize a candle that has burned out. Focus on the cold and hard wax that has accumulated at the base of the candle. Now visualize the wax slowly softening—becoming first gooey, then soft like butter, then totally liquid as the wax warms and melts.

4. Visualize yourself on a loud city corner. It's windy and cold, very busy, and very noisy. Feel people buffet you as they rush by, hear the noise of cars and trucks, and smell the fumes as buses drive by. Right beside you is a construction site, and a jackhammer goes off without warning. It is so loud that your ears hurt and your body vibrates with the noise and concussions as it tears up the concrete. Slowly, ease yourself away so you are lying on your back on a grassy knoll by a sparkling blue lake. The sun warms your face and body, and a gentle breeze creates small ripples on the water. Listen as the jackhammer fades into a woodpecker gently rapping on a tree.

5. Now focus inwardly on yourself. You have released the knots and relaxed your body. You have softened and then melted the tension of your day. You have transformed the bustle and noise in your life into pleasant sounds of nature. By doing this, you have gained control over your mind and body. Remind yourself now that you have the ability to gain control of your thoughts and feelings through creative visualization. Affirm your personal power to choose to think and feel well, and to believe in your ability to transform your life in productive ways.

6. Refocus now on your breathing, and repeat the following affirmation each time you exhale: "My body is relaxed and open" (wait 30 seconds). Now change that affirmation (each time you exhale) to: "I choose to think and be well" (wait 30–50 seconds). Feel pride in yourself and your abilities, and reinforce to yourself now that you have the power each day to manage how you think and feel. Take time each day to relax your body, melt away the tension, and quiet the noise in your life.

(Fanning, 1988)

Increasing self-awareness. By systematically practicing imagery, athletes can become more aware of what is taking place within and around them by relaxing and paying attention to sensory details. A runner may learn much about a previously run race by vividly re-creating it in her mind. A member of the U.S. Nordic ski team was having problems sustaining the level of concentration she needed throughout her races. By imagining her past races in vivid detail, she suddenly became aware that she was shifting attention to the wrong things at the end of her races. She made a tactical correction in her race plan, and then mentally practiced her new strategy using imagery.

Aiding in the recovery from injury. Because injured athletes typically cannot participate in physical training, imagery allows them to mentally practice skills and strategies during their recovery. Injured athletes should attend team training sessions and imagine themselves running through the drills and workouts just as though they were physically performing them. Athletes should be challenged to use their time recovering from injuries to engage in mental training, and to maintain a focused, productive-thinking, strong-willed mind-set toward recovery. Among other things, athletes can set progressive rehabilitation goals and vividly imagine attaining these goals. They can also use the ISI exercise to work toward full recovery of their competitive self-image. Productive, goal-oriented imagery is essential to facilitate the critical mind–body link that has been shown to enhance the healing process. Consider the following experience of a professional (NHL) hockey goalie:

> The best example I've had . . . of the effects of positive imagery was the season with the lockout and then, being injured for eight weeks, and coming back, having to play in midseason form after a layoff of close to eight months. I came back and immediately played well that year, largely due to the visualization and my belief that I was going to be ready and I was going to play well with very little practice time. There is really no better proof than that. So I know it works . . . and if you start off slow, I know it will work for you. (Orlick, 1998, p. 74)

Times to Use Imagery

You now know some specific uses for imagery. But when is the most effective time to use it? Staying with our cookbook design, we offer three suggestions about when to use imagery.

Daily practice.   To be systematic, daily imagery practice is advised. As you will see in the sample programs at the end of the chapter, this may require only 5–10 minutes per day.

- Before actual physical practice sessions. This fits imagery into the athletes' routine and may get them into the proper frame of mind for practice.

- After actual physical practice sessions. This has been successful with groups in reaffirming the points emphasized in practice that day. Also, athletes are more relaxed at the end of practice and may be more receptive to imagery at that time.

- During practice. For example, if a basketball coach implements an imagery program to practice free throws, he or she may build in time for imagery practice prior to shooting free throws in practice. This is especially helpful in developing kinesthetic imagery ability.

Preperformance routine.   It is helpful for athletes to go through a preperformance imagery routine *before every contest*. This routine should be individualized for each athlete and practiced in preperformance situations. To facilitate developing a routine, it is helpful to have a quiet, comfortable room available to all athletes prior to competition. However, if no room is available, imagery can be practiced anywhere. In this case, athletes could use the Energy Room image suggested earlier to mentally prepare for competition. Suggestions about the content of these precompetitive routines are included with the sample programs at the end of the chapter.

Also, certain skills in sport are conducive to a preperformance imagery routine before actually performing the skill. Closed skills such as free throw shooting, field goal kicking, ski jumping, volleyball serving, or gymnastic vaulting are more easily practiced in this way, as opposed to open skills such as broken field running in football or executing a fast break in basketball.

Postperformance review.   Another appropriate time to use imagery is after competition. Again, this should be an individual exercise, but coaches can monitor it by having the athletes complete postcompetitive evaluation sheets based on their postperformance imagery. Using imagery at this time facilitates increased awareness of what actually happened during the competition.

Strategies to Enhance Imagery Practice

This section offers some additional strategies to make their imagery more effective.

Athletes should practice imagery in many different places and positions.   Most people envision mental training as something an athlete does when lying on a couch. Athletes may want to spend time developing their imagery skills in quiet, nondistractible settings but, once they have become proficient at imagery, they should engage in it in many different settings and positions. Athletes should be able to engage in imagery in the locker room, on the field, in the pool, during practice, during competition—in any type of setting! It helps if coaches incorporate imagery into practice sessions to make it habitual for athletes. Encourage athletes to practice imagery in many different positions. If they are mentally practicing a sport skill such as a gymnastics routine or a high jump, it might be useful for them to stand up or even walk through and move their body in certain ways that match the different segments of their images. They may want to hold the bat, club, or ball in their hands to facilitate their images as they repeat their imagery triggers to themselves to cue in perfect responses.

Training the inner winner

Tony DiCicco, former coach of the U.S. Women's Soccer national team, talks about the importance of developing the "inner winner" in athletes. He describes how he attempted to boost his athletes' confidence by helping them feel themselves being successful by using imagery:

> *In the middle of the day, with the sun beaming down after a hard training session, I would have the players lie down on the grass, relax, and do imagery training. I had them visualize performing their unique abilities on the soccer field over and over again. I would say, 'Imagine in your mind what you do well. If you're a great header, visualize yourself winning headers. If you're a great defender, visualize yourself stripping the ball from an attacking player. If you're a great passer of the ball, visualize yourself playing balls in. If you've got great speed, visualize yourself running by players and receiving the ball.' I made a special point of saying, 'Visualize the special skills that separate you from the rest— the skills that make your team better because you possess them.' (DiCicco, Hacker, & Salzberg, 2003, p. 112)*

Know when to use real-time, slow motion, and fast motion imagery. Athletes should make their images as realistic in timing as possible in relation to the actual timing of their physical performance. Timing is a critical performance factor in many sports; thus it becomes a key response characteristic that athletes want to stamp into their images. Elite swimmers and runners are typically able to imagine their races down to the fraction of a second in terms of their splits and final times. Indeed, elite gymnasts used real-time imagery when they wanted to really feel the rhythm and timing of the movements in their routines (Post & Wrisberg, 2012).

However, athletes report using slow-motion imagery when learning new skills, breaking down complex movements into smaller pieces, correcting bad habits, and focusing on one small part of their overall performance (O & Hall, 2009; Post & Wrisberg, 2012). Athletes also report using fast-motion imagery when they need only to remind themselves of how a mastered task is generally performed (O & Hall, 2009). This type of imagery might be useful in competitive situations where time is limited, and a brief speeded-up image could enhance focus and confidence.

Help athletes use technology to enhance their images. Some athletes find it useful to download commercially produced imagery scripts onto their personal electronic devices or make their own imagery scenarios that they record themselves. Sport psychology consultants are also able to record personalized imagery scripts for athletes that combine the practice of physical and mental skills. Imagery tapes made for athletes should be highly individualized with specific verbal triggers and symbolic images that are meaningful to each athlete.

The use of personal highlight videotapes has been shown to enhance the confidence and performance of basketball (Templin & Vernacchia, 1995), ice hockey (Halliwell, 1990), and soccer (Lieber, 1999) players. Athletes' peak performance moments are edited from competitive videotape and integrated with special effects and motivational music. These highlight videos can then be used in conjunction with imagery to enhance confidence in returning from injury or slumps.

Remember that athletes should imagine vivid mental, physiological, and behavioral responses to situations. Athletes must load their images with vivid responses. Remember that imagery works by helping athletes build and refine mental blueprints for perfect responses (bioinformational theory). Repeatedly remind athletes that their images should include their mental, physiological, and behavioral responses to competition—not just the stimulus characteristics of the situation. That is, when they imagine a big crowd and lots of noise and distractions, make sure they imagine how they will respond (e.g., using the energy as positive fuel, keeping focused in the "cocoon," and exuding confidence as they physically warm up for competition).

Image performance and outcome. Tennis players should imagine executing sharply paced passing shots and then see these shots hit in the corners of their opponent's court. Baseball players should imagine a strong and compact swing, and then see the ball driven as a line drive through the outfield. Golfers should envision and feel the swing they will use, and then see the trajectory the ball will take as well and exactly where it will land. Athletes should follow through on their imagery to see not only perfect performances, but also perfect outcomes.

Be specific in all uses of imagery. Imagery should be very specifically tailored to each athlete's individual needs. For example, consider a softball pitcher who generally pitches well until there are runners on base, which seems to distract her from throwing strikes. Have her set up many different situations to practice using imagery to build her confidence and concentration to pitch effectively in changing game situations. She should repeatedly envision herself in various situations with base runners, different counts and number of outs, and different game scores to develop strong and consistent mental and physical responses to the pressure of these situations. Athletes must consider their exact performance needs, so that their imagery practice is specific in helping them develop thoughts and behaviors that can overcome performance problems.

Imagery Cookbook for Coaches and Practitioners

You now have all the ingredients (uses, times, strategies) to cook up an effective and systematic imagery program for your athletes. Remember the KISS principle—keep it simple and systematic instead of trying to do too much at first. Carefully consider the types and methods of imagery that will work for you in your particular situation.

Sample imagery programs. Three sample imagery programs are provided next to give you a basic idea about the structure and progression of imagery programs for athletes. These program outlines are generic, and should be modified to meet the sport-specific and program-specific needs of your athletes.

Team Imagery Program

The coach or sport psychology consultant should begin the team imagery program well before the start of the competitive season so athletes are familiar with imagery and proficient in their imagery skills.

First three weeks of preseason

1. Introduce program (15–20 minutes).
2. Evaluate athletes' imagery ability (15 minutes).
3. Basic Training (three times per week for 10 minutes following practice). Begin Basic Training with the exercises suggested in this chapter, then add exercises that are appropriate for your team and sport (team tactics and strategies).
4. Provide individual imagery sessions for athletes who are interested. Also, invite athletes to meet with you individually to discuss personalized imagery training they can do on their own. Continue to provide individual sessions for athletes throughout the season if they want them.

Remainder of season (three times per week 10 minutes before, following, or during practice).

1. Repetitive practice of simple sport skills*—perform them perfectly!

2. Repetitive practice of advanced sport skills*—perform them perfectly!

3. Competitive tactics and strategies in relation to specific needs of team and upcoming opponents*

4. Re-create past successful performance

5. Goal programming for future success

Include in *all* sessions the imagery exercises marked with an asterisk. They are a warm-up for the other types of imagery. After these initial warm-up exercises, you can use any types of imagery exercises. Other suggested images might include the following:

- Confidence in fulfilling team role successfully

- Attentional focus (develop a team focus plan for different opponents)

- Using verbal triggers and symbolic images

- Energy management (Energy Room or similar image to feel control over arousal regulation)

- Correcting mistakes/practice refocusing plan

- Precompetitive routine (should be practiced at least twice a week)

Precompetitive imagery routine.   The suggested practice outline (the first five steps listed under "Remainder of Season") could be incorporated into individual precompetitive routines. Encourage each athlete to develop his or her own routine, and make available a pre-event imagery room or specified area in which imagery can be practiced privately.

Postgame imagery review. Devise an event evaluation sheet that athletes will complete after each game. This sheet should ask the athletes to evaluate their performance in the following areas: physical skills, strategies, fulfillment of role, achievement of goals, energy management, attentional focus, self-confidence, areas that need improvement, and strategies to improve these areas. Make the sheet concise and objective so the athletes will find it easy to complete (see Chapter 11 for a sample evaluation sheet).

Individual Imagery Program

1. Education about imagery to understand basics of imagery.

2. Evaluation of imagery ability (use questionnaire).

3. Basic Training (once a day for 10 minutes).

4. Regular imagery sessions (throughout competitive season)

   Prepractice (5 minutes): Technique work, goal programming for practice

   Postpractice (10 minutes): Re-create practice performance, mental skills practice (according to individual need), practice precompetitive imagery program

5. Competition day

   Pre-event imagery (10–20 minutes): Use format suggested in "Team Imagery Program"

   Postevent review (10–20 minutes): Design personal event evaluation sheet or log

Case studies

Now that you've read the "cookbook" and some sample programs, let's try your hand at planning imagery training programs for athletes. In this section, three case studies are presented that describe athletes who are having performance problems. Read through each case and use your knowledge from the chapter to plan an imagery intervention to help that athlete perform better. Write your plan for each athlete down on paper, and then go on to read the hypothetical imagery interventions that we suggest for each case. Don't look ahead until you plan your own imagery interventions for each athlete!

Molly

Molly, a 13-year-old figure skater, is attempting her senior freestyle test for the third time. Molly needs to pass this test to qualify for the highest level of national competition. In practice, Molly has completed all of the elements of her free-style program with ease, but she tends to choke during the test sessions. Her coach attempts to be patient and supportive by telling Molly that she just needs to try harder and practice more.

Mario

Mario is a collegiate ice hockey player who lacks consistency in his performance. He performs well until he becomes distracted by his anger in reaction to game events that he cannot control, such as poor officiating, rough play by opponents, or poor ice conditions. When asked about his inconsistency, Mario says, "I just can't concentrate on the game when things go wrong!" Mario's coach tells him that he'd better get a handle on his temper and focus on the game.

Dee

Dee is a gifted high school sprinter. She is in top physical condition and is expected to have a great senior season and earn a track scholarship to a major university. Dee injures her ankle before the first meet of the year, yet when she returns to competition a few weeks later, she does not perform as well as she or her coaches expected. Dee has recovered physically from the injury, but mentally she is worried about reinjury. She is not putting 100 percent effort into practice and her performance suffers as a result. Deep down, she is concerned that she will not make it back to her previous performance level, and she is worried that she will now fail to gain a scholarship.

Suggested Imagery Intervention Plans

Molly. Initially we got to know Molly and talked with her about her perceived strengths and weaknesses as a figure skater. We introduced the concept of imagery to her and guided her through imagery in which she imagined her performance during practice and during a test session. After imagining each scene, she wrote down the characteristics of the performances, including how she felt during the performance, what she said to

herself, how she prepared for the performances, and how she responded to mistakes. Based on an evaluation of Molly's imagery ability, we recommended some Basic Training exercises with an emphasis on arousal control and refocusing after mistakes.

We worked with Molly to develop a pretest imagery program in which she saw herself performing well, achieving her goals (goal programming), and refocusing after mistakes in her program. We developed an imagery script for Molly to use before test sessions focusing on arousal control and self-confidence. Here is an example of Molly's imagery script:

> I am calm, confident, and in control. My muscles are loose and relaxed, like flexible springs. I am breathing easily, feeling my lungs fill with energizing air. During my warm-up, I feel focused and confident. My blades cut into the ice with ease, making a crisp cutting noise. My jumps are snappy and explosive. My spins are centered and tight. My muscles are warm and elastic. As I step onto the ice for my program, I feel balanced and in control. I take my beginning position with a confident posture, feeling excited anticipation to perform my best. I know that I'm ready.

Molly practiced this pretest imagery program during simulated test sessions and during practice sessions to re-create the testing experience. Through imagery, Molly developed the mental skills to become more mentally tough and focused during pressure performances.

Mario. We first got to know Mario and talked with him about his perceived strengths and weaknesses as a hockey player. We introduced the concept of imagery to him and guided him through an imagery session in which he visualized his performance being negatively affected by anger. After the imagery, we specifically worked with Mario to identify the specific characteristics of the situation, such as what triggered his anger, his attitude before and after the trigger event, and his focus before and after the trigger. We evaluated Mario's imagery ability and recommended various Basic Training exercises, especially focusing on self-awareness and controllability.

We worked with Mario to develop a refocusing imagery program in which he saw himself refocusing after negative events, directing the anger in a productive way, and performing well after negative events. Mario imagined several different scenarios in which he typically loses his temper and his focus, such as after a poor call from an official or rough play by the opposing team. We worked with Mario to develop several imagery scripts incorporating imagery triggers, so he could mentally practice emotional control and refocusing. An excerpt from his emotional control script follows:

> [Trigger event] . . . Deep breath . . . Squeeze stick . . . Let anger swell up from the bottom of your toes, into your legs, all the way through your trunk and chest. Feel the anger flowing down out of your arms, feel the hot emotions bursting out of your fingers. Squeeze all of that anger into your stick. Take a deep breath. Relax your hands.

Mario was able to use his imagery scripts to practice emotional control and refocusing skills. He became more consistent in his ability to focus after negative events during games and continued to use imagery for refocusing.

Dee.   We first got to know Dee and discussed her physical and mental approach to competition. We guided her through several imagery sessions in which she imagined her performance both before and after her injury. We asked Dee to focus on how she felt, what she said to herself, and what her mental attitude was during both situations. We had her re-create through imagery the times before her injury in which she ran well, and also had her compare her thoughts, feelings, and behaviors to times after her injury. During this time, we also had Dee practice imagery to become more skilled at controlling her images.

We worked with Dee to develop an imagery program in which she re-created the feelings of confidence and competence she experienced prior to her injury. We had her keep a log of her mental states before, during, and after practices and meets. Additionally, Dee recorded any triggers that she associated with changes in her attitude or mood toward her ability. Initially, Dee's log indicated that she questioned her running ability. After a period of systematic and consistent use of imagery, Dee's attitude began to change. She began to feel more sure of herself and thus pushed herself harder during practice. The combination of her mental and physical training helped Dee to get back to her preinjury running level. Seeing *was* believing for Dee as she went on to become a successful collegiate runner and advocate for the power of imagery.

Summary

Imagery is using one's senses to re-create or create an experience in the mind. Both scientific and experiential accounts of the use of imagery to enhance sport performance report positive results. Key considerations in using imagery include developing both internal and external perspectives and understanding that imagery is a supplement to, not a replacement for, physical practice. The ability of athletes to engage in vivid and controlled images is critical to the effectiveness of imagery in enhancing performance.

Three conceptual explanations suggest how imagery may enhance performance. Bioinformational theory indicates that individuals respond to imagery with response characteristics that create psychophysiological changes in the body that positively influence performance. The functional equivalence explanation is based on the idea that imagery activates the same areas and processes in the brain as the actual physical execution of the movement. The mental readiness explanation suggests that imagery causes athletes to optimize arousal and confidence and to focus their attention on relevant cues prior to competition.

Setting up a systematic imagery program involves four steps. First, athletes are introduced to imagery. Second, athletes evaluate their imagery abilities to understand their strengths and areas that need improvement. Third, athletes should engage in Basic Training to develop and enhance their imagery skills. Finally, imagery should be integrated into a systematic program of physical and mental training.

Study Questions

1. Briefly describe some of the evidence supporting the positive influence of imagery on sport performance.

2. Describe the four phases of setting up an imagery training program.

3. Vividness, controllability, and self-awareness are three areas of Basic Training in the imagery training program. Define each of these and describe the role each plays in training an athlete to use an imagery program.

4. What are five different ways imagery can be used by athletes?

5. Identify and describe the three explanations provided in this chapter that address how imagery works to enhance sport performance.

6. Develop an imagery program for an athlete in your sport using the imagery cookbook.

7. Explain why and how imagery can be polysensory.

8. What are three different times imagery can be used optimally by athletes?

9. What is the difference between external and internal imagery, and how can athletes use each perspective?

10. Can imagery hurt athletes' performance? Explain and then identify how athletes can avoid this negative imagery effect.

References

Bakker, F. C., Boschker, M. S. J., & Chung, T. (1996). Changes in muscular activity while imagining weight lifting using stimulus or response propositions. *Journal of Sport & Exercise Psychology, 18,* 313–324.

Beilock, S. L., Afremow, J. A., Rabe, A. L., & Carr, T. H. (2001). "Don't miss!" The debilitating effects of suppressive imagery on golf putting performance. *Journal of Sport & Exercise Psychology, 23,* 200–221.

Bird, L. (1989). *Drive: The story of my life.* New York: Bantam.

Callow, N., Hardy, L., & Hall, C. (2001). The effects of a motivational general-mastery imagery intervention on the sport confidence of high-level badminton players. *Research Quarterly for Exercise and Sport, 72,* 389–400.

Callow, N., & Roberts, R. (2010). Imagery research: An investigation of three issues. *Psychology of Sport and Exercise, 11,* 325–329.

Calmels, C., Berthoumieux, C., & d'Arripe-Longueville, F. (2004). Effects of an imagery training program on selective attention of national softball players. *The Sport Psychologist, 18,* 272–296.

Calmels, C., d'Arripe-Longueville, F., Fournier, J. F., & Soulard, A. (2003). Competitive strategies among elite female gymnasts: An exploration of the relative influence of psychological skills training and natural learning experiences. *International Journal of Sport & Exercise Psychology, 1,* 327–352.

Cumming, J., Olphin, T., & Law, M. (2007). Self-reported psychological states and physiological responses to different types of motivational general imagery. *Journal of Sport & Exercise Psychology, 29,* 629–644.

DiCicco, T., Hacker, C., & Salzberg, C. (2003). *Catch them being good.* New York: Penguin.

Durand-Bush, N., & Salmela, J. H. (2002). The development and maintenance of expert athletic performance: Perceptions of world and Olympic champions. *Journal of Applied Sport Psychology, 14,* 154–171.

Fanning, P. (1988). *Visualization for change.* Oakland, CA: New Harbinger.

Gould, D., Guinan, D., Greenleaf, C., Medbery, R., & Peterson, K. (1999). Factors affecting Olympic performance: Perceptions of athletes and coaches from more and less successful teams. *The Sport Psychologist, 13,* 371–394.

Gould, D., Weinberg, R., & Jackson, A. (1980). Mental preparation strategies, cognitions, and strength performance. *Journal of Sport Psychology, 2,* 329–339.

Gregg, M., & Hall, C. (2006). The relationship of skill level and age to the use of imagery by golfers. *Journal of Applied Sport Psychology, 18,* 363–375.

Hall, C. R., & Rodgers, W. M. (1989). Enhancing coaching effectiveness in figure skating through a mental skills training program. *The Sport Psychologist, 2,* 142–154.

Halliwell, W. (1990). Providing sport psychology consulting services in professional hockey. *The Sport Psychologist, 4,* 369–377.

Hardy, L., & Callow, N. (1999). Efficacy of external and internal visual imagery perspectives for the enhancement of performance on tasks in which form is important. *Journal of Sport & Exercise Psychology, 21,* 95–112.

Hecker, J. E., & Kaczor, L. M. (1988). Application of imagery theory to sport psychology: Some preliminary findings. *Journal of Sport & Exercise Psychology, 10,* 363–373.

Holmes, P. S., & Collins, D. J. (2001). The PETTLEP approach to motor imagery: A functional equivalence model for sport psychologists. *Journal of Applied Sport Psychology, 13,* 60–83.

Jeannerod, M. (1994). The representing brain: Neural correlates of motor intention and imagery. *Behavioral and Brain Sciences, 17,* 187–202.

Kerr, G., & Leith, L. (1993). Stress management and athletic performance. *The Sport Psychologist, 1,* 221–231.

Lang, P. J. (1977). Imagery in therapy: An information processing analysis of fear. *Behavior Therapy, 8,* 862–886.

Lang, P. J. (1979). A bio-informational theory of emotional imagery. *Psychophysiology, 16,* 495–512.

Layden, Tim. (2010, February 8). Ready to rock. *Sports Illustrated, 112* (5). Retrieved from http://sportsillustrated.cnn.com/vault/cover/toc/11382/index.htm.

Lee, C. (1990). Psyching up for a muscular endurance task: Effects of image content on performance and mood state. *Journal of Sport & Exercise Psychology, 12,* 66–73.

Lidor, R., & Singer, R. M. (2003). Preperformance routines in self-paced tasks: Developmental and educational considerations. In R. Lidor & K. P. Henschen (Eds.), *The psychology of team sports* (pp. 69–98). Morgantown, WV: Fitness Information Technology.

Lieber, J. (1999, July 6). USA won't kick habit of believing. *USA Today,* pp. 1c–2c.

Mamassis, G., & Doganis, G. (2004). The effects of a mental training program on juniors pre-competitive anxiety, self-confidence, and tennis performance. *Journal of Applied Sport Psychology, 16,* 118–137.

Martin, K. A., & Hall, C. R. (1995). Using mental imagery to enhance intrinsic motivation. *Journal of Sport & Exercise Psychology, 17,* 54–69.

Martin, K. A., Moritz, S. E., & Hall, C. R. (1999). Imagery use in sport: A literature review and applied model. *The Sport Psychologist, 13,* 245–268.

McCallum, J. (2004, May 24). It's that time again. *Sports Illustrated,* pp. 54–65.

Morris, T., Spittle, M., & Watt, A. P. (2005). *Imagery in sport.* Champaign, IL: Human Kinetics.

Murphy, S. M., & Woolfolk, R. (1987). The effects of cognitive interventions on competitive anxiety and performance on a fine motor skill task. *International Journal of Sport Psychology, 18,* 152–166.

O, J., & Hall, C. (2009). A quantitative analysis of athletes' voluntary use of slow motion, real time, and fast motion images. *Journal of Applied Sport Psychology, 21,* 15–30.

Orlick, T. (1998). *Embracing your potential.* Champaign, IL: Human Kinetics.

Orlick, T., & Partington, J. (1988). Mental links to excellence. *The Sport Psychologist, 2,* 105–130.

Post, P. G., & Wrisberg, C. A. (2012). A phenomenological investigation of gymnasts' lived experience of imagery. *The Sport Psychologist, 26,* 98–121.

Ravizza, K. (1993). An interview with Peter Vidmar, member of the 1994 U.S. Olympic gymnastics team. *Contemporary Thought in Performance Enhancement, 2,* 93–100.

Reiter, B. (2006, July 17). Preparation. *Sports Illustrated,* p. 36.

Ryska, T. A. (1998). Cognitive-behavioral strategies and precompetitive anxiety among recreational athletes. *Psychological Record, 48,* 697–708.

Short, M. W. (2002). The effect of imagery function and imagery direction on self-efficacy and performance on a golf-putting task. *The Sport Psychologist, 16,* 48–67.

Short, S. E., Smiley, M., & Ross-Stewart, L. (2005). The relationship between efficacy beliefs and imagery use in coaches. *The Sport Psychologist, 19,* 380–394.

Simons, J. (2000). Doing imagery in the field. In M. Andersen (Ed.), *Doing sport psychology* (pp. 77–92). Champaign, IL: Human Kinetics.

Smith, D., & Collins, D. (2004). Mental practice, motor performance, and the late CNV. *Journal of Sport & Exercise Psychology, 26,* 412–426.

Smith, D., Collins, D., & Hale, B. (1998). Imagery perspectives and karate performance. *Journal of Sport Sciences, 16,* 103–104.

Smith, D., & Holmes, P. (2004). The effect of imagery modality on golf putting performance. *Journal of Sport & Exercise Psychology, 26,* 385–395.

Smith, D., Holmes, P., Whitemore, L., Collins, D., & Devenport, T. (2001). The effect of theoretically-based imagery scripts on hockey penalty flick performance. *Journal of Sport Behavior, 24,* 408–419.

Smith, D., Wright, C., Allsopp, A., & Westhead, H. (2007). It's all in the mind: PETTLEP-based imagery and sports performance. *Journal of Applied Sport Psychology, 19,* 80–92.

Suinn, R. M. (1980). Psychology and sport performance: Principles and applications. In R. M. Suinn (Ed.), *Psychology in sports: Methods and applications* (pp. 26–36). Minneapolis: Burgess.

Templin, D. P., & Vernacchia, R. A. (1995). The effect of highlight music videotapes upon the game performance of intercollegiate basketball players. *The Sport Psychologist, 9,* 41–50.

Thelwell, R. C., Greenlees, I. A., & Weston, N. J. V. (2006). Using psychological skills training to develop soccer performance. *Journal of Applied Sport Psychology, 18,* 2006.

Tynes, L. L., & McFatter, R. M. (1987). The efficacy of "psyching" strategies on a weightlifting task. *Cognitive Therapy and Research, 11,* 327–336.

Williams, S. E., Cooley, S. J., & Cumming, J. (2013). Layered stimulus response training improves motor imagery ability and movement execution. *Journal of Sport & Exercise Psychology, 35,* 60–71.

Woolfolk, R., Parrish, W., & Murphy, S. M. (1985). The effects of positive and negative imagery on motor skill performance. *Cognitive Therapy and Research, 9,* 235–341.

Wright, C. J., & Smith, D. (2009). The effect of PETTLEP imagery on strength performance. *International Journal of Sport & Exercise Psychology, 7,* 18–31.

A

Sample Imagery Script for Competition Preparation

Get into a comfortable position and close your eyes. Focus on the center of your body and take several slow deep breaths. With each inhalation, imagine that you are pulling all of the tension from your body into your lungs. With each exhalation, imagine that you are releasing all of your tension and negative thoughts from your body. Continue this focused breathing until your body becomes relaxed and your mind is alert and open for productive thoughts. (Pause for 30 seconds.)

Imagine it is the night before an important competition or performance. You are preparing for the next day's event. As you are preparing to go to sleep, you are focusing on feeling calm, confident, and physically and emotionally in control. (Pause for 10 seconds.) You are excited and anticipatory about performing well tomorrow. (Pause for 10 seconds.) You sleep well and awaken feeling rested, excited, and focused. (Pause for 8 seconds.) You realize that you are well prepared, both physically and mentally, for the competition. Physically, you feel balanced and ready. Mentally, you are confident and focused. (Pause for 10 seconds.)

Now imagine that you are at home preparing to leave for the competition site. (Pause for 10 seconds.) You take some time to run through your mental warm-up by visualizing several repetitions of a few basic skills in your sport, such as a warm-up drill. (Pause for 30 seconds.) Now in your mind's eye, focus on the specific goals and strategies for this particular competition. Imagine yourself performing perfectly, achieving your goals for the competition and successfully executing specific strategies for this opponent. (Pause for 60 seconds.)

Now imagine yourself arriving at the competition site feeling confident in your physical and mental preparation. (Pause for 20 seconds.) You feel the nervous anticipation of competition and remind yourself that it is exhilarating to play your sport. You love it! (Pause for 10 seconds.) Imagine your feelings as you dress and go through any precompetitive preparations. (Pause for 20 seconds.) You feel confident in your preparation and clearly focused on your upcoming performance. Your breathing is calm and controlled. Your muscles feel warm and elastic, ready to explode with intensity and precision. You are ready! (Pause for 15 seconds.) Imagine going through your competition warm-up as you have done so many times in practice. (Pause for 30 seconds.) Your warm-up goes well, yet you remind yourself that you are ready for any unexpected problem or obstacle. You are confident in your refocusing ability and remind yourself that you are mentally tough. You feel optimally energized and ready to go. Enjoy it!

B

Sport Imagery Evaluation

As you complete this evaluation, remember that imagery is more than just visualizing something in your mind's eye. Vivid images may include many senses, such as seeing, hearing, feeling, touching, and smelling. Vivid images also may include feeling emotions or moods.

In this exercise you will read descriptions of general sport situations. You are to imagine the situation and provide as much detail from your imagination as possible to make the image as real as you can. Then you will be asked to rate your imagery in seven areas:

a. How vividly you *saw* or visualized the image.

b. How clearly you *heard* the sounds.

c. How vividly you *felt your body movements* during the activity.

d. How clearly you were aware of your mood or *felt your emotions* of the situation.

e. Whether you could see the image from *inside your body.*

f. Whether you could see the image from *outside your body.*

g. How well you could *control* the image.

After you read each description, think of a specific example of it—the skill, the people involved, the place, the time. Then close your eyes and try to imagine the situation as vividly as you can.

There are, of course, no right or wrong images. Use your imagery skills to create the most vivid and clear image that you can. After you have completed imagining each situation, rate your imagery skills using the following scales.

For items a–f:

1 = no image present

2 = not clear or vivid, but a recognizable image

3 = moderately clear and vivid image

4 = clear and vivid image

5 = extremely clear and vivid image

For item g:

1 = no control at all of image

2 = very hard to control

3 = moderate control of image

4 = good control of image

5 = complete control of image

Practicing Alone

Select one specific skill or activity in your sport, such as shooting free throws, performing a parallel bar routine, executing a takedown, throwing a pass, hitting a ball, or swimming the butterfly. Now imagine yourself performing this activity at the place where you normally practice (gym, pool, rink, field, court) without anyone else present. Close your eyes for about one minute and try to see yourself at this place, hear the sounds, feel your body perform the movement, and be aware of your state of mind or mood. Try to see yourself from behind your eyes or from inside your body. Then, try to see yourself from outside your body, as if you were watching a videotape of yourself performing.

a.	Rate how well you *saw* yourself doing the activity.	1	2	3	4	5
b.	Rate how well you *heard* the sounds of doing the activity.	1	2	3	4	5
c.	Rate how well you *felt yourself* making the movements.	1	2	3	4	5
d.	Rate how well you were aware of your *mood*.	1	2	3	4	5
e.	Rate how well you were able to see the image from *inside* your body.	1	2	3	4	5
f.	Rate how well you were able to see the image from *outside* your body.	1	2	3	4	5
g.	Rate how well you *controlled* the image.	1	2	3	4	5

Practicing with Others

You are doing the same activity, but now you are practicing the skill with your coach and teammates present. This time, however, you make a mistake that everyone notices. Close your eyes for about one minute to imagine making the error and the situation immediately afterward as vividly as you can. First, try to experience the feelings you have as you make the mistake. Then, quickly try to re-create the situation in your mind and imagine yourself correcting the mistake and performing perfectly. Try to see the image from behind your eyes or from inside your body as you correct the mistake. Next, try to see the image as if you were watching through a video camera as you correct the mistake.

a.	Rate how well you *saw* yourself in this situation.	1	2	3	4	5
b.	Rate how well you *heard* the sounds in this situation.	1	2	3	4	5
c.	Rate how well you *felt yourself* making the movements.	1	2	3	4	5
d.	Rate how well you *felt the emotions* of this situation.	1	2	3	4	5
e.	Rate how well you were able to see the image from *inside* your body.	1	2	3	4	5
f.	Rate how well you were able to see the image from *outside* your body.	1	2	3	4	5
g.	Rate how well you *controlled* the image.	1	2	3	4	5

Playing in a Contest

Imagine yourself performing the same or similar activity in competition, but imagine yourself doing the activity very skillfully and the spectators and teammates showing their appreciation. As you imagine the situation, try to see the crowd and hear the noise they are making. Imagine yourself feeling confident in your ability to perform, as well as your ability to handle the pressure. Now close your eyes for about 1 minute and imagine this situation as vividly as possible. Try to image yourself performing from inside your body, as if you were actually performing, as well as from outside your body, as if you were a spectator.

a.	Rate how well you *saw* yourself in this situation.	1	2	3	4	5
b.	Rate how well you *heard* the sounds in this situation.	1	2	3	4	5
c.	Rate how well you *felt yourself* making the movements.	1	2	3	4	5
d.	Rate how well you *felt the emotions* of this situation.	1	2	3	4	5
e.	Rate how well you were able to see the image from *inside* your body.	1	2	3	4	5
f.	Rate how well you were able to see the image from *out-side* your body.	1	2	3	4	5
g.	Rate how well you *controlled* the image.	1	2	3	4	5

Recalling a Peak Performance

Recall one of your all-time best performances—a performance in which you felt confident, in control, in the zone. Close your eyes for about one minute and try to see yourself in that situation, feel your emotions, and re-create the experience. Imagine your performance and re-create the feelings you experienced, both mentally and physically, during that performance. Try to see the image from within yourself, and then try to imagine the situation from outside yourself.

a.	Rate how well you *saw* yourself in this situation.	1	2	3	4	5
b.	Rate how well you *heard* the sounds in this situation.	1	2	3	4	5
c.	Rate how well you *felt yourself* making the movements.	1	2	3	4	5
d.	Rate how well you *felt the emotions* of this situation.	1	2	3	4	5
e.	Rate how well you were able to see the image from *inside* your body.	1	2	3	4	5
f.	Rate how well you were able to see the image from *out-side* your body.	1	2	3	4	5
g.	Rate how well you *controlled* the image.	1	2	3	4	5

Scoring

Now let's determine your imagery scores and see what they mean. Sum the ratings for each category and record them below.

Directions	Dimension	Score
Sum all *a* items	Visual	_____
Sum all *b* items	Auditory	_____
Sum all *c* items	Kinesthetic	_____
Sum all *d* items	Emotion	_____
Sum all *e* items	Internal perspective	_____
Sum all *f* items	External perspective	_____
Sum all *g* items	Controllability	_____

Interpret your scores in the visual, auditory, kinesthetic, emotion, and controllability categories based on the following scale: excellent (20–18), good (17–15), average (14–12), fair (11–8), and poor (7–4). Notice the categories in which your scores were low and refer to exercises in the chapter to increase your imagery ability in those areas. All of these categories are important for imagery training, so don't just rely on your visual sense. Work to improve the others! Remember, it takes practice but you *can* increase your imagery ability. Good luck!

Cognitive Techniques for Building Confidence and Enhancing Performance

Jean M. Williams, *University of Arizona, Emeritus*
Nate Zinsser, *United States Military Academy*
Linda Bunker, *University of Virginia, Emeritus*

If you think you can do a thing or think you can't do a thing, you're right.
　　　　　—Henry Ford, founder of Ford Motor Company and assembly line mass production

But with hard work, with belief, with confidence and trust in yourself and those around you, there are no limits.

　　　　　—Michael Phelps, winner of 18 Olympic gold medals

The most consistent finding in peak performance literature is the direct correlation between self-confidence and success (see Chapter 9). Athletes who are truly outstanding are self-confident. Their confidence has been developed over many years and is the direct result of factors such as effective thinking and frequent experiences in which they have been successful. Because developing confidence is such a high priority for athletes and coaches who wish to become successful, understanding confidence and how to enhance it is an equally high priority for sport psychologists working in applied settings.

What we think and say to ourselves in practice and competition is critical to performance. Confident athletes think about themselves and the action at hand in a different way than those who lack confidence. They have learned that the conscious mind is not always an ally, that it must be disciplined, just as their bodies have been disciplined. We all spend vast amounts of time talking to ourselves. Much of the time we are not even aware of this internal dialogue, much less its content. Nevertheless, thoughts directly affect feelings and ultimately actions:

THOUGHTS → FEELINGS → BEHAVIOR

Inappropriate or misguided thinking usually leads to negative feelings and poor performance, just as appropriate or positive thinking leads to enabling feelings and good performance (McPherson, 2000; Neil, Hanton, & Mellalieu, 2013; Thomas, Maynard, & Hanton, 2007b; Van Raalte et al., 1995).

Athletes who are truly outstanding are self-confident, and this confidence is not an accident. Vealey and colleagues (Vealey, Hayashi, Garner-Holman, & Giacobbi, 1998) proposed a Sport-Confidence Model that includes nine sources of confidence, sources such as mastery, demonstrations of ability, physical/mental preparation, social support, coaches' leadership, and situational favorableness. Their model, and efforts to test and review it (e.g., Machida, Ward, & Vealey; 2012; Vealey & Chase, 2008), provides excellent information for helping to understand sport confidence. So too does the confidence profiling process developed by Hays and colleagues (Hays, Thomas, & Maynard, 2010), which is an ideographic interview approach that enables the athlete to discuss confidence in his or her own words.

This chapter's focus, however, is to look at the relationship between thoughts and confidence. The central thesis is that self-talk and particular thinking habits are key factors that influence confidence, related constructs, feelings, and ultimately behavior, including performance. Confident athletes have thinking habits which, when consistently practiced until they become automatic and natural, enable them to retain and benefit from the experiences in which they have been successful and release or restructure the memories and feelings from their less successful experiences. Confident athletes think they can, and *they do*. They never give up. They typically are characterized by positive self-talk, images, and dreams.

If confidence is so critical to successful performance and personal growth, what can coaches and sport psychologists do to help promote self-confidence within their athletes? Many of the earlier chapters in this book have provided, either directly or indirectly, some answers to this question. For example, seeing improvement in physical skill and providing for a history of successful experiences builds both confidence and the expectation of future success. Coaches who observe the learning and performance guidelines outlined in Chapters 2 and 3 will be more likely to maximize successful skill development in their athletes. Effective coach–athlete interactions, as illustrated in Chapters 6, 7, and 8, are

likely to enhance each athlete's sense of self-worth and self-esteem. Practices that maximize such growth in athletes, whether the growth be in physical skills or personal development, lead to a more positive self-concept and increased self-confidence.

In this chapter we discuss techniques for improving confidence and performance by learning to use and control thoughts or cognitions appropriately. Developing and maintaining confidence for high-level competition requires that athletes become aware of and then deliberately step away from many of the dysfunctional thinking habits they may have developed over the years. It is important that athletes understand how the mind works, how it affects their feelings and actions, and ultimately how it can be disciplined. Initially thoughts may appear to occur spontaneously and involuntarily—thus, beyond control. With the skills of intentional thinking, athletes can control their thoughts. They can learn to use self-talk to facilitate learning and performance. They can also learn to replace self-defeating thoughts with positive ones—thoughts that build confidence and the expectation of success. Such positive thought processes become self-fulfilling prophecies.

Key Definitions: Confidence, Mental Toughness, Optimism, Self-Efficacy

Most dictionary definitions of *confidence* include phrases such as "feeling of self-assurance" and "a belief in one's powers." It is useful to think of sport confidence as a relatively global concept that refers to an individual's belief that they can do whatever it takes to be successful in their sport. The image of any great athlete (e.g., Tiger Woods, Serena Williams, LeBron James) is one that exudes this confidence,

The idea of "mental toughness" is certainly related to the concept of confidence. Through a series of interviews with international caliber athletes, Jones, Hanton, and Connaughton (2002) arrived at a definition of mental toughness as "the natural or developed psychological edge

. . . that enables you to cope better than your competitors with the demands of performance . . . and to remain more determined, focused, confident, and in control." Furthermore they identified the most important attribute of mental toughness as "an unshakable belief in your ability to achieve your competitive goals." Their later work affirmed that *belief* and *focus* (attitude/mind-set dimension) are the foundation for mental toughness development and maintenance (Connaughton, Hanton, & Jones, 2010). A related concept important to the understanding of confidence is optimism, which is the tendency to expect the best possible outcome or dwell on the most hopeful aspects of a situation. In the world of sport and competitive performance, the propensity to look for opportunities to score, to win, to excel, regardless of the circumstances, is indispensable for success. Most important, any athlete or performer can systematically cultivate and develop this optimistic tendency, as the following pages will describe.

A fourth related concept is self-efficacy (Bandura, 1997). Think of self-efficacy as a situational-specific type of confidence referring to one's expectation of succeeding at a specific task or meeting a particular challenge such as sinking this free throw or beating this opponent. See Chapter 4 for a discussion of self-efficacy and its role in motivation and performance. Taken together, the concepts of confidence, mental toughness, optimism, and self-efficacy make up both a global and a specific belief that "I can do it," which is essential for success, especially for athletic success. Without this belief, one automatically concedes an advantage to the opponent.

Perhaps the best example of the powerful impact of beliefs on performance occurred over a half century ago when Roger Bannister, a young English medical student, made history by breaking one of sport's most fabled physical and psychological barriers—running a mile in less than 4 minutes. Many today consider his run one of the defining athletic achievements of the 20th century. Until his 1954 race, it was considered physically and mentally impossible for the body to endure the punishment of such a feat. Individuals had even written treatises on why the body was physiologically incapable of running the mile in under 4 minutes. Bannister, however, believed that the mile could be run in under 4 minutes and, equally important, he was the person who would do it. He achieved the impossible not merely by physical practice but also by rehearsing in his head breaking through the 4-minute barrier so often and with so much emotional intensity that he programmed his mind and body to believe. What people do not realize, though, is that the greatest impact of his feat was on others. Within the next year, 37 runners broke the 4-minute barrier. The only thing that had changed was their belief system!

Common Misconceptions about Confidence

Misconception 1: Either You Have It or You Don't

Some people believe that confidence is an inherited disposition or trait that cannot be changed by training, practice, or experience. The truth is that the high self-confidence seen in outstanding athletes is not an accident or a random genetic occurrence over which athletes have no control. Instead, confidence is the result of the sources identified in Vealey's model and a consistently constructive thinking process.

Misconception 2: Only Positive Feedback Can Build Confidence

Although positive feedback from teammates, parents, and coaches certainly helps build confidence, it is possible to selectively perceive and reinterpret criticism, sarcasm, and negative comments as stimulating challenges and use them to build confidence. Instead of being mentally destroyed, athletes who choose to respond by reinterpreting the comments in a constructive way or using other active strategies to combat them may actually *gain* confidence.

Misconception 3: Success Always Builds Confidence

It is generally true that "nothing succeeds like success," but this is not the whole story.

Successful high school athletes do not always make an easy transition to college competition, despite their years of previous success. Other successful athletes may lose their confidence because past success becomes a form of pressure from which they cannot escape. Still other athletes who experience great success use their perceptual abilities to focus only on their weaknesses and to remember only their failures. Thus, successful athletes may limit their future success because they do not have the level of confidence that their accomplishments would suggest.

Logic would assert that confidence follows competence, that after having performed and accomplished at a certain level, confidence inevitably follows. Although seemingly obvious and often true (e.g., Connaughton et al., 2010), success or competence in no way guarantees confidence. Take the example of Michael Strahan, All-Pro defensive end for the New York Giants. Despite making 10 sacks and playing at his all-time best during the 1998 season, Strahan was plagued by self-doubt: "I thought I sucked, and we were losing. It was like I had no hope" (King, 2001). How could a player of such obvious and demonstrated competence be so lacking in confidence? The answer lies in the often illogical and irrational nature of the human mind. Strahan's mind was apparently focused on his mistakes, misses, and losses, rather than on his sacks, tackles, and successes, even though he had ample successes in his immediate past to draw strength and optimism from. Only when he disciplined his thinking with regular mental training sessions that incorporated visualizations of success did Strahan's confidence come back, and with that confidence his Pro Bowl season, and his long-term dominance, were virtually assured.

Misconception 4: Confidence Equals Outspoken Arrogance

Certain confident individuals in the world of sport are outspoken and brash, but there are just as many who have an equally powerful quiet confidence. Names such as Muhammad Ali, Charles Barkley, and Terrell Owens (TO) are associated with loud and often abrasive levels of confidence, but other great athletes such as Tim Duncan, Peyton Manning, and Missy Franklin are every bit as confident on the inside while conveying politeness and modesty on the outside. It is crucial for athletes to realize that they can be confident without being considered conceited or arrogant.

Misconception 5: Mistakes Inevitably Destroy Confidence

The greatest difficulty in gaining confidence is the fact that sports are played by imperfect human beings who often make mistakes. Too many athletes selectively attend more to the mistakes and errors that are inevitable in sport. Other athletes build confidence despite their failures because they selectively attend to whatever small improvements and positive experiences may also have occurred and they examine what went wrong in a constructive way.

Taken collectively, the preceding points all indicate that *confidence results from how one thinks, what one focuses on, and how one reacts to the events in one's life.*

Prerequisites for Gaining Confidence

Now that we have dispelled several myths about confidence and shown that confidence is within anyone's grasp, how does one gain confidence? The following four prerequisites provide a solid foundation for building confidence:

1. Understand the interaction of thought and performance.
2. Cultivate honest self-awareness.
3. Develop an optimistic explanatory style.
4. Embrace a psychology of excellence.

Understand the Interaction of Thought and Performance

The thoughts we have of our ability, of the demands we face, and of the environment we happen to be in determine to a large extent the way we feel at any given moment. Think "I have done this many times before," and you feel confident. Think "I am being taken advantage of," and you feel anger. Think "This practice is worthless," and you feel impatient and unmotivated. These immediate feelings, in turn, directly affect performance because they produce objectively verifiable changes in muscle tension, blood flow, hormone production, and attentional focus. For example, thoughts that anticipate failure lead to feelings of anxiety and, among other things, inappropriate muscle tension and attentional focus. The confident athlete deliberately directs his or her thoughts onto those aspects of the environment and self that produce powerful, confident feelings, so as to produce better and better performance.

Cultivate Honest Self-Awareness

Striving for control over one's thoughts and feelings is a process demanding honest self-awareness. Athletes must commit to becoming aware of what they say to themselves, what the circumstances are when the self-talk occurs, and what consequences follow from the self-talk. One must be willing to honestly pursue the question, "Am I really thinking in a way that will give me the best chance of success?" For most people who play sport the real opponent is within themselves in the form of ineffective cognitive habits. This is the most difficult battle that anyone will ever try to win, and it is also the challenge that makes sport such a great experience with so much potential for self-development and satisfaction.

Develop an Optimistic Explanatory Style

The term **explanatory style** refers to the way an athlete internally responds to and explains both the good and bad events that occur in his or her life. According to Seligman (1991), explanatory style is the hallmark of whether an individual is an optimist or a pessimist. This habitual style of interpreting events is developed in childhood and adolescence and "stems directly from your view of your place in the world, whether you think you are valuable and deserving, or worthless and hopeless" (Seligman, 1991, p. 98). In the often-hostile world of sport, explanatory style is a useful tool for helping athletes maintain optimism and confidence when facing the inevitable setbacks, obstacles, and disappointment.

Explanatory style can be broken into three dimensions. The first is **permanence**—the degree to which one feels events will repeat and continue to affect one's life either negatively or positively. An athlete with an optimistic explanatory style will usually assume that positive events, such as success, will repeat rather than be a fluke; and they respond to bad events or setbacks with the explanation that they will not continue to occur, they are isolated and rare. In contrast, an athlete with a negative explanatory style tends to think that good events will not repeat, but bad events will.

The second dimension is **pervasiveness**—the degree to which one feels that a particular experience will generalize to other contexts. The optimistic athlete tends to assume that a good event or a success in one aspect of his or her game will positively affect other aspects, but that mistakes and difficulties will remain confined to their original context. For example, success with the first serve bodes well for the net game and groundstrokes. The more pessimistic athlete tends to assume that a breakdown in one area of the game will spread to other areas and that successes will be limited to their original context.

The third dimension of explanatory style is **personalization**—the degree to which one sees him- or herself as the primary causal agent in events. Optimistic athletes take personal credit for successes and progress and protect their confidence by explaining failures as the result of forces beyond their control (e.g., exceptional play by the opponent) or forces within their control (e.g., effort) that they will change. More pessimistic athletes have the opposite tendency, to see success as a function of luck and circumstance rather than personal actions, but losses and setbacks as due to personal shortcomings.

An athlete's tendency to interpret events along the preceding dimensions is learned and reinforced through experience. By learning techniques of productive self-talk and selective perception, and then employing these techniques in practice and competition, athletes can systematically cultivate optimism and gain confidence.

The preceding does not mean that one ignores mistakes or adopts a totally unrealistic view of one's ability and circumstances. Taking notice of errors or shortcomings is a great way to grow, as long as it is done with an eye to the bigger question, "How do I use this to help me improve?" For example, watching a game film and noting technical errors is a good idea, as long as the athlete (a) simultaneously makes note of the good points revealed on the film, (b) decides right then and there what to do about those errors, and (c) *while correcting those errors remains focused on his or her good points and bright future.*

To summarize, an optimistic explanatory style is one in which errors are treated as temporary, specific to that one practice or game, or correctable, and atypical of one's potential, whereas one looks at successes as more permanent, more general, and certainly more indicative of one's true abilities.

> *"It's just these few mistakes that I'll soon correct, they don't affect the rest of my game, and they are balanced out by all these other things I did well."*
>
> (quote by optimist)

> *"I made tons of errors, they spoiled every part of my game, and they're going to keep on happening."*
>
> (quote by pessimist)

One caveat, however, for excessive optimism comes from a golf study by Kirschenbaum, O'Connor, and Owens (1999). They found that individuals could be overly optimistic, having such *positive illusions* about their skill and control that they make poor decisions. Across all skill levels, performance suffered on challenging holes because of too aggressive shot selection.

An intervention in which golfers were taught more conservative and realistic shot selection led to better performance. A useful guideline here is the phrase "conservative strategy and cocky execution" (Rotella, 1995). This refers to setting realistic, short-term expectations and game plans; and then totally, completely, and utterly committing oneself to following them through.

Embrace a Psychology of Excellence

Here are a few components of an approach, an overall psychology of excellence that has a better chance of resulting in a pattern of constructive thinking, energy, optimism, and enthusiasm:

1. *Go for your dreams.* Get excited about doing the best that you can, even things that few people have ever done before. Believe that great things are possible.

2. *Focus on your successes.* Deliberately use your capacity for free will to dwell on and emphasize your day-by-day accomplishments, improvements, and episodes of great effort. After every practice session or competition (not just after the successful ones), file away in a training journal at least one instance of success, one instance of improvement, and one instance of great effort.

3. *Be your own best friend, biggest fan, and greatest coach.* Give yourself the same helpful advice and total support you routinely give to your very best friends. At the end of each day create the image of the most positive and helpful person you have ever known and talk to yourself the way that person would.

4. *Create your own reality.* Interpret the events in your sport in a way that opens you to greater and greater chances for success. If your performance early in a contest (e.g., first at bat, first field goal attempt) does not go well, take it as a signal that you are getting all the kinks out and expect to do better as the game continues. Conversely, if performance in the early rounds is good, take it as a signal that you are in a great groove and expect it to continue.

All athletes searching for the "mental edge" that will take their game to the next level must honestly look inside and understand the source of their thinking habits, explanatory style, emotional tendencies, and beliefs about themselves. Are those habits of mind determined by a perspective that encourages mediocrity, or are those habits of mind based on a personal perspective dedicated to success, achievement, and the realization of potential? This is an ongoing personal mental battle that athletes must enter and win to realize their dreams. The remainder of this chapter is devoted to learning the skills that will make this possible.

Self-Talk

The key to cognitive control is **self-talk.** The frequency and content of thoughts vary from person to person and situation to situation. You engage in self-talk any time you carry on an internal dialogue with yourself, such as giving yourself instructions and reinforcement or interpreting what you are feeling or perceiving (Hackfort & Schwenkmezger, 1993). This dialogue can occur out loud (e.g., mumbling to yourself) or inside your head. Self-talk becomes an asset when it enhances self-worth and performance. Such talk can help the athlete change cognitions, generate positive emotions, stay appropriately focused, and cope with difficulties. For example, Gould, Eklund, and Jackson's (1992a, 1992b) studies of Olympic wrestlers indicated that self-talk was a technique that the wrestlers used to foster positive expectancies and appropriately focus attention. These wrestlers also reported more positive expectancies and task-specific self-talk prior to their best versus worst performances. In another qualitative study, Gould, Finch, and Jackson (1993) investigated the stress-coping strategies of U.S. national champion figure skaters and found that their two most common coping strategies were (a) rational thinking and self-talk and (b) positive focus and orientation maintenance.

Self-talk becomes a liability when it is perceived as negative, distracting to the task at hand, or so frequent that it disrupts the automatic performance of skills. For example, studies of observed self-talk and behavioral assessments with junior and competitive adult tennis players found that negative self-talk led to performing worse (Van Raalte, Brewer, Rivera, & Petitpas, 1994; Van Raalte, Cornelius, Hatten, & Brewer, 2000). Similar results have occurred in the laboratory with a dart-throwing task (e.g., Peters & Williams, 2006) and when told to say (and see) planned, destructive self-talk (i.e., "I will miss the bull's eye") (Cumming, Nordin, Horton, & Reynolds, 2006). Other experimental studies found that positive self-talk led to better performance than negative self-talk for individuals completing fairly simple tasks (Dagrou, Gauvin, & Halliwell, 1992; Van Raalte et al., 1995) and complex tasks such as bowling and golfing (Johnston-O'Conner & Kirschenbaum, 1986; Kirschenbaum, Ordman, Tomarken, & Holtzbauer, 1982).

In contrast, a review of self-talk studies (Tod, Hardy, & Oliver, 2011) reported no evidence (only 4 studies) for negative self-talk impeding performance. Review selection criteria, however, kept all studies from being included, plus no consideration could be given to the influence of negative self-talk that is illustrated in anecdotal reports in the media and the reported self-talk of individual athletes in qualitative studies nor the rich source of data from cognitive-behavioral interventions (e.g., Cotterill, Sanders, & Collins, 2010; Gaudiano, 2008; Hanton & Jones, 1999; McArdle & Moore, 2012; Neil et al., 2013; Thomas, Hanton, & Maynard, 2007a; Thomas, et al, 2007b). Although the reviewers recommended continued investigations before firm conclusions could be drawn, they also questioned the value of using thought-stopping interventions to decrease negative self-talk. We, however, see sufficient evidence for negative self-talk impeding performance, but also recognize that there is individual variability.

Coaches influence athletes' self-talk, and need to behave accordingly. Athletes exposed to supportive coaching behaviors had more positive self-talk (one sample) and less negative self-talk (both samples) and exposure to negative coaching behaviors correlated with more negative self-talk (both samples) and less positive self-talk (one sample) (Zourbanos, Hatzigeorgiadis, Tsiakaras, Chroni, & Theodorakis, 2013).

The use of negative self-talk by athletes affects self-esteem. Raising self-esteem through effective self-talk, however, takes time and patience. Although evidence exists for cognitive-behavioral techniques effectively enhancing and maintaining self-esteem (Branden, 1994; McKay & Fanning, 1994), doing so is more complex than it might appear (see Wood, Perunovic, & Lee, 2009). By fostering healthy self-esteem, sport psychologists can enhance the personal growth and development of athletes as well as their performance. See http://www.mayoclinic.com/health/self-esteem/MH00129 for great suggestions on how to harness your own thoughts and beliefs to change how you feel about yourself.

Before we address how specific types of self-talk can be used in different situations to help achieve excellence in learning and performance and to promote confidence and self-esteem, we want to remind you that the interview research reported in Chapter 9 found many athletes stating that their best sport performances occurred when they had no thoughts at all. The athletes were so immersed in the action that it just seemed to happen without conscious thought. Tim Gallwey, author of *The Inner Game of Tennis* (1974), Bob Rotella, author of *Golf Is a Game of Confidence* (1996), and others have stressed that peak performance does not occur when athletes are thinking about it. They emphasize learning to turn performance over to unconscious or automatic functions—functions that are free from the interference of thought.

> *"I'm not thinking . . . I block everything else out."*
>
> Michael Phelps, who won 18 Olympic gold medals in swimming, describing his preparation for races (cited in Whitworth, 2008, p. 25).

It may be desirable to strive for such thought-free performance, but athletes usually *do* think when performing. In fact, they engage in sport related self-talk outside of practice as well as before, during, and after both practice and competition (Hardy, Gammage, & Hall, 2001). There is even evidence that more self-talk occurs in competition settings than in practice settings and that the greatest use occurs *during* competition compared to before or after performance (Hardy, Hall, & Hardy, 2005). In addition, individual sport and skilled athletes use self-talk more frequently than team sport and less skilled athletes (Hardy, Hall, & Hardy, 2004). This self-talk affects athletes' self-concept, self-confidence, emotions, and behavior. Therefore, it is important that coaches and sport psychologists teach athletes to recognize and control their thoughts. Once successful, these athletes are far more likely to experience those desirable episodes of unconscious immersion. The question should not be whether to think but what, when, and how to think. The rest will take care of itself.

Self-Talk for Skill Acquisition and Performance

In their review of 47 self-talk studies, Tod, Hardy, and Oliver (2011) concluded that performance benefits occurred with the use of positive, instructional, and motivational self-talk, with the latter two equally effective on precision and conditioning-based skills. The nature and desirability of self-talk changes as performers become more proficient. During early learning, skill acquisition is usually aided when instructional self-talk is used to remind the performer of key aspects of the movement. For example, cue words such as "step, swing" in tennis and "step, drop, step, kick" for a soccer punt foster cognitive associations that aid in learning proper physical execution. Even on the beginning level, self-talk should be kept as brief and minimal as possible. Oververbalization by the coach or athlete can cause paralysis by analysis. As skill acquisition improves, the goal is to reduce conscious control and promote the automatic execution of the skill. Thus, as skills are mastered, self-talk becomes shorter, less frequent, and even non-existent. Once skillful, shifting focus to what the performer wants to achieve (e.g., "deep outside corner" when serving or "high and inside" if pitching) rather than physical mechanics may also prove helpful (Bunker and Young, 1995).

The content and timing of self-talk is influenced by whether skills are self-paced or externally paced. Skills that are self-paced—that is, initiated by the performer when he or she is ready and without interference from other performers (e.g., pitching, shooting free throws, bowling, archery, golf, serving) provide more opportunities for pre-programming successful execution with self-talk. With reactive, externally paced skills such as spiking in volleyball, the fast break in basketball, or volleying in tennis, the performer needs to use naturally occurring pauses in the game (e.g., changing sides of the court, time-outs, out-of-bounds) as opportunities to focus their self-talk on what they want to do when the action begins again. That said, if done appropriately, self-talk can be used effectively during the actual performance of externally paced skills (Johnson, Hrycaiko, Johnson, & Halas, 2004; Landin & Hebert, 1999; Rogerson & Hrycaiko, 2002). For example, skilled tennis players improved their volleying performance after they were taught a two-word *(split, turn)* self-talk sequence in which they separately said the words and timed each to specific reactions and movement on the court (Landin & Hebert, 1999). The players attributed the success of the self-talk to its directing their attentional focus. They also reported increased confidence.

Self-Talk for Changing Bad Habits

Athletes will need to use self-talk when they want to change a well-learned skill or habit. To change a bad habit, it is usually necessary to intentionally force conscious control over the previously automatic execution and to then direct attention to the replacement movement. Self-talk can facilitate this process. The more drastic the change, the more detailed the self-talk in the relearning phase.

When an athlete uses self-talk in this way, it is essential that the content of the statements focus on what they want to happen rather than what they want to avoid because the head fills

with the negative image when focusing on the error, making the appropriate actions even more difficult to execute. A cue such as "step-hit" rather than, "don't stay on your back foot," could be used if inadequate weight transfer occurs when hitting a backhand. An additional bonus with this type of short but "desired action-oriented" self-talk is that it reinforces the habit of making thoughts positive. Remember, "Winners say what they want to happen; losers say what they fear might happen."

Self-Talk for Attention Control

Distractions abound during competition and practice. Even focusing on the past ("If I had only made that last putt") or the future ("If I birdie the next hole, I'll be leading the field") distracts from executing the present skill. Once again, focusing the mind on what is desired *right now* (e.g., "head down, smooth") gives the athlete the best chance of success. Several books, including *Golf Is a Game of Confidence* (Rotella, 1996), have emphasized the importance of remaining in the present tense (see Chapter 15). Self-talk can help athletes control their attention (e.g., Gould et al., 1992a, 1992b; Hardy et al., 2001; Landin & Hebert, 1999, Neil, et al., 2013). Athletes often report using self-talk cues to improve concentration; and the influence of self-talk on concentration/attention is so powerful that Hardy, Oliver, and Tod (2009) proposed that it is one of the mediating mechanisms that help explain the self-talk/performance relationship.

Self-Talk for Creating Affect/Mood and Controlling Effort

Affective cues can enhance performance. For example, runners who say "fast" or "quick" have been found to increase their speed (Meichenbaum, 1975). A sprinter in the starting blocks will get a faster start by saying "explode" than by thinking about hearing the gun because such a cue directly triggers the desired affect and movement when the gun sounds (Silva, 1982). For a long-distance run, a runner may wish to shift word cues throughout the race so that each is linked to the appropriate movement quality or intent at that phase in the run (Meichenbaum, 1975).

Motivational self-talk is particularly effective for psyching up and maximizing effort and persistence (Hatzigeorgiadis, Galanis, Zourbanos, & Theodorakis, 2013). Finn (1985) advised underaroused athletes to use a combination of self-talk and rapid breathing to reach a desired emotional state. Statements like "Come on, rev up, go all out!" combined with rapid breathing will increase the athlete's heart rate and produce a mood state more favorable for peak performance. Novice and expert martial arts participants increased their handgrip strength when they added a loud, guttural yell (kiap), which presumably increased arousal (Welch & Tschampl, 2012).

It may be difficult for some athletes to get started in the morning, at practice, or in the first few moments of a contest. Others may have difficulty changing tempo or maintaining effort. Phrases such as "go for it," "easy," "pace," "pick it up," "cool it," "push," "stay," and so forth can be very effective in controlling effort (Harris & Harris, 1984). Research supports using self-talk to sustain effort (Tod, Iredale, & Gill, 2003; Thellwell & Greenlee, 2003), such as during a tedious or fatiguing practice. An emphasis on effort control is particularly beneficial because it helps athletes recognize the importance of hard work in achieving success. And if by chance the athletes do not succeed, they are more likely to attribute failure to insufficient effort and therefore want to work harder in the future. Coaches should note that this is a much more productive attribution strategy than blaming lack of success on factors such as luck, poor officiating, or lack of skill.

Self-Talk for Changing Affect/Mood and the Effect of Emotions

In a similar manner, the use of appropriate self-talk can help an athlete change his or her mood to achieve a desired emotional state. Both anecdotal and research data support this conclusion. Golf legend Sam Snead learned in high school that simply recalling the phrase "cool-mad" helped him control his temper so that it worked for him rather than against him. Experimental

data indicates that a motivational self-talk intervention significantly decreased cognitive anxiety (Hatzigeorgiadis, Zourbanos, Mpoumpaki, & Theodorakis (2009). Hanton and Jones (1999) demonstrated that competitive swimmers who perceived their precompetitive anxiety symptoms as debilitative could be taught to use self-talk interventions to reinterpret them as facilitative and thereby enhance their performance. Similar intervention results occurred with elite golfers who were selected initially because they interpreted the emotions they experienced as debilitative toward performance (Neil et al., 2013). See Chapter 12 for a further discussion of how to change anxiety and/or its effect on performance.

Self-Talk for Building Self-Efficacy and Confidence

Studies have shown that athletes with high self-efficacy and/or confidence outperform those with lower levels (Feltz, Short, & Sullivan, 2008; Hatzigeorgiadis et al., 2009; Weinberg, Gould, Jackson, 1979). Correspondingly, performance accomplishment is a predictor of self-efficacy (Bruton, Mellalieu, Shearer, Roderique-Davies, & Hall, 2013) and sport confidence (Vealey & Chase, 2008), which adds credence to Bandura's (1997) proposal that past successful experiences are the strongest predictor of self-efficacy and the inclusion of mastery, physical/mental preparation, and demonstration of ability as sources of sport confidence (Vealey et al., 1998). In addition to the benefits of providing an expectation of success, self-efficacy affects performance by influencing how much effort is expended on a task and how long one persists when confronted with setbacks and obstacles (Bandura, 1997). Efficacy beliefs are vulnerable and need constant reinforcement when confronted with failures (Rongian, 2007) and efficacy lowers when imaging being unconfident (Nordin & Cumming, 2005). These findings illustrate the value of interventions to enhance self-efficacy and confidence.

According to Bandura (1977), self-efficacy is also influenced by verbal persuasion, both from others and from self in the form of self-talk. Self-talk intervention studies have supported this conclusion as well as shown an improvement in performance (e.g., Hatzigeorgiadis, Zourbanos, Goltsios, & Theodorakis, 2008; Zetou, Vernadakis, Bebetsos, & Makraki, 2012). Further support for the influence of self-talk comes from elite college and national team coaches who rated the encouragement of positive self-talk as the third most effective strategy for developing self-efficacy, ranking physical practice first and modeling confidence by the coach second (Gould, Hodge, Peterson, & Gianni, 1989). Furthermore, interventions that include self-talk enhance self-confidence (e.g., Hatzigeorgiadis et al., 2009; Thomas et al., 2007b). Not only did Hatzigeorgiadis et al. find that self-talk enhanced self-confidence, they found evidence that this effect may be a mechanism that explains the facilitating effects of self-talk on performance.

Self-Talk for Adoption and Maintenance of Exercise Behavior

Many studies in the area of exercise behavior have implicated self-efficacy cognitions as a significant factor in predicting adoption and adherence to an exercise program (see Chapter 24 and McAuley and Blissmer, 2000, for a review). Self-efficacy cognitions are a mediator of behavior change, that is, the mechanism by which interventions affect exercise behavior (Dishman, et al., 2004). These findings suggest that appropriately modifying self-efficacy cognitions toward exercise contributes to exercise adoption or adherence. The nature of exercisers' self-talk is also important in that positive self-talk (e.g., I went one block farther than last time) can promote greater confidence in one's exercise activity and can increase commitment whereas negative self-talk (e.g., I'm too fat to walk) can do the opposite.

Identifying Self-Talk

Appropriate use of the preceding kinds of self-talk will enhance self-worth and performance. The first step in gaining control of self-talk is to become aware of what you say to yourself. Surprisingly enough, most people are not aware of

their thoughts, much less the powerful impact they have on their feelings and behavior. By getting athletes to review carefully the way in which they talk to themselves in different types of situations, the athletes and the coach or sport psychologist will identify what kind of thinking helps, what thoughts appear to be harmful, and what situations or events are associated with this talk. Once athletes develop this awareness, they usually discover that their self-talk varies from short cue words and phrases to extremely complex monologues, with the overall content ranging from self-enhancing to self-defeating. The key is to know both when and how to talk to yourself.

Identifying the thoughts that typically prepare an athlete to perform well and to cope successfully with problems during performance can provide a repertoire of cognitive tools for the enhancement of performance. The use of these same thoughts in future performance environments should create similar feelings of confidence and direct performance in much the same way. When an athlete can re-create these positive thoughts and bring them to the new environment, the athlete can be said to be *taking control* of his or her mind.

Most athletes discover that during an unsuccessful performance their mind actually programmed failure through self-doubt and negative statements. The body merely performed what the mind was thinking. Examples might include, "I never swim well in this pool" or "I always play poorly against this opponent" and then going on to swim or compete exactly as prophesied. Obviously, future performance would be enhanced if athletes could eliminate dysfunctional and self-defeating thoughts, but before such thoughts can be eliminated, they need to be identified. Three of the most effective tools for identifying self-talk are retrospection, imagery, and keeping a self-talk log.

Retrospection

By reflecting on situations in which they performed particularly well or particularly poorly and trying to re-create the thoughts and feelings that occurred prior to and during these performances, many athletes are able to identify typical thoughts and common themes associated with both good and bad performance. It is also beneficial to recall the specific situation, or circumstances, that led to the thoughts and resulting performance. Viewing videotapes or DVDs of actual past performances helps the athlete recount the action by heightening the memory of the event. If this technique is used, also film the time before and right after the contest and the time-outs or breaks during the contest. Thoughts during all of these times play a major role in determining the quality of one's present performance, one's expectations regarding future performance, and even one's feelings of self-esteem.

Imagery

Another technique is to have athletes relax as deeply as possible and then try reliving a past performance through imagery, re-creating all relevant sensory experiences, such as how a moment felt or sounded. Obviously, this technique is more effective if athletes have been trained in imagery (see Chapter 13 for suggestions). Athletes who are effective at imagery can usually describe exactly what happened during the competition and what thoughts and feelings preceded, accompanied, and followed the performance. It may be helpful to have them write down the recalled thoughts, situations, and outcomes or, if it is not disruptive, talk into a tape recorder as they are imaging.

Self-Talk Log

Not all athletes can use retrospection and imagery to remember accurately how they thought and felt or what circumstances triggered their thoughts and feelings. Even athletes who are comfortable using these tools run the risk that time and personal impressions may distort their memory of actual thoughts and circumstances. Research has shown that keeping a thought awareness logbook provides insights into the content of an athlete's self-talk, the situations that prompt negative self-talk, and the

consequences of using negative self-talk (Hardy, Roberts, & Hardy, 2009. Thoughts should be transcribed as soon after they occur as possible. Athletes in sports such as golf, archery, rowing, and running have found it beneficial to have a recorder present while they perform so they can directly tape their thoughts and a description of the situation as it occurs.

When keeping a log, the athlete should address such questions as, What do I say before, during, and following my good and poor performances? Not only what thoughts, but how frequently am I talking to myself? What is said after teammates perform poorly, after having difficulty performing a new skill or strategy, when fatigued, and after the coach criticizes performance? Do I stay in the present moment, or revert to dwelling on past performance or future outcome? Does the content of self-talk center on how I feel about myself, how others feel about me, or on letting down my friends and teammates, or how unlucky I am?

If there is a problem in thinking, the goal is to identify the problem and its boundary points in specific terms. To do so specify the initial cue that caused starting to think negatively and when such thinking stopped. For example, if fouled, do I start worrying from the moment the whistle blows or only after I walk to the free throw line? This detailed knowledge will help in planning an optimal intervention. For instance, if worry begins with the referee's whistle, then this is the cue with which to link an alternate thought pattern.

Monitoring thought and behavior patterns during practice is as important as during competition. Often the pattern of thoughts found during competition is merely a reflection of what occurs during practice, thus learning to recognize and control self-talk during practices provides the foundation for effective thinking during competition.

Exercise 1

For three days carry a notebook or your laptop and record, immediately if possible, self-talk that you perceive as negative or dysfunctional. Note the circumstances in which the self-talk occurred and how it affected your feelings and behavior. What did you learn from the self-talk log? Then design and implement an appropriate intervention from the techniques for controlling self-talk. Critique its effectiveness.

Techniques for Controlling Self-Talk

Using the preceding self-monitoring tools is just the *first step* in the process necessary for producing performance-enhancing thoughts and eliminating disabling thoughts. In fact, paying too much attention to undesirable thoughts can be detrimental if not linked to some action or change process; thus, once awareness is heightened, the coach or sport psychologist should immediately instruct the athlete in how to start dealing with them. Similarly, when good performance is analyzed, it should be with the intent of trying to purposefully duplicate it in the future.

In this section we present techniques for controlling self-talk. The empirical support for the effectiveness of these techniques is well documented. In fact, a meta-analysis by Meyers, Whelan, and Murphy (1996) calculated a greater effect size for cognitive restructuring interventions ($n = 4$, $d = .79$, $SD = .36$) than that found for goal setting ($n = 3$, $d = .54$, $SD = .15$), mental rehearsal ($n = 28$, $d = .57$, $SD = .75$), and relaxation interventions ($n = 25$, $d = .73$, $SD = 1.65$). A more recent meta-analysis of 32 self-talk studies yielded a positive moderate effect size of .48 (Hatzigeorgiadis, Zourbanos, Galanis, & Theodorakis, 2011). Their analyses also found that systematic training in and practice of the self-talk routine is crucial to maximizing the effectiveness of the self-talk technique. In fact, training was the strongest moderator of intervention effectiveness. Techniques for controlling self-talk include:

Thought-stoppage

Changing negative thoughts to positive thoughts

Countering

Reframing

ABC cognitive restructuring

Affirmation statements

Mastery and coping tapes

Video technology

"There were no thoughts about 'this is for the Open' . . . I stroked it in."

> *Quote from Padraig Harrington (triple-major champion golfer) describing his thoughts as he prepared for his final putt in a playoff against Sergio Garcia to win the 2007 Open Championship (cited in Jones, 2007, p.12).*

Thought Stoppage

If an athlete's self-talk is too frequent and thus distracting, or if the talk is detrimental to performance, it must be terminated. Getting rid of such thoughts often makes it possible to break the link that leads to negative feelings and behaviors and an inappropriate attentional focus. The technique of **thought stoppage** provides one method for eliminating counterproductive thoughts (Meyers & Schleser, 1980). The technique begins with awareness of the unwanted thought and uses a trigger to interrupt or stop the undesirable thought. The trigger can be a word such as *stop* or a physical action such as snapping the fingers or clapping one hand against the thigh. Each athlete should choose the most natural trigger and use it consistently.

Thought stoppage will not work unless the athlete first recognizes undesirable thoughts and then is motivated to stop them. Developing the commitment necessary to improve the quality of an athlete's self-talk is not as easy for the coach and sport psychologist to accomplish as it sounds. For example, even after using tools to create awareness of thoughts, one young professional golfer would not admit negative statements were affecting her golf. To convince her of the severity of the problem, she was asked to empty a box of 100 paper clips into her pocket.

Each time she had a negative thought, she had to move a clip to her back pocket. At the end of the golf round she had shot an 84 and had 87 paper clips in her back pocket! The process of actually counting paper clips, each of which represented a self-defeating thought, made her dramatically aware of her problem and motivated her to change (Owens & Bunker, 1989).

Thought stoppage is a skill, and, as with any other skill, it is best to first practice it before use in competition. An effective way to practice is to combine it with imagery of past performance. Instruct the athletes to select a typical dysfunctional thought, or thought pattern, they would like to eliminate. Next close your eyes and as vividly as possible imagine being in the situation in which you usually have those thoughts. Once the situation is re-created, practice interrupting the thought with the trigger selected for thought stoppage. Repeat until you can effortlessly and automatically eliminate dysfunctional talk and accompanying feelings of worry and anxiety, and then move on to using thought stoppage during actual physical practice.

During the earlier stages of practicing thought stoppage, athletes may want to visibly use their trigger, such as saying "stop" out loud. Doing so makes athletes more conscious of their wish to stop dysfunctional talk and also helps coaches and sport psychologists to monitor usage. If body language shows frustration or disgust with play, the thoughts probably are frustrating too. When coaches and sport psychologists see no visible thought-stoppage trigger during these circumstances, they should directly confront the athlete as to what thoughts are occurring. This approach serves to reinforce awareness and the need to stop such talk immediately. The other advantage of visible practicing is that athletes realize they are not alone in their need to deal more effectively with self-talk. The technique is particularly effective if becoming more positive is a team effort and responsibility. When one high school basketball coach instituted such a program halfway through his season, he was so impressed with the outcome that he attributed turning a losing season into a winning season to his athletes' learning to control negative talk and body language and to becoming supportive toward one another rather than critical and sarcastic.

Even with practice it may be difficult for some to suppress an unwanted thought (e.g., "Don't think about the umpire"). In fact, studies by Wegner and his colleagues (see Wegner, 1994 and 2009, for a review) have demonstrated that individuals deliberately trying to suppress unwanted thoughts often find themselves even more preoccupied by the thoughts they are trying to escape, particularly so when under stress, time pressure, or distraction conditions. Similar cognitive results have occurred within sport research (Dugdale and Ecklund, 2002; Wenzlaff & Wegner, 2000; Janelle, 1999) and also with trying to suppress action (Wegner, Ansfield, & Pilloff, 1998; Woodman & Davis, 2008). That is, participants were more likely to overshoot the hole when putting, particularly under the stress of cognitive load, when they received instructions to *avoid* overhitting the hole, but only with repressors (individuals who report low cognitive anxiety, but have high physiological arousal) in the Woodman and Davis study. Wegner (1994) explained these failures (i.e., doing the opposite of what one intends) with the theory of ironic processes of mental control. For an interesting discussion of the implications this theory has for sport psychology research and interventions, see Janelle (1999) and Hall, Hardy, and Gammage (1999).

These findings indicate how important it is for athletes to use undesirable thoughts as the stimulus or trigger to deliberately focus the mind on a desired process or outcome. This leads to the next technique for controlling thoughts—changing self-defeating thoughts to self-enhancing thoughts.

Changing Negative Thoughts to Positive Thoughts

Although it makes sense to stop negative thoughts altogether, sometimes this cannot be accomplished. An alternative is to learn to couple any negative thought with a positive thought that either provides encouragement and support or appropriately redirects attention. The coach or sport psychologist should instruct athletes to switch to a positive or more appropriate thought as soon as they are aware of a dysfunctional self-statement. For example, when a gymnast finds himself saying, "This new move is really hard—I'll never get it right!" he could immediately follow the phrase with, "I've learned hard moves before, if I'm persistent I'll learn this one too."

One advantage of teaching this technique after thought stoppage is that it takes pressure off athletes who initially doubt their ability to control their thoughts. Although these athletes think they cannot control what thoughts first enter their head, they usually will accept their ability to control the thoughts that follow. An example is the golfer who used the "paper clip" technique to become aware of her many self-defeating thoughts. Her goal in working with cognitions was simply to reduce the dysfunctional statements that were not followed by self-enhancing statements. Not having to worry about the occurrence of a self-defeating statement took considerable pressure off her. Each day she was able to reduce the number of paper clips that stood for negative thoughts not followed by positive thoughts, and in time she was able to rid herself of the recurring pattern of dysfunctional talk.

"Just little key words like 'come on,' 'think head down,' 'stay low and hard.' I'm saying things like that to myself when warming up. That's all it needs, just some key words, something positive just to get me focused and overcome the negative thoughts."

(elite field hockey player, cited in Thomas et al., 2007a)

Learning to turn off negative or inappropriate thoughts takes time, particularly when negative thought patterns have become the athlete's habitual mode of response to adversity (Cautela & Wisocki, 1977). Frustration over the recurrence of negative thoughts may be lessened if the coach or sport psychologist draws the parallel to

trying to unlearn well-established errors in physical technique. We change old habits slowly, whether they are physical or cognitive, and only with considerable motivation and practice.

A good way to first implement this technique is for athletes to make a list of self-defeating things they typically say and would like to change. The self-talk log can be a good source for generating this list. Meichenbaum (1977) emphasized that athletes should specify when they make these statements and what causes them. The goal is to recognize the situation involved and why the thought occurred. Athletes should then identify a substitute positive statement. It may be helpful to make a list with each self-defeating thought on one side and the preferred self-enhancing statement directly opposite the negative thought (see Table 14-1).

Notice that the self-enhancing statements in the table always bring the athlete back to the present time and personal control of the situation. Coupling some type of relaxation with this technique may prove helpful considering negative thoughts often occur when an individual is stressed and likely overaroused physiologically. For example, athletes might stop their negative thought, take a deep breath, and substitute the self-enhancing thought as they feel relaxation spreading with the long exhalation.

There is nothing unusual about having negative thoughts, and even the greatest athletes have anxious or negative thoughts on occasion. Tennis legend Arthur Ashe once feared "he wouldn't get a single serve in the court" just before his U.S. Open championship. Bobby Jones, the famous golfer, was standing over a 2-foot putt that would allow him to win the U.S. Open when he had the thought, "What if I stub my putter into the ground and miss the ball entirely and lose the tournament?" These champions, however, did not store their negative thoughts away where they could build into a mental block. Instead, Ashe and Jones replaced those thoughts with constructive ones. The key is not to allow negative thoughts to control and dominate the mind. Make the last thought in any string or sequence of thoughts self-enhancing.

Table 14-1 Examples of Changing Negative Thoughts to Positive Thoughts

Self-Defeating Thoughts	Change to Self-Enhancing Thoughts
I can't believe it's raining. I have to play in the rain.	No one likes the rain, but I can play as well in it as anyone else.
You dumb jerk.	Ease off. Everyone makes mistakes. Sluff it off and put your mind on what you want to do.
There's no sense in practicing. I have no natural talent.	I've seen good players who had to work hard to be successful. I can get better if I practice correctly.
This officiating stinks; we'll never win.	There's nothing we can do about the officiating, so let's just concentrate on what we want to do. If we play well, the officiating won't matter.
Why did they foul me in the last minute of play—I'm so nervous, I'll probably choke and miss everything.	My heart is beating fast. That's OK, I've sunk free throws a hundred times. Just breathe and swish.
We'll win the meet only if I get a 9.0 on this routine.	Stop worrying about the score; just concentrate on how you're going to execute the routine.
The coach must think I'm hopeless. He never helps me.	That's not fair. He has a whole team to coach. Tomorrow I'll ask what he thinks I need to work on the most.
I don't want to fail.	Nothing was ever gained by being afraid to take risks. As long as I give my best, I'll never be a failure.
I'll take it easy today and go hard next workout.	The next workout will be easier if I go hard now.
Who cares how well I do anyway?	I care, and I'll be happier if I push myself.
This hurts; I don't know if it's worth it.	Of course it hurts, but the rewards are worth it.

Although their purpose was not changing negative to positive self-talk, intervention studies by Hatzigeorgiadis and colleagues found that teaching swimmers self-talk cues that had either an attentional or anxiety control (2007) or instructional or motivational focus (2004) resulted in not only improving performance, but also in a significant deterioration in the frequency of interfering thoughts. These findings suggest that simply diverting attention to a desirable self-talk cue may lessen dysfunctional self-talk.

The recommendations presented above are based on research conducted with athletes and nonathletes from individualistic cultures (e.g., the United States, Western Europe). Some research suggests that the relationship of self-talk to performance may be different for individuals from collectivist cultures (e.g., China, Singapore) and, if true, self-talk interventions such as stopping negative thoughts or changing them to positive thoughts may not be appropriate for them. This concern comes from the finding by Peters and Williams (2006) that Asians had significantly more negative self-talk than European Americans during dart-throwing performance and that their negative self-talk related to better performance. Conversely, as previously found, the opposite occurred for European Americans. Additionally, cross-cultural research suggests that a self-critical versus self-enhancing orientation is a characteristic of collectivist individuals' self-concepts, and is necessary for self-improvement (Kitayama, 2002).

Countering

Changing negative to positive self-statements probably will not achieve the expected behavioral outcome if the athlete still *believes* in the negative statements. Athletes will rarely be able to accomplish something if they truly believe they cannot. Furthermore, the motivation even to try will be eroded if there is no belief that one's efforts will ultimately yield success. Bell (1983) proposes that in such instances merely directing one's thoughts toward desired actions may not be enough. Instead, the athlete may have to identify and build a case against the negative self-statements that are interfering with effective performance. Bell suggests using the tool of countering under these circumstances. **Countering** is an internal dialogue that uses facts and reasons to refute the underlying beliefs and assumptions that led to negative thinking. Rather than blindly accepting the negative voice in the back of his head, the athlete argues against it.

"I'm not sure how much I really believe what I'm trying to say to myself. I know that what I feel is negative and that it's not going to help. . . I tell myself 'come on,' 'I've done it before,' and 'I am good enough.' But then I have this big question: 'just because I did it then does it mean that I'll be able to do it today?' And the answer is 'no'. . .")

(athlete debilitator, cited in Thomas et al., 2007a).

When learning to use counters, it is important to describe the evidence necessary to change an attitude or belief. In the preceding example, the coach or sport psychologist might try helping the athlete identify issues such as, What makes me think I am slow? Have I ever in the past played with good speed? Am I as fast as any of the other athletes? If yes, are they successful at running this offense? What might be causing my slowness, and can I do anything to change it? If I am not quite as fast as some of my teammates, do I have any other talents that might compensate for this, such as being able to read the situation faster so I can react more quickly? What

other skills do I have that might help me learn this offensive pattern?

Look for evidence that refutes either the athlete's slowness or the importance of just speed in the successful execution of the offensive pattern. The more evidence and logic there is to refute the negative belief structure, the more effective the counters will be in getting the athlete to accept the positive statement. Later it may be possible for the athlete to identify the negative or irrational thought and simply dismiss it with phrases such as "That's not right," "Who says I can't?" or just plain "Bull."

In his discussion of countering, Bell (1983) makes another excellent point. Sometimes thoughts are neither correct nor incorrect—they cannot be verified. Bell suggests that what is more important is determining whether a given thought *helps* an athlete reach his or her goals. Encourage athletes to ask themselves, "Is this thinking in my best interest? Does this thinking help me feel the way I need to or does it make me worried and tense? When athletes realize that thinking certain thoughts can only be detrimental, it becomes sensible, and thus easier, to stop them or change them.

Reframing

Another effective technique for dealing with negative self-talk is **reframing,** described by Gauron (1984) as the process of creating alternative frames of reference or different ways of looking at the world. Because the world is literally what we make it, reframing allows us to transform what appears at first to be a weakness or difficulty into a strength or possibility, simply by looking at it from a different point of view. Gauron encourages athletes to cultivate the skill of reframing because it helps athletes control their internal dialogue in a positive, self-enhancing manner. Almost any self-defeating statement or negative thought can be reframed, or interpreted from a different perspective, so that it aids rather than hinders the athlete.

An important element of reframing is that it does not deny or downplay what the athlete is experiencing or encourage the athlete to ignore something troublesome. Instead, by reframing, the athlete acknowledges what is happening and decides to use it to his or her best advantage. For example, if an athlete was saying, "I'm feeling tense and anxious about playing today," he can reframe the statement to "I'm feeling excited and ready." Similarly, an athlete dwelling on the *problems* of improving a skill or the *struggle* of a performance slump can turn these situations to his advantage and maintain a positive attitude by focusing on the *possibilities* of achieving a new level of skill and the *opportunity* present in each new performance.

Research support for the positive effects of reframing comes from a study that compared the mental preparation of teams who met or exceeded their goals in the 1996 Atlanta Olympics to teams that failed to meet expectations at the games (Gould, Guinan, Greenleaf, Medbery, & Pederson, 1999). Gould et al. found that members of the more successful teams reported that they were able to "reframe negative events in a positive light." Additional support comes from research by Hanton and Jones (1999) who improved performance in nonelite swimmers by teaching them to reframe their anxiety symptoms as facilitative rather than debilitative to performance. See Chapter 12 for similar examples.

Identifying Irrational and Distorted Thinking

In addition to dealing with negative self-talk and self-doubt, athletes need to realize that they may also be engaging in cognitive distortions and irrational thinking. According to Albert Ellis (1982), a prominent cognitive behavioral psychologist, athletes fail to reach their goals and perform below their ability primarily because they accept and endorse self-defeating, irrational beliefs. Ellis identifies four basic irrational beliefs that negatively affect athletes' performance. If athletes accept any of these beliefs (let alone two or three of them), or any of their variations, their progress and satisfaction will be blocked. These four irrational beliefs are (1) I *must* at all times perform outstandingly well, (2) others who are significant to me (e.g., teammates and coaches) *have to* approve and love me, (3) everyone has *got to* treat me kindly and fairly, and (4) the conditions of my life, particularly my life in sports, absolutely *must* be arranged so that I get what I want when I want.

Such thinking is counterproductive because it negatively influences self-concept, self-confidence, and performance. Once identified—a task that may take considerable soul searching—these self-defeating types of beliefs need to be modified. Here are some irrational thoughts and cognitive distortions that are common among athletes (most are from Gauron, 1984):

- Perfection is essential
- Catastrophizing
- Worth depends on achievement
- Personalization
- Fallacy of fairness
- Blaming
- Polarized thinking and labeling
- One-trial generalizations
- Shoulds
- Emotional reasoning

Let's take a look at each of these thought patterns along with some suggestions for modifying such irrational and distorted thinking.

Perfection is essential.   One of the most debilitating irrational ideas for athletes (coaches too) is that one must be thoroughly competent and successful and achieve everything attempted. No one can consistently achieve perfection. Individuals who believe they should will blame themselves for every defeat, every setback. Their self-concept will likely suffer and they may start a fear-of-failure syndrome. Furthermore, they will put such pressures on themselves to do well that both their enjoyment and performance will likely suffer. There is always value in *striving* for perfection, but nothing is gained by *demanding* perfection.

Catastrophizing (awfulizing).   Catastrophizing often accompanies perfectionistic tendencies, as the athlete believes that any failure will be a humiliating disaster. Catastrophizers expect the worst possible thing to happen. Unfortunately, expecting disaster often leads to disaster! Individuals become plagued by what-ifs. "What if I lose today?" "What if my parents are embarrassed when I strike out?" Realistic evaluations of the actual situation and setting appropriate goals help combat perfectionistic thinking and catastrophizing.

Worth depends on achievement. Too many athletes believe they are only as good as their accomplishments, what they win. Correspondingly, they think they must excel in order to please others. Try asking an athlete or coach to describe who he or she is without mentioning his or her sport success rate! Athletes must learn to value themselves for more than what they do in sport; worth as a human being is based on factors other than achievement outcome.

Personalization. Athletes who personalize believe they are the cause and focus of activities and actions around them. They think that everything people do or say is some kind of reaction to them. They also have a tendency to frequently make comparison to others, trying to determine who is better, who gets more playing time, and so forth.

Fallacy of fairness and ideal conditions. You feel resentful because you think you know what is fair but other people do not agree. "Fair" is often a disguise for just wanting your own way. "Ideal conditions" means that coaches should carve out the easiest possible path for athletes to follow. It is irrational to think that things will come easily or that the world of sport, and life, should somehow be fair—that each investment of time and energy should deliver an equitable level of success, or that everyone should be treated the same. Holding these expectations produces frustration, because in reality coaches do treat players differently; one's efforts, improvements, and achievements are not always noticed; and the breaks of the game, and life, are often unfair. Coming to grips with unfairness and learning to stay composed is one of sport's great lessons.

Blaming. This takes two forms—you hold other people responsible for your actions and feelings, or you blame yourself for every problem or outcome. Making excuses or assigning fault to others gains nothing. Athletes must learn to replace external attributions with attributions that are within their control: "Success comes from effort and working hard, whereas failure comes from lack of effort or insufficient practice of key fundamentals." Athletes often learn their attributions from coaches. If coaches blame failure on factors outside one's control, athletes will too. Coaches and sport psychologists should provide appropriate internal attributions for successes and failures. When athletes realize they are responsible for and in control of their performance, their confidence will grow after a good performance and they will have more confidence in turning current failures into future successes. Accepting complete responsibility for everything, however, is equally nonproductive. "We lost because I missed that last free throw." This irrational blame can lead to potential problems such as loss of confidence and the thought, "The coach and my teammates must really hate me." Instead, help athletes to be realistic and honest in evaluating performance outcome.

All-or-nothing thinking and labeling. Seeing things as black or white, all good or bad, e.g., "If I fail to win this tournament, I am a total failure and an inadequate person." Such thinking can also lead to judgmental labeling—the identification or description of something or someone with an extreme evaluative word or phrase, such as "choker," "butterfingers," "airbrain," "loser." Once established and internalized, these negative labels are difficult to erase—*labeling is disabling.* Coaches and sport psychologists should instead set a good example and stress that athletes avoid any kind of negative evaluative language, judgmentalism, and absolute thinking.

One-trial generalizations. This cognitive distortion results from reaching a general conclusion based on a single incident or piece of evidence. For example, if you play poorly the first time you golf in the rain, you might expect it to happen again when similar circumstances present. If these conclusions are based on only one or two experiences, careful analysis can usually lead to negating them. If based on many experiences, largely because of the expectation, then practicing under perceived negative conditions until success is achieved will often produce evidence to repudiate the initial negative generalization.

Shoulds. These people have a list of ironclad rules/expectations about how they and other people should act. People who break the rules anger them and they feel guilty when they break the rules. Avoid should and must statements because they put unreasonable demands on yourself and others.

Emotional reasoning. You mistake feelings for facts. If you *feel* stupid and boring, then you must *be* stupid and boring. Such people are more likely to have problems with adverse emotions because they tend to generalize them as personal characteristics versus just a transitory emotion.

Modifying Irrational and Distorted Thinking: ABC Cognitive Restructuring

Irrational beliefs often underlie much of the stress and resulting self-defeating thoughts and feelings athletes experience during athletic performance and in life in general. Unfortunately, athletes often are unaware that the culprit is maladaptive beliefs and thinking. Instead they think the circumstance or event caused the deleterious emotional reaction and behavior. For example, a basketball player misses a critical free throw in the final seconds of a game and ends up feeling worthless and fearing similar circumstances in the future. The typical athlete probably thinks his missed free throw caused the thoughts and anxiety (see Figure 14-1). In actuality, the *assumptions* the athlete made are the cause. In this case, irrational assumptions such as perfectionism, worth depends on achievement, or personalization may have been the culprit.

The coach or sport psychologist can help athletes identify and dispute their irrational assumptions. One excellent way to do so is to use Albert Ellis's Rational Emotive Behavior Therapy (REBT) (Ellis & Dryden, 1987), sometimes referred to as ABC cognitive restructuring. The process begins by keeping a daily record in which athletes record not only their upsetting thoughts but also the resulting feelings and behavior and the negative events that triggered them (see Figure 14-1). In column A briefly describe the activating event in terms of what happened, what one saw and heard. In column B record the exact content of whatever dysfunctional self-talk one thought or said out loud. In column C record the resulting emotional and behavioral consequences. To help determine what dysfunctional talk to record, use Steinmetz, Blankenship, and Brown's (1980) five criteria for deciding whether self-talk and underlying beliefs are rational or irrational, productive or unproductive.

1. Are the beliefs based on objective reality? Would other people see the event the way you perceived it, are there other explanations, did you exaggerate and personalize experiences?

2. Are they helpful to you? Self-destructive thoughts are usually irrational.

3. Are they useful in reducing conflicts with other people, or do you set up a me versus them situation?

4. Do they help you reach your short- and long-term goals, or do they get in the way?

5. Do they reduce emotional conflict and help you feel the way you want to feel?

After completing the ABC steps across a designated number of days, implement the next critical step, which entails trying to rebut or dispute self-criticism, etc. The first step is to reexamine the self-talk under column B to determine if irrational beliefs or distortions in thinking might underlie what appeared, on the surface, to be automatic statements. Record the underlying beliefs in column B after the dysfunctional self-talk statement. In many cases, more than one thinking error may have led to the self-talk. For example, see Figure 14-1 for what occurred when the athlete missed the free throw.

ABC Cognitive Restructuring

A. Activating Event	B. Beliefs or Interpretations	C. Consequences	D. Dispute
Briefly describe the actual event that led to the feelings and behavior	Record the actual dysfunctional self-talk and, if appropriate, include mental pictures	Identify feelings, bodily reactions, and behavior	Write rational response(s) to the automatic thoughts
Fouled in final ten seconds with game tied – missed free throw	"I lost the game for the team." *(personalization)* *(blaming)* "I always choke in pressure situations." *(overgeneralizations)* *(catastrophizing)*	Depressed, tensed up, blew defensive assignment after free throw	"Hey, I'm disappointed but that was just one point out of 40 minutes of play." "I missed this shot, but there are other times when I've come through under pressure. I'll put extra time into free throw practice and work on staying loose and positive."

Figure 14-1 **Example of how to use ABC cognitive restructuring to identify and modify irrational and distorted thinking**

Identifying the underlying irrational beliefs and thinking distortions helps athletes discover the erroneous or illogical aspects of their initial self-talk. Once done, substitute more rational and productive thoughts in column D. If a particular dysfunctional thought often occurs (e.g., saying "I always screw up" or something equivalent after every disappointment), the person will want to frequently repeat the substituted rational statement until it is believed. Believability might increase if you incorporate one of the quick relaxation techniques discussed in Chapter 12. For example, take a complete breath and with the exhalation say, "Lighten up! It's human to make mistakes. Learn from it and move on." The preceding may be difficult, but it gets easier and easier with practice. The ultimate goal is to create such awareness that athletes immediately recognize and dispute dysfunctional self-talk.

Support for REBT and Beck's cognitive behavior therapy (CBT, which is similar to REBT) exists within a sport milieu (e.g., McArdle & Moore, 2012; Thomas et al., 2007b; Turner & Barker, 2013). Using the preceding ABCD framework with four elite youth cricketers, Turner and Barker found visual and statistical analyses indicated a change from irrational beliefs to rational beliefs and a reduction in cognitive anxiety. McArdle & Moore successfully used CBT to address an elite rugby player's disabling perfectionism ("I should perform exceptionally well at all times because doing things perfectly means success." p. 306) and catastrophizing ("I made a mistake; I'm going to lose my place on the team" p. 304).

> "... he appreciates he is a good player, and is not worried he will be judged on bad performances." "He now thinks through how he is feeling before and after and tries to rationalize." "He thinks about positives and uses self-talk." "He has become more relaxed, confident as the sessions have developed."
>
> *(quotes from parents and a coach about the effects of REBT, cited in Turner and Barker, 2013, pp. 141–142)*

Less enlightened coaches and athletes might fear that modifying irrational beliefs such as perfectionistic demands and taking excessive responsibility for performance outcome may take the edge off an athlete's competitiveness. This fear is unfounded. Reflecting back to an athlete's best moments in competition almost always reveals the opposite. Helping athletes eliminate irrational beliefs and develop more adaptive thoughts will go a long way toward improving performance and, perhaps more important, personal growth.

Constructing Affirmation Statements

Feelings of confidence, efficacy, and personal control will be enhanced if coaches and sport psychologists assist athletes in constructing personal affirmation statements. **Affirmations** are statements that reflect positive attitudes or thoughts about oneself. They are statements about what you want, *phrased as if you already had it.* For example, in 1985 Ivan Lendl had a record of 9 wins and 12 losses against John McEnroe. Lendl then started writing each day in a notebook, "I look forward to playing John McEnroe." By early 1991 his record against McEnroe had improved to 19 wins and 15 losses, and Lendl had won the last 10 straight matches (Wishful Inking, 1991).

The most effective affirmations are both *potentially* believable and vivid. A good source of affirmations is positive statements that might naturally have occurred with previous successful performance. Affirmations should capture the desired feelings: "I am strong as a bull," "I fly down the finish line," "I really come through under pressure."

Slogans can also serve as affirmations: "Winners think they can and they do"; "See it, think it, believe it, do it"; "Say yes to success." Each slogan can become a recipe or formula for success provided it is internalized. Another way to build and accept affirmations is to have each athlete make a self-esteem list and a success list (Gauron, 1984). The **self-esteem list** contains all of one's positive attributes—all of his or her perceived assets, strengths, and positive qualities. The **success list** contains all of one's successes thus far.

These lists serve to remind athletes of how capable and deserving they are of success. Now is not the time for modesty, but for honest reflection on all positive qualities and successes. Rushall (1979) has emphasized that once this positive frame of reference is established, the athlete should write specific affirmation statements that are *positive action-oriented* self-statements affirming capabilities and what he or she would like to do: "I play well under pressure" rather than "I know I can play well under pressure." Affirmations should be in the present tense and worded in a way that avoids perfectionist statements such as "I always . . ." or "I never . . . ."

Once formulated, how can these statements be best used to foster confidence and the desired goal of the affirmation? Gauron (1984) suggests having a number-one affirmation to work on each day, especially when feeling bummed or going into a slump. Write the statement 10 to 20 times each day on a piece of paper or on a card that can be carried around and pulled out and read during free moments. Once the affirmation becomes so integrated into the conscious mind that it is completely believed and made automatically, select another affirmation on which to work. Other techniques for utilizing affirmations are to post them (singularly or in combination) in places such as one's bedroom, bathroom, locker, or screen saver. Consider recording affirmations on cassette tapes and playing them whenever possible, such as between classes or before going to bed.

Exercise 2

Write three affirmation statements that reflect what you would like to be true about yourself, but currently are not, e.g., "I prepare for each class, listen carefully in class, and take good notes." Plan and implement a strategy to help your affirmations become true.

Make a self-esteem list and a success list. Now is not the time for modesty!

Designing Coping and Mastery Self-Talk Tapes or Files

Every individual has the capacity to program his or her mind for successful thoughts. Some athletes do it naturally; others must learn how to be effective thinkers. One very effective method for training the mind to think in a confident, success-oriented way is through the use of mastery and coping tapes or digital audio files such as an MP3 or an iPod. For a mastery tape or file the athlete records his or her own voice describing an outstanding performance in which events proceed precisely as desired, including the ideal thoughts, feelings, and emotions experienced just before, during, and after performance. Recalling a past outstanding performance may help the athlete get started in this process. Feedback from the coach might help in preparing the script. If the technology is available, put the voice-over on a video of their performing exactly as wanted, maybe with a musical background that creates the desired emotions.

The concept with the mastery tape or file is to be playing the best game possible and be in complete control of the situation. Speak slowly and provide pauses when recording the self-talk to allow the mind time to fully visualize each of the described or depicted scenes. Listening or watching a mastery rendition of perfect performances over and over helps program the conscious and subconscious mind for success.

Because obstacles and setbacks are likely to occur in even the best of circumstances, producing and listening to a **coping tape or file** is an effective way of programming the mind to maintain confidence, control, and focus in the face of difficulties. Coping tapes or files allow the athlete to practice dealing with all the potential things that could go wrong. The situation might be one in which the athlete makes a foolish mistake and loses mental or emotional control.

The athlete then rehearses the strategies needed to regain control and confidence. This is an excellent opportunity to practice not only this chapter's cognitive techniques, but also arousal/anxiety control, imagery, and concentration techniques.

It should be stressed that the emphasis on a coping tape or file is not on the stressful or distracting situation described but on the process by which the athlete regains control and confidence when confronted with these situations. Listening or watching over and over to you successfully coping helps create a sense of confidence and control so that if the same situation occurs in real life the athlete can effectively deal with it.

Use Highlight Videotapes, CDs, or DVDs to Enhance Performance

Modern video technology can also be used to help athletes gain confidence and improve skills (Ives, Straub, & Shelley, 2002). Video cameras are now so easy to use, and so common, that almost any athlete or team has access to enough raw footage from which a personal or team highlight video can be created. All that is necessary is to identify the beginning and ending points of a few scenes of peak performance. It is particularly desirable to select performances in which athletes can see themselves excelling at the skills or strategies that currently need emphasis. An audio input can add an athlete's or teams favorite musical selection to serve as the sound track. Watching well-executed play while recalling the self-talk, emotions, and sensations that accompanied the scenes enhances confidence and self-efficacy and serves as a form of imagery rehearsal, which programs the body/mind in many positive ways (see Chapter 13). The examples of NCAA and Olympic champions using highlight tapes are too numerous to mention.

Summary

There is a direct correlation between self-confidence and success. Confident athletes think about themselves and the action at hand in a different way from those who lack confidence. The difference is that the confident athlete's self-talk and internal imagery are consistently positive and enthusiastic. This self-enhancing thinking is likely to lead to enabling feelings and good performance, just as the inappropriate or misguided thinking of athletes lacking in confidence is likely to lead to negative feelings and poor performance. Athletes can learn to use self-talk to build confidence and self-efficacy, to appropriately direct attentional focus and thus to facilitate learning and performance. The first step in gaining control of thinking is to monitor self-talk to become aware of what kind of thinking helps, what thoughts are occurring that appear to be harmful, and what situations or events are associated with the talk. Three of the most effective tools for identifying self-talk are retrospection, imagery, and keeping a self-talk log.

Once awareness of self-talk and feelings, particularly of dysfunctional talk, is heightened the coach or sport psychologist can instruct the athlete in how to start dealing with these thoughts. Techniques such as thought stoppage, changing negative thoughts to positive thoughts, countering, reframing, cognitive restructuring of irrational and distorted thinking, and constructing affirmation statements are possible tools for producing performance-enhancing thoughts and eliminating disabling thoughts. Mastery and coping tapes or files and video technology can also enhance confidence and performance.

Using these interventions will require an investment of time and faith on the part of the athlete, and there is no guarantee of immediate improvements. As with any other training method that truly enhances performance and personal growth, the results will emerge gradually, in precise correlation to the athlete's persistence and commitment (Brewer & Shillinglaw, 1992). Athletes who invest in improving their self-talk will find their efforts well rewarded.

Study Questions

1. Describe how the self-talk of a successful athlete is different from that of an unsuccessful athlete. Give five examples of self-talk from each.

2. What is the relationship between (a) self-talk and self-esteem and (b) self-confidence and self-efficacy?

3. Compare and contrast optimistic and pessimistic explanatory styles in terms of the three dimensions of explanatory style. How would you rate yourself on each of these?

4. Name and describe the seven uses for self-talk. Using any sport or exercise setting, provide an example of each.

5. Susie, a varsity golfer, is concerned that her self-talk may be having an adverse effect on her play. What three techniques could she use to become more aware of her self-talk and how might she use them?

6. Describe how a coach or sport psychologist might help athletes use the techniques of thought stoppage and changing negative thoughts to positive thoughts.

7. How does countering a negative self-statement differ from reframing? Give examples of both in response to the statement "I'm always getting beaten on my opponent's first serve", or an equivalent statement from your own experiences.

8. List and describe at least eight types of irrational and distorted thinking. Provide an example for how you can use the ABC cognitive restructuring intervention to help an athlete modify his or her irrational and distorted thinking.

9. When John monitors his self-talk, what five criteria should he use to determine whether his self-talk and underlying beliefs are rational or irrational?

10. What are the guidelines for determining and using affirmations?

11. How does a mastery tape or file help an athlete develop appropriate self-talk?

12. What is the purpose of a coping tape or file, and how is this purpose accomplished?

13. How might a videotape, CD, or DVD be designed and used to enhance an athlete's confidence and performance?

References

Bandura, A. (1997). *Self-efficacy: The exercise of control*, New York: W. H. Freeman and Company.

Bell, K. E. (1983). *Championship thinking: The athlete's guide to winning performance in all sports*. Englewood Cliffs, NJ: Prentice-Hall.

Branden, N. (1994). *The six pillars of self-esteem*. New York: Bantam.

Brewer, B. S., & Shillinglaw, R. (1992). Evaluation of a psychological skills training workshop for male intercollegiate lacrosse players. *The Sport Psychologist, 6*, 139–147.

Bruton, A. M., Mellalieu, S. D., Shearer, D., Roderique-Davies, G., & Hall, R. (2013). Performance accomplishment information as predictors of self-efficacy as a function of skill level in amateur golf. *Journal of Applied Sport Psychology, 25*, 197–208.

Bunker, L. K., & Young, B. (1995). *The courtside coach*. Charlottesville, VA: Links.

Cautela, J. R., & Wisocki, P. A. (1977). Thought stoppage procedure: Description, application and learning theory interpretations. *Psychological Record, 27*, 255–264.

Connaughton, D.; Hanton, S., & Jones, G. (2010). Development and maintenance of mental toughness in the world's best performers. *The Sport Psychologist, 24*, 168–193.

Cotterill, S. T., Sanders, S., & Collins, D. (2010). Developing effective pre-performance routines in golf: Why don't we ask the golfer? *Journal of Applied Sport Psychology, 22*, 51–64.

Cumming, J., Nordin, S. M., Horton, R., & Reynolds, S. (2006). Examining the direction of imagery and self-talk on dart-throwing performance and self-efficacy. *The Sport Psychologist, 20*, 257–274.

Dagrou, E., Gauvin, L., & Halliwell, W. (1992). Effets du langage positif, négatif, et neutre sur la performance motrice. [Effects of positive, negative, and neutral language on motor performance.] *Canadian Journal of Sport Sciences, 17*, 145–147.

Dishman, R. K., Motl, R. W., Saunders, R., Felton, G., Ward, D. S., Dowda, M., & Pate, R. R. (2004). Self-efficacy partially mediates the effect of a school-based physical-activity intervention among adolescent girls. *Preventive Medicine, 38,* 628–636.

Ellis, A. (1982). Self-direction in sport and life. In T. Orlick, J. Partington, & J. Salmela (Eds.), *Mental training for coaches and athletes* (pp. 10–17). Ottawa, ON: Coaching Association of Canada.

Ellis, A., & Dryden, W. (1987). *The practice of rational emotive therapy.* New York: Springer.

Feltz, D. L., Short, S. E., & Sullivan, P. S. (2008). *Self-efficacy in sport: Research and strategies for working with athletes, teams, and coaches,* Champaign, IL: Human Kinetics.

Finn, J. (1985). Competitive excellence: It's a matter of mind and body. *Physician and Sports Medicine, 13,* 61–72.

Gallwey, W. T. (1974). *The inner game of tennis.* New York: Random House.

Gaudiano, B. A. (2008). Cognitive-behavioral therapies: Achievements and challenges. *Evidence Based Mental Health, 11,* 5–7.

Gauron, E. F. (1984). *Mental training for peak performance.* Lansing, NY: Sport Science Associates.

Gould, D., Eklund, R. C., & Jackson, S. A. (1992a). 1988 U.S. Olympic wrestling excellence: I. Mental preparation, precompetitive cognition, and affect. *The Sport Psychologist, 6,* 358–382.

Gould, D., Eklund. R. C., & Jackson, S. A. (1992b). 1988 U.S. Olympic wrestling excellence: II. Thoughts and affect occurring during competition. *The Sport Psychologist, 6,* 383–402.

Gould, D., Finch, L. M., & Jackson, S. A. (1993). Coping strategies used by national champion figure skaters. *Research Quarterly for Exercise and Sport, 64,* 453–468.

Gould, D., Guinan, D., Greenleaf, C., Medbery, R., & Pederson, K. (1999). Factors affecting Olympic performance perceptions of athletes and coaches from more or less successful teams. *The Sport Psychologist, 13,* 371–394.

Gould, D., Hodge, K., Peterson, K., & Gianni, J. (1989). An exploratory examination of strategies used by elite coaches to enhance self-efficacy in athletes. *Journal of Sport and Exercise Psychology, 11,* 128–140.

Hackfort, D., & Schwenkmezger, P. (1993). In R. N. Singer, M. Murphey, and L. K. Tennant (Eds.), *Handbook of research on sport psychology* (pp. 328–364). New York: MacMillan.

Hall, C. R., Hardy, J., & Gammage, K. L. (1999). About hitting golf balls in the water: Comments on Janelle's (1999) article on ironic processes. *The Sport Psychologist, 13,* 221–224.

Hanton, S., & Jones G. (1999) The effects of a multimodal intervention program on performers: II. Training the butterflies to fly in formation. *The Sport Psychologist, 13,* 22–41.

Hardy, J., Gammage, K., & Hall, C. (2001). A descriptive study of athlete self-talk. *The Sport Psychologist, 15,* 306–318.

Hardy, J., Hall, C. R., & Hardy, L. (2004). A note on athletes' use of self-talk. *Journal of Applied Sport Psychology, 16,* 251–257.

Hardy, J., Hall, C. R., & Hardy, L. (2005). Quantifying athlete self-talk. *Journal of Sports Science, 23,* 905–917.

Hardy, J., Oliver, E., & Tod, D. (2009). A framework for the study and application of self-talk within sport. In S. D. Mellalieu & S. Hanton (Eds.), *Advances in applied sport psychology: A review* (pp. 37–74). London: Routledge.

Hardy, J., Roberts, R., & Hardy, L. (2009) Awareness and motivation to change negative self-talk. *The Sport Psychologist, 23,* 435–450.

Harris, D. V., & Harris, B. L. (1984). *The athlete's guide to sports psychology: Mental skills for physical people.* West Point, NY: Leisure Press.

Hatzigeorgiadis, A., Theodorakis, & Zourbanos, N. (2004). Self-talk in the swimming pool: the effects of self-talk on thought content and performance on water-polo tasks. *Journal of Applied Sport Psychology, 16,* 138–150.

Hatzigeorgiadis, A., Zourbanos, N., & Theodorakis, Y. (2007). The moderating effects of self-talk content on self-talk functions. *Journal of Applied Sport Psychology, 19,* 240–251.

Hatzigeorgiadis, A., Galanis, E., Zourbanos, N., & Theodorakis, Y. (in press). Self-talk and competitive sport performance. *Journal of Applied Sport Psychology.*

Hatzigeorgiadis, A., Zourbanos, N., Galanis, E., & Theodorakis, Y. (2011). Self-talk and sports performance: A meta-analysis. *Perspectives on Psychological Science, 6,* 348–356.

Hatzigeorgiadis, A., Zourbanos, N., Goltsios, C., & Theodorakis, Y. (2008). Investigating the functions of self-talk: The effects of motivational self-talk on self-efficacy and performance in young tennis players. *The Sport Psychologist, 22,* 458–471.

Hatzigeorgiadis, A., Zourbanos, N., Mpoumpaki, S., & Theodorakis, Y. (2009). Mechanisms underlying the self-talk-performance relationship: The effects of motivational self-talk on self-confidence and anxiety. *Psychology of Sport and Exercise, 10,* 186–192.

Hays, K., Thomas, O., Butt, J., & Maynard, I. (2010). The development of confidence profiling for sport. *The Sport Psychologist, 18,* 373–392.

Ives, J. C., Straub, W. F., Shelley, G. A. (2002). Enhancing athletic performance using digital video in consulting. *Journal of Applied Sport Psychology, 14,* 237–245.

Janelle, C. (1999). Ironic mental processes in sport: Implications for sport psychologists. *The Sport Psychologist, 13,* 201–220.

Johnson, J. J. M., Hrycaiko, D. W., Johnson, G. V., & Halas, J. M. (2004). Self-talk and female youth soccer performance. *The Sport Psychologist, 18,* 44–59.

Johnston-O'Conner, E. J., & Kirschenbaum, D. S. (1986). Something succeeds like success: Positive self-monitoring for unskilled golfers. *Cognitive Therapy and Research, 6,* 335–342.

Jones, G., Hanton, S., & Connaughton, D. (2002). What is this thing called mental toughness?: An investigation of elite sport performers. *Journal of Applied Sport Psychology, 14,* 205–218.

Jones, M. (2007, December 23). Open minded. *Mad About Sport, (9),* 10–13 (supplement to the *Sunday Tribune*).

King, P. (2001, January 29). Who let this dog out? *Sports Illustrated,* 46–50.

Kirschenbaum, D. S., O'Connor, E. A., & Owens, D. (1999). Smart golf: Preliminary evaluation of a simple, yet comprehensive, approach to improving and scoring the mental game. *The Sport Psychologist, 12,* 271–282.

Kirschenbaum, D. S., Ordman, A. M., Tomarken, A. J., & Holtzbauer, R. (1982). Effects of differential self-monitoring and level of mastery on sports performance: Brain power bowling. *Cognitive Therapy and Research, 6,* 335–342.

Kitayama, S. (2002). Cultural psychology of the self: A renewed look at independence and interdependence. In C. Hofsten & L. Backman (Eds.), *Psychology at the turn of the millennium* (Vol. 2, pp. 305–322). Florence, KY: Taylor & Frances/Routledge.

Landin, D., & Hebert, E. P. (1999). The influence of self-talk on the performance of skilled female tennis players. *Journal of Applied Sport Psychology, 11,* 263–282.

Machida, M., Ward, R. M., & Vealey, R. S. (2012). Predictors of sources of self-confidence in collegiate athletes. *International Journal of Sport and Exercise Psychology, 10,* 172–185.

McArdle, S., & Moore (2012). Applying evidence-based principles from CBT to sport psychology. *The Sport Psychologist, 26,* 299–310.

McAuley, E., & Blissmer, B. (2000). Self-efficacy determinants and consequences of physical activity. *Exercise and Sport Sciences Reviews, 28,* 85–88.

McKay, M., Fanning, P. (1994). *Self-esteem* (2nd ed.). Oakland, CA: New Harbinger.

McPherson, S. L. (2000). Expert-novice differences in planning strategies during collegiate singles tennis competition. *Journal of Sport and Exercise Psychology, 22,* 39–62.

Meichenbaum, D. (1975). Toward a cognitive theory of self-control. In G. Schwartz & D. Shapiro (Eds.), *Consciousness and self-regulation: Advances in research.* New York: Plenum.

Meichenbaum, D. (1977). *Cognitive behavior modification: An integrative approach.* New York: Plenum.

Meyers, A. W., & Schleser, R. A. (1980). A cognitive behavioral intervention for improving basketball performance. *Journal of Sport Psychology, 2,* 69–73.

Meyers, A. W., Whelan, J. P., & Murphy, S. M. (1996). Cognitive behavioral strategies in athletic performance enhancement. In M. Hersen, R. M. Eisler, & P. M. Miller (Eds.), *Progress in behavior modification* (pp. 53–65). New York: Plenum Press.

Neil, R., Hanton, S., & Mellalieu, S. D. (2013). Seeing things in a different light: Assessing the effects of a cognitive-behavioral intervention upon the further appraisals and performance of golfers. *Journal of Applied Sport Psychology, 25,* 106–130.

Owens, D., & Bunker, L. K. (1989). *Golf: Steps to success.* Champaign, IL: Human Kinetics.

Perkos, S., Theodorakis, Y., & Chroni, S., (2002). Enhancing performance and still acquisition in novice basketball players with instructional self-talk. *Sport Psychologist, 16,* 368–383.

Peters, H. J., & Williams, J. M. (2006). Moving cultural background to the foreground: An investigation of self-talk, performance, and persistence following feedback. *Journal of Applied Sport Psychology, 18,* 240–253.

Rogerson, L. J., & Hrycaiko, D. W. (2002). Enhancing competitive performance of ice hockey goaltenders using centering and self-talk. *Journal of Applied Sport Psychology, 14,* 14–26.

Rongian, L. T. (2007). Building and communicating collective efficacy: A season-long in-depth study of an elite sport team. *The Sport Psychologist, 21,* 8–93.

Rotella, R. (1995). *Golf is not a game of perfect.* New York: Simon & Schuster.

Rotella, R. (1996). *Golf is a game of confidence.* New York: Simon & Schuster.

Rushall, B. S. (1979). *Psyching in sports.* London: Pelham.

Seligman, M. (1991). *Learned optimism.* New York: Knopf.

Silva, J. (1982). Performance enhancement through cognitive intervention. *Behavioral Modification, 6,* 443–463.

Steinmetz, J., Blankenship, J., & Brown, L. (1980). *Managing stress before it manages you.* Palo Alto, CA: Bull.

Thellwell, R., & Greenlee, I. (2003). Developing competitive endurance performance using mental skills training. *Sport Psychologist, 17,* 208–225.

Tod, D., Hardy, J., Oliver, E. (2011). Effects of self-talk: A systematic review. *Journal of Sport & Exercise Psychology, 33,* 666–687.

Tod, D., Iredale, F., & Gill, N. (2003). Psyching-up and muscular force production. *Sports Medicine, 33,* 47–59.

Thomas, O., Hanton, S., & Maynard, I. (2007a). Anxiety responses and psychological skill use during the time leading up to competition: Theory to practice I. *Journal of applied sport psychology, 19,* 379–397.

Thomas, O., Maynard, I., & Hanton, S. (2007b). Intervening with athletes during the time leading up to competition: Theory to practice II. *Journal of Applied Sport Psychology, 19,* 398–418.

Turner, M., & Barker, J. B. (2013). Examining the efficacy of Rational-Emotive Behavior Therapy (REBT) on irrational beliefs and anxiety in elite youth cricketers. *Journal of Applied Sport Psychology, 25,* 131–147.

Van Raalte, J. L., Brewer, B. W., Lewis, B. P., Linder, D. E., Wildman, G., & Kozimor, J. (1995). Cork! The effects of positive and negative self-talk on dart throwing performance. *Journal of Sport Behavior, 18,* 50–57.

Van Raalte, J. L., Brewer, B. W., Rivera, P. M., & Petitpas, A. J. (1994). The relationship between observable self-talk and competitive junior tennis players' match performance. *Journal of Sport & Exercise Psychology, 16,* 400–415.

Van Raalte, J. L., Cornelius, A. E., Hatten, S. J., & Brewer, B. W. (2000). The antecedents and consequences of self-talk in competitive tennis. *Journal of Sport & Exercise Psychology, 22,* 345–356.

Vealey, R. S., & Chase, M. A. (2008). Self-confidence in sport: Conceptual and research advances. In T. S. Horn (Ed.), *Advances in sport psychology* (3rd ed., pp. 65–97). Champaign, IL: Human Kinetics.

Vealey, R. S., Hayashi, S. W., Garner-Holman, M., & Giacobbi, P. (1998). Sources of sport-confidence: Conceptualization and instrument development. *Journal of Sport & Exercise Psychology, 20,* 54–80.

Wegner, D. M. (1994). Ironic processes of mental control. *Psychological Review, 16,* 34–52.

Wegner, D. M. (2009). How to think, say, or do precisely the worst thing for any occasion. *Science, 325,* 48–50.

Wegner, D. M., Ansfield, M., & Pilloff, D. (1998). The putt and the pendulum: Ironic effects of mental control of action. *Psychological Science, 9,* 196–199.

Weinberg, R. S., Gould, D., & Jackson, A. (1979). Expectations and performance: An empirical test of Bandura's self-efficacy theory. *Journal of Sport Psychology, 3,* 320–331.

Welch, A. S. & Tschampl, M. (2012). Something to shout about: A simple, quick performance enhancement technique improved strength in both experts and novices. *Journal of Applied Sport Psychology, 24,* 418–428.

Wenzlaff, R. M., & Wegner, D. M. (2000). Thought suppression. *Annual Review of Psychology, 51,* 39–91.

Whitworth, D. (2008, September 13). On the waterfront. *The Times (Magazine).* 20–25.

Wishful Inking. (1991, January). *Special Report: On Sports,* p. 24.

Wood, J. V., Perunovic, W. Q. E., & Lee, J. W. (2009). Positive self-statements: Power for some, peril for others. *Psychological Science, 20,* 860–867.

Woodman, T., & Davis, P. A. The role of repression in the incidence of ironic errors. *The Sport Psychologist, 22,* 183–196.

Zetou, E., Vernadakis, N., Bebetsos, E., Makraki, E. (2012). The effect of self-talk in learning the volleyball service skill and self-efficacy improvement. *Journal of Human Sport and Exercise, 7,* 794–805.

Zourbanos, N., Hatzigeorgiadis, A., Tsiakaras, N., Chroni, S., Theodorakis, Y. (2010). A multimethod examination of the relationship between coaching behavior and athletes'inherent self-talk. *Journal of Sport and Exercise Psychology, 32,* 764–785.

15

Concentration and Strategies for Controlling It

Jean M. Williams, *University of Arizona, Emeritus*
Robert M. Nideffer, *Enhanced Performance Systems*
Vietta E. Wilson, *York University, Senior Scholar, Emeritus*
Marc-Simon Sagal, *The Winning Mind*

When I'm focused, there is not one single thing, person, anything that can stand in the way of my doing something.

—Michael Phelps, 2008, Winner of 18 Olympic gold medals

If I had stood at the free-throw line and thought about 10 million people watching me on the other side of the camera lens, I couldn't have made anything, so I mentally tried to put myself in a familiar place. I thought about all those times I shot free throws in practice and went through the same motion, the same technique that I had used thousands of times. You forget about the outcome.

—Michael Jordan, 1998

Concentration is essential for performing one's best whether the performer is an athlete, student, surgeon, musician, or something else. Few areas in sport psychology are as important to overall performance as the area of concentration or attention.[1] Effective concentration entails attending to the right things at the right time and in the right way. Unless concentration skills have been mastered, and the performer

[1]The words *concentration* and *attention* are used interchangeably in this chapter.

knows what to attend to, performance will almost always suffer.

When someone performs badly, one of the most frequently heard comments is "I couldn't concentrate" or "I lost my focus." What do we mean by good concentration? The major component of concentration is the ability to selectively attend to appropriate cues, such as some aspect of the environment or internal stimuli, while screening out irrelevant and distracting external and internal stimuli such as an audience booing, bad officiating calls, or thinking, "I blew it!"

Under maximally demanding conditions, good concentration entails 100 percent attention to the task at hand. The goal is total absorption in the experience. For example, Walsh and Spelman (1983) reported that conductor Carlos Kleiber never noticed the earthquake rattling a giant chandelier when he was conducting Strauss's *Der Rosenkavalier* at La Scala. Less than 100 percent attention will work when conditions are not maximally demanding. For example, most of the time people can safely drive a car while also carrying on a conversation or even eating. That said, performance often suffers because we fail to give appropriate attention resources to the demands of the task. Perhaps failing to remember someone's name upon being introduced because rather than sufficiently focusing on the name and trying to associate it with something we could remember, we minimally listened or thought instead about the impression we were making.

The best concentration, and greatest prospect of succeeding, occurs from total immersion in the *here and now*, in the present (Hermansson & Hodge, 2012). When our minds drift into the past (e.g., a mistake) or future (e.g., potential outcome), present performance can suffer. To illustrate, when the University of Arizona men's basketball team was up by 15 points with only minutes to play in an NCAA tournament game that would have sent them to the final four, someone brought courtside boxes of celebratory "final four" T-shirts and caps. Obviously many factors contributed to Arizona's loss, including possibly the distraction of projecting into the future.

> "I was thinking about exactly what I needed to do and kind of staying in the present, thinking about what I was doing now and not about negative past experiences and I wasn't thinking about the outcome."
>
> (Elite golfer after intervention, cited in Neil, Hanton, & Mellalieu, 2013, p. 123)

Optimal concentration also requires keeping an appropriate focus over an appropriate length of time and the ability to shift attention based upon changing performance demands. It is not enough to start with the appropriate focus; it must be maintained as long as needed. Correspondingly, for many tasks, the athlete must be able to shift his or her focus of attention in response to changing performance demands.

Based upon the preceding, you have lost concentration when you attend to irrelevant cues, have inappropriate divided attention, or leave the here and now. Becoming aware of gaps in experience is another sign of lost concentration. One of the best examples comes from studying. How often have you *read* a chapter that was boring or with something else on your mind only to discover that you've been turning the pages and have no idea what you read? Finally, although not always, when performance level is suffering there is a good chance you have lost optimal concentration. A first step in regaining concentration is to increase your awareness of these signs of having lost it.

In what situations are we most likely to not have or to lose concentration? There are many possible answers, but the most likely ones are after mistakes, when stressed out, when not sufficiently motivated, or when overmotivated. Motivation and stress play a major role in determining physiological arousal level and thereby influence attentional focus. See Chapters 4 and 11 for relevant discussions and interventions. It is impossible to perform one's best in the present moment when ruminating about a previous mistake. Instead, if there is time, quickly learn from the mistake and let it go. If there is no time to learn, let it go and deal with it later. This sounds simple, but is often difficult to do. Later, we present exercises designed to increase your ability to control focus.

The next few sections discuss Robert Nideffer's conceptualization of concentration and his principles for attention control training. This work provides an excellent operational definition of concentration and foundation for training concentration, including clarifying the relationship between arousal and focus of concentration and how and why choking occurs.

Attention Control Training Principles

Attention control training (ACT) is based on a theory of attentional and interpersonal style (Nideffer, 1976). The principles underlying the application of ACT to performance enhancement are outlined here.

1. Athletes need to be able to engage in at least four different types of concentration.

2. Different sport situations will make different attentional demands on an athlete. Accordingly, the athlete must be able to shift to the appropriate type of concentration to match changing attentional demands.

3. Under optimal conditions, the average person can meet the concentration demands of a wide variety of performance situations.

4. Individual differences exist in attentional abilities; thus individual athletes have different attentional strengths and weaknesses. Attentional characteristics are at times traitlike, having predictive utility in any number of situations. At other times they are statelike, situationally determined and modifiable through training. Factors that determine the extent to which a given individual's attentional skills are traitlike include biological or genetic predispositions and alterations in arousal. As arousal moves out of the moderate range, individuals are more likely to go to their dominant attentional focus or style (Hull, 1951). Thus, the individual's dominant attentional style becomes more traitlike and more predictive of behavior when arousal levels are higher.

5. The individual's ability to perform effectively depends on two factors: (1) the appropriateness of the dominant attentional style, and (2) the level of confidence within the particular performance situation (Carver & Scheier, 1989).

6. The phenomenon of choking—of having performance progressively and uncontrollably

deteriorate—occurs as physiological arousal increases well beyond the desired level, causing attention to involuntarily narrow and become more internally focused. This results in alterations in perception; time seems speeded up, which contributes to a tendency to rush (e.g., to start to throw the ball before completing the catch). Muscles antagonistic to performance begin to tighten, interfering with weight transfer, timing, and coordination.

7. Alterations in physiological arousal affect concentration. Thus, the systematic manipulation of physiological arousal is one way of gaining some control over concentration.

8. Alterations in the focus of attention will also affect physiological arousal. Thus, the systematic manipulation of concentration is one way to gain some control over arousal (e.g., muscular tension levels, heart rate, and respiration rate).

Different Types of Concentration

All too often a coach just shouts, "Concentrate!" at an athlete. The athlete is more likely to respond effectively to the instruction if the coach specifically defines the type of concentration or focus to which he or she would like the athlete to engage. To do this, it helps to think of attention as requiring at least two different types of focus. First, the athlete will need to control the *width* of his or her attentional focus. Certain sports, such as basketball and hockey, require a broad focus of attention. Other sports, such as sprints, diving, and shooting, require a narrow focus. The second type of focus that needs to be controlled relates to the *direction* of the athlete's attention. In some situations, attention must be directed internally to make adjustments in technique, muscle tension or to problem solve and strategize. At other times, attention must be focused externally, such as on the implement, ball, opponents, or sound of the starting gun. Figure 15-1 presents the four general types of concentration that result when considering the combinations of both width and direction of attention, and Figure 15-2 presents examples of each.

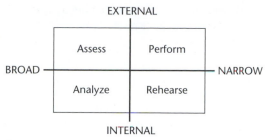

EXTERNAL

Assess	Perform
Analyze	Rehearse

BROAD — — NARROW

INTERNAL

Figure 15-1 **Dimensions of attention**

Shifting Attention

Recall the second principle underlying attention control training: Different sport situations make different attentional demands. A quarterback in football has a greater need to develop a broad external focus of attention (e.g., awareness of the entire field) than a guard who needs a narrower type of external concentration (e.g., opposing player he intends to block). Often there are many demands for shifting attention within a particular sport or skill. An example from golf illustrates the point.

When golfers walk up to the ball, they need a broad external type of attention in order to take in information such as the placement of hazards (e.g., trees, sand traps, out-of-bounds markers, water) and various conditions (e.g., slope and dryness of the terrain, speed and direction of the wind). Once this external information is garnered, golfers shift to a broad internal focus to plan their shot. They recall how they played past similar situations and what the results were, and anything that might modify how they should now play. Analyzing all of this information enables golfers to determine what shot to hit and what club it will take.

After formulating a plan, golfers take their set-up position where attention usually shifts to a narrow internal type of concentration in order to do things such as monitor tension and mentally rehearse the shot. Before starting the swing, golfers typically shift attention to the ball or club, a narrow external focus. Evaluation after the shot takes golfers back to a broad internal focus.

Thus, athletes are continually required to shift attentional focus even though some sports or positions require more of one type of attention than others. Research shows that attentional focusing can be improved with attention control training that entails drills in which athletes have to shift their attention (e.g., Ziegler, 1994).

In addition, in some sport situations coaches and other athletes can make up for attentional deficiencies of some players. As an illustration, a football coach can select the plays for the quarterback, thus limiting the quarterback's need to develop a broad internal type of attention. An increasingly important role for the sport psychologist and coach is to assist athletes in knowing

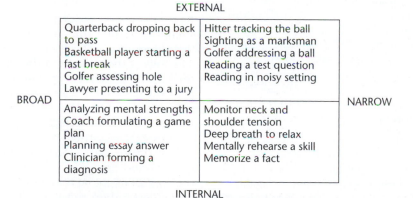

EXTERNAL

Quarterback dropping back to pass Basketball player starting a fast break Golfer assessing hole Lawyer presenting to a jury	Hitter tracking the ball Sighting as a marksman Golfer addressing a ball Reading a test question Reading in noisy setting
Analyzing mental strengths Coach formulating a game plan Planning essay answer Clinician forming a diagnosis	Monitor neck and shoulder tension Deep breath to relax Mentally rehearse a skill Memorize a fact

BROAD   NARROW

INTERNAL

Figure 15-2 **Examples of dimensions of attention**

what is most important to focus on at a particular time, and to assess and develop their ability to appropriately shift from one type of attention to another. Our consulting work with athletes, even skilled ones, has indicated that they often do not know exactly on what they should be focusing.

Individual Differences

The third principle indicates that if individuals are appropriately motivated, trained in what to do (including focus), and have control over their level of arousal (neither too high nor too low), they are capable of effective concentration. They can control the width and direction of attention enough to be effective because the actual attentional demands of most tasks are not so extreme that the average person cannot meet them.

At the same time, the fourth principle indicates individual differences in attentional abilities and dominant attentional style. Further, as physiological arousal increases beyond an athlete's optimal level, athletes tend to rely more heavily on their most highly developed attentional ability. Research on attentional processes suggests the following differences, among others.

1. Individuals have different capacities for developing a broad internal type of attention. Thus, some individuals are better suited to analyzing large amounts of information than others.

2. Certain individuals appear to be more sensitive to environmental (external) information than others. The former read and react to the environment (e.g., other people) more effectively. They have an ability to deal with a great deal of information and not become overloaded and confused. This helps them to be more resistant to pressure and to perform in critical situations.

3. Some individuals are more capable of developing a narrow, nondistractible type of attention. This is especially true of world-class performers in sport (Nideffer, Sagal, Lowry, & Bond, 2000). Their ability to focus narrowly makes it easier to follow through

on a task, and also to be as selfish as they must be to make it to the top.

Thus, another important role for the sport psychologist and coach is helping athletes identify their relative attentional strengths and weaknesses. This assessment will aid the majority of athletes in developing concentration skills and compensating for any attentional problems they may have. An effective way to accomplish this objective is the Attentional and Interpersonal Style (TAIS) inventory Nideffer developed and used in his attention-control training programs (Nideffer, 1976, 2003; Nideffer & Sagal, 2001). TAIS measures relevant concentration skills and interpersonal characteristics such as an athlete's attentional strengths, the types of situations likely to interfere with his or her performance, and the most likely performance errors. See Table 15-1 for a description of the attentional scales and Nideffer (1976) for the interpersonal scales. TAIS results provide the basis for a situation-specific focus for an attention-control training program, but interviews, behavior rating scales, observations, and other assessment tools also help assess the concentration and interpersonal skills required by different performance situations. See McGraw-Hill's Instructor's Web site for this book for two case histories developed by Nideffer and Sagal to illustrate both use of the TAIS and their entire attention-control training processes.

Playing to One's Attentional Strength

An individual's tendency to play to their strengths as pressure increases is beneficial if their dominant attentional style matches the demands of the task and if they are confident in their ability to perform. In contrast, performance may suffer with increased pressure when individuals are not attentionally suited to the task or they overuse their strength.

For example, there is an unproven assumption in sport that good athletes do not make good coaches and vice versa. If this is true, one of the reasons might be that coaching makes a very heavy demand on thinking and analyzing, that is, a broad internal type of attention. In contrast,

Table 15-1 Attentional Scales from the Test of Attentional and Interpersonal Style

Scale	Scale Description
BET	*Broad External Attention:* High scores indicate good environmental awareness and assessment skills (street sense).
OET	*Overloaded by External Information:* High scores are associated with errors because attention is inappropriately focused on irrelevant external stimuli.
BIT	*Broad Internal Attention:* High scores indicate good analytical planning skills.
OIT	*Overloaded by Internal Information:* High scores are associated with errors due to distractions from irrelevant internal sources (e.g., thoughts and feelings).
NAR	*Narrow-Focused Attention:* High scores indicate the ability to remain task oriented, to avoid distractions, and to stay focused on a single job.
RED	*Reduced Attention:* High scores are associated with errors due to a failure to shift attention from an external focus to an internal one, or vice versa.

many sporting situations require athletes to shut off their analyzing. If they do not, we see the paralysis by analysis that coaches are so fond of talking about. Athletes who ultimately become coaches are often the ones who were continually analyzing. They are not the brilliant broken-field runners who reacted instinctively.

Take the pressure off most coaches and athletes and they can be either analytical or instinctive. Put them under pressure, however, and they play to their strengths, including overdoing it. Analytical coaches become *too* analytical and, worse, they attempt to communicate that analysis to their athletes, getting them to think too much. Instinctive athletes have a tendency to react too quickly. When too pressured (i.e., physiological arousal too high), they may fail to analyze and plan when it is needed. They lose their capacity to make adjustments, getting faked out by the same moves time and time again, not learning from their own mistakes. Sport psychologists can sensitize coaches and athletes to their own and others' relative attentional strengths and weaknesses and help them train to better control their focus and plan alternative ways to behave.

As an example, consider a situation in which a coach tends to be more analytical and more assertive than the athletes (a normally ideal situation). As pressure increases, the coach becomes even more analytical and more assertive and the

athletes less so. At a certain point the athletes should confront the coach regarding being overloaded with instructions; instead they behave in an even more outwardly compliant way, nodding their heads to show agreement even when they are not hearing or are confused. The coach, sensing a willing, even enthusiastic audience, feels encouraged to give still more information. The sport psychologist can help athletes recognize their confusion and provide them with the support they need to confront the coach (e.g., "Coach, I can't take all of this right now.") Then all work together to develop ways of minimizing the problem. Sometimes insight is all the coach needs to decrease the amount of information he or she gives. When not so, the sport psychologist can usually give the coach suggestions for communicating the same information in a more simplified and structured way.

Operationally Defining Choking

A perfect example of the sixth principle underlying ACT comes from a sport psychologist who worked with a football quarterback. The coach referred the player because his play was outstanding in practice, but he often blew it (choked) when under pressure in big games. The quarterback told the sport psychologist that he became so stressed during big games he could literally feel his heart thumping and he kept thinking he

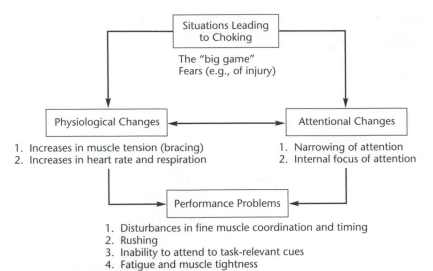

Figure 15-3 **Interaction between physiological and attentional processes under highly stressful conditions**

was going to blow it. Worse, when he dropped back to pass, it was like looking for the receiver through the hole in a roll of toilet paper. Before we examine the sixth principle, we must define operationally the term **choking.** Given what we do know about the interaction between thought process (what we say and attend to) and physiological process, it is possible to come up with a definition of choking that can be very useful to coaches, athletes, sport psychology practitioners, and researchers alike.

Behaviorally, we can infer that athletes are choking when there is a significant drop in performance, they "blow it" under high stress and, more often than not, they cannot regain control without some outside assistance. Examples would be that quarterback or possibly a too stressed golfer trying to sink what should be an easy putt to win the tournament or athletes who let an earlier mistake upset them to the point of making additional errors on subsequent actions. In all cases of "choking," the athlete becomes focused on the increasing pressure and physiological arousal gets too high.

Figure 15-3 illustrates the interaction that occurs between physiological and attentional processes under highly stressful conditions. The figure also shows how the changes that occur affect performance. By using Figure 15-3 and the section that follows, coaches should gain a more useful understanding of the choking process—an understanding that can help increase their ability to understand, predict, and control behavior in sport situations. Also see Chapter 12 for a discussion of attentional-based mechanistic explanations that might underlie choking.

Prevention and Treatment of Choking

The seventh and eighth principles underlying attention control training suggest that by creating changes in what is going on either physiologically or attentionally athletes can break the downward spiral associated with choking. Thus, if they eliminate the physical feelings associated with excessive tension (e.g., tight muscles, pounding heart), they will reduce the number of attentional distractions and improve their ability to concentrate.

Likewise, if coaches can get the athletes to either ignore or reinterpret their physical feelings (e.g., give a positive interpretation to being aroused, such as "I'm ready"), the physical activation might lower and, if not, it no longer is a negative distraction. To illustrate how important the preceding is, Abernethy (2001) and Zaichkowsky and Naylor (2005) have advocated that a foundation of psychological skills training relative to performance is increasing athletes' awareness of their arousal level as it relates to the construct of attention.

An unrealistic goal of some sport psychology programs is to prevent choking by teaching athletes some type of relaxation, rehearsal, and/or focusing procedure. In truth, we probably can reduce the frequency of choking through better training, but we cannot eliminate it, thus learning to recover once choking has occurred may be even more critical than trying to eliminate choking altogether.

> "When it comes to choking, the bottom line is that everyone does it. The question isn't whether you choke or not, but how—when you choke—you are going to handle it. Choking is a big part of every sport, and a part of being a champion is being able to cope with it better than everyone else."
>
> (John McEnroe, former top professional tennis player, cited in Goffi, 1984, pp. 61–62)

When providing interventions dealing with choking, we are likely to be successful only if the program has a performance-specific training focus. For example, teaching an athlete to use relaxation and to then appropriately focus attention at a particular time (e.g., at bat one might take a deep relaxing breath and then focus attention on the pitcher), and to provide training to rehearse doing so in particular performance situations (e.g., hitting under certain conditions).

Research has shown that incorporating detailed pre-performance routines is another way to prevent and treat choking (Hill, Hanton, Matthews, & Fleming, 2011; Mesagno, Marchant, & Morris, 2008; Mesagno & Mullane-Grant, 2010). For example, in a study with bowlers predisposed to choke under pressure, they found accuracy improved and more relevant, task-focused attention occurred when bowlers were taught before each delivery to use a pre-performance routine that included modifying arousal to optimal levels and that used behavioral steps, attention control (e.g., focusing on a target), and cue words. They demonstrated that the intervention alleviated choking through the prevention of self-focus and distraction. The Hill study, on the premise that effective interventions are multimodal, also included process goals, cognitive restructuring, imagery, and simulated practice; and emphasized the importance of designing the interventions to meet the individual needs of the athlete. The interventions were based on their earlier work that revealed, "self-confidence, focus, anxiety management and perceived control were the psychological constructs that required enhancement to prevent choking" (Hill, Hanton, Matthews, & Fleming, 2011, p. 468)

In the sections that follow we address other concentration training exercises that have proven helpful in enhancing athletes' ability to appropriately focus and, when necessary, refocus.

Process versus Outcome

During practice and one's free time, especially in sports that require a great deal of training and sacrifice on the part of the athlete, individuals often motivate themselves by thinking about outcome: "I am working this hard because I want to win a gold medal." "By making these sacrifices I can get the recognition and financial rewards I want." Once the competition begins, however, an outcome focus can generate physical and attentional changes that interfere with performance. For example, Hill, Hanton, Matthews, and Fleming (2010) found that during critical competitions thinking about the outcome, the importance of winning, created pressure. The chokers in their study maintained this outcome focus (e.g., focused on impressing others), but the participants who excelled adopted a task-orientated approach (e.g., the use of process goals). The coaches they studied also identified the importance of a task-focused approach during critical events.

"The pressure comes from me and wanting to win. But I just work on the processes of the game . . . that is all I think about."

(Competitor who excelled under pressure, cited in Hill et al., 2010, p. 226)

"I use to care so much about hitting it close . . . So there is no point worrying about the outcome. I just focus on the process."

(Post-intervention quote from professional golfer who previously had frequently choked under pressure, cited in Hill et al., 2011, p. 476.)

"You have to take away winning and the consequences of winning, and [just] focus on the processes."

(Quote from coach, cited in Hill et al., 2010, p. 226)

Sport psychologists and coaches can train vulnerable athletes to recognize their tendency toward placing too much importance on outcome (during the competition) and to use those thoughts, when they occur, as signals to attend to the process. **Process cues** are related to the process of performing as opposed to the outcome. Later we discuss growing evidence that cues such as an external movement effect (e.g., pendulum-like motion of the golf club when pitching) are particularly beneficial. If, however, athletes are not sufficiently motivated during a competition, they can think about outcome to get arousal levels and focus up to an optimal level.

Increasing Awareness of Types of Attention

Earlier we identified the different types of attention or concentration athletes use in athletic situations. These types were described along two dimensions: broad versus narrow and internal versus external. In concentration training, knowing what to focus on is as critical as knowing how to control one's focus. Athletes may have excellent concentration skills, but if they focus on the wrong things, the skills will not be very helpful. Additionally, they must know when to switch from one focus to another in a very short time period, sometimes even changing attentional style. Fortunately, the brain is capable of responding in milliseconds (one thousandth of a second) and extremely complex skills can be done almost instantaneously if switching attention is practiced correctly.

The first step in training for better control of concentration involves coaches and sport psychologists assisting athletes in identifying the different attentional styles and when to use them (see Figures 15-1 and 15-2), including the specific application within their sport. Our experience is that confusion often exists, even amongst coaches and physical educators, regarding the optimal attentional focus at any given time in the learning and performance of sport skills and strategies. Until somewhat recently, we lacked research to provide guidance in making these decisions. That deficit has improved, but more research is needed. We will later discuss some of the recent findings.

To familiarize athletes with the different attentional styles and to get them to experience them, a starting point might be an "expanding awareness" exercise developed by Gauron (1984). Below we present some of his exercises as well as some of our own.

1. Narrow-external drills. Focus on an object across the room, noticing just it and observing every detail. Do the same with a different object. Now pay attention to what you hear by taking each separate sound, identifying and mentally labeling it, such as footsteps, voices, or a cough. Focus on only one sound at a time.

In some sports, one way to enhance a narrow external focus is for the coach to place different numbers on a ball or puck and have the players yell out the number as the ball or puck approaches them (e.g., receiving a served volleyball). Another version puts different colors on the balls or pucks and instructs players to hit to a different location depending on the color. Because players have a tendency to become too aroused during these drills, we suggest reminding them to relax the shoulder muscles and keep the knees bent so they can move quickly.

2.   Broad-external drills. Look straight ahead, see as much of the room as your peripheral vision will allow. Simultaneously note all the objects in the room. In some team sports, coaches can enhance this experience by making a game of FREEZE out of it. The coach yells *FREEZE;* players immediately stop and close their eyes, and then the coach asks the players or a selected player where everyone was on the floor or field and where the ball or puck was.

3.   Narrow-to-broad external drills. Extend both arms in front of you with thumbs up approximately 4 inches apart framing some "main focus" in the distance. See the main focus in as much detail as you can. While maintaining that focus, slowly move your arms to the side and notice everything between the thumbs. Repeat several times, staying relaxed and passive. Many athletes report this drill enables them to see the primary focus while also clearly picking up the broader field. A variation is to have athletes think of their external focus as a zoom lens; practice zooming in and out, narrowing or broadening (panoramic), according to their wishes, thus practicing what often occurs within athletic skills and situations.

4.   Narrow-internal drills. Focus on your breathing for a few breaths. Notice how the abdominal region rises as the air comes in and how it gently falls as the air goes out. Now pause after the inhalation and make the exhalation longer than the inhalation, letting all the air effortlessly come out. It is as if the breathing is being done for you, you are a mere spectator. Next switch the focus to any tension in your shoulders (or pick another muscle group). Release that tension and contrast your relaxed versus tense shoulders. Attend now only to an emotion or thought. Let each thought or emotion appear gently, without being forced. Identify the nature of it and remain calm no matter how pleasant or unpleasant it was. Stop and attend to another. Now try to empty yourself of all thoughts and feelings. Let them go. If this is

not possible, tune in to only one and hold your attention there.

Have individuals of similar size pair-up and stand facing each other. One extends his or her dominant arm with the palm up and wrist resting on the partner's opposite shoulder. The individual with the extended arm focuses on contracting the muscles to make the arm as strong as possible while the other cups his or her hands over the elbow and slowly pulls downward to bend the elbow. (Note: palm must be up to prevent elbow injury.) Repeat, only this time the individual with the extended arm focuses on staying relaxed and creating an image such as the arm is a solid steel bar that extends through the wall. Signal when the image is created, and the partner will begin slowly increasing force on the elbow, trying to bend it. In most cases, the arm will not bend as easily. This exercise demonstrates the power of imagery through a narrowly focused mind that directs energy and creates great strength.

5.   Broad-internal drills. Think of times in which you solved a problem. What processes did you go through? Do a quick assessment of your mental strengths and weaknesses in problem solving.

Have athletes perform an important sport skill in a low-stress environment. Instruct them to focus on every body sensation while simultaneously attending to what they might be feeling or thinking. Emphasize keeping a passive, open awareness. Repeat the exercise but do it when performing in a higher-stress environment. Contrasting these two experiences can help athletes identify the subtle changes that sometimes occur in stress conditions that can lead to poorer performance. It is okay if athletes, either during or after the exercise, shift to a narrow-internal focus in order to zoom in on a particularly relevant sensation.

6.   Narrow-to-broad internal drill. Become aware of bodily sensations such as the feeling of where the chair or floor supports your body. Before moving on to another sensation, let each sensation linger for a moment while you examine it; consider its nature and source. Next, experience all these sensations simultaneously without identifying or labeling any particular one. Doing so necessitates the broadest possible internal body awareness.

7. Intention leads to attention. Intentions are psychological processes that affect our effort and attention and consequently our performance and physiological responses. Goal setting is one example of intention. We suggest that equally important is the intent behind *every* drill, skill, and movement; and every intention to focus. The intent is what **primes** attention. To illustrate how intention leads to attention do the following: For one minute, scan the room and find everything that is green. . . . Now close your eyes and describe how many things in the room are blue. You may not remember any. The same effect occurs in sport. If we are primed by our attentional focus to look for something, we are more likely to see it and see it in more detail. Although the preceding exercise does not practice a specific attentional style, it illustrates the danger of having the wrong intention and, ergo, attention.

As we mentioned earlier, coaches should not assume their athletes automatically know where to look and how to focus when they tell them to concentrate. Instead, tell athletes specifically what to focus on, and then create drills similar to some of the preceding exercises so the athletes experience the optimal focus, if one exists. If it does not, coaches should create drills that help athletes find the focus that best suits them. For example, in football most coaches would agree that focusing on the hips (or center) rather the head of an opponent that one has to guard is better because it lessens the risk of being "faked" into the wrong movement. In running or swimming where speed out of the blocks is important, the specific attentional focus is not so clear cut. Such athletes need to try all possible attentional strategies while getting accurate feedback (e.g., reaction time and correct takeoff for runners and sprinters) to determine what is the best focus. Before reaching a final decision, athletes must test the attentional focus at competitions as reactions often differ between practice and

stress-filled conditions. In general, for all drills that train what to focus on, once athletes have learned the appropriate focus in a relatively stress-free environment, progressively add challenges so athletes can practice the skill in an overload situation.

The preceding sounds fairly straightforward, but the optimal attentional focus may not be what the coach and sport psychologist think. There is growing evidence that instructing individuals to focus on an external movement effect, as opposed to one's own movements or an external cue not related to the movement effect, leads to the best learning and performance; probably by allowing automatic control processes to mediate movement. For example, researchers found that when learning to hit a pitch shot in golf, better results occur from focusing on the pendulum-like motion of the club (an external movement effect focus) rather than the swing of their arms (an internal focus) or the dimples on the ball (an external focus not related to the effect). In hitting a backhand cross-court shot in tennis, focusing on the trajectory of the ball and its landing point leads to greater accuracy than focusing on the backswing and the racket-ball contact point. Thus, the distance of the external movement effect also appears relevant, with best results occurring with an external focus far enough away to be easily distinguishable from body movements, but not so far that the performer cannot relate the effect to the movement technique. Although not universal, these results have been found with novices and experts and with diverse tasks such as a ski simulator, basketball shooting, dart throwing, volleyball serves, soccer passes, and various balance tasks. See Kee et al. (2012) and Wulf (2007) for a review of this literature. That said, view the preceding as a starting point. Treat athletes as individuals because optimal attentional focus for the same task might vary across performers, and there are always limitations and exceptions to research results.

In the remainder of this chapter we provide specific strategies and techniques that coaches and sport psychologists can use to train better concentration control in athletes. These strategies are divided into two sections: strategies to control distracting external factors and strategies to control internal distractions. The categorization is somewhat arbitrary because external and internal stimuli continually affect each other. Because of this interaction, strategies in one category may be effective in correcting apparent lack of concentration in the other category.

External Factors: Strategies to Minimize External Distractions

The novelty of the competitive environment, compared to the practice environment, tends to reduce performance. Research by Orlick and Partington (1988) found that the ability to control distractibility was closely associated with superior performance at the Olympic Games. Athletes, therefore, need to be trained not to react (orient) to irrelevant external stimuli. In a competition these stimuli are situational factors that coaches often expect the athletes to have learned to control by trial and error in previous competitive experiences. This "previous experience" strategy for developing concentration control has obvious limitations and false assumptions. Coaches need to realize that athletes can be systematically trained before a competition to be situationally independent. The concept underlying training is based on Pavlovian conditioning. Through training, the novelty of the competitive environment can be minimized when athletes practice their physical skills while being exposed to all possible external stimuli that can occur during a real competition, but realize that not all unusual events can be anticipated, so also prepare a "coping plan" to deal with the unexpected. What follows are three strategies that reduce the competition novelty effect upon performance.

Strategy 1: Dress Rehearsal

Dress rehearsal is a particularly effective strategy for sports such as gymnastics, diving, synchronized swimming, and figure skating. Dress rehearsal is based on the concept that ease in skillful competitive performance is unconsciously conditioned by the external and internal stimuli that surround athletes during practice. The greater the number of different stimuli present during competition compared to practice, the more likely performance quality will decrease. Stimuli can include things such as the athletes' uniforms, background illumination, announcers' voices, and music and applause. Ironically, to make a good impression during the competitive event, athletes usually wear uniforms or costumes different from the ones they wear during practice. This means that an unconscious stimulus (the practice uniform) associated with the performance of the skill (response) is not elicited during the competition and also that wearing a different uniform is a new stimulus that may inhibit performance. Dress rehearsal in which the athlete wears the competition uniform and goes through the same sequence of events as in competition, including factors such as scoring and judging, needs to be conducted frequently after athletes have mastered their skills and are practicing the whole routine for performance.

The reverse of this strategy can also be applied when an athlete is in a slump. In this case the athletes ceremoniously discard their uniforms and thereby symbolically disconnect from the slump associations while now practicing with a new uniform that has no failure associations. The athlete is metaphorically and ritualistically reborn. Athletes and coaches should not lose sight of the fact that these rituals are not the underlying reasons for nonperformance. Often it is more productive for the coach and athlete to maintain their traditional patterns with an understanding that performance is typically not linear but, rather, up and down.

Strategy 2: Rehearsal of Simulated Competition Experiences

Simulated competition experiences enable performers to become so familiar with the stimuli associated with competition, or some performance situation, that they no longer become distracted. They are trained to concentrate and dissociate from the disruptive stimuli. Research is limited, but does support the effectiveness of simulation training (Hill et al., 2011; Oudejans & Pijpers, 2010). For example, Oudejans and Pijpers found that training novices under conditions designed to increase anxiety helped to prevent choking when performing under a highly pressurized test environment compared to novices who trained with no anxiety and who had deteriorated performance. The Hill study, on the premise that effective interventions are multimodal, also included process goals, cognitive restructuring, imagery, and pre/post-performance routines; and emphasized the importance of designing the interventions to meet the individual needs of the athlete.

> *"As for the [simulated] practice . . . I would start off chipping from a fluffy lie, then a patch of mud, then a lie that I would have on the course. The pressure would start to build, and I got confidence from it."*
>
> *(Post-intervention quote from professional golfer who had frequently choked under pressure, cited in Hill et al., 2011, p. 476.)*

There are numerous anecdotal accounts of simulation training. Gymnasts might rehearse their routines with a loud recording of a previous meet played over the public address system. This tape could include other gymnasts' music, audience applause, and so on. A similar example for team sports such as football, basketball, and volleyball would be holding the week's practice before an away game with the public address system loudly playing hostile crowd noises and the opposing team's fight song. Such exercises reduce the effect of competition-induced novelty, which tends to interfere with performance. The goal is to make the practice workouts seem just like the competitive experience.

When using this strategy, coaches and sport psychologists should overtrain athletes in these simulated practices of the worst possible scenario, such as having a basketball player wait the length of a time-out before shooting a free throw. In football, many psychologically astute coaches turn the sprinklers on before practice and then soak the ball between plays to prepare for a game in which rain is likely. Pilots and astronauts spend a significant amount of time practicing in realistic flight simulators to help them maintain concentration and appropriate responses in the face of disruptions or emergencies. Lacking equivalent simulators for sport, creative coaches can simulate many competition situations by judiciously springing novelty situations in practice. Athletes generally look forward to these challenges as long as they provide an opportunity for learning and are not used to punish or embarrass. Just as learning a physical skill takes time, learning the mental control of concentrating on the task while not reacting to external stimuli takes many hours of training.

Strategy 3: Mental Rehearsal

Use mental rehearsal to create the high stress and external distractions that often occur in competition and then image effectively performing and concentrating under those conditions. Obviously, athletes cannot use this strategy until they have learned relaxation and imagery skills. A variation of such rehearsal is to have athletes form pairs in which one member of the pair mentally rehearses a sport skill while the other attempts to distract the performer from the mental rehearsal. The distraction can be anything except touching. The goal is to stay relaxed and focused on performing by tuning out the distractions. After this type of mental rehearsal, have the athlete rate his achieved concentration on a 0–6 scale. Thereafter the athletes reverse roles.

In a study involving members of the U.S. national rhythmic gymnastic team (Schmid & Peper, 1982), the gymnasts practiced this imagery pair distraction exercise daily for 5 days. On the first and fifth days they rated their concentration, with the results indicating a significant improvement. Through this type of exercise, athletes learn how to detach and dissociate themselves from external distractions and resulting unwanted internal reactions (stimuli) while focusing on the task of mentally rehearsing their sport. In his Basic Mental Training program, Unestahl (1983) uses dissociation and detachment exercises. He teaches athletes to screen out distractions either by building a mental wall around themselves, a wall that cannot be penetrated, or by accepting the distraction but not judging it. Let it pass by and continue on its way. These strategies can all be employed during regular physical practice sessions. Athletes are responsive to them and especially enjoy being involved in generating the distracting stimuli.

Internal Factors: Strategies to Stay Focused

The coach or sport psychologist must help train the athlete's mind to exert control because concentration inhibits distraction. Lapses in concentration invite fear and self-doubt, and the resulting worry and anxiety lead to further increases in lack of concentration, thus creating a vicious cycle that ultimately leads to failure. The effect of internal factors becomes more pronounced in high-pressure situations. As an analogy, what would happen if you walked on a board 4 inches wide, 15 feet long, and 9 inches above the ground (like a practice beam in gymnastics). You probably could do this without hesitation. In contrast, if the board were 60 feet off the ground, you might become paralyzed by the fear of falling. Such fear inhibits performance and increases the possibility of failing. Ironically, there is no difference in the physical skill required. The difference is in the psychological response to the perceived stressful event, and as a result, your attention is on fear and trying not to fall instead of just walking across the beam. In addition, if you had previously fallen off a beam, then every time you thought about it or related the experience to someone, you might have unknowingly rehearsed all of the cognitive and motor events that led to failure.

Similar psychological processes occur during competition. For example, a field-goal kicker who normally hits his short kicks during practice may react quite differently during competition when he attempts a short field goal with only a few seconds left on the clock and his team behind by 2 points. He is even more likely to fear "blowing it" if he has recently missed a kick in similar circumstances. One professional football player, while kicking under such a high-pressure situation, described the goal posts as looking as though they had narrowed to less than a foot apart. It does not take much insight to figure out what happened to his kick!

One way to improve concentration is to reduce self-doubts and competitive anxiety and their resulting physical manifestations (e.g., increased physiological arousal, including muscle tension). Unless an athlete has control over internal dialogue, his or her focus of attention will not be congruent with good performance, let alone peak performance. In addition to the specific arousal and cognition techniques found in Chapters 12 and 14, in our work with performers we have found the following strategies helpful in controlling internal dialogue and facilitating concentration and performance.

Strategy 1: Attentional Cues and Triggers

Athletes can use visual, verbal, and kinesthetic cues to focus their concentration and to refocus concentration once it has been lost. These cues help athletes center their attention on the most appropriate focus within the task at hand and thus help them to avoid distracting thoughts and feelings (Neil et al., 2013; Schmid, 1982). Similar observations have been confirmed by Nideffer (1981, 1987), who reported case histories in which athletes benefited from centering and using task-relevant cues.

> *"When I count to 100 three times [counting steps], it's a mile. It helps me to focus on the moment and not to think about how many miles I have to go. I concentrate on breathing and striding, and I go within myself."*
>
> *(Paula Radcliffe, winner of 2007 New York City Marathon, cited in Kolata, 2007, p. 1)*

Generally, it is best to find cues that focus on positives rather than negatives, the present (current or upcoming moment) rather than the past or the future, and the process (proper form or execution) or external factors (e.g., ball, racquet head) rather than the score. During a television interview on September 1, 1984, Greg Louganis, the Olympic diving champion, gave some excellent examples of attentional cues that he uses to appropriately control focus. He said, "I picture my dive as the judge will see it, then as I see it." In his forward three-and-one-half somersault dive, he used the following word cues: "Relax, see the platform, spot the water, spot the water, spot the water, kick out, spot the water again." Coaches and sport psychologists should work with athletes to help them establish effective cues for triggering optimal concentration and performance. Such cues must be individualized because what is effective for one athlete may not be for another. Similarly, some athletes perform best with frequent cues and others with few.

Strategy 2: Centering

Centering is an excellent technique for controlling physiological arousal and for ignoring negative and task-irrelevant stimuli. It reduces arousal and stops negative or task-irrelevant focus because it shifts focus to relevant performance cues. To understand centering, you need first to understand three terms: *center of mass, centered,* and *centering.* Imagine a vertical line from your head to your toes, dividing your body into two equal parts; and then a horizontal line so that half your weight is above and half below it. Where those two lines intersect (somewhere behind your navel) is your **center of mass.** You are **centered** within a performance situation when your body weight is distributed about your center of mass in a way that feels comfortable (e.g., body seems to communicate a physical readiness to perform). Exactly how your center of mass should be distributed varies from situation to situation. When you need more aggressiveness and alertness, your center of mass is raised and slightly forward. The more relaxed and immovable you need to be, the lower your center of mass.

Centering is a conscious process used to adjust weight about your center of mass so you feel centered and in control. It entails directing attention inward to your center of mass and then altering breathing and tension levels in various muscle groups (e.g., deep, relaxing breath from abdomen and relax neck and shoulder muscles). Time the centering technique as closely as possible to the beginning of the motor sequence so that attention can be directed immediately afterward (perhaps with attentional cues) to the task at hand.

Nideffer and Sagal provide an example of centering with a stressed baseball player in one of the case studies on the instructor's Web site. The player was instructed to use the centering technique immediately prior to each pitch when he was hitting with men on base. He was to time the end of his centering breath so that it was as close to the time the pitcher began his windup as possible. On the exhalation he used two words to create the physical feelings and mental focus he wanted, i.e., *loose* to create the feelings he wanted in his hands as he held the bat and *focused* to remind him to "pick up the ball on release." Research supports the effectiveness of a centering breath from adolescent to adult and unskilled to elite performers (Haddad, & Tremayne, 2009; Halliwell, 1990; Rogerson & Hrycaiko, 2002).

Strategy 3: TIC-TOC

Another effective strategy for switching attention from nonproductive to productive thoughts, feelings, or actions is an exercise that uses the words TIC and TOC to trigger the response (Burns, 1993). Simply stated, any self-statement, feeling, or action that is irrelevant or harmful to what you need to be doing right now is a TIC, and should be immediately recognized. Then switch to a task relevant focus (e.g., desired effect of the action such as optimal ball flight) or a TOC. In both sport and nonsport situations, become aware of TICs and immediately make them TOCs.

Strategy 4: Turning Failure into Success

Many athletes report that they commonly lose concentration after making a mistake. One way to deal with this problem is to train athletes to turn failure into success. This is a cognitive habit by which athletes mentally rehearse successful performance after a failure. Rather than dwelling on the error, as soon as possible mentally rehearse executing the same skill perfectly. One component of successful performance is to avoid self-judgment or blaming others, which disrupts concentration, and to instead refocus on imaging success.

More harmful than making a performance error is ruminating on the failed event. The verbal retelling to others or the chronic rumination on why one made a mistake is a type of global visual-motor behavior rehearsal in which the athlete conditions the mind to perform the same failure behavior again. Instead of reciting the error, athletes might ask: "What was the problem and how do I fix it?" "How could I have performed differently in the same situation?" or "What other skills do I need?" Then athletes can mentally rehearse the previous conditions leading to the error, but now change their behavior so that they imagine themselves performing the skill perfectly.

Strategy 5: Use of Brain Biofeedback (Neurofeedback) to Enhance Attention

Previously, the influence of attention and concentration on performance has primarily depended on behavioral observations, interview data, case studies, and the self-report of performers, but sport psychologists are now directly measuring brain activity, using electroencephalography (EEG), to determine how athletes attend to information from the outside, process information internally, and the relationship of each of these to performance (for additional information see Edmonds & Tenenbaum, 2012; Hatfield, Haufler, & Spaulding, 2006; and Strack, Linden, & Wilson, 2011). Although simplified, EEG findings indicate that as one becomes more skilled less brain activity is needed in the relevant brain regions to produce the correct response.

The EEG can identify athletes with superior brain efficiency (e.g., Wilson & Shaw, 2011), and those who would benefit from training to enhance their attentional abilities. The athlete trains using his or her brain waves to become aware of the attentional state needed to control the display on the computer and, with practice, this attentional awareness and control transfers to the sport setting. Neurofeedback is also an excellent method to demonstrate the effects of emotions on the ability to pay and sustain attention and to refocus. Although use of neurofeedback is becoming more widespread, disadvantages are the cost, time required, and need for a highly trained clinician. For sport skills where attention is paramount, such as with shooters, batters, goalies, and others, neurofeedback may be the attention training of choice in the future.

Strategy 6: Increasing Focusing and Refocusing Skills

Focus training teaches performers to gently hold their attention on a predetermined task and, if the attention wanders, to gently bring the attention back. The dynamics of this strategy are similar to those of meditative practices, such as Raja yoga meditation in which a person focuses on a mantra and each time the attention wanders from the mantra the person gently guides the attention back to it. Using a similar approach, the following exercises can help performers improve their focusing skills.

Exercise A: Mindfulness. Sit quietly, close your eyes, and see how long you can focus on a single thought. For many activities this is very important. Next athletes can enhance locking in their concentration by practicing focusing in the sport location. For example, some tennis players focus only on their strings prior to a serve and then transfer this narrow focus to what they need to do in the next moment. For serving, they might focus on what is necessary for them to execute their ideal serve (such as a cue word, feeling of power, or looking at a spot where the ball is to go).

Exercise B: One pointing. Look at an action photo or an object from your sport. For example, if your sport is baseball, softball, or tennis, you might focus on the ball. If distracting thoughts enter your mind, bring your attention back to the ball. Don't shut out the thoughts or continue to explore the disruptive thoughts or feelings. Just gently bring your attention back to the ball. This exercise also can be done with watching a second hand or digital display on a watch "tick off" the seconds for one minute. How many times did you lose your concentration?

Have athletes practice Exercises A and B daily for 5 minutes and chart their progress. Get them to time how long they can focus their attention before becoming distracted. It is our experience that these home mindfulness practices help athletes eliminate their concentration-breaking thoughts. Note, however, that one research study found that a higher dispositional susceptibility to mindfulness was a prerequisite for such training to enhance performance and affect attentional focus strategies (Kee, Chatzisarantis, Kong, Chow, & Chen, 2012).

Exercise C: Grid exercise. Another training exercise for practicing focusing ability is the grid exercise (Harris & Harris, 1984). It requires a 10-by-10 block grid with each block containing a two-digit number ranging from 00 to 99 (see Figure 15-4 for a sample grid). The purpose of this exercise is to scan the grid and within a given time (usually 1 to 2 minutes) find and put a slash through as many numbers as possible in numerical sequence starting with number 00. The same form can be reused by starting with a number above the highest number reached on the first attempt. New grids can be developed easily by simply relocating the numbers. According to Harris and Harris, athletes who have the ability to concentrate, scan, and store relevant cues will usually score in the upper 20s and into the 30s during a 1-minute timed trial.

After an initial practice, increase the difficulty of the exercise by creating distractions such as loud noises and verbal harassment by a partner. This exercise helps create awareness of when focus breaks down by attending to irrelevant information, leaving the here and now, or not staying fully immersed in the task. Besides training focusing

skills, Harris and Harris reported the extensive use of this exercise in Eastern Bloc countries as a precompetition screening device to select athletes most ready to compete on the team.

Exercise D: Video games. Many video games increase reaction speed, hand–eye coordination, and concentration. For example, Michele Mitchell, the 1984 and 1988 Olympic silver medalist in women's platform diving, attributed her consistent performance to good concentration enhanced by playing computer video games. As she said: "It helped me to be in the present." The advantage of many video games is that momentary lapses in concentration result in immediate feedback—you *lose*. Most early games involved only hand movements and had little similarity to real sport, but the newer technology and games often involve total body movement and are sport specific. The closer the video game's reactions and movements parallel sport demands, the more likely it will transfer to the sport setting.

Strategy 7: Developing Pre-performance and Performance Protocols

Many athletes develop the ability to tune in to their ideal performance state by associating concentration with certain performance rituals. Preset behavioral protocols should be established for warm-ups, practice, and specific times during actual competition, including unexpected events that might occur. These protocols should cue both body and mind. It will take time to help each athlete identify his or her own ideal pre-performance routine. Once a routine is developed, it should be thoroughly practiced. Over time these protocols will serve automatically to trigger the optimal arousal, thinking, and focused concentration athletes need for good performance, and, if for some reason attention lapses, using the protocols will help refocus attention. See the discussion of pre-performance routines under the earlier section on prevention and treatment of choking.

GRID CONCENTRATION EXERCISE

Directions:
Beginning with 00, put a slash through each number in the proper sequence.

84	27	51	78	59	52	13	85	61	55
28	60	92	04	97	90	31	57	29	33
32	96	65	39	80	77	49	86	18	70
76	87	71	95	98	81	01	46	88	00
48	82	89	47	35	17	10	42	62	34
44	67	93	11	07	43	72	94	69	56
53	79	05	22	54	74	58	14	91	02
06	68	99	75	26	15	41	66	20	40
50	09	64	08	38	30	36	45	83	24
03	73	21	23	16	37	25	19	12	63

Comments:

Figure 15-4 Sample grid exercise form for training and assessing the ability to concentrate

Summary

Concentration is the ability to direct attention to appropriate cues in the present task instead of being controlled by irrelevant external or internal stimuli. The ability to control thoughts, arousal, and attentional focus is the common denominator in the concentration of winning competitors. Most top athletes have developed their own mental strategies for doing this. These strategies are often perceived as a component of natural athletic ability, but, in fact, they are primarily learned through regular practice just as any difficult physical skill is learned.

Because of genetic makeup, early life experiences, and different opportunities for training the mind and body, every athlete will have individual attentional strengths and weaknesses. These influence the ease with which the athlete can utilize the appropriate focus. They influence the types of situations that are likely to be stressful, the specific behaviors that are likely to occur under pressure, and the types of errors that occur within a performance situation (e.g., susceptible to internal versus external distractions, the tendency to become tentative when leading or to choke when under high pressure).

Nideffer's conceptualization of concentration and his principles for attention control training provide a foundation for understanding and training concentration, including clarifying the relationship between arousal and focus of attention, how and why choking occurs, and how to prevent or deal with it. Because of athlete variability concentration training should include the development of individualized, situation-specific training exercises.

The initial education phase begins with differentiating the types of concentration (width and direction of focus) required within a particular sport and recognizing when to shift from one focus to another. Next comes assessment of the athletes' strengths and weaknesses and then training. To achieve consistency in performance, athletes need to develop and practice their concentration skills in practice sessions and then practice them in competitive or equivalent settings. The following is a general guideline for training:

1. Learn personal strategies to attain optimal arousal for performance.

2. Learn to practice with a positive attitude and specified intention.

3. Learn which attentional focus is best for you in given situations, how to switch focus, and when to "park" thoughts.

4. Learn and practice the attentional strategies that are best for specific situations within your particular sport.

5. Associate concentration with certain triggers such as visual, verbal, and kinesthetic cues. Practice finding TICs and making them TOCs. If arousal is an issue, learn centering and implement it according to the recommended guidelines.

6. If needed, practice the focusing and refocusing skills and desensitize yourself to the novelty effect of competition by practicing the external control strategies.

7. Develop performance and pre-performance protocols or rituals to focus concentration and refocus when you "lose it."

Study Questions

1. Under maximally demanding conditions, what five components are entailed in good concentration?

2. What five factors help determine if you have lost attention?

3. Under what circumstances are you most likely to lose or not have appropriate concentration?

4. Describe the eight principles that underlie attention control training.

5. Diagram the figure depicting the four different types of attentional focus, distinguish conceptually among the four (including when to use each), and give an example of each.

6. What does it mean to play to one's attentional strength and when are you most likely to do so?

7. How does arousal level influence attentional focus?

8. How is choking defined in terms of attentional focus?

9. Describe how to prevent and treat choking.

10. Explain the process versus outcome notion in regard to attentional phenomena.

11. Describe the techniques of dress rehearsal, rehearsal of simulated competition, and mental rehearsal, give an example of each, and discuss the premise behind why they are effective strategies to keep concentration.

12. How can attentional cues and triggers and the TIC-TOC exercise be used to either focus or refocus concentration?

13. What is centering, why would you use it, and how is it done?

14. Provide an example of how the technique of "turning failure into success" might be used and a brief description of why the strategy might be effective.

15. Briefly describe the four exercises under the section "Increasing Focusing and Refocusing Skills."

16. Provide two examples of when and how developing performing protocols might be used to improve concentration.

References

Abernethy, B. (2001). Attention. In R. N. Singer, H. A. Hausenblaus, and C. M. Janelle, (Eds.), *Handbook of sport psychology* (pp. 53–85). New York: John Wiley & Sons.

Burns, D. (1993). *Ten days to self esteem.* New York: William Morrow.

Carver, C. S., & Scheier, M. F. (1989). A control-process perspective on anxiety. *Anxiety Research, 1,* 17–22.

Edmonds, W. A., & Tenenbaum, G. (2012). *Case studies in applied psychophysiology: Neurofeedback and biofeedback treatments for advances in human performance.* London: John Wiley & Sons, Ltd.

Goffi, C. (1984). *Tournament tough.* London: Ebury Press.

Haddad, K., & Tremayne, P. (2009). The effects of centering on the free-throw shooting performance of young athletes. *The Sport Psychologist, 23,* 118–136.

Halliwell, W. (1990). Providing sport psychology consulting services in professional hockey. *The Sport Psychologist, 4,* 368–377.

Harris, D. V., & Harris. B. L. (1984). *The athlete's guide to sports psychology: Mental skills for physical people.* New York: Leisure Press.

Hatfield, B. D., Haufler, A. J., & Spaulding, T. W. (2006). A cognitive neuroscience perspective on sport performance. In E. Acevedo & P. E. Kekakis (Eds.) *Psychobiology of physical activity* (pp. 221–240). Champaign, IL: Human Kinetics.

Hermansson, G., & Hodge, K. (2012). Uncontrollable outcomes: Managing expectations at the Olympics. *Journal of Sport Psychology in Action, 3,* 127–138.

Hill, D. M., Hanton, S., Matthews, N., & Fleming, S. (2010). A qualitative exploration of choking in elite golf. *Journal of Clinical Sport Psychology, 4,* 221–240.

Hill, D. M., Hanton, S., Matthews, N., & Fleming, S. (2011). Alleviation of choking under pressure in elite golf: An action research study. *The Sport Psychologist, 25,* 465–488.

Hull, C. L. (1951). *Essentials of behavior.* New Haven, CT: Yale University Press.

Kee, Y. H., Chatzisarantis, N. N. L. D., Kong, P. W., Chow, J. Y., & Chen, L. H. (2012). Mindfulness, movement control, and attentional focus strategies: Effects of mindfulness on a postural balance task. *Journal of Sport & Exercise Psychology, 34,* 561–579.

Kolata, P. (2007, December 6). I'm not really running, I'm not really running. . .*The New York Times,* as cited in Moran, A. (2012, p. 127) Concentration: attention and performance. In S. M. Murphy (Ed.) *The Oxford Handbook of Sport and Performance Psychology,* Oxford University Press.

Mesagno, C., Marchant, D., & Morris, T. (2008). A pre-performance routine to alleviate choking in "choking-susceptible" athletes. *The Sport Psychologist, 22,* 439–457.

Neil, R., Hanton, S., & Mellalieu, S. D. (2013). Seeing things in a different light: Assessing the effects of a cognitive-behavioral intervention upon the further appraisals and performance of golfers. *Journal of Applied Sport Psychology, 25,* 106–130.

Nideffer, R. M. (1976). Test of attentional and inter-personal style. *Journal of Personality and Social Psychology, 34,* 394–404.

Nideffer, R. M. (1981). *The ethics and practice of applied sport psychology.* Ithaca, NY: Mouvement Publications.

Nideffer, R. M. (1987). Psychological preparation of the highly competitive athlete. *The Physician and Sports Medicine, 15* (10), 85–92.

Nideffer, R. M. (1990). Use of the test of attentional and interpersonal style in sport. *The Sport Psychologist, 4,* 285–300.

Nideffer, R. M. (2003). Theory of attentional and interpersonal style vs. Test of Attentional and Interpersonal Style (TAIS). http://www.enhanced-performance.com/articles/tais.pdf

Nideffer, R. M., & Sagal, M. S. (2001). *Assessment in sport psychology.* Morgantown, WV: Fitness Information Technology.

Nideffer, R. M., Sagal, M. S., Lowry, M., & Bond, J. (2000). Identifying and developing world class performers. In *The practice of sport and exercise psychology: International perspectives*. Morgantown, WV: Fitness Information Technology.

Orlick, T., & Partington, J. (1988). Mental links to excellence. *The Sport Psychologist, 2,* 105–130.

Oudejans, R. R. D., & Pijpers, J. R. (2010). Training with mild anxiety may prevent choking under higher levels of anxiety. *Psychology of Sport and Exercise, 11,* 44–50.

Phelps, M., & Abrahamson, A. (2008). *No limits: The will to succeed.* New York: Free Press.

Rogerson, L. J., & Hrycaiko, D. W. (2002). Enhancing competitive performance of ice hockey goaltenders using centering and self-talk. *Journal of Applied Sport Psychology, 14,* 14–26.

Schmid, A. B. (1982). Coach's reaction to Dr. A. B. Frederick's coaching strategies based upon tension research. In L. D. Zaichkowsky & W. E. Sime (Eds.), *Stress management for sport* (pp. 95–100). Reston, VA: AAHPERD.

Schmid, A. B., & Peper, E. (1982). *Mental preparation for optimal performance in rhythmic gymnastics.* Paper presented at the Western Society for Physical Education of College Women Conference, Asilomar, CA.

Strack, B. W., Linden, J. K., & Wilson, V. E. (Eds.) (2011). *Biofeedback and neurofeedback in sport psychology.* Wheatridge, CO: AAPB.

Unestahl, L. E. (1983). *Inner mental training.* Orebro, Sweden: Veje.

Walsh, M., & Spelman, F. (1983, June 13). Unvarnished symphonies. *Time,* p. 75.

Wilson, V. E., & Shaw, L. (2011). Clinical use of a one hertz bin Electroencephalography assessment to distinguish elite from less elite and typical from atypical athlete profiles. *Biofeedback, 39,* 78–84.

Wulf, G. (2007). *Attention and motor skill learning.* Champaign, IL: Human Kinetics.

Wulf, G., & Su, J. (2007). An external focus of attention enhances golf shot accuracy in beginners and experts. *Research Quarterly for Exercise and Sport, 78,* 384–389.

Zaichkowsky, L. D., & Naylor, A. H. (2005). Arousal in sport. *Encyclopedia of applied psychology, 1* (pp. 155–161). Elsevier, Inc.

Implementing Training Programs

Integrating and Implementing a Psychological Skills Training Program

Robert S. Weinberg, *Miami University*
Jean M. Williams, *University of Arizona, Emeritus*

The authors of Chapters 9 through 15 have discussed peak performance characteristics, psychological theory, and exercises for training specific psychological skills. When sport psychologists began employing psychological skills interventions in the early 1980s, not many empirical data or controlled studies were available to help guide these initial attempts to improve performance. However, the last 25 to 30 years have produced a number of field-based studies that have investigated the effectiveness of different psychological interventions to enhance performance. Some of these studies have investigated questions such as: How old and skillful should athletes be before beginning psychological skills training? Who should conduct the training program—the sport psychologist or the coach? Is there an ideal time during the year for implementing a psychological skills training program? How much time is needed for psychological skills training? What specific components should be incorporated in training, and how should those components be sequenced and integrated? What ethical considerations should one be aware of when implementing a program? In this chapter we address these questions and others, but first we must recognize that in some cases only preliminary data exist regarding these questions. Therefore, caution must be observed until more definitive studies are conducted.

Most comprehensive mental training programs stress the development of psychological skills and techniques such as goal setting, arousal control, anxiety management, imagery, confidence, self-talk control, concentration, and routines (just to name a few). The multitude of possibilities makes it very difficult to integrate all the components into one comprehensive mental training program. In essence, situational constraints (e.g., the athlete or team only has a few weeks to learn and implement a psychological skills training program) do not always permit the implementation of a comprehensive mental training program, and thus it is often necessary, and desirable, to plan an abbreviated program individualized to the specific needs of the athlete(s) and situation. Furthermore, when does a performance enhancement issue become a clinical issue that requires special training from a clinical psychologist? Moore (2012) offers some thoughtful discussion of when an athlete in distress might simply be suffering from "normal" performance anxiety versus when this distress requires special psychological/clinical knowledge.

Unfortunately, there are no ready-made solutions to questions of how coaches and sport psychologists can integrate and implement a psychological skills-training program. The database is expanding, but many questions still remain and only partial answers exist for other implementation questions. Nonetheless, if a mental training program is to be effective, strategies for putting all of the different components into place must be planned and well thought out. In this chapter we offer some suggestions and practical pointers for implementing mental skills training and for integrating various psychological skill components into these programs. Unless otherwise noted, these guidelines are the same for either the coach or sport psychologist, although we will discuss the pros and cons of taking on a dual role of coach/sport psychologist. Finally, we again caution you to view these recommendations only as suggested guidelines.

Are Psychological Interventions Effective in Improving Sport Performance?

Probably the most important question that sport psychology consultants need to ask themselves revolves around the effectiveness of their psychological interventions in enhancing performance and personal growth. It is the same problem that has plagued clinical psychologists and counselors over the years—demonstrating that what they do makes a difference in the behavior and well-being of their clients. Defending the effectiveness of psychological skills-training programs in improving sport performance and well-being requires the accumulation of well-controlled, outcome-based intervention studies conducted in competitive sport environments. These are traditionally difficult to carry out because of time and money constraints, unwillingness of coaches and athletes to participate, and inability to adequately control the environment.

Fortunately, sport psychology researchers have been working hard to establish a database concerning the effectiveness of these psychological interventions in improving performance. Reviews by Greenspan and Feltz (1989), Vealey (1994), and Weinberg and Comar (1994) identified 45 studies employing psychological interventions in competitive sport settings, including such diverse sports as golf, karate, skiing, boxing, basketball, volleyball, gymnastics, baseball, tennis, and figure skating. Of the 45 studies, 38 (85 percent) found positive performance effects. Many of these studies employed a variety of psychological techniques as part of the total program package. In addition, Meyers, Whelan, and Murphy (1996) conducted a meta-analysis of psychological interventions to enhance sport performance. Their analysis of 90 interventions indicated moderate positive effects on performance for interventions such as goal setting, mental rehearsal, anxiety management, cognitive restructuring, attentional focusing, and multiple components.

An even greater percentage of the more recent studies have shown positive effects of psychological interventions (e.g., Fournier, Calmels, Durand-Bush, & Salmela, 2005;); this is likely attributable to the more in-depth, multimodal approach taken in recent years, which combines different types of psychological skills (e.g., imagery, relaxation, self-talk, goal setting) in a packaged approach. Furthermore, international-caliber athletes use mental training more often, as well as employ more elaborate and complex mental strategies and techniques than national-level athletes (Calmels, d'Arripe-Longueville, Fournier, & Soulard, 2003). Applied sport psychologists have begun to understand that to be effective, a psychological intervention must be carried out in an individualized, systematic manner over time, often using a variety of psychological techniques to form an integrated program.

Models of Sport Psychology Delivery and Practice

Now that we know sport psychology interventions can be effective, the next step for a sport psychology consultant is determining which model of delivery to employ. Fortunately, Aoyagi and Poczwardowski (2012) have reviewed the major models used in delivering sport psychology interventions to athletes. It is beyond the scope of the present chapter to review all these models. However, a brief listing of them along with references will allow the reader to access them in more detail. The models (specific to sport) are broken into three general categories with one category (psychological skills training) broken into two, given the diversity of models falling into this category. The categories and some specific examples of delivery systems are noted below.

Psychological Skills Training (Sport Psychology Service Delivery)

- *Sport Psychology Service Delivery Heuristic* (Poczwardowski et al. (1998). This model focuses on common features in the consultant "toolbox" applicable to the process of consultation (as opposed to performance enhancement) such as professional boundaries, professional philosophy, making contact, assessment, and consultant evaluation.

- *Cognitive-Behavioral Consultation Model (Perna et al., 1995).* This involves eight steps including consultation orientation, sport familiarization, evaluation and assessment, goal identification, group intervention, individual intervention, outcome evaluation, and reassessment of goals.

Psychological Skills Training (Nurturing Athletic Excellence)

- *Individual Zones of Optimal Functioning* (Hanin, 2007). This model takes an idiographic approach, focusing on an understanding of positive and negative emotions and their effects on performance and identifying the optimal range of each emotion for best performance.

- *Resonance Performance Model* (Newburg et al., 2002). This model attempts to combine performance enhancement goals with ones of personal balance and fulfillment, which accounts for the model's unique potential to become a truly holistic tool in sport psychology practice.

Counseling

- *Life Development Intervention* (Danish et al., 1995). This is a psychoeducational-developmental approach to sport psychology that emphasizes continuous growth and change.

Interdisciplinary

- *Periodization of Mental Training* (Holiday et al., 2008). This model parallels periodized physical training in using the same principles in manipulation of the training volume (e.g., number of mental training sessions and skills) and intensity (e.g., difficulty, complexity and specificity of mental skills) across the training cycles.

- *Educational Model* (Weiss, 1995). This model combines performance enhancement and developmental needs with a primary focus on personal development and healthy lifestyle through positive sport experiences.

Who Will Benefit from Psychological Skills Training?

Highly skilled athletes certainly benefit from systematic psychological skills training programs. As athletes start to excel, physical differences tend to become smaller. At this level, minute adjustments and differences in the mental game can literally mean the difference between winning and losing. For example, Orlick (2000) provides a number of case studies of Olympic athletes who systematically employed a mental training program. The athletes reported that their mental training and discipline were a critical component of their success. Their comments generally reflect the notion that everybody they were competing against was physically talented. The key difference was in their consistency of mental preparation and training.

That said, too many coaches and athletes think mental training strategies are only applicable to elite athletes or for fine-tuning the performance of the already highly skilled. In actuality, psychological skills training is appropriate for all athletes; including young developing athletes (Camire, Forneris, Trudel, & Bernard, 2011; Chase, 2013), the vast number of competitive recreational athletes (Whelan Meyers, & Donovan, 1995), and special populations such as people who are mentally disabled/intellectually challenged (Gregg, 2013), physically challenged (Martin, 2013), or hearing impaired (Vose, Clark, & Sachs, 2013).

The ideal time for initially implementing training may be when individuals are just beginning to participate in sport. As any experienced teacher or coach knows, it is far easier to develop proper physical technique in a beginner than it is to modify poor technique in a more experienced athlete. Although never empirically tested, the same phenomenon may be true for psychological skills. Furthermore, early implementation ensures the establishment of a psychological skills foundation that will facilitate future achievement of full athletic potential, enjoyment, and personal growth. Special adjustments may be needed, however, based on the population of athletes. For example, very young athletes may need fewer goals, shorter training sessions, simpler verbal instruction, and turning the exercises into games, but these athletes can still benefit from some sort of mental skills training provided they are interested in receiving it (Visek, Harrism & Blom, 2013).

Who Should Conduct the Psychological Skills Training Program?

Ideally, a psychological skills training program should be planned, implemented, and supervised by a qualified consulting sport psychologist. The sport psychologist has the advantage of having more extensive special training and experience than a coach. Also, athletes may be more open in discussing difficulties with the psychological aspects of play because the sport psychologist does not decide who stays on the team and who gets to play. Even though it is desirable to have a sport psychologist administer the program, this is rarely feasible except perhaps at the highest levels of competition (and even here it

is still a rarity for a sport psychologist to work and travel with a team throughout a season). The basic premise of this book is that it is also the responsibility of the coach to provide mental skills training and reinforce optimal psychological states; after all, who knows the athletes better and who works more closely with them?

When the mental training program is to be implemented by a sport psychologist, the selection of that person is critical. Who is qualified to be a sport psychologist? In 1991 the Association for Applied Sport Psychology (*AASP Newsletter,* 1991) adopted criteria for certification of individuals working in the area of applied sport psychology. Their certification requirements include a background in sport sciences, psychological sciences, sport psychology, and supervised experience implementing psychological skills with sport and exercise participants (see Chapter 1 for more detail). The USOC now requires AASP certification to become part of its sport psychology registry. Having an individual who is certified by AASP ensures a certain experience, background, and competence in applied sport psychology. However, just because an individual is certified does not necessarily mean he or she has the type of orientation or experiential background that would best meet the needs of a specific team or athlete. For example, will the person's focus be on dealing with personal and emotional problems (i.e., clinical approach) or teaching mental skills for enhancing performance (performance enhancement approach)? Does the person have experience with younger athletes or primarily elite athletes? Is he or she sufficiently knowledgeable about the sport in which the psychological skills are to be applied? How much time does the person have to spend with the team? Does the person have references from prior clients? These and other questions guide the selection of the sport psychologist who best suits the athletes' specific needs and goals.

If a sport psychology consultant conducts the program, we recommend that the coach, or coaching staff, attend most, or all, of the initial group training sessions for a number of reasons. First, the coach's presence tells the athletes that the coach thinks the sessions are important.

Second, the sport psychologist will not be present during most of the physical practices and competitions; a knowledgeable coach can be a key person in ensuring the effectiveness of mental skills training by seeing that appropriate application of such training occurs. Ideally, the sport psychologist and coach should have special meetings, whether formal or informal, to discuss ways for the coach to apply and reinforce whatever the sport psychologist emphasizes in mental skills training sessions. Third, misunderstandings regarding what the sport psychologist is doing will not occur because the coach will know exactly what is happening and will be providing feedback regarding what needs to be done.

Our understanding about how to conduct psychological skills training programs with athletes has increased rapidly over the years. Along these lines, a number of sport psychologists have written about their consulting experiences with athletes and teams. In fact, as far back as 1989, separate issues of *The Sport Psychologist* (1989, #4; 1990, #4; 1991, #4) were devoted to psychological interventions with a variety of sports as well as with physically and mentally disabled athletes. More recently, the *Journal of Sport Psychology in Action* (2012, v. 2, #1) focused on delivering psychological skills as a sport psychology team (collaboration) at the Olympic Games.

Petitpas, Giges, and Danish (1999) have argued that the effectiveness of psychological interventions is closely tied to the quality of the relationship between athlete and sport psychologist. They draw on the counseling psychology literature, which has demonstrated that of all the techniques and variables examined the only one that has consistently related to positive therapeutic outcomes has been the counselor-client relationship (Sexton & Whitson, 1994). Sport psychology research also indicates that the ability to build rapport and create a positive environment is highly correlated with successful sport psychology interventions (e.g., Gould, Murphy, Tammen, & May, 1991; Martin, Wrisberg, Beitel, & Lounsbury, 1997). Plus, a recent study (Sharp & Hodge, 2011) reported that sport psychology consultants felt the three most important

characteristics for an effective consultant were (a) building a connection with the athlete to create positive change, (b) building a professional consulting relationship with the athlete, and (c) assuring that the consulting relationship meets the needs of the athlete.

Interestingly, new sport psychology consultants tend to be rigid and take a problem-solving approach; whereas with more experience they focus on developing relationships with clients and being more adaptive in their approach (Tod, Andersen, & Marchant, 2008). Murphy and Murphy (2013) provide some excellent suggestions for developing attending and listening skills, which are critical to creating a positive consultant-client relationship.

In addition, certain counseling competencies have been rated as essential for sport psychologists working with athletes (Ward, Sandstedt, Cox, & Beck, 2005). These include such competencies as recognizing limits of competency or expertise, respecting confidentiality, recognizing how one's own values and biases may impact psychological processes, making appropriate referrals, understanding the unique athlete culture, understanding the influence of the athletic environment on athletes, and considering cultural differences when working with athletes. As to the last point, Barber and Krane (2005) demonstrated that sensitivity to ethnic and racial diversity and sexual orientation in applied sport psychology settings enhances the quality of the relationship. More sport psychologists of color are needed and, Butryn (2002) argues, more multicultural training programs for sport psychology consultants working with diverse athlete populations.

Of course, the philosophy and implementation of mental training programs differ somewhat from one sport psychologist to the next. Each person has to understand the nature of the team or individual athletes he or she is working with and integrate that with his or her own background, training, and orientation. It's important for the sport psychologist to communicate his or her philosophy to the athletes and coaches at the outset and to make sure that everyone understands the parameters of the consultation.

When Should You Implement a Psychological Skills Training Program?

It is generally agreed that the *least* desirable time to implement a psychological skills program is after the competitive season has started, when the athlete is facing a string of competitions in quick succession. At this time, mental training often amounts to no more than a quick-fix, bandage approach and consequently is rarely, if ever, effective. One of the underlying principles of this book is that psychological skills are learned and therefore need to be practiced systematically, just like physical skills. To draw an analogy, golfers or tennis players would not change their grip on the club or racket right before a tournament without extensively using the new grip in practice for several weeks or even months. Similarly, we should not expect athletes to be able to learn new psychological skills in such a short period of time.

For these reasons, most sport psychology consultants believe the best time to initially implement psychological skills training is during the off-season or the preseason. During this period there is more time to learn new skills, and it is easier to try new ideas because athletes are not so pressured with winning. Some athletes have reported that it took several months to a year to fully understand and integrate their new psychological skills into actual competitions. This underscores the importance of viewing mental training as an ongoing process that needs to be integrated with physical practice. Regardless of when initial implementation occurs, we strongly believe that one-shot or occasional psychological skills training, no matter how competently carried out, cannot be as effective as that provided on a continuous basis over time.

Although most sport psychology consultants believe in initially starting PST programs in the off-season or preseason, there is precedent for elite athletes integrating mental skills into their training regimen one week prior to a match and showing enhanced performance, as well as increased self-confidence, decreased anxiety, and more positive reinterpretation of anxiety symptoms (Thomas, Maynard, & Hanton, 2007). However, in this situation, the athletes engaged in intensive mental skills training 5 to 7 days before, 1 or 2 days before, and on the day of competition, for a total of almost 20 hours of mental practice. Such training is not likely feasible in most situations, but might be possible with dedicated high level-athletes.

When Should Athletes Practice Psychological Skills?

The rudiments of most psychological skills should first be taught and systematically practiced during special training sessions. The first or last 15 to 30 minutes of practice is often a good time for training. The content of the particular session will determine whether it is better held at the beginning or end of practice (see earlier chapters for suggestions on which training exercises are better practiced before or after physical workouts). Homework assignments also can be given, but unless the athletes are self-directed, it is better to have most mental training practice occur under someone's supervision.

As soon as possible, the psychological skills practice should be integrated with physical skills practice; with the integration having a performance-specific focus. For example, once athletes have learned the skill of relaxation and recognizing tension, they should be instructed to scan their muscles for harmful tension and practice appropriate differential relaxation, or perhaps a tense and relax, while performing. Specific performance times should be identified—for example, always scan and relax before pitching, shooting a free throw, serving a tennis ball, or taking a shot in golf. Once relaxation skills have been effectively integrated into physical workouts, they should be tried during simulated or practice competition and later during actual competition. It is important not to proceed too quickly from learning to competition because the psychological skills may not be fully integrated and therefore performance decrements could occur.

This progressive method of practice is also psychologically sound from a learning standpoint because it allows athletes to gain knowledge and competence in using each mental skill as environmental demands slowly become more variable, challenging, and applicable. The ultimate goal is for the practice of mental skills to become such an integral part of all physical practices that the training program does not appear to be something extra. This type of systematic, consistent practice of mental skills is likely to achieve lasting optimal results rather than short-term placebo effects.

Let us provide a concrete illustration of integrating psychological skills into actual physical practice. A tennis player is having trouble hitting the ball short, thus allowing his opponent to take the offensive. Set up a practice drill where his goal is to get 20 balls in a row over the net between the service line and baseline to work on his depth of shot. If he misses, he has to start over from zero. Instruct him to use a cue word like "lift" when he swings to make sure that he follows through on the shot and lifts his racquet after impact. With this type of drill the player practices his concentration skills by using a concentration cue and setting the conditions of practice to require extreme concentration. In addition, this drill creates pressure. The player will typically start to get a little tight as he approaches the goal of 20 consecutive shots because he doesn't want to miss and have to start all over at that point, thus an opportunity to recognize the tension and appropriately relax.

How Much Time Should Be Spent in Mental Training?

By now it should be obvious that the time needed for practicing mental skills varies according to what is being practiced and how well it is learned. If a new mental skill is being introduced, special 15- to 30-minute training sessions 3 to 5 days per week may be needed. As athletes become more proficient, fewer special training sessions are necessary. However, special sessions still may be advisable for individual athletes who

are experiencing difficulty learning the mental skills.

When separate times are not being designated solely for mental training, it is very important that the coaching staff or sport psychologist provide verbal reminders for integrating mental skills practice with physical skills practice. In addition, appropriate reinforcement for the use of these mental skills during practice is crucial for athletes' motivation because they are attempting to develop new habits and possibly break old bad habits. This can be a difficult task, and a positive approach is important to keep spirits up, as well as providing informative feedback to help athletes integrate the mental skills into their physical performance.

The time frame we have just recommended may not be desirable if a sport psychology consultant is implementing the training, particularly when the sport psychologist has to spend time traveling to reach the team. Under such circumstances, fewer and longer mental training sessions are usually held unless a coach or other organization member is trained to carry out the mental training program. Most of the initial meetings should be group sessions to best use the sport psychologist's time. However, individual sessions and individualized training programs are needed to optimize the effectiveness of mental training programs. It is particularly critical that athletes be assigned training exercises to practice during the times the sport psychologist is not with the team. The traveling sport psychology consultant must design practice exercises in such a way that maximum feedback occurs from participation and that adherence to training is likely to occur. In the absence of the consultant, the coach or an individual designated by the coach can play a major role in ensuring compliance and feedback, particularly if he or she assumes responsibility for personally conducting the training exercises. If this is not possible, the coach or designated individual should remind athletes of their homework assignments and briefly discuss the athletes' reactions to the exercises once the homework has been completed.

A logical question that arises after a mental training program has been put in place is, "When can athletes stop mental skills training?" In the truest sense, mental skills training continues as long as athletes participate in sport. In this sense, mental skills are no different from physical skills. Retention will not occur without continued practice. When we hear the names of such athletes as Peyton Manning, Roger Federer, Tiger Woods, Anika Sorenstam, LeBron James, Candice Parker, and Michael Phelps (just to name a few), we think of individuals who are highly skilled and great competitors. However, these same athletes are also known for their great practice habits, especially making sure that the mental aspects of their respective sports are integrated into their physical practice on an ongoing basis.

If athletes never stop mental skills training, what is the ideal length of time for their first exposure to a formal mental skills training program? Most sport psychology consultants would recommend an average of between 3 and 6 months because it takes time to learn these new mental skills, use them in practice, and then integrate them into actual competitive situations. The specific sport, time available, existing mental skills, and commitment of individuals are all factors to consider in determining actual length of time. For example, we have worked with athletes who simply needed to change a small part of their mental approach and were able to do that in under 2 months. In contrast, Orlick (1986) has noted that many of the Canadian Olympic athletes he has consulted with developed psychological plans and mental preparation that were extremely detailed and precise, as seen in the example provided in Table 16-1 for an Olympic alpine skier (Orlick, 1986, p. 34).

Setting Up a Mental Skills Training Program

Thus far we have discussed some important questions surrounding the use of mental training programs, including who will benefit, who should conduct the program, when to implement the training program, when to actually practice the mental skills, and how much time to spend on mental training. Although this information is

important in understanding mental training programs, it does not really tell us exactly what to do in setting up such a program; therefore, we will attempt to outline some of these critical components.

Self-Regulation: A Key to Effective Mental Training

One of the critical aspects of successfully implementing a mental training program is the use of self-regulation. Self-regulation encompasses the processes by which people manage their own behaviors that are directed toward specific goals. These processes include goal setting, planning, observing, and evaluating behaviors (Kirschenbaum, 1997). Being able to regulate and control one's behavior is an essential part of any athlete's mental training plan, and this process has five specific phases.

Begin with *problem identification*. This phase encourages you to evaluate progress in your sport thoroughly and to remain open to new suggestions about all aspects of performance. For example, you might become aware that you lose your concentration by thinking negatively at critical junctures during competition. This awareness is a critical first step on the road to improvement. The second step is to establish *commitment to change*. This usually involves developing specific plans and setting goals. After problems are identified and commitments are made, actions must be initiated so that positive steps toward goal attainment can occur. This *execution* of self-regulated change is the third step. It can be viewed as a feedback loop with self-monitoring leading to self-evaluation, which in turn leads to self-consequation (Kirschenbaum, 1997). For example, you might monitor progress toward a goal of improving your average golf score from 85 to 80. After several rounds, you could evaluate whether you achieved your goal. If you did, you might treat yourself to a great dinner; this would be an example of positive consequation. Although self-regulation implies a solitary pursuit of goals, in sport you also have to *manage the environment* (step 4), which might include teammates, friends, and coaches as well as specific

Table 16-1 **Prerace Mental Preparation Plan**

General Warm-Up	Start Preparation
Physical and Mental	*Physical and Mental*

Night Before Race

- Receive number, determine how many minutes after start I race.
- Figure out what time to awaken and leave for hill in the morning and approximately how many free runs or training course runs to have before start.
- Estimate how long to put number on, stretch inside lodge.
- Spend ideally no more than 20 to 25 minutes in start area.

- Arrive at start 20 minutes prior to my start.
- First get race skis in snow, check them to see if all is ready; see rep (equipment person).
- Begin stretching, running; think happy, relaxed thoughts.
- Apply these comments to mental imagery.

Morning of Race

- Light run, exercises, begin the morning on a positive or high note.
- Wake up feeling good about myself, be optimistic, flow.
- Important for me not to project (e.g., about outcomes); just feel good about myself for myself.
- Free skiing and training courses to feel aggressive and pumped, yet calm and relaxed.
- Focused and concentrated while skiing.
- Mental imagery (to know course and feel good about myself on the course).

- Heavier physical preparation.
- Get into skis, binding check.
- More imagery of race focus and feeling—include correction imagery if needed.
- Quicker physical activity.
- 1 minute: Take coat, warm-ups off, intense, focused on task.
- 30 seconds: Ready myself in start, think only of course and of myself.
- Explosive start.

playing and practice conditions. The long-term goal of self-regulation is to maintain behavior change over time and across different situations. This fifth step is called *generalization.* It is often difficult to achieve because it requires dedicated, consistent, systematic practice of mental skills over time.

Discuss Your Approach—What You Do and What You Don't Do

Many athletes are still fairly naive or uninformed about what sport psychology is and what sport psychologists do. Therefore, spell out these parameters right at the outset of the initial meeting. Although most athletes typically view sport psychology solely in terms of performance enhancement, they also should be made to understand its mental health aspects and potential for application outside of sport. In fact, as reflected in the title of this text, sport psychology has as much to do with personal growth issues as it does with achieving maximum performance.

In addition to conducting a brief discussion on what sport psychology is, it is equally critical that sport psychologists clarify their specific approach in dealing with psychological problems in sport and exercise. Sport psychologists use two approaches when working with athletes: clinical and educational. Research and experience have indicated that the large majority of athletes consulting with sport psychologists typically require an educational versus clinical approach. They need to develop psychological skills such as improving concentration or managing anxiety rather than to deal with a deep-seated, severe psychological problem. Therefore, we will focus on the educational approach, but it should be made clear that if an educational sport psychologist or coach comes across an athlete who has such a serious psychological problem that it is beyond his or her skills to treat, then the athlete should be referred to a qualified individual or counseling center. (See Chapter 19 for a discussion of when it may be appropriate to refer athletes for counseling or psychotherapy.)

Thus, the sport psychology consultant should tell the athlete what he or she does and does not do, as many people still believe that if athletes see a sport psychologist then something must be psychologically wrong with them. This is especially true of younger athletes, who can be extra sensitive to the idea that they "have to see a shrink." Rather, we try to emphasize that if an athlete stayed after practice to work with the coach on a particular move or physical technique most people would applaud this extra effort to improve. Similarly, if an athlete realizes that he or she needs to work on some aspect of the mental game such as concentration skills, then this also should be applauded.

In discussing your philosophy or approach, a contemporary way of making initial contact with athletes is through electronic methods such as e-mail or Web pages. More and more people are using the Internet as a communication tool, and it is at least as good as, and in several cases superior to, traditional contact (e.g., phone, in-person contact methods). For example, when Zizzi and Perna (2002) compared traditional versus electronic contact, they found that the electronic group completed more contacts and assessments compared to the traditional group one month after taking a workshop.

Emphasize the Importance of Mental Training

Another important component to an initial meeting with athletes is convincing them of the need for systematic mental training. This can be done in many ways. One way to have athletes identify how important their state of mind is in achieving success is to have them decide what percentage of their game is mental. Then compare this percentage to the actual percentage of practice time spent training mental skills. The disparity is usually because the mental side of sport is recognized as very important, yet little or no time is spent specifically practicing these mental aspects.

Providing anecdotes about the importance of mental preparation from relevant, well-known amateur and professional athletes is another effective way to increase receptivity. Along these lines, a study from the U.S. Olympic Training Center (Murphy, Jowdy, & Durtschi, 1990) revealed that more than 90 percent of Olympic athletes surveyed regularly used some sort of mental preparation and training in preparing for competition. This type of information can help athletes realize that mental training does work and that it is being used by most of our very best athletes, although athletes of all ability levels can benefit from such training.

Fortunately, the popularity of applied sport psychology has evolved to the point that it is becoming easier to sell a mental skills training program to most athletes. Nevertheless, some athletes still will refuse to accept mental skills training. Most sport psychologists recommend not forcing unreceptive athletes to participate. Conversely, there also can be problems with athletes who are highly enthusiastic about mental training. Occasionally this enthusiasm can lead to unreasonable expectations. Athletes, coaches, and sport psychologists must realize that no amount of mental training will substitute for poor mechanics, lack of practice, or limited physical aptitude.

Assess Psychological Strengths and Weaknesses

Once athletes know the approach the sport psychologist plans to take and are convinced of the importance of mental training, the next step is to determine the athletes' psychological strengths and weaknesses as related specifically to sport. A needs assessment helps reveal those psychological skills that are deficient or appear to have the most adverse effect on performance and personal satisfaction. It also reveals the athlete's mental strong points. When something is bothering athletes, or they are struggling with a specific problem, they often overlook all the things that they do well, and these should not be forgotten.

In conducting the initial evaluation of athletes' psychological strengths and weaknesses, it is important that sport psychology consultants understand that factors outside the psychological realm influence performance. These include such things as physiological conditioning, biomechanics (technique), strategy, and equipment. For example, a golfer who has developed a flaw in his or her swing may attribute the resulting poor performance to negative self-talk, whereas the underlying problem is biomechanical., thus an intervention to modify the self-talk will not be effective.

In terms of the actual psychological skills evaluation, one procedure we recommend is the combination of an oral interview, written psychological inventories, and behavioral observation. With this procedure the athlete has a chance to tell his or her story face to face as well as to respond to some objective questionnaires. It also enables the consultant to spot consistencies (and inconsistencies) between oral and written statements.

There are various approaches to conducting an initial interview, but the one we recommend is the semi-structured interview, which Orlick (2000) outlines in detail. Some general steps/questions provide structure (see the following), but there is leeway to use the athlete's responses to form other follow-up questions.

- Summarize your involvement in your sport, noting important events both positive and negative (this is a good starting point as it lets athletes talk about themselves and become more comfortable).

- Describe what you believe to be your greatest psychological strength and your biggest weakness.

- Describe the boundaries of any specific psychological problem you are currently having (i.e., when, why, how).

- What is your relationship with your coach?

It is our experience that this interview typically lasts approximately one hour. The initial interview is very important not only to find out where the athlete needs help but also as a place to start building the trust that is critical for any therapeutic relationship. For a sport psychology consultant to be maximally effective, the athlete needs to feel comfortable and believe that the consultant not only is competent but also cares about the athlete's particular situation. One thing that we have found important is that the consultant needs good conceptual knowledge of the sport to be effective and build credibility with the athletes. Simons (2013) provides some thoughtful commentary on conducting an intake interview, especially noting the need for a more integrative view that also notes the culture and context in which the athlete is performing, what physical/physiological limitations might be relevant, and what is the training regimen of the athlete.

In addition to the interview, between 63 and 75 percent of sport psychology consultants use paper and pencil questionnaires (O'Conner, 2004) to assess psychological traits/states and skills related to sport and more general mood states. Woodcock et al. (2012) provide some excellent recommendations for effective psychometric assessment to help practitioners more accurately assess athletes' mental skills. Although many different inventories are utilized, some of the more popular ones include the following: Sport Competition Anxiety Test (Martens, 1977), Competitive State Anxiety Inventory-2 (Martens, Vealey, & Burton, 1990) and its revised (Cox, Martens, & Russell, 2003) and modified version (assesses whether a facilitative or debilitative effect on performance, Jones & Swain, 1992), Sport Anxiety Scale (Smith, Smoll, & Schutz, 1990), Test of Attentional and Interpersonal Style (Nideffer, 1976,) Athletic Coping Skills Inventory-28 (Smith, Schutz, Smoll, & Ptacek, 1995), and Trait-State Sport Confidence

Inventory (Vealey, 1986). In addition, the Ottawa Mental Skills Assessment Tool (OMSAT-3) has been developed by Durand-Bush, Salmela, and Green-Demers (2001) to assist consultants and coaches in their designing of appropriate and individualized mental training programs as well as to help researchers assess the effectiveness of interventions with sport performers.

It should be noted that applied sport psychology consultants should consider a number of factors before administering questionnaires or other formal assessments to athletes (Beckman & Kellmann, 2003). For example, to be used effectively, assessment instruments need to be reliable and valid for the individual athlete or sport group in question, be seen as useful by the athlete(s), and be completed honestly by the athlete(s). In addition, sport psychology consultants need to provide athletes with a clear identification of the purpose of the assessment, and make sure that the athlete and coach (if applicable) are committed to the assessment. Marchant (2013) provides a good discussion of factors to consider when determining what psychological tests to give, including tests that might be considered more clinical in nature that would need special training to interpret.

Once the interview and psychological inventories have been completed, we recommend that written feedback be provided to each athlete that highlights his or her psychological strengths and weaknesses as they relate to sport performance and participation. This assessment should be given to athletes in a second one-on-one meeting and athletes should be provided with an opportunity to react to it. This provides an opportunity to get consensual validation from athletes in terms of the evaluation of the sport psychology consultant. At times we have found the oral interview and written assessments to be contrary, and this is a good time to bring any discrepancy up and have the athlete resolve it. The assessment should conclude with recommendations for the type of skills and intervention program that the consultant thinks would best suit the athlete's needs.

One weakness of using interviews, questionnaires, and behavioral observation to determine an athlete's psychological strengths and weaknesses is that the athlete plays a relatively passive role in the process. Motivation and adherence problems will occur in the psychological skills training program if the athlete does not fully accept the decisions reached in the needs assessment. Butler and Hardy (1992) propose that using performance profiling resolves this problem, and an increasing number of sport psychology consultants are using the approach and finding it very effective. For these reasons, we recommend performance profiling as an alternative approach to assessing psychological strengths and weaknesses. When using performance profiling, the athlete, with his or her own labels and definitions, determines the psychological skills needed for success. Once done, the athlete rates him- or herself on each of the identified constructs. Butler and Hardy (1992) propose that the rating use a 0–10 scale anchored with "not at all" and "very much." The athlete's resulting constructs are then displayed in the form of performance profiles. See Figure 16-1 for one example of plotting and using a performance profile to determine psychological needs and goals.

In this particular example, an athlete client of one of the authors had the goal of making the national team. Four months before the qualifying competition, the athlete, with the help of the sport psychologist, determined what psychological skills he would need, and their relative importance, in order to make the national team (see the dark bars depicting long-term goals). The athlete then assessed his present weakness and strength specific to each of the constructs he identified (see the shaded bars). This information was displayed pictorially and together the athlete and the sport psychologist determined what progress the athlete wanted to make in the next month and exactly what he would have to do to reach each of his psychological skills goals. See the clear bars added later to represent the athlete's short-term goals. (Note: The athlete had previously received some psychological skills training and was adamant that he simultaneously works on all the constructs.)

The performance profiling sheet also has the advantage of providing a format for the athlete

Figure 16-1 **Example of using performance profiling to determine psychological needs and goals**

and sport psychology consultant to periodically assess and record the athlete's progress in using interventions to reach his or her goals, which is done by using that same 10-point rating scale. Once done, draw a new bar to depict the rating, or you can extend or shade in the existing bar depicting starting status (labeled "present") and short-term goals. When using performance profiling in this way, we also recommend modifying the sheet in Figure 17-1 to allow sufficient room for comments after listing each construct.

The sport psychology consultant and coach can assess the psychological strengths and weakness of teams by using essentially the same profiling procedure as that described for the individual athlete. We recommend putting the team members into groups of three to five players. Have each group take 5 to 10 minutes to identify the constructs that they perceive as important to reach the team's goal. Then have a team discussion regarding each construct identified by the groups, with the goal of reaching

consensus regarding what psychological skills to include. After identifying the resulting constructs and their relative importance, have the small groups use the 10-point scale to rate the present status of the team on each of the constructs. Also ask the groups to provide a rationale for their decision. Once finished, have all team members discuss each group's ratings and rationale until some consensus is reached regarding a final rating.

Recent empirical research has investigated the benefits of performance profiling from both athlete and sport psychologist perspectives (Weston, Greenlees, & Thelwell, 2011). From the sport psychology consultant perspective, the benefits include the following:

- provides a basis for goal setting
- identifies athlete mental strengths and weaknesses
- raises athlete awareness

- evaluates and monitors athlete performance
- facilitates discussion, communication, and interaction within teams

From an athlete perspective, the benefits include the following:

- raises self-awareness
- helps decide what to work on
- motivates to improve
- sets goals
- monitors and evaluates performance
- encourages more responsibility for development

Regardless of the approach used to assess psychological strengths and weaknesses, if a sport psychology consultant is working with an entire team, it is essential that the coach be involved in the needs assessment because he or she is more likely to know the team's mental strengths and weaknesses over a period of time. This might, in turn, require different psychological approaches based on the team's history. For example, quite different psychological needs would probably be perceived for a team with a long history of losing compared to a team that climbed to the top and has the pressure of maintaining number-one status.

An obvious implication of this discussion on needs assessment is that the coach should be wary of anyone who suggests a canned mental training program that does not provide for the specific needs of a given athlete or group of athletes. Although such a program may be better than nothing, the more attention that is paid to the individual needs and the maturation and experiences of the given group, the more likely it is that the program will be successful.

Analyze Demands of the Sport

Every sport has unique physical, technical, and logistical demands that require special preparation by participating athletes. These characteristics that distinguish different sports also affect the type of mental preparation and training an athlete may employ. Thus, sport psychologists need a detailed understanding of important aspects of the sport in which they are working.

For example, sports that involve explosiveness and anaerobic power (e.g., 100-yard dash) will differ greatly from those requiring endurance and aerobic conditioning (e.g., long-distance running and cycling). Similarly, a sport or sport skill requiring great precision (e.g., golf putting) might differ from one requiring more gross motor movements (e.g., power lifting). Furthermore, a sport or performance that lasts a very short time (figure skating) would require a different set of psychological skills than one that lasts hours (e.g., a marathon). Whether a sport or sport skill is self or externally paced influences optimal mental training interventions (e.g., see Lidor, 2007, for preparatory routines in self-paced events). Self-paced skills are ones in which the environment is relatively stable and predictable and the performer, within a few limitations, can initiate the activity when ready (e.g., free throw shot, tennis or volleyball serve, soccer penalty kick, golf). Externally paced skills typically occur when the performer has to react to an unstable and unpredictable environment (e.g., tennis and volleyball except for serving, most team sport skills). In essence, the demands of the sport or sport skill need to be carefully analyzed and considered when devising a mental skills training program.

Along these lines, it is important to observe athletes while they are competing and practicing their sport throughout the consultation process. These observations not only provide the consultant with important information regarding how athletes are reacting in different situations, but they also help clarify the sport demands and build the relationship between consultant and athlete as it demonstrates the commitment the consultant has to the athlete. Watson and Shannon (2013) provide excellent guidelines for conducting systematic observations including when, where, and what to observe for both individual and team sport athletes.

Determining What Skills to Include

Once psychological assessment is complete and all needed psychological skills have been identified, the coach or sport psychologist must decide how many of these skills to emphasize. This decision should be based on when the program is first being implemented (e.g., preseason, practice season, competitive season) and how much time the athletes and coach are willing to devote to mental skills training. Several questions are pertinent at this point:

- How much practice time will be given on average each week to mental skills training?

- How many weeks of practice are available?

- Will there still be time to practice mental skills after the competitive season starts, or after the first couple of losses?

- How interested are the athletes in receiving mental skills training?

The answers to these questions will help provide a realistic perspective on the commitment to mental skills training and the time available for accomplishing psychological skill objectives. When there is not adequate time or commitment for a comprehensive training program, it is better to prioritize objectives and emphasize a few to work on initially rather than work superficially on all of the needed skills. The coach or sport psychologist may even wish to develop a 2-to3-year plan (Gould, 1983; Orlick, 1986).

Although there is certainly no definitive answer as to what a psychological skills training program should include or in what sequence these skills should be taught, Vealey (2007) provides a thoughtful analysis of the nature of psychological skills training programs. Specifically, Vealey (2007) proposes a number of skills that can and should be developed in a well-rounded program (see Table 16-2). It's important to note that these skills reflect areas related to personal development as well as performance enhancement.

The most basic skills, termed **foundation skills,** represent those qualities that are basic and necessary psychological skills. The first foundation skill is *achievement drive,* which is the compelling desire to overcome obstacles to accomplish something worthwhile. The second foundation skill is *self-awareness.* Before athletes

Table 16-2 Mental Skills for Athletes

Foundation Skills:	Achievement drive
	Self-awareness
	Productive-thinking
	Self-confidence
Performance Skills:	Perceptual-cognitive skill
	Attentional focus
	Energy management
Personal Development Skills:	Identity achievement
	Interpersonal competence
Team Skills:	Leadership
	Communication
	Cohesion
	Team Confidence

Source: Vealey, 2007.

can start changing some of their previous bad habits, they need to understand and become aware of exactly when and where their problem behaviors occur and what they are thinking and feeling at that time. In addition, athletes need to be aware of what they typically think and feel when performing at their best. That is, do they have an ideal performance state that is associated with peak performance (see Chapter 9)? Keeping a sport journal is one way to increase awareness of performance states and to understand how different situations bring about different emotional reactions (see Chapter 10 for journaling guidelines and other techniques for increasing awareness.) The third and fourth foundation skills are *productive thinking* and *self-confidence,* which not only are critical to sport performance (see Chapters 9 and 14) but also are central to a wide array of behaviors outside the world of sport and physical activity (Bandura, 1986). Thus, it would appear inappropriate to begin other psychological skills training until individuals learn a certain level of proficiency in the foundation skills.

The **performance skills** in Vealey's (2007) model are some of the traditional psychological skills that most sport psychology consultants attempt to teach including *energy management* (e.g., arousal regulation), *attentional focus,* and *perceptual-cognitive skills* (e.g., decision-making skills). These skills are addressed in detail in various chapters throughout this text. The premise is that exceptional performance is most likely to occur when these skills are learned and integrated into an athlete's actual competitive performance.

"Personal development skills are mental skills that represent significant maturational markers of personal development, and that allow for high-level psychological functioning through clarity of self-concept, feelings of well-being, and a sense of relatedness to others" (Vealey, 2007, p. 290). Two personal development skills that Vealey (2007) feels are especially important are *identity achievement* (establishing a clear sense of identity) and *interpersonal competence* (interacting effectively with others). Taking a life skills approach is an example of a mental training intervention that focuses on personal development skills.

The final category of mental skills is **team skills,** which are collective qualities of the team that are instrumental to an effective team environment and overall team success. Team skills are made up of (a) *team confidence*—the belief that the team has the collective resources or team abilities to achieve team success, (b) *cohesion*—the team's ability to stick together and remain united in the pursuit of its goals (see Chapter 7), (c) *communication*— the process of interpersonal interaction within the team that facilitates team success and athletes' well-being, (see Chapter 8) and (d) *leadership*—the ability of individuals to influence others on the team to think and act in ways that facilitate team success and the quality of the team's social-psychological environment (see Chapter 6).

Sport psychology consultants have a wide variety of methods and techniques that they can choose from to develop and enhance the preceding psychological skills. The most commonly used methods are the four traditional techniques of goal setting (Chapter 11), imagery (Chapter 14), physical relaxation and arousal regulation (Chapter 12), and thought control (Chapter 14).

Regardless of the specific skills and methods included in the psychological skills training program, it will be more effective if psychological objectives appropriate to the athletes are identified and if these objectives are defined in easily understood and measurable terms; Table 16-3

Table 16-3 A Sample of Psychological Skills Objectives and Outcomes

Objective 1	Objective 2	Objective 3
Positive Mental Attitude	*Coping With Mistakes and Failures*	*Handling the High-Stress Situation*
Don't make negative statements at games or practices.	Accept the fact that mistakes and failures are a necessary part of the learning process.	Learn to interpret the situation as a challenge rather than a threat.
Change "I can't" statements to "I can" statements.	Don't make excuses. Appropriately accepting responsibility will help turn failures into success.	Recognize too much tension. Achieve appropriate differential relaxation.
Always give 100% effort.	Stay positive even after a stupid mistake.	Keep thoughts positive and focused on the task at hand.
Don't talk while coaches talk.	Be supportive of teammates even when they are making mistakes.	Image goal of performing well under high-stress situations.
Hustle during all plays and drills.	Keep focused concentration rather than dwelling on mistakes.	Focus concentration on appropriate cues.

provides some examples. Such definitions help clarify exactly what the objective means and what outcomes are expected once it is achieved. The definitions also provide a clear foundation for planning strategies to accomplish the objectives and for assessing how effective the strategies were in achieving the objective.

Evaluation of Program Effectiveness

It is not easy to evaluate the impact of a psychology skills training program, yet evaluation is essential for improving a training program and the skills of the person in charge of the program. In fact, evaluation should be an essential feature of any organizational as well as individualized intervention. Aside from the accountability demands that ethically oblige sport psychology consultants to evaluate the effectiveness of what they do (see Smith, 1989), practical considerations are also important.

First, program evaluation provides consultants and coaches with the information needed to gauge the effectiveness of the various components of their programs and to make modifications where needed. Second, an evaluation provides consumers with an opportunity to provide feedback concerning areas that they feel weren't included or to suggest changes in the way the program was conducted. Third, evaluation is the only way we can objectively judge whether the program achieved its intended goals in changing some aspects of the individual's or team's behavior or performance.

It is important to note that evaluation should be a continuous process. Sport psychology consultants should assess the strengths and weaknesses of the content and delivery of each of their sessions, especially team sessions. Questions such as the following might be addressed: Did the session accomplish its objective(s)? Were explanations of psychological concepts and directions for practicing the training exercises adequate? What techniques appeared to work best? Was time allotted appropriately during the session? Are any additions or deletions warranted? How

responsive did the athletes appear to be? Writing a critique is more beneficial than simply trying to remember strengths and weaknesses. Plans for future sessions may need to be modified on the basis of the results of each session evaluation.

A more formal, total evaluation should occur at the end of the mental skills training program. This evaluation might include team and individual discussions as well as written evaluations by the athletes and coaches. The evaluation should focus on the players' assessment of the value of the program from both a psychological and performance perspective. Objective performance data should be used in addition to subjective reports from coaches and athletes. For example, one recommended objective data system entails behavioral assessment, which involves collecting and analyzing information and data relevant to the behaviors targeted for change (see Tkachuk, Leslie-Toogood, & Martin, 2003). In addition, athletes should be asked how often they actually practiced their skills. When psychological skills programs don't work, one of the major reasons is simply because athletes did not systematically practice what they were being taught. The following questions are also helpful: What did athletes see as the major strengths and weaknesses of the mental skills training? What mental skills improved the most? What exercises and handouts were the most helpful? What suggestions do athletes have to make the program even better in the future?

Other authors provide good guidance on conducting program evaluation. See Partington and Orlick (1987a, 1987b) for a sample sport psychology evaluation form and data on what makes a consultant effective from both the coaches' and athletes' point of view. Luiselli (2012), noting the similarities of cognitive-behavioral theory and applied behavioral analysis, provides suggestions for program evaluation including intervention integrity, social validity, and assessment. Anderson, Miles, Mahoney, and Robinson (2002) suggest employing four distinct categories of effectiveness indicators when conducting an evaluation. These include the quality of support (e.g., consultant effectiveness), psychological skill and well-being (e.g., anxiety control, happiness), response to support (e.g., changes in knowledge and attitude), and performance (objective, subjective). This approach presents a more well-rounded view of evaluation than simply performance (bottom line), which is the focus of many interventions.

Practical Pointers for Teaching Mental Skills

In the preceding chapters on mental skills training the authors have presented many excellent pointers for teaching specific mental skills. The following pointers apply either to the entire psychological training program or to its components.

Provide the What, Why, When, and How of Training

For mental skills to be of maximum value, the athlete must consciously and continually choose to utilize mental training methods. This necessitates a high level of commitment, an understanding of proper execution, and ultimately the ability to be self-sufficient in mental preparation. This can be accomplished in a number of ways. Athletes who are taught the what, why, when, and how of mental skills training are much more likely to acquire the necessary knowledge base to become self-sufficient in mental training as well as the motivation to follow through with the program. It is critical that the initial educational aspect of the program provides the athletes with an understanding of what principles the program is based on and how it works. At the beginning of each special mental training session, the coach or sport psychologist should outline for the athletes the purpose, content, and approximate length of the session. It is also a good idea to allot time for discussion and questions after practicing each exercise and at the end of each session. In addition to enhancing forthright self-examination and the learning process, the sharing that occurs in these discussions often improves communication and understanding among teammates and leads to better group support and more team cohesiveness.

Stress Personal Responsibility

When it comes to performance, some athletes have the attitude "When you're hot, you're hot, and when you're not, you're not." They view peak performance as more a consequence of fate than something under their own personal control. Implementers of mental skills training should teach the opposite attitude. Peak performance is not fate or mysterious; it is a product of the body and mind, both of which can be controlled. This is why, with the right physical and mental training, athletes can learn to repeat their best performances more consistently. This means learning to be in control of oneself instead of letting the environment or others do the controlling. The athlete must ultimately accept the fact that only he or she can take responsibility for being physically and mentally ready to compete.

Be Flexible and Individualized

When teaching mental skills to a group of athletes, the best approach is to be flexible and individualized. All athletes do not learn mental skills in the same way and at the same pace any more than they do physical skills. Within reasonable time constraints, a variety of techniques should be introduced and practiced. Do not force everyone into a fixed pattern. Instead, encourage athletes to modify or combine techniques until they derive the most effective method for them. A backup technique should also be identified and practiced for those times when the preferred one fails to accomplish its objective.

Providing handouts and cassette or CD recordings of exercises and specific concepts, including the ones in this book, is another way to ensure that athletes have a variety of exercises to use and the knowledge base for making modifications and application. Although many athletes like to use recordings and handouts when they practice, be sure they do not become so dependent on them that they cannot practice the mental skills without such props.

Use Goal Setting and Journal Assignments

You can also enhance and individualize the teaching of specific mental skills by using goal setting and journal assignments. This is one reason many

Case Study

John, a cross country runner, after having been taught to recognize tension and to relax, identifies that he grimaces and his neck and shoulder muscles tighten when he runs under poor weather conditions, after experiencing the first signs of fatigue, and when a steep hill is coming up. He records this in his journal. Next, John sets a reasonable goal for correcting the problem: "In one week, I will run a workout over hilly terrain keeping my face, neck, and shoulder muscles relaxed throughout the run." After he records the goal, he plans and records a strategy for reaching the goal: "(1) Do 5 minutes of progressive relaxation (PR) each day on just the face, neck, and shoulder muscles. (2) After PR practice, visualize running fluidly over hilly terrain. (3) When running, frequently scan the face for tension—if needed, relax the face so the forehead is smooth as glass and the jaw is slack. When the face is relaxed, scan neck and shoulders for unwanted tension. If tense, relax by slowly rolling the head and/or dropping the shoulders." Each day John records his progress in achieving the goal. Once John feels he is consistently achieving the goal, he may want to establish a slightly more difficult goal and repeat the process.

sport psychology consultants suggest that athletes be encouraged to keep a journal (see Chapter 10) and set goals (see Chapter 11) early in a training program. The following case study is an example of their use and the desired self-sufficiency outcome for a mental skills training program.

Precompetition and Competition Plans

The ultimate goal of psychological skills training is for each athlete to learn how to create consistently at competition time the ideal performance state (thoughts, feelings, bodily responses) typically associated with his or her peak performance. Rarely will this occur if precompetition preparation and competition behaviors are left to chance or good and bad breaks. Athletes get ready for competition in a variety of ways, but more often than not they fail to have a consistent pattern of readying procedures. Performance is likely to be enhanced if an athlete's preparation becomes more systematic.

One of the objectives of precompetition planning is to arrange the external and internal world in a way that maximizes the athlete's feelings of control. The athlete's **external world** consists of the actual physical surroundings, what is happening in these surroundings, and the physical things the athlete does. The **internal world** is

the athlete's physical state, thoughts, feelings, mental images, and attentional focus. The greater the familiarity, routine, and structure in the external environment, the easier it is for the athlete to be in control of his or her internal world. The external world can be stabilized in a number of ways—for example, eating similar meals the same amount of time before each competition; always arriving at the contest site with a set amount of time for precompetition preparation; establishing a set dressing ritual; and following the same equipment check, taping, and warm-up procedures.

Maintaining a constant and familiar external world is even more critical with away competitions. This is more easily accomplished when athletes diligently adhere to elaborate and consistent precompetition plans before both home and away games. The coach can also increase familiarity by taking the athletes to the site of away games before the competition begins, ideally at least a day before. Some coaches and sport psychology consultants even advocate getting films of the away facility, including the locker rooms, and showing these films to their athletes well before a competition

The best precompetition and competition plans consist of procedures that ready the athlete physically and mentally for competition. The typical physical preparations should be supplemented with emotional and cognitive readying procedures if athletes are to maximize their chances of being ready to peak at competition time. This entails planning procedures for monitoring and controlling the task at hand as competition nears. It also means monitoring and controlling emotions so that the energy and excitement for competing build slowly.

Mental monitoring and readying procedures should be integrated with certain external markers such as waking up the morning of competition, traveling to the competition, arriving at the competition site, getting dressed, doing warm-up exercises and technique drills, and dealing with the short time between physical warm-ups and the beginning of competition. When some athletes arrive at a competition site, they like to find a quiet place where they can practice 5 to 10 minutes of relaxation exercises such as deep breathing or passive progressive relaxation. Such athletes believe these relaxation procedures have the benefit of bringing them to the same starting point prior to each competition before they begin the rest of their on-site preparation. Other athletes combine their dressing ritual with cognitive focusing techniques designed to narrow attentional focus to what the athletes want to do during the competition. Often athletes end their dressing ritual or precede their physical warm-up with a 5-to-10-minute imagery exercise of exactly what they want to feel and perform during competition. Some athletes even use *all* of these readying procedures.

Some interesting qualitative research by Gould, Eklund, and Jackson (1992) and Eklund, Gould, and Jackson (1993) on thoughts and cognitions of Olympic wrestlers highlights the importance of precompetition and competition plans as well as individual variability. First, some between-group differences among medalists and nonmedalists revealed that medalists had competition plans firmly in their minds and did not spontaneously second-guess these plans during matches, whereas nonmedalists reported spontaneous deviations from their competition plans and often a resulting negative consequence (i.e., poorer performance). In addition, medalists had very systematic preperformance routines that they consistently adhered to throughout the Olympics, whereas nonmedalists reported

deviating from their preperformance routines, especially in matches considered less challenging or important.

Despite these differences between medalists and nonmedalists, interviews revealed individual differences and variations among the medalists. For example, one medalist placed great importance on prematch focus. "I just try to think about the techniques I am going to use and what strategies I am going to do and get that into my mind before I go out on the mat so I am focused on what I am going to do" (Eklund et al., 1993, p. 43). Conversely, another medalist deemphasized preperformance routines and strategy, feeling that they made him "too programmed." This orientation is captured in the following quotation: "I don't worry about strategy and technique. I try to keep my mind clear of getting caught up in all that stuff. . . I just keep my mind clear and when I get out there, I just react" (Eklund et al., 1993, p. 44).

Some excellent examples of precompetition and competition planning come from the work of Orlick (1986) with Canadian Olympic athletes. His athletes develop precompetition and competition *refocusing* plans in case things don't go exactly as they originally planned. And, as Jack Donohue, Canadian Olympic basketball coach, says, "What happens to you is nowhere near as important as how you react to what happens to you." A refocusing plan is aimed at helping athletes refocus away from unwanted external distractions or internal distractions such as worries, self-doubt, and self-put-downs. Table 16-4 provides a good example of precompetition and competition refocusing plans for an Olympic speed skater.

Stress Application to Other Life Pursuits

One tremendous bonus that comes from implementing a mental training program is that the skills learned are applicable to life in general, and the benefits last long after the competitive year is over. Sport psychology consultants need to play a role in maximizing this transfer. For example, suggest that athletes learn to do their homework more quickly by using mental training concentration skills. Use them to become more aware of when one's mind is wandering and then refocus

Table 16-4 Refocusing Plans for an Olympic Speedskater

Worries about Competitors before the Race

- They are human just like me. We'll see what they can do in the race, not in warm-ups or in training. I need to focus on my *own* preparation.
- All I can do is my best. Nobody can take that away from me. If my performance is good, I'll be happy. If it's not so good and I try, I shouldn't be disappointed.
- I'm racing for *me*. It's *my* max that I want.

Worry about Competitors during the Race

- If I start to think about others during the race, I'll shift my concentration to *my* race, *my* technique— "Stay low, race your race."
- "I have the potion—I have the motion."

Pre-Event Hassles

- Skate blades don't cut the ice—carry a small sharpening stone to pass over the blades.
- Delay in start—if I'm already on the ice and it's likely to be a short delay, jog around, keep moving, stay warm, do a mini warm-up with some accelerations. Follow normal prerace plan when approaching the line.
- Windy or snowy conditions—it's the same for everyone. Just go out and do what you can do.

Worries during Competition

- Poor start—no problem, it can happen. It's not the start that determines the final results. Follow your race plan. Push your max.
- Not hearing a split time—it's okay. Just skate well and race your race.
- Pain in legs—shift focus to the specifics of the task to be done, the steps in the turn, pushing the blade to the side, pushing hard to the finish line.

Source: Reprinted by permission from T. Orlick, 1986, *Psyching for Sport* (Champaign, IL: Human Kinetics Publishers), pp. 165–166.

on the task at hand. If an athlete gets so uptight before tests that he or she cannot remember what was learned, suggest that the same relaxation and positive thinking skills taught to control competitive anxiety can be used for test-taking anxiety and other stressful situations they face.

An issue of the *Journal of Applied Sport Psychology* (2002, #4) focused on the application of psychological skills typically used in sport and exercise settings to other settings and endeavors such as business, medicine, space travel, and special forces. More and more sport psychology consultants are practicing in areas outside of sport, fueled in part by interest in the psychology of excellence. For example, Loehr and Schwartz (2001) have discussed the similarities of high performers, whether they are elite athletes or CEOs working for a Fortune 500 company. Similarly, Murphy (1996) discusses the transfer from working with elite athletes at the Olympic Training Center to working with performers in the corporate arena. Murphy reports that his clients (whether sport or nonsport) tell him that the skills they are taught help them achieve their best under pressure, allow them to stay focused during difficult tasks, and enable them to enjoy even the most challenging assignments. More recently, the army has been hiring individuals trained in sport psychology to teach soldiers psychological skills, on the premise such training will be more effective than their previous focus on teaching primarily physical skills Thus, the transfer from sport to other areas of life seems to be a fertile ground for future practitioners and researchers. Finally, Fletcher (2010) provides an extensive bibliography and narrative commentary of applying sport psychology to business.

Practice It Before Teaching It

Before teaching any of the mental training exercises to athletes, sport psychology consultants and coaches should take the time to practice each technique themselves. Personally experiencing an exercise is an excellent way to increase one's ability to teach a specific technique and to answer any questions athletes may have about it. An additional bonus of practicing the exercises, particularly if the practice is systematic and long term, is that the practitioner will accrue psychological benefits similar to those the athletes receive from the practice and they can better lead by example.

Teach by Example

In regard to psychological control—or any type of behavior—good coaches and sport psychology consultants teach and lead by example. The coach who appears calm, confident, and in control during a competition usually has athletes who act the same way. The next time you see athletes consistently losing control and concentration after poor officiating calls, look to the bench, and you probably will see the coach behaving similarly. Watch how athletes react to poor performance. Athletes who become negative or rattled after mistakes are often led by coaches who react similarly. For psychological training to be maximally effective, the coaches and sport psychology consultants must exemplify in the behavior they expect from athletes.

Observe Practices and Competitions Whenever Possible

As noted earlier, one of the disadvantages of sport psychology consultants conducting mental training programs with teams is their lack of day-to-day availability. Despite this limitation, it is critical that consultants attempt to attend some practices and competitions. We have found that this is particularly important at the beginning stages of the intervention. This firsthand view can provide consultants with critical information that might not be evident from an interview or paper-and-pencil measure. As noted earlier, the problem might be biomechanical or physical in nature rather than psychological, and this would not likely show up in an interview or a test. Survey research also indicates that the amount of time observing athletes directly affected building trust between athletes and consultants and was a critical component to the perceived effectiveness of sport psychology consultants (Gould, Tammen, Murphy, & May, 1989; Partington & Orlick, 1987a).

Emphasize Strengths as Competition Nears

Behavior by the coach and sport psychology consultant prior to and during competition is particularly critical. The nearer the time to competition, the more important it is that they are reassuring and complimentary toward athletes. This is not the time to be critical of technique or anything else. Besides, it is too late to change weaknesses, so there is no reason to focus on them. Instead, if at all possible, get athletes to think they are looking great and help build their confidence. In short, now is the time to build from what is positive, to play to strengths rather than weaknesses.

The preceding recommendation is particularly critical with athletes who have higher anxiety and lower self-confidence. Williams et al. (2003) found that when these athletes perceived the coach to lose emotional control, become negative, or fail to be supportive, this was likely to lead to poorer performance and more difficulty maintaining optimal mental states and focus. Using the self-monitoring or outside monitoring described in the next section should help coaches and sport psychology consultants assess their behavior prior to and during competition.

Monitor Your Behavior

In Chapter 10, Ravizza and Fifer suggest that athletes become more aware of their behavior, thoughts, and feelings through self-monitoring. The same awareness on the part of coaches and sport psychology consultants can help them become more effective in working with athletes. For example, by means of self-monitoring, coaches and sport psychology consultants can become more conscious of how they communicate with athletes during different situations. They should ask themselves such questions as "How is my behavior likely to change in certain situations?" "Am I a good role model for the mental discipline and psychological control I wish to teach?" The awareness created by conscientious and objective self-monitoring is a necessary first step in becoming more effective in working with athletes.

There also is merit in having someone observe and evaluate one's behavior. For example, if a coach has a sport psychology consultant working with the team, he or she would be an ideal person to observe the coach's behavior during practices and games. Coaching behaviors should be analyzed on the basis of the principles for desirable behavior elaborated in earlier chapters. Evaluation would be facilitated if special forms were employed, such as that used by Smith, Smoll, & Hunt (1977). Once awareness is created and shortcomings identified, use the information presented in earlier chapters to plan a specific strategy for modifying behavior in a direction that is more likely to facilitate the performance and personal growth of one's athletes.

Ethical Considerations for the Coach and Sport Psychology Consultant

The purpose of this section is to call attention to some basic ethical concerns involved in implementing mental skills training. A more thorough discussion of these topics can be found in Moore (2003) and Whelan, Meyers, and Elkin (1996). To better understand specific situations and circumstances perceived as particularly difficult and possibly controversial from an ethical perspective, Petitpas, Brewer, Rivera, and Van Raalte (1994) administered surveys to individuals practicing applied sport psychology. Four classifications of behaviors were identified as requiring the most difficult ethical judgments or were perceived as controversial:

- conflicts with confidentiality (e.g., reporting recruiting violations to appropriate officials)

- conflicts between personal values and professional ethics (e.g., working with an athlete who uses steroids)

- conflicts with dual relationships (e.g., socializing with clients)

- conflicts with self-presentation or advertising (e.g., including athlete testimonials in advertising)

To help guide professionals working in applied sport psychology settings deal with ethical dilemmas more effectively, sport psychology associations such as the Association for Applied Sport Psychology, the North American Society for the Psychology of Sport and Physical Activity, and the Canadian Society for Psychomotor Learning and Sport Psychology have developed modifications of the American Psychological Association's Ethical Standards (1992). At the core of these standards is the general philosophy that sport psychology consultants respect the dignity and worth of the individual and honor the preservation and protection of fundamental human rights. In addition, consultants are committed to increasing the knowledge of human behavior and of people's understanding of themselves and others in sport environments. The essence of this philosophy is that the athlete's welfare must be foremost. For a more detailed discussion of ethical principles please consult the American Psychological Association's ethical guidelines (1992). In addition, McCann, Jowdy, and Van Raalte (2002) provide ethical guidelines especially for assessments.

Potential Problem Areas

Although the potential benefits of implementing a psychological skills training program are clearly demonstrable, each situation also offers its own unique set of problems. For example, working one on one with individual athletes is quite different from working with an entire team. Working with Olympic or professional athletes might present an entirely different set of problems than working with high school athletes just as would working with largely minority athletes versus exclusively Caucasian athletes. If the consultant or coach does not adequately anticipate and plan for the different sets of problems that come from working with different populations, he or she can severely reduce the effectiveness of the program. In addition, they need to plan for commonly occurring problems such as the following:

- Overcoming player reluctance about participating in a mental training program.
- Spending too little time with individual athletes in a team setting.
- Gaining the trust of the athletes.
- Making sure athletes systematically practice their skills.
- Lacking knowledge about the specific sport.

- Maintaining contact with athletes throughout a competitive season.
- Getting full cooperation from the coaching staff or organization.

A sport psychology consultant needs to be aware of these potential problem areas and ready to deal with them if necessary. It has taken most of us several years to learn many of these things by trial and error. We made mistakes in our early years of consulting because we simply weren't aware of, or hadn't experienced, many of these nuances of setting up and implementing a mental training program. However, with good preparation, careful thought, and a sense of commitment, this can be a very rewarding experience.

Summary

In this chapter we have addressed many general issues relating to the integration and implementation of a psychological skills training program. In summary, (1) there are advantages to having either a coach or a sport psychologist implement a psychological skills training program, (2) athletes of all types and age and skill levels can benefit from mental training, (3) mental skills training should continue for as long as an athlete participates in sport, (4) the initial mental skills training program should probably last 3 to 6 months and start in the off-season or preseason, (5) a psychological skills needs assessment should be made to determine the specific components to be incorporated in training and the psychological objectives to be achieved, (6) there is no one best way to sequence and integrate psychological components even though one was proposed, (7) once basic mental skills are acquired they should have a performance-specific focus and be integrated with practice of physical skills, and (8) real benefits from psychological skills training will occur only with long-term systematic practice.

We have also suggested practical teaching pointers that apply either to the entire psychological training program or to many of its components. Stress that athletes accept responsibility for their mental state. Be flexible, eclectic, and individualized in planning training techniques. Stress personal growth and how to use mental skills in nonathletic settings. Practice techniques before teaching them. Teach by personally exemplifying the mental skills being taught. Finally, we concluded the chapter with ethical considerations that all psychological training implementers need to be aware of and observe in their own behavior.

Study Questions

1. Discuss three different models of sport psychology practice/intervention.

2. Are psychological skills intervention programs effective in enhancing performance? Provide evidence to support your answer.

3. Based on research, discuss three things a consultant can do to enhance his/her effectiveness.

4. Discuss who will benefit most from psychological skills training.

5. What are some advantages and disadvantages of a coach or sport psychology consultant conducting a mental training program?

6. How much time should be spent in mental training?

7. When is the best time to practice psychological skills?

8. When is the best time to implement a psychological skills training program?

9. Discuss what would be covered in a first interview with an athlete.

10. Discuss the use of psychological inventories to help assess athletes' psychological skills.

11. Discuss the benefits of Performance Profiling from a sport psychology consultant and athlete's point of view?

12. Discuss Vealey's distinction between psychological methods and psychological skills. What are the different categories of psychological skills? What impact does this distinction between methods and skills have on the implementation of a psychological skills training program?

13. John, a golfer, goes to a sport psychologist because his play is "erratic." One of the sport psychologist's observations is that he has no consistent preshot readying procedure. How might the sport psychologist help John develop a preshot routine, what might it include, and why should this intervention improve John's performance?

14. Discuss how a psychological skills program might be evaluated.

15. Discuss five practical pointers that may help make a psychological skills program more effective. Cite specific practical examples and research to support your points.

References

Aoyagi, M., & Poczwardoski, A. (2012). Models of sport psychology practice and delivery. In S. Hanton & S. Mellalieu (Eds.). *Professional practice in sport psychology: A review,* pp. 5–30. New York, Routledge.

American Psychological Association. (1992). Ethical principles and code of conduct. *American Psychologist, 47,* 1597–1611.

Anderson, A., Miles, A., Mahoney, C., & Robinson, P. (2002). Evaluating the effectiveness of applied sport psychology practice: Making the case for a case study approach. *The Sport Psychologist, 16,* 432–453.

Aoyagi, M., & Poczwardoski, A. (2012). Models of sport psychology practice and delivery. In S. Hanton & S. Mellalieu (Eds.). Professional practice in sport psychology: A review, pp. 5–21. London: Routledge.

Association for the Advancement of Applied Sport Psychology Newsletter 6 (Winter 1991).

Bandura, A. (1986). *Social foundations of thought and action: A social cognitive theory.* Englewood Cliffs, NJ: Prentice Hall.

Barber, H., & Krane, V. (2005). The elephant in the locker room: Opening the dialogue about sexual orientation on women's sports teams. In M. Andersen (Ed.). *Sport psychology in practice.* Champaign, IL: Human Kinetics.

Beckman, J., & Kellmann, M. (2003). Procedures and principles of sport psychological assessment. *The Sport Psychologist, 17,* 338–350.

Butler, R. J., & Hardy, L. (1992). The performance profile: Theory and application. *The Sport Psychologist, 6,* 253–264.

Butryn, T. (2002). Critically examining white racial identity and privilege in sport psychology consulting. *The Sport Psychologist, 16,* 316–336.

Calmels, C., d'Arripe-Longueville, Fournier, J., & Soulard, A. (2003). Competitive strategies among elite female gymnasts: An exploration of the relative influence of psychological skills training and natural learning experiences. *International Journal of Sport and Exercise Psychology, 1,* 327–352.

Camire, M., Forneris, T., Trudel, P., & Bernard, D. (2011). Strategies for helping coaches facilitate positive youth development through sport. *Journal of Sport Psychology in Action, 2,* 92–99.

Chase, M. (2013). Children. In S. Hanrahan & M. Andersen (Eds.). *Routledge handbook of applied sport psychology: A comprehensive guide for students and practitioners,* (pp. 377–386) New York: Routledge.

Cox, R. H., Martens, M. P., & Russell, W. D. (2003). Measuring anxiety in athletics: The revised Competitive State Anxiety Inventory-2. *Journal of Sport and Exercise Psychology, 25,* 519–533.

Danish, S., Petitpas, A., & Hale, B. (1995). Psychological interventions: A life developmental model. In S. Murphy (Ed.) *Sport psychology interventions* (pp.19–28). Champaign, IL: Human Kinetics Press.

Durand-Bush, N., Salmela, J., & Green-Demers, I. (2001). The Ottawa mental skills assessment tool (OMSAT3). *The Sport Psychologist, 15,* 1–19.

Eklund, R. C., Gould, D., & Jackson, S. A. (1993). Psychological foundations of Olympic wrestling excellence: Reconciling individual differences and nomothetic characterization. *Journal of Applied Sport Psychology, 5,* 35–47.

Fletcher, D. (2010). Applying sport psychology in business: A narrative commentary and bibliography. *Journal of Sport Psychology in Action, 1,* 139–149.

Fournier, J., Calmels, C., Durand-Bush, N., & Salmela, J. (2005). Effects of a season-long PST program on gymnastic performance and on psychological skill development. *International Journal of Sport and Exercise Psychology, 3*, 59–78.

Gould, D. (1983). Developing psychological skills in young athletes. In N. Wood (Ed.), *Coaching science update*. Ottawa, ON: Coaching Association of Canada.

Gould, D., Eklund, R. C., & Jackson, S. A. (1992). 1988 U.S. Olympic wrestling excellence I. Mental preparation, precompetition cognition, and affect. *The Sport Psychologist, 6*, 358–382.

Gould, D., Murphy, S., Tammen, V., & May, J. (1991). An evaluation of Olympic sport psychology consultant effectiveness. *The Sport Psychologist, 5*, 111–127.

Gould, D., Tammen, V., Murphy, S., & May, J. (1989). An examination of the U.S. Olympic sport psychology consultants and the services they provide. *The Sport Psychologist, 3*, 300–312.

Gregg, M. (2013) Working with athletes with intellectual disabilities. In S. Hanrahan & M. Andersen (Eds.) Routledge handbook of applied sport psychology: a comprehensive guide for students and practitioners, (pp.441–449). New York: Routledge.

Greenspan, M. J., & Feltz, D. F. (1989). Psychological interventions with athletes in competitive situations: A review. *The Sport Psychologist, 3*, 219–236.

Hanin, Y. (2007). Emotions in sport: Current issues and perspectives. In G. Tenenbaum & R. Eklund (Eds.), Handbook of sport psychology (3rd ed.) Hoboken, NJ: John Wiley & Sons.

Jones, G., & Swain, A. B. J. (1992). Intensity and direction dimensions of competitive state anxiety and relationships with competitiveness. *Perceptual and Motor Skills, 74*, 467–472.

Kirschenbaum, D. (1997). *Mind matters: 7 steps to smarter sport performance*. Carmel, IN: Cooper Publishing.

Lidor, R. (2007). Preparatory routines in self-paced events. In. G. Tenenbaum & R. C. Eklund (Eds.). *Handbook of research in sport psychology* (3rd ed., pp. 445–465). Hoboken, NJ: John Wiley & Sons.

Loehr, J., & Schwartz, T. (January 2001). The making of the corporate athlete. *Harvard Business Review*, pp. 120–128.

Luiselli, J. (2012). Behavioral sport psychology consulting: A review of some practice concerns and recommendations, *Journal of Sport Psychology in Action, 3*, 41–51.

Marchant, D. (2013). Objective/self-report measures. In S. Hanrahan & M. Andersen (Eds.). *Routledge handbook of applied sport psychology: A comprehensive guide for students and practitioners*, pp. 111–119). New York: Routledge.

Martens, R. (1977). *Sport competition anxiety test*. Champaign, IL: Human Kinetics.

Martens, R., Vealey, R. S., & Burton, D. (1990). *Competitive anxiety in sport*. Champaign, IL: Human Kinetics.

Martin, J. (2013). Athletes with physical disabilities. In S. Hanrahan & M. Andersen (Eds.) *Routledge handbook of applied sport psychology: a comprehensive guide for students and practitioners* (pp. 432–440). New York: Routledge.

Martin, S. B., Wrisberg, C. A., Beitel, P. A., & Lounsbury, J. (1997). NCAA Division 1 athletes' attitudes toward seeking sport psychology consultation: The development of an objective instrument. *The Sport Psychologist, 11*, 201–218.

McCann, S., Jowdy, D., & Van Raalte, J. (2002). Assessment in sport and exercise psychology. In J. Van Raalte and B. Brewer (Eds.), *Exploring sport and exercise psychology* (2nd ed., pp. 291–305). Washington, DC: American Psychological Association.

Moore, Z. (2012). Counseling performers in distress. In S. Murphy (Ed.), *The Oxford Handbook of Sport and Performance Psychology* (pp. 527–544). New York: Oxford Press.

Meyers, A. W., Whelan, J. P., & Murphy, S. M. (1996). Cognitive behavioral strategies in athletic performance enhancement. In M. Hersen, R. M. Eisler, & P. M. Miller (Eds.), *Progress in behavior modification,* Vol. 30 (pp. 137–164). Pacific Grove, CA: Brooks/Cole.

Moore, Z. E. (2003). Ethical dilemmas in sport psychology: Discussion and recommendations for practice. *Professional Psychology: Research and Practice, 34,* 601–610.

Murphy, S. (1995). *Sport psychology intervention.* Champaign, IL: Human Kinetics.

Murphy, S. (1996). *The achievement zone.* New York: Putnam.

Murphy, S., Jowdy, D., & Durtschi, S. (1990). *Imagery perspective survey.* Colorado Springs, CO: U.S. Olympic Training Center.

Murphy, S., & Murphy, A. (2013). Attending and listening. In S. Hanrahan & M. Andersen (Eds.), *Routledge handbook of applied sport psychology: A comprehensive guide for students and practitioners* (pp. 12–20). New York: Routledge.

Newburg, D. (2002). The role of resonance in performance excellence and life engagement. *Journal of Applied Sport Psychology, 14,* 249–267.

Nideffer, R. M. (1976). Test of attentional and interpersonal style. *Journal of Personality and Social Psychology, 34,* 394–404.

Nideffer, R. M. (1989). Psychological services for the U.S. track and field team. *The Sport Psychologist, 3,* 350–357.

O'Connor, E. (2004). Which questionnaire? Assessment practices of sport psychology consultants, *The Sport Psychologist, 18,* 464–468.

Orlick, T. (2000*). In pursuit of excellence: How to win in sport and life through mental training* (3rd ed.). Champaign, IL: Human Kinetics.

Partington, J., & Orlick, T. (1987a). The sport psychology consultant: Olympic coaches' views. *The Sport Psychologist, 1,* 95–102.

Partington, J., & Orlick, T. (1987b). The sport psychology consultant evaluation form. *The Sport Psychologist, 1,* 309–317.

Petitpas, A., Brewer, B., Rivera, P., & Van Raalte, J. (1994). Ethical beliefs and behaviors in applied sport psychology: The AAASP ethics survey. *Journal of Applied Sport Psychology, 6,* 135–151.

Petitpas, A. J., Giges, B., & Danish, S. J. (1999). The sport psychologist-athlete relationship: Implications for training. *The Sport Psychologist, 13,* 344–357.

Perna, F. Neyer, M., Murphy, S., Ogilvie, B., & Murphy, A. (1995). Consultations with sport organizations: A cognitive-behavioral model. In S. Murphy (Ed.) *Sport psychology interventions,* pp. 235–252. Champaign, IL: Human Kinetics Press.

Sexton, T. L., & Whitson, S. C. (1994). The status of the counseling relationship: An empirical review, theoretical implications, and research directions. *The Counseling Psychologist, 22*, 6–78.

Sharp, L., & Hodge, K. (2011). Sport psychology consulting effectiveness: The sport psychology consultant's perspective. *Journal of Applied Sport Psychology, 23*, 360–376.

Simons, J. (2013). The applied sport psychology intake. In S. Hanrahan & M. Andersen (Eds.). *Routledge handbook of applied sport psychology: A comprehensive guide for students and practitioners* (pp. 81–89). New York: Routledge

Smith, R. E. (1989). Applied sport psychology in the age of accountability. *Journal of Applied Sport Psychology, 1*, 166–180.

Smith, R. E., Schutz, R. W., Smoll, F. L., & Ptacek, J. T. (1995). Development and validation of a multi-dimensional measure of sport-specific psychological skills: The Athletic Coping Skills Inventory–28. *Journal of Sport and Exercise Psychology, 17*, 379–387.

Smith, R. E., Smoll, F. L., & Hunt, E. (1977). A system for the behavioral assessment of athletic coaches. *Research Quarterly, 48*, 401–407.

Smith, R. E., Smoll, F. L., & Schutz, R. W. (1990). Measurement and correlates of sport-specific cognitive and somatic trait anxiety: The Sport Anxiety Scale. *Anxiety Research, 2*, 263–280.

Thomas, O., Maynard, I., & Hanton, S. (2007). Intervening with athletes during the time leading up to competition: Theory to practice II. *Journal of Applied Sport Psychology, 19*, 398–418.

Tkachuk, G., Leslie-Toogood, A., & Martin, G. (2003). Behavioral assessment in sport psychology. *The Sport Psychologist, 17*, 104–117.

Tod, D., Andersen, M., & Marchant, D. (2008). A longitudinal examination of neophyte applied sport psychologists' development. *Journal of Applied Sport Psychology, 21*, S1–S16.

Vealey, R. S. (1986). Conceptualization of sport-confidence and competitive orientation: Preliminary investigation and instrument development. *Journal of Sport Psychology, 8*, 221–246.

Vealey, R. S. (1988). Future directions in psychological skills training. *The Sport Psychologist, 2*, 318–336.

Vealey, R. (1994). Current status and prominent issues in sport psychology interventions. *Medicine and Science in Sport and Exercise*, 495–502.

Vealey, R. S. (2007). Mental skills training in sport. In G. Tenenbaum & R. Eklund (Eds.). *Handbook of sport psychology* (3rd ed., pp. 287–309.) New York: Wiley.

Visek, A., Harris, B., & Blom, L. (2013). Mental training with your sport teams: Developmental considerations and best practice recommendations. *Journal of Sport Psychology in Action, 4*, 45–55.

Vose, J., Clark, R., & Sachs, M. (2013). Athletes who are blind/visually impaired or deaf/hard of hearing. In S. Hanrahan & M. Andersen (Eds.) *Routledge handbook of applied sport psychology: a comprehensive guide for students and practitioners* (pp. 450–459). NewYork: Routledge.

Ward, D., Sandstedt, S., Cox, R., & Beck, N. (2005). Athlete-counseling competencies for U.S. psychologists working with athletes. *The Sport Psychologist, 19*, 318–334.

Watson, J., & Shannon, V. (2013). Individual and group observations: purposes and processes. In S. Hanrahan & M. Andersen, Eds. *Routledge handbook of applied sport psychology* (pp. 90–100). NewYork : Routledge

Weinberg, R. S., & Comar, W. (1994). The effectiveness of psychological interventions in competitive sport. *Sports Medicine Journal, 18,* 406–418.

Weiss, M. R. (1995). Children in sport: An educational model. In S. Murphy (Ed.) *Sport psychology interventions* (pp. 39–69). Champaign, IL: Human Kinetics.

Weston, N., Greenlees, I., & Thelwell, R. (2013). A review of Butler and Hardy's (1992) performance profiling procedure within sport. *International Review of Sport and Exercise Psychology, 6,* 1–21.

Whelan, J. P., Meyers, A. W., & Donovan, C. (1995). Competitive recreational athletes: A multisystemic model. In S. Murphy (Ed.), *Sport Psychology Interventions* (pp. 71–116). Champaign, IL: Human Kinetics.

Whelan, J. P., Meyers, A. W., & Elkin, D. (1996). Ethics in sport and exercise psychology. In J. L. Van Raalte and S. Brewer (Eds.), *Exploring sport and exercise psychology* (pp. 431–447). Washington, DC: American Psychological Association.

Williams, J. M., Jerome, G. J., Kenow, L. J., Rogers, T., Sartain, A., & Darland, G. (2003). Factoring structure of the coaching behavior questionnaire and its relationship to athlete variables. *The Sport Psychologist, 17,* 16–34.

Woodcock, C., Duda, J., Cumming, J., Sharp, L., & Holland, M. (2012). Assessing mental skill and technique use in applied interventions: Recognizing and minimizing threats to the psychometric properties of the TOPS. *The Sport Psychologist, 26,* 1–15.

Zizzi, S., & Perna, F. (2002). Integrating web pages and e-mail into sport psychology consultations. *The Sport Psychologist, 16,* 416–431.

Conducting Evidence Based Coach-Training Programs: A Social-Cognitive Approach

Frank L. Smoll, *University of Washington*
Ronald E. Smith, *University of Washington*

In this game, you're either a winner or a loser. Success means winning championships. Anything else is failure.

—*George Allen, Pro Football Hall of Fame coach*

Success is peace of mind which is a direct result of self-satisfaction in knowing you made the effort to do the best of which you are capable.

—*John Wooden, Basketball Hall of Fame player and coach*

There are several routes to knowledge and sound practice in sport psychology. One is personal experience. Indeed, informal observations are typically the first stage in the process of scientific inquiry. People notice something of interest and try to figure out why it occurred, or they draw conclusions from their personal observations. This is a good starting point, but *experiential knowledge* cannot be the end point for an ethically grounded science of sport psychology. The reason is that personal judgment and conclusions are likely tainted by various sources of error, including self-serving biases that selectively reinforce already-existing beliefs and mental operations that cause us to make misjudgments about probabilities. For example, psychologist Daniel Kahneman won the 2002

Nobel Prize in Economics for his pioneering research on the fallibility of human judgment, even by so-called experts in their fields. And for more than 60 years, psychologists have known that simple mathematical formulas for combining clinical data to arrive at decisions generally almost always trump expert judgment by even highly experienced professionals (Grove & Meehl, 1996).

Given the fallibility of human observation and decision making, we cringe when some sport psychology practitioners reject the need for scientific study of an intervention based on the faulty notion that, "I don't need to test it, because I know it works from my own experience." The pages of history illustrate well the folly that can result from this way of "knowing."

For instance, in the history of medicine, experiential knowledge has served as the basis for procedures that physicians "knew" were effective from their clinical experience, including purging, blood-letting, blistering, and lobotomies. Unfortunately for their patients, these treatments were later shown through empirical research not only to be ineffective, but also dangerous and sometimes fatal. Today, all major medical and psychological organizations champion *evidence-based practice* (see Institute of Medicine, 2001; McHugh & Barlow, 2010). This means that all interventions (whether medical or behavioral) should be based on firm empirical evidence and should have demonstrated efficacy based on outcome research.

Most coaches are fairly well versed in the technical aspects of their sport, but they rarely have had any formal training in creating a healthy psychological environment for athletes. It is here that sport psychologists are capable of making significant contributions, by developing and conducting educational programs that positively affect coaching behaviors and thereby increase the likelihood that athletes will have positive experiences. Relative to evaluation of coach-training programs, qualitative testimonials from coaches and practitioners are of interest. However, as affirmed above, they are no substitute for experimental demonstrations of program efficacy. Our research has shown that coaches have limited awareness of how they behave, so their reports are not as compelling as observed behavioral evidence of change (Smith, Smoll, & Curtis, 1978). Likewise, programs that are promoted as "scientifically based" because they are founded on scientific data obtained in other areas of psychology cannot be considered to be *evidence based* until the program itself is evaluated in carefully controlled research.

This chapter begins with an overview of the development and systematic evaluation of two interventions designed to assist coaches in relating more effectively to young athletes. Consideration is then given to cognitive-behavioral principles and techniques for implementing psychologically oriented coach-training programs. Although the focus throughout is on youth sports, the various methods and approaches are applicable to sport psychology workshops for coaches at virtually all levels of competition, including the professional ranks (Smith & Johnson, 1990).

Developing Coach-Training Programs

A crucial first step in developing training programs is to determine *what* is to be presented. In addressing this issue, our work was guided by a fundamental assumption that training programs should be based on scientific evidence rather than on intuition or what we "know" on the basis of informal observation. An empirical foundation for coaching guidelines not only enhances their validity and potential value, but also increases their credibility in the eyes of consumers.

Theoretical Model and Research Paradigm

Recognition of the potential impact of coaches on athletes' psychological welfare prompted us to develop a cognitive-mediational model of coach–athlete interactions (Smoll, Smith, Curtis, & Hunt, 1978). The basic elements of the model are represented as follows:

> COACH BEHAVIORS → ATHLETES'
> PERCEPTIONS AND RECALL → ATHLETES'
> EVALUATIVE REACTIONS

This model stipulates that the ultimate effects of coaching behaviors are mediated by the athletes' recall and the meaning they attribute to the coach's actions. In other words, what athletes remember about their coach's behaviors and how they interpret these actions affect the way athletes evaluate their sport experiences. Furthermore, a complex of cognitive and affective processes is involved at this mediational level. These processes are likely to be affected not only by the coach's behaviors but also by other factors, such as the athlete's age, what he or she expects of coaches (normative beliefs and expectations), and certain personality variables such as self-esteem and anxiety. The basic three-element model was expanded to reflect these factors (Smoll & Smith, 1989). The more comprehensive model specifies a number of situational as well as coach and athlete individual difference variables that are expected to influence coach behaviors and the perceptions and reactions of athletes to them.

In accordance with the model, we have sought to determine how observed coaching behaviors, athletes' perception and recall of the coach's behaviors, and athlete attitudes are interrelated. We have also explored the manner in which athlete and coach individual difference variables might serve as moderator variables and influence basic behavior–attitude relations. An overview of our basic and applied research is presented below. A more detailed account appears elsewhere (Smith & Smoll, 2011), and abstracts of the studies are posted on the Youth Enrichment in Sports Web site (www.y-e-sports.com).

Measurement of Coaching Behaviors

To measure leadership behaviors, we developed the Coaching Behavior Assessment System (CBAS) to permit the direct observation and coding of coaches' actions during practices and games (Smith, Smoll, & Hunt, 1977). The behavioral categories, derived from content analyses of observers' verbal descriptions of coach behavior-situation units using a time-sampling procedure, are shown in Table 17-1.

The 12 CBAS categories are divided into two major classes of behaviors. *Reactive* (elicited) behaviors are responses to immediately preceding athlete or team behaviors, whereas *spontaneous* (emitted) behaviors are initiated by the coach and are not a response to a discernible preceding event. Use of the CBAS in observing and coding coaching behaviors in a variety of sports indicates that the scoring system is sufficiently comprehensive to incorporate the vast majority of overt leader behaviors, that high interrater reliability can be obtained, and that individual

differences in behavioral patterns can be discerned (see Smith, Smoll, & Christensen, 1996).

Coaching Behaviors and Children's Evaluative Reactions

Following development of the CBAS, a systematic program of research was carried out over a period of several years (Curtis, Smith, & Smoll, 1979; Smith & Smoll, 1990; Smith et al., 1978; Smith, Zane, Smoll, & Coppel, 1983; Smoll et al.,). This involved pursuing several questions concerning the potential impact of youth coaches on athletes' psychological welfare. For example, how frequently do coaches engage in behaviors such as encouragement, punishment, instruction, and organization, and how are observable coaching behaviors related to children's reactions to their organized athletic experiences? Answers to such questions not only were a first step in describing the behavioral ecology of one aspect of the youth sport setting, but also provided an empirical basis for the development of a psychologically oriented intervention program.

The results indicated that the typical baseball or basketball coach engages in more than 200 codable actions during an average game. We were thus able to generate behavioral profiles of up to several thousand responses over the course of a season. In large-scale observational studies, we coded more than 80,000 behaviors of some 70 male youth coaches, then interviewed and administered questionnaires after the season to nearly 1,000 children in their homes to measure their recall of their coaches' behaviors and their evaluative reactions to the coach, their sport experiences, and themselves. We also obtained coaches' postseason ratings of how frequently they engaged in each of the observed behaviors.

These data provided clear evidence for the crucial role of the coach. We found that win-loss records bore little relation to our psychosocial outcome measure (i.e., reactions to coach, enjoyment, and self-esteem); virtually all of the systematic variance was accounted for by differences in coaching behaviors. Not surprisingly, we found that the most positive outcomes occurred when children played for coaches who

Table 17-1 Response Categories of the Coaching Behavior Assessment System

Response Category	Behavioral Description
Class I: Reactive (Elicited) Behaviors	
Responses to desirable performance	
Reinforcement	A positive, rewarding reaction (verbal or nonverbal) to a good play or good effort
Nonreinforcement	Failure to respond to a good performance
Responses to mistakes	
Mistake-contingent encouragement	Encouragement given to an athlete following a mistake
Mistake-contingent technical instruction	Instructing or demonstrating to an athlete how to correct a mistake
Punishment	A negative reaction (verbal or nonverbal) following a mistake
Punitive technical instruction	Technical instruction following a mistake given in a punitive or hostile manner
Ignoring mistakes	Failure to respond to an athlete's mistake
Responses to misbehavior	
Keeping control	Reactions intended to restore or maintain order among team members
Class II: Spontaneous (Emitted) Behaviors	
Game related	
General technical instruction	Spontaneous instruction in the techniques and strategies of the sport (not following a mistake)
General encouragement	Spontaneous encouragement that does not follow a mistake
Organization	Administrative behavior that sets the stage for play by assigning, for example, duties, responsibilities, positions
Game irrelevant	
General communication	Interactions with athletes unrelated to the game/practice

Source: Adapted from Smith, Smoll, and Hunt, 1977.

engaged in high levels of positive reinforcement for both desirable performance and effort, who responded to mistakes with encouragement and technical instruction, and who emphasized the importance of fun and personal improvement over winning. Not only did the children who had such coaches like their coaches more and have more fun, but they also liked their teammates more.

A study of 268 male and female youth basketball players yielded similar results to those discussed earlier (Cumming, Smoll, Smith, & Grossbard, 2007). The athletes' attitudes toward the coach were positively associated with perceptions of a supportive, learning-oriented sport environment and negatively associated with perceptions of a coaching climate that emphasized gaining superiority over others. Win-loss percentages positively predicted players' evaluations of their coach's knowledge and teaching ability, but accounted for far less attitudinal variance than did measures of the coaching climate. Moreover, young athletes' sport enjoyment and evaluations of their coach were more strongly related to coaching behaviors than to their team's win-loss record. Indeed, in terms of athletes' ratings of how much fun they had and how much they liked playing for their coach, our results showed that a positive coaching climate was about 10 times more influential than was the team's win-loss record.

Another important issue concerns the degree of accuracy with which coaches perceive their own behaviors. Correlations between CBAS-observed behaviors and coaches' ratings of how frequently they performed the behaviors were generally low and nonsignificant. The only actions on their self-report measure that correlated significantly (around .50) with the observational measures were the punitive behaviors. Overall, we found that children's ratings on the same perceived behavior scales correlated much more highly with CBAS measures than did the coaches' own reports! It thus appears that coaches were, for the most part, blissfully unaware of how they behaved and that athletes were more accurate perceivers of actual coach behaviors. Because behavior change requires an awareness of how one currently is behaving, this finding clearly indicated the need to increase coaches' self-awareness when developing an intervention program.

The data from one of our field studies were also used to test a hypothesis derived from a self-enhancement model of self-esteem (Smith & Smoll, 1990). This model posits that people who are low in self-esteem are particularly responsive to variations in supportiveness from others because they have a strong need for positive feedback from others (or, alternatively, because they find a lack of support to be highly aversive). This hypothesis was strongly supported by the data; the greatest difference in liking for supportive (reinforcing and encouraging) versus nonsupportive coaches was found for children who were low in self-esteem. Also consistent with a self-enhancement model, boys with low self-esteem showed the greatest difference in attraction toward (i.e., liking for) coaches who were either quite high or quite low on a behavioral dimension identified through factor analysis as instructiveness (general technical instruction and mistake-contingent technical

instruction versus general communication and general encouragement). Instructiveness should be relevant to self-enhancement because athletes are likely to perceive such behaviors as contributing to skill increments that would increase positive self-regard.

Assessing the Efficacy of a Coach-Training Program

Sweeping conclusions are often drawn about the efficacy of intervention programs in the absence of anything approximating acceptable scientific evidence. We therefore felt it was important not only to develop an empirical foundation for a coach-training program but also to measure its effects on coaches and the youngsters who play for them.

Our intervention, which is known as Coach Effectiveness Training (CET), was conceptualized within a cognitive-behavioral framework (Bandura, 1986). It was specifically designed to train coaches to provide a more positive and socially supportive athletic environment for their young athletes. In an initial field experiment (Smith, Smoll, & Curtis, 1979), 31 Little League Baseball coaches were randomly assigned either to an experimental (training) group or to a no-treatment control group. During a preseason CET workshop, behavioral guidelines derived from our earlier research were presented and modeled by the trainers. In addition to the information-modeling portion of the program, behavioral feedback and self-monitoring procedures were employed in an attempt to increase the coaches' self-awareness of their behaviors and to encourage them to comply with the coaching guidelines. To provide behavioral feedback, observers trained in the use of the CBAS observed experimental group coaches for two complete games. Behavioral profiles for each coach were derived from these observations and were then mailed to the coaches so that they were able to see the distribution of their own behaviors. Trained coaches were also given brief self-monitoring forms that they completed immediately after the first 10 games of the season.

To assess the effects of the experimental program, CBAS data were collected throughout the season, and behavioral profiles were generated for each coach in the experimental and control groups. Postseason outcome measures were obtained from 325 children in individual data collection sessions in their homes. On both observed behavior and player perception measures, the trained coaches differed from the controls in a manner consistent with the coaching guidelines. The trained coaches gave more reinforcement in response to good performance and effort, and they responded to mistakes with more encouragement and technical instruction and with fewer punitive responses. These behavioral differences were, in turn, reflected in their players' attitudes. Although the average win-loss percentages of the two groups of coaches did not differ, the trained coaches were better liked and were rated as better teachers. Additionally, players on their teams liked one another more and enjoyed their sport experiences more. These results seemingly reflect the more socially supportive environment created by the trained coaches. Perhaps most encouraging was the fact that children who played for the trained coaches exhibited a significant increase on a measure of general self-esteem compared to scores obtained a year earlier, while those who played for the untrained coaches showed no significant change.

Replication of our research on the efficacy of CET has been conducted with the inclusion of several additional outcome measures. The study included 18 coaches and 152 children who participated in three Little League Baseball programs. Using a quasi-experimental design, one league (eight teams) was designated as the experimental group. The no-treatment control group included 10 teams from two other leagues. Prior to the season, the experimental group coaches participated in CET. The control coaches participated in a technical skills training workshop conducted by the Seattle Mariners baseball team. To assess the effects of CET, preseason and postseason data were collected for 62 and 90 children in the experimental and control groups, respectively. The study yielded four major results.

- CET intervention resulted in player-perceived behavioral differences between trained and untrained coaches that were consistent with the behavioral guidelines. Thus, as in previous research (Smith et al., 1979), the experimental manipulation was successful in promoting a more desirable pattern of coaching behaviors.

- Behavioral differences resulting from the CET program were accompanied by player evaluative responses that favored the trained coaches. They were better liked and rated as better teachers; and their players reported more fun playing baseball, and a higher level of attraction among teammates, despite the fact that their teams did not differ from controls in win-loss records.

- Consistent with a self-esteem enhancement model, children with low self-esteem who played for the trained coaches exhibited a significant increase in general self-esteem over the course of the season; youngsters with low self-esteem in the control group did not change (Smoll, Smith, Barnett, & Everett, 1993).

- Children who played for the CET coaches manifested lower levels of performance anxiety than did the control children (Smith, Smoll, & Barnett, 1995).

An extension of the above study was completed one year after the CET intervention. At the beginning of the next baseball season, dropout rates were assessed for youngsters who had played for the two groups of coaches. The results showed a 26 percent dropout rate among the control group, a figure that was quite consistent with previous reports of 22 to 59 percent annual attrition rates in youth sport programs (Gould, 1987). In contrast, only 5 percent of the children who had played for the CET-trained coaches failed to return to the sport program in the next season (Barnett, Smoll, & Smith, 1992).

Other sport psychologists have utilized our research findings and CET principles in developing psychologically oriented training programs for youth sport coaches. Evaluations of the derivative interventions have shown positive changes in both observed and athlete-perceived coaching behaviors that are consistent with the interventions' behavioral guidelines. Moreover, evidence indicates that young athletes who played for trained coaches experienced beneficial effects as reflected by measures of their psychosocial development (e.g., Coatsworth & Conroy, 2006; Conroy & Coatsworth, 2004; Sousa, Cruz, Torregrosa, Vilches, & Viladrich, 2006; Sousa, Smith, & Cruz, 2008).

Achievement Goals, Motivational Climate, and Coaching

The sport environment is inherently a competence and achievement context. Consequently, motivational factors play an important role in determining the ultimate effects of participation on psychosocial development. As a theoretical framework, achievement goal theory provides an appropriate vantage point from which to explore factors (e.g., coach behaviors) that might affect motivated behavior in youth sports. Achievement goal theory (Ames, 1992a; Dweck, 1999; Nicholls, 1989) focuses on understanding the function and the meaning of goal directed actions, based on how participants define ability and how they judge whether or not they have demonstrated competence. Although a variety of variables are incorporated into achievement goal theory (e.g., goal states, attributions, fear of failure, self-perceived competence, incremental and entity implicit theories of competence), two of the central constructs have received particular attention in the sport literature namely, individual *goal orientations* that guide achievement perceptions and behavior, and the *motivational climate* created within adult-controlled achievement settings. An overview of these constructs as related to coach-athlete interactions follows. Comprehensive discussions of achievement goal theory and its implications for coaching practice appear elsewhere (e.g., Chapter 4; Duda & Balaguer, 2007; Duda & Ntoumanis, 2005; Roberts, Treasure, & Conroy, 2007).

Goal orientations.   In essence, goal orientations involve the criteria individuals use to define success. This dispositional variable is a product of and contributes to (along with situational factors) goal involvement states in achievement situations.

Achievement goal theory focuses on mastery and ego orientations and states. When an individual is in a mastery state, success is defined in a self-referenced manner and is focused on skill development, task mastery, and exerting maximum effort. In a sense, mastery-oriented people compare themselves with themselves. They can feel success and satisfaction when they have learned something new, witnessed skill improvement in themselves, or given maximum effort.

In an ego state, social comparison plays a major role in self-perceived success, and the emphasis is on outperforming others in order to attain recognition and status. Thus, ego-oriented people define success as winning or being better than others. They are always comparing themselves with others and don't feel successful unless they view themselves as performing better than others. Anything short of victory is failure and indicates to them that they are inferior.

Historically, several different labels have been attached to the two major classes of achievement goal orientations. *Mastery* and *task* have been used interchangeably by various theorists and researchers, as have *ego* and *performance* (e.g., Ames, 1992a, 1992b; Duda & Whitehead, 1998; Dweck, 1986; Midgely et al., 2000; Nicholls, 1989; Roberts, Treasure, & Kavussanu, 1997). We find the terms *mastery* and *ego* to be more semantically meaningful in relation to the underlying constructs, as well as the characteristics of the measures developed to assess them (Cumming, Smith, Smoll, Standage, & Grossbard, 2008; Smith, Cumming, & Smoll, 2008). Thus, we have chosen these labels for use in our work.

Motivational climate.   Achievement goal theory also addresses environmental factors that foster mastery or ego involvement. Because achievement behavior is influenced by interacting personal and situational factors, situational factors can predispose individuals to enter particular goal states and, over time, to acquire a disposition toward experiencing mastery or ego goal states. This is influenced, however, by the way in which relevant adults structure the situation and define success (Ames, 1992a, 1992b). A mastery climate is one in which teachers, coaches, or parents define success in terms of self-improvement, task mastery, and exhibiting maximum effort and dedication. In such a climate, students and athletes tend to adopt adaptive achievement strategies such as selecting challenging tasks, giving maximum effort, persisting in the face of setbacks, and taking pride in personal improvement. In both academic and sport settings, a wide range of salutary outcomes have been linked to a mastery-involving motivational climate, including a stronger mastery orientation on the part of participants, greater enjoyment and satisfaction, stronger intrinsic and self-determination motivation, group cohesion, and lower levels of performance anxiety.

In contrast, an ego-involving climate promotes social comparison as a basis for success judgments and tends to foster an ego achievement orientation. When coaches create an ego climate, they tend to give differential attention and concentrate positive reinforcement on athletes who are most competent and instrumental to winning, the importance of which is emphasized. Rivalry among teammates may be encouraged by comparing them openly with one another. Inadequate performance or mistakes are often punished with criticism, teaching athletes that mistakes are to be avoided at all costs and thereby building fear of failure. Another unfortunate outcome associated with ego environments is the willingness to win at all costs, even if rule-breaking is required to gain the needed advantage.

The Mastery Approach to Coaching

Inspired in part by the impressive research outcomes associated with a mastery-oriented climate, we redesigned CET to fit the framework of achievement goal theory. The new program, which is called the Mastery Approach to Coaching (MAC), incorporates content on goal orientations and motivational climate and includes specific guidelines on how to create a mastery climate. Accordingly, MAC behavioral guidelines focus on two major themes. First, it strongly emphasizes the distinction between positive versus aversive control of behavior (see Chapter 3).

In a series of coaching *do's* and *don'ts* derived from the foundational research on coaching behaviors and their effects, coaches are encouraged to increase four specific behaviors—positive reinforcement, mistake-contingent encouragement, corrective instruction given in a positive and encouraging fashion, and sound technical instruction. Coaches are urged to avoid nonreinforcement of positive behaviors, punishment for mistakes, and punitive technical instruction following mistakes. They are also instructed how to establish team rules and reinforce compliance with them to avoid discipline problems, and to reinforce socially supportive behaviors among team members. These guidelines, which are summarized in Appendix A, are designed to increase positive coach–athlete interactions, enhance team solidarity, reduce fear of failure, and promote a positive atmosphere for skill development (Smith & Smoll, 2012).

The second important theme in MAC guidelines, derived from CET and also from achievement goal theory and research, is a conception of success as giving maximum effort and becoming the best one can be, rather than an emphasis on winning or outperforming others. Coaches are encouraged to emphasize and reinforce effort as well as outcome, to help their athletes become the best they can be by giving individualized attention to all athletes and by setting personalized goals for improvement, to define success as maximizing one's athletic potential, and to emphasize the importance of having fun and getting better as opposed to winning at all costs. Like the guidelines that foster positive coach–athlete relations and team solidarity, these guidelines are designed to reduce fear of failure, to foster self-esteem enhancement by allowing athletes to take personal pride in effort and improvement, and to create a more enjoyable learning environment that increases intrinsic motivation for the activity. The behavioral guidelines are thus consistent with the procedures designed by Ames (1992a, 1992b) and Epstein (1988, 1989) to create a mastery learning climate in the classroom.

In the tradition of CET, a field experiment was conducted to assess the effects of the newly evolved intervention on coaches' behaviors and on the athletes who played for them (Smith, Smoll, & Cumming, 2007; Smoll, Smith, & Cumming, 2007). Prior to the season, an experimental group of 20 basketball coaches participated in a 75-minute version of MAC. A control group of 16 coaches received no training. A total sample of 225 boys and girls, ranging in age from 10 to 14 years, responded to a variety of measures prior to and at the end of the season. Hierarchical linear modeling (multilevel modeling) analyses revealed several major findings.

- Late-season differences in athletes' reports of the coach-initiated motivational climate clearly supported the efficacy of the MAC intervention. In this regard, coaches in the experimental condition received significantly higher mastery-climate scores and lower ego-climate scores.

- In line with previous research on sport attrition (Barnett et al., 1992), youth who played for trained coaches were more likely to stay engaged on a daily basis in the program.

- Differential patterns of change occurred in achievement goal orientations over the course of the season. Athletes who played for MAC-trained coaches exhibited increases in mastery goal orientation scores and significant decreases in ego orientation scores. In contrast, athletes who played for control group coaches did not change in their goal orientations from preseason to late season.

- Paralleling a significant difference between intervention and control groups in sport-related mastery scores, a significant group difference was found on the mastery score of an academic achievement goal scale. This result suggests the importance of assessing generalization effects of sport-related interventions on athletes' functioning in other life domains.

- Young athletes who played for MAC-trained coaches showed significant decreases in both physical and mental components of sport anxiety, whereas control group youngsters increased in these measures across the season.

- The MAC intervention had equally positive effects on boys' and girls' teams.

Finally, some issues regarding experimental design deserve mention. In our initial CET field experiment, coaches were randomly assigned to the conditions (Smith et al., 1979). Fortunately, there was no difference in the mean win-loss percentages of teams coached by the experimental and control group coaches. Team success (winning) was thus ruled out as a plausible explanation for the differences obtained in the outcome variables. In the replication and extension studies, assignment to the experimental or control group was made by league rather than within leagues (Barnett et al., 1992; Smoll et al., 1993; Smith et al., 1995). Similarly, a matched quasi-experimental design was utilized in our evaluation of MAC (Smith et al., 2007; Smoll et al., 2007). Use of separate, intact groups helped to ensure the integrity of the intervention by reducing the possibility of contamination (communication of training guidelines to control coaches). Moreover, this procedure guaranteed that the average win-loss records of the teams in the experimental and control conditions would be an identical 50 percent.

Implementing Sport Psychology Workshops for Coaches

Creating a Positive Learning Environment

The most basic objectives of MAC and other sport psychology training programs are to communicate coaching principles in a way that is easy to understand and to maximize the likelihood that coaches will adopt the information. Because of this, the importance of creating a positive learning environment cannot be overemphasized. Even the very best program is of little value if presented in a way that creates antagonism and defensiveness on the part of coaches.

There are several considerations in setting the stage for a successful session. The primary key is to convey respect for the participating coaches. They really deserve it! Indeed, without their unselfish involvement, there could be no organized youth sports.

Next, at the very outset of a training session we emphasize that the coaches themselves have a great deal to offer as a result of their own experiences and associated practical knowledge. We attempt to take advantage of their expertise by encouraging them to share it with the group. In conducting a MAC workshop as a two-way sharing of information, coaches are treated as an integral part of the session rather than a mere audience. The open atmosphere for exchange promotes active rather than passive learning, and the dialogue serves to enhance the participants' interest and involvement in the learning process.

A final key to successful program implementation is to put a considerable amount of sincere enthusiasm into leading the session. When a trainer truly enjoys his or her pedagogical role, the pleasurable feeling ultimately carries over to the coaches. In such an atmosphere, attention and audience involvement is likely to be enhanced, increasing the enjoyment of coaches and trainer alike.

In contrast to the above, three strategies are virtually guaranteed to create hostility and resistance from coaches. One is to approach coaches in a condescending manner. In other words, the thing *not* to do is communicate how much you think you know and how little they know. An associated implication concerns the way a trainer is introduced at the beginning of a session. We recommend against presenting an extensive list of credentials and professional accomplishments, which tends to convey an air of elitism. Another contraindicated approach is to intimate that your training program is designed to protect athletes from coaches. Indeed, most volunteer coaches have commendable motives for coaching (Martens & Gould, 1979; Smith et al., 1978), and they generally make positive contributions to children's well-being. A final breach is to convey the impression that what the coaches have been doing is incorrect. Rather, we emphasize that many options are available for dealing with particular coaching situations, and although all of these tactics may work in *some* cases, certain procedures have a greater likelihood than others of being successful. By counteracting the notion of "right versus wrong," we stress the importance of flexibility and thus attempt to make coaches receptive to alternative ways of responding to specific circumstances.

Orientation to the Psychology of Coaching and a Mastery-Oriented Philosophy of Winning

In introducing the psychology of coaching, workshop participants should first be made aware of the importance of their role as coaches. Some coaches underestimate their influence, and they must be reminded of the many ways they can affect young athletes. Information and increased awareness of what they are doing can help them optimize the desirable effects they can have on young athletes.

It is generally believed that young athletes can learn from both winning and losing. But for this to occur, winning must be placed in a *healthy* perspective. We have therefore developed a four-part philosophy of winning that is taught in MAC (Smith & Smoll, 2012, pp. 27-28):

1. *Winning isn't everything, nor is it the only thing.* Young athletes cannot get the most out of sports if they think that the only objective is to beat their opponents. Although winning is an important goal, it is not the most important objective.

2. *Failure is not the same thing as losing.* It is important that athletes do not view losing as a sign of failure or as a threat to their personal value.

3. *Success is not equivalent to winning.* Neither success nor failure need depend on the outcome of a contest or on a win-loss record. Winning and losing pertain to the outcome of a contest, whereas success and failure do not.

4. *Athletes should be taught that success is found in striving for victory (that is, success is related to commitment and effort).* Athletes should be taught that they are never "losers" if they give maximum effort.

This philosophy is designed to maximize young athletes' enjoyment of sport and their chances of deriving the benefits of participation, partly as a result of combating competitive anxiety (Smith, Smoll, & Passer, 2002). Although seeking victory is encouraged, the ultimate importance of winning is reduced relative to other participation motives. In recognition of the inverse relation between enjoyment and postcompetition stress, *fun* is highlighted as the paramount objective. The philosophy also promotes separation of the athlete's feelings of self-worth from the game's outcome, which serves to help overcome fear of failure.

Because they tend to project adult values onto children, many coaches seem to believe that how their athletes feel about them hinges on how successfully the team performs. Yet, as noted earlier, our own research has shown that differences in coaching behaviors consistently accounted for significantly more variance in player attitudes toward the coach than did win-loss records (Cumming, Smoll, et al., 2007; Smith et al., 1978). Stressing this finding to coaches tends to make them more receptive to the philosophy of winning that we espouse.

Presenting an Empirical Basis for Coach-Training Programs

We believe in the importance of establishing an empirical foundation for training guidelines, but we also feel that the ability to present supportive evidence increases the credibility of the guidelines for the coaches. A MAC workshop therefore includes a description of the differences between a mastery- and ego-oriented motivational climate. The creation of a mastery climate is strongly recommended, and a list of salutary effects of such a climate is presented.

A number of considerations underlie our commitment to presenting empirical results. First of all, expertise (special knowledge) and trustworthiness (the quality of meriting confidence) are two critically important variables in communicating credibility (Hovland, Janis, & Kelley, 1953; Petty & Wegener, 1998). Both are enhanced when data are presented rather than

intuitive beliefs. Coaches have greater confidence in a training program when they know the content is not merely composed of armchair psychology or athletic folklore. Second, the presence of empirical data arouses the curiosity and involvement of the participants. Coaches show a great deal of interest in the research, which stimulates their active involvement in the workshop. Also, presentation of unexpected results prevents either the trainer or the coaches from believing they already know all the answers. Third, the ability to demonstrate empirically that certain behaviors have positive effects on children serves to arouse the expectation that the coaches can produce similar effects if they themselves apply the behavioral guidelines. This may increase their motivation to learn and apply the information.

There are some practical points to be aware of in presenting empirical results. Trainers should use lay terms and avoid scientific jargon. It is best to present data as simply as possible and to avoid technical details. In addition, appropriate use of visual aids enhances any presentation. Diagrams and cartoons illustrating certain concepts, and tables summarizing important principles, serve to facilitate comprehension and retention.

Behavioral Guidelines and Their Presentation

The core of a MAC training session consists of a series of empirically derived behavioral guidelines. As discussed earlier, the coaching guidelines are based primarily on (a) social influence techniques that involve principles of positive control rather than aversive control, and (b) a mastery-oriented philosophy of winning.

Didactic procedures. In a MAC workshop, behavioral guidelines are presented both verbally and in a printed manual given to the coaches. The manual (Smoll & Smith, 2009) supplements the guidelines with concrete suggestions for communicating effectively with young athletes, gaining their respect, and relating effectively to their parents. The importance of sensitivity and being responsive to individual differences among athletes is also stressed. The manual eliminates the need for coaches to take notes; it facilitates their understanding of the information; and it gives coaches a tangible resource to refer to in the future.

Audiovisual aids to a presentation are necessary for providing a multisensory stimulus and for countering the potential influence of "verbalism"—the tendency to place excessive reliance on words. In MAC, animated PowerPoint slides and cartoons illustrating important points are used to present key principles and add to the organizational quality of the session. A word of caution is in order here. We have witnessed the collapse of several commendable presentations because of the failure of one or more electronic devices. Murphy's Law—if anything can go wrong it will—should be taken seriously when preparing to give a coaching workshop that includes audio or visual aids. An essential *preworkshop* procedure should thus include an operational check of each piece of equipment. (See Howell and Borman [1997] for an overview of audio and visual aids and their use.)

In introducing coaching guidelines, we emphasize that they should not be viewed as a "magic formula" and that mere knowledge of the principles is not sufficient. We stress that the challenge is not so much in learning the principles; they are relatively simple. Rather, the challenge is for the coach to integrate the guidelines into his or her own coaching style. When coaches believe that adoption of the guidelines is a result of their own dedication and effort, they are more likely to attribute behavioral changes to themselves rather than to the trainer. This approach is supported by evidence that self-attributed behavioral changes are more enduring than those attributed to some outside causal agent (Deci & Ryan, 1987).

As noted earlier, MAC workshops are conducted with an interactive format to encourage active participatory learning (Brookfield, 2004). Efforts are made to draw coaches into a discussion of the guidelines as opposed to using an exclusively lecture-type approach. This is accomplished by directing questions to the coaches and then relating their responses to the written

materials. To use this instructional style, a trainer must be well versed in the practical ramifications of the guidelines, their applicability to various kinds of coaching situations, and the kinds of questions they are likely to elicit from coaches.

A practical problem occurs when coaches ask questions that are unrelated to the topic being covered. For example, during a discussion of principles of reinforcement, a coach might inquire about formulating team rules. Our experience indicates that answering such questions disrupts the sequencing and continuity of concepts, which causes confusion for some coaches. A tactful procedure is to politely ask the coach to write down the question and to indicate when he or she should repeat the query.

What are the secrets of effective, engaging presentations? In answering this question, Chamberlin (2000) interviewed six university faculty members, each of whom was known for delivering outstanding lectures. Their recommendations are presented here, along with comments by the professors.

- *Prepare, prepare, prepare.* Practicing the workshop is an excellent way to thoroughly learn the material and feel comfortable speaking and answering questions about the content. "Saying it out loud will highlight the sticky points and give you a chance to smooth those out beforehand. It feels like you run the risk of making the lecture stale, but the energy in the classroom will bring it to life and you feel like you are doing it for the first time" (p. 63). Some experienced teachers bring notes or a script to every class—even for those they have done dozens of times—and advise against trying to conduct a session cold. As one expert states, "I may never look at my typed notes, but I always have them there as a security blanket" (p. 63).

- *Find your style.* Seasoned lecturers warn about the mistake of emulating a mentor or favorite instructor. Rather, they emphasize the importance of performing in a way that reflects your own style. "Your personality is a part of your lecturing so you have to lecture in a way that is comfortable to your personality"

(p. 63). In other words, do what feels right. And, as noted earlier, whatever your approach, make enthusiasm a big part of it. "Enthusiasm is infectious. If you're not excited about the material, they're not going to be either" (p. 63).

- *Spice it up.* The use of intermittent stories and anecdotes can enliven your presentation. Weaving in personal sport stories or linking coaching principles to current research and events helps keep workshop participants engaged. One trap to avoid is relying solely on computer graphics and technology to add flavor to a workshop. As a master teacher claims, "I have sat through far too many sleep-inducing PowerPoint presentations that have had a lot of power and no point" (p. 63).

- *Cover less, not more.* Another pitfall is packing too much content into a workshop because of the fear that coaches will not learn certain material if it is not included in the session. Trainers who try to cover too much inevitably end up going too fast. In this regard, "Less is more. . . . Go slowly and thoughtfully through the material" (p. 64). Additionally, one of the benefits of providing participants with a workshop manual is that they can obtain considerable information by reading on their own.

- *Make improvements.* Avoid doing the same thing over and over, even though it is not working. If your presentation style is not effective, be committed and courageous enough to change it. An initial step toward improvement is to find out how you are doing by asking coaches for feedback, especially if you feel they are not responding well to your style or are not learning. Furthermore, do not get discouraged when you have a bad workshop. With sufficient dedication and effort, you will nail it and feel great the next time.

Credibility and persuasiveness. A primary goal of our instructional approach is to change coaches' attitudes about some of their roles and responsibilities and about their use of certain coaching behaviors. Several aspects of the persuasion process, such as credibility, trustworthiness, likeability, and novelty, are utilized and have proven to be effective in a variety of intervention contexts (see Petty & Wegener, 1998; Taylor, Peplau, & Sears, 2005; Worchel, Cooper, & Goethals, 1991). In terms of personal characteristics, a highly *credible* communicator is more effective in changing attitudes than one with low credibility. As Galbraith (2004) emphasized, "common sense tells us that being technically proficient in the content area within the teaching and learning encounter is paramount if it is going to have some meaning and value" (p. 4). Although the best-qualified workshop presenter would be a certified sport psychologist/consultant (e.g., through the Association for Applied Sport Psychology), a well-structured "train the trainer" program should allow a youth sport administrator to present a satisfactory version. However, this hypothesis requires empirical validation.

Credibility is a multifaceted concept that seems to be a function of at least *expertise* and *trustworthiness*. As stated earlier, we endeavor to establish expertise in MAC by substantiating the content with empirical evidence from our own work and from the research of other sport psychologists as well. With respect to trusting a communicator's intentions, credibility increases when the communicator does not appear to be purposefully trying to persuade the target (i.e., coaches in this case). We therefore present information and coaching guidelines objectively, and as noted earlier, we specifically avoid a "right versus wrong" orientation. In addition, because unexpected positions are generally seen as more trustworthy, we inform coaches that although we have been studying coach–athlete interactions for more than 30 years we simply do not have all the answers, and in some cases one must be willing to say, "I don't know." The honesty of such disclosures likely contributes to credibility.

The perceived *similarity* between a communicator and the target of the message affects the power of persuasion. To increase the degree of perceived similarity with coaches, we customarily dress in a fairly casual style. More important, while leading discussions, we share examples from our own experiences as athletes and coaches, and we often phrase comments with a "we" versus "you" perspective.

The communicator's *likability* also affects the efficacy of persuasion. Because liking works by identification, we try to create a warm, friendly rapport with coaches—partly by showing enjoyment in being with them and by expressing caring for them. Empirical work from the communication studies literature suggests that teachers' behavioral cues of interpersonal warmth and students' perceptions of those behaviors are predictive of a variety of desirable learning outcomes, including students' liking for the material and their intentions to act on what they have learned (Friedrich & Douglass, 1998). Accordingly, we strive to be more persuasive agents by honestly and sincerely engaging in behaviors that are known to communicate caring for learners, such as gesturing while lecturing, modulating one's voice, making eye contact, smiling, and self-disclosing. Reciprocity is another factor that increases liking: People tend to like those who like them. We communicate our high esteem for coaches by praising their commitment to providing high-quality sport experiences for young athletes. Listening ability is yet another factor in being likable. By encouraging coaches to express themselves freely, and by listening attentively to them when they do, we are better able to conduct a MAC workshop as a mutual sharing of information.

In addition to characteristics of the communicator, several facets of the message affect its persuasiveness. Coaches are generally not opposed to the points of view advocated in MAC, so we usually present *one-sided* communications. In some instances, however, we use *two-sided* presentation. This involves more than just acknowledging that another side exists. Rather, this approach analyzes contrary perspectives to point out their deficiencies and thus strengthen our position. For example, in discussing recommendations relative to reinforcement, the coaching guidelines are developed fully, and their beneficial effects are substantiated with empirical evidence. Then, when aversive control is considered, we proceed to point out the disadvantages of using punitive coaching behaviors. (See Chapter 3 for a discussion of the negative side effects of punishment.)

Using *rhetorical questions* is another way of influencing attitudes. We ask coaches rhetorical questions (questions to which no answer is expected) to stimulate their thinking and to make them pay closer attention to a communication. For example, "What is the best way to maintain order and teach self-discipline?"

Novelty of information also affects the message's impact. Some coaches may have had previous exposure to some of MAC's behavioral guidelines. We attempt to make the principles seem unique by using diagrams, charts, and cartoons for their presentation.

Finally, *humor* can enhance the persuasiveness of messages. If used properly, humor can loosen up a potentially tense atmosphere, make people feel good, increase their responsiveness, and reveal a more human side of the speaker (Barker & Gaut, 2002). Moreover, research suggests that humor produces psychological and physiological benefits that help students learn (Stambor, 2006). We use humorous anecdotes whenever possible—not primarily for entertainment but as an educational tool to help emphasize certain points and make concepts memorable. This objective is best accomplished by strongly establishing the link between humor and the point to be made such that coaches remember the key point, not just the good joke or story (Farrah, 2004).

Modeling. The instructional procedures described above contain many *verbal* modeling cues that essentially tell coaches what to do. Information is also transmitted through *behavioral* modeling cues (i.e., demonstrations showing coaches how to behave in desirable ways). In MAC such cues are presented by a live model (the trainer) and by symbolic models (animated coach cartoons), as many forms of modeling have been shown to be highly effective in changing behavior (Bandura, 1986; Perry & Furukawa, 1986).

Role playing. Coaches are kept actively involved in the training process through presentation of critical situations and opportunities for them to role-play appropriate ways of responding. This form of behavioral rehearsal has great promise in enhancing acquisition of desired behaviors, in providing the opportunity to practice the behaviors, and in establishing an increased level of participant involvement during the workshops.

Increasing Self-Awareness and Compliance with Coaching Guidelines

One of the striking findings from our basic research was that coaches had very limited awareness of how often they behaved in various ways (Smith et al., 1978). Thus, an important goal of MAC is to increase coaches' awareness of what they are doing, for no change is likely to occur without it. MAC coaches are taught the use of two proven behavioral-change techniques, namely, behavioral feedback and self-monitoring.

Behavioral feedback.   To obtain feedback, coaches are encouraged to work with their assistants as a team and share descriptions of each other's behaviors (Edelstein & Eisler, 1976; Huberman & O'Brien, 1999). They can discuss alternate ways of dealing with difficult situations and athletes and prepare themselves for dealing with similar situations in the future. Other potential feedback procedures include coaches soliciting input from athletes and provision of feedback by a league committee.

Self-monitoring.   Another behavioral-change technique that has the potential for increasing coaches' awareness of their own behavioral patterns and encouraging their compliance with the guidelines is self-monitoring (observing and recording one's own behavior). This method of self-regulation has proved to be an effective behavioral-change procedure in a variety of intervention contexts (Crews, Lochbaum, & Karoly, 2001; Kanfer & Gaelick-Buys, 1991). Because it is impractical to have coaches monitor and record their own behavior during practices or games, the workshop manual contains a brief self-monitoring form. To achieve optimal results, coaches are encouraged to complete the form on a regular basis after practices and games (see Appendix B).

A Final Word

Given the ever-expanding nature of youth sports, the need for effective coach-training programs is obvious. Likewise, the large coach turnover from year to year creates a continuing demand for intervention. Our experience in offering workshops has shown that youth coaches are committed to providing positive experiences for youngsters; they are willing to spend time to acquire additional information, and they do take advantage of the availability of workshops. An important feature of MAC is that it is a brief program that focuses on a relatively small number of critical principles and guidelines that clearly make a difference.

In concluding this chapter, it is appropriate to reaffirm that coach-training programs *must* be evidence based. Indeed, the justification presented earlier can be expanded with respect to the issue of social accountability/responsibility. Coach training has become a large-scale commercial enterprise in the United States—most notably the American Sport Education Program (www.asep.com), the National Youth Sports Coaches Association program (www.nays.com), and the Positive Coaching Alliance (www.positivecoach.org). Unfortunately, however, virtually nothing is known about what effects these programs have on coaches and athletes and how well they achieve their objectives. The absence of empirical attention is understandable, as proprietors of these programs have focused primarily on dissemination rather than evaluation, and they have not had the benefit of research grants to support their work. We firmly believe that evaluation research is not only desirable, but essential. In the words of Lipsey and Cordray (2000), "the overarching goal of the program evaluation enterprise is to contribute to the improvement of social conditions by providing scientifically credible information and balanced judgment to legitimate social agents about the effectiveness of interventions intended to produce social benefits" (p. 346). It follows that efforts to improve the quality of coaching are best achieved by delivering evidence-based programs, and we strongly encourage sport psychologists to do this.

Summary

We have described the development and evaluation of an empirically supported intervention designed to assist coaches in providing a more positive and growth-inducing athletic experience for athletes. This chapter provides guidelines in how to present such a program. We describe the principles and ways we have found successful in presenting them with maximum positive impact. As noted in the chapter, there are several virtues of presenting a program that is based on scientific data rather than on experiential knowledge or speculation. First, you can have greater confidence in the principles you are presenting. Even more important is the approach you can take in presenting the principles. You can present your workshop as informational in nature. In other words, you can play to coaches' desires to provide the best possible experience for youngsters (the prevailing motivation for most volunteer coaches). You are not telling them what they "should do," but rather what research has shown to be effective in helping them meet their goals and how they can incorporate these findings into their own coaching style. We have always found coaches receptive to this approach. By communicating simple but sound principles and showing coaches how to implement them and become more self-aware, you provide tools that they can apply immediately. Once they begin doing so, the positive responses from athletes and the reduced need to maintain discipline through punitive means provide powerful sources of reinforcement that strengthen and maintain the new behaviors. Many a coach has reported that applying the MAC principles resulted in the most enjoyable season they had experienced in their coaching tenures, an outcome that is highly reinforcing to the trainer as well.

Study Questions

1. Explain why *evidence-based* coach-training programs are superior to interventions that are primarily founded on *experiential knowledge*.

2. Describe the three basic elements of the mediational model of coach–athlete interactions that served to guide the coaching-behavior research.

3. What are the two major classes of behaviors included in the CBAS, and what is the difference between them?

4. Following development of the CBAS, field studies were conducted to establish relations between coaching behaviors and children's evaluative reactions. Describe the basic research procedures, and discuss the major findings with respect to (a) the role of winning relative to athletes' psychosocial outcome measures, (b) relations between coaching behaviors and athletes' attitudinal responses, (c) the degree of accuracy with which coaches perceived their own behaviors, and (d) the role of self-esteem as a mediator variable in coaching behavior athlete-attitude relations.

5. Describe the research design and methodology incorporated in the studies that tested the efficacy of CET. What were the results with respect to (a) behavioral differences between trained and untrained coaches, (b) win-loss records, (c) players' evaluative reactions to trained and untrained coaches, (d) self-esteem effects, (e) competitive anxiety

differences between youngsters who played for trained and untrained coaches, and (f) dropout rates?

6. With respect to achievement goal theory, what are the distinctions between (a) mastery and ego goal orientations, and (b) mastery and ego motivational climates?

7. Briefly describe the (a) major behavioral guidelines (i.e., coaching *do's* and *don'ts*), and (b) mastery-oriented philosophy of winning that are emphasized in the MAC program.

8. For the field experiment that was conducted to assess the efficacy of MAC, what were the results with respect to (a) differences between the motivational climates created by trained and untrained coaches, (b) differences in sport attrition for athletes who played for trained versus untrained coaches, (c) differential patterns of change in athletes' achievement goal orientations, (d) group differences in athletes' academic achievement goals, (e) group differences in athletes' sport performance anxiety, and (f) differential effects for male and female athletes?

9. In implementing sport psychology workshops for coaches, the trainer should create a positive learning environment. What are some ways to foster a receptive and cooperative attitude on the part of coaches? What approaches should be avoided?

10. Describe the components of the healthy philosophy of winning that is taught in MAC, and indicate how this orientation is designed to combat competitive anxiety.

11. In conducting a MAC workshop, what is the rationale/justification for presenting empirical results to coaches?

12. What are the advantages of conducting coach-training programs with an interactive format, and how might this be accomplished?

13. Discuss the key points associated with the following recommendations for making effective presentations: (a) prepare, prepare, prepare; (b) find your style; (c) spice it up; (d) cover less, not more; and (e) make improvements.

14. With respect to changing coaches' attitudes during a training program, explain how the following aspects of the persuasion process might be taken into account: (a) credibility (expertise and trustworthiness) of the trainer, (b) perceived similarity between the trainer and the coaches, (c) likability of the trainer, (d) one-sided versus two-sided communications, (e) use of rhetorical questions, (f) novelty of information, and (g) use of humor.

15. Describe the procedures that can be utilized to increase coaches' self-awareness and their compliance with coaching guidelines.

References

Ames, C. (1992a). Classrooms: Goals, structures, and student motivation. *Journal of Educational Psychology, 84,* 261–271.

Ames, C. (1992b). Achievement goals and adaptive motivational patterns: The role of the environment. In G. C. Roberts (Ed.), *Motivation in sport and exercise* (pp. 161–176). Champaign, IL: Human Kinetics.

Bandura, A. (1986). *Social foundations of thought and action: A social cognitive theory.* Englewood Cliffs, NJ: Prentice Hall.

Barker, L. L., & Gaut, D. R. (2002). *Communication* (8th ed.). Upper Saddle River, NJ: Pearson.

Barnett, N. P., Smoll, F. L., & Smith, R. E. (1992). Effects of enhancing coach–athlete relationships on youth sport attrition. *The Sport Psychologist, 6,* 111–127.

Brookfield, S. D. (2004). Discussion. In M. W. Galbraith (Ed.), *Adult learning methods: A guide for effective instruction* (3rd ed., pp. 209–226). Malabar, FL: Krieger.

Chamberlin, J. (2000, December). Stand and deliver. *Monitor on Psychology, 31,* 62–64.

Coatsworth, J. D., & Conroy, D. E. (2006). Enhancing the self-esteem of youth swimmers through coach training: Gender and age effects. *Psychology of Sport and Exercise, 7,* 173–192.

Conroy, D. E., & Coatsworth, J. D. (2004). The effects of coach training on fear of failure in youth swimmers: A latent growth curve analysis from a randomized, controlled trial. *Journal of Applied Developmental Psychology, 25,* 193–214.

Crews, D. J., Lochbaum, M. R., & Karoly, P. (2001). Self-regulation: Concepts, methods and strategies in sport and exercise. In R. N. Singer, H. A. Hausenblaus, & C. M. Janelle (Eds.), *Handbook of research on sport psychology* (2nd ed., pp. 566–584). New York: John Wiley & Sons.

Cumming, S. P., Smith, R. E., Smoll, F. L., Standage, M., & Grossbard, J. R. (2008). Development and validation of the Achievement Goal Scale for Youth Sports. *Psychology of Sport and Exercise, 9,* 686–703.

Cumming, S. P., Smoll, F. L., Smith, R. E., & Grossbard, J. R. (2007). Is winning everything? The relative contributions of motivational climate and won-lost percentage in youth sports. *Journal of Applied Sport Psychology, 19,* 322–336.

Curtis, B., Smith, R. E., & Smoll, F. L. (1979). Scrutinizing the skipper: A study of leadership behaviors in the dugout. *Journal of Applied Psychology, 64,* 391–400.

Deci, E. L., & Ryan, R. M. (1987). The support of autonomy and the control of behavior. *Journal of Personality and Social Psychology, 53,* 1024–1037.

Duda, J. L., & Balaguer, I. (2007). Coach-created motivational climate. In S. Jowett & D. Lavallee (Eds.), *Social psychology in sport* (pp. 117–130). Champaign, IL: Human Kinetics.

Duda, J. L., & Ntoumanis, N. (2005). After-school sport for children: Implications of task-involving motivational climate. In J. L. Mahoney, R. W. Larson, & J. S. Eccles (Eds.), *Organized activities as contexts of development: Extracurricular activities, after school, and community programs* (pp. 311–330). Mahwah, NJ: Erlbaum.

Duda J. L., & Whitehead, J. (1998). Measurement of goal perspectives in the physical domain. In J. L. Duda (Ed.), *Advances in sport and exercise psychology measurement* (pp. 21–48). Morgantown, WV: Fitness Information Technology.

Dweck, C. S. (1986). Motivational processes affecting learning. *American Psychologist, 41,* 1040–1048.

Dweck, C. S. (1999). *Self-theories and goals: Their role in motivation, personality, and development.* Philadelphia: Taylor & Francis.

Edelstein, B. A., & Eisler, R. M. (1976). Effects of modeling and modeling with instructions and feedback on the behavioral components of social skills. *Behavior Therapy, 7,* 382–389.

Epstein, J. (1988). Effective schools or effective students? Dealing with diversity. In R. Haskins & B. MacRae (Eds.), *Policies for America's schools* (pp. 89–126). Norwood, NJ: Ablex.

Epstein, J. (1989). Family structures and students motivation: A developmental perspective. In C. Ames & R. Ames (Eds.), *Research on motivation in education: Vol. 3. Goals and cognitions* (pp. 259–295). New York: Academic Press.

Farrah, S. J. (2004). Lecture. In M. W. Galbraith (Ed.), *Adult learning methods: A guide for effective instruction* (3rd ed., pp. 227–271). Malabar, FL: Krieger.

Friedrich, J., & Douglass, D. (1998). Ethics and the persuasive enterprise of teaching psychology. *American Psychologist, 53,* 549–562.

Galbraith, M. W. (2004). The teacher of adults. In M. W. Galbraith (Ed.), *Adult learning methods: A guide for effective instruction* (3rd ed., pp. 3–21). Malabar, FL: Krieger.

Gould, D. (1987). Understanding attrition in children's sport. In D. Gould & M. R. Weiss (Eds.), *Advances in pediatric sport sciences: Vol. 2. Behavioral issues* (pp. 61–85). Champaign, IL: Human Kinetics.

Grove, W. M., & Meehl, P. E. (1996). Comparative efficiency of informal (subjective, impressionistic) and formal (mechanical, algorithmic) prediction procedures: The clinical-statistical controversy. *Psychology: Public Policy and Law, 2,* 293–323.

Hovland, C. I., Janis, I. L., & Kelley, H. H. (1953). *Communication and persuasion.* New Haven, CT: Yale University Press.

Howell. W. S., & Borman, E. G. (1997). *The process of presentational speaking* (2nd ed.), Boston: Allyn and Bacon.

Huberman, W. L., & O'Brien, R. M. (1999). Improving therapist and patient performance in chronic psychiatric group homes through goal-setting, feedback, and positive reinforcement. *Journal of Organizational Behavior Management, 19,* 13–36.

Institute of Medicine (2001). *Crossing the quality chasm: A new health system for the 21st century.* Washington, DC: Author.

Kanfer, F. H., & Gaelick-Buys, L. (1991). Self-management methods. In F. H. Kanfer & A. P. Goldstein (Eds.), *Helping people change: A textbook of methods* (4th ed., pp. 305–360). Boston: Allyn and Bacon.

Lipsey, M. W., & Cordray, D. S. (2000). Evaluation methods for social intervention. *Annual Review of Psychology, 51,* 345–376.

Martens, R., & Gould, D. (1979). Why do adults volunteer to coach children's sports? In G. C. Roberts & K. M. Newell (Eds.), *Psychology of motor behavior and sport, 1978* (pp. 79–89). Champaign, IL: Human Kinetics.

McHugh, R. K., & Barlow, D. H. (2010). The dissemination and implementation of evidence-based psychological treatments. *American Psychologist, 65,* 73–84.

Midgley, C., Maehr, M. M., Hruda, L. M., Anderman, E., Anderman, L., Freeman, K. E., et al. (2000). *Manual for the Patterns of Adaptive Learning Scales.* Ann Arbor, MI: University of Michigan School of Education. Retrieved February 2, 2004, from http://www.umich.edu/~pals/pals

Nicholls, J. G. (1989). *The competitive ethos and democratic education.* Cambidge, MA: Harvard University Press.

Perry, M. A., & Furukawa, M. J. (1986). Modeling methods. In F. H. Kanfer & A. P. Goldstein (Eds.), *Helping people change: A textbook of methods* (3rd ed., pp. 66–110). New York: Pergamon.

Petty, R. E., & Wegener, D. T. (1998). Attitude change: Multiple roles for persuasion variables. In D. T. Gilbert, S. T. Fiske, & G. Lindzey (Eds.), *The handbook of social psychology, Vol. I* (4th ed., pp. 323–390). Boston: McGraw-Hill.

Roberts, G. C., Treasure, D. C., & Conroy, D. (2007). Understanding the dynamics of motivation in sport and physical activity: An achievement goal interpretation. In G. Tenenbaum & R. C. Eklund (Eds.), *Handbook of sport psychology* (3rd ed., pp. 3–30). Hoboken, NJ: Wiley.

Roberts, G. C., Treasure, D. C., & Kavussanu, M. (1997). Motivation in physical activity contexts: An achievement goal perspective. In M. L. Maehr & P. R. Pintrich (Eds.), *Advances in motivation and achievement* (Vol. 10, pp. 413–447). Greenwich, CT: JAI Press.

Smith, R. E., Cumming, S. P., & Smoll, F. L., (2008). Development and validation of the Motivational Climate Scale for Youth Sports. *Journal of Applied Sport Psychology, 20,* 116–136.

Smith, R. E., & Johnson, J. (1990). An organizational empowerment approach to consultation in professional baseball. *The Sport Psychologist, 4,* 347–357.

Smith, R. E., & Smoll, F. L. (1990). Self-esteem and children's reactions to youth sport coaching behaviors: A field study of self-enhancement processes. *Developmental Psychology, 26,* 987–993.

Smith, R. E., & Smoll, F. L. (2011). Cognitive-behavioral coach training: A translational approach to theory, research, and intervention. In J. K. Luiselli & D. D. Reed (Eds.), *Behavioral sport psychology: Evidence-based approaches to performance enhancement* (pp. 227–248). New York: Springer.

Smith, R. E., & Smoll, F. L. (2012). *Sport psychology for youth coaches: Developing champions in sports and life.* Lanham, MD: Rowman & Littlefield.

Smith, R. E., Smoll, F. L., & Barnett, N. P. (1995). Reduction of children's sport performance anxiety through social support and stress-reduction training for coaches. *Journal of Applied Developmental Psychology, 16,* 125–142.

Smith, R. E., Smoll. F. L., & Christensen, D. S. (1996). Behavioral assessment and interventions in youth sports. *Behavior Modification, 20,* 3–44.

Smith, R. E., Smoll, F. L., Cumming, S. P., & Grossbard, J. R. (2006). Measurement of multidimensional sport performance anxiety in children and adults: The Sport Anxiety Scale-2. *Journal of Sport & Exercise Psychology, 28,* 479–501.

Smith, R. E., Smoll, F. L., & Cumming, S. P. (2007). Effects of a motivational climate intervention for coaches on young athletes' sport performance anxiety. *Journal of Sport & Exercise Psychology, 29,* 39–59.

Smith, R. E., Smoll, F. L., & Curtis, B. (1978). Coaching behaviors in Little League Baseball. In F. L. Smoll & R. E. Smith (Eds.), *Psychological perspectives in youth sports* (pp. 173–201). Washington, DC: Hemisphere.

Smith, R. E., Smoll, F. L., & Curtis, B. (1979). Coach effectiveness training: A cognitive-behavioral approach to enhancing relationship skills in youth sport coaches. *Journal of Sport Psychology, 1,* 59–75.

Smith, R. E., Smoll, F. L., & Hunt, E. B. (1977). A system for the behavioral assessment of athletic coaches. *Research Quarterly, 48,* 401–407.

Smith, R. E., Smoll, F. L., & Passer, M. P. (2002). Sport performance anxiety in young athletes. In F. L. Smoll & R. E. Smith (Eds.), *Children and youth in sport: A biopsychosocial perspective* (2nd ed., pp. 501–536). Dubuque, IA: Kendall/Hunt.

Smith, R. E., Zane, N. W. S., Smoll, F. L., & Coppel, D. B. (1983). Behavioral assessment in youth sports: Coaching behaviors and children's attitudes. *Medicine and Science in Sports and Exercise, 15,* 208–214.

Smoll, F. L., & Smith. R. E. (1989). Leadership behaviors in sport: A theoretical model and research paradigm. *Journal of Applied Social Psychology, 19,* 1522–1551.

Smoll, F. L., & Smith, R. E. (2009). *Mastery Approach to Coaching: A leadership guide for youth sports.* Seattle, WA: Youth Enrichment in Sports.

Smoll, F. L., Smith, R. E., Barnett. N. P., & Everett, J. J. (1993). Enhancement of children's self-esteem through social support training for youth sport coaches. *Journal of Applied Psychology, 78,* 602–610.

Smoll, F. L., Smith, R. E., & Cumming, S. P. (2007). Effects of a motivational climate intervention for coaches on changes in young athletes' achievement goal orientations. *Journal of Clinical Sport Psychology, 1,* 23–46.

Smoll, F. L., Smith, R. E., Curtis, B., & Hunt, E. (1978). Toward a mediational model of coach–player relationships. *Research Quarterly, 49,* 528–541.

Sousa, C., Cruz, J., Torregrosa, M., Vilches, D., & Viladrich, C. (2006). Behavioral assessment and individual counseling programme for coaches of young athletes. *Revista de Psicologia del Deporte, 15,* 263–278.

Sousa, C., Smith, R.E., & Cruz, J. (2008). An individualized behavioral goal-setting program for coaches: Impact on observed, athlete-perceived, and coach-perceived behaviors. *Journal of Clinical Sport Psychology, 2,* 258–277.

Stambor, Z. (2006, June). How laughing leads to learning. *Monitor on Psychology, 37,* 62–64.

Taylor, S. E., Peplau, L. A., & Sears, D. O. (2005). *Social psychology* (12th ed.). Upper Saddle River, NJ: Prentice Hall.

Worchel, S., Cooper, J., & Goethals, G. R. (1991). *Understanding social psychology* (5th ed.). Pacific Grove, CA: Brooks/Cole.

Summary of Coaching Guidelines

I. Reacting to Athlete Behaviors and Game Situations

A. Good plays

Do: Provide *reinforcement!* Do so immediately. Let the athletes know that you appreciate and value their efforts. Reinforce effort as much as you do results. Look for positive things, reinforce them, and you will see them increase. Remember, whether athletes show it or not, the positive things you say and do remain with them.

Don't: Take their efforts for granted.

B. Mistakes

Do: Give *encouragement* immediately after mistakes. That's when the youngster needs your support the most. If you are sure the athlete knows how to correct the mistake, then encouragement alone is sufficient. When appropriate, give *corrective instruction,* but always do so in an encouraging manner. Do this by emphasizing not the bad things that just happened but the good things that will happen if the athlete follows your instruction (the "why" of it). This will make the athlete positively self-motivated to correct the mistakes rather than negatively motivated to avoid failure and your disapproval.

Don't: Punish when things are going wrong! Punishment isn't just yelling. It can be tone of voice, action, or any indication of disapproval. Athletes respond much better to a positive approach. Fear of failure is reduced if you work to reduce fear of punishment. Indications of displeasure should be limited to clear cases of lack of effort; but, even here, criticize the lack of effort rather than the athlete as a person.

Don't: Give corrective instruction in a hostile, demeaning, or harsh manner. That is, avoid *punitive instruction.* This is more likely to increase frustration and create resentment than to improve performance. Don't let your good intentions in giving instruction be self-defeating.

C. Misbehaviors, lack of attention

Do Maintain order by establishing clear expectations. Emphasize that during a game all members of the team are part of the activity, even those on the bench. Use reinforcement to strengthen team participation. In other words, try to prevent misbehaviors by using the positive approach to strengthen their opposites.

Don't: Get into the position of having to constantly nag or threaten athletes to prevent chaos. Don't be a drill sergeant. If an athlete refuses to cooperate, deprive him or her of something valued. Don't use physical measures, such as running laps. The idea here is that if you establish clear behavioral guidelines early and work to build team spirit in achieving them, you can avoid having to repeatedly *keep control.* Youngsters want clear guidelines and expectations, but they don't want to be regimented. Try to achieve a healthy balance.

II. Getting Positive Things to Happen and Creating a Good Learning Atmosphere

Do: Give *technical instruction*. Establish your role as a caring and competent teacher. Try to structure participation as a learning experience in which you are going to help the athletes become the best they can be. Always give instruction in a positive way. Satisfy your athletes' desire to improve their skills. Give instruction in a clear, concise manner and, if possible, demonstrate how to do skills correctly.

Do: Give encouragement. Encourage effort, don't demand results. Use encouragement selectively so that it is meaningful. Be supportive without acting like a cheerleader.

Do: Concentrate on the activity. Be "in the game" with the athletes. Set a good example for team unity.

Don't: Give either instruction or encouragement in a sarcastic or degrading manner. Make a point, then leave it. Don't let "encouragement" become irritating to the athletes.

Note: These guidelines were excerpted from the manual that is given to MAC workshop participants (Smoll & Smith, 2009).

Coach Self-Report Form

Complete this form as soon as possible after a practice or game. Think about what you did, but also about the kinds of situations in which the actions occurred and the kinds of athletes who were involved.

1. When athletes made good plays, approximately what percent of the time did you respond with REINFORCEMENT? _____%

2. When athletes gave good effort (regardless of the outcome), what percent of the time did you respond with REINFORCEMENT? _____%

3. About how many times did you reinforce athletes for displaying good sportsmanship, supporting teammates, and complying with team rules? _____

4. When athletes made mistakes, approximately what percent of the time did you respond with:

   A. Encouragement only _____%

   B. Corrective instruction given in an encouraging manner _____%

   (Sum of A and B should not exceed 100%)

5. When mistakes were made, did you stress the importance of learning from them? _____Yes _____No

6. Did you emphasize the importance of having fun while practicing or competing? _____Yes _____No

7. Did you tell your athletes that doing their best is all you expect of them? _____Yes _____No

8. Did you communicate that winning is important, but working to improve skills is even more important? _____Yes _____No

9. Did you do or say anything to help your athletes apply what they learned today to other parts of their life (for example, doing the right things in school, family, or social life)? _____Yes _____No

10. Something to think about: Is there anything you might do differently if you had a chance to coach this practice or game again?

This form was excerpted from the manual that is given to MAC workshop participants (Smoll & Smith, 2009).

Gender, Diversity, and Cultural Competence

Diane L. Gill, Ph.D., *University of North Carolina at Greensboro*
Cindra S. Kamphoff, Ph.D., *Minnesota State University, Mankato*

How many goodly creatures are there here! How beauteous mankind is! O brave new world that has such people in it!

—*From William Shakespeare's The Tempest, V, 1, 182*

One size does NOT fit all!

Both our larger world and our sport world do indeed include a wondrous diversity of people. Just as clearly—one size does NOT fit all—whether we are considering clothing, policies, institutions, or applied sport psychology. Gender and cultural diversity issues are real and powerful. As applied sport psychologists, whether in teaching, research, or consulting with athletes, it is imperative that we recognize the possibilities and constraints of cultural diversity and keep reminding ourselves that one size does not fit all. Attention to gender and cultural diversity is vital to our scholarship, and cultural competence is essential to professional practice. We hope this chapter will encourage more scholarship on diversity issues and greater emphasis on cultural competencies in professional practice.

Overview and Framework

This chapter begins with a guiding multicultural framework, examines gender and cultural diversity in sport, and then focuses on applied sport psychology research and professional practice. Throughout the chapter we include examples, as well as suggestions for promoting cultural competence in applied sport psychology. We interpret sport broadly, including all levels and forms of sport, and we intentionally advocate *sport for all*. That is, applied sport psychology can best address gender and cultural diversity by promoting safe, inclusive physical activity and by highlighting cultural competence in professional practice.

Multicultural Psychology

Although gender and cultural diversity are seldom central themes in applied sport psychology, the larger field of psychology, and particularly the American Psychological Association (APA), has developed a scholarly base and professional resources on multicultural psychology. The continuing work in gender psychology and the rapidly growing multicultural psychology scholarship provide a framework for this chapter, help clarify terminology, and provide guidelines for professional practice.

In one representative text, *multicultural psychology* is defined as the *"systematic study of behavior, cognition, and affect in many cultures"* (Mio, Barker-Hackett, & Tumambing, 2006, p. 3). *Culture,* however, is complex and not easily defined. As Mio et al. note, narrow definitions emphasize ethnicity, but a broader definition refers to *shared values, beliefs, and practices of an identifiable group of people.* With that broader, encompassing definition, gender is part of culture. Because gender is so prominent in sport we devote a large section in this chapter to gender. Thus, culture includes gender, race and ethnicity, language, spirituality, sexuality, many other social characteristics, and of particular relevance here, *physicality* (physical abilities and characteristics).

This chapter draws from that expanding multicultural psychology scholarship along with the feminist and cultural sport studies literature. These sources converge on the following common themes that form the guiding framework for this chapter:

> *Multiple, intersecting cultural identities.* We all have gender, race and ethnicity, and multiple cultural identities, with the mix varying across individuals, time, and contexts.

> *Power relations.* Culture relations involve power and privilege. Who makes the rules? Who is *left out?*

> *Action and advocacy.* Multicultural perspectives demand action for social justice.

Culturally competent applied sport psychology professionals develop their own multicultural competencies and also advocate sport for all.

Gender and Multiple Identities

Psychology has been addressing gender issues in both research and practice for some time. More recently, recognizing the diversity among women, and noting that disparities still persist despite tremendous gains for women in many areas, the APA (2007) developed and approved Guidelines for Psychological Practice with Girls and Women that "will enhance gender- and culture-sensitive psychological practice with women and girls from all social classes, ethnic and racial groups, sexual orientations, and ability/disability statuses in the United States" (APA, 2007, p. 950). These guidelines draw from similar APA guidelines, clearly take a multicultural perspective, and include definitions that are relevant to this chapter. First, the guidelines clarify the distinction between sex and gender, with *sex* referring to biological aspects of being male or female, and *gender* referring to psychological, social, and cultural experiences and characteristics associated with being male or female. Moreover, individuals vary in how they identify with and express their gender. Rather than defining culture, the guidelines define the broader term, *social identities,* as encompassing personal and group definitions embedded in social groups and statuses including gender, race, ability level, culture, ethnicity, geographic location, intellectual ability, sexual orientation, gender identity, class, age, body size, religious affiliation, acculturation status, socioeconomic status, and other sociodemographic variables. The guidelines explicitly note the complex and dynamic interactions of identities.

Exercise 1: Identify Your Own Multiple Identities

List as many as you can of your own social identities (gender, race and ethnicity, social class, sexuality, spirituality/religion, physicality, etc.). You should have a long list. Try to mark three identities that are especially salient or influential for you (that won't be easy, as different identities are more or less salient in different situations). Now, select a profession in which you might be working with sport participants, such as sport psychology consultant, athletic trainer, coach, or fitness leader. How will your own multiple, intersecting identities impact your work and interactions with participants?

The APA (2007) guidelines define *oppression* as discrimination against and/or systematic denial of resources to members of groups who are identified as different, inferior, or less deserving than others. *Privilege* refers to social status, power, or institutionalized advantage gained by virtue of valued social identities. Privilege typically is experienced by those with dominant social identities (e.g., white, male, upper/middle class), and privilege often is unrecognized by those people who have it. Privilege is more easily recognized by individuals who don't have it and experience oppression. For example, the 25-year-old Latino son of one of my faculty colleagues (both are U.S. citizens) was asked for identification at a worksite, and then detained when he could not produce it (he'd left it at home). No doubt he recognized the power relations in that situation even if his white colleagues did not. Most people experience both privilege and oppression; you likely have some characteristics that convey privilege and others that do not. Think about all of your multiple identities from Exercise 1. In what ways do you experience power and privilege? That's a tough question; it may be easier to first think of how you experience oppression. If you have ever been the only person like you (the only girl on the team, the only athlete in an advanced academic class) you likely recognized the power relations in the situation. Continuing to think about how you experience both privilege and oppression will help you recognize cultural power relations. The APA (2007) guidelines clearly recognize connections and interactions of multiple identities and power relations, and they emphasize social justice and advocacy in the specific guidelines for psychological practice.

By adopting the approach of the APA (2007) guidelines, and the multicultural framework of this chapter, applied sport psychology can advance our understanding of gender and cultural diversity, and promote cultural competence in professional practice—but that's no easy task. Sport psychology is explicitly context-dependent, and sport culture is unique in many ways. As multicultural psychologists advocate, applied sport psychologists must pay attention to power relations (e.g., how relationships with those in power such as coaches, athletic directors, and owners impact the athlete) and social context in sport (e.g., the environment), but they also must retain concern for the individual. The combined focus on the individual and cultural relations is the essence of cultural competence in applied sport psychology—and promoting inclusive and empowering sport for all.

The Cultural Context of Sport

Before examining the scholarship on gender and cultural diversity, consider the cultural context of sport. Specifically consider gender and culture in the following exercise.

Exercise 2: Gender and Culture Influence in Sport

Chris, the most talented 12-year old soccer player on the team, often loses focus and has angry outbursts on the field. The coach wants to help Chris develop emotional control and asks your advice. Before moving into a psychological skills training program, consider how gender and culture might affect Chris, the coach, and your advice. Specifically, would you expect different behaviors or reactions from Christine and Christopher? Do you think others (parents, teammates) would react the same way to both of them? What if Chris's parents were immigrants from a non-Western culture? What if Chris were not so talented?

Gender and culture are embedded in sport. If you try to be nonsexist or nonracist and treat everyone the same, you will have difficulty; everyone is not the same and cultural identities are relevant. Moreover, power and privilege are involved; trying to treat everyone the same may well do a disservice to participants. Invariably, identical treatment means treating everyone as if they were part of the dominant (privileged) group without considering cultural and individual differences. Our world is shaped by gender and culture. Gender influence is particularly powerful in sport, with some unique features. Sport participants are diverse, but not as diverse as the broader population. Sport is male-dominated and elite sport programs clearly reflect gender and cultural restrictions. For example, Sabo and Veliz' (2012), in a nationwide study of high schools, found that overall boys have more sport opportunities than girls. Geographic region and social class further impacted sport opportunities with urban schools and those with the least economic resources offering fewer athletic opportunities for all students.

Exercise 3: Treating Everyone the Same

As a physical educator or coach, you likely want to be fair and treat all of your students and athletes the same. How might that be problematic? How might treating everyone the same do a disservice to athletes? How might considering gender, race, ethnicity, or social class help you better understand a student or athlete?

Gender and Sport

Society and social institutions are clearly gendered, and sport has a unique gender context. Long before the women's movement of the 1970s early women leaders advocated putting athletes first, preventing exploitation, downplaying competition while emphasizing enjoyment and sportsmanship, and promoting activity for all rather than an elite few, as expressed in the classic statement, *"A game for every girl and every girl in a game"* (National Amateur Athletic Federation [NAAF], 1930, p. 41). The 1972 passage of Title IX of the Educational Amendments Act, which is the U.S. federal law that prohibited sex discrimination in federal funded educational programs or activities, marked the beginning of the move away from that model toward today's competitive women's sport programs. Indeed,

female athletic participation has exploded in the last generation. Still, the numbers of female and male participants are not equal. More important, female athletes are not the same as male athletes. To understand gender and sport we must look beyond dichotomous biological sex differences to the social context. *Citius, Altius, Fortius*—the Olympic motto—translates as "swifter, higher, stronger," underscoring that sport is competitive and hierarchical as well as physical. The average male may be taller, faster, and stronger than the average female, but biological sex is only part of the gender mix. All the meanings, social roles, and expectations related to gender are constructed in the sport context, and the sport context varies across cultures.

Cultural Diversity in Sport

In considering cultural diversity, we must go beyond numbers to consider power and privilege—*"who makes the rules."* Derald Wing Sue (2004) illustrated the power differential in noting that while White males make up just 33 percent of the U.S. population, they hold 80 percent of tenured faculty positions, 92 percent of Forbes 400 CEO-level positions, 80 percent of the House of Representatives and 84 percent of the U.S. Senate, and of special interest here, *99 percent of the athletic team owners*. As Sue (2004) noted, privileged people often are unaware of power relations, and "color blindness" often denies opportunity to others. Sue argued that psychology must recognize white privilege and the culture-bound nature of our scholarship and practice to advance psychology's mission and enhance the health and well-being of all people. The following quote from Muhammad Ali clearly illustrates that White privilege is quite visible to those who are not so privileged:

> We were taught when we were little children that Mary had a little lamb, its fleece was white as snow. Then we heard about Snow White, White Owl cigars. White Swan soap. White Cloud tissue. White Rain hair rings. White Tornado floor wax. White Plus toothpaste. All the good cowboys ride white horses and wear white hats. The President lives in the White House. Jesus was White. The Last Supper was White.

The angels is White. Miss America is White. Even, Tarzan, the King of the Jungle in Africa is White.

—*Muhammad Ali,* 1967. (cited in Hauser, 1996, p. 76; McDonald, 2005, p. 245)

The Ali quote is 45 years old, and Sue's numbers are over 10 years old, but white privilege remains and the numbers haven't changed much. Richard Lapchick's annual *Racial and Gender Report Cards* clearly show persistent racial and gender inequities in U.S. sport, with little progress. In the 2011 report card (Lapchick, 2011), African Americans are slightly over-represented in U.S. college sports, but other cultural minorities are clearly under-represented.

When we consider power positions, cultural diversity drops dramatically. The Racial and Gender Report Card (Lapchick, 2011) indicated that whites hold approximately 90 percent of the head coaching positions in U.S. college athletics, and about 90 percent of Division I athletics directors are white and only 8.2 percent are women. Before Title IX was enacted (1972) over 90 percent of U.S. women's college athletic teams were coached by women and had a woman athletic director. Vivian Acosta and Linda Carpenter have documented the decline in the number of women coaches since then. Their most recent 2012 update (Acosta & Carpenter, 2012) indicates that while participation of female athletes has increased, the percentage of female coaches remains under 50 percent of women's teams. The proportion of female athletic directors, head athletic trainers, and sports information directors is even lower and far below male numbers.

Although international data are lacking, the under-representation of women coaches at the elite level is likely a global trend (Marshall, 2010; Norman, 2010), and the limited data available suggest even fewer women coaches at the youth level than at the collegiate and elite levels (Kamphoff & LaVoi, 2013; Messner, 2007). For example, Kamphoff and LaVoi report that 27 percent of all high school coaches are female, with females coaching 39.6 percent of girls' teams and only 7.5 percent of boys' teams. The 2012 London Olympics showcased women athletes, and also demonstrated intersecting cultural identities

and power relations. The United States sent more female than male athletes to London, but women were vastly under-represented in several delegations. Power relations were also evident; although we saw more women and athletes from varied cultural backgrounds, coaching positions are heavily dominated by men, and Olympic officials are not as diverse as the athletes. Clearly, elite sport is culturally elite.

Gender bias and white male privilege may not totally explain the declining numbers of women coaches, but Kamphoff's (2010) research clearly shows that women coaches within collegiate athletics experience marginalization, devaluation, and homophobia. The former women coaches that she interviewed suggested they received fewer resources, lower salaries, more responsibilities, and less administrative support than their male counterparts. For example, several women mentioned outdated facilities, wide disparities in salaries, and added responsibilities that male coaches were not expected to take on. They also had difficulty balancing work and family, and reported that others saw them "distracted by motherhood" if they had children. As one coach commented:

> When I resigned, I remember [the athletic director] telling me, "You know, I often wondered how you could juggle being a wife, and having two kids." . . . Are you kidding me? He wouldn't say that to a man. (A former collegiate coach, Kamphoff, 2010, p. 367)

Cultural Diversity in Exercise and Physical Activity

Perhaps exercise and physical activity are more diverse than elite sport—or perhaps not. Do the fitness centers and activity programs in your community reflect the population diversity? U.S. census data and public health reports indicate that physical activity is limited by gender, race, age and socioeconomic status. Physical activity decreases across the adult lifespan, with men more active than women, and racial and ethnic minorities less active across all age groups. The Centers for Disease Control (CDC) tracks physical activity, and the CDC Web site (http://www.cdc.gov/) provides data on those trends as well as helpful information.

Cultural Diversity in Sport Psychology

Despite the diversity of participants and the need for cultural competence, sport psychology has not adopted multicultural perspectives in research or professional practice. Duda and Allison (1990) first identified the lack of research, reporting that only 7 of 186 empirical papers (less than 4 percent) considered race and ethnicity, and most of those were sample descriptions. Ram, Starek, and Johnson (2004) updated that report by reviewing articles in sport and exercise psychology research journals between 1987 and 2000 for both race and ethnicity and sexual orientation content. They confirmed the persistent void in the scholarly literature, finding that only 20 percent of the articles made reference to race or ethnicity and 1.2 percent to sexual orientation. More important, those few articles provided few insights to advance our understanding. Ram et al. concluded that there is no systematic attempt to include the experiences of marginalized groups.

Exercise 4: Lack of Research on Cultural Diversity

Research reviews (Duda & Allison, 1990; Kamphoff, Gill, Araki & Hammond, 2010; Ram et al., 2004) demonstrate a lack of culturally diverse samples in sport psychology research. Assume that you want to study psychological skills and motivation in sport. How might you design a study to include a culturally diverse sample? Which specific aspects of diversity will you include in your study? How and why? What research questions will the study address?

Kamphoff, Gill, Araki, and Hammond (2010) surveyed the Association for Applied Sport Psychology (AASP) conference programs from the first conference in 1986 to 2007 and found only about 10 percent of all abstracts addressed cultural diversity issues, with most of those being simple comparisons of gender differences. Almost no abstracts addressed race, ethnicity,

sexual orientation, social class, physical disabilities, or any other cultural diversity issue. AASP program content extends beyond the research to professional issues, but our findings suggest a continuing gap in applied sport psychology with little attention to the wider range of participants or multicultural issues.

Butryn (2002), taking a critical perspective, examined white privilege in sport psychology consulting. Butryn specifically argued that "confronting the invisible knapsack of white privilege" is essential for effective sport psychology consulting. Butryn used Peggy McIntosh's (1988) term "invisible knapsack" to describe the invisible privileges that come with having white skin including that if a white person goes shopping, he or she will not be followed or harassed. Butryn emphasized that we must consider these privileges when consulting. He further reminded us that race is not just black and white; we must expand the discourse on race and privilege to the wider range of racial and ethnic identities.

To expand our worldview, sport psychology must expand the research base on cultural diversity, and adopt multicultural competencies for professional practice. To get started, we can draw from related multicultural psychology scholarship.

Exercise 5: White Privilege in Sport Psychology

Sue discussed "invisible whiteness" and Butryn (2002) examined white privilege in sport psychology, arguing that we should confront the often "taken for granted" notion of race. Check the Association of Applied Sport Psychology's Web site, and specifically the Certified Consultants link (http://appliedsportpsych.org/consultants/consultant-websites) and http://appliedsportpsych.org/consultants). What do these Web sites and the consultant's bios and pictures tell you about cultural diversity in applied sport psychology? How do these Web sites help us to examine white privilege in applied sport psychology?

Gender and Sexuality

Gender Scholarship

Gender is a clear and powerful cultural force in society, and a particularly powerful and persistent influence in sport. Gender scholarship in sport psychology largely follows gender scholarship within psychology, which has shifted from sex differences, to gender role and personality, to emphasis on social context and processes, and most recently to a multicultural perspective, but sport psychology is lagging behind.

Much sport psychology research on gender emphasizes differences, such as early work (e.g., Harris & Jennings, 1977; Spence & Helmreich, 1978) reporting that female collegiate athletes were more masculine than nonathlete college females who were more often classified as feminine. One study (Koca & Asci, 2005) expands our cultural perspective by surveying a large Turkish sample. As with Western samples, Turkish female athletes scored higher on masculinity, and the authors suggested that both female and male athletes must be competitive, assertive, independent, and willing to take risks. Overall, this research suggests that female athletes possess more masculine personality characteristics than do female nonathletes, but this is not particularly enlightening. Sport psychology research must follow psychology to move beyond the male–female and masculine–feminine dichotomies to more complex developmental, social, and multicultural models to advance our understanding.

Gender Stereotypes

Gender stereotypes did not fade away with the implementation of Title IX in 1972. Messner and Cooky's (2010) research, for example, indicates that media coverage continues to reflect gender bias. Female athletes receive much less coverage than males, and different coverage, with the emphasis on athletic ability and accomplishments for men, but on femininity and physical attractiveness for women. In their recent update on televised sports from 1989–2009, Messner and Cooky (2010) indicated no progress, and in fact a decline in women's sport coverage on major networks from 6.3 percent in 2004 (hardly a mark to strive for) to an all-time low of 1.6 percent in 2009. On a positive note, they did report far less portrayal of women athletes in sexist or demeaning ways.

Stereotypes are a concern because we act on them, exaggerating minimal gender differences and restricting opportunities for everyone. Psychological research confirms that how people *think* males and females differ is more important than how they actually differ. If children think that dance is for girls, boys will stand aside while girls dance. Children see female gymnasts and male baseball players as role models; peers gravitate to sex-segregated activities; and parents, teachers, and coaches support gender-appropriate activities of children.

Exercise 6: Gender Stereotyping in the Media

Follow the coverage of both men's and women's intercollegiate basketball for a week in a newspaper, television news sport report, sport magazine, or sport Web site. Do men and women receive different amounts of time or space? Does the type of coverage differ (e.g., references to accomplishments, appearance, personal lives)? If so, how does the coverage differ? Do you find gender stereotyping or bias?

Sexuality

Sexuality and sexual orientation are clearly linked with gender, and especially so in sport contexts. In her early work on gender roles, discussed in the previous section, Bem noted that we often (and incorrectly) conflate biological sex, gender roles, and sexual orientation. For example, it often is assumed that a biological male football player must have masculine personality characteristics and be heterosexual. As research shows, and as most people recognize, that is not necessarily true. Furthermore, the male–female biological sex, masculine–feminine personality, and homosexual–heterosexual categories are not the clear, dichotomous binaries that we often assume. By binaries, we mean a pair of related terms that most people think are opposite in meaning (e.g., male/female, masculine/feminine). For example, biological sex (e.g., male/female) is not the clear dichotomy that we assume, as many individuals (about 1 in 2000) are born intersex, which includes a variety of conditions in which a person's sexual anatomy does not match the typical definitions of male and female (from Intersex Society of North America: www.isna.org). Clearly individuals' gender identities, gender expressions, and sexual orientations are even more varied, and not necessarily linked. Still, when people step out of those binaries, or when biological sex, gender roles, and sexual orientation do not line up with our stereotypes, people face discrimination. Discrimination and prejudice on the basis of sexual orientation is often described as homophobia, but Herek (2000), a leading psychology scholar on lesbian/gay/bisexual (LGB) issues, prefers *sexual prejudice*. As Herek notes, sexual prejudice is an attitude (evaluation), directed at a social group, involving hostility or dislike. *Homophobia* is typically understood as an irrational fear, and the term implies psychopathology. *Heterosexism* refers to the institutionalized oppression of nonheterosexual people (Kauer & Krane, in press). Sexual prejudice is used here, but related scholarship also refers to homophobia and heterosexism.

Messner (2002) argues that sexual prejudice is particularly powerful in sport and leads all boys and men (gay or straight) to conform to a narrow definition of masculinity; real men compete and avoid anything feminine that might lead them to be branded a sissy. More recent work (e.g., Anderson, 2011) suggests that sportsmen, and particularly gay men, may have more latitude in sports today, but some sport settings are still spaces of restricted masculinity and hostility toward sexual minorities (Kauer & Krane, 2013). Thomae and Kamphoff (2013) is one of the only studies we know of to examine gay male coaches' experiences; they specifically examined gay collegiate coaches' experiences negotiating their multiple identities as gay men, males,

coaches, and members of the college staff. The majority of the coaches had come out about their sexuality to their team, and most felt supported by their athletes, collegiate department, and university, but some talked about harassment and bullying, especially as assistant coaches. Still, sexual prejudice in sport typically is discussed in relation to women's athletics. We stereotypically assume that sport attracts lesbians (of course, not gay men), but no research or logic supports any inherent relationship between sexual orientation and sport. The former women coaches that Kamphoff (2010) interviewed provided examples of rampant sexual prejudice in U.S. collegiate coaching, and they clearly felt pressure to act in a heterosexual way to fit into the collegiate system.

> *I know of a specific case of a lesbian coach that was asked to leave and . . . they said, "We want to change the face of the coaching staff." So, what does that mean? A lesbian coach, of course, is going to take that as you want a straight coach. You are saying it without saying it.* (A former collegiate coach, Kamphoff, 2010, p. 368)

Vikki Krane and her colleagues draw connections among gender, sexism, and heterosexism using social identity as a theoretical framework (e.g., Krane, 2001; Krane & Barber, 2003). Barber and Krane (2005) have taken social identity perspective in examining the experiences of lesbian coaches and found that these women worked in an implicitly heterosexist and homonegative environment. The lesbian coaches used several strategies to remain productive and successful at the collegiate level including compartmentalizing their lives, engaging in behaviors to protect themselves, and remaining silent. The lesbian coaches did what they could to create a more positive, accepting environment on their teams including emphasizing respect for individual differences and constructively addressing homonegative comments or incidences on their teams to create a safe space for all athletes.

Sport psychology scholarship on sexual orientation focuses on competitive athletics, with little research on sexual prejudice in other physical activity settings. Although research is limited, reports from the Gay, Lesbian, Straight Education Network (GLSEN) national surveys (Kosciw, Greytak, Bartkiewicz, Boesen, & Palmer, 2012) suggest that sport is a particularly hostile environment for LGBT youth. In one of the few empirical studies, Morrow and Gill (2003) reported that both physical education teachers and students witnessed high levels of homophobic and heterosexist behaviors in public schools, but teachers failed to confront those behaviors. Gill, Morrow, Collins, Lucey, and Schultz (2006) found that attitudes of our preprofessional students were markedly more negative for both gay men and lesbians than for other minority groups, with males especially negative toward gay men. In 2013, GLSEN released a research brief on the experiences of LGBT students in school sport based on their 2011 national school survey data. The brief confirms that LGBT students face discrimination and bullying in physical education and school athletics, and do not feel supported by school officials. In response to the continuing reports, in 2011, GLSEN developed "Changing the Game: The GLSEN Sports Project" (available at: http://sports.glsen.org/) to assist kindergarten through high schools with creating safe and respectful sports and physical education environments for LGBT students.

In the short time from the last edition of this chapter to the current time, the situation for lesbian, gay, bisexual, and transsexual (LGBT) people has changed in society, and even in sport. More professional LGBT athletes have come out (e.g., Sheryl Swoops, John Amaechi, Amelie Mausesmo), although usually after their professional careers have ended. The recent (2013) widely publicized coming out of NBA basketball player Jason Collins and 2012–2013 collegiate basketball player of the year and top WNBA selection Brittney Griner clearly show changing times. The most common response to Jason Collins' *Sports Illustrated* (May 6, 2013) cover story was muted, but positive. Griner's announcement received far less fanfare. In her *NY Times* essay (May 5, 2013) and a video for the "It gets better" project, she expressed optimism and pride, even after describing the bullying and harassment she had faced in earlier years.

Exercise 7: Consider Intersections of Gender, Culture and Sexuality

NBA basketball player Jason Collins and top WNBA selection Brittney Griner are both talented Black athletes who came out as gay/lesbian in May 2013 with a great deal of public attention. Consider how gender, culture, and sexuality interact to affect their behaviors, media reports, and the reactions of others. How does gender affect the situation and reactions? What if they had been White or Asian? What if they were not so talented? What other aspects of their cultural identities might affect their behaviors or reactions of others?

Sexual Harassment

Considerable research demonstrates the prevalence of sexual harassment, in all types of settings, but prior to the important work of Kari Fasting of Norway and Celia Brackenridge of the United Kingdom, the sport psychology literature was silent on this topic. Related research in sport indicates that the sport climate fosters sexual harassment and abuse; that young, elite female athletes are particularly vulnerable; that neither athletes nor coaches have education or training about the issues; and that both research and professional development are needed to address the issues (Brackenridge, 2001; Brackenridge & Fasting, 2002; Fasting, Brackenridge & Sundgot-Borgen, 2004; Fasting, Brackenridge & Walseth, 2007). That research comes from several European countries and Australia, and recently, Rodriguez and Gill (2011) reported similar findings with former Puerto Rican women athletes. The International Olympic Committee (IOC) recognized the problem, and defines sexual harassment as "behavior towards an individual or group that involves sexualized verbal, nonverbal or physical behavior, whether intended or unintended, legal or illegal, that is based on an abuse of power and trust and that is considered by the victim or a bystander to be unwanted or coerced" (p. 3). Women are more likely to be harassed and men are more likely to be harassers, although it is not exclusively men harassing women—as the highly publicized Sandusky case at Penn State in the U.S. illustrates. Clearly more research is needed, and sport psychology consultants, coaches, and other sport professionals who are aware of gender and cultural dynamics might be quicker to recognize and prevent sexual harassment.

Race and Ethnicity

Race and ethnicity are just as salient as gender and sexuality in the ever-changing cultural context of sport, but have received far less attention in the sport psychology literature. As noted earlier, the striking void in sport psychology research on race and ethnicity persists despite the increased multicultural diversity in society and in sport.

The psychology scholarship on race and ethnicity is growing and beginning to take a multicultural perspective. Much of that work addresses health disparities, which refer to any health differences linked with social or economic disadvantages. Health disparities are well documented and reports indicate that health care access and quality is suboptimal for minorities and low-income people (2011 National Health Quality and Disparities Reports; available at: www.ahrq.gov). For example, racial and ethnic minorities are more likely to be poor or near poor, and Blacks, Native Americans, and Hispanics/Latinos all had poorer quality of care and worse access to health care than Whites with no significant change over time. Given that physical activity is a key health behavior, and that disparities in physical activity parallel disparities in health, sport psychology professionals who are aware of the health disparities research are better positioned to provide guidance on promoting physical activity for health and well-being.

Steele's (1997) extensive research on stereotypes and *stereotype threat*—the fear of confirming negative stereotypes—indicates that stereotypes affect all of us. That research, largely in academic settings, indicates that the most devastating effects are on those minority group members who have abilities and are motivated to succeed. On the positive side, Steele's research also suggests that even simple manipulations that take away the stereotype threat (e.g., telling students the test is not related to race or gender) can help. Beilock and McConnell (2004) reviewed the related sport psychology literature, concluding that negative stereotypes are common in sport (e.g., White men can't jump, girls can't throw) and lead to performance decrements.

The prevalence of negative stereotypes for racial and ethnic minorities, particularly Black athletes, is well-documented. For example, Black athletes are assumed to have natural talent, whereas White athletes are assumed to be smarter. Stone, Perry, and Darley (1997) found that individuals who listened to a college basketball game rated Black players more athletic and White players as having more basketball intelligence. Stone and colleagues (1999) later confirmed stereotype threat in a study in which Black participants did worse when told a test was of sports intelligence, while white participants performed worse when told the test was of natural ability.

As Beilock and McConnell (2004) concluded, we know less about stereotype threat in physical domains than in cognitive areas. They also pointed out that people are members of multiple groups, and how they think about their group membership is critical. Ruth Hall, who is particularly eloquent on intersections of gender, race, and class in sport and exercise, began a discussion of women of color in sport (Hall, 2001) with a commentary in "She Got Game: A Celebration of Women's Sports" that claimed:

> Race and gender are firecrackers that ignite America's social conscience, rattle the cages that bind us—cages that block our passage to equality. It's a double whammy for African American female athletes since we aren't the dominant norm—we're not white. Race and racism loom large and throw a level playing field off kilter.
>
> Many of us don't fit the Anglo mold. We stretch the parameters of gender roles by our presence, our physical appearance, and sometimes unorthodox style. We aren't "feminine" they say. Commentators describe figure skaters Debbie Thomas and Surya Bonaly and the tennis star Venus Williams as

"athletic" and "muscular" meaning not feminine. We create dissonance with our skin color, body type, and facial features. We are the other. . . . (p. 386–387)

Physicality and Cultural Diversity

Sport psychology professionals deal with physical activities, and thus, physical abilities and characteristics are prominent. Moreover, opportunity is limited by physical abilities, physical skills, physical size, physical fitness, and physical appearance—collectively referred to here as *physicality*. Elite sport implies physically elite performers. Persons with disabilities certainly are among the "left outs" in sport and exercise settings, and the increasing public attention on obesity has created a negative culture for overweight and obese persons. Indeed, exclusion on the basis of physicality is nearly universal in sport and exercise, and this exclusion is a public health issue. Rimmer (2005) notes that people with physical disabilities are among the most inactive segments of the population; he further argues that rather than physical barriers, organizational policies, discrimination, and social attitudes are the real barriers.

Gill, Morrow, Collins, Lucey, and Schultz (2005) examined the climate for minority groups (racial and ethnic minorities; gay, lesbian, and bisexual people; older adults; and people with disabilities) in organized sport, exercise, and recreational settings, and found the climate most exclusionary for those with disabilities. Testimony from people who have faced discrimination because of physicality speaks clearly. Pain and Wiles (2006) conducted in-depth interviews with obese and disabled individuals; consider these quotes from three of the participants:

> *I am frightened to go back about this wheelchair because they're always going on about my weight.*

> *They think that because you are in a wheelchair you haven't got a brain.*

> *I have got to say that actually every time you go outside your front door, life's really difficult. . . . Barriers all the way along, really.*

(each of these quotes is from an obese and disabled person, Pain & Wiles, 2006, p. 4)

Physicality is particularly relevant to applied sport psychology. Physical skill, strength, and fitness are key sources of restrictions and stereotyping. Physical appearance influences outcomes in subjectively judged sports such as gymnastics—and perhaps in some that are not so subjectively judged. Physical size, particularly obesity, is a clear source of social stigma and oppression, and a particular concern in physical activity and health promotion.

Many studies (e.g., Puhl & Heuer, 2011) document clear and consistent stigmatization of obese individuals in employment, education, and health care. And, several studies indicate that sport and physical activity professionals hold negative stereotypes and biases. Greenleaf and Weiller (2005) found that physical education teachers held anti-fat bias and strong personal weight control beliefs (obese individuals are responsible for their obesity). Chambliss, Finley, and Blair (2004) found a strong anti-fat bias among U.S. exercise science students, and Robertson and Vohora (2008) found a strong anti-fat bias among fitness professionals and regular exercisers in England. Negative stereotypes about obese people are so prevalent that we may not realize our biases. That is, we may have implicit, or unconscious, biases even if we do not explicitly recognize those biases. A great deal of research has been done on implicit biases and their effects (see Project Implicit Web site: https://implicit.harvard.edu/implicit/) and check your own implicit biases in Exercise 7). Implicit biases are particularly likely with weight and size given the media coverage. Research confirms that obese individuals are targets for teasing, more likely to engage in unhealthy eating behaviors, and less likely to engage in physical activity (Puhl & Wharton, 2007). Check the Yale Rudd Center Web site (http://yaleruddcenter.org/) for resources and information on weight bias in health and educational settings.

Exercise 8: Test your Implicit Biases

Go to the Implicit Attitude Test (IAT) at the Project Implicit Web site at Harvard University (https://implicit.harvard.edu/implicit/) and take the IAT on weight demonstration test to assess your own implicit attitudes about obesity. Most likely you will find that you have some implicit bias. Implicit bias does not necessarily suggest that you are prejudiced, but it does indicate the power of the negative stereotypes and associations that are so prevalent that we don't recognize them. Think about those implicit assumptions and cultural biases that may affect your behaviors and interactions in sport. Specifically, how might you counter that implicit bias to make a youth sport program more welcoming for youth who are overweight or not physically skilled? Check information on the Project Implicit Web site, Puhl and Wharton's (2007) article, and Rudd Center (http://yaleruddcenter.org/) for ideas.

Cultural Sport Psychology

Although the earlier sections show a lack of attention to cultural diversity in sport psychology, a few dedicated scholars have been developing *cultural sport psychology* over the last 10 years. Fisher, Butryn, and Roper (2003) advocated cultural studies as a promising perspective for sport psychology, and the publication of Schinke and Hanrahan's (2008) edited text, *Cultural Sport Psychology,* suggests that cultural sport psychology is now a recognized area. Recently, two of our journals have devoted special issues to cultural sport psychology. The *International Journal of Sport and Exercise Psychology* special issue (Ryba & Schinke, 2009) highlighted the dominance of the western worldview in our research and practice. The *Journal of Clinical Sport Psychology* special issue (Schinke & Moore, 2011) on culturally informed sport psychology called for understanding, respect, and integration of culture in professional practice. The continuing work of these scholars gives culture and cultural diversity a greater presence in sport psychology and fits with the framework of this chapter. Cultural sport psychology calls for awareness of (and a critical look at) our own cultural identity, continuing reflection to gain a deeper understanding of culture within sport psychology, and, in line with the third theme, cultural sport psychology

calls for action. That brings us to the topic of cultural competence.

Cultural Competence in Sport Psychology

Cultural competence takes gender and cultural diversity directly into professional practice. Culturally competent professionals act to empower participants, challenge restrictions, and advocate for social justice. Indeed, cultural competence is a professional competency required in psychology and many health professions, and applied sport psychology might well follow that lead. Cultural competence includes both understanding and action, and is needed at both the individual and organizational level. That is, sport psychology professionals not only develop their own cultural competence, but also work to ensure that their educational programs, professional practices, and organizations are culturally competent.

Psychology has resources and actively promotes multicultural competence, which may be described as: *the ability to work effectively with individuals who are of a different culture.* Most psychology resources adopt a model of cultural competence developed by Stanley Sue (2006), one of the leading scholars in multicultural psychology. Cultural competence has three key components: (a) awareness of one's own cultural values and biases, (b) understanding of other worldviews, and (c) development of culturally appropriate skills. Culturally competent sport psychology professionals would, therefore, work to be conscious and mindful of their personal reactions, biases, and prejudices to people who are different (i.e., awareness); recognize their client's worldview or perspective given their culture and background (i.e., understand); and develop abilities that allow them to work effectively with people who are different from them (i.e., skills). We include a few exercises for sport psychology professionals in the remainder of the chapter for them to examine their biases and prejudices. Sport psychology professionals work with a wide range of people who are culturally different and similar to themselves, therefore, establishing avenues for learning about the cultures of their clients is essential. Sport psychology professionals also should consult with supervisors or colleagues for feedback on their style and how it might impede or enhance their cultural competence. Cultural competence is not static and it requires frequent learning, relearning, and unlearning about diversity and culture.

The American Psychological Association (APA) followed that model in developing the APA (2003) Multicultural Guidelines, which call on psychologists to develop and apply knowledge and awareness of cultural diversity, and to promote culturally informed organizational policies and practices.

Exercise 9: Becoming Aware of Your Own Worldview

Becoming aware of your own limited worldviews is the first step to becoming culturally competent. Consider your own perceptions and stereotypes about one specific marginalized group (e.g., women, Asians, gay athletes). Be sure to check for implicit biases. For each perception or stereotype consider (a) why do you believe this? And, (b) how might this perception influence a client–consultant relationship and/or one's research?

The AASP Ethical Guidelines, Principle D (Respect for People's Rights and Dignity) clearly call for cultural competence within applied sport psychology in stating "AASP members are aware of cultural, individual, and role differences, including those due to age, gender, race, ethnicity, national origin, religion, sexual orientation, disability, language, and socioeconomic status. AASP members try to eliminate the effect on their work of biases based on those factors, and they do not knowingly participate in or condone unfair discriminatory practices" (AASP, 2006; available at: http://appliedsportpsych.org).

Most recently the International Society of Sport Psychology (ISSP) developed and published an ISSP position stand on culturally competent research and practice in sport and exercise psychology (Ryba, Stambulova, Si, & Schinke, 2013). That article includes an excellent review of the relevant cultural sport psychology scholarship as well as guidelines and recommendations for culturally competent research and practice in sport psychology. In the closing section, they describe three major areas of cultural competence for sport psychology practitioners as: (a) cultural awareness and reflexivity, (b) culturally competent communication, and (c) culturally competent interventions. Awareness and reflectivity refers to recognition between and within culture variations as well as reflection on both the client and one's own cultural background. Culturally competent communication involves meaningful dialogue and shared language—much as Parham (2011) suggested with "less of me and more of thee" in conversation. Culturally competent interventions recognize culture while avoiding stereotyping, take an idiosyncratic approach, and stand for social justice.

William Parham (2005), a leader in APA's multicultural efforts as well as an active sport psychology professional, offers useful guidelines based on his professional practice, including the following three guiding premises:

Context is everything. When working with diverse individuals (and all sport psychology professionals work with diverse individuals) history, economics, family, and social context are all relevant.

Culture, race, and ethnicity as separate indexes do little to inform us. Parham reminds us that cultural groups are not homogeneous, and every individual has a unique mix of cultural identities.

Using paradigms reflecting differing worldviews. The typical U.S. worldview emphasizes independence, competitiveness, and individual striving. Emphasis on connectedness rather than separation, deference to higher power, mind–body interrelatedness rather than control, and a sense of "spirit-driven energy" may be more prominent in another's worldview.

More recently, Parham (2011) offered further helpful guides, and proposed consideration of the immediate and historical cultural context of both parties in the communication. Overall, Parham calls for "more of thee and less of me" in research and practice. That is, professionals are listening as much as (or more than) talking while engaging in culturally informed interactions.

Hazel Markus and colleagues (Markus, Uchida, Omoregie, Townsend, & Kitayama, 2006) provided evidence for diverse worldviews with their study of Japanese and American explanations of Olympic performances. They found that in Japanese contexts, agency (and performance) is construed as jointly due to athletes' personal attributes, background, and social-emotional experience. In American contexts, agency is construed as disjoint, separate from background or social-emotional experience; performance is primarily due to personal characteristics. They further note that these differing explanations are reflected and fostered in the culture, particularly television reports. As Markus et al. (2006) suggest, we may all "go for the gold" but we go for it in different ways, and we value gold in different ways. We all live, act, and engage in sport within a cultural context, and that context affects our perceptions and interpretations (our worldview) as well as our performance.

Exercise 10: Working with Diverse Clients

Assume that you are a professional sport psychology consultant. You begin working with a client from a culture about which you have limited knowledge (e.g., an Australian indigenous athlete, a Muslim athlete, an athlete from China). What could you do to increase your understanding and work more effectively with this client? List three ways you can learn more about the athlete's culture and enhance your cultural competence. What personal or professional limitations given this discussion on cultural competence might warrant the referral of this client to another sport psychology professional?

Cultural Competence for Sport Psychology Professionals

Cultural competence is integral to quality programs and effective practice, not only for sport psychology but for all sport and physical activity professionals. Sport psychology specialists can play an important role in helping all sport professionals develop multicultural competencies.

As part of a project to develop more inclusive physical activity programs, we (Gill, Jamieson, & Kamphoff, 2005) found professionals rated their ability to deal with students of other cultural backgrounds as good, but they seldom took any proactive steps to promote inclusion. While the professionals saw the need for cultural competence, the work has barely begun. We suggested Cross, Bazron, Dennis, and Isaacs' (1999) continuum of cultural competence to be a helpful starting place. Considering cultural competence as a developmental process, the continuum presents steps moving from cultural ineptness to cultural proficiency:

Cultural destructiveness—characterized by policies, actions, and beliefs that are damaging to cultures.

Cultural incapacity—not intending to be culturally destructive, but lacking ability to respond effectively to diverse people (e.g., bias in hiring practices, lowered expectations).

Cultural blindness—philosophy of being unbiased and that all people are the same (e.g., encouraging assimilation, blaming individuals for not "fitting in").

Cultural precompetence—desire but no clear plan to achieve cultural competence.

Cultural competence—respect and recognition for diversity, genuine understanding of cultural differences (e.g., seek training and knowledge to prevent biases from affecting work, collaboration with diverse communities, willingness to make adaptations, continued training, and commitment to work effectively with diverse groups).

Cultural proficiency—culture held in high esteem and it is understood to be an integral part of who we are (e.g., conducting research to add to knowledge base, disseminating information on proven practices and interventions, engage in advocacy with diverse groups that support the culturally competent system).

Although the emphasis is on health services rather than psychology, the Cross et al. (1999) model and APA multicultural guidelines reflect similar themes. That is, professionals including sport psychology professionals, must recognize and value cultural diversity, continually seek to develop their multicultural knowledge and skills, translate those understandings into practice, and extend their efforts to advocacy by promoting organizational change and social justice. The Office of Minority Health Web site (http://minorityhealth.hhs.gov/) includes terminology and resources on assessing cultural competence, and the National Center for Cultural Competence (http://nccc.georgetown.edu/) has a wealth of resources related to cultural and linguistic competence that sport psychology professionals can use.

Sport psychology professionals must continuously examine their own cultural competence to ensure their practices support their diverse clients. Sport psychology professionals can extend their services to a wider population—including those who may not have access to our services. Sport psychology professionals could also help other physical activity professionals in developing their cultural competencies, and advocate sport and physical activity programs that are open to all.

Exercise 11: Consider Your Own Cultural Competence

How culturally competent are you? Review the six points on the continuum of cultural competence and think about your current or possible applied sport psychology activities. Are you culturally proficient or competent? How so? Are any of your activities culturally destructive or incapacitating? Where does your school, agency, or program fit on this continuum? How could you move "up" the cultural competence continuum? List two specific things you could do.

Summary

Gender and cultural diversity characterize sport and influence all sport participants. Culturally competent sport psychology professionals cannot simply treat everyone the same. Gender and culture are dynamic social influences best understood within a multicultural framework that recognizes multiple, intersecting identities, power relations, and the need for social action. Sport psychology has barely begun to address multicultural issues in research and professional practice. To date most scholarship focuses on gender issues, with few truly multicultural frameworks. Multicultural perspectives and cultural competence are especially needed for sport psychology in the real world. To advance sport psychology research and professional practice, we must develop our multicultural competencies, expand our reach to the marginalized "left outs," and promote sport for all.

Study Questions

1. Identify and briefly explain the three themes in the multicultural framework for this chapter.
2. Describe the impact of Title IX on girls' and women's participation in athletics and in coaching and administration positions.
3. Explain the terms *invisible whiteness* and *white privilege.* Give two specific examples to demonstrate white privilege in sport.
4. Define the terms *sexual prejudice, heterosexism,* and *homophobia,* and explain how sexual prejudice might affect sport participants.
5. Define stereotype threat and explain how stereotype threat might operate in sport.
6. Describe the research on stereotypes and biases related to obesity, and explain how such bias might affect participants and professionals in physical activity programs.
7. Define *cultural competence* and identify the three general areas of multicultural competencies.
8. Identify the steps or levels on the cultural competence continuum. Give two specific things a sport psychology professional could do to move up to a higher level of cultural competence. Describe how sport psychology professionals might promote organizational change and social justice in sport.

References

Acosta, V. R., & Carpenter, L. J. (2012). *Women in intercollegiate sport: A longitudinal, national study thirty-five year update 1977–2012.* Retrieved from: http://www.acostacarpenter.org/.

Anderson, E. (2011). Masculinities and sexualities in sport and physical culture: three decades of evolving research. *Journal of Homosexuality, 58*(5), 565–578.

American Psychological Association (2003). Guidelines on multicultural education, training, research, practice and organizational change for psychologists. *American Psychologist, 58,* 377–402. (available online at APA PI directorate: http://www.apa.org/pi).

American Psychological Association (2007). Guidelines for psychological practice with girls and women. *American Psychologist, 62,* 949–979 (available online at APA PI directorate women's programs office: http://www.apa.org/pi/wpo).

Barber, H., & Krane, V. (2005). The elephant in the locker room: Opening the dialogue about sexual orientation on women's sport teams. In M. B. Anderson (Ed.), *Sport psychology in practice* (pp. 265–285). Champaign, IL: Human Kinetics.

Beilock, S. L., & McConnell, A. R. (2004). Stereotype threat and sport: Can athletic performance be threatened? *Journal of Sport and Exercise Psychology, 26,* 597–609.

Brackenridge, C. (2001). *Spoilsports: Understanding and preventing sexual exploitation in sport.* New York: Routledge.

Brackenridge, C. H., & Fasting, K. (Eds.) (2002) *Sexual harassment and abuse in sport: International research and policy perspectives.* London: Whiting and Birch.

Butryn, T. M. (2002). Critically examining White racial identity and privilege in sport psychology consulting. *The Sport Psychologist, 16,* 316–336.

Chambliss, H. O., Finley, C. E., & Blair, S. N. (2004). Attitudes toward obese individuals among exercise science students. *Medicine and Science in Sports & Exercise, 36,* 468–474.

Conception, R. Y., & Ebbeck, V. (2005). Examining the physical activity experience of survivors of domestic violence in relation to self-views. *Journal of Sport and Exercise Psychology, 27,* 197–211.

Cross, T., Bazron, B., Dennis, K., & Isaacs, M. (1999). *Towards a culturally competent system of care.* Washington, D. C. National Institute of Mental Health, Child and Adolescent Service System Program Technical Assistance Center, Georgetown University Child Development Center.

Duda, J. L., & Allison, M. T. (1990). Cross-cultural analysis in exercise and sport psychology: A void in the field. *Journal of Sport & Exercise Psychology, 12,* 114–131.

Fasting, K., Brackenridge, C., & Sundgot-Borgen, J. (2004). Prevalence of sexual harassment among Norwegian female elite athletes in relation to sport type. *International Review for the Sociology of Sport, 39,* 373–386.

Fasting, K., Brackenridge, C., & Walseth, K. (2007). Women athletes' personal responses to sexual harassment in sport. *Journal of Applied Sport Psychology, 19,* 419–433.

Fisher, L. A., Butryn, T. M., & Roper, E. A. (2003). Diversifying (and politicizing) sport psychology through cultural studies: A promising perspective. *The Sport Psychologist, 17,* 391–405.

Gill, D. L., Jamieson, K. M., & Kamphoff, C. (2005). *Final report: Promoting cultural competence among physical activity professionals.* American Association of University Women.

Gill, D. L., Morrow, R. G., Collins, K. E., Lucey, A. B., & Schultz, A. M. (2005). Climate for minorities in exercise and sport settings. *Journal of Sport & Exercise Psychology, 27,* Suppl. S68.

Gill, D. L., Morrow, R. G., Collins, K. E., Lucey, A. B., & Schultz, A. M. (2006). Attitudes and sexual prejudice in sport and physical activity. *Journal of Sport Management, 20,* 554–564.

GLSEN (2013). *The Experiences of LGBT Students in School Athletics* (Research Brief). New York: GLSEN. Retrieved from http://www.glsen.org/binary-data/GLSEN_ATTACHMENTS/file/000/002/2140-1.pdf.

Greenleaf, C., & Weiller, K. (2005). Perceptions of youth obesity among physical educators. *Social Psychology of Education, 8,* 407–423.

Hall, R. L. (2001). Shaking the foundation: Women of color in sport. *The Sport Psychologist, 15,* 386–400.

Harris, D. V., & Jennings, S. E. (1977). Self-perceptions of female distance runners. *Annals of the New York Academy of Sciences, 301,* 808–815.

Herek, G. M. (2000). Psychology of sexual prejudice. *Current directions in psychological science, 9,* 19–22.

International Olympic Committee (IOC) (2007, February). IOC adopts consensus statement on "sexual harassment and abuse." Retrieved June 2, 2013 from http://www.olympic.org/Documents/Reports/EN/en_report_1125.pdf.

Kamphoff, C. S. (2010). Bargaining with patriarchy: Former female coaches' experiences and their decision to leave collegiate coaching. *Research Quarterly for Exercise and Sport, 81,* 360–372.

Kamphoff, C. S., Gill, D. L., Araki, K., & Hammond, C. C. (2010). A Content Analysis of Cultural Diversity in the Association for Applied Sport Psychology's Conference Programs. *Journal of Applied Sport Psychology, 22,* 231–245.

Kamphoff, C. S., & LaVoi, N. (2013). *Females in positions of power within U.S. high school sports.* Presentation at the American Alliance of Health, Physical Education, Recreation, and Dance. Charlotte, NC.

Kauer, K. J. & Krane, V. (2013). Sexual identity and sport. In E. Roper (Ed.), *Gender relations in sport* (pp. 53–72). Boston: Sense Publishers.

Koca, C., & Asci, F. H. (2005). Gender role orientation in Turkish female athletes and nonathletes. *Women in Sport and Physical Activity Journal, 14,* 86–94.

Kosciw, J. G., Greytak, E. A., Bartkiewicz, M. J., Boesen, M. J., & Palmer, N. A. (2012). *The 2011 National School Climate Survey: The experiences of lesbian, gay, bisexual and transgender youth in our nation's schools.* New York: GLSEN. (available at www.glsen.org/research)

Krane, V. (2001). One lesbian feminist epistemology: Integrating feminist standpoint, queer theory, and feminist cultural studies. *The Sport Psychologist, 15,* 401–411.

Krane, V., & Barber, H. (2003). Lesbian experiences in sport: A social identity perspective. *Quest, 55,* 328–346.

Lapchick, R. (2011) The 2010 Racial and Gender Report Card. Retrieved from http://www.tidesport.org/rgrc/2010/2010_college_rgrc_final.pdf.

McIntosh, P. (1988). *White privilege and male privilege: A personal account of coming to see correspondences through work in Women's Studies.* Wellesley College, Center for Research on Women. Retrieved from http://www.nymbp.org/reference/WhitePrivilege.pdf.

Markus, H. R., Uchida, Y., Omoregie, H., Townsend, S. S. M., & Kitayama, S. (2006). Going for gold: Models of agency in Japanese and American context. *Psychological Science, 17,* 103–112.

Marshall, D. (2010). Introduction. In S. Robertson (Ed.), *Taking the lead: Strategies and solutions from female coaches* (pp. xv–1). Edmonton: The University of Alberta Press.

McDonald, M. G. (2005). Mapping whiteness and sport: An introduction. *Sociology of Sport Journal, 22,* 245–255.

Messner, M. A. (2002). *Taking the field: Women, men, and sports.* Minneapolis: University of Minnesota Press.

Messner, M. A. (2007). *It's all for the kids: Gender, families, and youth sports.* Berkeley, CA: University of California Press.

Messner, M. A., & Cooky, C. (2010, June). *Gender in televised sports: News and highlights shows, 1989–2009.* Center for Feminist Research, University of Southern California. Retrieved from: http://dornsife.usc.edu/cfr/gender-in-televised-sports/.

Mio, J. S., Barker-Hackett, L., & Tumambing, J. (2006). *Multicultural psychology: Understanding our diverse communities.* Boston: McGraw-Hill.

Morrow, R. G., & Gill, D. L. (2003). Perceptions of homophobia and heterosexism in physical education. *Research Quarterly for Exercise and Sport, 74,* 205–214.

Norman, L. (2010). The UK coaching system is failing women coaches. *International Journal of Sports Science and Coaching, 3,* 447–467.

Pain, H., & Wiles, R. (2006). The experience of being disabled and obese. *Disability and Rehabilitation, 28*, 1211–1220.

Parham, W. D. (2005). Raising the bar: Developing an understanding of athletes from racially, culturally, and ethnically diverse backgrounds. In M. B. Anderson (Ed.), *Sport psychology in practice* (pp. 201–215). Champaign, IL: Human Kinetics.

Parham, W. D. (2011). Research vs. me-search: Thinking more of thee and less of me when working within the context of culture. *Journal of Clinical Sport Psychology, 5*, 311–324.

Puhl, R., & Heuer, C. A. (2011). Obesity stigma: Important considerations for public health. *American Journal of Public Health, 100*, 1019–1028.

Puhl, R. M., & Wharton, C. M. (2007). Weight bias: A primer for the fitness Industry. *ACSM's Health & Fitness Journal, 11* (3), 7–11.

Ram, N., Starek, J., & Johnson, J. (2004). Race, ethnicity, and sexual orientation: Still a void in sport and exercise psychology. *Journal of Sport & Exercise Psychology, 26*, 250–268.

Rimmer, J. H. (2005). The conspicuous absence of people with disabilities in public fitness and recreation facilities: Lack of interest or lack of access? *American Journal of Health Promotion, 19*, 327–329.

Robertson, N., & Vohora, R. (2008). Fitness vs. fatness: Implicit bias towards obesity among fitness professionals and regular exercisers. *Psychology of Sport and Exercise, 9*, 547–557.

Rodriguez, E. A., & Gill, D. L. (2011). Sexual harassment perceptions among Puerto Rican female former athletes. *International Journal of Sport and Exercise Psychology, 9*, 323–337.

Ryba, T. V., Stambulova, N. B., Si, G., & Schinke, R. J. (2013). ISSP position stand: Culturally competent research and practice in sport and exercise psychology. *International Journal of Sport and Exercise Psychology, 11*, 123–142, http://dx.doi.org/10.1080/1612197X.2013.779812.

Sabo, D., & Veliz, P. (2012). *Decade of decline: Gender equity in high school sports.* Ann Arbor, MI: SHARP Center for Women and Girls.

Schinke, R., & Hanrahan, S. (2008). *Cultural sport psychology.* Champaign, IL: Human Kinetics.

Schinke, R., & Moore, Z. E. (2011). Culturally informed sport psychology: Introduction to the special issue. *Journal of Clinical Sport Psychology, 5*, 283–294.

Spence, J. T., & Helmreich, R. L. (1978). *Masculinity and femininity.* Austin, TX: University of Texas Press.

Steele, C. M. (1997). A threat in the air: How stereotypes shape intellectual identity and performance. *American Psychologist, 52*, 613–629.

Stone, J., Lynch, C. I., Sjomeling, M., & Darley, J. M. (1999). Stereotype threat effects on black and white athletic performance. *Journal of Personality and Social Psychology, 77*, 1213–1227.

Stone, J., Perry, Z. W., & Darley, J. M. (1997). "White men can't jump": Evidence for the perceptual confirmation of racial stereotypes following a basketball game. *Basic and Applied Social Psychology, 19*, 291–306.

Sue, D. W. (2004). Whiteness and ethnocentric monoculturalism: Making the "invisible" visible. *American Psychologist, 59*, 761–769.

Sue, S. (2006). Cultural competency: From philosophy to research and practice. *Journal of Community Psychology, 34*, 237–245.

Thomae, J., & Kamphoff, C. (2013). *Emerging from silence: Experiences of gay male coaches in the NCAA.* Under review.

Enhancing Health and Well-Being

When to Refer Athletes for Counseling or Psychotherapy

David Tod, *University of the Sunshine Coast*
Mark B. Andersen, *Victoria University*

Canst thou not minister to a mind diseas'd, Pluck from the memory a rooted sorrow, Raze out the written troubles of the brain, And with some sweet oblivious antidote Cleanse the stuff'd bosom of that perilous stuff Which weighs upon the heart?

—*Macbeth, act V, scene iii*

A sport psychology practitioner had been working with a gifted collegiate male hammer thrower for about three months. A close trusting relationship had formed, and together they had addressed a number of performance and communication issues. Recently, however, the thrower started to miss sessions, although he always contacted the psychologist and rescheduled. The practitioner was concerned because he also had noticed the athlete had been losing weight. One day when the young man failed to attend a session and did not call, the psychologist tried to contact him and left a message. After not hearing from the thrower for two days, the sport psychologist attended practice and found out from the coach that the thrower had missed the last two days of training because of the flu. Later that evening the practitioner finally made contact with the athlete via the telephone. The thrower was very apologetic and also scared because he

had lied to his coach; he did not have the flu. On further discussion, the athlete admitted that he had not been able to train, go to school, or even bring himself to eat. He had fallen into a dark place, and he wanted to go to sleep without waking up. The psychologist, recognizing the signs of depression, and realizing the associated risk of suicide, managed to convince the athlete to come to his office straight away.

Depression is "the common cold" of mental health disorders among the general population (Andersen, 2004), and sport psychology practitioners will invariably come across athletes displaying some signs and symptoms, such as those in the above example. Athletes often experience depressed moods following losses or failures to perform as hoped or expected. If depressed moods are particularly severe or seem to last longer than usual, athletes may need help to get through the sense of loss or disappointment. In many cases, individuals hide their depression from others or may self-medicate through the use of alcohol or other substances. Individuals experiencing depression may show social withdrawal, hopelessness, or loss of self-esteem. Lethargy is also a common symptom and may prevent sports participants from training. Verbalizations indicating depression, hopelessness, or poor self-esteem should be red flags for coaches and sport psychology practitioners alike. Overt and covert signs may signal a call for help. With depression there is often the possibility of suicide, which may take the form of unusual risk taking (Cogan, 2000). Treatment may include psychotherapy and antidepressant medication, and unless the sport psychology practitioner is competent and qualified to deal with depressed athletes, a referral to another professional is needed. Referral is a sensitive issue, and practitioners need to show compassion and care (see Andersen & Van Raalte, 2005, for how the above case example was successfully resolved). In general, when a sport psychologist is faced with an athlete or coach whose presenting concern is outside the practitioner's realm of expertise (or in need of medication) then the practitioner needs to: (a) refer the client to another therapist (or physician to prescribe medication) for treatment, and (b) might consider upskilling through training courses, professional development, workshops, clinical supervision, and self-study, along with gaining any necessary qualifications, to become recognized as competent to work with future athletes presenting with the issue.

Most athletes' requests for assistance with performance issues, such as prerace anxieties, will not necessitate referral to professionals trained to help individuals with clinical, deep-seated, or severe emotional difficulties. Over time, however, sport psychology practitioners and coaches will come into contact with athletes they are not equipped to help, and in these situations referral is the ethical path to follow. The goal of this chapter is to provide a set of guidelines that people working with athletes and exercise participants can use for referring individuals for professional counseling or psychotherapy. We also will provide suggestions about making

suitable referrals for varying circumstances, and we will present dialogue from a referral session. Referring athletes to mental health practitioners does not mean sport psychology practitioners need to stop working with their clients. There are no ethical violations or professional problems when performance enhancement sport psychology practitioners and clinical or counseling psychologists work with athletes at the same time, as long as all parties are informed with the clients' consent. In many cases, a team approach can be the optimal way to deliver services. In the space of a chapter it is impossible to describe the symptoms, methods for assessment, and suitable interventions for the many possible mental health issues athletes may present. Such information already exists, and readers are referred to the American Psychiatric Association's (2013) *Diagnostic and Statistical Manual for Mental Disorders-V* for information on specific issues. Instead, we provide some information on many of the more common issues for referral to clinical and counseling practitioners that might arise in sport settings.

The False Dichotomy of Performance Enhancement Versus Problematic Personal Issues

In many (probably most) instances it may not be possible to disentangle performance from personal issues, and sometimes they may be one and the same. Imagine, for example, that a performance enhancement practitioner has worked with an athlete for several months, and the client's skill level has improved to the point that making an international team is now a realistic possibility. The athlete's life may have changed considerably; she is now living her dream, her self-worth has risen, and her relationships with her coach, parents, and siblings have improved. She has become a happier person. A useful question is: "How does performance fit in the rest of the athlete's life?" Performance enhancement techniques, such as goal setting and self-talk, may be of limited value if the athlete's life is a jumble of confusion and conflict. For an athlete experiencing prerace anxiety that is intimately tied to parental love and acceptance, or feelings of worthiness as a human being, relaxation may prove to be an inadequate Band-Aid for what are deeper issues than prerace nerves.

In much of the performance enhancement literature, problems in performance are related to issues such as competition anxiety, motivational problems, poor self-talk, and lapses in concentration. Determining whether other factors might be involved requires understanding a number of interrelated issues. An athlete coming to a coach or sport psychology practitioner may be uncomfortable if an interview probes personal areas. Likewise, the practitioner may be reluctant to ask highly personal questions. It is possible, however, to get at least a feel for some of the salient issues in typical discussions of sport performance factors. It is natural for the sport psychologist or coach to build rapport by asking athletes about themselves. Getting athletes to talk about their lives can lead to understanding their performance or motivational problems, as well as the whole person.

Often, many requests for assistance with performance enhancement will be just what they appear to be, and practitioners with supervised experience and adequate sport psychology training will be able to assist the athletes with whom they interact. In some cases, however, athletes will present with issues outside the realm of practitioners' expertise, and sometimes those concerns will emerge after the sport psychologist and athlete have worked together for a while. The next few paragraphs provide some guidelines to allow practitioners to decide if an issue warrants additional professional assistance to help the athlete.

First, how long a problem has existed, its severity, and its relationship to other issues in the person's life becomes important. A problem that is relatively recent, that is not severe in its emotional implications, and that does not have substantial overlap with other aspects of a person's life is less likely to require professional assistance. For example, an athlete who is facing a tough competitive situation and who experiences mild to moderate anxiety and negative self-talk is not likely to require referral. A person for whom each athletic competition becomes an all-or-nothing battle for a sense of self, whose emotional state is dependent on performance outcomes, and where strong anxiety, depressive states, or substance abuse may also be involved is more likely to need a referral, although performance-related issues can still be addressed by the performance enhancement sport psychology practitioner.

Second, unusual emotional reactions may also need to be considered. Anxiety that generalizes to situations beyond the athletic arena may signal that other issues are present and that interventions may be needed to help deal with other areas of the person's life. Anger or aggression is likely to be an issue presented by an athlete only if it has become a problem to others. Unfortunately, it may take the form of fights with strangers, which sometimes involve legal complications, as well as familial abuse issues. In other cases, an athlete may lose control within the competitive context. This emotional reaction may inhibit otherwise good performance or be a performance threat in that the person becomes a liability in terms of penalties or ejections from the game.

Third, it may also be important to examine the effectiveness of traditional performance enhancement interventions. For example, perhaps an athlete has not disclosed the full extent of the issue or is not aware of it. It may be that the person working with the athlete did not come to understand the nature and extent of the problem. If traditional interventions, such as self-talk and imagery, do not seem to be working, there are several possibilities to consider. Perhaps the athlete did not respond to the particular intervention; for example, many individuals are not naturally adept at imagery. It may also be that the sport-related problem was not accurately assessed or was stronger than initially assumed. It may also be, however, that the sport-related concern is intimately tied to other issues in the person's life and may have deeper, stronger, or more chronic patterns than the practitioner first believed.

Considerations for Helping to Decide if an Issue Warrants Referral

1. *How long has the issue existed?*
2. *What is the severity of the issue?*
3. *How does the issue relate to other factors in the person's life?*
4. *Does the person display unusual emotions or behaviors around the issue?*
5. *How well is the athlete using existing interventions or coping strategies?*
6. *Does the practitioner have the knowledge, skills, and competencies to address the issue?*

How to Start the Referral Process

The referral process is not usually a straightforward one. If trust and rapport have been built between the sport psychologist and the athlete, sending the athlete directly to someone else when material comes up that the practitioner does not feel competent to handle may not be the optimal choice. Instead of referring out, *referring in* may be the better choice (Van Raalte & Andersen, 2013). Bringing in a qualified professional and having all three parties sit down and discuss a plan may be less threatening to the athlete and help ease the individual into the therapeutic process. Referring in may be the best way to keep that therapeutic process going.

Most articles on referring athletes to other practitioners (Andersen & Van Raalte, 2005; Van Raalte & Andersen, 2013) focus on what to do (and what not to do), and what should happen. The question of many students is, "how do you do it?" There is probably no better way (except for a live role play) to demonstrate how to do a referral than through dialogue and commentary. The second author's (Mark Andersen's) experiences when he knew he was not qualified to work with an athlete with an eating disorder illustrate the issue.

Quite early in my career, I (Mark) had been seeing a swimmer, Angela, for about two months, working with her primarily on self-talk

and arousal regulation. When she arrived at our eighth meeting, I could see something was wrong. We had built a strong working alliance, so when she answered my question about how things were going with a flat "Okay, I guess," I jumped in:

Mark (M): From over here, it doesn't look like things are okay. It looks like something not very good is going on.

Angela (A): I don't know Doc, I'm just kind of worried. [I kept silent to see if she would go on, but she just sighed.]

M: So, what's troubling you, Angela?

A: [beginning to have tears in her eyes] I am just outta control [now full tears flowing].

M: I can see that this is really painful; tell me what's going on.

A: You'd be disgusted with me.

M: We've worked together for about two months, and I think we've built up a good relationship. I don't know everything about you, but what I know is that you are a fine person. I can't imagine that anything you could tell me would put me off. So let's look at what's going on and see if we can figure out what to do.

At this point, I know something big is coming. Angela is having trouble talking to me about the problem for a variety of reasons. First, she is disgusted with herself and thinks I will be disgusted too. Because of our strong working alliance and her positive transference to me, she does not want to say anything that will disappoint me (see Tod & Andersen, 2012). I am trying to reassure her of my unconditional positive regard and to remind her that we are in this endeavor together and that we will look for solutions. Angela then began to tell me of being stressed with swimming, her weight, and school pressures and how her long-standing once-a-week binge–purge episodes had turned into an almost daily occurrence.

A: How can I do that to myself? Don't you think it's terrible?

M: No, I don't think it's terrible. In fact, right now I am feeling really proud of you for having the courage to talk about all this. I know it's gotta be one of the harder things you've done. . . . I want to do everything I can to help, but Angela, to tell you the truth, I am not trained in eating problems. I think we need to talk to an expert.

A: But I don't want to talk to anyone else. I want to talk to you. Those people over in Student Health don't understand athletes.

M: I know what you mean, but I know a great psychologist over there who is a runner herself and competed in college. She is a major sweetheart and really understands eating problems and weight concerns in sport.

A: I just hate going over there, and I don't want to go to sports medicine. If I did that, I know it would get back to the coach.

M: Nothing is going to get back to the coach unless you want it to. I have an idea. How about if I ask Dr. Kerstner [the expert] to come over here and you and she and I all sit down together? We could meet right here in my office just like our usual appointment. How's that sound?

A: I guess that would be okay. I just feel comfortable with you.

M: I'll be there with you all the way, and I know you and Dr. Kerstner will hit it off.

A: Can I still keep seeing you?

M: Of course! I am your sport psychologist as long as you want me to be. We can keep working on your swimming, and I'll be checking in with you and Dr. Kerstner occasionally on how things are going. How's that?

A: Okay, ask her to come over.

M: I'll get hold of her right after our session.

A: Doc, could we do a nice long autogenic thing today? I'm kind of frazzled.

M: You bet, you know the drill. All right, get yourself in a comfortable position and take a nice deep breath. . . .

This interchange contains many different processes, all directed at making the referral an acceptable option. First, I assure Angela that instead of seeing her problem as terrible (and disgusting), I am proud of her. I am letting her know that my opinion of her has changed only for the better because of what she has told me. Next, I introduce the idea of referral, but she is quite resistant. Athletes at large North American universities (from my experience) often feel that services on "main campus" are not geared for their needs. I attempt to overcome the resistance by telling her a little bit about the psychologist's sport background and by letting her know that I think quite highly of Dr. Kerstner. This last point illustrates the importance of having a referral network of health care professionals who are sensitive to athletes' issues. Angela is coming around, but she still wants to stay with me. Her reaction is understandable; our relationship has been built to this intimate point, a point where she is able to talk about truly painful issues in her life. Getting here was a long process, and she may not want to tell her problems to a stranger. I address Angela's lingering resistance by suggesting that we see Dr. Kerstner on familiar turf (my office) and by letting her know I will be with her all the way.

At the end of this emotionally draining session (for athlete and psychologist both), Angela wants to return to the familiar and the soothing, so we do something together that we have done several times before—we relax. In time, other professionals (e.g., a physician or nutritionist) would be called in to help Angela (see Petrie & Sherman, 2000, for a description of a team approach to eating disorders). This first, and largest, referral step helped Angela get on the path of treatment. No two referrals are alike, and some referrals are easier than others. But almost all referrals are complex and sensitive in nature.

When Referrals Don't Go Smoothly

Some athletes may not follow their sport psychologists' advice to seek assistance from other professionals. Van Raalte & Andersen, (2013) presented a list of *dos* and *don'ts* for the referral process that provide some indications of why athletes may not follow their practitioners' suggestions. First, sport psychologists and athletes may not have sound working alliances. In the absence of close relationships, athletes may not trust that their sport psychologists have their best interests at heart. Practitioners' recommendations, for example, might be interpreted as attempts to rid themselves of their athletes and pass them on to other professionals. From such interpretations, athletes might infer they are damaged goods and possibly unworthy.

Second, if handled insensitively, athletes might feel unsupported and believe their trepidations regarding referral have been ignored. One fear might be that the mental health practitioners will take away from athletes what made them high achievers in sports. Confidentiality is important as well; if word gets around that athletes are seeing other practitioners, they might feel they have lost some of their dignity. Although society has become more psychologically aware in recent years, there are those who still stigmatize people seeking counseling.

Third, practitioners may not have prepared athletes adequately for the referral process. Sport psychologists need to inform athletes about what referrals involve, whom the other helpers include, why they might help, and what the implications are for the existing sport psychologist–athlete relationships. Practitioners can begin preparation right from the start by signaling to athletes in their first sessions together that referral might be a possibility in the future. Athletes poorly prepared for referral may have unrealistic expectations about how helpful the new practitioners might be, particularly if sport psychology practitioners have oversold the benefits to convince athletes to seek help.

Fourth, in the absence of any follow-up or facilitation, athletes might never contact the recommended practitioners or may not persist after the initial meetings. The match between the athlete and the helper may not be close enough for benefits to accrue. Also, it may have been a huge step for athletes to share sensitive material with their sport psychology practitioners, who may be among the few trusted people in their lives. Athletes may not be ready to establish new relationships with other strangers.

When faced with referrals that do not appear to be working well, sport psychologists can still keep in contact with athletes. To maintain a close relationship, the perception that the sport psychology practitioner's continued help is conditional on the athlete meeting with the external helper needs to be avoided. It is probably inadvisable, and impractical, to force athletes to meet with other professionals if they are uncomfortable, except in situations where there is a threat of harm to self or others. Then practitioners have ethical (and legal) obligations to consider. Sport psychologists who maintain their relationships with their athletes can continue to provide performance enhancement assistance and can still initiate the referral process in the future if athletes change their minds.

Some Specific Athlete-Related Issues

Sometimes, in addition to performance issues, or related to them, other concerns confronting athletes may surface. Insights into depression were presented at the start of this chapter; let's now look at some other issues in more detail.

Identity Issues

One of the most problematic issues for many athletes is that sometimes their whole sense of self has revolved around their roles as athletes (Balague, 1999), the development of which may begin in childhood (Carless & Douglas, 2013). This overidentification may be particularly salient for competitors at elite levels or in more glamorous sports, but it can occur for any person in any sport. Often the athlete's hopes for the future, and social support from others, may revolve around the sport and competitive success. For someone working with these issues, attempts at performance enhancement may take on an extreme urgency, because the athlete's sense of self may well be riding on performance outcomes. When individuals identify with the role of athlete exclusively, they are said to have *foreclosed* their identities (Miller & Kerr, 2003). Petitpas and Danish (1995) have discussed psychological identity foreclosure:

> In psychological foreclosure people rigidly adhere to their identities to maintain security or to cope with intrapsychic anxiety. This might be seen in athletes who are adult children of an alcoholic parent. They may be resistant to change and more vulnerable to threats of identity loss because their method of coping with their life situations is to seek approval through their athletic successes. The loss of their athletic role would compromise their entire defensive structure. (p. 263)

Major threats to identity can come through athletic injury and through career terminations (Brewer, 2010; Park, Lavallee, & Tod, 2013). Brewer and Petrie (2002) have reported that 5 to 24 percent of athletes who sustain an injury experience clinically significant levels of psychological distress. For an example of this distress, see the Brewer and Petitpas (2005) chapter that contains an in-depth case study about an international skier who had experienced repeated knee injuries.

Although we normally think of the identity of athletes as something both individuals and peer groups see as positive, valuable, and rewarding, there are also versions that become negative identities (Erikson, 1968). In essence, a *negative identity* is the acceptance and valuing of an identity that is generally disapproved of by society. For example, the dumb jock is one such negative identity. Individuals and subgroups may hold opinions that athletes shouldn't care about school or shouldn't do well, and so forth. This negative identity, although disapproved of by many, may become important to an individual or subgroup. Similarly, the tough jock identity is problematic. For many, being an athlete means being tough, and it often involves intimidating others verbally or physically. Substance abuse issues also can become part of negative identity patterns. To be a successful jock one may need to be able to consume a great deal of alcohol or other drugs. In some cases such activity is done covertly, with an eye to the clean-cut image that has to be maintained for public relations purposes.

As with many other human affairs, unless individuals see these identity issues as areas that are problematic and that they would like to change, it may only be possible for coaches or sport psychologists to communicate concern for these areas and to point athletes in the direction of those who can help them work on these difficulties.

Sexual Orientation and Abusive Environments

Athletes' sexual orientation, especially for lesbian, gay, bisexual, and transsexual (LGBT) athletes, has received limited attention in the sport psychology literature (Krane, Waldron, Kauer, & Semerjian, 2010; Martens & Mobley, 2005), and one must go to sociological and popular writings to learn about LGBT athletes' experiences and the culture of abuse and discrimination in sport (e.g., Louganis & Marcus, 1996). Although LGBT athletes may struggle with the "coming out" process, for most of these sports participants their sexuality is not their primary issue. The abuse and discrimination present in the sporting world is usually a far more serious concern, and it raises fears in athletes about getting less playing time, being kicked off teams, being harassed, and being physically abused if their orientations were made public. Reactions to the abusive environments of sport may manifest in anxiety disorders, relationship problems, depression, and even suicidal ideation. All of these potential problems may require referral to clinical professionals. If sport psychology practitioners are uncomfortable interacting with LGBT athletes or are not sensitive to the abusive environments and issues these athletes experience, then referral may be the optimal and ethical decision. LGBT athletes are likely to feel more comfortable talking with professionals who can empathize with them and offer specific assistance.

Sex- and Health-Related Issues

Most athletic careers start seriously sometime during adolescence and usually end somewhere in the mid-20s to late 30s. In Erikson's (1968) language, many athletes are in the middle of the challenges of either "identity versus role confusion" or "intimacy versus isolation." Both these times are periods of experimentation, exploration, and finding out about oneself. For some athletes the exploration of self and intimate relationships may involve risk-taking behavior, especially in the realm of sex. The number of sexually transmitted diseases (STDs) is overwhelming. HIV is only the most obvious. Other potentially lethal or debilitating STDs include hepatitis B and C, gonorrhea, and syphilis. Athletes may approach sport psychology practitioners to talk about risky sexual behaviors they have engaged in that have made them quite anxious about their health status. If a professional is uncomfortable discussing intimate behavior or is just not knowledgeable about STDs, referral to a counselor with expertise in sexual health is most appropriate.

Butki, Andersen, and Heyman (1996) revealed that collegiate athletes and nonathletes alike use condoms irregularly, but athletes in general engage in sexual behavior more frequently and have more partners than their nonathlete peers. Student athletes may be at greater risk for a variety of STDs than students in general. In addition to sexual behaviors, sharing needles is also a high-risk factor for hepatitis B and C and HIV infection. Steroids can be injected, for example, and often in gyms or locker rooms several athletes may use the same syringe. Again, athletes or sport participants may need to talk with someone about their behaviors and their fears. This person should be knowledgeable and able to make referrals for more specific issues.

Eating Disorders

Because of the complexities of eating disorders and the psychological, physical, and physiological effects that accompany them, referral to a variety of health care professionals (e.g., dieticians, gastroenterologists, psychologists, team doctors) is becoming the norm. Eating disorders among athletes have received much attention in the sports medicine and sport psychology fields (Reel & Galli, 2012). Reported prevalence rates

for eating disorders among athletes vary considerably depending on the sport and who is doing the study. For example, Sundgot-Borgen (1994) found that 8 percent of elite female Norwegian athletes were diagnosable as having eating disorders, but Burckes-Miller and Black (1988) found a huge prevalence rate (39 percent) for U.S. female collegiate athletes.

Although estimates of eating disorder incidence in men vary greatly, from 0.2 to 20 percent depending on the study cited, the rate may be increasing (Petrie & Greenleaf, 2007; Reel & Galli, 2012). Eating disorders historically have been considered a "female" concern, and so there is probably significant underreporting of the prevalence and incidence in males (Baum, 2006). Compared to women, however, men may have a higher age of onset (Braun, Sunday, Huang, & Halmi, 1999), seek therapeutic help less often (Olivardia, Pope, Mangweth, & Hudson, 1995), and have less chance of successful outcomes (Oyebode, Boodhoo, & Schapira, 1988). In controlling weight, men may be more likely to use saunas, steam baths, and exercise, whereas women may resort to purging, diet pills, and laxatives (Braun et al., 1999).

A central feature of eating disorders is often a disturbance in body image, and over the last two decades interest in the ways men view their physiques has grown. Increasingly, men are feeling as if they need to attain a highly muscular mesomorphic body shape (Edwards, Tod, Morrison, & Molnar, 2012). In addition to eating disorders, body dissatisfaction has been related with body dysmorphia, some forms of somatic delusional disorders, poor self-esteem, depression, social anxiety, inhibition, sexual dysfunction, and a variety of health-risk behaviors, such as excessive exercise and steroid use (Edwards et al., 2012; Tod & Lavallee, 2010).

The etiologies for eating disorders and body dissatisfaction in the general public and in athletes are probably, in some cases, dissimilar. Andersen and Fawkner (2005) identified a number of reasons why athletes may experience disturbed eating and body dissatisfaction. First, although poor body image might motivate exercise and sports participation, there may be no changes in some anatomical features, and, hence, the source of the dissatisfaction may not be alleviated. Second, some sports and types of exercise may not produce desired body changes. Third, participation in sport and exercise may raise expectations beyond what is realistically or genetically possible. Fourth, comparing oneself against others may result in a negative evaluation. The chance of dissatisfaction may be heightened in sports where comparisons are part of the competitive process, especially in sports such as diving or gymnastics. Fifth, participants may be reinforced for developing an excessive preoccupation with their weight and physique, notably those athletes whose coaches dwell on body appearance. Disturbed body image may continue past an athletic career into retirement (Park et al., 2013). Sixth, individual, psychosocial, and cultural factors also need consideration. For example, men with stronger affiliations to the gay community experience greater body dissatisfaction compared to those with weaker affiliations (Beren, Hayden, Wilfley, & Grilo, 1996). Andersen and Fawkner suggested that individual, psychosocial, and cultural factors need more empirical and clinical examination if a better understanding of the relationships between exercise participation, sports involvement, body dissatisfaction, and eating disorders is to be achieved.

Athletes with eating disorders should be referred for treatment if the sport psychologist is not knowledgeable regarding these disorders and how best to treat them. A more important question in sports, however, is whether the pathogenic sport environment should be the object of treatment. I (Mark Andersen) worked with a collegiate gymnast whose disordered eating was essentially environmentally dependent. When she was away from school and away from the coach and the gym, her bulimic behavior dropped to zero. After returning from semester break, she said, "I was just fine at home; it didn't happen, not even once. But as soon as I get back here—Blam!—it's starting all over again." I met this gymnast in her senior year and we worked together on some cognitive-behavioral interventions to decrease the frequency of her bulimic behavior. She was successful at reducing the frequency of the bulimic behaviors, but the eating disorder did not go into full remission until she finished her competitive career and left the sport at the end of her senior year.

Eating disorders are difficult to treat, and eating disorders among athletes, more than many other referrals, bring up the question of whom or what is really in need of referral. Stimulated by the previously mentioned case (and others), the Eating Disorders Team at my (Mark's) university (composed of general practitioners, a psychiatrist, psychologists, a dietician, and a sport psychologist from the student mental health center) ran educational seminars in the athletics department. These seminars were aimed at increasing the coaches', administrators', and sports medicine personnel's awareness of the signs and symptoms of eating disorders and helping them make referrals to appropriate services. The athletics department was receptive to these interventions, in part, because they and the university were facing litigation from a former student athlete who claimed she arrived at the university healthy and left with an eating disorder directly related to her sport.

There is an extensive body of literature that coaches and psychologists can read to learn how to help athletes with eating disorders (Arthur-Cameselle & Baltzell, 2012), such as how to identify warning signs. Some warning signs of eating disorders to watch for include a marked loss in weight, preoccupation with weight, avoidance of team and other socially related functions involving food, eating very little at such functions, visits to the bathroom after meals, bloodshot eyes after bathroom visits, a decrease in energy level and ability to concentrate, chronic gastrointestinal complaints, and increased mood swings. Eating disorders among athletes is a topic deserving an entire chapter on its own, and entire books have been written on the subject (e.g., Dosil, 2008).

Alcohol and Substance Abuse Issues

Due to the public fascination with celebrities' problems with alcohol and drugs, this domain is one in which athletes' problems have received extensive attention (Backhouse, 2012; Stainback

& Taylor, 2005). The association in the United States and other Western countries between masculinity and drinking (as well as the ability to consume large amounts of other substances) may make some athletes more vulnerable to developing problems in this area. Research suggests that student-athletes are a high-risk group (Doumas, Haustveit, & Coll, 2010): they consume more alcohol, start drinking earlier, and engage more frequently in alcohol-related risk behaviors (e.g., driving after drinking) than their nonsporting counterparts (Hildebrand, Johnson, & Bogle, 2001). Research also indicates that athletes' alcohol consumption may vary with different sports and at various times during the competitive year (Doumas, Turrisi, & Wright, 2006; Martens, Dams-O'Connor, & Duffy-Paiement, 2006). In addition, individuals inclined to take risks, or "sensation seekers" (Zuckerman, 1979), are also likely to indulge in greater amounts of alcohol and drug use. Certain sports may disproportionately attract sensation seekers.

Someone working with athletes should recognize the general symptoms of excessive alcohol or drug use. Most commonly these signs involve chronic use or binges, centering major events around drug and alcohol usage, personality changes during usage, and usage interfering with other life activities or relationships. Unfortunately, high school and college life in general, and often the athletic environment, will cloak problem usage with different forms of social acceptability. Given denial and defensiveness around alcohol and drug use, coaches or sport psychology practitioners concerned about these issues can note their concerns, but not in lecturing or threatening ways. It is important to have sources for referral available, particularly if athletes become concerned about their usage and would like to seek help.

Anger and Aggression Control

In many competitive sports, coaches and players encourage psychological attributes of toughness and competitiveness and portray opponents as enemies to be defeated. In contact sports in particular, but in other sports as well, physical aggression is sanctioned. Most athletes are able to control their anger and aggression both on the field and off, although some require a little time after competition for the behavioral controls to reset.

For some individuals, however, who experience difficulty with anger or aggression control, a referral might be appropriate. Some individuals may have always had a reputation for conflict. For men, this tendency may have a negative identity component that cloaks the problem in an acceptable way for a peer group. The athlete may be tough on and off the field, someone "not to mess with." Unfortunately, the frequency and severity of conflicts may escalate to harmful levels.

In other cases, someone going through a personally difficult time may be less able to control anger or aggression. This difficulty may be expressed either on or off the field. Particularly when anger and aggression have not been issues for a person before, they might be discussed with the athlete and a referral made.

Alcohol and drug use may also be related to such behaviors. In general, when people are intoxicated, bottled-up anger or rage may be expressed more easily than when sober. In recent years, in addition, *roid rages,* or violent reactions in some individuals who are taking steroids, have been noted (Backhouse, 2012).

There are ways to help individuals deal with anger and aggression (Novaco, 1975). It is easier to help individuals resolve conflicts and reestablish controls if they have had a reasonably good history of anger and aggression control. Helping athletes with more problematic histories is possible, but it may be a slower process.

Romantic and Family Relationship Issues

Athletes and sport participants are likely to have relationship problems similar to those of others in their peer groups. Some problems, however, might be unique to athletes, although similar to others who are celebrities or who are dedicated to demanding activities in which their partners may not be involved.

Many athletes have to be away from friends or family for extended periods of time. This absence can cause loneliness, anxiety, and depression, for both the athlete and family members.

There may be conflicts in the relationship, or fears or suspicions, and these problems can manifest themselves in decreased performance, increased anger and aggression, or a number of other ways. At the same time, practice and competition place demands on the athlete's time at home, and this pressure, too, may be problematic for the partner. For many marathoners, who may not be elite or competitive athletes, for example, the months taken to train may disrupt family or relationship patterns. Someone who spends years involved in training and competition may need an understanding or mutually involved partner. Also, given the amount of time that teams and squad spend together, intrateam romantic relationships issues may surface (Van Raalte et al., 2011).

The glamour and celebrity-like status that can surround athletes, as well as long travels away from home, offer opportunities for infidelity. Even when an athlete is not unfaithful, the partner may have fears about straying when the athlete is away, or the athlete may have anxiety about the partner left behind.

It is not always easy to identify these issues. In some cases, when performance becomes problematic, the athlete will indicate that the source is an interpersonal or relationship problem. In other cases, a relationship problem may manifest itself in changes in mood; the expression of anger, depression, or anxiety; or increases in alcohol or drug use. Often teammates will be told of the situation, and they may discuss it with a coach or others.

The athlete or sport participant may need to talk with someone individually to come to understand personal reactions and to make decisions about commitments and behaviors. In other cases, marital, relationship, or family counseling or therapy might be the best referrals.

Professional Development Tasks for Practitioners and Students

Practitioners and students can engage in numerous professional development tasks to help make referral processes go smoothly and to ensure that athletes feel accepted and supported. Becoming familiar with the psychopathology of various mental health problems is a valuable first step, particularly for those individuals without clinical backgrounds. Practitioners with knowledge about the origins and manifestations of mental and behavioral disorders are well placed to recognize when athletes are experiencing serious difficulties and be able to direct them to suitable professionals. Knowledge of psychopharmacology is also relevant because practitioners need to be familiar with what drugs are prescribed for various disorders and their typical side effects. For example, some anxiolytic drugs may lower blood pressure, and if relaxation treatment is also being used, blood pressure may drop to unhealthy levels. Also, sport psychology practitioners, coaches, and athletes need to be aware of what medications are prohibited by national and international sport governing agencies (e.g., the World Anti-Doping Agency, WADA, at http://www.wada-ama.org/en/). Sport psychologists, well informed about psychopathology and pharmacology, may have a keen appreciation of what life is like for people with mental health concerns, and they may be able to use that empathic understanding to maintain helpful working relationships with their athletes. Being able to talk knowledgeably and nonjudgmentally about mental disorders with athletes will help practitioners support their clients and prepare them for referrals to recommended mental health professionals. Texts and chapters (American Psychiatric Association, 2013; Andersen, 2004) contain useful information for practitioners' continuing education, and sport psychologists can supplement their technical knowledge by reading biographies of athletes who have experienced mental health issues (Fussell, 1991; Louganis & Marcus, 1996). Many NCAA institutions in the United States are seeking licensed clinical sport psychologists who can assist athletes with performance enhancement and address a range of clinical issues (Gardner, 2007). If such a trend continues, then individuals who are trained in sport and exercise science departments may find it worthwhile considering further training to become licensed psychologists.

Another way students and practitioners can prepare themselves for handling future referrals well is by identifying professionals they know and trust. Sport psychologists can select from a range of suitable individuals, depending on athletes' needs. These professionals include psychiatrists, clinical and counseling psychologists, social workers, pastoral care providers, marriage and family therapists, substance abuse counselors, and career guidance experts. Many athletes' concerns may not be related to mental health, but instead to other domains such as nutrition or physical well-being. Sport psychologists' networks could include nutritionists, biomechanists, sports medicine specialists, and exercise physiologists. Understanding the sporting backgrounds of the individuals in sport psychologists' professional networks will help practitioners suggest experts who are best suited to helping and forming working alliances with athletes. For example, a clinical psychologist who has participated in track and field events may be a good choice for the depressed hammer thrower mentioned at the start of this chapter.

Sport psychology practitioners and students also can engage in role plays to prepare themselves for making referrals (Tod, 2007). By rehearsing the referral process, sport psychologists can practice ways to interact with athletes in a caring and compassionate manner. For example, an athlete may feel threatened by meeting a clinical or counseling psychologist, and role playing helping the athlete overcome those anxieties adds another dimension to the sport psychologist's repertoire. Peer-group supervision is an ideal place to conduct role plays because fellow practitioners can receive feedback from their colleagues in a safe, problem-solving environment.

Supervision, generally, can be an ideal place for practitioners to seek guidance from senior practitioners and colleagues about specific athletes whom they are unsure if they can help. Seeking advice and guidance from others may be instrumental in deciding if referral is suitable and how best to handle such instances. Supervision is also a place where practitioners can self-reflect and develop their skills. Practitioners who do not examine their own attitudes and behaviors may not be in a position to help others. A person who is open and accepting of others, however, will convey an important message to athletes and will increase the likelihood of the athlete agreeing to referral procedures.

Professional Development Tasks for Practitioners

1. *Become familiar with the psychopathology of various mental health issues*

2. *Increase awareness of various other physical, medical, and social challenges*

3. *Develop knowledge of psychopharmacology*

4. *Enhance awareness of currently banned substances, their consequences, and their side effects*

5. *Read about athletes' experiences with mental health issues*

6. *Develop a network of professionals from various disciplines*

7. *Engage in career-long supervision with mentors and colleagues*

8. *Role-play possible scenarios and receive feedback*

9. *Undertake reflective practice*

Summary

Throughout this chapter, we have tried to address a variety of issues involved in deciding when to refer an athlete for professional counseling or psychotherapy. We hope that this chapter has provided helpful information for recognizing when athletes present issues beyond the scope of the usual performance enhancement realm. It is also important, however, for individuals working on performance-enhancement issues to recognize the need for sensitivity towards the athlete's other life issues in making appropriate referrals. These helping individuals should also be cognizant of their own issues and values because they might affect their ability to work with and to be sensitive to the issues others might have.

This chapter has been a difficult one to write (and rewrite) because referral involves many complex issues that should be discussed, or at least acknowledged. Many of these topics, such as career termination or injury rehabilitation, merit chapters on their own (see Chapters 23 and 22). This chapter has explored ways to help those not trained in counseling or psychotherapy to recognize these issues and to facilitate sensitive and caring referrals.

Study Questions

1. From the dialogue in the chapter, what are some important issues to be sensitive to when making a referral?

2. What are three patterns someone might note as indicating other serious problems when working with an athlete on performance enhancement?

3. What are some reasons why the hammer thrower presented at the beginning of this chapter may not meet with a mental health practitioner?

4. How does homophobia in society and in the sport world contribute to problems for athletes that may manifest in mental and behavioral disorders?

5. How might a concern with food or weight gain reflect a serious eating disorder problem?

6. What can sport psychologists do to prepare themselves for making referrals?

7. What are some signs that aggressiveness in an athlete has become problematic? Is it likely that an athlete who has been driven by anger will become less successful if underlying conflicts are resolved?

8. What factors related to sport can cause or exacerbate relationship problems for athletes?

9. How might a coach or sport psychologist find professionals to whom to refer athletes for counseling or psychotherapy?

10. What might you do if an athlete currently does not want to take your referral advice?

References

American Psychiatric Association. (2013). *Diagnostic and statistical manual of mental disorders* (5th ed.). Washington, DC: Author.

Andersen, M. B. (2004). Recognizing psychopathology. In G. S. Kolt & M. B. Andersen (Eds.), *Psychology in the physical and manual therapies* (pp. 81–92). Edinburgh, Scotland: Churchill Livingstone.

Andersen, M. B., & Fawkner, H. J. (2005). The skin game: Extra points for looking good. In M. B. Andersen (Ed.), *Sport psychology in practice* (pp. 77–92). Champaign, IL: Human Kinetics.

Andersen, M. B., & Van Raalte, J. L. (2005). Over one's head: Referral processes. In M. B. Andersen (Ed.), *Sport psychology in practice* (pp. 159–169). Champaign, IL: Human Kinetics.

Arthur-Cameselle, J. N., & Baltzell, A. (2012). Learning from collegiate athletes who have recovered from eating disorders: Advice to coaches, parents, and others athletes with eating disorders. *Journal of Applied Sport Psychology, 24,* 1–9. doi: 10.1080/10413200.2011.572949

Backhouse, S. H. (2012). The misuse of anabolic-androgenic steroids. In D. Tod & D. Lavallee (Eds.), *Psychology of strength and conditioning* (pp. 195–218). London: Routledge.

Balague, G. (1999). Understanding identity, value, and meaning when working with elite athletes. *The Sport Psychologist, 13,* 89–98.

Baum, A. (2006). Eating disorders in the male athlete. *Sports Medicine, 36,* 1–6. doi: 10.2165/00007256-200636010-00001

Beren, S. E., Hayden, H. A., Wilfley, D. E., & Grilo, C. M. (1996). The influence of sexual orientation on body dissatisfaction in adult men and women. *International Journal of Eating Disorders, 20,* 135–141. doi: 10.1002/(SICI)1098-108X(199609)

Braun, D. L., Sunday, S. R., Huang, A., & Halmi, K. A. (1999). More males seek treatment for eating disorders. *International Journal of Eating Disorders, 25,* 415–424. doi: 10.1002/(SICI)1098-108X(199905)

Brewer, B. W. (2010). The role of psychological factors in sport rehabilitation outcomes. *International Review of Sport and Exercise Psychology, 3,* 40–61. doi: 10.1080/17509840903301207

Brewer, B. W., & Petitpas, A. J. (2005). Returning to self: The anxieties of coming back after injury. In M. B. Andersen (Ed.), *Sport psychology in practice* (pp. 93–108). Champaign, IL: Human Kinetics.

Brewer, B. W., & Petrie, T. A. (2002). Psychopathology in sport and exercise. In J. L. Van Raalte & B. W. Brewer (Eds.), *Exploring sport and exercise psychology* (2nd ed., pp. 307–323). Washington, DC: American Psychological Association.

Burckes-Miller, M. E., & Black, D. R. (1988). Male and female college athletes: Prevalence of anorexia nervosa and bulimia nervosa. *Athletic Training, 23,* 137–140.

Butki, B. D., Andersen, M. B., & Heyman, S. R. (1996). Knowledge of AIDS and risky sexual behavior among athletes. *Academic Athletic Journal, 11*(1), 29–36.

Carless, D., & Douglas, K. (2013). "In the boat" but "selling myself short": Stories, narratives, and identity development in elite sport. *The Sport Psychologist, 27,* 27–39.

Cogan, K. D. (2000). The sadness in sport: Working with a depressed and suicidal athlete. In M. B. Andersen (Ed.), *Doing sport psychology* (pp. 107–119). Champaign, IL: Human Kinetics.

Dosil, J. (2008). *Eating disorders in athletes.* Chichester, England: Wiley.

Doumas, D. M., Haustveit, T., & Coll, K. M. (2010). Reducing heavy drinking among first year intercollegiate athletes: A randomized controlled trial of web-based normative feedback. *Journal of Applied Sport Psychology, 22,* 247–261. doi: 10.1080/10413201003666454

Doumas, D. M., Turrisi, R., & Wright, D. A. (2006). Risk factors for heavy drinking in college freshman: Athletic status and adult attachment. *The Sport Psychologist, 20,* 419–434.

Edwards, C., Tod, D., Morrison, T. G., & Molnar, G. (2012). Drive for muscularity. In D. Tod & D. Lavallee (Eds.), *Psychology of strength and conditioning* (pp. 148–172). London: Routledge.

Erikson, E. H. (1968). *Identity: Youth and Crisis.* London: Faber & Faber.

Fussell, S. W. (1991). *Muscle: Confessions of an unlikely bodybuilder.* New York: Avon.

Gardner, F. L. (2007). Introduction to the special issue: Clinical sport psychology in American intercollegiate athletics. *Journal of Clinical Sport Psychology, 1,* 207–209.

Hildebrand, K. M., Johnson, D. J., & Bogle, K. (2001). Comparison of patterns of alcohol use between high school and college athletes and non-athletes. *College Student Journal, 35,* 358–365.

Krane, V., Waldron, J. J., Kauer, K. J., & Semerjian, T. (2010). Queering sport psychology. In T. Ryba, R. Schinke, & G. Tenenbaum (Eds.), *The cultural turn in sport and exercise psychology* (pp. 153–180). Morgantown, WV: Fitness Information Technology.

Louganis, G., & Marcus, E. (1996). *Breaking the surface.* New York: Penguin Putnam.

Martens, M. P., Dams-O'Connor, K., & Duffy-Paiement, C. (2006). Comparing off-season with in-season alcohol consumption among intercollegiate athletes. *Journal of Sport & Exercise Psychology, 28,* 502–510.

Martens, M. P., & Mobley, M. (2005). Straight guys working with gay guys: Homophobia and sport psychology service. In M. B. Andersen (Ed.), *Sport psychology in practice* (pp. 249–263). Champaign, IL: Human Kinetics.

Miller, P. S., & Kerr, G. A. (2003). The role of experimentation of intercollegiate student athletes. *The Sport Psychologist, 17,* 196–219.

Novaco, R. W. (1975). *Anger control: The development and evaluation of an experimental treatment.* Lexington, MA: Heath.

Olivardia, R., Pope, H. G., Jr., Mangweth, B., & Hudson, J. I. (1995). Eating disorders in college men. *American Journal of Psychiatry, 152,* 1279–1285.

Oyebode, F., Boodhoo, J. A., & Schapira, K. (1988). Anorexia nervosa in males: Clinical features and outcome. *International Journal of Eating Disorders, 7,* 121–124. doi: 10.1002/1098-108X(198801)

Park, S., Lavallee, D., & Tod, D. (2013). Athletes' career transition out of sport: A systematic review. *International Review for Sport and Exercise Psychology, 6,* 22–53. doi: 10.1080/1750984X.2012.687053

Petitpas, A., & Danish, S. J. (1995). Caring for injured athletes. In S. M. Murphy (Ed.), *Sport psychology interventions* (pp. 255–281). Champaign, IL: Human Kinetics.

Petrie, T. A., & Greenleaf, C. A. (2007). Eating disorders in sport: From theory to research to intervention. In G. Tenenbaum & R. C. Eklund (Eds.), *Handbook of sport psychology* (3rd ed., pp. 352–378). Hoboken, NJ: Wiley.

Petrie, T. A., & Sherman, R. T. (2000). Counseling athletes with eating disorders: A case example. In M. B. Andersen (Ed.), *Doing sport psychology* (pp. 121–137). Champaign, IL: Human Kinetics.

Reel, J. J., & Galli, N. (2012). Eating disorders in sport. In D. Tod & D. Lavallee (Eds.), *Psychology of strength and conditioning* (pp. 173–194). London: Routledge.

Stainback, R. D., & Taylor, R. E. (2005). Facilitating change: Alcohol and violence among athletes. In M. B. Andersen (Ed.), *Sport psychology in practice* (pp. 135–158). Champaign, Il: Human Kinetics.

Sundgot-Borgen, J. (1994). Risk and trigger factors for the development of eating disorders in female elite athletes. *Medicine and Science in Sports and Exercise, 26,* 414–419. doi: 10.1249/00005768-199404000-00003

Tod, D. (2007). The long and winding road: Professional development in sport psychology. *The Sport Psychologist, 21,* 94–108.

Tod, D., & Andersen, M. B. (2012). Practitioner-client relationships. In S. Hanton & S. D. Mellalieu (Eds.), *Professional practice issues in sport psychology: A review* (pp. 273–306). Oxon, England: Routledge.

Tod, D., & Lavallee, D. (2010). Towards a conceptual understanding of muscle dysmorphia development and sustainment. *International Review of Sport and Exercise Psychology, 3,* 111–131. doi: 10.1080/17509840903428513

Van Raalte, J. L., & Andersen, M. B. (2013). Referral processes in sport psychology. In J. L. Van Raalte & B. W. Brewer (Eds.), *Exploring sport and exercise psychology* (3rd ed. pp. 337–350). Washington, DC: American Psychological Association.

Van Raalte, J. L., Petitpas, A. J., Krieger, L., Lide, C., Thorpe, C., & Brewer, B. W. (2011). Looking for love in all the wrong (?) places: Intrateam romantic relationships. *The Sport Psychologist, 25,* 382–395.

Zuckerman, M. (1979). *Sensation seeking: Beyond the optimal level of arousal.* Hillsdale, NJ: Erlbaum.

Drug Abuse in Sport: Causes and Cures

Mark H. Anshel, *Middle Tennessee State University*

"It's a good day for baseball. Nobody wants an uneven playing field. I'm glad this happened. You want everybody on the same page. We shouldn't be competing against guys who use drugs like that. You always want to compete on the same level. That's all I want. That's all everyone else wants. Today is bad for baseball and the fans. But as a player, this is what you want."

Boston Red Sox star Dustin Pedroia in response to the suspensions by Major League Baseball of 13 players for using performance enhancing drugs.

The use of banned substances in elite sport—both professional and amateur—has received more media attention than ever in recent years. For example, two clinics, the Bay Area Laboratory Co-Operative (BALCO) and Biogenesis, have been exposed as providing performance enhancement drugs to Olympic, professional, and other elite athletes. Athletes such as professional baseball player Alex Rodriguez, U.S. Olympic track athlete Marianne Jones, and numerous other professional baseball, track, and American football players have been implicated, suspended, or had their careers ended because of their connections to these labs. The Tour de France and professional bicycling also have been rocked by confessions of blood doping, most notably by Lance Armstrong, seven-time winner of the race, as well as by several other former champions. Figures reported by the World Anti-Doping Agency (WADA, http://www.wada ama.org) revealed that the percentage of adverse atypical findings for 2011 and 2012 were the highest compared to the past 5 years. (An adverse atypical finding indicates "the presence of a prohibited substance or its metabolites or markers" but "does not necessarily lead to an anti-doping rule violation, since an athlete may have a therapeutic use exemption for this particular substance"; WADA, 2011).

The use of drugs in sport is not new. Greek athletes in the third century B.C. ingested substances to improve their performance. In the 1970s performance-enhancing drugs were used by medal winners from the Soviet Union and other Eastern European countries, most notably East Germany, but it was not until the 1976 Olympic Games held in Montreal that the International Olympic Committee (IOC) started widespread drug testing and penalized athletes for testing positive. Even with more rigorous testing for banned substances at the Olympics, the problem of ingesting banned substances and engaging in other inappropriate behaviors continues among both the world's best and less elite athletes. For example, just prior to the 2012 Olympic Games in London, nine track and field athletes were suspended and could not compete due to failed drug tests (Manning, 2012).

Perhaps engaging in unethical actions in sport is not surprising, even if it means facing severe penalties if tests confirm the use of banned substances that provide a performance edge. Considering the emphasis put on winning, and that winning is often tied to an athlete's self-esteem, it is not surprising that some athletes will do whatever it takes to succeed. The sport community must not let that happen, and this chapter explains the reasons for rules and the need for tough enforcement of those rules because drug education, alone, is ineffective in preventing drug abuse among sport competitors. In particular, this chapter will (a) present the different types of drugs that athletes are taking and other forms of banned behaviors (e.g., blood doping) in which athletes are engaging to gain a performance edge, (b) describe the reasons these substances and actions are banned, including the negative, even possibly fatal, effects on the athlete's physical and mental health, and (c) suggest strategies that coaches, sport administrators, and sport psychology consultants may use to reduce the likelihood of drug-taking in sport.

Why are certain substances banned from competitive sport, and why should sport administrators, coaches, parents of athletes, and athletes themselves be concerned about the use of drugs categorized as "performance-enhancing"? These behaviors by athletes (a) may cause physical and psychological harm, (b) often violate state and federal laws, (c) are cheating and violate the team rules and organizational policies of almost every sport, and (d) contaminate performance results, which are obtained by unnatural means. Only when causes for drug usage are identified can we devise cognitive and behavioral strategies to help prevent and perhaps eliminate this problem.

The word *drug* means different things to different people. The two most common categories of drug use among competitive athletes are performance-enhancing drugs, such as anabolic steroids, and drugs referred to as "recreational" such as cocaine or marijuana. The objective of recreational drug users is to alter the state of mind, with no intention of improving performance. The different rationales for

ingesting performance-enhancing and recreational drugs must be taken into account when developing strategies to reduce or eliminate such behaviors.

How prevalent is drug use among competitive athletes? Regarding performance-enhancing drugs, Backhouse, McKenna, Robinson, and Atkin (2007) projected that between 6 and up to possibly 34 percent of elite athletes use them. A recent study of competitive Hungarian athletes revealed that 14.6 percent admitted to using performance-enhancement drugs and 31.7 percent used recreational drugs (Uvacsek et al., 2011). The most recent National Collegiate Athletic Association (NCAA, 2012) study reported findings from a survey of 20,474 student-athletes across 23 sports and showed that within the past 12 months:

- 3.7 percent of the respondents admitted using amphetamines

- 0.4 percent of the respondents indicated using anabolic steroids

- Less than 1 percent used ephedrine

- 83 percent drank alcohol

- 22.6 percent reported using marijuana

- 3.3 percent of the respondents indicated use of narcotics

- 6.4 percent noted they used Adderall or Ritalin (used to treat attention deficit disorder, ADD) without a prescription

- 4.9 percent used Vicodin, Oxycontin or Percocet without a prescription

A study of 2516 middle and high school students revealed that 1.4 percent of the females and 1.7 percent of the males admitted to steroid use (Van Den Berg, Neumark-Sztainer, Cafri, & Wall, 2007). While this study did not specifically focus on athletes, the researchers found that the desire for a larger body size in boys and participation in weight-related sports for girls were predictors of steroid use. A more recent study of "muscle-enhancing behaviors" with 2,793 adolescents revealed that 5.9 percent reported using steroids while 34.7 percent used protein powders or shakes (Eisenberg, Wall, & Neumark-Sztainer, 2012). The athletes in this study were "significantly more likely to report more muscle-enhancing behaviors than those not involved in sports" (p. 1022). The authors concluded that prevention programs were needed, especially those aimed at sport teams, coaches, and parents.

Important to recognize across these studies, is that underreporting is an inherent limitation of any self-report study that requires acknowledging behavior that may be considered undesirable or illegal. Relatively few athletes will admit to engaging in a behavior that they know is either illegal or unethical, such as drug use. One approach to overcoming this problem is to ask athletes about the behaviors of "others" rather than themselves.

Review of Drugs Banned in Sport

The IOC refers to the act of ingesting banned drugs as "doping" (Prokop, 1990). **Doping** has been defined as "the administering or use of substances in any form alien to the body or of physiological substances in abnormal amounts and with abnormal methods by healthy persons with the exclusive aim of attaining an artificial and unfair increase of performance in competition" (p. 5). The World Anti-Doping Agency (WADA), established in 1999, has set international standards and coordinates anti-doping efforts, including drug testing, for Olympic sport. A current list of substances banned by WADA can be found at their Web site (http://www.wada-ama.org/en/World-Anti-Doping-Program/Sports-and-Anti-Doping-Organizations/International-Standards/Prohibited-List/).

Not banned by most sport organizations, at least for mature-age athletes, are alcohol, nicotine (e.g., tobacco products), diet regimens (e.g., carbohydrate loading or any other food-ingestion habits), amino acids, caffeine (within limits), antidepressants, and vitamins (Lennehan, 2003; Williams, 1998). Additional supplements such as creatine, human growth hormone (HGH), and tetrahydrogestrinone (THG) have been banned by some sport organizations.

Anabolic Steroids

Anabolic steroids are the best-known category of performance-enhancing drugs. Of course, any potential benefit of steroid use to sport performance depends on the type of skills and physical demands required of that sport. Perhaps the most salient advantage of steroid use on sport performance is improved strength and power (Mazzeo & Ascione, 2013), thus aiding performance in sports such as football and track and field. This is because the function of anabolic steroids is to increase the male hormone androgen and decrease the female hormone estrogen. Increased strength occurs because steroids promote the synthesis of proteins that are used to build skeletal muscle tissue (Mazzeo & Ascione, 2013). Anabolic steroids also are used for medicinal purposes, most notably, to promote muscle growth and tissue repair as part of injury rehabilitation.

The harmful side-effects of prolonged steroid use are extensive (see Mazzeo & Ascione, 2013). High testosterone levels in females can increase facial and body hair, lower the voice, increase muscularity and strength, and interfere with reproductive function. When testosterone levels become too high, the hypothalamus in the brain starts to shut down the body processes involving the hormone. These processes include stimulation and maintenance of the sex organs for males, leading to reduced facial and body hair, reduced sperm production, and impotence. All users may experience temporary or permanent sterility. In addition, tendons and ligaments may not strengthen at the same rate as muscle tissue, thus increasing risk of injury. The negative side effects of prolonged steroid use are even greater for individuals who have not yet reached physiological maturity. For example, adolescent abusers may incur reduced bone growth because of premature fusion of the epiphysis of long bones; the result is permanently stunted growth (Miller, Barnes, Sabo, Melnick, & Farrell, 2002).

More ominously, prolonged heavy steroid users risk cancerous liver cell tumors, high blood pressure (i.e., hypertension), premature heart disease, myocardial infarction (heart attack), and stroke. Some chronic steroid users experience what popularly is referred to as **roid rage,** which is heightened, uncontrolled aggression, and may include criminal acts of violence (e.g., child abuse, domestic violence, suicide, and attempted murder) (Mazzeo & Ascione, 2013).

Another concern about steroid use is its addictive properties, both psychologically and physiologically (Mazzeo & Ascione, 2013). From a psychological perspective, the individual may feel dependent on steroids for maintaining a sense of well-being, perceived strength and musculature, and a performance edge. Failing to maintain the steroid regimen may result in lost confidence, fear of failure, irritability, and depression. Physiological addiction may reflect the body's dependence on molecular substances for protein synthesis, which builds skeletal tissue. Symptoms of sudden withdrawal of prolonged steroid ingestion include changes in heart rate, blood pressure, tension, and fatigue (Leccese, 1991). When chronic steroid use is suddenly stopped, clinical depression often results. Other symptoms during withdrawal may include fatigue, restlessness, insomnia, headache, dissatisfaction with physical appearance, and possibly suicide (Mazzeo & Ascione, 2013).

> I lied. I lied to you. I lied to my family. I lied to a lot of people for a lot of years when I said I didn't use steroids. I started taking anabolic steroids in 1969, and I never stopped. Not when I retired from the NFL in 1985. Not ever. I couldn't, and then I made things worse by using human growth hormone, too. I had my mind set, and I did what I wanted to do. So many people tried to talk me out of what I was doing, and I wouldn't listen. And now I'm sick. I've got cancer—a brain lymphoma—and I'm in the fight of my life.
>
> —Lyle Alzado, former All-Pro American football player (Alzado, 1991)

According to Schlaadt and Shannon (1994), athletes may attempt to overcome these problems by taking "drug holidays" between periods of use by "pyramiding" or "stacking." Pyramiding consists of beginning with a lower dose, then increasing the amount progressively until the maximum dose is reached, then tapering the dosage until the drug is completely withdrawn. Stacking consists of using numerous drugs and varying the dosage throughout the cycle. The authors conclude, however, that "no scientific evidence supports the idea that

'stacking' or 'pyramiding' the drugs is more effective than other methods of using them or that it minimizes the harmful side effects of steroid use" (p. 50).

To find detailed information about steroids and their effects, read the National Institute on Drug Abuse Research Report Series, which is sponsored by the National Institutes of Health and can be obtained at http://www.drugabuse.gov/publications/research-reports/anabolic-steroid-abuse.

Stimulants

Stimulant drugs increase the rate and, hence, the work capacity of the heart, central nervous system, and respiratory system. Stimulants are divided into four groups: **psychomotor** (e.g., amphetamines, cocaine, and most diet suppressants); **sympathomimetic amines,** which stimulate the sympathetic and autonomic nervous systems; **hallucinogens,** often referred to as recreational, mind-altering, or street drugs (Martens et al., 2007); and miscellaneous **central nervous system (CNS) stimulants** such as ephedrine that are found in many prescription and over-the-counter cold remedies. Ostensibly these drugs improve athletic performance by increasing alertness through inhibition of mental and physical fatigue. However, on the minus—and very dangerous—side, some stimulants (e.g., cocaine) may result in death due to seizures, damage to the heart muscle, or stroke (Doweiko, 1996).

Hallucinogens, often referred to as "recreational" or "mind-altering" drugs, influence the individual's perceptions of incoming stimuli by slowing response and decision-making time, and inhibiting attentional focusing. Hallucinogens are categorized as either stimulants (e.g., cocaine), which increase somatic arousal (e.g., heart or respiration rate), or narcotic analgesics (e.g., marijuana, LSD, PCP), which can reduce pain (as an anti-inflammatory) and anxiety (as a sedative). Not surprisingly, this category of drug actually impairs, not promotes, sport performance. Most sport organizations ban all types of hallucinogens. The use of these drugs is also against the laws of most countries.

Narcotic Analgesics (Anti-Inflammatories)

Narcotic analgesics, discussed briefly in the previous paragraph, are used by athletes as pain suppressants and enable an injured competitor to continue playing despite tissue damage and injury. Anti-inflammatories can reduce performance effectiveness in some sports due to their sedative effect. All analgesics are toxic and addictive in large doses (Doweiko, 1996). Examples of narcotic analgesics include codeine, heroin, morphine, and opium. Harmful effects of analgesics include gastrointestinal disturbances, physical and psychological dependence, and depressed respiration, including respiratory arrest. Non-narcotic analgesics such as aspirin and acetaminophen, which are not habit forming, do not affect the central nervous system and are not banned.

Beta-Adrenergic Blockers

Perhaps best known for the treatment of high blood pressure and some forms of heart disease, **beta-blockers** aid performance by slowing the heart rate, decreasing anxiety, and steadying natural body tremors. These are desirable outcomes in sports such as rifle and pistol shooting, archery, bowling, and golf, which are why their use creates an unfair advantage. Adverse effects of beta-blockers include bronchospasms, CNS disturbances, hypotension, and impotence. In addition, beta-blockers may negatively affect high-intensity, longer endurance tasks.

Diuretics

Diuretics increase the rate at which water and salts leave the body as urine. Athletes such as jockeys, wrestlers, and boxers use diuretics to make weight for a competition. Other athletes use diuretics to overcome fluid retention—often to modify the excretion rate of urine to alter the urinary concentrations of banned drugs such as anabolic steroids. The rapid depletion of body fluids in general and of potassium in particular can produce heart arrhythmias. Nausea, heat exhaustion, or stroke from impaired thermoregulatory control, blood clotting, reduced blood volume, and muscle cramps are other possible outcomes (Russell, 1990).

Additional Banned Performance Aids

Caffeine is another type of central nervous system (CNS) stimulant that is banned by WADA if ingested beyond moderation. How much caffeine intake is too much? Moderate caffeine intake commensurate with less than 18 ounces of coffee is not prohibited by the IOC. Caffeine increases alertness and arousal, thereby preventing or overcoming mental and physical fatigue. These effects may improve forms of athletic performance that depend on heightened CNS activity. Excessive amounts of caffeine can prolong endurance performance and high-intensity short-duration exercise, creating an unfair advantage in competitive sport. However, excessive caffeine may also adversely affect thermoregulation (i.e., internal body temperature). As a diuretic, caffeine increases urination. Combined with insufficient water intake, the athlete's internal body temperature rises, inducing premature fatigue and, at dangerous levels, heat-related illnesses.

Blood Doping

Blood doping involves removing approximately one liter (about two units) of the athlete's blood one to two months before the competition and appropriately freezing and storing it. The athlete's frozen red blood cells are then infused back into the competitor shortly before competition, thus increasing red cell mass and hemoglobin up to 15 percent. This technique increases oxygen uptake—the blood's oxygen-carrying capacity—thereby improving aerobic (endurance) performance. The effect may last as long as two weeks. Blood doping has few medical dangers if a careful and knowledgeable physician performs it. Yet, there is the possibility of being infected by hepatitis B, hepatitis C, and HIV (AIDS) due to mishandling or mislabeling of blood products. As Williams (1998) indicates, "an incompatible blood transfusion could be fatal" (p. 143).

Erythropoietin

Another form of blood doping may occur by ingesting the hormone erythropoietin (EPO). EPO is a hormone secreted by the kidneys in response to hypoxia—a lack of oxygen in the blood—that stimulates production of red blood cells (hemoglobin). As Branch explained (2002), "an increase in hemoglobin and the circulating red blood cell mass by doping would increase the oxygen content in arterial blood and enhance the body's ability to transport oxygen to peripheral exercising muscle (p. 61). Typically, EPO is used clinically to treat anemia in hemodialysis patients; however, world-class endurance athletes also have been known to ingest EPO. For example, a number of world class cyclists who competed in the Tour de France, including Lance Armstrong, have admitted to using EPO (Keller, 2013). EPO reduces the onset of muscular fatigue and may improve regulation of the internal body temperature, thus providing an unfair advantage to endurance athletes who use it. The American College of Sports Medicine (ACSM) considers blood doping unethical, and readers are referred to Sawka et al. (2010) for the ACSM's position paper on the use of blood doping.

Creatine

Creatine has become increasingly popular since St. Louis Cardinals' home run slugger Mark McGuire admitted using it during the 1998 season in which he hit 70 home runs (he has since discontinued using creatine according to media reports). Creatine is classified as a physiological sports ergogenic, although it also is regarded as a nutritional sports ergogenic (Williams, Kreider, & Branch, 1999). Ostensibly, its function is to increase muscular power and speed in sports events (Williams, 1998). It is a popular substance because it is not considered an anabolic steroid and is perceived as safe, and it is legally available in drug and health food stores and fitness clubs around the world.

How effective is it? The results of studies are equivocal. Williams et al. (1999) has concluded that "short-term creatine supplementation may contribute to increased total body mass, at least in males, although much of the increase in body mass may be attributed to water retention rather than increased contractile protein. Chronic

creatine supplementation, combined with resistance training, may increase lean body mass, but more supportive research is desirable to determine efficacy and the possible underlying mechanism" (p. 194). Williams (1998), however, also reports that "creatine supplementation might be detrimental to performance in events dependent primarily on the oxygen energy system. Creatine phosphate is not a very important energy source for prolonged aerobic exercise" (p. 180). Williams concludes that creatine supplementation may have a beneficial effect only in certain types of performance (e.g., repetitive, high-intensity, very short-term tasks with brief recovery periods).

Human Growth Hormone and Gamma-Hydroxybutyrate

Human Growth Hormone (HGH), banned by WADA, is naturally secreted by the pituitary gland. More recently, it has been created by recombinant DNA technology, but it remains very expensive. Clinically, HGH is prescribed to overcome pituitary deficiency in children. In adults, HGH increases lean body mass and decreases fat mass. Mark McGuire (Major League Baseball player with one of the best single season home run records) has admitted to using HGH and it was the primary steroid used by the late professional football player, Lyle Alzado, quoted earlier, who died at age 42 of two brain tumors.

Banned by many sport organizations, HGH is medically used to treat HGH deficiency, Turner's syndrome, and for relief from excessive burns by stimulating growth (Saugy et al., 2006). In addition, the U.S. national media reported in 2004 that HGH has been taken by 20,000 to 30,000 nonathletes in the United States to prevent aging at a cost of $1,000 per month (*The Tennessean,* January 16, 2007). Although this anabolic outcome may appear to have a beneficial effect related to sport performance, the results of past studies have indicated that the use of HGH for 6 months produces less than 5 pounds of muscle mass and a similar decrease in fat. This outcome is similar following resistance training, but without the use of HGH. Thus, the effect of HGH on physical performance seems negligible in contrast to regular exercise. It can also cause the skull to thicken and the forehead and eyebrow ridge to become especially prominent. One's hands and feet grow out of proportion with the rest of the body, causing a condition called acromegaly. If a patient is young enough that his or her bones are still growing, exposure to excessive HGH will result in gigantism.

A related hormone that ostensibly has an ergogenic effect is *gamma-hydroxybutyrate (GHB)*. Although the body produces this substance naturally, too much can lead to distorted physical characteristics, which is why it sometimes is referred to as "Frankenstein's syndrome." GHB stimulates the release of human growth hormone and can lead to a coma and death. WADA also bans GHB.

Rationale for an Antidrug Policy in Sport

There are several reasons for controlling drug intake in competitive sport. These are categorized as legal, ethical, and medical. **Legal** considerations reflect federal and state laws that ban the use or sale of selected substances, such as hallucinogenic drugs, and the illegal use of steroids, narcotic analgesics, and beta-blockers. **Ethical** issues form the core reason for banning drug use in sport: it creates an unfair advantage; thus, it's cheating. In addition, most reasonable persons would agree that allowing athletes to ruin their health for short-term gain is immoral. **Medical** factors that include the long-term harmful effects of prolonged drug use among athletes are severe and well known (e.g., Martens et al., 2007). These outcomes include dehydration, heatstroke, cardiac arrest, liver cancer, lymphoma, cardiovascular disease, kidney stones, irregular heartbeat, sterility, and hypertension. Psychological problems include heightened anxiety, suicidal tendencies, short attention span, depression, aggression, and schizophrenia (Pope & Katz, 1994; Weinhold, 1991). Finally, most drugs are addictive.

How Widespread Is Drug Abuse in Sport?

It is impossible to determine the exact extent of drug abuse in sport. The two primary sources of information about drug usage, anecdotal evidence and scientific research studies, have serious limitations. Anecdotal reports, among other serious shortcomings, fail to provide concrete evidence documenting the usage of drugs. Scientific studies suffer from underreporting because ethical and legal considerations make drug taking a largely clandestine behavior. Keep these limitations in mind when examining the following information.

Anecdotal Evidence

Anecdotal evidence consists of information provided by individuals based on their own experiences or perceptions. For example, former U.S. Olympic gold medal hurdler Edwin Moses (1988) asserted that "at least 50 percent of the athletes in high-performance sports such as track and field, cycling, and rowing would be disqualified if they weren't so adept at beating the tests" (p. 57). Other anecdotal evidence exists to show that some coaches actually sanction drug use, either *passively*, by failing to warn their athletes against it, or *actively*, by encouraging athletes to use steroids and ways to avoid positive drug tests. For example, Kelli White (American world champion sprinter) stated,

> I want to explain what it takes for the whole system to work . . . It not only took [Nick] Conte's [founder of BALCO] help, it took my coach making me believe it was O.K. I think a lot of the time, what happens to athletes is that people make you believe that what you are doing is O.K. because everyone else is doing it. (Nazzaro, 2013, p. 10)

Encouragement to take banned substances can be direct, as in the example above, or indirect (e.g., requiring that the participant reach an unrealistic body weight by a certain time, requiring a particularly demanding performance goal, or ignoring drug-taking behavior and thus sanctioning its use). For example, Canadian world-class sprinter Ben Johnson, after having his gold medal taken away, strongly asserted to a Canadian government inquiry that his coach knowingly gave him a substance that was banned by international sport organizations (*Time*, 1989).

Anecdotal evidence indicates team physicians also have contributed to drug abuse among athletes. For example, Ye Qiaobo, a Chinese speed skater, was sent home in disgrace from the 1988 Olympics after testing positive for steroids. A later inquiry revealed that she unknowingly had been taking steroids prescribed by the team doctor. Television's coverage of the 1992 (Madrid), 1996 (Atlanta), and 2000 (Sydney) Olympics revealed the extensiveness, as far back as preparation for the 1976 Olympics, of experimentation with steroids by many countries. In the former East Germany, for example, team doctors, under orders from the highest political powers, prescribed steroids for athletes, even 13-year-old girls, and then kept careful records regarding the effects of different dosages on performance and the length of time needed to test clean.

In recent high profile cases (CNN, 2013), Major League Baseball contended that Alex Rodriguez, an all-star who at the time was the highest-paid player in the league, has used performance enhancing drugs. While *Rodriguez*'s 211 regular-season game suspension is being appealed, 12 additional players have accepted 50-game suspensions for their connections to Biogenesis, a lab found to be supplying performance-enhancing drugs. Also in 2013, Former American world champion sprinter Tyson Gay tested positive for a banned substance and pulled out of the world championships. After admitting to using performance-enhancing drugs, American cyclist Tyler Hamilton was disqualified and retroactively stripped of his gold medal from the 2004 Athens Olympic Games. Additionally, professional team employees have played roles in athletes' use of performance-enhancing drugs (CNN, 2013). Richard Rydze, former team doctor for the Pittsburgh Steelers, was arrested for distributing steroids, HGH, and painkillers. Also, Kirk Radomski, who was a NY Mets clubhouse employee, pled guilty to distributing steroids between 1995 and 2005.

Scientific Evidence

Scientific research on drug use in sport has centered primarily on performance-enhancing drugs, particularly anabolic steroids. Pope, Katz, and Champoux (1988) found that only 17 of 1,010 (1.7 percent) U.S. college male athletes reported using anabolic steroids. The motive for using steroids of all but four of these men was to improve sport performance. In another study, Yesalis et al. (1988) distributed surveys about steroid use to 60 elite U.S. male body builders. Of the 45 competitors who returned the survey, 15 (33 percent) admitted to anabolic steroid use. Perhaps no sport has experienced greater use of anabolic steroids than weight lifting.

Grogan and colleagues (2006) conducted in-depth interviews with five male and six female body builders to examine their motives for steroid use and the subsequent effects of prolonged steroid use. These users believed steroids used in moderation were safe, and that serious side effects were not significant disincentives. Perhaps not surprisingly, the researchers found that competitors deemphasized serious side effects relative to short-term gains. This result has widespread implications for athletes in other sports in which more immediate concerns about performance enhancement is more important than possible long-term risks. While the use of performance-enhancing drugs does not seem to be going away any time soon, what is unknown at this time is the extent to which these drugs are used at various levels of competitive sport.

The seriousness of ingesting steroids in sport is apparently a concern to coaches. BlueCross BlueShield of Tennessee and the Tennessee Secondary School Athletic Association surveyed 462 high school coaches in Tennessee (*Daily News Journal*, November 18, 2005). They found that 90 percent of the coaches perceived performance-enhancing drugs as a problem among high school athletes, with 18 percent concluding it is a "serious" problem. In addition, while 98 percent of the coaches believed that educating students about performance-enhancing drugs is important, 54 percent of the coaches did not believe students understand the long-term effects of using such drugs, and 65 percent said they have warned the athletes against using them. These data, if accurate and generalizable to other samples, represents a turning point for coaches to acknowledge the seriousness and pervasiveness of drug usage in sport.

In one study, Anshel (1991a) conducted personal interviews with U.S. university athletes, 94 males and 32 females, competing in nine sports. To overcome the inherent dangers of underreporting found in related literature, information about the participants' personal use of drugs was not solicited. Over half of the athletes surveyed (64 percent) revealed "known" drug use on their team. More specifically, 72 percent of the males and 40 percent of the females contended that teammates took a drug the user knew was illegal or banned from their sport. Forty-three percent (494 of the athletes' 1,156 responses) acknowledged that athletes use drugs for the purpose of enhancing performance as opposed to recreational use.

Melia, Pipe, and Greenberg (1996) attempted to determine the prevalence of use of anabolic steroids and other performance-enhancing drugs among 16,119 Canadian students from grades 6–12 representing five regions of Canada. They found that 2.8 percent of this sample ($N = 4,513$) ingested these banned substances in attempts to improve sport performance or to improve body build. To some extent, there appears to be a gender gap in drug taking among athletes. Doweiko (1996), supporting earlier findings by Anshel (1991a), concluded from his review of literature that more males than females abuse anabolic steroids.

Despite numerous attempts to ascertain the prevalence of drug taking among competitive athletes, the results of these studies must be viewed cautiously. Asking athletes to acknowledge their own unethical behavior is very difficult, if not impossible. This is one reason well-publicized antidrug policies by sports organizations and coaches, a strong drug testing program that has consequences, continuous drug education, and close monitoring of athlete behavior by coaches and parents are of extreme importance, issues that will be addressed later.

Likely Causes of Drug Abuse in Sport

Based on a review of the anecdotal and scientific literature the causes of drug use lie within three categories: physical (performance enhancement), psychological and emotional, and social.

Physical Causes

Enhance sport performance.   The most common physical reason for athlete drug use is attempting to enhance sport performance. As indicated earlier, coaches and sponsors can and often do contribute to the competitors' dilemma by reinforcing the need to win at any cost. The expectations of parents, media, teammates, and peers only fuel the pressure to maximize performance and may lead to ingesting banned substances (Williams, 1989). Depending on the drug being taken, the athlete may be seeking benefits such as increased strength, endurance, alertness, and aggression; decreased fatigue, anxiety, and muscle tremor; or faster recovery from injury.

For example, in a rare study in this area, Laure and Reinsberger (1995) attempted to identify the reasons elite race walkers used anabolic steroids. Improving performance, the wish—and pressure—to win, and financial incentives (e.g., commercial contracts and product endorsements) were the three principal motives to use banned performance-enhancing drugs. Forty-one percent of these athletes had heard of endurance walkers using such drugs. Apparently, the pressure of performing well in international events can exacerbate the problem.

Cope with pain and injury rehabilitation.   Athletes also ingest drugs to cope psychologically with physical discomfort and to expedite recovery from injury (English, 1987). For example, athletes may feel that medical treatment is not sufficient to eliminate pain. They will take drugs to attenuate pain with no prescription and without the coach's knowledge, usually to avoid disappointing the coach or losing starting status (a tendency more typical of the male athletes) (Anshel, 1991a).

Weight control. Amphetamines often are used to control appetite, while diuretics reduce fluid weight. This allows the athlete to compete in a lower weight group, which the athlete feels is more likely to lead to success (Donald, 1983).

Psychological Causes

By far the most common rationale for using recreational drugs among athletes is psychological and emotional (Anshel, 1991a). Several psychological reasons promote taking banned drugs.

Stress and anxiety. Emotions such as stress, tension, and anxiety may be antecedent causes of ingesting drugs, particularly hallucinogens and beta-blockers. The need to control anxiety and other undesirable emotions in sport is widely known, but these artificial means provide an unfair advantage. Recreational drugs also have been used to help athletes manage stress and anxiety, which is both unethical and illegal (Anshel, 1991a). Instead, athletes can be taught mental skills for controlling emotions.

Boredom. Recreational drugs, which, of course, are illegal, might be ingested to help overcome boredom (Julien, 1981), which is more prevalent on weekends, when teams travel, or when team-related activities are unplanned (Anshel, 1991b).

Personal problems. A variety of personal, non-sport issues may lead an athlete to use drugs. The athlete's personal life may be in turmoil (e.g., poor school grades, an unhappy or dysfunctional home life). Drugs, then, may be a coping mechanism or a means of escape in dealing with personal difficulties away from the sport venue (Gardner & Moore, 2006).

Low self-confidence and self-esteem. Athletes may use drugs, either performance-enhancing to build self-confidence or recreational, due to a lack of self-confidence (Anshel, 1991a). Perhaps the athlete doubts his or her skills or is worried about the perceived superior skills of an opponent (e.g., "They make me feel better about my ability," "I'm sure 'so and so' is taking them," "If I'm going to perform at 'X' speed, I have to take

these"). These feelings may reflect a personality trait called low *self-esteem,* which is a person's evaluation of the picture they hold about themselves (Sonstroem, 1997). Drug use may be perceived to increase self-esteem or confidence.

The Superman (Adonis) Complex. The Superman, or Adonis, Complex is a condition in which some athletes feel impervious to the known harmful effects of drugs, even after obtaining valid information about possible detrimental effects to their health (Anshel, 1993). According to Don Weiss, executive director of the National Football League: "It is not easy to convince pro football players that they are vulnerable to the negative health effects of steroids. Some of these young men are such great physical specimens with such great athletic ability that they think they'll be like that forever" (Shroyer, 1990, p. 115). Also worrisome is that the Superman/Adonis Complex can prompt adolescent *nonathletes* to use steroids to improve their physique (Pope, 2002).

What may change these perceptions of invincibility are the publicized stories of high-profile athletes whose health has significantly deteriorated or who have died because of the prolonged use of anabolic steroids. This was the exact reaction to the death of former Denver Broncos football player Lyle Alzado in 1989 at age 42. Alzado died from cancer that he (and his doctors) attributed to prolonged, extensive use of steroids and human growth hormone (HGH). In an article published in *Sports Illustrated* (Alzado, 1991) entitled, "I'm sick and I'm scared," Alzado asserted, "If I had known that I would be this sick now, I would have tried to make it in football on my own—naturally. Whoever is doing this stuff, if you stay on it too long or maybe if you get on it at all, you're going to get something bad from it. . . . It is a wrong thing to do" (p. 25).

Negative perfectionism. Some individuals are never pleased with their accomplishments, even with the appropriate recognition and adulation of others. For these people, "good" is never quite good enough. A **perfectionist** is someone who has trouble discriminating between realistic and idealized standards (Flett & Hewitt, 2002). He or she bypasses attainable excellence in pursuit of unattainable perfection. Using performance-enhancing drugs provides a means to overcome the self-doubt and anxiety associated with failing to meet excessively high standards, a condition called neurotic perfectionism (Hewitt & Flett, 2002). Although researchers have increased their attention to perfectionism in recent years (Stoll, Lau, & Stoeber, 2007), additional research is needed to determine its connection to drug use in sport.

Social Causes

Perhaps there is no greater cause of succumbing to drug ingestion than response to social—and societal—pressures.

Peer pressure and acceptance. Pressure from peers, the need to gain group acceptance, or the natural need to be accepted and admired by others are likely causes of drug use. Athletes who have a strong need for social approval may use recreational or performance-enhancing drugs if they believe that is what is expected by their teammates (Waldron & Krane, 2005). In their eagerness to attain social acceptance, athletes become aware of the types of approval-earning behaviors—the need to please other people—that will facilitate popularity.

Models. If sports stars are known to ingest steroids, will younger, less skilled athletes be copycats? Modeling occurs when we learn by demonstration or change our behavior to imitate behaviors we have observed (Gill & Williams, 2008). Modeling has a particularly influential effect during adolescence. Accordingly, the development of appropriate (e.g., training and effort) and inappropriate (e.g., cheating, drug taking) behavior of young athletes often is derived from the modeling of older, more experienced counterparts. The modeling effect is reinforced by media reports that publicize incidences of drug abuse by professional athletes. For example, the Mitchell Report (2007) on steroid use in Major League Baseball highlighted the increased proliferation of steroid use by adolescents, both athletes and non-athletes, and partly attributed the problem to the perception that professional athletes are also taking these drugs.

Strategies for Controlling Drug Abuse

The effectiveness of strategies to prevent or eliminate drug taking in sport is often a function of factors such as the individual's perceived needs for using drugs (e.g., gaining self-confidence, overcoming pain, improving strength or performance), the type of drug usage (e.g., performance-enhancing versus mind-altering), the sport's physical demands (e.g., those requiring improved aerobic capacity, strength, or steadiness), and situational factors (e.g., boredom, stress, endorsements, the high expectations of others). However, because athletes share similar psychological demands and performance requirements, many of the issues described here can be applied to competitors from various sports, skill levels, genders, and cultures.

An array of techniques is available in the antidrug arsenal (see Anshel, 1991b, 1993, 2005, for extensive reviews of drug prevention and control strategies). Strategies for eliminating the intake of banned substances are only as effective as the policy makers, sport organizations, coaches, consultants, and parents who help implement them. Strict policies by sport organizations to which the athlete belongs form a formidable obstacle to drug abuse in sport, as evidenced by organizations representing elite sports (e.g., IOC, USOC, NCAA, professional sport organizations). Regulating drug use, therefore, starts with organizational policy. The coach, however, is the one person who has the most credibility with the athlete and who is the most important agent in preventing drug use on the team (Anshel, 1990, 1993) yet coaches, and the organizations that employ them, have traditionally seemed disconnected from the seriousness of this problem.

The two approaches offered in this chapter for combating drug use center on cognitive and behavioral strategies. **Cognitive** strategies deal with influencing the athlete's behaviors and attitudes intellectually and psychologically through verbal and nonverbal communication. **Behavioral** techniques involve two components: (a) setting up situations that foster certain desirable responses from the athletes, including instituting organization and team policies that prohibit drug use, and (b) using verbal and nonverbal techniques that reinforce favorable behaviors or performance outcomes (Martin & Lumsden, 1987). The following suggestions were derived from anecdotal and scientific literature, media reports, and my own experiences as a sport psychology consultant.

Cognitive Approaches

Provide education. Education is the most widely used strategy for preventing drug abuse. Traditionally, the primary objective of drug education programs was to disseminate accurate information about the negative consequences of drug taking. Two underlying factors may explain the limited success of educational programs in controlling drug use. First, education is based on the tenet that people use drugs because they have little knowledge of their deleterious effects (Nicholson, 1989). Supposedly, after being educated about these deleterious effects, the individual is expected to develop a negative attitude toward drug use that, in turn, will dictate desirable behavior. However, the effectiveness of drug education programs on drug-taking behaviors has been less than optimum. For example, Heitzinger and Associates (1986) indicated that "drug education deterred [only] about 5% of the regular users from experimenting with drugs; drug testing and knowledge of punishment deterred 5% of the social users" (p. 158). Numerous studies have shown that increased knowledge about the harmful effects of drugs and drug education programs do not lead to reduced drug use (e.g., Anshel & Russell, 1997; Hanson, 1980; Marcello, Danish, & Stolberg, 1989). This could be due to poor judgment about drug use by most drug users (Perko et al., 1995). Yesalis and Cowart (1998), however, contend that providing information about the potential *benefits* of anabolic steroids provides greater credibility for disclosing its harmful effects.

Discuss ethical issues. It is generally known that drug taking has three effects on compromising the integrity of sport competition: (a) The athlete will never know his or her real full potential, (b) drug use has a health risk, and (c) athletes who use drugs are quitting on themselves; they are relying on a foreign substance to reach peak performance rather than on their own physical and mental training and nutritional habits. Sports administrators, coaches, and parents can send a joint message that drug taking is cheating, and this dishonesty deprives athletes and others of knowing the true victor at the risk of one's health. Ethical concerns may not be a primary motive that influences drug-taking behavior in sport, however. For example, Martin and Anshel (1991) found that Australian athletes were more likely to use a banned performance-enhancing drug if drug testing could not detect it than if the athlete thought it could be detected. While effective communication and education strategies appear to be needed that address ethical considerations of drug use in sport, additional strategies also should be used.

Recognize the athletes' use of drugs. To think "it can't happen on my team (or to me)" is not only naive but also irresponsible. To be effective, coaches and parents must detect signs and symptoms of drug ingestion—even legal drugs that are against team rules, such as alcohol and tobacco—before it becomes addictive and has long-lasting negative consequences to good health. Unfortunately, according to at least one study (Hanson & Gould, 1988), parents and coaches cannot always detect athletes' thoughts, emotions, and signals of certain behavioral patterns. Coaches and team consultants (e.g., athletic trainers, sport psychology consultants, academic tutors) should be sensitive to various aspects of athletes' lives. Examples include a newly divorced or deceased parent, poor school grades, high absentee rate, a personal crisis, frequent illnesses, short-term change in physical features, heightened aggression, frequent bouts of anger, and unwarranted challenges to authority (Damm, 1991).

Attempts to stop the drug-taking behavior must be enacted immediately. While sensitivity toward the athlete's condition is needed at this time, strict limit setting about the offending—and perhaps illegal—behavior is also required. This is why organizational and team policy on drug taking (discussed later in the chapter) is so necessary. Physical, emotional, behavioral, and cognitive signs of drug use are listed in Table 20-1.

Build confidence and self-esteem. Athletes who doubt their ability to succeed are more susceptible to performance-enhancing drugs than their more confident counterparts. As such, athletes can be taught to believe in their ability to perform to their capability by continually learning new skills and strategies, and through hard physical and mental training. Sport psychologists can help athletes with low self-confidence by teaching them the cognitive techniques found in Chapter 16.

Professional counseling. An athlete's decision to ingest steroids, particularly over a prolonged period of time, usually has a psychological explanation. Low self-esteem, irrational thinking, depression, pressure to meet abnormally high expectations (both their own and those of others, a condition associated with neurotic perfectionism), chronic anxiety, pressure to achieve, need for peer approval and acceptance by others, or feelings of helplessness and low personal control are all reasons for athletes to obtain professional counseling. Possible reasons for an athlete's drug-taking habit should be addressed immediately (Ringhofer & Harding, 1996).

Coaches do not typically have training in counseling, but the coach is often the first—and most important—person to whom an athlete comes to discuss personal or team-related concerns (Rosenfeld et al., 1989). Team members need private and confidential access to their coach. The sport psychology consultant can be another effective confidant and facilitator in helping athletes deal with their pressures and problems. Addressing the issues surrounding drug-taking behavior may warrant referral to a licensed mental health professional (see Chapter 19 for guidelines on referral).

Motivational Interviewing (MI). Miller and Rollnick (2002) have developed a client-centered directive method to increase a client's intrinsic

Table 20-1 Physical, Behavioral, Emotional, and Cognitive Signs of Drug Use

Physical Signs
- Bloodshot eyes
- Dark circles under eyes
- Profuse sweating
- Heightened sensitivity to touch, smell, and sound
- Chronic fatigue
- Trouble maintaining normal body temperature (always feeling too hot or cold)

Behavioral Signs
- Unusually secretive behavior
- Increased tardiness to practice and school
- Apathetic attitude about school
- Poor school performance
- Social isolation
- Often broke or out of money
- Irresponsible
- High risk-taking behaviors
- Change in dress style
- New circle of friends
- Marked changes in usual or normal ways of behaving (e.g., unwarranted challenges to authority, isolation, increased arguments, new friends)

Emotional Signs
- Extreme mood swings
- Irritability
- Highly reactive
- Less affectionate
- Chronic physical fatigue
- Heightened aggression/hostility
- Recurrent depressive episodes

Cognitive Signs
- Decreased mental capabilities
- Disordered thinking
- Increased forgetfulness
- Paranoid thoughts that others are out to get him or her
- Denial of problems
- Superman complex (i.e., sense of invulnerability)
- Shortened attention span
- Thoughts of suicide

motivation for health behavior change by exploring and resolving ambivalence. MI could perform three essential functions with respect to reducing or eliminating drug use in sport: (a) collaborating with the athlete to create a safe, supportive, and nonjudgmental environment within which to influence the athlete to avoid drug use, (b) exploring with the athlete reasons for and against drug use, the goal of which is to resolve ambivalence, and (c) developing the athlete's sense of autonomy, or responsibility, for changing the decision to take drugs. One study using MI for health behavior change indicated significant improvements in fitness, exercise adherence, and blood lipids (i.e., changes in diet) among Tennessee police officers (Anshel & Kang, 2008).

Behavioral Strategies

As indicated earlier, the primary objective of a behavioral approach is to shape the environment to control and influence subsequent behavior, a system referred to as "contingency management" (see Martin & Lumsden, 1987, for guidelines). Specifically, behavioral techniques involve (a) setting up situations that foster certain desirable responses from the athletes, and (b) using verbal or nonverbal techniques that reinforce favorable behaviors or performance outcomes.

Teach sport skills and offer positive feedback. Athletes, perhaps more than most other individuals, are driven to achieve the virtually impossible task of performing consistent and error-free skilled movements. Experiencing improved performance will give the athletes fewer reasons to take banned substances. Offering high quality, proper conditioning programs can result in improved performance with better training. Good coaches are good teachers. The key objectives for the coach include skill and conditioning improvement and positive reinforcements of desirable performance changes through verbal and nonverbal communication (Martin & Lumsden, 1987).

Develop and implement a drug policy and plan of action. This strategy is of particular importance, especially given the recent drug scandals that have plagued professional sports. Sport organizations at all levels of competition starting with preadolescents should include widespread information about the dangers of drugs in sport. Teams and sport organizations must develop a drug policy, including consequences for taking them, education, and a process for seeking assistance and/or counseling. Failure to do so, in effect, actually sanctions drug use—or gives the impression that sport leaders do not care. For example, a study conducted by *USA Today* (February 1, 1990) showed that "only 54 percent of coaches said their school has an anti-steroids drug policy" (p. 1B). Although this study is not new, there is reason to believe, it according to the Mitchell Report's (2007).

The results of research support this contention. Fields, Lange, Kreiter, and Fudala (1994) examined current and proposed drug-testing policies from 288 athletic directors across the United States. Of the 245 respondents, 29 percent reported drug testing of their student athletes, mostly conducted on a random basis. Surprisingly, however, most of the tests covered cocaine (85 percent) and amphetamines (83 percent), with only 56 percent of tests for using performance-enhancing drugs such as anabolic steroids. Referral for treatment rather than immediate termination from the team or school was the most common consequence for testing positive.

Athletes need to know the boundaries between acceptable and unacceptable behaviors. The coach and parents must jointly assert that taking drugs is not allowed. Strict limit setting is equally important for responding effectively to an infringement of the team's policy. This is especially relevant following a positive drug test. The team's response to breaking team rules is the most important element in protecting each player and maintaining the coach's (and organization's) integrity.

A strict sport organization and team drug policy also relieves athletes of feeling pressured to engage in behaviors that are illegal, unethical, and detrimental to their physical and mental health. Drug policies have become more stringent at the professional level as well. For example, in the National Hockey League (NHL), a player who fails his random drug testing is suspended for 20 games without pay for the first incident (NHL, 2013).

If a drug-taking incident occurs, coaches should know whom to call—physicians, school administrative personnel, a counselor, a legal advisor, perhaps a religious leader. For example, should parents be notified if their son or daughter is involved in taking banned substances of any kind? All team leaders and athletes should know *in advance* the necessary steps in responding to a player's drug problem or the results of a positive drug test. This policy should be an integral part of an overall crisis management plan. Medical and psychological support services should be in place and ready to respond in an emergency 24 hours a day. A management-by-crisis approach must be avoided.

Respecting the competitor's confidentiality and privacy is another important ingredient to an effective plan of action. Cases of drug abuse need not be publicized or handled publicly. The objective of an effective response to drug abuse is to extinguish the probability of future undesirable behaviors by responding efficiently to an emergency. Effective crisis management consists of anticipating the likelihood of a drug problem and being ready to react accordingly (Wilkerson, 1995).

Have a continuous random drug-testing program. Drug policies and educational programs should also emphasize drug testing. Drug-testing programs in sports have become a more common reality for intercollegiate and elite athletes—probably so much so that, in some settings, drug-testing programs and sanctions now contribute to the effective prevention of drug use. Drug testing, especially if used randomly so the athletes do not anticipate it, can be a particularly powerful behavioral controller when the threat of dismissal or some other serious penalty accompanies a positive test.

The results of studies show that drug testing effectively reduces the likelihood of drug abuse among athletes. For example, Albrecht, Anderson, McGrew, McKeag, and Hough (1992) found, in their study of 2,282 college athletes, that "among those athletes participating at colleges and universities with institutionally based drug-testing programs, individuals who are aware of the fact they are susceptible to periodic testing are more inclined to view such procedures as an effective deterrent to drug use" (p. 245). These results can be generalized to adolescent athletes as well (Martin & Anshel, 1991).

Perhaps nowhere has drug testing become more expected, persistent, and sophisticated than at the Olympic Games. Drug-testing programs at the Olympics include short- or no-notice testing during training periods, testing at qualifying competitions, and testing at the Olympic Games. In their review of these procedures, Catlin and Murray (1996) report that the 1996 Games in Atlanta included testing urine samples for stimulants, narcotics, anabolic agents (particularly steroids), diuretics, peptides, and glycoprotein hormones, as well as prohibited methods of enhancing performance, including blood-doping and pharmacological, chemical, and physical manipulation of urine.

Four principles contribute to an effective drug-testing program.

1. *Announce the policy in advance.* All team personnel should become aware of the team's or league's rules and guidelines from the first day of participation. Only in this way can participants effectively be held accountable for their actions. However, the actual testing procedure should *not* be announced in advance. To reduce costs, **random testing**—in which only a percentage of the team's athletes, rather than all players, are selected—has been shown to deter, though not necessarily eliminate, drug abuse (Martens et al., 2007).

2. *Be consistent in implementing the policy.* The least effective approach to enacting a drug policy is responding to one athlete differently than to others. Unfortunately, group members will likely test team rules. If the coach or league officials are serious about drug abuse prevention and control, they must react vigorously and consistently to the team's most and least talented players. Otherwise, any credibility the policy has will be destroyed.

3. *Have an independent organization responsible for testing.* Anti-doping tests can be conducted

by an external agency, such as the World Anti-Doping Agency (WADA).

4. *Link test results to sanctions.* Strong and swift sanctions can act as a deterrent for some athletes. Accordingly, rules need to be perceived as fair by the athletes, which includes having a reasonable appeal process.

Use behavioral contracting. A **contract system,** often called a performance contract, is among the most sophisticated forms of contingency management. It is a preplanned agreement between two parties (the coach or administrative unit and athlete in this case) that a specified reinforcement will occur to the athlete following the occurrence of a particular action (Martin & Lumsden, 1987; Rushall & Siedentop, 1972). Contracts can be verbal or, perhaps more effectively, in written form and signed by the parties involved. Of course, in professional sports in the United States, player unions and team contracts stipulate drug-testing procedures and penalties.

Use a support group. Results of research on the effectiveness of educational programs on drug (Palmer, 1989) and alcohol prevention (Werch, Carlson, Pappas, Edemon, & DiClemente, 2000) revealed that high school seniors serve as excellent peer educators and role models in drug prevention among fellow student athletes and nonathletes. Among the first structured attempts at dealing with drug abuse on a sports team, particularly at the elite level, was one conducted by the Cleveland Browns football team (Collins et al., 1984). In addition to medical and psychological treatment programs, the team owner hired a psychiatrist to conduct group and individual therapies and to establish self-help meetings for players and their wives. The core of the program consisted of a subgroup called The Inner Circle, which included of a group of identified drug-involved players. According to Collins et al.:

> Group discussions typically dealt with who was relapsing and why and the need for changes in the individual's lifestyle to support staying "clean." . . . Rather than participating in cover-ups and deceptions, the players saw that

relapses were "contagious," and that when one member was in trouble, others would soon follow. . . . The group eventually became responsible for much of its own therapeutic work in keeping its individual members away from drugs (p. 490).

Invite guest speakers. Sometimes athletes become *coach deaf*—they are so accustomed to the voice of their coach (or, for that matter, their parents) that they tune him or her out. Guest speakers bring to the team a renewed sense of authority, expertise, credibility, and respect. Examples of guest speakers include pharmacists, retired athletes, former coaches, physicians, lawyers, religious leaders, and individuals whose personal history may benefit the listeners (e.g., the medical problems of a former steroid abuser, former champion athletes who can reveal their commitment and dedication to become successful). Kelli White was the first athlete implicated in the BALCO scandal (Nazzaro, 2013). She also was the first athlete to join efforts by the United States Anti-Doping Agency (USADA) in working to reduce drug use in sport. White now speaks publicly about the dangers of doping and her message is very powerful. As Travis Tygart, the chief executive of USADA stated, "Kelli's contributions to antidoping . . . will have a much longer-lasting and beneficial impact for athletes and sport than anything she ever did on the track" (Nazzaro, 2013, p. 15).

Two Intervention Models for Regulating Drug Use in Sport

Two models, which have similar components, have been published that have direct implications for reducing or eliminating drug use in sport. The Drugs in Sport Deterrence Model (DSDM; Strelan & Boeckman, 2003) applies deterrence theory whereas the Disconnected Values Model (Anshel & Kang, 2007) emphasizes an examination of athletes' values. Both models warrant additional research related to drug-taking behaviors in sport.

Drugs in Sport Deterrence Model. The DSDM provides an attempt at influencing the athlete's decision about using banned substances using deterrence theory by providing athletes with extensive information about the possible—even likely—consequences of using banned substances. Ostensibly, the athlete's acknowledgement of consequences will provide an adequate deterrent to drug taking. Identifying the downside of a behavior pattern has more credibility to the client, however, if the advantages, or benefits, of the inappropriate behavior are also determined.

The authors contend that the DSDM provides "a theoretical framework for some much-needed systematic research into understanding performance-enhancing drug use decisions by elite athletes . . . and has important implications for the way in which future drug deterrence policies are framed and funded" (Strelan & Boeckman, 2003, p. 181). More studies are needed to examine the efficacy of this model on influencing the decision-making process on using banned substances in sport.

Disconnected Values Model. The pressures to succeed in sport, especially at elite levels, are too great to expect athletes to regulate their own personal behavior. And, as indicated earlier, frequently the athletes' self-esteem is dependent on their sport success—at virtually any cost. In addition, typical of human nature, most athletes do not associate a negative, unhealthy habit with longer-term harmful outcomes. Short-term benefits prevail over long-term consequences. A unique approach to behavioral change among athletes and nonathletes that appeals to the very core of the athletes' reasons for competing— their deepest values and beliefs—is the *Disconnected Values Model* (Anshel & Kang, 2007).

The primary purpose of the DVM is to assist athletes in acknowledging that taking drugs, whether it is for performance-enhancing or recreational purposes, is a negative habit that has benefits, but also dire costs and long-term consequences, similar to Strelan and Boeckman's (2003) DSDM. The model is driven by the athletes' willingness to become aware of the contradiction between their deepest values and beliefs and their actions, in this case, taking banned substances. For example, athletes may acknowledge a disconnect, or inconsistency, between their values of competitiveness, integrity, fairness, health, honesty, and faith and their conscious decision to ingest substances they know to be illegal in society, unhealthy to long-term health, or against the team's or sport organization's rules. Does the athlete find this disconnect acceptable? If the athlete acknowledges the disconnect, yet deems it acceptable, the negative habit (i.e., drug-taking) will continue. The ability to act in a way that is consistent with one's deepest values and beliefs is referred to as expanding spiritual capacity (Loehr & Schwartz, 2003). The model, presented in Figure 20-1, depicts the intervention stages. Research findings have indicated that, used as an intervention, the DVM significantly improved cardiovascular and strength fitness, exercise adherence, and blood lipids profile of university faculty (Anshel & Kang, 2007) and police officers (Anshel & Kang, 2008). Investigation on the model's effectiveness in changing attitudes and behaviors related to drug use in sport, in particular, is needed.

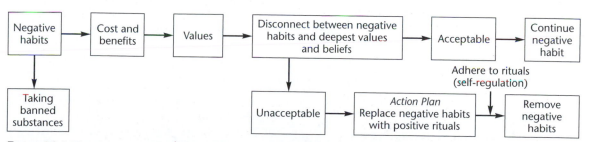

Figure 20-1 **The disconnected values intervention model for drug use in sport**

Summary

The causes of drug taking among athletes are multidimensional and lead to taking performance-enhancing and recreational drugs. Although personal characteristics play a relevant role in drug taking, situational and environmental issues also contribute by exacerbating the pressures placed on athletes to achieve sport success. Examples include: unreasonable expectations by others, particularly the coach; peer pressure; the perception of social acceptance through media reports of high-profile athletes who take drugs; and, at the elite level, the financial incentives for success.

Protection from sport pressures must come from their coach, sport organizational policies, sport psychology consultants whose expertise includes teaching effective mental skills, and licensed psychologists who are trained to deal with pathological issues related to the athlete's irrational thinking, various disorders, addictions, and personal traits and characteristics that make the athlete vulnerable to drug use. It is unrealistic to expect athletes to eliminate the problem of drug abuse without external support.

The various national and international sporting organizations have to show a high degree of consistency and unanimity in fighting drugs in sport. Clearly, additional research is needed on the effectiveness of various cognitive and behavioral interventions on changing the attitudes and actions of athletes, coaches, and sports organizations about drug use in sport. Two models were reviewed, the Drugs in Sport Deterrence Model and the Disconnected Values Model, that are intended to deter athletes from ingesting banned substances. Further research is needed to examine the efficacy of these models on influencing drug-taking behavior in sport. The fight against illegal and unethical drug use in sport must be aggressive to protect the integrity and future of competitive sport.

Study Questions

1. What is doping and why does it occur?

2. Give examples of drugs that athletes may use to enhance their performance and why athletes might take each drug.

3. Identify the different health concerns for different forms of doping.

4. Develop a rationale for an antidrug policy in sport. Consider if the policy should be different for high school versus professional sport versus other competitive levels.

5. Using both anecdotal reports and evidence from scientific studies, give some indication of the extensiveness of drug abuse in sport.

6. Discuss the physical, psychological and emotional, and social causes of drug abuse in sport.

7. Distinguish between cognitive approaches and behavioral strategies in controlling drug abuse in athletes. Provide examples of both types of interventions.

8. If you were the team's head coach, describe the cognitive and behavioral strategies you would use with your team to prevent and respond to the use of anabolic steroids.

9. Discuss the three main components of an effective drug-testing program and how to help ensure an effective testing program.

10. Should sports administrators and coaches institute drug-taking policies? Why not simply allow athletes to take any substance they wish, if they thought it would help their performance?

11. What strategies can *parents* of athletes use to reduce the chance their child athlete will use anabolic steroids and other banned substances?

References

Albrecht, R. R., Anderson, W. A., McGrew, C. A., McKeag, D. B., & Hough, D. O. (1992). NCAA institutionally based drug testing: Do our athletes know the rules of *this* game? *Medicine and Science in Sport and Exercise, 24,* 242–246.

Alzado, L. (1991, July 8). I'm sick and I'm scared. *Sports Illustrated, 75,* 21–25.

Anshel, M. H. (1990). Commentary on the national drugs in sport conference—1989. Testing the causes and symptoms. *Australian Journal of Science and Medicine in Sport, 22,* 49–56.

Anshel, M. H. (1991a). Causes for drug abuse in sport: A survey of intercollegiate athletes. *Journal of Sport Behavior, 14,* 283–307.

Anshel, M. H. (1991b). Cognitive and behavioral strategies for combating drug abuse in sport: Implications for coaches and sport psychology consultants. *Sport Psychologist, 5,* 152–166.

Anshel, M. H. (1993). Psychology of drug use in sport. In R. N. Singer, M. Murphey, & L. K. Tennant (Eds.), *Handbook of research on sport psychology* (pp. 851–876). New York: Macmillan.

Anshel, M. H. (2005). Substance use: Chemical roulette in sport. In S. Murphy (Ed.), *The sport psych handbook* (pp. 255–276). Champaign, IL: Human Kinetics.

Anshel, M. H., & Kang, M. (2007). Effect of an intervention on replacing negative habits with positive routines for improving full engagement at work: A test of the Disconnected Values Model. *Journal of Consulting Psychology: Practice and Research, 59,* 110–125.

Anshel, M. H., & Kang, M. (2008). Effectiveness of motivational interviewing techniques on changes in fitness, blood lipids, and exercise adherence of police officers: An outcome-based action study. *Journal of Correctional Health Care, 14,* 48–62.

Anshel, M. H., & Russell, K. (1997). Effect of an educational program on knowledge and attitudes toward ingesting anabolic steroids among track and field athletes. *Journal of Drug Education, 27,* 172–187.

Backhouse S., McKenna J., Robinson S., Atkin A. (2007). Attitudes, behaviours, knowledge and education – drugs in sport: Past, present and future. Available at http://www.wada-ama.org/rtecontent/document/backhouse_et_al_full_report.pdf

Branch, J. D. (2002). Performance-enhancing drugs and ergogenic aids. In L. L. Mostofsky & L. D. Zaichkowsky (Eds.), *Medical and psychological aspects of sport and exercise* (pp. 55–71). Morgantown, WV: Fitness Information Technology.

Catlin, D. H., & Murray, T. H. (1996, July 17). Performance-enhancing drugs, fair competition, and Olympic sport. *Journal of the American Medical Association, 276,* 231–237.

Chu, D. (1982). *Dimensions of sport studies.* New York: Wiley.

CNN Library. (2013, August 17). *Performance enhancing drugs in sports fast facts.* http://www.cnn.com/2013/06/06/us/performance-enhancing-drugs-in-sports-fast-facts

Collins, G. B., Pippenger, C. E., & Janesz, J. W. (1984). Links in the chain: An approach to the treatment of drug abuse on a professional football team. *Cleveland Clinic Quarterly, 51,* 485–492.

Damm, J. (1991). Drugs and the college student-athlete. In E. F. Etzel, A. B. Ferraute, & J. W. Pinkney (Eds.), *Counseling college student-athletes: Issues and interventions* (pp. 151–174). Morgantown, WV: Fitness Information Technology.

Donald, K. (1983). *The doping game.* Brisbane, Australia: Boolarang.

Doweiko, H. E. (1996). *Concepts of chemical dependency* (3rd ed.). Pacific Grove, CA: Brooks/Cole.

Eisenberg, M., Wall, M., & Neumark-Sztainer, D. (2012). Muscle-enhancing behaviors among adolescent girls and boys. *Pediatrics, 130,* 1019–1026.

English, G. (1987). A theoretical explanation of why athletes choose to use steroids, and the role of the coach in influencing behavior. *National Strength and Conditioning Association Journal, 9,* 53–56.

Fields, L., Lange, W. R., Kreiter, N. A., & Fudala, P. J. (1994). *Medicine and Science in Sports and Exercise, 26,* 682–686.

Flett, G. L., & Hewitt, P. L. (2002). Perfectionism and maladjustment: An overview of theoretical, definitional, and treatment issues. In G. L. Flett & P. L. Hewitt (Eds.), *Perfectionism: Theory, research, and treatment* (pp. 5–32). Washington, DC: American Psychological Association.

Gardner, F., & Moore, Z. (2006). *Clinical sport psychology.* Champaign, IL: Human Kinetics.

Gill, D. L., & Williams, L. (2008). *Psychological dynamics of sport and exercise* (3rd ed.). Champaign, IL.

Grogan, S., Shepherd, S., Evans, R., Wright, S., & Hunter, G. (2006). Experiences of anabolic steroid use: In-depth interviews with men and women body builders. *Journal of Health Psychology, 11,* 845–856.

Hanson, D. (1980). Drugs education, does it work? In F. Scarpitti & S. Datesman (Eds.), *Drugs and youth culture: Annual reviews of drug and alcohol abuse* (Vol. 4, pp. 212–236), Beverly Hills, CA: Sage.

Hanson, T. W., & Gould, D. (1988). Factors affecting the ability of coaches to estimate their athletes' trait and state anxiety levels. *Sport Psychologist, 2,* 298–313.

Heitzinger & Associates. (1986). *1981–1986 data collection and analysis: High school, college, professional athletes alcohol/drug survey.* Madison, WI.

Hewitt, P. L., & Flett, G. L. (2002). Perfectionism and stress processes in psychopathology. In G. L. Flett & P. L. Hewitt (Eds.), *Perfectionism: Theory, research, and treatment* (pp. 255–284). Washington, DC: American Psychological Association.

IOC. (2013). Factsheet: The fight against doping and promotion of athletes' health update. Retrieved from http://www.olympic.org/Documents/Reference_documents_Factsheets/Fight_against_doping.pdf

Julien, R. M. (1981). *A primer of drug action* (3rd ed.). San Francisco: Freeman.

Kandel, D. B. (1978). *Longitudinal research on drug use: Empirical findings and methodological issues*. Washington, DC: Hemisphere-Wiley.

Keller, G. (2013, August 22). Tour de France winners Pantani and Ullrich took EPO. *The Scotsman*. Retrieved from http://www.scotsman.com/sport/more-sport/other/tour-de-france-winners-pantani-and-ullrich-took-epo-1-3013919

Laure, P., & Reinsberger, H. (1995). Doping and high-level endurance walkers—knowledge and representation: A prohibited practice. *Journal of Sports Medicine & Physical Fitness, 35,* 228–231.

Leccese, A. P. (1991). *Drugs and society: Behavioral medicines and abusable drugs*. Upper Saddle River, NJ: Prentice Hall.

Lennehan, P. (2003). *Anabolic steroids*. London: Taylor & Francis.

Loehr, J., & Schwartz, T. (2003). *The power of full engagement*. New York: Free Press.

Manning, S. (2012, July 26). Nine athletes fail drugs tests on eve of Olympic Games. *The Independent*. http://www.independent.co.uk/sport/olympics/athletics/nine-athletes-fail-drugs-tests-on-eve-of-olympic-games-7976834.html

Marcello, R. J., Danish, S. J., & Stolberg, A. L. (1989). An evaluation of strategies developed to prevent substance abuse among student-athletes. *The Sport Psychologist, 3,* 196–211.

Martens, M., Dams-O'Connor, K., & Kilmer, J. R. (2007). Alcohol and drug abuse among athletes. In G. Tenenbaum & R. C. Eklund (Eds.)., *Handbook of research in sport psychology* (3rd ed., pp. 859–878). Hoboken, NJ: John Wiley & Sons.

Martin, G. L., & Lumsden, J. A. (1987). *Coaching: An effective behavioral approach*. St. Louis, MO: Times Mirror/Mosby.

Martin, M. B., & Anshel, M. H. (1991). Attitudes of elite junior athletes on drug-taking behaviors: Implications for drug prevention programs. *Drug Education Journal of Australia, 5,* 223–238.

Mazzeo, F., & Ascione, A. (2013). Anabolic androgenic steroids and doping in sport. *Medicina Sportivâ, 9,* 2009–2020.

Meilman, P. W., Crace, R. K., Presley, C. A., & Lyerla, R. (1995). Beyond performance enhancement: Polypharmacy among collegiate users of steroids. *Journal of American College Health, 44,* 98–104.

Melia, P., Pipe, A., & Greenberg, L. (1996). The use of anabolic-androgenic steroids by Canadian students. *Clinical Journal of Sport Medicine, 6,* 9–14.

Miller, K. E., Barnes, G. M., Sabo, D., Melnick, M. J., & Farrell, M. P. (2002). Anabolic-androgenic steroid use and other adolescent problem behaviors: Rethinking the male athlete assumption. *Sociological Perspectives, 45,* 467–489.

Miller, W. R., & Rollnick, S. (2002). *Motivational interviewing: Preparing people for change* (2nd ed.). New York: Guilford Press.

Mitchell, G. J. (December 13, 2007). *Report to the Commissioner of baseball of an independent investigation into the illegal use of steroids and other performance enhancing substances by players in major league baseball.* Presented to the Commissioner of Major League Baseball.

Moses, E. (1988, October 10). An athlete's Rx for the drug problem. *Newsweek,* p. 57.

National Collegiate Athletic Association (2012). *National study of substance use trends among NCAA college student-athletes.* Indianapolis: IN. Retrieved from http://www.ncaapublications .com/productdownloads/SAHS09.pdf

National Hockey League (NHL, 2013). NHL, NHLPA team up against performance-enhancing substances. Retrieved from http://www.nhl.com/ice/page.htm?id=26397

Nazarro, M. N. (2013). Out of track's doping scandal, redemption and progress. *New York Times.* Retrieved from http://www.nytimes.com/2013/08/18/sports/olympics/out-of-a-doping-scandal-redemption-for-Kelli-White-and-progress-for-track.html?pagewanted=all&_r=0

Nicholson, N., (1989). The role of drug education. In S. Haynes & M. H. Anshel (Eds.), *Proceedings of the 1989 National Drugs in Sport Conference—Treating the causes and symptoms* (pp. 48–57). University of Wollongong, Wollongong, NSW, Australia.

Palmer, J. (1989). High school senior athletes as peer educators and role models: An innovative approach to drug prevention. *Journal of Alcohol and Drug Education, 35,* 23–27.

Perko, M. A., Cowdery, J., Wang, M. Q., & Yesalis, C. S. (1995). Associations between academic performance of Division I college athletes and their perceptions of the effects of anabolic steroids. *Perceptual Motor Skills, 80,* 284–286.

Pope, H. G. (2002). *The Adonis complex: How to identify, treat, and prevent body obsession in men and boys.* New York: Free Press.

Pope, H. G., & Katz, D. L. (1994). Psychiatric and medical effects of anabolic-androgenic steroid use. A controlled study of 160 athletes. *Archives of General Psychiatry, 51,* 375–382.

Pope, H. G., Katz, D. L., & Champoux, R. (1988, July). Anabolic-androgenic steroid use among 1,010 college men. *The Physician and Sportsmedicine, 16,* 75–77, 80–81.

Prokop, L. (1990). The history of doping. In J. Park (Ed.), *Proceedings of the International Symposium on Drug Abuse in Sport (doping)* (pp. 1–9). Seoul: Korea Institute of Science and Technology.

Ringhofer, K. R., & Harding, M. E. (1996). *Coaches guide to drugs and sport.* Champaign, IL: Human Kinetics.

Rosenfeld, L. B., Richman, J. M., & Hardy, C. J. (1989). Examining social support networks among athletes: Description and relationship to stress. *Sport Psychologist, 3,* 23–33.

Rushall, B. S., & Siedentop, D. (1972). *The development and control of behavior in sport and physical education.* Philadelphia: Lea & Febiger.

Russell, D. G. (1990). *Drugs and medicines in sport.* Wellington, NZ: Royal Society of New Zealand.

Saugy, M. M., Robinson, N. N., Saudan, C. C., Baume, N. N., Avois, L. L., & Mangin, P. P. (2006). Human growth hormone doping in sport. *British Journal of Sports Medicine, 40,* i35–i39.

Sawka, M. N., Joyner, M. J., Miles, D. S., Robertson, R. J., Spriet, L. L., & Young, A. J. (2010). *ACSM position stand: The use of blood doping as an ergogenic aid.* Retrieved from http://www.medscape.com/viewarticle/716353_1

Schlaadt, R. G., & Shannon, P. T. (1994). *Drugs: Use, misuse, and abuse.* Upper Saddle River, NJ: Prentice Hall.

Shroyer, J. (1990). Getting tough on anabolic steroids. Can we win the battle? *The Physician and Sportsmedicine, 18,* 106, 108–110, 115, 118.

Sonstroem, R. J. (1997). Physical activity and self-esteem. In W. P. Morgan (Ed.), *Physical activity and mental health* (pp. 127–143). Washington, DC: Taylor & Francis.

Stoll, O., Lau, A., & Stoeber, J. (2007). Perfectionism and performance in a new basketball training task: Does striving for perfection enhance or undermine performance? *Psychology of Sport and Exercise, 9,* 111–129.

Strelan, P., & Boeckman, R. J. (2003). A new model for understanding performance-enhancing drug use by elite athletes. *Journal of Applied Sport Psychology, 15,* 176–183.

Uvacsek, M., Nepusz, T., Naughton, D., Mazanov, J., Ránky, M., & Petróczi, A. (2011). Self-admitted behavior and perceived use of performance-enhancing vs. psychoactive drugs among competitive athletes. *Scandinavian Journal of Medicine & Science in Sports, 21,* 224–234.

Van Den Berg, P., Neumark-Sztainer, D., Cafri, G., & Wall, M. (2007). Steroid use among adolescents: longitudinal findings from Project EAT. *Pediatrics, 119,* 476–486.

WADA (2011). *Anti-doping glossary.* http://www.wada-ama.org/en/Resources/Anti-Doping-Glossary/

Waldron, J. J., & Krane, V. (2005). Whatever it takes: Health compromising behaviors in female athletes. *Quest, 57,* 315–329.

Weinhold, L. L. (1991). Steroid and drug use by athletes. In L. Diamant (Ed.), *Psychology of sport, exercise, and fitness: Social and personal issues.* New York: Hemisphere.

Werch, C. E., Carlson, J. M., Pappas, D. M., Edemon, P., & DiClemente, C. C. (2000). Effects of a brief alcohol preventive intervention for youth attending school sports physical examinations. *Substance Use and Misuse, 35,* 421–432.

Wilkerson, L. A. (1995). Taking a strong stance against anabolic steroid use [editorial]. *Journal of the American Osteopathic Association, 95,* 468–470.

Williams, M. H. (1989). *Beyond training: How athletes enhance performance legally and illegally.* Champaign, IL: Leisure Press.

Williams, M. H. (1998). *The ergogenics edge: Pushing the limits of sports performance.* Champaign, IL: Human Kinetics.

Williams, M. H., Kreider, R. B., & Branch, J. D. (1999). *Creatine: The power supplement.* Champaign, IL: Human Kinetics.

Yesalis, C. E., & Cowart, V. S. (1998). *The steroids game.* Champaign, IL: Human Kinetics.

Yesalis, C. E., Herrick, R. T., Buckley, W. E., Friedl, K. E., Brannon, D., & Wright, J. E. (1988). Self-reported use of anabolic-androgenic steroids by elite power-lifters. *The Physician and Sportsmedicine, 16,* 91–94; 96–98.

Athlete Burnout: An Individual and Organizational Phenomenon

J.D. DeFreese, *University of North Carolina at Chapel Hill*
Thomas D. Raedeke, *East Carolina University*
Alan L. Smith, *Michigan State University*

"No kid should have to go through what she went through," said Kenny, a past president of the American Volleyball Coaches Association. "Adults need to pay attention. It's a problem in youth sports. These kids are burned out. From 12 to 18, I bet Elena can count on her hands the amount of weekends she didn't have anything to do related to sport. She's missed the opportunity to be a kid."

Regarding Elena Delle Donne—former burnout case and current WNBA player

—In Longman, 2008

Athlete burnout can be perplexing and frustrating for coaches, sport psychology practitioners, and athletes alike due to the wide range of meanings for the term in popular culture, the negative impact it has on athletes, and the complexity in understanding what causes it (Eklund & Cresswell, 2007; Maslach, Schaufeli, & Leiter, 2001). The vast array of potential individual and environmental contributors to burnout, along with the consequences associated with it, can be difficult to digest and ultimately address with interventions. Thus, unsurprisingly it can be a challenge for practitioners to address this phenomenon. Understanding what burnout is (and is not) as well as its key psychosocial antecedents is important for those who wish to combat this maladaptive athlete experience and to safeguard athlete performance and enhance well-being.

In this chapter we provide an overview of the athlete burnout knowledge base to inform evidence-based practice. Specifically, we summarize existing theory and research on athlete burnout with an emphasis on how theory can inform practice. We also illustrate how individual and organizational factors together are central to the development of athlete burnout. Successful prevention and treatment of athlete burnout requires multifaceted strategies. We strive to arm sport psychology practitioners with the knowledge to pursue evidence-based athlete burnout interventions that consider both the individual and the organization.

What Is Athlete Burnout?

Before gaining empirical interest in sport, Freudenberger (1974) first described burnout among highly dedicated individuals working in free health clinics who became exhausted due to the chronic strain associated with their role. Around the same time, Maslach (1976; 1978) recognized a similar phenomenon in healthcare professionals and in 1982 operationalized burnout as a multidimensional psychological syndrome involving emotional exhaustion, depersonalization, and reduced personal accomplishment among individuals who work in human service settings (e.g., social workers, nurses, teachers). Because sport is a highly effort-driven activity and was a source of anecdotal accounts of burnout in the media, sport scientists recognized the need to systematically understand and address this phenomenon in competitive sport (Dale & Weinberg, 1990; Fender, 1989).

To understand athlete burnout a clear operational definition was needed. Adapting Maslach's (1982) framework to sport, Raedeke (1997; Raedeke & Smith, 2001; 2009) defined athlete burnout as a multidimensional, cognitive-affective syndrome characterized by emotional and physical exhaustion, reduced sense of accomplishment, and sport devaluation. Definitions and symptoms for these dimensions are found in Table 21-1. Physical exhaustion was added to Maslach's definition of worker burnout to account for the physical demands of sport participation and depersonalization was adapted to devaluation because the athlete–sport (rather than the worker–patient) connection is of principal interest in competitive sport. Raedeke's definition addressed the multifaceted nature of athlete burnout and enabled researchers to best coordinate their efforts to measure and understand this maladaptive athlete experience.

Determining the prevalence of athlete burnout is challenging, allowing only for very tentative estimates ranging from approximately 1 to 10 percent of athletes (see Eklund & Cresswell, 2007; Gustafsson, Kenttä, Hassmén, & Lundqvist, 2007; Raedeke & Smith, 2009). The lack of consistent diagnostic criteria is a key limitation of efforts to assess athlete burnout prevalence. Notwithstanding this limitation, even the most conservative estimates suggest that burnout can take a toll on the performance and well-being of numerous athletes worldwide. The negative impact of burnout on athletes includes performance decrements, decreased motivation, potential dropout, and troubled social relations

Table 21-1 Athlete Burnout Dimensions, Definitions, and Symptoms

Dimension	Definition	Symptoms
Emotional & Physical Exhaustion	Emotional and physical fatigue stemming from the psychological and physical demands associated with training and competing	Excessively tired or lethargic Emotionally "drained" Unable to perform nonsport activities due to fatigue
Reduced Sense of Accomplishment	Inefficacy and a tendency to evaluate oneself negatively in terms of sport performance and accomplishments	Decreased feelings of sport achievement Performing below personal standards Consistent negative self-evaluation
Sport Devaluation	Negative, detached attitude toward sport reflected by lack of concern for sport and performance quality	Reduced concern for sport and performance quality Question the value/meaning of sport Resentful attitude toward sport

that negatively impact team climate. Burn-out also can negatively impact mental (anxiety, depression, eating disorders) and physical (illness susceptibility, substance abuse) health (Gustafsson, Hassmén, Kenttä, & Johansson, 2008). Sport medicine physicians describe athlete burnout as an important issue addressed with their patients (Brenner, 2007; Mann, Grana, Indelicato, O'Neill, & George, 2007). Altogether, this suggests that burnout is of epidemiological significance and that continued athlete burnout education, research, and practice efforts are warranted.

What Is Not Athlete Burnout?

Athlete burnout is distinct from depression and sport dropout. Confusion between the psychological outcomes of burnout and depression is not surprising as both represent negative affective experiences (Cresswell & Eklund, 2006a). However, carefully designed research has shown these two maladaptive outcomes to be related yet distinct psychological constructs (Cresswell & Eklund, 2006b; Raedeke, Arce, de Francisco, Seoane, & Ferraces, in press). Depression is distinguished from burnout by its more pervasive affective symptomology, as opposed to burnout's central (but not sole) link to the sport experience (Cresswell & Eklund, 2006b). Drawing from longitudinal research in organizational psychology, athletes suffering from burnout may be at risk for experiencing depression (Hakanen & Schaufeli, 2012). Thus, it is important to consider the potential existence of depressive symptoms (see Chapter 19) when assessing and treating burnout in athletes.

Though some early burnout conceptualizations confound burnout and dropout, they represent distinct potential outcomes of chronic sport involvement (Smith, 1986). Burnout causes some athletes to quit sport, but not all burned-out athletes will quit (Raedeke, 1997). Moreover, sport dropout can result from reasons other than burnout. These reasons include time constraints, personal choice, switching sports, or pursuing alternative activities. Accordingly,

differentiating athlete burnout and sport dropout is important for practitioners, as burned-out athletes may not outwardly manifest behaviors or attitudes that suggest a desire to leave sport.

In sum, it is crucial to distinguish athlete burnout from other maladaptive athlete experiences (depression) and participatory decisions (dropout). Distinguishing athlete burnout from its potential consequences helps researchers, practitioners, and athletes best understand when burnout may be occurring and best tailor prevention and treatment efforts.

Why Does Burnout Occur? A Review of Theoretically Informed Burnout Antecedents

Understanding what causes burnout is necessary to develop effective prevention and treatment strategies. Burnout is considered a reaction to chronic stress and therefore has been explained within overtraining and psychosocial stress perspectives. Burnout also is considered a motivational phenomenon and has been examined within self-determination and entrapment frameworks. A brief review of these prominent conceptualizations highlights key antecedents of athlete burnout (Eklund & Cresswell, 2007; Gould & Whitley, 2009). Notably, such a review points to both individual and organizational contributors to this maladaptive syndrome.

Overtraining

The simplest explanation for athlete burnout may be that it is a maladaptive psychophysiological response to high training loads, especially in conditioning intensive sports. In other words, burnout may result from overtraining. Overtraining commonly is viewed as an imbalance between training and recovery, often combined with other training and non-training stressors. Within the overtraining perspective, athletes are considered to be in a state of **overreaching** when they experience elevated fatigue and performance decrements that they can recover from within days to a few weeks. Overreaching can be intentional as part of training periodization. However, when not carefully planned or when athletes respond to performance plateaus caused by overreaching with intensified training, the overtraining syndrome can develop. The **overtraining syndrome** is characterized by performance decrements and exhaustion that fail to improve even with rest or reduced training and represents the repeated failure of the body's adaptive mechanisms to cope with chronic training stress (for reviews see Fry, Morton, & Keast, 1991; Kuipers, 1998; Kuipers & Keizer, 1988; Meeusen et al., 2013; Raglin & Wilson, 2000). The overtraining syndrome can take months to years to recover from and presently there is no evidence that the overtraining syndrome can be treated aside from prolonged rest and taking time away from sport (Meeusen et al., 2013). Although conceptually distinct, the overtraining syndrome and burnout share considerable overlap in that both are chronic states and that athletes are exhausted, have lowered motivation, and report negative feelings about sport. One pathway to burnout is through high training demands that result in the development of the overtraining syndrome.

Although coaches and athletes focus much attention on training loads, recovery processes are often overlooked. **Recovery** is integral to training periodization and represents the mechanism by which a higher level of function is achieved following intense training by reducing fatigue and regaining vitality (Kenttä & Hassmén, 2002). It is important for athletes and coaches to maintain a balance between rest and training stress in sport. In fact, some scholars highlight that underrecovery, rather than excessive training per se, results in the overtraining syndrome (Budgett, 1998; Kellmann, 2002). Thus, it is important to monitor not only training loads, but also recovery and what athletes do to recover. Although the most common forms of recovery are passive activities like rest, recovery is multifaceted and involves more than passive rest and time away from sport. It also involves more active strategies including light activity, proper nutrition, hydration, quality sleep, mental and physical relaxation, stretching, and warm-down. Recovery also can involve activities such as interacting with supportive others (e.g., peers, family members) or engaging experiences (e.g., spending time in nature, hobbies) that bring life balance, increase feelings of vitality, and provide a mental break from sport (Kenttä & Hassmén, 2002; Kellmann, 2002).

Beyond excessive training stress and inadequate recovery, life stress outside of sport can potentially impact how athletes respond to intense training according to the overtraining perspective. Athletes who experience high amounts of stress outside of sport are less able to handle high training volumes compared to those experiencing less outside stress (Tenenbaum, Jones, Kitsantas, Sacks, & Berwick, 2003). Collectively, the key variables of training volume, recovery, and life stress are important considerations when seeking to address burnout.

Psychosocial Sport Stress

Although overtraining can be a contributor, burnout also is thought to be a reaction to chronic sport-based psychosocial stressors (Smith, 1986). **Psychosocial stress** occurs when athletes perceive an imbalance between sport demands and their ability to meet those demands. Athletes with high sport demands yet insufficient resources to meet those demands experience elevated stress and are more susceptible to burnout. Supporting this perspective, a systematic review of the burnout literature found perceived stress to consistently and positively associate with athlete burnout perceptions (Goodger, Gorely, Lavallee, & Harwood, 2007).

Many potential sources of athlete stress have been described in interviews with coaches and athletes, including high training and competitive demands and the time requirements of sport participation (Gould, Tuffey, Udry, & Loehr, 1997; Raedeke, Lunney, & Venables, 2002). Stress can also stem from interpersonal sources such as social interactions and the performance emphasis of sport (e.g., pressure from coaches/teammates, family dynamics surrounding sport). Indeed, research supports an association between negative sport-based social interactions and athlete burnout (Smith, Gustafsson, & Hassmén, 2010; Udry, Gould, Bridges, & Tuffey, 1997). In addition to negative interactions, social influences can be more subtle such as when parents are supportive but family dynamics revolve excessively around sport (Raedeke et al., 2002).

Beyond outside sources, high demands can come from internal sources. Dispositional factors including self-esteem based on performance accomplishments, trait anxiety, dispositional negative affect, and perfectionism (i.e., overly high performance expectations, concerns about others' evaluations, and critical self-evaluations) can contribute to athlete burnout perceptions (DeFreese, 2012; Goodger et al., 2007; Hall, Hill, & Appleton, 2012). Importantly, these dispositional factors create potential psychological vulnerability whereas more adaptive athlete traits (e.g., dispositional optimism, hope, resiliency) can reduce vulnerability and, therefore, help athletes combat stress and burnout.

Finally, this perspective asserts the importance of sport-based resources in decreasing stress and alleviating burnout. For example, coping resources including lifestyle management (e.g., proper nutrition, adequate sleep; Raedeke & Smith, 2004) as well as social support (e.g., from teammates, parents, coaches; Cresswell, 2009; DeFreese & Smith, 2013b) are negatively associated with athlete burnout perceptions. This suggests that beyond lowering sport-based demands, increasing resources can be effective in deterring athlete burnout.

Self-Determination Theory

Although athlete burnout is a reaction to chronic sport stress, it is also tied to athlete motivation. **Self-determination theory** (SDT; Deci & Ryan, 1985; Ryan & Deci, 2000) is a prominent theory of human motivation that has been used to understand athlete burnout. According to SDT, psychological outcomes are influenced by the nature of one's motivation. The most adaptive motivation is self-determined in nature, resulting predominantly from individual choice rather than internal pressures (e.g., guilt, obligation) or

external pressures (e.g., rewards, punishments, expectations of others). More self-determined motivation is associated with lower burnout risk whereas less self-determined motivation is associated with greater burnout risk. SDT further posits that motivation is influenced by the psychological needs of autonomy, competence, and relatedness.

- Autonomy – feelings of personal choice or control

- Competence – sense of success and being effective in one's environment

- Relatedness – social connection to others reflected by feelings of acceptance and belonging

When needs for autonomy, competence, and relatedness are met by the social environment of sport, more self-determined motivation is expected. This yields the most adaptive outcomes for athletes. Athletes who do not feel autonomous, competent, or related with others in sport will be motivated for less self-determined reasons and more prone to experiencing burnout perceptions.

Research on athlete burnout has supported the tenets of SDT (see Li, Wang, Pyun, & Kee, 2013). Burnout-related perceptions have been shown to positively associate with less self-determined forms of sport motivation and/or negatively associate with more self-determined motivation (e.g., Cresswell & Eklund, 2005; Curran, Appleton, Hill, & Hall, 2011; Lemyre, Roberts, & Stray-Gundersen, 2007; Lonsdale, Hodge, & Rose, 2009). Additionally, in a longitudinal study of elite swimmers, Lemyre, Treasure, and Roberts (2006) found that shifts from more to less self-determined forms of motivation across a season predicted elevated burnout perceptions. Thus, changes in athlete motivation may precede burnout development. Also consistent with SDT, athlete autonomy, competence, and relatedness perceptions are negatively associated with burnout (e.g., Amorose, Anderson-Butcher, & Cooper, 2009; Hodge, Lonsdale, & Ng, 2008; Perreault, Gaudreau, Lapointe, & Lacroix, 2007; Quested & Duda, 2011). Research has also at least partially supported models specifying a sequence whereby psychological needs predict self-determined motivation for sport, which in turn predicts burnout-related perceptions in athletes (Lonsdale et al., 2009). This highlights the importance of understanding athlete need satisfaction and motivation in tandem as contributors to burnout.

Overall, burnout research within an SDT framework suggests that structuring sport to support satisfaction of psychological needs and increase self-determined motivation for athletes is helpful for burnout prevention. A variety of social-contextual factors including the team motivational climate, organizational structure, and coach and parent behaviors are important as they impact need satisfaction and motivation. For that reason, they warrant specific attention in burnout prevention efforts (Isoard-Gautheur, Guillet-Descas, & Lemyre, 2012).

Sport Entrapment

Reflecting that burnout is both stress and motivation related, a common belief is that burnout occurs only when highly motivated individuals become disillusioned with their involvement (e.g., Pines, 1993). Expanding on this idea, Schmidt and Stein (1991) and Coakley (1992) offer complementary perspectives emphasizing that burnout occurs when individuals feel trapped into the role of being an athlete in part because of the social structure of sport.

Schmidt and Stein (1991) characterized two faces of commitment. Adaptive commitment is when athletes maintain sport involvement because of passion and intrinsic motivation. These athletes are committed because they want to be an athlete and report high enjoyment and concomitantly high benefits (positive aspects of being an athlete) and low costs (negative aspects of being an athlete) connected to sport. They also invest a great deal of time and energy into sport because they enjoy it and feel sport is more attractive than other alternatives they could pursue. The other face of commitment is maladaptive and characterized by athletes who feel entrapped by sport and that they "have to"

maintain involvement. This occurs when they have decreasing sport attraction corresponding with decreasing benefits and increasing costs. Nonetheless, they maintain involvement because they have too much invested to quit (e.g., potential scholarship), perceive high social constraints (e.g., not wanting to disappoint significant others), and see few, if any, attractive alternatives to being an athlete. From a commitment perspective, burnout occurs when athletes experience **sport entrapment** and maintain involvement not because they *want to*, but because they feel they *have to*, remain in sport.

From a sociological perspective, Coakley (1992) concurs that burnout arises when highly motivated athletes begin to question the value of sport and feel trapped in the role of being an athlete. Athletes believe they are missing out on life opportunities due to the social structure of sport, yet still feel they have to stay in sport. As an integral part of normal adolescent development, young people sample a variety of activities and roles and through that process develop multi-faceted identities. However, the social structure of sport may discourage athletes from this exploration and foster unidimensional identities centered on athletics. As a result, athletes feel trapped in their athletic role. Additionally, adolescence is a developmental period in which athletes seek autonomy and control of their lives. Although athletes may have initially decided to participate in sport, the social structure of sport limits their autonomy because much of their sport experience is controlled by others. From Coakley's perspective, the development of a unidimensional identity combined with low autonomy results in feelings of sport entrapment when athletes begin to question the value of sport in their lives and ultimately results in burnout.

Though few investigators have examined them, entrapment-based perspectives have received empirical support (e.g., Black & Smith, 2007; Raedeke, 1997). For example, Raedeke (1997) examined athlete burnout via the integration of Schmidt and Stein's (1991) commitment model and Coakley's (1992) sociological perspective. In competitive age-group swimmers, Raedeke found that athletes endorsing entrapment profiles of sport commitment exhibited higher burnout compared to those experiencing more adaptive or low sport commitment profiles. Entrapment-based perspectives highlight that athlete burnout experiences are most appropriately considered within the sport structures that contribute to their occurrence.

Integrating the Burnout Knowledge Base: How the Individual and Organization Fit

The extant theoretical perspectives applied to athlete burnout highlight several well-studied antecedents to consider when establishing evidence-based guidelines for athlete burnout recognition, prevention, and treatment. Table 21-2 summarizes important burnout antecedent variables from the perspectives reviewed in this chapter. The table also includes example intervention strategies that tie to these variables and that are well suited for athlete populations. Efficacious interventions will be multi-faceted in nature and address a range of antecedents from the aforementioned perspectives. They will also be designed in consideration of the highly individualized nature of athlete burnout (Gould et al., 1997; Gustafsson, Kenttä, Hassmén, Lundqvist, & Durand-Bush, 2007). Finally, given the chronic nature of burnout, the most effective interventions will have a prevention, rather than treatment, focus. Within such a multi-faceted intervention strategy, individual and organizational antecedents should jointly be considered for each case. Indeed, adopting a framework of individual–organization fit may be especially fruitful for the prevention of burnout and the promotion of the more adaptive psychosocial outcomes in athletes.

Ultimately, the experience of burnout is neither the sole result of an individual problem nor exclusively charged to the organizational (or team) environment surrounding the individual. The fit of these elements is important for understanding burnout development. Much

contemporary research on worker burnout has been framed within the job–person fit model of burnout and engagement (see Maslach & Leiter, 1997; 1999; Leiter & Maslach, 2004). This model emphasizes individual perceptions of the six areas of worklife described below:

• Workload – demands relative to one's personal limits and resources

• Control – ability to influence decisions, autonomy, and access to the resources necessary for performance

• Reward – incentives (monetary, social, intrinsic) consistent with expectations

• Community – social interaction in the form of closeness, teamwork, and lack of conflict

• Fairness – fairness and respectfulness of decisions and treatment

• Values – correspondence between personal and organizational goals and behavioral expectations

According to the model, the perceived congruence of individual needs and organizational resources couched within these six domains is critical to well-being. With less congruence, a greater likelihood of experiencing burnout is expected. Conversely, with greater congruence on these variables, the likelihood of experiencing engagement is increased.

Engagement represents a distinct positive response in contrast to burnout. Specifically, **engagement** is a positive psychological experience characterized by (a) confidence in contrast to a reduced sense of accomplishment, (b) dedication in contrast to devaluation, and (c) vigor and enthusiasm in contrast to exhaustion (Lonsdale, Hodge, & Jackson, 2007). Creating sport experiences that foster engagement will not only prevent burnout but will also result in positive benefits for athletes including enhanced motivation, performance, and well-being.

Investigation of the areas of worklife and engagement in sport is in its infancy. Adopting a positive psychology approach (Gould, 2002; Seligman, & Csikszentmihalyi, 2000),

Table 21-2 Athlete Burnout Perspectives, Key Variables, and Intervention Strategies

Perspective	Key Variables	Intervention Strategies
Overtraining	Training Volume	Ensure developmentally appropriate training loads based on athlete age, physical maturity, and skill level.
		Continuously monitor individual athlete training responses and feeling states. Prolonged fatigue and mood disturbance are warning signs.
		Avoid a "one size fits all" approach to the design of athlete training programs.
	Recovery	Reduce training loads after a period of intense training or if athletes are experiencing prolonged fatigue.
		Educate athletes about maladaptive responses to training and emphasize the importance of recovery.
		Ensure that athletes receive adequate recovery, including passive rest and more active forms of recovery.
		Ensure that athletes engage in pursuits outside of sport that increase vitality.
	Nonsport Stress	Provide resources and training in strategies to cope with sources of stress beyond sport (e.g., schoolwork, family life, romantic relationships).
		Do not increase training loads when nonsport stressors are on the rise.
Psychosocial Sport Stress	Demands	Identify key stressors and develop a plan for dealing effectively with them.
		Adopt a positive coaching style and help parents maintain realistic expectations and positive support of their children.
		Emphasize that skill development is a continuous process with highs and lows.
	Resources	Increase coping resources such as through effective lifestyle management.
		Encourage athletes to form strong social support networks.
		Build self-regulation skills through mental skills training.
Self-Determination Theory	Self-Determined Motivation	Promote a stimulating sport climate that emphasizes effort, learning, accomplishment, and enjoyment of the sport.
	Autonomy	Allow athletes choices in their practice, competition, and treatment plans.
		Provide a rationale for decisions so athletes understand why they are doing things a certain way.
		Employ democratic coaching that involves group decisions when appropriate.
	Competence	Structure sport so athletes have opportunities to succeed with effort.
		Aid athletes in focusing on successes as well as areas in need of improvement.
		Establish effective goal-setting strategies.
		Continuously develop fundamental physical and mental sport skills by reinforcing effort, learning, and improvement as well as treating mistakes as part of the learning process.

(continued)

Perspective	Key Variables	Intervention Strategies
	Relatedness	Foster a productive and supportive coach–athlete relationship as well as positive relationships between athletes.
		Provide pre- and during-season programming that builds teammate relationships and supports positive social interactions.
		Incorporate team building activities within the practice structure and encourage outside social activities.
Sport Entrapment	Benefits	Help athletes recognize the benefits of their sport involvement that may not be evident to them or that they overlook.
		Assess what makes sport rewarding to athletes and incorporate those elements into the sport experience.
	Costs	Acknowledge personal costs of sport involvement and help athletes develop strategies for managing them effectively.
		Explore alternatives for athletes in dysfunctional training or competition environments.
	Enjoyment	Ensure practice variety and limit the monotony of training.
		Structure sport to be exciting and to foster competence, autonomy, and relatedness. Refer to self-determination theory in above section of the table.
	Investments	While recognizing the time and energy required by sport, encourage athletes to maintain nonsport interests and hobbies so they do not feel that they are missing out on other important life opportunities.
	Social Constraints	Promote athlete social relationships with both sport and nonsport associates.
		Ensure that coaches, parents, and peers are sources of support and not pressure.
	Attractiveness of Alternative Activities	Support athlete exploration of other sport and nonsport activities as a means of personal exploration and validation of sport involvement.
		Encourage athletes to reflect on the meaning and value of sport in their lives, including what they would miss if not an athlete.
	Athletic Identity	Communicate that one can strongly identify with multiple roles (e.g., athlete, student, responsible citizen).
		Encourage athletes to develop other aspects of their lives beyond sport and support their doing so.
		Help athletes put sport performance into proper life perspective.
	Sport Control	Refer to autonomy in above section of the table.

DeFreese and Smith (2013a) examined the areas of worklife as they relate to athlete burnout and engagement in a sample of collegiate athletes. Consistent with theoretical expectations, athlete endorsement of athlete–team congruence on the variables of workload, control, reward, community, fairness, and values was positively associated with athlete engagement and negatively associated with athlete burnout. Thus, striving to foster athlete–team congruence in these domains appears to be a promising approach that is innovative and comprehensive for enhancing engagement as well as preventing burnout.

Preventing Athlete Burnout: Individual and Organizational Intervention Strategies

In previous sections of the chapter, we reviewed theory and research on athlete burnout. In spite of the wealth of information on potential burnout antecedents, an important question remains for the practitioner: How can all of this information be used to recognize, prevent, and treat burnout in competitive athletes? We recommend an evidence-based approach that targets both individual and organizational burnout antecedents (see Table 21-2) as well as considers the fit between the individual (athlete) and organization (team or club). Specific antecedents and issues of fit will be more or less relevant to individual athlete cases. Therefore, rather than suggesting a "one size fits all" approach to athlete burnout intervention, we offer a guiding framework designed to help practitioners appropriately tailor prevention and/or treatment strategies.

Step 1: Assess the situation. It is important to establish whether burnout may be occurring or has the potential to develop. Evaluate whether potential symptoms of burnout exist. Gathering as much information as possible about the individual athlete and the organizational context will aid in understanding whether preventative or treatment strategies are necessary.

Step 2: Determine what individual and organizational factors are important. Extant theory showcases burnout as a complex maladaptive outcome associated with a combination of individual and organizational antecedents. Determining the specific individual and organizational factors that are currently impacting an athlete's burnout-related perceptions or that may create risk for future burnout is crucial for the design of effective intervention strategies.

Step 3: Design an intervention plan. The intervention plan should be multifaceted and target salient factors grounded in motivation and stress theory. Based on

the concept of athlete–organization fit, the congruence of individual characteristics with organizational structures impacting demands and resources should be targeted. Additionally, burnout may be stigmatized or considered an individual athlete flaw by some athletes and coaches. Therefore, an educational component that clearly describes and explains burnout to athletes, coaches, and significant others in user-friendly terms may be beneficial.

Step 4: Evaluate intervention effectiveness. Consistent with best practice, intervention strategies should be continuously evaluated to ensure their effectiveness. In the event specific strategies are unsuccessful or undesirable, they should be altered or new strategies (potentially targeting different burnout factors) should be implemented.

Based on the many ways individual burnout cases develop, a variety of individual and organizational options for burnout diagnosis, treatment, and prevention exist. In addition to being multifaceted, effective interventions will likely involve not only the athletes, but also parents, coaches, and sports medicine staff. We provide case studies below in order to help practitioners develop their skill in planning effective interventions through further study, discussion, and integration of the burnout knowledge base.

Case Studies as a Training Tool for Practitioners

The following case studies are fictional scenarios designed to simulate situations in which sport psychology practitioners may encounter burnout when working with athletes. We challenge you to work through these scenarios using the four-step evidence-based approach outlined above. First, **assess the situation** to establish whether burnout is occurring or has the potential to develop. Second, **determine what individual and organizational factors are important** in the given scenario. Third, **design an intervention plan** that addresses

Case Study 1

Mia

You are a sport psychologist consulting with a university athletics program. Mia is a first-year university soccer player referred to you by the athletic training staff (she has knee tendonitis) because she is struggling with her motivation. She is the first "blue chip" recruit of the soccer program, which was formed three years ago, and has a full scholarship. It is early October, and therefore Mia has been on campus about six weeks. Preseason and early season conditioning has been rigorous, and the competition schedule will soon heat up as the team plays conference opponents. Mia's performance has been subpar for her as she is not playing to the level expected nor is she improving. She tells you at your first meeting with her that she is "completely fried" from soccer. She also says that she is "going nowhere" with her soccer and that she can't imagine surviving the season let alone her entire four years. Mia's drive for soccer is not the same as it once was. Although the coach is disappointed with this, given the high expectations held for her, Mia overall feels the coach and other individuals linked to the team (e.g., administrators, training staff) are largely supportive of her. They are primarily concerned with improving her "attitude" and soccer experience this season. From working with this team and coach in the past, you have a very positive outlook on the way athletes are treated regarding training and as individuals. How will you proceed?

these targeted factors. Finally, consider how you will **evaluate intervention effectiveness** and make modifications if your initial intervention strategies are ineffective.

In each case, some symptoms of burnout are presented and many potential factors could be considered as contributing to burnout. A wide variety of potential intervention strategies exist that could be used. We offer progressively less guidance across the cases, encouraging you to frame the evaluation and discussion of them. In the first case, you are left to consider the symptoms of burnout, but we highlight some important individual and organizational factors and present a few potential solutions. You are encouraged to consider other potential factors and solutions that could have bearing on the case as ours are not comprehensive. In the second case, we highlight a few important individual and organizational factors and do not suggest potentially effective intervention strategies. In the third case, we neither identify factors that could be targeted in intervention design nor do we provide sample solutions. This weaning of guidance on potential

analysis and solutions supports the use of your expertise and creativity as well as your learning of the four-step evidenced-based approach to burnout intervention. In brainstorming intervention strategies, we encourage you to recall each theory and the concept of individual–organization fit and to develop a multifaceted intervention that targets the athlete as well as others (e.g., coaches, parents, organization). Initially, do not evaluate the quality of the intervention ideas—simply devise as many solutions as possible. Then, carefully evaluate each potential intervention idea to ensure both feasibility and effectiveness. We hope that these case studies foster helpful pedagogical discussion among coaches, sport psychology practitioners, and others interested in addressing athlete burnout.

Possible Case Study 1 Solutions

- As the team environment appears positive, potential intervention strategies will primarily address modifiable individual factors to promote an optimal individual–organization fit.

Case Study 2

Cal

Cal is an elite 12-year-old youth basketball player referred to you by his parents, who are extremely concerned with improving his performance. Cal is a gifted player for his age and was selected to be the "star" player on an elite travel basketball team which competes in tournaments all over the country. Cal performed extremely well at the team's initial tryout and pre-tournament practices, but his performance has declined to the point that he no longer is receiving playing time in important tournaments. His inability to compete at a high level has contributed to his team losing. Cal's parents feel that he is "mentally weak" and believe he would benefit from working with a sport psychologist to improve his mental toughness and ultimately his performance. During your initial meeting with Cal, he talks about how much he used to love the sport of basketball before joining this particular team. He very much enjoyed playing for his school team and practicing for hours on his own outside of the team environment. However, since joining the travel team things have changed. The team practices 4 days/ week and travels nearly every weekend to play in tournaments across the country. Cal says he feels "drained" and can't keep up mentally or physically with his coach's high standards. He has become so tired that he is behind on schoolwork and has trouble memorizing the team's plays. Cal says he is beginning to "hate basketball." He no longer practices by himself for fun because "he just doesn't see the point" if he will continue to perform poorly. He confides that he has also considered quitting because the sport he once loved now "makes him sad" and is causing friction with his parents. As a consultant hired by Cal's parents, how will you proceed?

- Key individual burnout factors for Mia may include overtraining, pressure associated with being a "blue chip" recruit, lack of recognition of sport benefits, low levels of self-determined (i.e., intrinsic) motivation for sport, and transitioning to college.

- Suggest Mia take some time off from soccer to focus on injury rehabilitation and participate in activities that promote psychological recovery. The benefits of this break will likely outweigh any performance/ conditioning decrements. These decisions should be made in collaboration with coaches and sports medicine staff.

- Provide Mia with training on the use of relaxation techniques (e.g., deep breath, progressive muscle relaxation). This will aid in her ability to cope with sport stress (see Chapter 13). Additionally, Mia should identify specific sport and nonsport stressors and construct a plan for dealing with them. This will help her manage the pressures of being a student-athlete.

- Initiate Mia creating a list of the benefits of her current sport involvement. This list should be exhaustive so as to showcase benefits she may not currently be considering.

- Mia's self-determined motivation for soccer will be increased by promoting feelings of competence, autonomy, and relatedness (see Chapter 4). Review past successful performances, particularly those in the collegiate environment, to build her sport competence. Also, help Mia realize that plateaus are a natural part of the training process and are normal when making the transition to a new environment.

Case Study 3

Judy

Judy is a competitive high school and club swimmer. She is visiting with you in compliance with her team requirement that all athletes meet with the club's sport psychology consultant (with the primary goal of performance enhancement) at least one time during the competitive season. In your initial meeting, Judy commented that she specialized at swimming at a young age where two-a-day practices and near year-round training were common. Although she believes that swimming prevents her from having a normal social life, she used to feel swimming success was worth the sacrifice. Now she is less sure of that. She also hints that she is extremely perfectionistic as well as singularly focused on winning. Even now others are describing her as the next Olympic hopeful. Because of that she feels pressure. She does not want to disappoint her coaches or parents as they have done a lot for her swimming career. Judy states that she continuously gets in extra workouts before and after practice, even when coaches insist that the athletes rest in order to best respond to a designed training taper. Despite her high level of focus and commitment, Judy also mentions that she is feeling much more lethargic than normal and does not seem to be performing as well as she did in previous seasons or even earlier in the present one. Further, she states that she often evaluates herself negatively, while simultaneously maintaining an image of confidence and positivity to her coach, teammates, and parents. Overall, your impression is that swimming is not really something that Judy enjoys, but rather is an activity she views as means to avoid disappointing others, gain recognition/approval, and maybe a college scholarship. From your knowledge of the training environment, you are aware that this particular club team has a very demanding regimen. This has allowed some athletes to excel and reach their goals of swimming in national competitions and receiving college scholarships. However, for others dropout and maladaptive psychological outcomes (e.g., burnout) are common. The coach states that she has a "survival of the fittest" approach to training. She guards her training regimens closely and does not "alter them for any athlete." Judy's parents were both former collegiate athletes and are personal friends with this coach. They believe that pushing Judy hard in swimming will benefit her character as well as help financially by landing her a college scholarship. You work regularly with this team to employ mental skills training for performance enhancement. How will you proceed?

- Initiate team-building activities such as a mentoring program to provide opportunities for Mia to develop relatedness with her teammates and to help make the transition to college.

Possible Case Study 2 Factors

- Considering Cal's enduring positive attitude and relatively young age, potential

intervention strategies may target modifiable organization factors to enhance individual–organization fit.

- Key organizational burnout factors may include parental and coach contributions to Cal's decreased basketball enjoyment, external sport control, unidimensional athletic identity, and insufficient recovery as well as nonsport stressors such as rigorous academic demands.

Summary

This chapter aims to provide sport psychology practitioners with clarity regarding the complex (and sometimes frustrating) phenomenon of athlete burnout. This multidimensional cognitive-affective syndrome is distinct from depression and dropout and is explained by several sport-based burnout theories. Accordingly, overtraining, psychosocial stress, motivation, and sport entrapment perspectives on burnout highlight key antecedents which inform evidence-based strategies for burnout treatment and prevention. Further, the host of burnout factors emphasized within these perspectives can be integrated within an individual–organization fit framework in sport.

As burnout is a multifaceted and individualized experience, the design and implementation of effective intervention strategies should be tailored accordingly. To facilitate best practice, we suggest a four-step evidence-based approach to burnout intervention that considers the fit between the athlete and the team on theoretically specified individual and organizational factors important to the athlete's burnout experience. Practitioners should 1) assess the situation, 2) determine what individual and organizational factors are important, 3) design an intervention, and 4) evaluate intervention effectiveness. We hope that this chapter aids sport psychologists in conceptualizing how to prevent and treat athlete burnout, which in turn enables athletes to achieve optimal performance and psychological health.

Study Questions

1. How is athlete burnout defined? What are its three dimensions?
2. How is burnout distinct from depression and sport dropout?
3. A coach mentions that burnout does not seem to be a very important issue in sport given its potentially low prevalence. How would you respond?
4. What key burnout antecedents are highlighted by an overtraining perspective? Can an athlete experience burnout without being overtrained? Why or why not?
5. How does a psychosocial sport stress perspective differ from an overtraining perspective on the causes of burnout?
6. What three psychological needs are showcased in self-determination theory? Describe an example athlete burnout intervention strategy tied to each of these three needs.
7. How does a sport entrapment perspective describe the development of burnout in athletes? Why don't "burned-out" athletes just leave sport altogether?
8. What is individual–organization fit? How can lack of congruence between the athlete and the team promote burnout and prevent engagement in sport?
9. What four steps should sport psychology practitioners consider when designing and implementing burnout prevention or treatment interventions?
10. A coach you are working with believes that burnout is a sign of weakness in an athlete. How would you respond to this coach? What information could you provide her?
11. Your initial intervention program for an adolescent track athlete experiencing burnout does not seem to be working well. You originally suggested a brief (2-week) break from training and competition. However, after returning from this break he is still feeling "burnedout". What will you recommend next? What non-training factors could be playing a role?

References

Amorose, A. J., Anderson-Butcher, D., & Cooper, J. (2009). Predicting changes in athletes' well being from changes in need satisfaction over the course of a competitive season. *Research Quarterly for Exercise and Sport, 80,* 386–392.

Black, J. M., & Smith, A. L. (2007). An examination of Coakley's perspective on identity, control, and burnout among adolescent athletes. *International Journal of Sport Psychology, 38,* 417–436.

Brenner, J. S. (2007). Overuse injuries, overtraining, and burnout in child and adolescent athletes. *Pediatrics, 119,* 1242–1245.

Budgett, R. (1998). Fatigue and underperformance in athletes: The overtraining syndrome. *British Journal of Sports Medicine, 32,* 107–110.

Coakley, J. (1992). Burnout among adolescent athletes: A personal failure or social problem? *Sociology of Sport Journal, 9,* 271–285.

Cresswell, S. L. (2009). Possible early signs of athlete burnout: A prospective study. *Journal of Science and Medicine in Sport, 12,* 393–398.

Cresswell, S. L., & Eklund, R. C. (2005). Changes in athlete burnout and motivation over a 12-week league tournament. *Medicine & Science in Sports & Exercise, 37,* 1957–1966.

Cresswell, S. L., & Eklund, R. C. (2006a). Athlete burnout: Conceptual confusion, current research and future directions. In S. Hanton & S. D. Mellalieu (Eds.), *Literature reviews in sport psychology* (pp. 91–126). New York, NY: Nova Science Publishers, Inc.

Cresswell, S. L., & Eklund, R. C. (2006b). The convergent and discriminant validity of burnout measures in sport: A multi-trait/multi-method analysis. *Journal of Sports Sciences, 24,* 209–220.

Curran, T., Appleton, P. R., Hill, A. P., & Hall, H. K. (2011). Passion and burnout in elite junior soccer players: The mediating role of self-determined motivation. *Psychology of Sport and Exercise, 12,* 655–661.

Dale, J., & Weinberg, R. (1990). Burnout in sport: A review and critique. *Journal of Applied Sport Psychology, 2,* 67–83.

Deci, E. L., & Ryan, R. M. (1985). *Intrinsic motivation and self-determined human behavior.* New York: Plenum Press.

DeFreese, J. D. (2012). *The association of positive and negative social interactions with athlete burnout and well-being* (Doctoral dissertation). Retrieved from ProQuest, UMI Dissertations Publishing (3556191).

DeFreese, J. D., & Smith, A. L. (2013a). Areas of worklife and the athlete burnout–engagement relationship. *Journal of Applied Sport Psychology, 25,* 180–196.

DeFreese, J. D., & Smith, A. L. (2013b). Teammate social support, burnout, and self-determined motivation in collegiate athletes. *Psychology of Sport and Exercise, 14,* 258–265.

Eklund, R. C., & Cresswell, S. L. (2007). Athlete burnout. In G. Tenenbaum & R. C. Eklund (Eds.), *Handbook of sport psychology* (3rd ed., pp. 621–641). Hoboken, NJ: Wiley.

Fender, L.K. (1989). Athlete burnout: Potential for research and intervention strategies. *The Sport Psychologist, 3,* 63–71.

Freudenberger, H. J. (1974). Staff burnout. *Journal of Social Issues, 30,* 159–165.

Fry, R. W., Morton, A. R., & Keast, D. (1991). Overtraining in athletes. *Sports Medicine, 12,* 32–65.

Goodger, K., Gorely, T., Lavallee, D., & Harwood, C. (2007). Burnout in sport: A systematic review. *The Sport Psychologist, 21,* 127–151.

Gould, D. (2002). Sport psychology in the new millennium: The psychology of athletic excellence and beyond. *Journal of Applied Sport Psychology, 14,* 137–139.

Gould, D., Tuffey, S., Udry, E., & Loehr, J. (1997). Burnout in competitive junior tennis players: III. Individual differences in the burnout experience. *The Sport Psychologist, 11,* 256–276.

Gould, D., & Whitley, M. A. (2009). Sources and consequences of athletic burnout among college athletes. *Journal of Intercollegiate Sports, 2,* 16–30.

Gustafsson, H., Hassmén, P., Kenttä, G., & Johansson, M. (2008). A qualitative analysis of burnout in elite Swedish athletes. *Psychology of Sport and Exercise, 9,* 800–816.

Gustafsson, H., Kenttä, G., Hassmén, P., & Lundqvist, C. (2007). Prevalence of burnout in competitive adolescent athletes. *The Sport Psychologist, 21,* 21–37.

Gustafsson, H., Kenttä, G., Hassmén, P., Lundqvist, C., & Durand-Bush, N. (2007). The process of burnout: A multiple case study of three elite endurance athletes. *International Journal of Sport Psychology, 38,* 388–416.

Hakanen J. J., & Schaufeli, W. B. (2012). Do burnout and work engagement predict depressive symptoms and life satisfaction? A three-wave seven-year prospective study. *Journal of Affective Disorders, 141,* 415–424.

Hall, H. K., Hill, A. P., & Appleton, P. R. (2012). Perfectionism: A foundation for sporting excellence or an uneasy pathway toward purgatory? In G. C. Roberts & D. C. Treasure (Eds.), *Advances in motivation in sport and exercise* (3rd ed., pp. 129–168). Champaign, IL: Human Kinetics.

Hodge, K., Lonsdale, C., & Ng, J. Y. (2008). Burnout in elite rugby: Relationships with basic psychological needs fulfillment. *Journal of Sports Sciences, 26,* 835–844.

Isoard-Gautheur, S., Guillet-Descas, E., & Lemyre, P.-N. (2012). A prospective study of the influence of perceived coaching style on burnout propensity in high level young athletes: Using a self-determination theory perspective. *The Sport Psychologist, 26,* 282–298.

Kellmann, M. (2002). Underrecovery and overtraining: Different concepts–similar impact? In M. Kellmann (Ed.), *Enhancing recovery: Preventing underperformance in athletes* (pp. 3–24). Champaign, IL: Human Kinetics.

Kenttä, G., & Hassmén, P. (2002). Underrecovery and overtraining: A conceptual model. In M. Kellmann (Ed.), *Enhancing recovery: Preventing underperformance in athletes* (pp. 57–79). Champaign, IL: Human Kinetics.

Kuipers, H. (1998). Training and overtraining: An introduction. *Medicine & Science in Sports & Exercise, 30,* 1137–1139.

Kuipers, H., & Keizer, H. A. (1988). Overtraining in elite athletes: Review and directions for the future. *Sports Medicine, 6,* 79–92.

Leiter, M. P., & Maslach, C. (2004). Areas of worklife: A structured approach to organizational predictors of job burnout. In P. L. Perrewe & D. C. Ganster (Eds.), *Research in Occupational Stress and Well-Being*. Oxford, UK: Elsevier.

Lemyre, P.-N., Roberts, G. C., & Stray-Gundersen, J. (2007). Motivation, overtraining, and burnout: Can self-determined motivation predict overtraining and burnout in elite athletes? *European Journal of Sport Science, 7,* 115–126.

Lemyre, P.-N., Treasure, D. C., & Roberts, G. C. (2006). Influence of variability in motivation and affect on elite athlete burnout susceptibility. *Journal of Sport & Exercise Psychology, 28,* 32–48.

Li, C., Wang, C. K. J., Pyun, D. Y., & Kee, Y. H. (2013). Burnout and its relations with basic psychological needs and motivation among athletes: A systematic review and meta-analysis. *Psychology of Sport & Exercise, 14,* 692–700.

Longman, J. (2008, October 18). At pinnacle, stepping away from basketball. *The New York Times*. Retrieved from http://www.nytimes.com

Lonsdale, C., Hodge, K., & Jackson, S. A. (2007). Athlete engagement: II. Development and initial validation of the Athlete Engagement Questionnaire. *International Journal of Sport Psychology, 38,* 471–492.

Lonsdale, C., Hodge, K., & Rose, E. (2009). Athlete burnout in elite sport: A self-determination perspective. *Journal of Sports Sciences, 27,* 785–795.

Mann, B. J., Grana, W. A., Indelicato, P. A., O'Neill, D. F., & George, S. Z. (2007). A survey of sports medicine physicians regarding psychological issues in patient-athletes. *The American Journal of Sports Medicine, 35,* 2140–2147.

Maslach, C. (1976). Burned-out. *Human Behavior, 5,* 16–22.

Maslach, C. (1978). The client role in staff burnout. *Journal of Social Issues, 34,* 111–124.

Maslach, C. (1982). *Burnout - The cost of caring*. Englewood Cliffs, NJ: Prentice-Hall.

Maslach, C., & Leiter, M. P. (1997). *The truth about burnout: How organizations cause personal stress and what to do about it.* San Francisco: Josey-Bass.

Maslach, C., & Leiter, M. P. (1999). Burnout and engagement in the workplace: A contextual analysis. *Advances in motivation and achievement, 11,* 275–302.

Maslach, C., Schaufeli, W. B., & Leiter, W. B. (2001). Job burnout. *Annual Review of Psychology, 52,* 397–422.

Meeusen, R., Duclos, M., Foster, C., Fry, A., Gleeson, M., Nieman, D., . . . & Urhausen, A. (2013). Prevention, diagnosis and treatment of the overtraining syndrome: Joint consensus statement of the European College of Sport Science (ECSS) and the American College of Sports Medicine (ACSM). *European Journal of Sport Science, 13,* 1–24.

Perreault, S., Gaudreau, P., Lapointe, M.-C., & Lacroix, C. (2007). Does it take three to tango? Psychological need satisfaction and athlete burnout. *International Journal of Sport Psychology, 38,* 437–450.

Pines, A. M. (1993). Burnout: An existential perspective. In W. B. Schaufeli, C. Maslach, & T. Marek, (Eds.), *Professional burnout: Recent developments in theory and research* (pp. 33–51). Washington, DC: Taylor & Francis.

Quested, E., & Duda, J. L. (2011). Antecedents of burnout among elite dancers: A longitudinal test of basic needs theory. *Psychology of Sport and Exercise, 12,* 159–167.

Raedeke, T. D. (1997). Is athlete burnout more than just stress? A sport commitment perspective. *Journal of Sport & Exercise Psychology, 19,* 396–417.

Raedeke, T. D., Arce, C., de Francisco, C., Seoane G., & Ferraces, M. J. (2013). The construct validity of the Spanish version of the ABQ using a multi-trait/multi-method approach. *Anales de Psicologia, 29,* 693–700.

Raedeke, T. D., Lunney, K., & Venables, K. (2002). Understanding athlete burnout: Coach perspectives. *Journal of Sport Behavior, 25,* 181–206.

Raedeke, T. D., & Smith, A. L. (2001). Development and preliminary validation of an athlete burnout measure. *Journal of Sport & Exercise Psychology, 23,* 281–306.

Raedeke, T. D., & Smith, A. L. (2004). Coping resources and athlete burnout: An examination of stress mediated and moderation hypotheses. *Journal of Sport & Exercise Psychology, 26,* 525–541.

Raedeke, T. D., & Smith, A. L. (2009). *The Athlete Burnout Questionnaire Manual.* Morgantown, WV: West Virginia University.

Raglin, J. S., & Wilson, G. S. (2000). Overtraining in athletes. In Y. L. Hanin (Ed.), *Emotions in sport* (pp. 191–207). Champaign, IL: Human Kinetics.

Ryan, R. M., & Deci, E. L. (2000). Self-determination theory and the facilitation of intrinsic motivation, social development, and well-being. *American Psychologist, 55,* 68–78.

Schmidt, G. W., & Stein, G. L. (1991). Sport commitment: A model integrating enjoyment, dropout, and burnout. *Journal of Sport & Exercise Psychology, 13,* 254–265.

Seligman, M. E. P., & Csikszentmihalyi, M. (2000). Positive psychology: An introduction. *American Psychologist, 55,* 5–14.

Smith, A. L., Gustafsson, H., & Hassmén, P. (2010). Peer motivational climate and burnout perceptions of adolescent athletes. *Psychology of Sport and Exercise, 11,* 453–460.

Smith, R. E. (1986). Toward a cognitive-affective model of athletic burnout. *Journal of Sport Psychology, 8,* 36–50.

Tenenbaum, G., Jones, C. M., Kitsantas, A., Sacks, D. N., & Berwick, J. P. (2003). Failure adaptation: Psychological conceptualization of the stress response process in sport. *International Journal of Sport Psychology, 34,* 1–26.

Udry, E., Gould, D., Bridges, D., & Tuffey, S. (1997). People helping people? Examining the social ties of athletes coping with burnout and injury stress. *Journal of Sport & Exercise Psychology, 19,* 368–395.

Injury Risk and Rehabilitation: Psychological Considerations

Jean M. Williams, *University of Arizona*, Emeritus

Carrie B. Scherzer, *Mount Royal University*

I knew I was in trouble when I heard snap, crackle and pop, and I wasn't having a bowl of cereal.
—Nick Kypreos, Toronto Maple Leaf player (in McDonell, 2004, p. 96)

Sport injuries frequently occur and often have a devastating impact on the injured athlete, team performance, and health care costs. Although many of the causes for injury are undoubtedly physical in nature (e.g., level of conditioning, equipment failure, poor playing surface, faulty biomechanics) or just plain bad luck, psychosocial factors also play a role. This chapter reviews research on both psychosocial factors that influence risk of injury and psychological reactions to injury and it also provides examples of how to implement psychological interventions to reduce injury risk and to enhance the physical and psychological recovery of the injured athlete. It is beyond the scope of this chapter to discuss the psychological issues involved when injuries are so severe that return to sport is impossible, but the reader is directed to Chapter 23 in this volume and to a book on injured athletes edited by Pargman (2007).

Factors That Predispose Athletes to Injury

Research with recreational to elite competitive athletes has found that certain psychosocial factors predispose individuals to injury, whereas other psychosocial factors help protect them from injury. The best understanding of how this influence occurs comes from a theoretical model put forward by Andersen and Williams (1988) and their later modification of it (Williams & Andersen, 1998). They proposed that most psychosocial variables, if they influence injury outcome at all, probably do so through a linkage with stress and a resulting stress response. The central hypothesis of their stress–injury model is that athletes with a history of many stressors, personality characteristics that intensify the stress response, and few or maladaptive coping resources will,

Case Study 1: Is one of these players more vulnerable to injury?

John is a freshman football player at a California college. He came from New York and is missing his family and friends, plus is worried about his mother who just began treatment for breast cancer. Used to being the star on the team, he's having difficulty accepting his role and is frustrated with the coaches. He feels pressure to perform and is losing his confidence, both on the field and in the classroom. He's become moody and pessimistic.

Manuel, another freshman, has his best friend from high school on the team. He too is frustrated with less playing time, but is excited about his teammates and coaches pushing his game to a higher level. His optimistic nature and work with a sport psychologist is helping him to stay positive and focused, both on the field and in the classroom.

when placed in a stressful situation such as a demanding practice or crucial competition, be more likely to appraise the situation as stressful and to exhibit greater physiological activation and attentional disruptions (see Figure 22-1). The severity of the resulting stress response, caused by the increased stress reactivity, is what predisposes the athletes to injury. Considerable support exists for all facets of the stress–injury

model (see Williams and Andersen, 1998 and 2007, for a more thorough review of research testing the model).

The stress response reflects a bidirectional relationship between cognitive appraisal of and physiological and attentional responses to potentially demanding athletic situations. If an athlete views a competitive situation as challenging, exciting, and fun, the resulting "good" stress

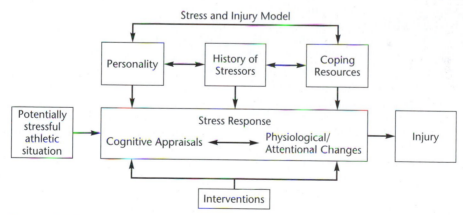

Figure 22-1 **Revised version of the stress and injury model**
From Williams and Andersen (1998)

(eustress) may help the athlete stay focused and his/her play to successfully "flow." Injury risk in this situation is low, but it would be higher when the athlete feels "bad" stress (distress), such as appraising the competition as ego threatening or anxiety producing and becoming too tense and distracted. This latter interpretation most likely occurs when athletes perceive inadequate resources to meet the demands of the situation and potential dire consequences for failure to meet the demands.

Whether the cognitive appraisal is accurate or distorted by irrational beliefs or other maladaptive thought patterns (see Chapter 14) is unimportant. Correspondingly, these cognitive appraisals and physiological and attentional responses to stress constantly modify each other. An example is that relaxing the body can help calm the mind just as stopping anxious thoughts can lower the physical stress response. The resulting individual differences in stress responsivity due to differences in psychosocial variables may either help inoculate the athlete against injury or exacerbate his or her risk.

Of the myriad physiological and attentional changes that occur during the stress response, Andersen and Williams (1988) hypothesized that increases in generalized muscle tension, narrowing of the visual field (the revised model added auditory cues), and increased distractibility were the primary culprits in the stress–injury relationship. Generalized muscle tension can lead to fatigue and reduced flexibility, motor coordination difficulties, and muscle inefficiency, thereby creating a greater risk for incurring injuries such as sprains, strains, and other musculoskeletal injuries. Narrowing of peripheral vision could lead to not picking up or responding in time to dangerous cues in the periphery such as an outside linebacker rushing the quarterback. Increased distractibility during stress, often due to attention to task-irrelevant cues, may also result in failure to detect or respond quickly enough to relevant cues in the central field of vision such as when a batter fails to avoid a pitch coming directly at his head.

"Coming into the game my concentration was divided, due to unforeseen incidents . . . before the game started. I recall that I was not in the best mental state for playing."

(Quote in study assessing why athletes thought they were injured, Johnson, 2011, p. 106)

Considerable support (seven studies) exists for individuals with a high- versus low-risk psychosocial profile reporting higher state anxiety and experiencing greater peripheral narrowing under stressful laboratory or real-life athletic situations compared to low-stress situations. Even more important, Rogers and Landers (2005) found support for the model's hypothesis that peripheral narrowing during stress is one of the mechanisms by which athletes with high life stress increase their likelihood of athletic injury, as did Andersen and Williams (1999). Only Williams and Andersen (1997) examined central field of vision and they found a greater susceptibility to attention disruptions (e.g., missed or delayed responses) for athletes with a high injury-risk profile when they performed under higher stress. The one study that examined the connection between psychosocial factors and muscle tension found increased muscle tension during the stress condition for the total group, but failed to support the hypothesis of even greater muscle tension for individuals with a high-risk profile. The results may have been influenced by studying the general population rather than a high-risk subpopulation.

Before addressing the implications of these findings for designing interventions to decrease injury risk, we will discuss how history of stressors, personality factors, and coping resources influence stress and injury. These variables may contribute interactively or in isolation in influencing the stress response and, ultimately, injury occurrence and severity. The original stress–injury model hypothesized that an athlete's history of stressors contributes directly to the stress response, whereas personality factors and coping resources act on the stress response either directly or by attenuating the negative effects of the history of stressors. Ten years later, when Williams and Andersen (1998) critiqued and modified their stress–injury model, they proposed bidirectional arrows between each of these three predictor categories.

History of Stressors

This category of injury risk variables includes major life change events, daily hassles, and previous injury.

> *"It was a very chaotic period in life, all the time new things to do and stress everywhere. So much training and obligations and hardly any time to socialize with family and friends outside the team. It really made me feel bad. I think this was the main reason behind my injury."*
>
> *(Johnson, 2011, p. 105)*

The most support exists for the detrimental effects of experiencing major life events—typically assessed as the amount of change and upset that athletes experienced in the year prior to a competitive season. Examples of general life events are incidents such as the breakup of a relationship, change in residence, and death of a loved one, whereas major events related to sports include eligibility difficulties, trouble with coaches, and change in playing status. Over 50 studies have examined life event stress and injuries. Approximately 90 percent of them found a positive relationship between high life stress and injury with the most frequent association occurring with negative life stressors and/or total life stressors. The most extensive evidence involves football (seven studies), but similar findings have occurred across activities as diverse as Alpine skiing, race walking, figure skating, baseball, gymnastics, soccer, field hockey, tennis, wrestling, track and field, and ballet. Injuries tended to occur two to five times more frequently in athletes with high compared to low life stress and risk of injury tended to increase in direct proportion to the level of life stress.

Researchers failed to support daily hassles (e.g., minor daily problems, irritations, or changes) as a contributor to injury risk (e.g.,

Smith, Smoll, & Ptacek, 1990; Van Mechelen et al., 1996) when they assessed hassles only once. Better designed studies that measured hassles on a weekly basis and used the hassle score for the one or two week period prior to injury found the hypothesized relationship (Fawkner, McMurray, & Summers, 1999; Ivarsson and Johnson, 2010; Ivarsson, Johnson, & Podlog, 2013). Moreover, Ivarsson et al. found that experiencing more major negative life events led to more frequent daily hassles, which in turn had a direct effect on injury frequency.

Personality and Coping Resources

The presence of desirable personality attributes and coping resources may buffer individuals from stress and injury by helping them to perceive fewer situations and events as stressful or by helping them cope more effectively with their history of stressors. Conversely, the lack of desirable personality characteristics and coping resources, or the presence of undesirable ones, may leave individuals vulnerable to higher stress (acute and chronic) and, presumably, greater injury risk.

It would be useful to have a specific personality test that predicts injury-prone athletes, but none exists so researchers examined specific variables of interest. A number of researchers studied some type of trait anxiety, or concept related to it. **Trait anxiety** is a general disposition or tendency to perceive situations as threatening and to react with an anxiety response. When assessing global trait anxiety, no relationship to injury occurred with nonsport tools (e.g., Kerr & Minden, 1988), but did with sport-specific tools. Athletes scoring higher on competitive trait anxiety (e.g., Hanson, McCullagh, & Tonymon, 1992; Petrie, 1993) incurred more injuries or had more severe injuries. In contrast, similar somatic trait anxiety results occurred with both nonsport (Ivarsson & Johnson, 2010; Johnson & Ivarsson, 2011) and sport-specific assessment (Smith, Ptacek, & Patterson, 2000). The injured athletes in the Ivarsson and Johnson studies also scored higher on stress susceptibility, suggesting that they might experience more athletic situations as stressful or have higher levels of stress in those situations.

In other promising personality research, dispositional optimism and hardiness was examined. Individuals high in optimism anticipate that good rather than bad things will happen to them whereas individuals high in hardiness feel deeply committed to the activities in their lives, believe they have at least partial control over the events they experience, and consider change an exciting challenge that furthers development. As hypothesized by the stress–injury model, researchers found that being optimistic and hardy correlated with fewer injury problems and, in some of the studies, that these variables moderated the greater injury effects of higher life stress (e.g., Ford, Eklund, and Gordon, 2000; Wadey, Evans, Hanton, & Neil, 2012a, 2013). Wadey and colleagues (2012b) follow-up qualitative study sought to find the mechanisms by which athletes high or low in hardiness exacerbated or attenuated their injury risk and the effects of life stress. They found that athletes high in hardiness possessed a repertoire of problem- and emotion-focused coping strategies that lowered strain and facilitated a plan of action to resolve stressful events/situations while athletes low in hardiness used avoidance coping strategies such as denial and mental disengagement that had long-term negative implications.

Other researchers also have tested whether personality variables might interact with history of stressors or with other personality and coping variables in influencing injury risk. Smith et al. (2000) found that the combination of high daily life stress and high cognitive or somatic trait anxiety predicted high injury time-loss in ballet dancers affiliated with a major ballet company. In another study (Smith, Ptacek, & Smoll, 1992), only athletes who scored low in sensation seeking had a significant positive relationship between major negative life events and subsequent injury time-loss. According to Zuckerman (1979), sensation avoiders, unlike sensation seekers, have a lower tolerance for arousal

and, therefore, do not care for change, avoid the unfamiliar, and stay away from risky activities. Also, although they found that sensation avoiders reported poorer stress management coping skills, no support existed for differences in coping skills mediating the injury vulnerability differences.

"I was not in the mood for anything. I was simply depressed and just wanted to quit playing soccer, but something still kept me going. This was obviously a wrong decision. However, it is easy to be wise after an injury happens."

(Johnson, 2011, p. 107)

In addition to personality traits, mood states also influence injury risk. Findings support the premise that positive states of mind might buffer the effects of potentially stressful sport situations, thereby creating less stress and fewer injuries, just as negative states might do the opposite. Williams, Hogan, and Andersen (1993) found that intercollegiate football, volleyball, and cross-country athletes who experienced positive states of mind (e.g., ability to stay focused, keep relaxed, share with others) early in the season incurred significantly fewer injuries compared to athletes with less positive states of mind. Negative states such as tension/anxiety, competitive cognitive and somatic anxiety, and/or total negative mood state correlated with a higher rate of injury and/or severity of injury (Alizadeh, Pashabadi, Hosseini, & Shahbazi, 2012; Lavallee and Flint, 1996). Fawkner (1995) noted significant increases in mood disturbance in the measurement immediately prior to injury and Kleinert (2007) reported risk of serious injuries with mood disturbance three hours to three days before tournament play.

When it comes to research on coping resources (e.g., general coping behaviors, social support systems, psychological coping skills such as stress management techniques and mental skills), the results are equivocal, largely due to differences in design, statistics, or sample sizes, but there is sufficient support of the stress–injury model's predictions that coping resources need to be considered when trying to understand injury vulnerability and how to decrease it. Researchers have found that social support influences injury outcome directly and/or by lessening the negative effects of high life-event stress (e.g., Hardy, O'Connor, & Geisler, 1990; Petrie, 1992; Johnson, 2011; Williams, Tonymon, & Wadsworth, 1986). These findings suggest that increasing social support from family, friends, and significant others—a group likely to include coaches and teammates—is one way to reduce injury risk. Richman, Hardy, Rosenfeld, and Callahan (1989) offer an excellent source for a variety of strategies coaches and sport psychologists could implement to enhance social support in student athletes.

Although a greater number of supportive relationships is desired, the *quality* of such relationships is also important. For example, an athlete with fairly strong religious values felt he had to go out, drink, and chase women with his teammates to receive their support and friendship. Although he achieved an external measure of support, the relationships added to his level of stress. It was, in fact, through a classroom discussion of stress that the athlete sought someone with whom to discuss his conflicts. The athlete successfully resolved the conflicts, and may well have been an accident that *did not* happen.

Findings from studies such as Smith et al. (1990), Rogers and Landers (2005), and Devantier (2011) suggest that increasing psychological coping skills (e.g., the ability to control arousal and to think clearly and stay focused under pressure) might decrease injury risk. Smith et al., by far the best-designed psychology of injury study, found that the most injuries occurred in athletes who experienced high negative life events and who lacked both social support and psychological coping skills. In contrast, having either moderate to high social support or psychological coping skills eliminated the relationship between high life stress and injury. Having ineffective coping strategies, such as self-blame, also puts athletes at higher injury risk (Ivarsson & Johnson, 2010).

Interventions to Reduce Injury Vulnerability

Researchers have shown that it is possible to reduce sports injuries through psychological skills training. Strengthening coping skills and controlling emotional states was the common theme in most of the intervention studies.

Exercise 1

In Case Study 1 at the beginning of this chapter, which athlete is more likely to benefit from an intervention to reduce injury vulnerability and why is that athlete more likely to become injured based upon what you just read? Describe how to use one of the following interventions to reduce his injury risk.

The stress–injury model proposes a two-pronged approach to prevent injuries from increased stress reactivity due to the individual's psychosocial profile. One set of interventions aims to change the cognitive appraisal of potentially stressful events (see Chapter 14 for techniques to eliminate or modify cognitions that cause stress) and the second to modify the physiological/attentional aspects of the stress response. Chapter 12 describes relaxation techniques such as progressive muscle relaxation, meditation, and breathing exercises, and Chapter 15 presents techniques to decrease distractibility and to keep an appropriate attentional focus. Also included on the cognitive appraisal side of the stress response are interventions for fostering realistic expectations, a sense of belonging (e.g., team cohesiveness), and optimal coach–athlete communication. For example, if coaches clearly communicate athletes' capabilities and potential, athletes should more realistically appraise potentially stressful situations. See Chapters 6–8 and 11 for suggestions to enhance communication, cohesiveness, and realistic goal setting. In addition, interventions can be designed to directly influence some of the variables under coping resources and personality factors.

Considerable support exists, both direct and indirect, for the interventions portion of the model. DeWitt (1980) found that her basketball and football players detected a noticeable decrease in minor injuries in addition to performance-enhancing effects and greater arousal control after participation in a cognitive and physiological (biofeedback) training program. Although reducing injuries was not his focus, when Murphy (1988) conducted relaxation sessions after every workout until competition with 12 members of a team at the 1987 Olympic Sports Festival, he found that all were able to compete when, at the start, five had minor injuries and two, serious injuries.

Davis (1991) reported an archival review of injury data from athletic trainers for the season before and when two university teams practiced progressive relaxation and technique/strategy imagery during team workouts. A reduction in injuries of 52 percent for the swimmers and 33 percent for the football players occurred during the intervention season. Another favorable intervention study that led to reduced injuries, increased self-confidence, and enhanced self-control comes from May and Brown (1989). They used techniques such as attention control, imagery, and other mental practice skills in their interventions with U.S. alpine skiers in the Calgary Olympics. They also employed team building, communication, relationship orientations, and crisis interventions.

Kerr and Goss (1996) offer more experimentally sound support for reducing life stress and injuries through a stress management program. Participants included 24 gymnasts who competed on the national and international level. They were matched in pairs according to sex, age, and performance and then randomly assigned to a control or experimental group. Across an 8-month time period, each gymnast in the experimental group met individually for 16 one-hour, biweekly stress management sessions. Meichenbaum's stress inoculation training program provided the framework for the intervention, which included skills such as cognitive restructuring, thought control, imagery, and simulations. The intervention group reported less negative athletic stress, less total negative stress, and half the amount of time injured (5 versus 10 days) compared to the control group.

In a similar randomized, single-blind clinical trial with collegiate athletes, a seven-session cognitive behavioral stress management program (e.g., relaxation, visualization, cognitive restructuring, and emotional relief) that used a stress-inoculation training format found significant reductions in the number of injury days in the intervention group compared to athletes in the control group (Perna, Antoni, Baum, Gordon, & Schneiderman, 2003). Similar intervention findings were found in a population of rugby players (Maddison & Prapavessis, 2005), football players (Edvardsson, Ivarsson, & Johnson, 2012), and dancers (Noh, Morris, & Andersen, 2007).

The injury benefits from the preceding intervention programs are even more impressive considering none targeted athletes at risk of injury (they targeted athletes in general). Two more recent studies, however, did identify and target at-risk athletes. Johnson, Ekengren, and Andersen (2005) provided six intervention sessions and two telephone contacts consisting of treatments such as stress management skills, somatic and cognitive relaxation, goal-setting skills, and attribution and self-confidence training. Findings indicated 10 of 13 in the experimental group remained injury free, in contrast to only 3 of 16 in the control group. Maddison and Prapavessis (2005) also found less time-loss due to injury for rugby players in their cognitive behavioral stress management group. In addition, these athletes reported an increase in coping resources and a decrease in worry following the intervention program.

The success of these interventions in reducing injuries suggests that coaches, sport psychologists, and athletic trainers may want to implement them with athletes they suspect are predisposed to injury due to psychosocial variables. Recognize, however, that it would be most egregious to think that all individuals in an at-risk group will experience injury or that none will in a low-risk group. Identifying athletes most predisposed to injury simply allows targeting specific interventions to those most likely to benefit from them.

To identify at-risk athletes, coaches and others must be aware of what is happening in athletes' lives and the presence of personal characteristics identified in the at-risk profile. Sport psychologists or others trained in the use of psychological tests may even want to employ the questionnaires used in injury research as screening instruments. Coaches also should consider reducing exposure to high-risk activities, such as learning a new and potentially dangerous vault or dive, with athletes who meet the high-risk profile and/or who appear to be in a stressed or distracted state. Where levels of stress appear to be extreme and coping skills minimal, professional counseling may be necessary (see Chapter 19).

Athletes' Reactions to Injury

Regardless of the best efforts of athletes, coaches, and athletic trainers, injuries still occur; and the consequences are both physical and psychological. Historically, sport medicine specialists have been most concerned with the physical aspects of injury rehabilitation, assuming that completing physical rehabilitation prepared the athlete for a safe and successful return to competition. But some athletes, despite physical readiness, are not psychologically ready to return to competition. To them even the suggestion of returning creates unmanageable stress from fears such as reinjury and embarrassing performance. As a result, optimal injury rehabilitation often requires both physical and psychological components. When done well, injuries often heal faster, psychological adjustment is healthier, and higher levels of performance occur more quickly. This entails gaining an understanding and appreciation of the psychology of injury rehabilitation, which is the focus of the remainder of this chapter.

Psychological Reactions to Injury

Athletes perceive injury in various ways. Some view it as disaster; some as an opportunity to display courage; others welcome it as relief from the drudgery of practice or the embarrassment and frustration of poor performance or lack of playing time; and still others see it as an opportunity to focus on other aspects of their life. It is not uncommon for injured athletes to be concerned about whether they will ever completely recover and return to their previous form. Understanding the emotional response of injured athletes can lead to more effective interventions. Injured athletes are often uncertain if they will be facing a quick return to action, a long rehabilitation process, or the end of their career. Athletes may also underestimate the seriousness of their injury initially, which may impact their emotional response (de Heredia, Munoz, & Artaza, 2004). Athletes have good reason to be upset when injured but, as one athletic trainer stated, "I know it's frustrating for athletes to be injured, but I found that those who have the negative attitudes or poor mood state, that they are the ones who are continuously in rehab, and having problems making it to rehab" (Granito, 2001, p. 78). A positive and enthusiastic response will ensure the best possible chance of complete rehabilitation both physically and mentally.

A study by Mainwaring et al. (2004) sheds some light on athletes' reactions to injury. Following concussion, athletes experienced depression, confusion, and overall total mood disturbance. The authors postulate that mood changes are due to the injury itself and not just the removal from sport, as they experienced a normalization of mood before their return to sport; this finding has been supported by other research as well (Hutchison, Mainwaring, Comper, Richards, & Bisschop, 2009).

Others also notice changes in injured athletes. According to a survey of 482 certified athletic trainers, 47 percent believed that every injured athlete suffers negative psychological effects such as stress and anxiety, anger, treatment compliance problems, depression, problems with concentration/attention, and exercise addiction (Larson, Starkey, & Zaichkowsky, 1996). In addition, 24 percent of their trainers referred an athlete for counseling for situations related to their injury. Unfortunately, 75 percent of athletic trainers in the United States do not have access to a sport psychologist (Cramer Roh & Perna, 2000). Sports medicine physicians are also aware of the problems that arise from injury—in a survey of 827 practitioners, 80 percent reported discussing psychological issues with injured athletes (Mann, Grana, Indelicato, O'Neill, & George, 2007). These practitioners also noted a lack of sport psychologists in their geographic areas, and 75 percent rarely or never referred athletes to sport psychologists (Mann et al., 2007).

Initially, sport psychologists (e.g., Pederson, 1986; Rotella, 1984) believed that, following injury, athletes experienced a sequence of predictable psychological reactions like those outlined by Kubler-Ross in *On Death and Dying* (1969). These reactions include (1) disbelief, denial, and isolation; (2) anger; (3) bargaining; (4) depression; and (5) acceptance and resignation while remaining hopeful about the eventual return to competition. Grief models, in which injured athletes proceed sequentially through a series of stages on the way to recovery, have not been empirically supported (Brewer, 1994). Quinn and Fallon (1999) found that athletes experience many emotions (e.g., tension, depression, anger) postinjury, and all of these improve as rehabilitation progresses. Brewer posited that cognitive appraisal models provide a better conceptualization of the

process of coping with athletic injury. For individuals still inclined toward a grief approach, Evans and Hardy's (1995) article provides a better understanding of grief models.

Cognitive Appraisal Models

Brewer (1994) identified five cognitive appraisal models relevant to psychological responses to athletic injury. Each model (Figure 22-2) is rooted in the literature on stress and coping; athletic injury is conceptualized as a stressor to the athlete, who then evaluates or *appraises* the stressor in accordance with personal and situational factors. Cognitive appraisal models account for individual differences in response to athletic injury. The response to injury comes from how the athlete perceives the injury. This cognitive appraisal determines the emotional response (e.g., anger, depression, relief), which determines the behavioral response to injury rehabilitation (e.g., adherence to rehabilitation regimens).

Personal factors. Personal factors contribute to cognitive appraisal and emotional and behavioral responses to athletic injury. For example,

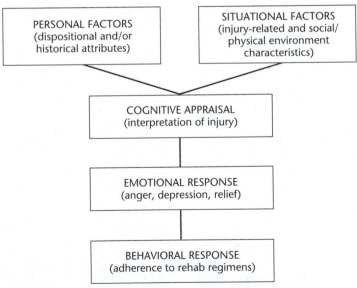

Figure 22-2 Cognitive appraisal model of psychological adjustment to athletic injury

Brewer (1994) reported that Shaffer (1992) found that a history of successful rehabilitation positively affected assessments of ability to manage a subsequent injury. This rehabilitation self-efficacy, in turn, related positively to physical recovery. Grove, Stewart, and Gordon (1990) documented a positive relationship between pessimistic explanatory style and depression and anger for the first month of knee rehabilitation. In contrast, hardiness was negatively associated with total mood disturbance. More recent research on hardiness shows that athletes who are higher in hardiness tend to have a lower risk of becoming injured, and when they do, they are more successful at rehabilitation (Wadey et al., 2012a). Brewer (1993) found that physical self-esteem may buffer the negative effects of athletic injury on mood. Brewer (1994) reported that adherence to injury rehabilitation programs was linked to personal factors such as self-motivation (Duda, Smart, & Tappe, 1989; Fisher, Domm, & Wuest, 1988), task involvement (Duda et al., 1989), pain tolerance, and perceived exertion (Fisher et al., 1988).

Tracey (2003) examined the emotional response of athletes to moderate to severe injuries. She found that at the onset of injury, the type and severity did not matter as much as the injury itself and that athletes experienced a myriad of emotions. Frustration was the primary negative affect one week postinjury. Three weeks postinjury, emotions were more positive. Four main themes describe the interplay of cognitions on the emotional response: (1) internal thoughts, (2) injury and rehabilitation concerns, (3) concern for and comparison to others, and (4) looking ahead to the future (Tracey, 2003). Overall, the athletes focused on healing and return to sport, not the possibility of reinjury, and they also saw their injury as a learning opportunity. These findings reinforce the importance of cognitive appraisal of the injury and rehabilitation process.

One of the most supported personal factors is the influence an athlete's psychological investment in sport has on his or her adjustment to athletic injury (e.g., Brewer, 1993; Brewer, Van Raalte, & Linder, 1993). For many athletes, particularly those who are intensely involved with their sport and/or achieve notable success, the whole focus of their identity may be as an athlete (see Case Study 2). Many of the issues athletes face with injury parallel those that occur with career termination or retirement (see Chapter 23).

The more narrowly focused an injured athlete's sense of self is, the more threatened the athlete will be. Such a person appears more likely to appraise his or her injury in terms of threat or loss (Brewer et al., 1993) and to experience feelings of anxiety, depression, or hopelessness (Brewer, 1993; Smith, Scott, O'Fallon, & Young, 1990). Athletes who are more involved in sport before injury may be confused during rehabilitation and may perceive a lesser degree of recovery at the end of rehabilitation (Johnston & Carroll, 2000). He or she might be more motivated to return to sport, possibly prematurely. Eric Lindros, a former player in the national hockey league (NHL), is a prime example. He was a standout player in juniors and he was a dominant force for the Philadelphia Flyers and was named the league's most valuable player in 1994–1995. Lindros's career was marred with injuries, though, concussions in particular. In January 2004, while playing for the New York Rangers, he suffered his eighth concussion. He played for two other teams over the next two seasons (ESPN.com, 2007a), but after failing to sign with a team, in November 2007 Lindros announced his retirement (ESPN.com, 2007b). Over the years, Lindros had public feuds with the Flyers over the treatment he received and pressure to return to the game.

The coach, athletic trainer, or others involved during rehabilitation should be sensitive to these issues and help the athlete see himself or herself more fully as a person, with many potentials, and to explore other possibilities—not to replace the sport or athlete identity, but to complement it. The development of the NCAA CHAMPS/Life Skills program and books to help athletes plan for careers, such as the one by Petitpas, Champagne, Chartrand, Danish, and Murphy (1997), help athletes develop in other realms. Highlighting past athletic success may be helpful in establishing careers after sport. For example, Tim Horton, a former NHL player,

Case Study 2

An Athlete Reacting to Injury

Beth was a two-time all-state performer who had already accepted a full athletic scholarship to a major college soccer powerhouse. During the winter months, Beth was a starter on the varsity basketball team. During the third game of the season she severely injured her right knee diving for a loose ball. The injury required surgery to repair torn ligaments, and the doctors told Beth that with hard work she would be as good as new in a few months.

This was Beth's first major injury. She was afraid, and she was angry at herself for getting injured because she felt it was a stupid play on her part. She also felt that she had let her parents and friends down because of what might happen if she didn't fully recover. She asked herself many of the same questions she heard her friends asking: Would she lose her scholarship? Would she be able to play as well as before? Did she make a mistake by playing basketball this year?

Up to this point, it seemed that the anger, guilt, and other feelings that resulted from the injury caused Beth to doubt herself and her ability to cope with the situation. She found it easier to be alone than to deal with family and friends. Although withdrawing from people brought her temporary relief from her feelings, it also kept her away from the support she needed to get through this unexpected transition.

During her rehabilitation, Beth refused to go to basketball games or social events that she normally attended. She was very moody and seemed to become angry at the smallest thing. Her boyfriend would come over to visit, but these meetings usually ended in a fight because Beth would say he didn't know what she was going through. She was becoming frustrated at her progress in physical therapy, even though she was reaching her therapist's treatment goals. She would be particularly demanding of her therapist if her strength or range of motion had not improved from day to day. Her frustration led her to ignore her therapist's recommendations. She pushed her exercises so hard that she cried from the pain and then became angry at herself for not being tough enough. Instead of getting better, Beth suffered a setback.

Although Beth was trying to deal with her feelings, she found herself pushing away the people who were trying to help her. At the same time her fear caused her to make some poor decisions about her rehabilitation program. Fortunately, Beth was able to get the support she needed to work through her feelings.

Beth's physical therapist introduced her to a counselor who worked in the training room. The counselor listened to Beth's story and tried to understand what she was going through. For the first time Beth was able to voice her anger and sadness. After this, the counselor helped Beth identify the skills that she had used to become a good athlete and showed her how to use them to deal with her injury. Beth had not been prepared for her injury, and her emotions kept her from using the goal-setting and imagery techniques that she used to improve her sport skills.

Beth had also failed to seek help from others. Before her injury, she had always sought out the best coaches for advice and had often talked with players she admired to learn more about game strategies and techniques. She withdrew from this type of support while she was injured. Once Beth learned to use her skills and the support of others, she made better decisions about her rehabilitation and made a quick recovery.

opened a doughnut shop that has expanded into one of the most recognized chains in Canada. Other athletes have gone on to careers in sport broadcasting (e.g., Bill Walton, Sean Elliot), owning a business (e.g., ex–Cleveland Brown Clay Matthews's Ford dealership), and developing the next generation of athletes (e.g., Justine Henin's tennis academy).

In addition to helping athletes understand the implications of their injury, counseling or therapy can also give athletes the opportunity to discover *positive* implications of the injury (Ermler & Thomas, 1990). Ermler and Thomas note that individuals who develop positive meanings from injury adjust and cope better than those who do not.

Researchers (Udry, Gould, Bridges, & Beck, 1997; Wadey, Evans, Evans, & Mitchell, 2011) have assessed the benefits perceived by athletes following injury. Udry et al.'s participants identified four general dimensions: personal growth, psychologically based performance, physical and technical development, and none. Wadey et al. (2011) found that there were multiple benefits at different points (i.e., injury onset, rehabilitation, return to competitive sport). Some of the benefits were improvements in social networks, increased knowledge of anatomy, and becoming more resilient. Helping injured athletes discover positive aspects of their injury may help them through the rehabilitation period and once they return to sport.

The question of referral for counseling can be problematic (see Chapter 19 for when to refer). Not all sport psychologists are trained counselors, and not all counselors are aware of the particular issues confronting athletes. One alternative is to have athletic trainers take a more active role in providing sport psychology in the athletic training room. Several authors have suggested that athletic trainers are perfectly positioned to train athletes to use psychological skills (e.g., goal-setting, imagery), as they frequently see injured athletes and possess a wealth of knowledge about injuries (e.g., Cramer Roh & Perna, 2000; Misasi, Redmond, & Kemler, 1998). Tracey (2008) found that physical therapists and athletic trainers see themselves as filling the role

of building rapport, educating, and communicating with injured athletes, which supports Misasi et al. (1998), who point out that "the athletic therapist cannot avoid the need to be an effective counselor or helper" (p. 36). Scherzer and Williams (2008) found that when athletic trainers are given additional training in sport psychology, they perceive themselves as more skilled at using the various techniques and they think that they use the skills more. Additional training does not have to be extensive to be effective, either. Clement and Shannon (2009) found that athletic training students increased their sport psychology behaviors following a 75 minute workshop.

Situational factors. Many potential situational factors influence cognitive appraisal and emotional and behavioral responses to injury. For example, Wiese-Bjornstal and colleagues (1998) enumerated three types of situational factors: (1) sport factors (e.g., time in season, playing status); (2) social factors (e.g., coach and sports medicine team influences); and (3) environmental factors (e.g., accessibility to rehabilitation). Granito (2001) conducted focus groups with injured athletes and found that athletes' reactions to injury fell into seven categories: (1) personal factors (e.g., athlete's personality, role on team); (2) effects on relationships (e.g., with coaches, parents, teammates); (3) sociological aspects (i.e., gender differences, athletic subculture); (4) physical factors (e.g., pain and use of painkillers); (5) daily hassles (i.e., stress); (6) feelings associated with injury (e.g., frustration, depression, tension); and (7) rehabilitation (i.e., adherence, ease of receiving treatment). Granito's investigation provides support that many factors contribute to an athlete's response to injury. More recently, Evans, Wadey, Hanton, and Mitchell (2012) examined situational factors at different points in the injury process. They found that athletes are impacted by medical/physical, sport-related, social, and financial demands at the time of injury and during rehabilitation, however, only medical/physical and sport-related demands impacted return to competitive sport.

Other models. Other researchers (Striegel, Hedgpeth, & Sowa, 1996) proposed a model that incorporates both the grief stage model and the individual nature of the stress response as encompassed in cognitive appraisal models. Striegel and colleagues' model proposes that cognitive appraisal is incorporated in short- (i.e., first two weeks of recovery) and long-term rehabilitation (i.e., anything beyond two weeks) and the Kubler-Ross (1969) grief stage model is incorporated when an injured athlete is facing termination of participation in sport. Their model suggests that there are differences in psychological reaction of athletes who will be injured for two weeks versus athletes who will never compete again (Striegel et al., 1996).

Another model, proposed by Hagger, Chatzisarantis, Griffin, and Thatcher (2005), suggests that self-regulation theory, in which people form a representation of their injury on the basis of (1) general information available about the injury, (2) information obtained from expert sources (e.g., athletic trainer, physician), and (3) current and past experiences with injury, may explain the reactions of injured athletes. In their study of 220 injured athletes, they found that emotional representations predicted both positive and negative affect and that some cognitive representations were predictors of physical function, while others predicted sports function. For a more thorough description of self-regulation theory and its applicability to athletic injury, we recommend Hagger, Chatzisarantis, and Griffin's (2004) chapter.

Brewer, Andersen, and Van Raalte (2002) put forward a biopsychosocial model to explain the way seven components occur in concert and influence each other through the rehabilitation process. They suggest that psychological factors play a key role, particularly in terms of reciprocal interaction with biological and social/contextual factors. The other factors in this model are injury, sociodemographic factors, biological factors, intermediate biopsychological outcomes, and sport injury rehabilitation outcomes (Brewer et al., 2002).

Potentially Dangerous Attitudes

While developing athletes into successful competitors, many coaches and athletic trainers have unknowingly fostered erroneous attitudes concerning successful injury rehabilitation. Understanding these potentially dangerous attitudes is crucial to appreciating the psychological aspects of injury and rehabilitation.

Act tough and always give 110 percent. Athletes have been systematically taught that mental toughness and giving 110 percent are necessary for athletic success. Although mental toughness and giving one's best are important, we must realize that when taken to *extremes* these actions can foster injury and failure. Curt Schilling's performance in the 2004 World Series epitomizes these beliefs. Schilling suffered an ankle injury during the Division Series that affected his performance in Game 1 of the league's championship series against the New York Yankees. Rather than succumbing to his injury, the Boston Red Sox medical team devised a method to stabilize his tendon that allowed him to pitch again in Game 6 of the series, which he won. On the morning of his scheduled start in Game 2 of the World Series, Schilling was prepared to tell the team he couldn't pitch. Again, the medical staff found a solution that enabled Schilling to take to the mound (MacMullan, 2004). In both outings in which his tendon was stabilized by stitches, Schilling truly wore a red sock for the Red Sox—his socks turned red from blood oozing from his injury. Schilling needed ankle surgery during the off-season and in 2005 began the season on the disabled list. He then rebounded and helped lead the Red Sox to a second World Championship in 2007 ("Curt Schilling," 2007).

Athletes must be capable of "playing through" some kinds of pain. Seldom do we educate athletes about which kinds of pain to ignore and which kinds of pain to respond to appropriately. Both the Schilling example and research findings indicate that sports medicine practitioners can be complicit in this culture of risk. Safai (2003) interviewed physicians, physiotherapists, and intercollegiate athletes at a Canadian university and found that sports medicine practitioners seem to understand why athletes endorse the sport ethic of playing through pain and they help them play again as quickly as possible, even before an injury is healed.

> *"You may get skinned knees and elbows, but it's worth it if you score a spectacular goal."*
>
> Mia Hamm, U.S. Women's Soccer Team (1987–2004) ("Mia Hamm," 2013; Searchquotes.com, 2013).

How is this sport ethic learned, and is it pervasive at all levels of sport? Malcom (2006) observed girls aged 11-16 in a softball league over three years. Most of the injuries tended to be minor, but how the girls learned to react was fascinating. Some girls would initially react to injuries to gain attention, while others would try to move out of harm's way to avoid injury. As the season(s) wore on, coaches and other players taught the girls to play through the injuries by ignoring complaints of injuries, teasing girls about injuries, or modeling acting tough (e.g., a coach would catch a line drive without a glove and not react). Malcom demonstrated that the sport ethic is learned through participation in sport, though it is not directly taught. Other researchers (Liston, Reacher, Smith, & Waddington, 2006) were curious whether the sport ethic would be found in nonelite rugby, reasoning that professional athletes might be more willing to play through pain due to financial and commercial pressures. They found that the sport ethic was present and identified two codes in rugby: (1) a willingness to be hurt, and (2) playing when hurt for the good of the team. It seems the sport ethic of playing in pain permeates every strata of athletics.

Injured athletes are worthless. Some coaches believe that the best way to foster a rapid recovery from injury is to make injured athletes feel unimportant, which communicates that they care for them only as performers and encourages the athlete to ignore the precautions needed for a full recovery. Leaders must realize that the time when athletes are recovering from injury is crucial for either developing or destroying trust. During this time leaders have a chance to demonstrate care and concern and show that they are as committed to their athletes as they ask their athletes to be.

Leaders must help injured athletes realize that attitudes such as desire, pride, and commitment are beneficial at the right time, but these attitudes may be hazardous to present and future health if taken to the extreme. Athletes become extremely vulnerable and totally unprepared for the incapacitating injury or lifelong pain that may follow inappropriate reactions to pain and injury. Attitude change is required to ensure adaptation to injury and life. Sport professionals must realize the hazards of these mistaken attitudes before they can fully use the psychological strategies that we present later in this chapter. Leaders have to do what is in the *best interest* of injured athletes. When this approach is followed, athletes, coaches, and teams alike will have the best possible chance of attaining their fullest potential.

Whole-Person Philosophy

Reaction to an injured athlete can spring from old-school attitudes such as the preceding or can proceed naturally from a whole-person philosophy. The first reaction can impede an athlete's recuperation and can even *predispose* an athlete to sport accidents. The second reaction deals with short- and long-term aspects of an injury situation in a way that increases the chances of an athlete's return to healthy sport participation. Reactions to Kevin Ware's injury, the Louisville guard who experienced a serious fracture during a 2013 Elite Eight round of the NCAA Men's Basketball tournament, exemplify a whole-person philosophy. Ware's injury has been called one of the most gruesome in sport, but it didn't stop Kevin from being part of the team. Ware had surgery on his leg and was with the team when they won the semi-final and championship games of one week later. The net at the Georgia Dome was lowered so that Ware could cut a piece of the net after the victory.

> *"The bone's 6 inches out of his leg and all he's yelling is, 'Win the game, win the game,' I've not seen that in my life. . . . Pretty special young man."*
>
> (Rick Pitino, coach of Kevin Ware, ESPN.com, 2013).

"I'm not taking this rehabilitation off,. . . As soon as this bone heals and the doctor clears me to get on that court, I'm getting on that court full-speed. I know it's going to take a lot of time, a lot of patience, and it will be frustrating at times."

(Kevin Ware, cited in Armstrong, 2013).

Ware has stated his intention to play again next year, and posted pictures of himself online riding a stationary bike as part of his rehabilitation program two weeks after his injury (Ringo, 2013).

Danish (1986) makes an excellent point when he reminds us to respond to athletes as people, not just injuries. An athlete with an injury is no less of an athlete, no less of a person than before the injury. Danish describes a helping skill model that can be used when working with athletes.

Social support. Social support is critical in the rehabilitation process, particularly with moderate to severe injuries. Having the support of others can contribute to injured athletes having a better sense of well-being, particularly for those athletes who report having less hope (Lu & Hsu, 2013). Family and friends may respond to the athletes primarily as athletes, and in many cases friendships are based along these lines, particularly with teammates or other athletes. Suddenly these important ties may be ruptured. Activities around which their lives centered now move along without them. No one quite knows how to relate to these athletes except perhaps in terms of their past glory or possible future—but not to the injured people in the present. Too often, when athletes are kept away because of injury, they feel that their teammates and time have marched on.

Giving athletes the option to rejoin the team when injured might be a good starting point. We would go so far as to say that as soon as athletes can rejoin a team—even if on crutches or bandaged—they should do so. It is sometimes too much to ask someone to get back on a horse after being thrown, but a modified approach allows a gradual remount while preventing the consolidation of fears of overwhelming obstacles. Asking an injured athlete to help the coaching staff or to mentor younger players provides

ways in which an injured athlete can still be a contributing member. But it is important to consider that attending practice while injured may have a negative impact on an athlete's emotional state. Some of the athletes Tracey (2003) interviewed explained that it was really difficult to be at practice while injured; in fact, 6 of the 10 participants chose not to attend practice.

Coaches and sport psychologists must help ensure that normal contacts are maintained. They should be reassuring about recovery of past abilities, and they should encourage injured athletes to discover other bases of support. Some athletes note a lack of support from their coaches, and even go so far as to say that coaches can be pushy when athletes are injured (Ruddock-Hudson, O'Halloran, & Murphy, 2012), which underscores that athletes do need support from their coaches as they move toward recovery (Peterson, 2001). Athletic trainers can also be good sources of social support (Clement & Shannon, 2011). In particular, athletes will benefit from informational support (i.e., information about the injury) and emotional support (i.e., helping the athlete express emotions and feel understood) from coaches and athletic trainers throughout the injury and recovery processes.

With athletes whose rehabilitation will take longer than two weeks, Striegel, Hedgpeth, and Sowa (1996) suggest two additional forms of social support: peer mentors and injury support groups. Peer mentor relationships are opportunities for an injured athlete to talk with an athlete who has successfully rehabilitated a similar injury. Injury support groups provide injured athletes with a forum to talk about their injury, rehabilitation, and anything else with others who are in the same position. Both these forms of support may help motivate injured athletes during rehabilitation and give athletes a sense of community.

Although social support and the reintegration of the injured athlete are important parts of the rehabilitation process, there are two problems with this "double-edged crutch." First, an injured athlete may present a conscious or unconscious threat to others: "If it could happen to them, it could happen to me." This fear may evoke anything from a mild feeling of discomfort to an almost phobic avoidance of the injured player. When this type of situation develops, it is important for sport personnel to show that the injured person should not be feared and relay the message that the injured athlete will recover and rejoin the team.

Second, although cooperation and cohesion are part of teamwork, so is competition. An athlete's injury may present an opportunity to another person. The second-string player, for example, may have a chance for glory. This is what happened in the New England Patriots organization. Early in the 2000–2001 football season, the Patriots' starting quarterback, Drew Bledsoe, was injured. The starting job was turned over to an unknown, Tom Brady. With Brady as quarterback, the Patriots won seven games and were in contention for the playoffs. Even when Bledsoe was cleared to play, Coach Bill Belichick started Brady. When Brady got hurt in the AFC championship game, Bledsoe stepped in and got the win. Belichick had to decide who to start in the Super Bowl—should he start his high-profile, high-salary quarterback or his young breakout star? Brady was healthy, got the start, and the Patriots won the first of what would be three NFL championships in four years, all with Brady as quarterback ("New England Patriots," 2007). Where possible, this type of competition should be focused on the athletic situation and not personalized. Tensions within the system should be brought to the surface and discussed. One cannot ignore the realities of competition. One can, however, try to maintain as positive a climate as possible.

To treat a knee and ignore the brain and emotions that direct the choreography of that knee is not consistent with total care of the patient.

G. J. Faris, "Psychological Aspects of
Athletic Rehabilitation," Clinics in Sports
Medicine, 4, 1985, p. 546

Addressing the whole person. When dealing with an injured athlete, one of the most crucial aspects entails understanding what the athlete is experiencing before trying to "fix" him or her (Petitpas & Danish, 1995). An injured athlete may experience all, some, or none of a range of effects including grief, identity loss, separation and loneliness, fear, loss of confidence, and performance decrements. If you try to address all of these issues, or some of them, without assessing what the individual athlete is experiencing, you risk frustrating the athlete. It can sometimes be difficult to remember that the injured athlete is a person and not just a broken leg. As Andersen (2000) put it, "We do not treat knees; we treat people" (p. 46). It is important to talk to the athlete about him or herself, not just the injury.

Petitpas and Danish suggest a series of steps to follow when working with an injured athlete. First, build rapport with the athlete. This allows you to understand what the athlete is experiencing with his or her injury. Education is next, when the athlete learns about the injury and rehabilitation process. The phases of skill development and practice and evaluation follow the general education phase. The opportunity to learn and use skills (e.g., goal setting, imagery) helps athletes with rehabilitation and with performance once they are "back in the game."

A case study highlights the importance of treating the whole person. Davis and Sime (2005) documented their work with a collegiate baseball player struggling to regain his form following an eye injury. He had lingering effects after his injury had healed medically; he was not hitting effectively, reported feeling anxious when he had two strikes during an at-bat, and felt as though his vision was not 100 percent. Davis and Sime used a mix of traditional (e.g., breathing and relaxation training, imagery) and nontraditional strategies (i.e., electroencephalograph biofeedback) to great success—the athlete had his most successful season following the interventions. This blended intervention demonstrates the possibilities created when considering the whole picture, and the whole person (i.e., his psychological fears and perceived visual losses). Heil, Wakefield, and Reed (1998) suggest that conceptualizing rehabilitation as an athletic challenge may help athletes through the rehabilitation process. By using this metaphor, the rehabilitation process encompasses familiar skills and rehabilitation becomes just another part of training for excellence rather than a setback in achieving athletic goals.

Teaching Specific Psychological Rehabilitation Strategies

The same mental skills and techniques that help athletes in sport (e.g., goal-setting, mental imagery) can play a role in rehabilitation from injury. Coaches, sport psychologists, and athletic trainers may need to teach athletes that it is reasonable to think the injury is unfortunate, untimely, and inconvenient and to feel irritated, frustrated, and disappointed when one occurs. It is *unreasonable* for athletes to convince themselves that the situation is hopeless, that injuries are a sign of weakness and should be hidden, or that their season or career is over.

Part of the learning is about the injury itself and the rehabilitation process. It is difficult for intelligent athletes to be positive and relaxed if they lack knowledge, are anxious, and wonder about what they are doing in the athletic training room. Athletes who realize the purpose of rehabilitation are more likely to work hard and to provide useful information about their progress.

When athletes are experiencing depressed mood, coaches or sport consultants must not negate disturbing feelings by urging athletes to "pick their spirits up"—these feelings are normal and a sign of progress toward recovery. To help overcome this depression, athletes may benefit from talking with those who have recovered from similar injuries and returned to competition. For more seriously injured athletes, support groups for sharing and discussing concerns, fears, and difficulties may be helpful (Granito, 2001; Striegel et al., 1996). If prolonged detachment, lack of spontaneity, and disinterest in activities and people persist, professional counseling or therapy may be necessary (Wehlage, 1980).

Two studies that examined psychosocial factors related to sports injury rehabilitation found that athletes who possess certain mental attributes and who use certain mental skills may recover faster from injury. In the first study by Ievleva and Orlick (1991), athletes who used more goal setting, healing mental imagery, and positive self-talk recovered faster than athletes who did not. A follow-up study by Loundagin and Fisher (1993) revealed a similar pattern of results and also that focus of attention and stress reduction significantly enhanced recovery time. In contrast, a study by Scherzer (1999) failed to find any correlation between using mental skills and recovery from knee surgery except for goal setting predicting one outcome measure. In a review of research on both preventive and rehabilitative psychological interventions for sport injury, Cupal (1998) concluded that psychological interventions significantly altered the rehabilitation outcome for injured athletes in terms of earlier gains in strength, increases in functional ability, and reduction of pain, state anxiety, and reinjury anxiety. A recent review by Schwab Reese, Pittsinger, and Yang (2012) concluded that imagery and relaxation were associated with better psychological coping during rehabilitation. Both research and extensive anecdotal information from consulting experiences offer support for teaching the following psychological interventions to injured athletes.

Thought stoppage and cognitive restructuring. What athletes say to themselves following an injury helps determine their subsequent behavior. Athletes can be taught coping skills to control their inner thoughts. Then, when self-defeating internal dialogues occur, they can use an intervention strategy such as thought stoppage or cognitive restructuring. (See Chapter 14 for more information on these and other techniques for controlling thoughts.) Thought stoppage and cognitive restructuring can be conceptualized as "self-talk" or how we speak to ourselves. Positive self-talk is thought to contribute to personal well-being and the enhancement of healing (Ievleva & Orlick, 1991).

As an example of the importance of inner dialogue, consider a situation in which an athlete is going through rehabilitation exercises while experiencing pain and little apparent improvement in the injured area. If her inner dialogue becomes self-defeating, the athlete worries and questions the benefit of treatment and exercise:

> This is awful. This hurts too much to be beneficial. These exercises will probably cause me more harm. Besides, I've been doing this for three days now, and I can't see any progress. It would be a lot easier to just let the injury heal on its own. I don't think I'll come tomorrow. It really doesn't matter if I get treatment.

The athlete does not get much out of today's treatment and begins to develop excuses for not continuing therapy.

On the other hand, if the athlete's inner dialogue is self-enhancing, she worries and questions the benefits of treatment and exercise but then thinks:

> Stop. These exercises hurt, but it's okay—they'll pay off. I'm lucky to have knowledgeable people helping me. I'll be competing soon because I'm doing these exercises. If the pain gets too severe, I'll ask my trainer if I am doing it right and, if I am, I'll live with it and think about how happy I'll be to be competing again.

The athlete has a good treatment session and prepares herself to continue for as long as necessary. By using cognitive techniques that promote positive self-talk, athletes can often reduce the time they need to rehabilitate from injury (Ievleva & Orlick, 1991; Loundagin & Fisher, 1993).

Imagery

Athletes' imaginations can greatly influence their response to injury. Athletes can learn to control their visual images and to direct them productively to reduce anxiety and to aid in rehabilitation and successful return to sport. See Chapter 13 for more detailed information on what imagery is and techniques that can be used to teach and enhance imagery skills.

> Mastery imagery: visual rehearsal of successfully completing tasks

> Emotive imagery: rehearsal of scenes that produce positive self-enhancing feelings such as enthusiasm, self-pride, and confidence.

> Healing imagery: envisioning what is happening to the injury internally during the rehabilitation process.

All three types of imagery can help athletes when they are rehabilitating an injury. Mastery imagery can help foster motivation for rehabilitation and confidence on return to competition. Injured athletes also can use coping rehearsal to visually rehearse anticipated problematic situations that may stand in the way of their successful return to competition and then rehearse effectively overcoming these obstacles. Such visual rehearsal methods can effectively prepare injured athletes for any number of competitive or practice situations, helping them maintain physical skills, retain confidence in their ability, and dissipate any lingering fears they may have of reinjury on return to competition (Ievleva & Orlick, 1993). Injured athletes can use emotive imagery to help feel secure and confident that rehabilitation will be successful. In order to successfully use healing imagery, athletes must receive a detailed explanation of their injury and how it will heal physiologically. Color pictures can help athletes develop a mental picture of the injury. After visualizing the healing process, athletes are asked to imagine in vivid color the healing occurring during treatment sessions and at intervals during the day. For example, athletes can imagine increased blood flow and warmth going to the injured area, or they can imagine the stretching necessary for enhancing range of motion. Research also supports the effectiveness of using imagery for pain management (Driediger, Hall, & Callow, 2006).

Despite research findings that imagery can help with recovery (e.g., Ievleva & Orlick, 1991), many athletes in the past did not use imagery extensively during rehabilitation (Driediger et al., 2006; Sordoni, Hall, & Forwell, 2000). A more recent study found that 68 percent of their participants ($n = 36$ injured athletes) reported using imagery during rehabilitation (Monsma, Mensch, & Farroll, 2009), however, those who were injured the longest were less likely to use imagery. In a study examining imagery use and rehabilitation adherence, Wesch and colleagues found that their participants' use of imagery remained stable over the 8-week period and was associated with adherence to rehabilitation (Wesch et al., 2012). When Milne, Hall, and Forwell (2005) sought to extend Sordoni et al.'s results (2000), they found that injured athletes used more motivational and cognitive imagery than healing imagery while rehabilitating. They suggest that athletes may need additional instruction in healing imagery if they are to use it. This concern is echoed by Evans, Hare, and Mullen (2006), who found that the athletes used imagery to control pain and enhance healing, but were more familiar with performance-related imagery.

Goal-setting   It is helpful for the rehabilitation team to work with the injured athlete at setting specific short- and long-term goals for recovery, return to practice and competition, and day-to-day rehabilitation throughout the rehabilitation process (DePalma & DePalma, 1989). Athletes should be actively involved in this process. (See Chapter 11 for specific suggestions on how to effectively set goals and implement a goal-setting program.)

The following example of a college pitcher who needed surgery on his throwing arm highlights the effective use of goals in a rehabilitation process designed to physically and psychologically prepare him for return to practice the following spring. He was reminded of how excited he would be on the first day of practice to be back on the field with his teammates and to see if he still "had it." He also was told that he would feel great and have an almost overpowering urge to try all his pitches and overthrow on the first day his arm felt good, but he would overcome the urges by being smart, disciplined, and emotionally controlled. The desire to help his teammates be successful and the thrill of getting back on stage and becoming a star again would be highly motivating.

Together, this athlete, his coaches, and his athletic trainers outlined a specific goal plan. They decided on a set number of throws each day, the distance of the throws, the approximate speed of the throws, and the kinds of throws. For the first three weeks the athlete's catcher and a coach would help make sure that the plan was adhered to on a daily basis. Short- and long-term goals were detailed so that by the fifth game of the year the athlete would be ready to return to the pitching mound for three innings of relief pitching. It is essential that these goals are important to the athlete (Danish, 1986), and this is best accomplished if the athlete understands the relationship between staying focused on and committed to agreed-upon goals.

A similar plan was detailed for physical treatments. Both plans were reinforced by coaches, athletic trainers, and teammates, as well as by daily visualization of the good feelings and results that would occur from sticking to the plan. Despite many days of questioning, doubt, and uncertainty, the athlete generally remained positive, stayed with the plan, and made a highly successful return to competition one week later than planned.

As with many other athletes, the process from injury to return to competition was a challenge to this athlete's mind and body. Because the process was managed properly, it allowed for a positive and bright future. Research by Filby, Maynard, and Graydon (1999) found support for the notion that setting multiple goals (e.g., outcome, process, and performance goals) improved task performance. Wayda, Armenth-Brothers, and Boyce (1998) further explain that if the injured athlete feels that he or she is part of the process (i.e., by taking an active role in goal-setting), he or she is more likely to be committed to the rehabilitation program.

Relaxation

Practicing any of the relaxation techniques (see Chapter 12) can play a role in reducing stress and speeding injury rehabilitation (Loundagin & Fisher, 1993). These results may occur for a number of reasons. Relaxation helps open the mind–body channels that regulate the body, enabling inner control over the body (Botterill, Flint, & Ievleva, 1996). Tension levels often increase in the injured area owing to the stress of being injured (Brewer, Van Raalte, & Linder, 1991). This tension can increase pain and work against the effectiveness of the rehabilitation exercises by, for example, reducing blood flow and range of motion. Practicing a relaxation routine can relieve the tension and enhance blood circulation. Injured athletes who participated in stress inoculation training (i.e., deep breathing, progressive muscular relaxation, imagery) experienced less anxiety, less pain, and fewer days to recovery than counterparts who received only physical therapy, demonstrating the effectiveness of adding relaxation training to physical rehabilitation protocols (Ross & Berger, 1996).

Summary

Sport psychologists have made great advances in understanding the psychological rehabilitation of athletes and the psychological factors that put athletes at risk of injury. Although some athletes have effective psychological responses, others do not. This chapter focuses on factors that may predispose athletes to injuries, patterns of negative reactions to injuries, and ways in which coaches and sport psychologists can help athletes respond psychologically to injuries in positive, growth-oriented ways.

Although no clear injury-prone personality has been identified, some factors such as high life stress and low social support and psychological coping skills are predictive of injury. Possible preventive interventions are available for these and other factors related to injury. Athletes can respond to injury in more and less adaptive ways. Using a cognitive appraisal model, we identify personal and situational factors that might influence an athlete's cognitive appraisal of the injury and his or her resulting emotional and behavioral responses to both the injury and injury rehabilitation. We agree with Brewer's (1994) conclusion that cognitive appraisal models offer a useful framework to guide both future empirical efforts and rehabilitation practice. Systems of social support, treatment of the whole person, and cognitive-behavioral interventions are ways to help injured athletes respond to injury in a more positive way.

Study Questions

1. What are key factors that may predispose some athletes to injury? How can the athlete and the sport or team environment be modified to reduce risk factors and enhance buffering factors?

2. List five responses that may occur as a result of anxiety and tension associated with an injury on an athlete's initial return to competition.

3. How and why might personal growth possibilities become an important part of the psychological rehabilitation of the injured athlete?

4. List five problematic results of an athlete returning to competition following an injury if not psychologically prepared.

5. Diagram the cognitive appraisal model of psychological adjustment to athletic injury and discuss the different components.

6. Explain the differences among mastery imagery, emotive imagery, and healing imagery.

7. Describe what other psychological strategies might be used to hasten rehabilitation and to prepare for returning to competition.

References

Alizadeh, M. H., Pashabadi, A., Hosseini, S. M., & Shahbazi, M. (2012). Injury occurrence and psychological risk factors in junior football players. *World Journal of Sport Sciences, 6,* 401–405.

Andersen, M. B. (2000). Supervision of athletic trainers; counseling encounters. *Athletic Therapy Today, 5,* 46–47.

Andersen, M. B., & Williams, J. M. (1988). A model of stress and athletic injury: Prediction and prevention. *Journal of Sport and Exercise Psychology, 10,* 294–306.

Andersen, M. B., & Williams, J. M. (1999). Athletic injury, psychosocial factors, and perceptual changes during stress. *Journal of Sports Sciences, 17,* 735–741.

Armstrong, K. (2013, April 9). Kevin Ware, injured Louisville guard, goes from low of shattered leg to cutting down the nets in NCAA title game. *New York Daily News.* Retrieved from http://www.nydailynews.com.

AskMen.com. (2004). *Eric Lindros.* Retrieved September 29, 2004, from http://www.askmen.com/men/sports/45_eric_lindros.html.

Botterill, C., Flint, F. A., & Ievleva, L. (1996). Psychology of the injured athlete. In J. E. Zachazewski, D. J. Magee, & W. S. Quillen (Eds.), *Athletic injuries and rehabilitation* (pp. 791–805). Philadelphia: W. B. Saunders.

Brewer, B. W. (1993). Self-identity and specific vulnerability to depressed mood. *Journal of Personality, 61,* 343–364.

Brewer, B. W. (1994). Review and critique of models of psychological adjustment to athletic injury. *Journal of Applied Sport Psychology, 6,* 87–100.

Brewer, B. W., Andersen, M. B., & Van Raalte, J. L. (2002). Psychological aspects of sport injury rehabilitation: Toward a biopsychosocial approach. In D. L. Mostofsky & L. D. Zaichkowsky (Eds.), *Medical and psychological aspects of sport and exercise* (pp. 41–54). Morgantown, WV: Fitness Information Technology.

Brewer, B. W., Van Raalte, J. L., & Linder, D. E. (1991). Role of the sport psychologist in treating injured athletes: A survey of sport medicine providers. *Journal of Applied Sport Psychology, 3,* 183–190.

Brewer, B. W., Van Raalte, J. L., & Linder, D. E. (1993). Athletic identity: Hercules' muscles or Achilles heel? *International Journal of Sport Psychology, 24,* 237–254.

Clement, D., & Shannon, V. (2009). The impact of a workshop on athletic training students' sport psychology behaviors. *The Sport Psychologist, 23,* 504–522.

Clement, D., & Shannon, V. (2011). Injured athletes' perceptions about social support. *Journal of Sport Rehabilitation, 20,* 457–470.

Cramer Roh, J. L., & Perna, F. M. (2000). Psychology/counseling: A universal competency in athletic training. *Journal of Athletic Training, 35,* 458–465.

Crossman, J., & Jamieson, J. (1985). Differences in perceptions of seriousness and disrupting effects of athletic injury as viewed by athletes and their trainer. *Perceptual and Motor Skills, 61,* 1131–1134.

Cupal, D. D. (1998). Psychological interventions in sport injury prevention and rehabilitation. *Journal of Applied Sport Psychology, 10,* 103–123.

Curt Schilling. (2007, November 4). In *Wikipedia, The Free Encyclopedia*. Retrieved November 4, 2007, from http://en.wikipedia.org/wiki/Curt_Schilling.

Danish, S. J. (1986). Psychological aspects in the care and treatment of athletic injuries. In P. E. Vinger & E. F. Hoerner (Eds.), *Sports injuries: The unthwarted epidemic* (pp. 345–353). Littleton, MA: PSG.

Davis, J. O. (1991). Sports injuries and stress management: An opportunity for research. *The Sport Psychologist, 5,* 175–182.

Davis, P. A., & Sime, W. E. (2005). Toward a psychophysiology of performance: Sport psychology principles dealing with anxiety. *International Journal of Stress Management, 12,* 363–378.

de Heredia, R. A. S., Munoz, A. R., & Artaza, J. L. (2004). The effect of psychological response on recovery of sport injury. *Research in Sports Medicine, 12,* 15–31.

DePalma, M. T., & DePalma, B. (1989). The use of instruction and the behavioral approach to facilitate injury rehabilitation. *Athletic Training, 24,* 217–219.

DeWitt, D. J. (1980). Cognitive and biofeedback training for stress reduction with university athletes. *Journal of Sport Psychology, 2,* 288–294.

Devantier, C. (2011). Psychological predictors of injury among professional soccer players. *Sport Science Review, 20,* 5–36.

Driediger, M., Hall, C., & Callow, N. (2006). Imagery use by injured athletes: A qualitative analysis. *Journal of Sport Sciences, 24,* 261–271.

Duda, J. L., Smart, A. E., & Tappe, M. K. (1989). Predictors of adherence in the rehabilitation of athletic injuries: An application of personal investment theory. *Journal of Sport Psychology, 11,* 367–381.

Edvardsson, A., Ivarsson, A., & Johnson, U. (2012). Is a cognitive-behavioral biofeedback intervention useful to reduce injury risk in junior football players? *Journal of Sports Science and Medicine, 11,* 331–338.

Ermler, K. L., & Thomas, C. E. (1990). Interventions for the alienating effect of injury. *Athletic Training, 25,* 269–271.

ESPN.com (2007a). *Eric Lindros*. Retrieved November 3, 2007, from http://sports.espn.go.com/nhl/players/stats?playerId=543.

ESPN.com (2007b). *Former MVP Lindros Announces Retirement After 13 NHL Seasons*. Retrieved November 16, 2007, from http://sports.espn.go.com/espn/wire?section=nhl&id=3100724.

ESPN.com (2013). *Kevin Ware breaks bone in leg*. Retrieved May 5, 2013 from http://espn.go.com/mens-college-basketball/tournament/2013/story/_/id/9118319/2013-ncaa-tournament-kevin-ware-louisville-cardinals-breaks-bone-leg-duke-blue-devils.

Evans, L., & Hardy, L. (1995). Sport injury and grief responses. A review. *Journal of Sport & Exercise Psychology, 17,* 227–245.

Evans, L., Hare, R., & Mullen, R. (2006). Imagery use during rehabilitation from injury. *Journal of Imagery Research in Sport and Physical Activity, 1,* 1–19.

Evans, L., Wadey, R., Hanton, S., & Mitchell, I. (2012). Stressors experienced by injured athletes. *Journal of Sport Sciences, 30,* 917–927.

Faris, G. J. (1985). Psychologic aspects of athletic rehabilitation. *Clinics in Sports Medicine, 4,* 545–551.

Fawkner, H. J. (1995). *Predisposition to injury in athletes: The role of psychosocial factors.* Unpublished master's thesis, University of Melbourne, Australia.

Fawkner, H. J., McMurray, N. E., & Summers, J. J. (1999). Athletic injury and minor life events: A prospective study. *Journal of Science and Medicine in Sport, 2,* 117–124.

Filby, W. C. D., Maynard, I. W., & Graydon, J. K. (1999). The effect of multiple-goal strategies on performance outcomes in training and competition. *Journal of Applied Sport Psychology, 11,* 230–246.

Fisher, A. C., Domm, M. A., & Wuest, D. A. (1988). Adherence to sports-injury rehabilitation programs. *The Physician and Sports medicine, 16,* 47–52.

Ford, I. A., Eklund, R. C., & Gordon, S. (2000). An examination of psychosocial variables moderating the relationship between life stress and injury time-loss among athletes of a high standard. *Journal of Sports Sciences, 18,* 301–312.

Granito, V. J. (2001). Athletic injury experience: A qualitative focus group approach. *Journal of Sport Behavior, 24,* 63–82.

Green, S. L., & Weinberg, R. S. (2001). Relationships among athletic identity, coping skills, social support, and the psychological impact of injury in recreational participants. *Journal of Applied Sport Psychology, 31,* 40–59.

Grove, J. R., Stewart, R. M. L., & Gordon, S. (1990, October). *Emotional reactions of athletes to knee rehabilitation.* Paper presented at the annual meeting of the Australian Sports Medicine Federation, Alice Springs, Australia.

Hagger, M. S., Chatzisarantis, N. L. D., & Griffin, M. (2004). Coping with sports injury: Testing a model of self-regulation in a sports setting. In D. Lavallee, J. Thatcher, & M. V. Jones (Eds.), *Coping and emotion in sport* (pp. 105–130). Hauppauge, NY: Nova Science Publishers.

Hagger, M. S., Chatzisarantis, N. L. D., Griffin, M., & Thatcher, J. (2005). Injury representations, coping, emotions, and functional outcomes in athletes with sports-related injuries: A test of self-regulation theory. *Journal of Applied Social Psychology, 35,* 2345–2374.

Hanson, S. J., McCullagh, P., & Tonymon, P. (1992). The relationship of personality characteristics, life stress, and coping resources to athletic injury. *Journal of Sport and Exercise Psychology, 14,* 262–272.

Hardy, C. J., O'Connor, K. A., & Geisler, P. R. (1990). The role of gender and social support in the life stress injury relationship. *Proceedings of the Association for the Advancement of Applied Sport Psychology, Fifth Annual Conference (Abstract),* 51.

Heil, J., Wakefield, C., & Reed, C. (1998). Patient as athlete: A metaphor for injury rehabilitation. In K. F. Hays (Ed.), Integrating exercise, sports, movement and mind: Therapeutic unity. Binghamton, NY: Haworth Press.

Hutchison, M., Mainwaring, L. M., Comper, P., Richards, D. W., & Bisschop, S. M. (2009). Differential emotional responses of varsity athletes to concussion and musculoskeletal injuries. *Clinical Journal of Sports Medicine, 19,* 13–19.

Ievleva, L., & Orlick, T. (1991). Mental links to enhanced healing: An exploratory study. *Sport Psychologist, 5,* 25–40.

Ievleva, L., & Orlick, T. (1993). Mental paths to enhanced recovery from a sports injury. In D. Pargman (Ed.), *Psychological bases of sport injuries* (pp. 219–245). Morgantown, WV: Fitness Information Technology.

Ivarsson, A., & Johnson, U. (2010). Psychological factors as predictors of injuries among senior soccer players. A prospective study. *Journal of Sports Science and Medicine, 9,* 347–352.

Ivarsson, A., Johnson, U., & Podlog, L. (2013). Psychological predictors of injury occurrence: A prospective investigation of professional Swedish soccer players. *Journal of Sport Rehabilitation, 22,* 19–26.

Johnson, U. (2011). Athletes' experiences of psychosocial risk factors preceding injury. *Qualitative Research in Sport, Exercise and Health, 3,* 99–115.

Johnson, U., Ekengren, J., & Andersen, M. B. (2005). Injury prevention in Sweden: Helping soccer players at risk. *Journal of Sport and Exercise Psychology, 27.*

Johnson, U., & Ivarsson, A. (2011). Psychological predictors of sport injuries among junior soccer players. *Scandinavian Journal of Medicine & Science in Sports, 21,* 129–136.

Johnston, L. H., & Carroll, D. (2000). The psychological impact of injury: Effects of prior sport and exercise involvement. *British Journal of Sports Medicine, 34,* 436–439.

Kerr, G., & Goss, J. (1996). The effects of a stress management program on injuries and stress levels. *Journal of Applied Sport Psychology, 8 ,* 109–117.

Kerr, G., & Minden, H. (1988). Psychological factors related to the occurrence of athletic injuries. *Journal of Sport and Exercise Physiology, 37,* 1–11.

Kleinert, J. (2007). Mood states and perceived physical states as short term predictors of sport injuries: Two prospective studies. *International Journal of Sport and Exercise Psychology, 5,* 340–351.

Kolt, G. S., Hume, P. A., Smith, P., & Williams, M. M. (2004). Effects of a stress-management program on injury and stress of competitive gymnasts. *Perceptual and Motor Skills, 99,* 195–207.

Kubler-Ross, E. (1969). *On death and dying.* New York: Macmillan.

Larson, G. A., Starkey, C., & Zaichkowsky, L. D. (1996). Psychological aspects of athletic injuries as perceived by athletic trainers. *Sport Psychologist, 10,* 37–47.

Lavallee, L., & Flint, F. (1996). The relationship of stress, competitive anxiety, mood state, and social support to athletic injury. *Journal of Athletic Training, 31,* 296–299.

Liston, K., Reacher, D., Smith, A., & Waddington, I. (2006). Managing pain and injury in nonelite rugby union and rugby league: A case study of players at a British university. *Sport in Society, 9,* 388–402.

Loundagin, C., & Fisher, L. (1993, October). *The relationship between mental skills and enhanced injury rehabilitation.* Paper presented at the annual meeting of the Association for the Advancement of Applied Sport Psychology, Montreal, Quebec.

Lu, F. J. H., & Hsu, Y. (2013). Injured athletes' rehabilitation beliefs and subjective well-being: The contribution of hope and social support. *Journal of Athletic Training, 48,* 92–98.

MacMullen, J. (2004, October 31). Schilling talked a good game—and was a man of his word. *Boston Globe.* Retrieved November 4, 2007, from http://www.boston.com.

Maddison, R., & Prapavessis, H. (2005). A psychological approach to the prediction and prevention of athletic injury. *Journal of Sport and Exercise Psychology, 27,* 289–310.

Mainwaring, L. M., Bisschop, S. M., Green, R. E. A., Antoniazzi, M., Comper, P., Kristman, V., et al. (2004). Emotional reaction of varsity athletes to sport-related concussion. *Journal of Sport and Exercise Psychology, 26,* 119–135.

Malcom, N. L. (2006). "Shaking it off" and "toughing it out." Socialization to pain and injury in girls' softball. *Journal of Contemporary Ethnography, 35,* 495–525.

Mann, B. J., Grana, W. A., Indelicato, P. A., O'Neill, D. F., & George, S. Z. (2007). A survey of sports medicine physicians regarding psychological issues in patient-athletes. *The American Journal of Sports Medicine, 35,* 2140–2147.

May, J. R., & Brown, L. (1989). Delivery of psychological services to the U.S. alpine ski team prior to and during the Olympics in Calgary. *Sport Psychologist, 3,* 320–329.

McDonald, S. A., & Hardy, C. J. (1990). Affective response patterns of the injured athlete: An exploratory analysis. *Sport Psychologist, 4,* 261–274.

McDonell, C. (2004). *Shooting from the lip.* Buffalo, NY: Firefly Books.

Mia Hamm. (2013, May 5). In *Wikipedia, The Free Encyclopedia.* Retrieved May 5, 2013, from http://en.wikipedia.org/wiki/Mia_Hamm.

Milne, M., Hall, C., & Forwell, L. (2005). Self-efficacy, imagery use, and adherence to rehabilitation by injured athletes. *Journal of Sport Rehabilitation, 14,* 150–167.

Misasi, S. P., Redmond, C. J., & Kemler, D. S. (1998). Counseling skills and the athletic therapist. *Athletic Therapy Today, 3,* 35–38.

Monsma, E., Mensch, J., & Farroll, J. (2009). Keeping your head in the game: Sport-specific imagery and anxiety among injured athletes. *Journal of Athletic Training, 44,* 410–417.

Murphy, S. M. (1988). The on-site provision of sport psychology services at the U.S. Olympic Festival. *Sport Psychologist, 2,* 337–350.

New England Patriots. (2007, November 3). In *Wikipedia, The Free Encyclopedia.* Retrieved November 3, 2007, from http://en.wikipedia.org/wiki/New_England_Patriots.

Noh, Y. E., Morris, T., & Andersen, M. B. (2007) Psychological intervention programs for reduction of injury in ballet dancers. *Research in Sports Medicine 15,* 13–32.

Pargman, D., (Ed.). (2007). *Psychological bases of sports injuries* (3rd ed.). Morgantown, WV: Fitness Information Technology.

Pedersen, P. (1986). The grief response and injury: A special challenge for athletes and athletic trainers. *Athletic Training, 21,* 312–314.

Perna, F. M., Antoni, M. H., Baum, A., Gordon, P., & Schneiderman, N. (2003). Cognitive behavioral stress management effects on injury and illness among competitive athletes: A randomized clinical trial. *Annals of Behavioral Medicine, 25,* 66–73.

Peterson, K. (2001). Supporting athletes during injury rehab. *Olympic Coach, 11,* 7–9.

Petitpas, A., Champagne, D., Chartrand, J., Danish, S., & Murphy, S. (1997). *Athlete's guide to career planning.* Champaign, IL: Human Kinetics.

Petitpas, A., & Danish, S. J. (1995). Caring for injured athletes. In S. M. Murphy (Ed.), *Sport psychology interventions* (pp. 255–281). Champaign, IL: Human Kinetics.

Petrie, T. A. (1992). Psychosocial antecedents of athletic injury: The effects of life stress and social support on female collegiate gymnasts. *Behavioral Medicine, 18,* 127–138.

Petrie, T. A. (1993). Coping skills, competitive trait anxiety, and playing status: Moderating effects of the life stress-injury relationship. *Journal of Sport and Exercise Psychology, 15,* 261–274.

Quinn, A. M., & Fallon, B. J. (1999). The changes in psychological characteristics and reactions of elite athletes from injury onset until full recovery. *Journal of Applied Sport Psychology, 11,* 210–229.

Richman, J. M., Hardy, C. J., Rosenfeld, L. B., & Callahan, A. E. (1989). Strategies for enhancing social support networks in sport: A brainstorming experience. *Journal of Applied Sport Psychology, 1,* 150–159.

Ringo, K. (2013, April 15). Resilient Kevin Ware already rehabilitating gruesome leg injury, encouraging others [Web log post]. Retrieved from http://sports.yahoo.com/blogs/ncaab-the-dagger/resilient-kevin-ware-already-rehabilitating-gruesome-leg-injury-221816567--ncaab.html.

Rogers, T.J., Alderman, B.L., & Landers, D.M. (2003). Effects of life event stress and hardiness on peripheral vision in a real-life stress situation. *Behavioral Medicine, 29,* 21–26.

Rogers, T. J., & Landers, D. M. (2005). Mediating effects of peripheral vision in the life event stress/athletic injury relationship. *Journal of Sport and Exercise Psychology, 27,* 271–288.

Ross, M. J., & Berger, R. S. (1996). Effects of stress inoculation training on athletes' postsurgical pain and rehabilitation after orthopedic injury. *Journal of Consulting and Clinical Psychology, 64,* 406–410.

Rotella, R. (1984). Psychological care of the injured athlete. In L. Bunker, R. J. Rotella, & A. S. Reilly (Eds.), *Sport psychology: Psychological considerations in maximizing sport performance.* Ithaca, NY: Mouvement Publications.

Ruddock-Hudson, M., O'Halloran, P., & Murphy, G. (2012). Exploring psychological reactions to injury in the Australian Football League (AFL). *Journal of Applied Sport Psychology, 24,* 375–390.

Safai, P. (2003). Healing the body in the "Culture of Risk": Examining the negotiation of treatment between sport medicine clinicians and injured athletes from Canadian intercollegiate sport. *Sociology of Sport Journal, 20,* 127–146.

Scherzer, C. B. (1999). *Using psychological skills in rehabilitation following knee surgery.* Unpublished master's thesis, Springfield College, Springfield, MA.

Scherzer, C. B., & Williams, J. M. (2008). Bringing sport psychology into the athletic training room. *Athletic Therapy Today, 13,* 15–17.

Schwab Reese, L. M., Pittsinger, R., & Yang, J. (2012). Effectiveness of psychological intervention following sport injury. *Journal of Sport and Health Science, 1,* 71–79.

Searchquotes.com. (2013). *Mia Hamm.* Retrieved May 5, 2013, from http://www.searchquotes.com/search/Mia_Hamm/.

Shaffer, S. M. (1992). *Attributions and self-efficacy as predictors of rehabilitative success.* Unpublished master's thesis, University of Illinois, Champaign.

Smith, A. M., Scott, S. G., O'Fallon, W. M., & Young, M. L. (1990). Emotional responses of athletes to injury. *Mayo Clinic Proceedings, 65,* 38–50.

Smith, M. (2007). *Bledsoe retires, ends 14-year career.* Retrieved November 3, 2007, from http://sports.espn.go.com/nfl/news/story?id=2834191.

Smith, R. E., Ptacek, J. T., & Patterson, E. (2000). Moderator effects of cognitive and somatic trait anxiety on the relation between life stress and physical injuries. *Anxiety, Stress & Coping, 13,* 269–288.

Smith, R. E., Ptacek, J. T., & Smoll, F. L. (1992). Sensation seeking, stress, and adolescent injuries: A test of stress-buffering, risk-taking, and coping skills hypotheses. *Journal of Personality and Social Psychology, 62,* 1016–1024.

Smith, R. E., Smoll, F. L., & Ptacek, J. T. (1990). Conjunctive moderator variables in vulnerability and resiliency research: Life stress, social support and coping skills, and adolescent sport injuries. *Journal of Personality and Social Psychology, 58,* 360–369.

Sordoni, C., Hall, C., & Forwell, L. (2000). The use of imagery by athletes during injury rehabilitation. *Journal of Sport Rehabilitation, 9,* 329–338.

Striegel, D. A., Hedgpeth, E. G., & Sowa, C. J. (1996). Differential psychological treatment of injured athletes based on length of rehabilitation. *Journal of Sport Rehabilitation, 5,* 330–335.

Tracey, J. (2003). The emotional response to the injury and rehabilitation process. *Journal of Applied Sport Psychology, 15,* 279–293.

Tracey, J. (2008). Inside the clinic: Health professionals' role in their clients' psychological rehabilitation. *Journal of Sport Rehabilitation, 17,* 413–431.

Udry, E., Gould, D., Bridges, D., & Beck, L. (1997). Down but not out: Athlete responses to season-ending injuries. *Journal of Sport and Exercise Psychology, 19,* 229–248.

Van Mechelen, W., Twisk, J., Molendijk, A., Blom, B., Snel, J., & Kemper, H. C. G. (1996). Subject-related risk factors for sports injuries: A 1-yr prospective study in young adults. *Medicine and Science in Sports and Exercise, 28,* 1171–1179.

Wadey, R., Evans, L., Evans, K., & Mitchell, I. (2011). Perceived benefits following sport injury: A qualitative examination of their antecedents and underlying mechanisms. *Journal of Applied Sport Psychology, 23,* 142–158.

Wadey, R., Evans, L., Hanton, S., & Neil, R. (2012a). An examination of hardiness throughout the sport injury process. *British Journal of Health Psychology, 17,* 103–128.

Wadey, R., Evans, L., Hanton, S., & Neil, R. (2012b). An examination of hardiness throughout the sport-injury process: A qualitative follow-up study. *British Journal of Health Psychology, 17,* 872–893.

Wadey, R., Evans, L., Hanton, S., & Neil, R. (2013). Effect of dispositional optimism before and after injury. *Medicine and Science in Sports and Exercise, 45,* 387–394.

Wayda, V. K., Armenth-Brothers, F., & Boyce, B. A. (1998). Goal setting: A key to injury rehabilitation. *Athletic Therapy Today, 3,* 21–25.

Wehlage, D. F. (1980). Managing the emotional reaction to loss in athletics. *Athletic Training, 15,* 144–146.

Wesch, N., Hall, C., Prapavessis, H., Maddison, R., Bassett, S., Foley, L., Brooks, S., & Forwell, L. (2012). Self-efficacy, imagery use, and adherence during injury rehabilitation. *Scandanavian Journal of Medicine and Science in Sports, 22,* 695–703.

Wiese-Bjornstal, D. M., Smith, A. M., Shaffer, S. M., & Morrey, M. A. (1998). An integrated model of response to sport injury: Psychological and sociological dynamics. *Journal of Applied Sport Psychology, 10,* 46–69.

Williams, J. M. (2001). Psychology of injury risk and prevention. In R. N. Singer, H. A. Hausenblas, & C. M. Janelle (Eds.), *Handbook of research in sport psychology* (2nd ed., pp. 766–786). New York: Wiley.

Williams, J. M., & Andersen, M. B. (1997). Psychosocial influences on central and peripheral vision and reaction time during demanding tasks. *Behavioral Medicine, 26,* 160–167.

Williams, J. M., & Andersen, M. B. (1998). Psychosocial antecedents of sport injury: Review and critique of the stress and injury model. *Journal of Applied Sport Psychology, 10,* 5–25.

Williams, J. M., & Andersen, M. B. (2007). Psychosocial antecedents of sport injury and interventions for risk reduction. In G. Tenenbaum & R. C. Eklund (Eds.), *Handbook of research in sport psychology* (3rd ed., pp. 379–403), Hoboken, NJ: John Wiley & Sons.

Williams, J. M., Hogan, T. D., & Andersen, M. B. (1993). Positive states of mind and athletic injury risk. *Psychosomatic Medicine, 55,* 468–472.

Williams, J., Tonymon, P., & Wadsworth, W. A. (1986). Relationship of stress to injury in intercollegiate volleyball. *Journal of Human Stress, 12,* 38–43.

Zuckerman, M. (1979). *Sensation seeking: Beyond the optimal level of arousal.* Hillsdale, NJ: Erlbaum.

Career Transition among Athletes: Is There Life after Sports?

David Lavallee, *University of Stirling, UK*
Sunghee Park, *Kookmin University, South Korea*
Jim Taylor, *San Francisco*

I can't do it physically anymore, and that's really hard for me to say. It's hard to walk away. I can't explain in words how much everyone has meant to me. I'll never be able to fill the void of playing a football game. I don't look at it as a retirement. I look on it as graduation. You graduate from high school and you graduate from college. I'm graduating from pro football.

—John Elway, two-time Super Bowl–winning quarterback

During the course of athletes' careers, the primary focus of most sports administrators, coaches, and sport psychologists is on assisting athletes to maximize their competitive performances. This emphasis is expected, as athletes are their responsibilities during their competitive tenures, and when the athletes leave the team or sport organization, their attention has to turn to the current athletes under their charge. This system, unfortunately, tends to neglect what happens to athletes when they retire and must make the transition to another career and lifestyle.

Fortunately, interest is growing at many levels of sport and among many groups involved in sport in the issue of what has become known as "career transition" (Baillie & Danish, 1992). Popular accounts of this issue over the years have provided anecdotal depictions of professional athletes adjusting to life after sport (Park, Lavallee, & Tod, 2013). Even empirical studies in athletes' career transition have been increased; however, the study area still has more to explore because athletes' career transition is a complex and multidimensional process that is related to many different variables (Park et al., 2013).

History and Background

The issue of career transition gained the attention of sport psychologists just four decades ago. Leading professionals in the field in Europe such as Miroslav Vanek, Paul Kunath, Ferruccio Antonelli, Lars-Erik Unestahl, and John Kane, who were consultants for various national teams, began to discuss this issue, describe experiences they had in their work with athletes, and express concern about the athletes' adjustment to a life after sport. Additionally, the media (e.g., Bradley, 1976) and early scholarly, although anecdotal, writings (McPherson, 1980; Ogilvie & Howe, 1982) brought to light some of the significant concerns associated with career transition among athletes. Soon after these preliminary discussions began, research emerged investigating the issues raised by these professionals (e.g., Haerle, 1975; Hill & Lowe, 1974). This research studied the impact of career transition on athletes in different sports and at various levels of competition.

Over time the opportunity to study and address career transition needs of elite athletes has proven to be difficult for a variety of reasons. Typically, trained professionals such as sport psychologists and career counselors have had limited contact with athletes during their competitive careers, much less after they leave their sport. Until recently, sport administrators had little concern for athletes after they retire and sport psychologists rarely had the occasion to evaluate the need for such services to elite athletes. Additionally, the contact time that professionals had with athletes was not conducive to exploration of post-career concerns. For example, sport psychologists usually work with elite athletes at training camps and competitions, neither of which provide opportunities for discussion of career transition issues.

The divergent perspectives of administrators and coaches with respect to career transition also may have hindered further exploration of these concerns. For example, administrators either didn't see the need for career-transition services for their athletes or were limited because of budgetary constraints. Head coaches may have sabotaged career counseling programs because they interpreted them as distracting the athletes from their primary focus of winning. During the last 30 years, however, national sports federations in countries around the world have been establishing career transition programs for elite athletes, including the Athlete Career and Education (ACE) Program (Australia), Performance Lifestyle Program (the UK), and the Lifestyle Program (the Republic of Ireland; Stambulova & Ryba,

2013). In addition, since 2005, the International Olympic Committee (the IOC) has also provided athlete support programs via its Internet homepage (http://www.olympic.org/en/content/Olympic-Athletes/Elite-Athletes/). The program aims to enhance elite athletes' successful daily lives both inside and outside sport, and contains three major areas, including education (e.g., basic skills for enhancing academic achievement and time management), life skills (e.g., public speaking and problem-solving), and employment (e.g., CV writing and interview skills).

The academic interest in career transitions has also expanded. An international special-interest group of the European Federation of Sport Psychology (FEPSAC) has been initiated to exchange information on applied and investigative work in the area, and this organization has published Position Statements on Sports Career Termination and Sports Career Transitions as well as a monograph on the topic (Wylleman, Lavallee, & Alfermann, 1999). Recent review in the study area (Park et al., 2013) revealed that there have been 126 studies published in English, and among them, only 10 studies were published before 1990. The number of publications increased from 80 to 126 between 2000 and 2010. Park et al. (2013) also highlighted that the study area has been developed through examining athletes from various types of sports, a wide-range of age, and different cultural backgrounds.

Theoretical Perspectives on Career Transition

Since the onset of interest in the area of career transition for elite athletes, attempts have been made to provide a formal conceptualization of this process. Most investigators have drawn on retirement research outside of sport and tried to apply these models to the concerns of athletes.

Thanatology

Rosenberg (1982) originally suggested that retirement from sports is akin to social death, which is characterized as social isolation and rejection from the former in-group. This explanation has received support from anecdotal and fictitious accounts of athletes who have experienced similar reactions on retirement (Deford, 1981). The concept of social death also has, however, been widely criticized and there has been little empirical support for this position (Blinde & Greendorfer, 1985).

Social Gerontology

This view focuses on aging and considers life satisfaction as being dependent upon characteristics of the sports experience. Six social gerontological perspectives have been offered as the most applicable to sports retirement (Greendorfer & Blinde, 1985; Rosenberg, 1982). Disengagement theory (Cummings, Dean, Newell, & McCaffrey, 1960) posits that the person and society withdraw for the good of both, enabling younger people to enter the workforce and retired individuals to enjoy their remaining years. Subculture theory (Rose, 1962) asserts that people can be less active and well adjusted during retirement even if their situation is different from overall social norms. Activity theory (Havighurst & Albrecht, 1953) suggests that lost roles are replaced by new ones, so that people may maintain their overall level of activity. Continuity theory (Atchley, 1980) states that, if people have different roles, the time and energy from the earlier role may be reallocated to the remaining roles. Exchange theory (Homans, 1961) was developed to explain how aging individuals rearrange their activities so that their remaining energy generates maximum return. Finally, social breakdown theory (Kuypers & Bengston, 1973) proposes that retirement becomes associated with negative evaluation, which causes individuals to withdraw from the activity and internalize the negative evaluation.

Despite their intuitive appeal, these views have been criticized as inadequate when applied to athletic retirement. Specifically, early research by Arviko (1976), Greendorfer and Blinde (1985), and Lerch (1982) provided little support for any of the social gerontological approaches.

Retirement as Transition

A criticism of both thanatology and social gerontology theories is that they view retirement as a singular, abrupt event (Blinde & Greendorfer, 1985). In contrast, other researchers characterize retirement as a transition or process that involves development through life (Stambulova, 1994; Wylleman & Lavallee, 2004). Greendorfer and Blinde (1985) suggest that the focus should be on the continuation rather than the cessation of behaviors, the gradual alteration rather than relinquishment of goals and interests, and the emergence of few difficulties in adjustment.

Schlossberg's (1981) model of human adaptation to transition is one of the models most employed to investigate the athlete career transition process (e.g., Sinclair & Orlick, 1993; Swain, 1991). The model tries to explain all kinds of transitions that human beings experience during their life spans. Nowadays, researchers generally agree to see athletes' career transition as a process and findings from longitudinal studies also support this view (Lally, 2007; Park, Lavallee, & Tod, in press). Because of the lack of operational detail associated with the specific components as they relate to sport career transitions, the limitations of Schlossberg's model has also been discussed (e.g., Taylor & Ogilvie, 1994).

The Conceptual Model of Career Transition

To continue the evolutionary process in our understanding of career transition among elite athletes, Taylor and Ogilvie (1994) developed a conceptual model that attempted to integrate the theoretical and empirical investigations to date by incorporating aspects of earlier theorizing, taking into account the findings of previous empirical research, and considering their own applied work with athletes in career transition. What emerged was a model that addresses all relevant concerns from the initiation of career transition to its ultimate consequences (see Figure 23-1).

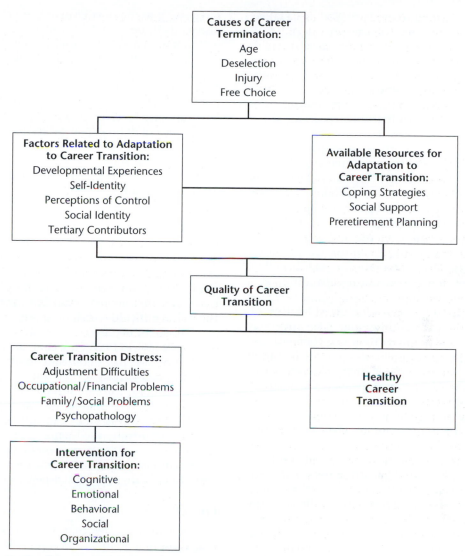

Figure 23-1 Conceptual model of adaptation to career transition

Stage 1: Causes of Career Termination

The causes for termination of an athletic career are found most frequently to be a function of four factors: age, deselection, the consequences of an injury, and free choice. These factors influence a variety of psychological, social, and physical issues that contribute to the likelihood of distress because of career transition.

Age

Age or, more specifically, the decline in performance because of advancing age, is a primary cause of retirement (e.g., Park, Tod, & Lavallee, 2012). The influence of age on career termination is a function of physiological, psychological, and social factors and has significant ramifications for both young and older athletes. For athletes competing in sports in which high-level performance occurs during adolescence, career termination may result when they are still teenagers. This will be particularly evident for those sports such as gymnastics in which puberty, and the accompanying physical changes, can restrict rather than contribute to motor development and performance. Similar difficulties with older athletes also are evident in sports such as baseball, football, and tennis, which require size, strength, and precise motor skills. Athletes' ability to continue to perform at an elite level depends on whether they can maintain their physical capabilities at a competitive level.

Age also has psychological influences on retirement. As athletes become older, they may lose their motivation to train and compete, and they may conclude that they have reached their competitive goals and/or their values may also change. (Cecić Erpič, Wylleman, & Zupančič, 2004). According to Cecić Erpič et al. (2004), finding life-long careers or becoming parents were reasons for Slovene athletes to leave their sporting careers.

Finally, age possesses a social element. "Aging" athletes, particularly those whose performances begin to diminish, can be devalued by fans, management, media, and other athletes. Sinclair and Orlick (1993) reported that elite-amateur athletes who retired because of declining competitive performance tended to have the most difficulties with loss of status and a lack of self-confidence.

Deselection

One of the most significant contributors to career termination is the nature of the selection process that occurs at every level of competitive sports (Munroe & Albinson, 1996). This process, which follows a Darwinian "survival of the fittest" philosophy, selects only those athletes capable of progressing to the next level of competition and disregards those who do not meet the necessary performance criteria. Organized youth programs still place the highest priority on winning and this same philosophy predominates throughout high school, university, and professional sport. Data indicates that only one in 10,000 scholastic athletes receives college scholarships and only 1 percent of those play professionally. Moreover, the typical career length of a professional player in sports such as football, basketball, and baseball is only 4 to 5 years (National Collegiate Athletic Association, 2003).

Injury

Research has shown that the occurrence of serious or chronic injury often forces athletes to end their athletic careers prematurely (Kadlcik & Flemr, 2008). Furthermore, it has been suggested that severe injuries may result in a variety of psychological difficulties including fear, anxiety, loss of self-esteem, depression, and substance abuse (Ogilvie & Howe, 1982; Park et al., in press).

Injury also has significant ramifications as retired athletes consider post-sport careers. It is not uncommon for elite athletes to leave their sport permanently disabled to varying degrees. These physical disabilities can influence retired athletes negatively, producing a range of psychological and emotional problems. Injuries sustained during their athletic careers also may limit them in their choices of new careers.

Free choice

Research has indicated that free choice is a common cause of retirement among elite amateur and professional athletes (Cecić Erpič et al., 2004). The impetus to end a career by choice is the most desirable of causes of retirement, because the decision resides wholly within the control of the athlete. Athletes choose to end their careers voluntarily for a variety of personal, social, and sport reasons. Athletes may choose to embark on a new direction in their lives and/or experience a change in values, motivations, and the desire to pursue new interests and goals (Cecić Erpič et al., 2004). For example, athletes in career transition may wish to spend more time with family and friends or seek out a new social milieu in which to immerse themselves. Lastly, athletes may have reached their sport-related goals or found their sports participation was no longer enjoyable and rewarding (Park et al., in press).

Athletic careers that end voluntarily do not necessarily preclude athletes from having transition difficulties. Kerr and Dacyshyn (2000) reported that some athletes who chose to retire described their retirement as difficult. The findings suggested that "voluntary" retirement is not always truly voluntary because some athletes argued that although their retirement decision was made by themselves, the main reasons for their sport career end were due to chronic injuries or bad relationships with coaches (Park et al., in press).

Finally, researchers (Park et al., 2013; Wylleman, Alfermann, & Lavallee, 2004) in athletes' career transition have also emphasized a need of examining differences in various kinds of retirement such as drop-out from sport or burn out in sport (see Chapter 21) rather than focus on voluntariness of retirement because the processes of drop-out and burn out could influence the quality of athletes' career transitions.

Athletes' retirement decision-making process

Some researchers (Cecić Erpič et al., 2004; Fernandez et al., 2006; Park et al., 2012) have interest in examining athletes' retirement decision-making process because it is an important part of overall retirement process. Kerr and Dacyshyn (2000) highlighted that athletes' retirement decision-making could be multidimensional and complex, and Park et al. (2012) revealed that athletes' experiences during their retirement decision-making process influence the quality of their career transition. For example, athletes tended to follow certain steps during the decision-making process,

including pre-decision, actual decision making and preparation for post-sport lives, and actual leaving from their sport. Athletes' decision was influenced by both internal (degree of athletic identity, perceived achievement in their sport) and external (post-sport career opportunities, team situation, and contract) variables rather than just reasons for their sport career end. In addition, athletes tended to develop their short-term and long-term plans during their decision-making process.

Other Causes of Career Termination

Other factors have been either suggested or reported to contribute to career termination. These causes include family reasons (Cecić Erpič et al., 2004), problems with coaches or the sports organization (Fernandez, Stephan, & Fouquereau, 2006; Park et al., 2012), and financial difficulties (Lavallee, Grove, & Gordon, 1997).

Stage 2: Factors Related to Adaptation to Career Transition

Athletes experiencing career transition may face a wide range of psychological, social, financial, and occupational changes. The extent of these changes and how athletes perceive them may dictate the quality of the adaptation they experience as a function of their retirement.

Developmental contributors. The presence and quality of adaptation to career transition may depend on developmental experiences that occurred since the inception of their athletic careers. The nature of these experiences will affect the emergence of self-perceptions and interpersonal skills that will influence how athletes adapt to retirement.

The often single-minded pursuit of excellence that accompanies elite sports participation has potential psychological and social dangers, and this quest is rooted in the earliest experiences athletes have in their youth sports participation. The personal investment in and the pursuit of elite athletic success, although a worthy goal, may lead to a restricted development.

Although there is substantial evidence demonstrating the debilitating effects of deselection in young athletes' self-esteem (e.g., Alfermann, 1995; Webb, Nasco, Riley, & Headrick, 1998), little consideration has been given to changing this process in a healthier direction. Most organized youth programs still appear to place the highest priority on winning with less concern for the positive development of young athletes.

To alleviate these difficulties at their source, the adoption of a more holistic approach to sports development can be beneficial early in the lives of athletes (Petitpas & Champagne, 2000; Wylleman & Lavallee, 2004). This perspective relies on a primary prevention model that emphasizes preventing problems prior to their occurrence (Pearson & Petitpas, 1990). The first step in the prevention process is to engender in parents and coaches involved in youth sport a belief that long-term personal and social development is more important than short-term athletic success (Ogilvie, 1987).

Self-identity. Most fundamental of the psychological issues that influence adaptation to career transition is the degree to which athletes define their self-worth in terms of their participation and achievement in sports (Lally, 2007). Athletes who have been immersed in their sport to the exclusion of other activities will have a self-identity that is composed almost exclusively of their sports involvement (Brewer, Van Raalte, & Petitpas, 2000). Without the input from their sport, retired athletes have little to support their sense of self-worth (Stephan, Bilard, Ninot, & Dilignieres, 2003).

Athletes who are disproportionately invested in their sports participation may be characterized as "unidimensional" people, in which their self-concept does not extend far beyond the limits of their sport (Warriner & Lavallee, 2008). These athletes often have few options in which

they can gain meaning and fulfillment from activities outside their sport (Park et al., in press). A one-year longitudinal study by Stephan and colleagues (2003) found that perceived physical condition, physical self-worth, and global self-esteem decreased during the first six months of transition out of elite sport. This was subsequently followed by a period of increase in these dimensions, as well as in perceived sports competence and physical strength.

It has been suggested that athletes with overly developed athletic identities are less prepared for post-sport careers (Baillie & Danish, 1992), have restricted career and educational plans, and typically experience retirement from sport as something very important that has been lost and will be hard to recover (Lally, 2007). Grove, Lavallee, and Gordon (1997) found that athletes who overly identified with their sports careers were most vulnerable to transition distress, and how effectively athletes adapted their identities in a healthy way following retirement is necessary to a positive reaction to distress over career termination.

Kerr and Dacyshyn (2000) suggest that the demands athletic retirement places on adolescent athletes can be excessive and destructive. Instead of adolescence being a time of identity formation (Erikson, 1963), it can actually be deconstructed, which may slow the identity formation process. Researchers (Kerr & Dacyshyn, 2000; Lavallee & Robinson, 2007) also emphasized that transition of young female athletes can be particularly difficult. Retirement at an early age, which is common among female athletes such as gymnasts, figure skaters, and swimmers, inhibits their ability to try out different roles and relationships, interferes with the development of autonomy and decision-making skills (Chickering & Reisser, 1993), and can distort perceptions related to body weight, body image, and eating habits (Stephan et al., 2003). They conclude that these issues have the cumulative effect of interfering with the healthy development of a mature self-identity in young female athletes.

Perceived control. Central to the issue of perceived control in career transition is whether athletes chose to leave their sport or were forced to retire (Kerr & Dacyshyn, 2000). The degree of perceived control that the athletes have with respect to the end of their careers also can impact how they respond to career transition (Park et al., 2013). The absence of control related to an event so intrinsically connected to athletes' self-identities may create a situation that is highly aversive and threatening (Lavallee & Robinson, 2007).

Both early and contemporary research examining Olympic-caliber and professional athletes has indicated that the causes of retirement for many athletes were beyond their control and that they experienced a decrease in their sense of personal control following retirement (Mihovilovic, 1968; McKenna & Thomas, 2007). Although this issue has not been addressed extensively in the sports literature, there is considerable research from the areas of clinical, social, and physiological psychology demonstrating that perceived control is related to many areas of human functioning including a sense of self-competence and the interpretation of self and other information. In addition, perceptions of control may influence individuals' feelings of helplessness, motivation, physiological changes, and self-confidence. Loss of control has been associated with a variety of pathologies including depression, anxiety, substance abuse, and dissociative disorders.

Social identity. The diversity of athletes' social identities can affect their adaptation to career transition (Gorbett, 1985). Researchers have associated retirement with a loss of status and social identity (Tuckman & Lorge, 1953). McPherson (1980) suggests that many athletes define themselves in terms of their popular status, although this recognition is typically short-lived. As a result, retired athletes may question their self-worth and feel the need to regain the lost public esteem (Stephan et al., 2003).

In addition, athletes whose socialization process occurred primarily in the sports environment may be characterized as "role restricted" (Park et al., in press). That is, these athletes have only learned to assume certain social roles specific to the athletic setting and are able to interact with others only within the narrow context of sports. As a result, their ability to assume other roles following retirement may be severely inhibited (Blinde & Greendorfer, 1985). Previous research findings (Kerr & Dacyshyn, 2000; Lally, 2007) indicate that athletes with a broad-based social identity that includes family, friendship, and educational and occupational components demonstrate better adaptation following sports career termination.

Tertiary contributors. In addition to the above intrapersonal factors, personal, social, and environmental variables may influence athletes' adaptation to retirement. These factors may be viewed as potential stressors whose presence will likely exacerbate the primary adaptive factors just discussed (Coakley, 1983).

Socioeconomic status may influence the adaptation process (Conzelmann & Nagel, 2003). Athletes who are financially dependent on their sports participation and possess few skills to earn a living outside of sport or have limited financial resources to fall back on may perceive retirement as more threatening and, as a result, may evidence distress (Koukouris, 1994; Lotysz & Short, 2004).

It has also been argued that marital status (Fernandez et al., 2006), competitive levels (Leung, Carre, & Fu, 2005), and age (Cecić Erpič et al., 2004) could affect the adaptation process because of differences in sport career achievement, degree of social support from partners, and timing of starting new careers. These factors are likely to be most significant when interacting with socioeconomic status and preretirement planning. The health of athletes at the time of retirement will further affect the quality of the adaptation (Kadlcik & Flemr, 2008).

Finally, as has been discussed in Chapter 18, similar to other areas of sport psychology, gender and cultural considerations could also influence athletes' quality of career transitions, in terms of role changes, post-sport career opportunities, and differences in sport context (Stambulova & Alfermann, 2009).

Stage 3: Available Resources for Adaptation to Career Transition

Athletes' adaptation to career transition depends largely on the resources they have available to surmount the difficulties that arise. Two of the most important factors that can influence people's ability to respond effectively to these problems include coping skills (Lazarus & Folkman, 1984; Meichenbaum, 1996) and social support (Rees & Freeman, 2012. In addition, recent review showed that another valuable resource, preretirement planning, may significantly influence adaptation to career transition (Park et al., 2013).

Coping strategies. During the course of retirement, athletes are faced with dramatic changes in their personal, social, and occupational lives. These changes will affect them cognitively, emotionally, and behaviorally. The quality of the adaptation to career transition athletes experience will depend on the manner in which they respond to these changes. The availability of effective coping strategies may facilitate this process and reduce the likelihood of difficulties. Research findings (e.g., Park et al., in press) reported that finding another focus of interest to replace their sports participation, keeping busy, maintaining their training and exercise regimens, talking with someone who listens, and staying in touch with their sport and friends in their sport were effective coping strategies for facilitating the transition process.

Cognitively, retiring athletes must alter their perceptions related to the career transition process, specifically with respect to self-identity, perceived control, and social identity (Lally, 2007). Athletes can use cognitive restructuring (Lazarus, 1972) and mental imagery (Smith, 1980) to reorient their thinking in a more positive direction, self-instructional training (Meichenbaum, 1996) to improve attention and problem solving, and goal setting to provide direction and motivation in their post-athletic careers (Bruning & Frew, 1987). These techniques have been used successfully to enhance adaptation in a variety of populations and activities (Meichenbaum & Cameron, 1973).

Similarly, relevant techniques could be used for emotional and physiological stressors.

Specifically, athletes in transition could employ anger and anxiety strategies such as time-out (Browning, 1983), relaxation training (May, House, & Kovacs, 1982), and health, exercise, and nutritional counseling (Bruning & Frew, 1987) to alleviate these difficulties. Finally, a regimen of behavior modification could deal with overt manifestations of distress associated with career transition. Techniques such as assertiveness training (Lange & Jakubowski, 1976), time management training (Bruning & Frew, 1987), and skills assessment and development (Taylor, 1987) could be effective in overcoming behavioral difficulties caused by retirement.

Previous findings indicated that elite athletes' commonly used coping strategies included seeking social support, searching for other interest outside sport, avoidance, keeping themselves busy, and acceptance (Park et al., 2013). Other studies (Lally, 2007; Park et al., in press) have also found that athletes who proactively diminished their athletic identity prior to retirement were able to adjust better following their career termination. This evidence, suggesting that athletes in transitions may employ various coping strategies as a function of their self-identity, provides a link between Step 2 and Step 3 of the present model.

Social support. Because of athletes' total psychological and social immersion in the sports world, the majority of their friends, acquaintances, and other associations are found in the sports environment and their social activities often revolve around their athletic lives (Petitpas & Champagne, 2000). Thus, athletes' primary social support system often will be derived from their athletic involvement (Park et al., in press).

When the athletes' careers end, they are no longer an integral part of the team or organization. Consequently, the social support that they received previously may no longer be present. Stephan and Brewer (2007) reported that because social identity is a big part of athletic identity, when athletes retire from their sport, missing the social aspects of their sport could be a source of difficulties during career transition. Moreover, in terms of their restricted social identity and the absence of alternative social support systems, they may become isolated, lonely, and unsustained socially, thus leading to significant distress (Lally, 2007). Therefore, nowadays, researchers have highlighted the importance of roles and influences of athletes' entourages in assisting athletes' career transition (Park et al., 2012).

Roles and influences of athletes' entourages and organizational culture in retirement from sport

Researchers have emphasized the importance of roles and influences of athletes' entourages and organizational culture in retirement from sport (Park et al., in press). Previous research (Chow, 2001; Kerr & Dacyshyn, 2000) showed that a good coach–athlete relationship is positively associated with the quality of athletes' career transitions because athletes tended to consider their coaches as mentors who had the same experiences as them and tried to get advice from the coaches. In addition, Park et al. (in press) revealed that athletes who had supportive coaches, families, and friends prepared for their post-sport lives better than those who did not have supportive close others. In regard to organizational culture, only a few study findings (Fernandez et al., 2006; Fleuriel & Vincent, 2009) have suggested relationships between organizational influences and the quality of athletes' career transitions. Fernandez et al. (2006) revealed that conflict between athletes and organizations could be one of the reasons for their retirement. Moreover, sport organizations might involve national team selection, which could lead athletes to experience forced retirement because of being cut from the team. Fleuriel and Vincent (2009) argued that organizations' lack of support could hinder elite athletes in the process of social, professional, and family reintegration after their retirement.

Preretirement planning. Of the available resources that are being discussed, preretirement planning appears to have the broadest influence on the quality of the career transition process (Murphy, 1995). Preretirement planning may include a variety of activities including continuing education, occupational and investment opportunities, and social networking. As a result, preretirement planning may significantly affect most of the factors previously discussed that are related to the adaptation process. For example, preretirement planning has been found to broaden an athlete's self-identity, enhance perceptions of control, and diversify his or her social identity (Lavallee & Robinson, 2007). Findings also indicated that athletes who had planned ahead showed feelings of comfort and seemed to have better adjustment for their post-sport career (Warriner & Lavallee, 2008). As for the tertiary contributors, socioeconomic status, financial dependency on the sport, and post-athletic occupational potential would all be positively influenced. Despite these benefits, a common theme that emerges from the literature on retirement outside of sports is the resistance on the part of individuals to plan for their lives after the end of their careers (Petitpas & Champagne, 2000). Gorely, Lavallee, Bruce, & Teale (2001) found that athletes often do not consider their career termination until it draws near. Yet, it is likely that this denial of the inevitable will have serious, potentially negative, and long-term implications for the athletes. A wide range of difficulties has been reported because of athletes' resistance to preretirement planning.

Structured preretirement planning that involves reading materials and workshops (Anderson & Morris, 2000) is a valuable opportunity for athletes to plan for and work toward meaningful lives following retirement. In addition, effective money management and long-term financial planning can provide athletes with financial stability following the conclusion of their careers (Menkehorst & van den Berg, 1997).

Increasingly, the incorporation of preretirement planning is becoming a part of collegiate, elite-amateur, and professional organizations (Sinclair & Hackfort, 2000). Empirical research findings (Redmond, Gordon, & Chambers, 2007; Torregrosa, Mateos, Sanchez, & Cruz, 2007) indicate that providing support programs helps athletes to plan their post-sport career and develop their life skills. The research clarifying the extent to which elite athletes use these services indicates that only a small proportion take advantage of them, however (Gorely et al., 2001).

Stage 4: Quality of Career Transition

Based on the present model to this point, it may be concluded that career transition from sports will not necessarily cause a distressful reaction on the part of athletes (Lally, 2007). Rather, the quality of athletes' adaptation to career transition will depend on the previous steps of the retirement process. It is at the point of retiring that the athlete's reaction to career transition will become evident. A variety of psychological, social, and environmental factors will determine the nature of the athlete's response. Specifically, the presence or absence of the contributing variables described in the early steps of the model will dictate whether athletes undergo a healthy transition following retirement or experience distress in response to the end of their competitive career.

Park et al. (2013) revealed that among 126 published studies related to athletes' career transition out of sport, participants from 86 studies discussed career transition difficulties or negative emotions or psychological responses such as identity crisis, feelings of loss, and distress. In addition, findings (Douglas & Carless, 2009; Fleuriel & Vincent, 2009; Wippert & Wippert, 2008) also indicated that some of the athletes experienced maladaptive reactions to their retirement such as alcohol dependence, increased smoking, committing suicide, drug use, or participation in criminal activities. The emergence of distress among elite-amateur and professional athletes is likely because of the significantly greater life investment in their sports and their commitment to their sports participation as a career into adulthood.

Students' exercise

Real World Example

For the exercise, find an article from a newspaper, magazine and/or the Internet within the last five years that focuses on the retirement of a professional athlete from any sport reflecting the diversity of people in sport. Consider the factors related to the athlete's adjustment to retirement that you feel are important in the case. These may include causes of career termination, factors related to adaptation to career termination, available resources for adaptation to career transition, and quality of career transition.

Stage 5: Intervention for Career Transition

Career transition may be characterized as a complex interaction of stressors. Whether the stressors are financial, social, psychological, or physical, their effects may produce some form of distress when athletes are confronted with the end of their careers. Despite the best efforts made in the prevention of career transition distress, difficulties may still arise when the reality of the end of an athletic career is recognized. The experience of career transition crises may adversely affect athletes cognitively, emotionally, behaviorally, and socially. As a result, it is important to address each of these areas in an active and constructive manner.

Unfortunately, as discussed earlier, there are significant organizational obstacles to the proper treatment of career transition difficulties (Sinclair & Hackfort, 2000; Thomas & Ermler, 1988). In particular, the limited involvement of sport psychologists at the elite level, where problems are most likely to occur, inhibits their ability to provide for the career transition needs of athletes. Also, the team psychologists typically associated with national governing bodies, collegiate teams, or professional organizations seldom have the opportunity to develop an extended relationship with team members. This limited contact rarely presents an opportunity to discuss issues related to career transition. Also, because retired athletes are no longer a part of a sports organization, treatment of the athletes may not be seen as being within the purview of the organization's psychologist (Sinclair & Hackfort, 2000). The retiring athletes themselves also may present their own obstacles to intervention. Surveys of former world-class amateur athletes indicate that they do not perceive personal counseling as a useful coping strategy during the career transition process (e.g., Sinclair & Orlick, 1993).

The treatment of distress related to career transition may occur at a variety of levels. As discussed earlier, the changes that result from retirement may detrimentally impact a person psychologically, emotionally, behaviorally, and socially. As a consequence, it is necessary for the sport psychologist to address each of these areas in the intervention process.

Perhaps the most important task in the transition process is to assist athletes in maintaining their sense of self-worth when establishing a new self-identity. The goal of this process is to adapt their perceptions about themselves and their world to their new roles in a way that will be maximally functional. The sport psychologist can assist them in identifying desirable non-sport identities and experiencing feelings of value and self-worth in this new personal conception. Van Raalte and Andersen (2007) have explained that people intimately involved in sport (sport psychologists included) may have a prejudice toward sport relative to other possible activities or goals. Because this bias may influence how sport psychologists listen to, interpret, and formulate athlete cases, they suggest that practitioners need to carefully manage bias.

Also, sport psychologists can aid athletes in working through any emotional distress they may experience during retirement (Grove, Lavallee, Gordon, & Harvey, 1998). Specifically, they can provide the athletes with the opportunity to express feelings of doubt, concern, or frustration relative to the end of their careers (Gorbett, 1985). Group counseling among retiring and

retired athletes may help them to gain empathy from each other because they may share similar concerns and difficulties (Park, Lavallee, & Tod, 2012). Lavallee (2005) also has evaluated the effectiveness of a life development intervention on career transition adjustment in retired professional athletes. Intervention and control groups were recruited for this study, both of which contained recently retired male professional soccer players. Results revealed significant post-intervention treatment group differences on career transition adjustment in favor of the life development intervention.

On a manifest level, the sport psychologist can help the athletes cope with the stress of the transition process (Gorbett, 1985). Traditional therapeutic strategies such as cognitive restructuring (Garfield & Bergin, 1978), stress management (Meichenbaum & Jaremko, 1983), and emotional expression (Yalom, 1980) can be used in this process. It also has been recommended that Shapiro's (1995) eye movement desensitization and reprocessing (EMDR) can be employed as a psychomotor technique to ameliorate undesirable beliefs and images associated with career-ending injuries (Sime, 1998). Also, athletes can be shown that the skills they used to master their sport can be used as effectively in overcoming the challenges of a new career and lifestyle (Meichenbaum & Jaremko, 1983).

Grove et al. (1998) have adapted Horowitz's (1986) model of coping with loss to retirement from sport. This perspective stresses a working-through process in the form of the construction of a narrative about the career termination experience, termed *account-making*. This account enables athletes to better understand their career transition, allows them to gain closure on their athletic careers, and encourages the adoption of an evolving self- and social identity that will foster growth in their post-athletic lives. Preliminary research indicates that account-making was directly related to athletes' success in coping with career termination (Lavallee et al., 1997).

Finally, the professional can help athletes at a social level. This goal may be accomplished by having athletes explore ways of broadening their social identity and role repertoire (Stephan

& Brewer, 2007). Additionally, athletes can be encouraged to expand their social support system to individuals and groups outside of the sports arena. The use of group therapy and the articulation of the athletes' potential social networks can be especially useful in aiding them in this process. Wolff and Lester (1989) propose a three-stage therapeutic process comprised of listening and confrontation, cognitive therapy, and vocational guidance to aid athletes in coping with their loss of self-identity and assist them in establishing a new identity.

Little empirical research has examined the significant factors in this process. Outside of sport, Roskin (1982) found that implementing a package of cognitive, affective, and social support interventions within didactic and small-group settings significantly reduced depression and anxiety among a high-stress group of individuals composed partly of retirees. Advances in the measurement of career transitions in sport in recent years, however, can assist practitioners, including the development of the *Athletes' Retirement Decision Inventory* (Fernandez et al., 2006), *Retirement Sports Survey* (Alfermann, Stambulova, & Zemaityte, 2004), *British Athletes Lifestyle Assessment*

Needs in Career and Education (BALANCE; Lavallee & Wylleman, 1999) *Scale, Athlete Retirement Questionnaire* (Sinclair & Orlick, 1993), *Australian Athletes Career Transition Inventory* (Hawkins & Blann, 1993), and *Professional Athletes Career Transition Inventory* (Blann & Zaichkowsky, 1989).

Intervention at the organizational level also can be a useful means of facilitating the career transition process. As indicated earlier, many elite-amateur and professional organizations offer some form of preretirement and career transition assistance. Reece, Wilder, and Mahanes (1996) suggest that such programs should emphasize the transferability of skills from sport to a new career. They further highlight the importance of identifying specific transferable skills and successful role models, and clarifying interests, values, and goals that will promote an effective career transition. Sinclair and Orlick (1993) recommend that sports organizations can facilitate the transition process by continuing financial support for a short time following retirement, encourage sports organizations to stay in contact with retired athletes, offer seminars on career transition issues, and establish a resource center for athletes in transition.

Summary

This chapter has reviewed the relevant literature pertaining to career transition among athletes. From this overview, several conclusions can be drawn. First, the extant research suggests that career transition difficulties are more likely to emerge with elite-amateur and professional athletes than with scholastic or collegiate athletes. This finding appears to be because of the greater ego involvement and personal investment of the former group of athletes and because transition from world-class and professional sports participation typically occurs outside of the normal developmental process. Second, distress because of career transition will not necessarily occur. Rather, problems emerge because of a variety of developmental, psychological, and social factors including early life experiences, coping strategies, perceptions of control, self and social identities, social support, and preretirement planning. Third, addressing career transition issues can begin at the earliest stages of sports participation. This process involves having parents, coaches, and youth sports administrators create an environment that will enable young athletes' sports involvement to be a meaningful vehicle that will engender healthy personal and social development. Finally, despite the best efforts to eliminate distress that may arise because of career transition, it may still occur when athletes fully recognize that their sports careers are over. This distress can manifest itself psychologically, emotionally, behaviorally, and socially. It is important that each of these areas is addressed directly and constructively by a trained professional.

Study Questions

1. Briefly describe theoretical perspectives in athletes' career transition research area.
2. Briefly describe the causes of career termination and indicate how each factor would affect athletes' adaptation to career transition.
3. Discuss the most prevalent factors to adaptation to career transition.
4. Discuss the interpersonal factors that affect athletes' reactions to career transition and how they are related to the athletes' adaptation.
5. Indicate the role that early development has on athletes' reactions to career transition and give an example of an ideal upbringing for healthy transition.
6. Describe the three primary resources available to athletes to help them during the career transition process and give examples of how they influence retiring athletes.
7. Discuss the difficulties that retiring athletes most often experience and what types of athletes are most likely to have these difficulties.
8. Provide the primary areas that sport psychologists must address in working with a retiring athlete and describe some of the techniques that could be used.

Situation Study

Sarah is a 25-year-old softball player who was informed earlier in the week that she was not selected for the Olympic Team. In terms of her deselection, she does not think that it is fair that the selectors suddenly decided that she could no longer do what she had trained so long and hard for. Sarah feels very frustrated and angry because this was going to be her first Olympics, and she is also disappointed that she will not compete alongside her teammates, who are some of her best friends. She also is concerned about what she is going to do next, as her philosophy has always been that she shouldn't concentrate on anything other than softball if she wanted to be the best and retain her place on the team.

1. *Based on the model presented in this chapter, what kind of reaction might you expect from her and why?*
2. *What are the primary issues that might affect the quality of her retirement?*
3. *What could she have done to alter her reaction?*
4. *Create an intervention plan to help Sarah through her transition.*

References

Alfermann, D. (1995). Career transitions of elite athletes: Drop-out and retirement. In R. Vanfraechem-Raway & Y. Vanden Auweele (Eds.), *Proceedings of the 9th European Congress of Sport Psychology* (pp. 828–833). Brussels: European Federation of Sports Psychology.

Alfermann, D., Stambulova, N., & Zemaityte, A. (2004). Reactions to sports career termination: A cross-cultural comparison of German, Lithuanian, and Russian athletes. *Psychology of Sport and Exercise, 5,* 61–75.

Anderson, D., & Morris, T. (2000) Athlete lifestyle programs. In D. Lavallee and P. Wylleman (Eds.), *Career transitions in sport: International perspectives* (pp. 59–81). Morgantown, WV: Fitness Information Technology.

Arviko, I. (1976). *Factors influencing the job and life satisfaction of retired baseball players.* Unpublished master's thesis, University of Waterloo, Ontario.

Atchley, R. C. (1980). *The social forces in later life.* Belmont, CA: Wadsworth.

Baillie, P. H. F., & Danish, S. J. (1992). Understanding the career transition of athletes. *The Sport Psychologist, 6,* 77–98.

Blann, F. W., & Zaichkowsky, L. (1989). *National Hockey League and Major League Baseball players' post sports career transition surveys.* Final report prepared for the National Hockey League Players' Association, USA.

Blinde, E. M., & Greendorfer, S. L. (1985). A reconceptualization of the process of leaving the role of competitive athlete. *International Review of Sport Sociology, 20,* 87–94.

Bradley, B. (1976). *Life on the run.* New York: Quadrangle/The New York Times.

Brewer, B. W., Van Raalte, J. L., & Petitpas, A. J. (2000) Self-identity issues in sport career transitions. In D. Lavallee & P. Wylleman (Eds.), *Career transitions in sport: International perspectives* (pp. 29–43). Morgantown, WV: Fitness Information Technology.

Browning, E. R. (1983). A memory pacer for improving stimulus generalization. *Journal of Autism and Developmental Disorders, 13,* 427–432.

Bruning, N. S., & Frew, D. R. (1987). Effects of exercise, relaxation, and management skills on physiological stress indicators: A field experiment. *Journal of Applied Psychology, 72,* 515–521.

Cecić Erpič, S., Wylleman, P., & Zupančič, M. (2004). The effect of athletic and non-athletic factors on the sports career termination process. *Psychology of Sport and Exercise, 5,* 45–59.

Chickering, A., & Reisser, L. (1993). *Education and identity* (2nd ed.). San Francisco: Jossey-Bass.

Chow, B. C. (2001). Moving on? Elite Hong Kong female athletes and retirement from competitive sport. *Women in Sport and Physical Activity Journal, 1,* 47–81.

Coakley, J. J. (1983). Leaving competitive sport: Retirement or rebirth. *Quest, 35,* 1–11.

Conzelmann, A., & Nagel, S. (2003). Professional careers of the German Olympic athletes. *International Review for the Sociology of Sport, 38,* 259–280.

Cummings, E., Dean, L. R., Newell, D. S., & McCaffrey, I. (1960). Disengagement: A tentative theory of aging. *Sociometry, 23,* 23–35.

Deford, F. (1981). *Everybody's All-American*. New York: The Viking Press.

Douglas, K., & Carless, D. (2009). Abandoning the performance narrative: Two women's stories of transition from professional sport. *Journal of Applied Psychology, 21*, 213–230.

Erikson. E. (1963). *Childhood and society*. New York: Norton.

Fernandez, A., Stephan, Y., & Fouquereau, E. (2006). Assessing reasons for sports career termination: Developing the Athletes' Retirement Decision Inventory. *Psychology of Sport and Exercise, 7*, 407–421.

Fleuriel, S., & Vincent, J. (2009). The quest for a successful career change among elite athletes in France: A case study of a French rugby player. *Leisure Studies, 28*, 173–188.

Garfield, S., & Bergin, A. (1978). *Handbook of psychotherapy and behavior change: An empirical analysis* (2nd ed.). New York: Wiley.

Gorbett, F. J. (1985). Psycho-social adjustment of athletes to retirement. In L. K. Bunker, R. J. Rotella, & A. Reilly (Eds.), *Sport psychology: Psychological considerations in maximizing sport performance* (pp. 288–294). Ithaca, NY: Mouvement Publications.

Gorely, T., Lavallee, D., Bruce, D., & Teale, B. (2001). An Evaluation of the Athlete Career and Education Program. *Athletic Academic Journal, 15*, 11–21.

Greendorfer, S. L., & Blinde, E. M. (1985). "Retirement" from intercollegiate sport: Theoretical and empirical considerations. *Sociology of Sport Journal, 2*, 101–110.

Grove, J. R., Lavallee, D., & Gordon, S. (1997). Coping with retirement from sport: The influence of athletic identity. *Journal of Applied Sport Psychology, 9*, 191–203.

Grove, J. R., Lavallee, D., Gordon, S., & Harvey, J. H. (1998). Account-making: A model of understanding and resolving distressful reactions to retirement from sport. *The Sport Psychologist, 12*, 52–67.

Haerle, R. K., Jr. (1975). Career patterns and career contingencies of professional baseball players: An occupational analysis. In D. Ball & J. Loy (Eds.), *Sport and social order* (pp. 461–519). Reading, MA: Addison-Wesley.

Havighurst, R. J., & Albrecht, R. (1953). *Older people*. New York: Longmans, Green.

Hawkins, K., & Blann, F. W. (1993). *Athlete/coach career development and transition*. Canberra: Australian Sports Commission.

Hill, P., & Lowe, B. (1974). The inevitable metathesis of the retiring athlete. *International Review of Sport Sociology, 4*, 5–29.

Homans, G. (1961). *Social behavior: Its elementary forms*. New York: Harcourt Brace Jovanovich.

Horowitz, M. J. (1986). *Stress response syndromes* (2nd ed.). Northvale, NJ: Jason Aronson.

International Olympic Committee (no publication date). Elite athletes: The IOC athlete career program [Internet; accessed 2013, April]. Retrieved from http://www.olympic.org/en/content/Olympic-Athletes/Elite-Athletes/.

Kadlcik, J., & Flemr, L. (2008). Athletic career termination model in the Czech Republic: A qualitative exploration. *International Review for the Sociology of Sport, 43*, 251–269.

Kerr, G., & Dacyshyn, A. (2000). The retirement experiences of elite, female gymnasts. *Journal of Applied Sport Psychology, 12,* 115–133.

Koukouris, K. (1994). Constructed case studies: athletes' perspectives of disengaging from organized competitive sport. *Sociology of Sport Journal, 11,* 114–139.

Kuypers, J. A., & Bengston, V. L. (1973). Social breakdown and competence: A model of normal aging. *Human Development, 16,* 181–120.

Lally, P. (2007). Identity and athletic retirement: A prospective study. *Psychology of Sport and Exercise, 8,* 85–99.

Lange, A. J., & Jakubowski, P. (1976). *Responsible assertive behavior.* Champaign, IL: Research Press.

Lavallee, D. (2005). The effect of a life development intervention on sport career transition adjustment. *The Sport Psychologist, 19,* 193–202.

Lavallee, D., Grove, J. R., & Gordon, S. (1997). The causes of career termination from sport and their relationship to post-retirement adjustment among elite-amateur athletes in Australia. *Australian Psychologist, 32,* 131–135.

Lavallee, D., & Robinson, H. (2007). In pursuit of an identity: A qualitative exploration of retirement from women's artistic gymnastics. *Psychology of Sport and Exercise, 8,* 119–141.

Lavallee, D., & Wylleman, P. (1999). Toward an instrument to assess the quality of adjustment to career transitions in sport: The British Athlete Lifestyle Assessment Needs in Career and Education (BALANCE) Scale. In V. Hosek, P. Tilinger, & L. Bilek (Eds.), *Psychology of sport and exercise: Enhancing the quality of life* (pp. 322–324). Prague: Charles University.

Lazarus, A. (1972). *Behavior theory and beyond.* New York: McGraw-Hill.

Lazarus, R. S., & Folkman, S. (1984). *Stress, appraisal, and coping.* New York: Springer.

Lerch, S. H. (1982). Athletic retirement as social death: An overview. In N. Theberge & P. Donnelly (Eds.), *Sport and the sociological imagination* (pp. 259–272). Fort Worth: Texas Christian University Press.

Leung, M. I., Carre, A., & Fu, F. H. (2005). Retirement rationale for Chinese female elite athletes. *International Journal of Eastern Sport and Physical Education, 3*(1), 87–94.

Lotysz, G. J., & Short, S. E. (2004). "What ever happened to. . . ." The effects of career termination from the National Football League. *Athletic Insight, 6,* 47–66.

May, E., House, W. C., & Kovacs, K. V. (1982). Group relaxation therapy to improve coping with stress. *Psychotherapy: Theory, research and practice, 19,* 102–109.

McKenna, J., & Thomas, H. (2007). Enduring injustice: A case study of retirement from professional rugby union. *Sport, Education, and Society, 12,* 19–35.

McPherson, B. P. (1980). Retirement from professional sport: The process and problems of occupational and psychological adjustment. *Sociological Symposium, 30,* 126–143.

Meichenbaum, D. (1996). Stress inoculation training for coping with stressors. *Clinical Psychologist, 49,* 4–7.

Meichenbaum, D., & Jaremko, M. (1983). *Stress reduction and prevention.* New York: Plenum.

Meichenbaum, D. H., & Cameron, R. (1973). Training schizophrenics to talk to themselves: A means of delivering attentional controls. *Behavior Therapy, 4,* 515–534.

Menkehorst, G. A. B. M., & van den Berg, F. J. (1997). Retirement from high-level competition: A new start. In R. Lidor & M. Bar-Eli (Eds.), *Proceedings of the IX World Congress on Sport Psychology* (pp. 487–489). Netanya, Israel: International Society of Sport Psychology.

Mihovilovic, M. (1968). The status of former sportsman. *International Review of Sport Sociology, 3,* 73–96.

Munroe, K. J., & Albinson, J. G., (1996, April). *Athletes' reactions immediately after and four months following involuntary disengagement at the varsity level.* Paper presented at the Joint Conference of the North American Society for the Psychology of Sport and Physical Activity and the Canadian Society for Psychomotor Learning and Sport Psychology, Ontario, Canada.

Murphy, S. M. (1995). Transition in competitive sport: Maximizing individual potential. In S. M. Murphy (Ed.), *Sport psychology interventions* (pp. 331–346). Champaign, IL: Human Kinetics.

National Collegiate Athletic Association (2003). *1981–2002 Sponsorship and participation report.* Indianapolis, IN: Author.

Ogilvie, B. C. (1987). Traumatic effects of sports career termination. *Proceedings of the National Conference of Sport Psychology, U.S. Olympic Committee.* Washington, DC.

Ogilvie, B. C., & Howe, M. (1982). Career crisis in sport. In T. Orlick, J. T. Partington, & J. H. Salmela (Eds.), *Proceedings of the Fifth World Congress of Sport Psychology* (pp. 176–183). Ottawa: Coaching Association of Canada.

Park, S., Lavallee, D., & Tod, D. (2012). The development of an athlete career transition support programme: A case study. *Qualitative Research in Psychology Bulletin, 13* (Spring), 11–19.

Park, S., Lavallee, D., & Tod, D. (2013). Athletes' career transition out of sport: a systematic review. *International Review of Sport and Exercise Psychology, 6,* 22–53.

Park, S., Lavallee, D., & Tod, D. (in press). A longitudinal qualitative exploration of elite Korean tennis players' career transition experiences. *Athletic Insight.*

Park, S., Tod, D., & Lavallee, D. (2012). Exploring the retirement from sport decision-making process based on the transtheoretical model. *Psychology of Sport and Exercise, 13,* 444–453.

Pearson, R., & Petitpas, A. (1990). Transition of athletes: Pitfalls and prevention. *Journal of Counseling and Development, 69,* 7–10.

Petitpas, A., & Champagne, D. (2000). Practical considerations in implementing sport career transition programs. In D. Lavallee & P. Wylleman (Eds.), *Career transitions in sport: International perspectives* (pp. 81–93). Morgantown, WV: Fitness Information Technology.

Piphers, M. (1994). *Reviving Ophelia: Saving the selves of adolescent girls.* New York: Ballantine Books.

Redmond, J., Gordon, S., & Chambers, T. (2007, September). *An in-depth evaluation of the Australian Athlete Career Education (ACE) program.* Paper presented at the 12th European Congress of Sport Psychology, Halkidiki, Greece.

Reece, S. D., Wilder, K. C., & Mahanes, J. R. (1996, October). *Program for athlete career transition*. Paper presented at Association for the Advancement of Applied Sport Psychology annual meetings, Williamsburg, Virginia.

Rees, T., & Freeman, P. (2012) Coping in sport through social support. In J. Thatcher, M. V. Jones, & D. Lavallee, (Eds.), *Coping and emotion in sport*. (2nd ed., pp. 102–117). New York: Routledge.

Rose, A. M. (1962). The subculture of aging: A topic for sociological research. *Gerontologist, 2*, 123–127.

Rosenberg, E. (1982). Athletic retirement as social death: Concepts and perspectives. In N. Theberge & P. Donnelly (Eds.), *Sport and the sociological imagination* (pp. 245–258). Fort Worth: Texas Christian University Press.

Roskin, M. (1982). Coping with life changes: A preventive social work approach. *American Journal of Community Psychology, 10*, 331–340.

Schlossberg, N. (1981). A model for analyzing human adaptation to transition. *Counseling Psychologist, 9*, 2–18.

Shapiro, F. (1995). *Eye movement desensitization and reprocessing: Basic principles, protocols, and procedures*. New York: Guilford Press.

Sime, W. E. (1998). Injury and career termination issues. In M. A. Thompson, R. A. Vernacchia, & W. E. Moore (Eds.), *Case studies in applied sport psychology: An educational approach* (pp. 195–226). Dubuque, IA: Kendall/Hunt.

Sinclair, D. A., & Hackfort, O. (2000). The role of the sport organization in the career transition process. In D. Lavallee & P. Wylleman (Eds.), *Career transitions in sport: International perspectives* (pp. 131–142). Morgantown, WV: Fitness Information Technology.

Sinclair, D. A., & Orlick, T. (1993). Positive transitions from high-performance sport. *Sport Psychologist, 7*, 138–150.

Stambulova, N. B. (1994). Developmental sports career investigations in Russia: A post-perestroika analysis. *Sport Psychologist, 8*, 221–237.

Stambulova, N., & Alfermann, D. (2009). Putting culture into context: Cultural and cross-cultural perspectives in career development and transition research and practice. *International Journal of Sport and Exercise Psychology, 7*, 292–308.

Stambulova, N., & Ryba, T. (Ed.). (2013). *Athletes' careers across the culture*. London: Routledge.

Stephan, Y., Bilard, J., Ninot, G., & Delignieres, D. (2003). Repercussions of transition out of elite sport on subjective well being: A one-year study. *Journal of Applied Sport Psychology, 15*, 354–371.

Stephan, Y., & Brewer, B. W. (2007). Perceived determinants of identification with the athlete role among elite competitors. *Journal of Applied Sport Psychology. 19*, 69–79.

Swain, D. A. (1991). Withdrawal from sport and Schlossberg's model of transitions. *Sociology of Sport Journal, 8*, 152–160.

Taylor, J. (1987, September). *The application of psychological skills for the enhancement of coaching effectiveness.* Presented at the Association for the Advancement of Applied Sport Psychology annual meetings, Newport Beach, California.

Taylor, J., & Ogilvie, B. C. (1994). A conceptual model of adaptation to retirement among athletes. *Journal of Applied Sport Psychology, 6,* 1–20.

Thomas, C. E., & Ermler, K. L. (1988). Institutional obligations in the athletic retirement process. *Quest, 40,* 137–150.

Torregrosa, M., Mateos, M., Sanchez, X., & Cruz, J. (2007, September). *Evaluation of a programme to combine elite sport and university education.* Paper presented at the 12th European Congress of Sport Psychology, Halkidiki, Greece.

Tuckman, J., & Lorge, I. (1953). *Retirement and the industrial worker.* New York: Macmillan.

Van Raalte, J. L., & Andersen, M. B. (2007). When Sport Psychology Consulting Is a Means to an End(ing): Roles and Agendas When Helping Athletes Leave Their Sports. *The Sport Psychologist, 21*(2), 227–242.

Warriner, K., & Lavallee, D. (2008). The retirement experiences of elite gymnasts: Self identity and the physical self. *Journal of Applied Sport Psychology, 20,* 301–317.

Webb, W. M., Nasco, S. A., Riley, S., & Headrick, B. (1998). *Journal of Sport Behavior, 21,* 338–362.

Wippert, P., & Wippert, J. (2008). Perceived stress and prevalence of traumatic stress symptoms following athletic career termination. *Journal of Clinical Sport Psychology, 2,* 1–16.

Wolff, R., & Lester, D. (1989). A theoretical basis for counseling the retired professional athlete. *Psychological Reports, 64,* 1043–1046.

Wylleman, P., Alfermann, D., (2004). Career transition in sport: European perspectives. *Psychology of Sport and Exercise, 5,* 7–20.

Wylleman, P., Lavallee, D., & Alfermann, D. (Eds). (1999). *Career transitions in competitive sports.* Biel, Switzerland: European Federation of Sport Psychology Monograph Series.

Yalom, I. D. (1980). *Existential psychotherapy.* New York: Harper/Collins.

Exercise Psychology

Rod K. Dishman, *University of Georgia*
Heather O. Chambliss, *University of Memphis*

Muscular vigor will . . . always be needed to furnish the background of sanity, serenity, and cheerfulness to life, . . . to round off the wiry edge of our fretfulness, and make us good-humored and easy of approach.

—*William James, 1899*

Physical inactivity is a public health burden in the United States and many other nations (Allender et al., 2007; Bauman & Craig, 2005; U.S. Department of Health & Human Services, 2010). Interest in physical activity for promotion of mental health continues to grow, especially for depression and cognitive function. Depression and dementia were among the 10 leading risk factors of disability-adjusted life expectancy in high-income nations worldwide during the past decade (Lopez et al., 2006), and they are projected to rank first and third by the year 2030 (Mathers & Loncar, 2006). In the United States, dementia and other disorders of the central nervous system are a leading cause of death, and mental disorders account for more than 40 percent of years lost to disability (Michaud et al., 2006) and 6.2 percent of all health care expenditures (Mark et al., 2007). Evidence supports that physical activity reduces odds of disorders such as depression, anxiety, and cognitive decline associated with aging, while promoting self-esteem, better sleep, and feelings of energy and well-being.

Despite the potential benefits of being physically active, 25 to 40 percent of adults in the United States are sedentary during their leisure time, and another 20 to 25 percent are not active enough to meet the levels recommended for health and fitness (Centers for Disease Control and Prevention, 2007). Physical activity decreases markedly between ages 9 to 15 years (Nader et al., 2008). In one national study, 42 percent of U.S. children 6–11 years of age were active at the recommended level of an hour each day, but only 8 percent of adolescents were active at that level (Troiano et al., 2008). Hence, understanding what motivates people to exercise is a high priority for public health.

The primary focus of exercise psychology has been to explain the social-cognitive and environmental antecedents of leisure-time physical activity and the psychological consequences of being physically active (Buckworth, Dishman, O'Connor, & Tomporowski, 2013). We have organized this chapter into two sections in which we describe the evidence for positive effects on mental health and address issues in physical activity behavior change and exercise adherence.

Exercise and Mental Health

Anxiety and Depression

Growing evidence from prospective cohort studies and randomized controlled trials supports that physical activity or exercise have favorable effects on mental health, especially for reducing symptoms of depression and some types of anxiety (Asmundson et al., 2013; Deboer et al., 2012; Physical Activity Guidelines Advisory Committee, 2008). About 18 percent of adults aged 18 years or older in the United States—about 23 million people—experience anxiety disorders each year (Kessler et al., 2005b), and 29 percent will have some type of anxiety disorder during their lifetimes (Kessler et al., 2005a). Estimates suggest that 8 percent of women and 4 percent of men have some form of depression at any point in time. About 20 percent of U.S. adults will have a mood disorder, mostly major depression, during their lifetime (Kessler et al., 2005a). Annually, anxiety and depression account for one-third of all mental health costs in the United States, about $85 billion each. These disorders not only affect quality of life, but also increase the risks for other chronic diseases, such as coronary heart disease (Stansfield & Marmot, 2002).

Anxiety

Population-based cross-sectional studies show that regular physical activity is associated with lower odds of experiencing anxiety symptoms (DeMoor et al., 2006; Strine, 2005; Taylor, 2004; Thorsen et al., 2005) or diagnosis of an anxiety disorder (i.e., specific phobia, social phobia, generalized anxiety, panic, and agoraphobia) by an average of about 30 percent after adjustment for other risk factors (Goodwin, 2003). At least four other studies used a prospective cohort design, which reduces the likelihood that the association is explainable by people becoming less active after they experience anxiety symptoms. The studies reported that the odds of developing any anxiety disorder or elevated symptoms were reduced by about one-fourth to one-half among physically active Australian adults (Beard et al., 2007), adolescents and young adults in Munich, Germany (Ströhle et al., 2007), recent college graduates in Spain (Sanchez-Villegas et al., 2008), and Swedish health professionals (Jonsdottir et al., 2010) when compared with inactive people.

Although very vigorous exercise can increase temporary feelings of tension or anxiety (i.e., state anxiety) in people without an anxiety disorder or other chronic illness (O'Connor, Petruzzello, Kubitz, & Robinson, 1995), state anxiety is typically reduced by about one-half of the baseline standard deviation (SD) after concluding an exercise session of moderate to vigorous intensity (Landers and Petruzzello, 1994). That is equivalent to increasing a grade from a C+ to a B in a course graded using a normal or bell-shaped curve.

Persistent feelings of anxiety (i.e., trait anxiety) are typically reduced by .40 SD (Long and van Stavel, 1995) to .50 SD (Conn, 2010) after exercise training in healthy adults. A recent meta-analysis of 40 randomized controlled trials including 2,914 patients with chronic medical conditions other than anxiety found that exercise training significantly reduced anxiety symptoms by about .30 SD when compared to control groups that did not exercise (Herring, O'Connor, Dishman, 2010). Anxiety reductions were greatest when sessions lasted at least 30 minutes and when people reported their experience of anxiety symptoms for more than the past week.

At least four small randomized controlled trials have shown a reduction in anxiety after exercise training among people who have an anxiety disorder (e.g., Broocks et al., 1998; Herring et al.,

2012; Jazaieri et al., 2012; Merom et al., 2008), encouraging larger trials with other types of anxiety (Abrantes et al., 2012).

Depression

Exercise has been recommended in treating depression for many centuries. Hippocrates prescribed exercise for depression, and clinical reports about using exercise in the psychiatric treatment of depression appeared as early as 1905. However, the first research efforts to discover the potential impact of exercise on depression did not begin until the early 1960s, led by William P. Morgan. Since then, a number of experimental, randomized controlled trials have been conducted.

A meta-analysis of a dozen studies by Lawlor & Hopker (2001) found that exercise groups decreased depression scores 1 SD more than comparison groups, but the authors noted several methodological limitations of the studies that have prevented clear interpretations of the results. Subsequent meta-analyses of randomized controlled trials of depressed patients conducted since that initial review have used more stringent standards of study quality and yielded smaller effects on average, ranging from about .80 SD (Mead et al., 2009) to .40 SD (Krogh et al., 2012). Some studies reported that reductions in symptoms met criteria for a clinically meaningful drop in symptoms (50 percent reduction) or remission (Blumenthal et al., 2007; Dunn et al., 2005; Pinchasov et al., 2000; Singh et al., 2005).

At least 30 population-based, prospective observational studies of physical activity and depression symptoms have been published worldwide (Physical Activity Guidelines Advisory Committee, 2008). Few studied adolescents (e.g., Motl et al., 2004) or the transition from adolescence to young adulthood (Ströhle et al., 2007). The average odds of experiencing symptoms were about 20% lower among active people compared with inactive people, after adjustment for other risk factors. Only seven of the studies examined whether the protective effects of physical activity vary according to the amount of physical activity. The adjusted odds were

reduced by about 15 percent in the lowest level of physical activity and by about 25 percent in each of the next two levels of physical activity. About a dozen studies suggest a 25 percent reduction in physician-diagnosed incident depression among people who were initially active, but those studies were limited to just one estimate of physical activity exposure measured by self-report. In the Aerobics Center Longitudinal Study, fitness and depression complaints to a physician were assessed at four clinic visits, each separated by two or three years, in 7,936 men and 1,261 women who had not complained of depression at their first clinic visit. After adjustment for age, time between visits, and confounders including co-morbid anxiety, each minute decline in treadmill time increased the odds of incident depression by approximately 2 and 5 percent in men and women (Dishman et al., 2012).

Randomized controlled trials in humans diagnosed with depression (e.g., Blumenthal et al., 1999; 2007; Brenes et al., 2007) have demonstrated that exercise training can reduce signs or symptoms of depression to a degree comparable to antidepressant drugs. Exercise has also been effective in patients who don't respond fully to drug treatment (Trivedi et al., 2006). There is no consensus, however, on the exercise prescription that is most effective for treating depression or anxiety (Dunn, Trivedi, & O'Neal, 2001). We know of only two controlled studies that addressed the dose response issue in depressed individuals. Dunn, Trivedi, Kampert, Clark, and Chambliss (2005) found that greater weekly energy expenditure (about 250-400 kcal per session) produced greater decreases in depressive symptoms after 12 weeks of aerobic training compared to a lower dose (about 100 to 150 kcal per session) and to an equal contact control. Singh et al. (2005) reported greater symptom reduction after resistance exercise at an intensity of 80 percent one repetition maximum (RM) compared to an intensity of 20 percent 1 RM 3 days per week for 8 weeks.

A systematic review of 90 randomized trials involving 10,534 adults with a chronic illness other than depression found that exercise training reduced depressive symptoms by a mean effect of 0.30 SD (Herring, Puetz, O'Connor, & Dishman, 2012). Larger antidepressant effects were obtained when (1) baseline depressive symptom scores were higher; (2) patients met recommended physical activity levels; and (3) the trial's primary health outcome was improved among patients with baseline depressive symptoms indicative of mild-to-moderate depression.

Distress and Well-Being

Psychological distress is a risk factor for psychiatric disorders and coronary heart disease (Stansfield & Marmot, 2002), and it is negatively associated with quality of life. Also, exaggerated physiological responses to mental stress are believed to play a role in the development of coronary heart disease and hypertension. Conversely, a feeling of well-being can reduce psychiatric risk and is an important feature of high life quality and health (Pressman & Cohen, 2005).

During the past decade, at least 15 prospective cohort studies and 30 randomized controlled trials of physical activity and feelings of distress or well-being have been published worldwide (Physical Activity Guidelines Advisory Committee, 2008). In the cohort studies, the odds favored active people by nearly 20 percent after adjustment for risk factors such as age, gender, socioeconomic status, smoking, alcohol or substance use, chronic health conditions, life events, job stress, and social support. The effects of exercise training were small, about .25 SD, and were not better than a placebo in many of the randomized controlled trials.

For the most part, the evidence for altered physiological responses during mental stress after exercise training is also ambiguous. A meta-analysis of the cumulative evidence published from 1965 to 2004 found that cardiorespiratory fitness was weakly associated with increased physiological reactivity, but quicker recovery, from laboratory stress (Jackson & Dishman, 2006). Also, responses such as heart rate and blood pressure were not affected in randomized exercise training studies that increased cardiorespiratory fitness. Despite negative findings,

vascular and blood flow responses, as well as their modulation by the autonomic nervous system, may be more important to health than gross measures of heart rate and blood pressure. For example, acute exercise increases flow-mediated dilation (a measure of vascular health) despite increased vascular resistance after neurovascular stress (Rooks, McCully, & Dishman, 2011). However, vascular responses during stress have been understudied (e.g., Dishman, Nakamura, Jackson, & Ray, 2003; Dishman, Jackson, Nakamura, Ray, 2013; Heydari, Boutcher, & Boutcher, 2013), especially in people with elevated risk of cardiovascular disease (e.g., Jackson & Dishman, 2002).

Sleep

According to reports from the National Institutes of Health's conference on sleep and sleep disorders (*Frontiers of Knowledge in Sleep & Sleep Disorders: Opportunities for Improving Health and Quality of Life,* March 2004), each year 50 to 70 million Americans experience some effects on their health from sleep disorders, sleep deprivation, and excessive daytime sleepiness. The annual prevalence of insomnia is nearly one-third of the adult population in the United States. The financial cost is approximately $65 billion, 50 billion of that in costs to industry from lost productivity. Only about 5 to 20 percent of people who suffer sleep disturbances will seek help from a primary care physician, and many will purchase over-the-counter sleep aids.

A meta-analysis on the acute effects of physical activity on sleep (Youngstedt, O'Connor, & Dishman, 1997) found statistically significant increases in total sleep time, slow wave sleep, and REM latency (the time before REM onset), with a decrease in REM, after an exercise session. However, the effects ranged from about .20 to .50 SD, which are small-to-moderately large effects statistically but equate to only a few minutes of sleep in each case, well within normal night-to-night variation. The subjects studied were good sleepers, so the effects may underestimate the potential efficacy of exercise among people with sleep disorders.

About a dozen epidemiological studies have reported an association between physical activity and good sleep based on questionnaires administered to population samples, but few studies have examined the long-term effects of exercise on sleep among people with sleep disorders (Youngstedt & Kline, 2006). There is some evidence that higher levels of usual physical activity appear to be protective against incident and chronic insomnia in older adults (Morgan, 2003), and a few randomized controlled trials have found that both aerobic (King et al., 1997) and resistance (Singh et al., 1997) exercise training led to improvements in self-rated sleep among older adults who had sleep problems. The long-term effects of exercise on polysomnographic measures of sleep among poor sleepers are not as yet known, but a few polysomnography studies have shown favorable results. Population-based studies found that men and women who exercised three or more hours per week had lower odds of sleep apnea (Peppard and Young, 2004; Quan et al., 2007), and randomized controlled trials of moderate intensity aerobic exercise reported quicker sleep onset, less awake time, and total sleep time (Passos et al., 2010), or more time in stage 2 sleep and fewer awakenings (King et al., 2008).

Feelings of Fatigue or Low Energy

Feelings of low energy and fatigue are a public health problem in the United States. Although less than 1 percent of the population suffers from "chronic fatigue syndrome," about 20 percent of adults say they have persistent feelings of fatigue (Wessely, Hotopf, & Sharp, 1998). Feelings of fatigue or low energy are common reasons for doctor visits, yet treatment is often inadequate (Lange, Cook, & Natelson, 2005). A dozen population-based observational studies, including four prospective cohorts published since 1995, suggest a protective effect of physical activity against feelings of fatigue or low energy (OR=0.61, 95% CI=0.52 to 0.72) (Puetz, 2006). Also, randomized trials of exercise with healthy adults and medical patients, including chronic fatigue syndrome (Fulcher and White, 1997;

Moss-Morris et al., 2005; Wallman et al., 2004), show a moderate reduction in symptoms of fatigue (Puetz, O'Connor, Dishman, 2006). These favorable chronic changes may result in part from the cumulative effects of improvements in transient feelings of energy and fatigue after repeated sessions of acute exercise (Dishman, Thom, Puetz, & O'Connor, 2012; Loy, O'Connor, & Dishman, 2013.

Self-Esteem

Enhanced self-esteem is important for mental health because it provides a feeling of value or worth and it is a general indicator of psychological adjustment (Pressman & Cohen, 2005). Symptoms of anxiety and depression often are associated with low self-esteem, and physical activities including sports may favorably mediate the association between self-esteem and depression (e.g., Dishman et al., 2006; Motl et al., 2005) and anxiety (Herring, O'Connor, Dishman, 2013). Positive changes in physical self-concept after exercise training are more likely to be observed than changes in self-esteem, but increased physical self-concept may contribute to enhanced self-esteem (Fox, 2000; Moore et al., 2011; Sonstroem, 1998; Sonstroem & Morgan, 1989; Moore et al., 2011). Changes in self-esteem with exercise are also more likely in children than adults, for whom self-esteem is more multidimensional.

A meta-analysis of eight randomized controlled trials of children and youths indicated a moderate (one-half SD) effect of physical activity (Ekeland et al., 2004). A recent meta-analysis of about 50 mostly small, randomized controlled trials reported an average increase in self-esteem of about .25 SD among adults (Spence et al., 2005). Self-esteem is increased among adults (Spence et al., 2005) and youths (Strong et al., 2005) when physical fitness is increased, more so than when the physical activity setting and study outcomes are focused on motor skills. However, the study designs used have not clarified the importance of the social context of the physical activity settings relative to features of physical activity, exercise, and fitness. Thus, it remains unclear whether it is exercise itself that increases self-esteem, or something in the social context of the exercise setting, including people's expectations of benefits (Desharnais, Jobin, Cote, Levesque, & Godin, 1993). The greatest gains in self-esteem can be expected for individuals with low initial levels, and for whom physical attributes have a relatively high value as a part of global self-concept.

Cognitive Function

Cognition involves the selection, manipulation, and storage of information and the use of that information to guide behavior. Cognitive function generally matures in childhood, peaks during young adulthood, and declines after middle age. Hence, there has been an interest in whether exercise or physical fitness moderates cognitive function during the lifespan. Early studies yielded mixed evidence about the benefits of regular exercise or cardiorespiratory fitness on cognitive functioning (e.g., Tomporowski & Ellis, 1986). Reevaluation of that evidence and more recent research suggest some positive effects of both acute and chronic exercise on selected features of cognitive function in children (Davis et al., 2007) and older adults (McAuley, Kramer, & Colcombe, 2004). Early studies of older adults found that fitness was more related to performance on tasks that were novel, complex, and required attention and fast processing speed (Chodzko-Zajko & Moore, 1994). More recent studies have shown that cardiorespiratory fitness and chronic aerobic exercise training facilitate executive control functions of cognition among older adults (Colcombe et al., 2004).

A review of 18 trials by Colcombe and Kramer (2003) indicated that aerobic exercise training had the greatest effect (.68 SD) for executive control tasks that measured goal-oriented decision-making behavior. Executive control includes response inhibition, attentional control, working memory, and rule discovery and is mainly regulated by neural activity in the prefrontal cortexes of the brain, areas that are further modulated by activity in the temporal and parietal cortexes, the hippocampus,

and several other brain areas involved with motivated behavior (Royall et al., 2002). A subsequent meta-analysis of randomized trials observed that eight out of 11 studies reported an average increase in aerobic fitness of 14 percent and also improvements in cognitive-motor function (1.17 SD) and auditory attention (0.50 SD). There were also small effects (one-fourth SD) for information-processing speed and visual attention (Angevaren et al., 2008). The cumulative evidence has indicated a small-to-moderately large positive effect, usually about one-third to one-half SD of both acute and chronic exercise on several indicators of cognitive performance (Etnier et al., 1997; Lambourne & Tomporowski, 2010; Sibley & Etnier, 2003). Whether those effects depend directly upon physical fitness remains unclear (Etnier et al., 2007).

At least 17 prospective population-based cohort studies assessed the relation between individuals' level of physical activity and the onset of age-related decline in cognitive functioning or incident cases of dementia or cognitive decline in healthy aging adults (Physical Activity Guidelines Advisory Committee, 2008). Of 11 studies of dementia, seven reported a protective effect of physical activity. The average risk reduction in the onset of dementia was nearly 40 percent. In a subsequent meta-analysis of those 11 cohort studies plus two others, the most active people in each study had 45 percent lower risk of Alzheimer's disease and 28 percent lower risk of all dementia compared to the least active groups (Hamer and Chida, 2009). No randomized trial has shown that regular exercise prevents dementia, but a few have shown improvement in some aspects of cognitive functioning in people with dementia, including Alzheimer's disease (Heyn, Abreu, & Ottenbacher, 2004; Rolland et al., 2007; 2010).

A meta-analysis of 44 studies found a small, cumulative effect of one-third SD on improved cognitive function after exercise training among children, regardless of whether the exercise was in physical education classes or special training to improve motor skills, muscular strength, or aerobic fitness training (Sibley and Etnier,

2003). Despite the encouraging early evidence in children, it is not yet known how the types of physical activities and their social context, the specific components of mental functioning, and the developmental maturity of children interact to directly influence cognitive function (Tomporowski et al., 2008).

Plausible Mediators or Mechanisms

The explanations of how physical activity improves mental health are largely unknown. However, the precise mechanisms for the therapeutic effect of psychotherapy and medications are also unclear. Cognitively based explanations for a beneficial effect of exercise on anxiety and depression include distractions from worries or symptoms, increased sense of mastery, improved self-perceptions, or a redefined subjective meaning of arousal. Improvements in mental health also may stem from increased opportunities for social interaction, meeting and reaching goals, or an enhanced sense of control or purpose.

Hypotheses about biological mechanisms for explaining reduced anxiety and depression after exercise have been incompletely developed because until recently few interested investigators had training in biological psychology or neuroscience or had access to brain neuroimaging or molecular biology techniques (Dishman, 1997; Dishman, Berthoud, Booth et al., 2006; Greenwood & Fleshner, 2011; Stranahan & Mattson, 2012; van Praag, 2008).

The thermogenic hypothesis that reduced anxiety after exercise is dependent on the increased body temperature typical of moderate-to-heavy exertion seems plausible but has received little support (Koltyn & Morgan, 1992; Youngstedt, Dishman, Cureton, & Peacock, 1993). Brain blood flow and oxygenation are increased during moderate-to-hard exercise (Rooks, Thom, McCully, & Dishman, 2010), but the effects so far have been limited to observations of the frontal cortex and regions involved with motor, sensory, and cardiovascular regulation (Secher et al., 2008), rather than deeper brain regions more specifically involved with emotional and motivational

responses (e.g., amygdala, hippocampus, central gray, ventral tegmentum, nucleus accumbens). Both acute and chronic exercise influences blood flow in the anterior cingulate and insular cortexes (areas that are involved with emotional processing, error detection/correction, response inhibition, and cardiovascular control) (Colcombe et al., 2004; Williamson, McColl, & Mathews, 2003). However, it remains to be determined whether such responses to exercise reflect emotional responding to exercise or sensory and cardiovascular responses to increased arousal. A brain neuroimaging study demonstrated decreased blood flow in the anterior cingulate among fit older adults during an executive function task requiring error detection, which was associated with their better performance (Colcombe et al., 2004). However, the altered blood flow could be the result of improved neural function rather than its cause.

Brain opioids such as enkephalin and dynorphin play a role in modulating dopamine neurons in parts of the brain involved with motivation and pleasure and could thus indirectly influence positive moods. (Dishman & O'Connor, 2009). An uncontrolled study reported a correlation between self-reports of euphoria and brain opioid binding measured by positron emission tomography in 10 experienced distance runners (Boecker et al., 2008). This is the first evidence that brain opioids are influenced by exercise in humans in a way that may help explain mood changes associated with running (Dishman & O'Conner, 2009).

Evidence from animal models of depression and anxiety points to exercise-induced changes in brain norepinephrine (NE) and serotonin, which are major modulators of brain neural activity, as potential mechanisms for the positive effects on mood or behavioral signs of anxiety or depression (Chambliss et al., 2004; Dishman et al., 1997; Dunn, Reigle, Youngstedt, Armstrong, & Dishman, 1996; Fox, Hammack, & Falls, 2008; Greenwood & Fleshner, 2011; Soares, Holmes, Renner, Edwards, Bunnell, & Dishman, 1999; Thom, Holmes, & Dishman, 2009; Yoo et al., 2000).

Hemispheric asymmetry in brain electroencephalographic (EEG) responses measured at anterior brain recording sites has been hypothesized as a correlate or possible mechanism for mood changes in response to acute exercise (e.g., Petruzzello, Hall, & Ekkekakis, 2001). However, support for this idea has been mixed (e.g., Crabbe, Smith, & Dishman, 2007), and the studies were limited to just a few recording sites rather than dense-array electrode mapping of the whole head. Most evidence indicates that EEG activity in all frequency bands increases in response to acute exercise regardless of hemispheric site (Crabbe & Dishman, 2004), suggesting that acute exercise increases EEG activity in a general way consistent with increased arousal, possibly from increased sensory and cardiovascular neural traffic to the thalamus processed through the brain stem.

New areas of research implicate other potential biological mechanisms for positive effects of exercise on mental health and cognitive function. For example, neurotrophic proteins such as brain-derived neurotrophic factor (BDNF) and VGF enhance the growth and maintenance of several neuronal systems, and might have an important role in the neuropathology and treatment of depression (Hunsberger et al., 2007; Russo-Neustadt, 2003). A large animal literature shows a strong effect of both acute and chronic physical activity on neural plasticity and the expression of BDNF in the hippocampus (Cotman & Berchtold, 2002), which appears dependent on noradrenergic function (Garcia et al., 2003; Ivy et al., 2003). Galanin, a neuropeptide that serves as both a neurotrophin and a neurotransmitter and is responsive to chronic exercise (O'Neal, Van Hoomissen, Holmes, & Dishman, 2001), has been hypothesized to be more important than BDNF for some types of learning and contextual memories (Van Hoomissen et al., 2004), and anxiety reduction after chronic exercise (Sciolino, Dishman, & Holmes, 2012).

Research Issues in Exercise and Mental Health

Some of the inconsistency in links between exercise and mental health can be traced to the quality of the research. Many studies did not quantify physical activity and exertion adequately, examine clearly defined clinical groups, control for subject expectancy or social interaction effects, or consider health and activity history of the participants (Tieman, Peacock, Cureton, & Dishman, 2001). Most studies of exercise and anxiety or depression have not used clinical diagnostic criteria or concomitantly measured biological signs that are common features of standard clinical diagnosis.

Current knowledge about dose-response relationships and biological plausibility for effects of exercise on mental health remains limited (Dishman, Berthoud, Booth et al., 2006; Dishman & O'Connor, 2009). Difficulties in defining a dose–response relationship also come from inconsistencies in mode, intensity, and duration of exercise treatment. The effects of different types of exercise haven't been fully studied. More studies of resistance training are needed, as are studies of other types of exercise, including milder forms such as Eastern health practices (e.g., Tai Chi and Qigong). Although evidence does not indicate that mental health benefits of physical activity depend upon changes in aerobic fitness, recommendations from the 2008 Physical Activity Guidelines for Americans suggest that people engage in moderate-intensity physical activity (e.g., brisk walking) for at least 150 minutes or 75 minutes of vigorous intensity activity each week. However, whether meeting that recommendation provides similar mental health benefits as participation at intensities and durations either lower or higher than the recommendation remains largely untested by experimental methods. Table 24-1 lists several practical applications of physical activity to improve mental health.

Physical Activity Behavior Change

Increased physical activity and fitness contribute to public health, but efforts to increase adoption and maintenance of an active lifestyle have yielded modest results. The proportion of adults who participated sufficiently in regular moderate or vigorous physical activity stayed at about 35 percent from 1997 to 2010, and didn't reach the Healthy People 2010 goal of 50 percent

Table 24-1 Coaching Points for Mental Health

- **General Well-Being**—Improved mental health is a short-term benefit that can be used to reinforce exercise training. Motivate clients and athletes by having them pay attention to benefits such as increased energy levels, lower stress, and improved mood after exercise. If an athlete shows a decline in psychological functioning with training, it may be useful to review the regimen to ensure that the athlete is not becoming stale.

- **Mood Disorders**—Anxiety and depression are common clinical disorders. Know the signs and symptoms, and have local referral resources available. If a client or athlete has a history of a mood disorder, exercise can be a useful adjunctive treatment. Don't encourage a person to discontinue medication or other prescribed treatment, but provide education on the mental health benefits of exercise.

- **Sleep**—Exercise may help regulate sleep patterns for some people. If a client or athlete complains of sleep problems, suggest that he or she experiment with the timing of the exercise routine to see what works best. In addition, light exposure from exercising outdoors may provide additional benefit.

- **Self-Esteem**—Exercise may improve self-esteem and physical self-concept, particularly among children and individuals with low initial self esteem. Help individuals by setting realistic goals and establishing an environment that promotes feelings of mastery, competence of new sport skills, and a positive body image.

- **Cognitive Function**—Exercising the body is good for the mind too. Even walking has been shown to reduce cognitive decline in older adults. Remind clients and athletes of this important benefit, and maximize the potential impact of exercise by creating stimulating learning environments. Create a brain and body workout—maximize the mental complexity of physical tasks, change up the exercise environment, or even pair athletic drills with memory tasks.

(Centers for Disease Control, 2005a; 2005b). When physical activity is measured directly using accelerometers, less than 10 percent of U.S. adults and adolescents are sufficiently active (Troiano et al., 2008). Without successful intervention, typical dropout or non-attendance rates in supervised exercise programs lasting 3–24 months have been 25–50 percent for the past 40 years.

Interventions to increase physical activity have usually shown modest, short-term improvements in children (Metcalf et al., 2012; van Sluijs et al., 2011) and adults (Dishman & Buckworth, 1996; Kahn et al., 2002; Heath et al., 2012) that often aren't sustainable. Understanding how to design more effective interventions will depend in part upon identifying key mediators (i.e., variables that transmit all or part of the effect of an independent variable on a dependent variable) and moderators (i.e., extraneous variables that modify that effect) of change in physical activity (Baranowski et al., 1998; MacKinnon, Fairchild, & Fritz, 2007; Luban, Foster, & Biddle, 2008; Rhodes & Pfaeffli, 2010).

There is no consensus about whether the most successful interventions will be those that change people or change their environments. Probably both are necessary. The following sections describe some of the main theories and methods that have been used.

Theories of Exercise Behavior

Several theories have been used to predict and explain exercise behavior (Buckworth, Dishman, O'Connor, Tomprowski, 2013; Rhodes & Pfaeffli, 2010). Many studies of exercise determinants and interventions have been based on social cognitive theories, including planned behavior and self-efficacy; self-determination theory; and the transtheoretical model, and various forms of behavior modification and cognitive behavior modification. In addition, the ecological model has gained support through efforts to implement multilevel multidimensional interventions with a focus on environmental influences.

Social cognitive.   Social cognitive theories conceptualize cognition, affect, and value-related variables as mediators in the choice of goals, intentions to act, and thus exercise behavior. The theories assume that personal factors, environmental events, and behavior function as interacting and reciprocal determinants of each other (Bandura, 1997).

The *Theory of Planned Behavior* (Ajzen, 2002) proposes that the direct cause of behavior is intention, which is determined by perceived behavioral control, attitude, and subjective norm. Perceived behavioral control includes efficacy beliefs about internal factors (e.g., skills, abilities, and willpower) and external factors (e.g., time, opportunity, obstacles, and dependence on other people) that are imposed on behavior (Rodgers & Murray, 2007). It also has a direct effect on behavior, independently of intention. The cumulative evidence from nonexperimental studies has supported those relations for understanding adults' and adolescents' intentions to be physically active and the relation of those intentions with physical activity, although those relations are modest in size (see Hagger & Chatzisarantis, 2009; Godin, 1994 for reviews). Most studies failed to model change in both physical activity and its predictors across time.

Self-efficacy conceptualizes a belief in personal capabilities to organize and execute the courses of action required to attain a behavioral goal (Bandura, 1997), similar to perceived behavioral control. Both perceived behavioral control and self-efficacy are distinguishable from *outcome expectancy,* which is the perceived likelihood that performing a behavior will result in a specific outcome. Bandura (1997) proposed that self-change operates through self-initiated reactions. For example, individuals dissatisfied with their current exercise or fitness who adopt challenging goals and are confident (i.e., have high self-efficacy) that they can attain their goals would have strong intentions and optimal motivation for maintaining exercise (Dishman et al., 2006). Consistent evidence indicates that self-efficacy is a mediator of behavior change, (e.g., Dishman et al., 2004). There is some longitudinal evidence that exercise self-efficacy increases as one moves from an established sedentary lifestyle to long-term maintenance of regular exercise (Dishman, Motl et al., 2004; McAuley & Blissmer, 2000). Four sources of efficacy information can be manipulated in interventions: performance accomplishments, vicarious experiences, verbal persuasion, and physiological/psychological states. Performance accomplishments refer to mastering a difficult or previously feared task and are the most potent strategy for increasing self-efficacy (Bandura, 1997). Someone who is successful meeting a reasonable but challenging short-term exercise goal will have a sense of accomplishment and increased efficacy. Vicarious experiences enable learning via observation of the success experienced by others. Modeling is an effective strategy if the model is similar to the participant and the model succeeds through effort with clear rewarding outcomes. Verbal persuasion entails encouragement or support to reinforce progress toward reaching the target behavior and fosters the attribution of accomplishments to the person's own behavior. Finally, unpleasant physiological responses to exercise might initially undermine confidence in a sedentary unfit person just starting an exercise program. Because high arousal impairs performance and decreases efficacy expectations, understanding that heavy breathing, increased heart rate, fatigue, and muscle discomfort are normal responses to exercise can help manage psychological arousal during exercise. Teaching individuals to reframe physical symptoms in a positive interpretation and notice positive psychological states with exercise (e.g., increased energy, lower stress) can foster immediate confidence in the person's ability to complete a physical activity task.

Self-determination.   Self-determination theory (Ryan & Deci, 2007) is complementary to other social-cognitive theories (Hagger & Chatzisarantis, 2009) and offers ideas about how intrinsic motives and self-regulation of behavior develop and how they interact with physical and social environments to influence physical activity of adults (Fortier, Duda, Guerin, & Teixeira, 2012; Teixeira et al., 2012), adolescents (Ntoumanis,

2012; Standage et al., 2012), and children (Dishman, McIver, Dowda et al., 2013). It assumes that people strive for autonomy (i.e., behavior as a personal choice), competence (i.e., a sense of mastery or efficacy), and relatedness (i.e., supportive and satisfying social relations) (Ryan & Deci, 2007). An essential distinction in SDT for understanding participation in physical activity is between autonomous motivation and controlled motivation. Autonomous motivation includes intrinsic motivation (fully volitional engagement in physical activity for its own sake), integrated regulation (the act of physical activity has been fully incorporated into the sense of self, i.e., core personal values, beliefs, and purpose), and identified regulation (partial internalization of physical activity outcomes as synonymous with personal values and self-identity) (Deci & Ryan, 1985). By contrast, controlled motivation includes introjected regulation (physical activity is motivated by the need to gain approval from others, to feel worthy or to ease guilt) and external regulation (physical activity depends on instrumental incentives or coercion). Amotivation denotes the absence of intent to be active.

Behavior modification. Behavior modification is the planned, systematic application of principles of learning to the modification of behavior. It proposes that changes in behavior result from associations between external stimuli and the consequences of a specific behavior and minimizes the role of thoughts, motives, and perceptions. The key to behavior change lies in the identification of the target behavior (e.g., walking at lunch or doing aerobics when the children take gymnastics) and effective cues and reinforcers. Behavioral approaches, such as written agreements, behavioral contracts, lotteries, and stimulus and reinforcement control have been successful in exercise intervention studies.

Cognitive-behavior modification. Cognitive behavior modification is based on the assumption that psychological variables are the mediators of behavior. A wide range of dysfunctional or maladaptive behaviors results from the individual's irrational, unproductive thoughts and incompletely formed cognitions. Learning or insight can serve to restructure, augment, or replace faulty thoughts with behaviorally effective beliefs and cognitive skills. People are educated about the relationship between cognitions, feelings, and behaviors and are taught skills to identify and control antecedents and consequences that prompt and reinforce behavior. Cognitive-behavioral approaches, including self-monitoring, goal setting, feedback, and decision making have been effective in increasing exercise adherence or health outcomes when used alone or when combined in intervention packages (Chambliss et al., 2011).

Transtheoretical model. The transtheoretical model, also known as the stages of change model, has been used to describe the processes of health behavior change and has been widely applied to exercise (Hutchinson et al., 2009; Marcus, Pinto, Simkin, Audrain, & Taylor, 1994; Marshall & Biddle, 2001; Rhodes & Pfaeffli, 2010; Spencer et al., 2006). Behavior change is seen as a dynamic process that occurs through a series of five interrelated stages: precontemplation, contemplation, preparation, action, and maintenance (Marcus & Simkin, 1994; Prochaska & Marcus, 1994). People in precontemplation are not thinking about starting an exercise program. Those in the contemplation stage are considering starting an exercise program. During the preparation stage, a plan has been made but not implemented. People in the action stage have started regular exercise within the past six months but are at greater risk of not adhering than someone in the maintenance stage, for whom exercise behavior is more established. Three components of the transtheoretical model that are proposed mediators of behavior change are self-efficacy, decisional balance (i.e., pros and cons), and processes of change. The processes of change include application of both cognitive strategies (e.g., consciousness raising, self-reevaluation) and behavioral strategies (e.g., stimulus control, reinforcement management) to different degrees depending on the stage of change. Contrary to the original theory, though, the stages are weakly related to maintenance of recommended physical activity (Dishman et al., 2009) and change in both experiential and behavioral processes, and their initial levels, seem to be related to moderate-to-vigorous physical activity (Dishman et al., 2010).

Nonetheless, marketing and media campaigns promoting exercise, as well as accurate, easy-to-understand information about how to start an exercise program, can help move people into the action stage. Other elements that can affect the intention to start exercising are role models, perceived barriers and benefits, and social-cognitive variables such as self-efficacy. Integrating decision theories with mass-reach social marketing strategies may be helpful for turning increased knowledge into intentions and then actions to adopt physical activity (Donovan & Owen, 1994; Kahn et al., 2002). In Canada's 30-year ParticipACTION campaign to promote physical activity, nearly 2,500 people from the 1981 Canada Fitness Survey were followed up in 1988. About 45 percent of them were tested again in 2002–2004 (Craig et al., 2010). Among those inactive in 1981, campaign awareness predicted positive attitudes toward physical activity, which predicted higher decision balance (i.e., more perceived benefits than costs), which predicted future intentions, which in turn mediated the relationship between decision balance and sufficient activity 20 years later.

Ecological models. Ecological models acknowledge that behavior can be influenced by intrapersonal, social environment, physical environment, and public policy variables (Sallis and Owen, 1999). Social environmental factors are supportive behaviors, social climate, culture, policies governing incentives for activity and inactivity, and policies governing resources and infrastructures related to activity and inactivity. Physical environmental factors are divided into natural and built environments. Natural environmental factors include weather and geography. Built environments include information, level of urbanization, architecture, and infrastructures for transportation, entertainment, and recreation. In the United States, *Healthy People 2020* (U.S. Department of Health and Human Services,

2010) has adopted this model, targeting physical activity change broadly through changing the environment and public policies regarding schools, personal transportation, and access to facilities.

Correlates of Physical Activity

The known correlates of physical activity, which might mediate the effects of interventions or moderate their effects, can be categorized as personal attributes, environmental features, and dimensions of physical activity itself (Bauman et al., 2012; Dishman, 1991; Dishman & Sallis, 1994).

Personal attributes. Personal attributes that might be mediators include cognitions, beliefs, attitudes, emotions, and values that can interact with environmental variables, such as social support and the weather. Personal attributes that might be moderators include smoking, education, income, ethnicity, age, gender, body fatness, or fitness, which can be markers of underlying habits or circumstances that reinforce sedentary living, thus predisposing people to be responsive or resistive to physical activity interventions. Also, there is wide variability in how people adapt to exercise programs, suggesting that genetic factors also influence people's natural tendency to be active (Strubbe et al., 2006) and their success at reaching their exercise goals (Dishman, 2008). There has been little research on personality traits and exercise adherence (De Moor et al., 2008; Rhodes & Smith, 2006).

Social and Environmental Features

Social influences in the form of social support (i.e., companionship, encouragement or help from someone) (Duncan et al., 2007; Wendel-Vos et al., 2007) and features of the built environment (e.g., access to equipment, facilities, parks, trails, street connectivity, walkable neighborhoods) are weak correlates of physical activity. However, most studies have used cross-sectional designs and self-reports of physical activity and people's self-assessments of social factors and the environment, rather than objective measures, so the true importance of the social and physical environments for promoting physical activity is not yet clear (Brownson et al., 2009). In studies with youths (Ferreira et al., 2007) and adults (Wendel-Vos et al., 2007) only 25 to 35 percent of associations were strong enough to be statistically significant. Objective features of the family and the built environment have been weakly associated with children's physical activity levels or change (Berge, 2009; Craggs et al., 2011; Ferreira et al., 2006; Kriemler et al., 2011; O'Connor et al., 2009; van Sluijs et al., 2011). This seems likely the case because differences among children in their beliefs and values about physical activity (Dishman, Dunn, Sallis et al., 2010; Dishman et al., 2013; Van Der Horst et al., 2007) that can mediate change or modify the influence of social and physical environments haven't been fully considered in environmental studies of children's leisure-time physical activity (e.g., Dowda et al., 2009). A meta-analysis of 30 cross-sectional studies found small positive associations between youths' physical activity levels and parental encouragement, modeling (i.e., parents being physically active), and instrumental behaviors (e.g., providing transportation or buying sports equipment) (Pugliese and Tinsley, 2007). However, parenting style wasn't predictive of change in physical activity in a large, five-year longitudinal study of 2,500 middle-school students from 31 schools in Minnesota (Berge et al., 2010).

A systematic review of 35 studies, including 14 randomized controlled trials, of physical activity in healthy youth that had a parental component concluded that there was little evidence for effectiveness of family involvement methods in programs for promoting physical activity in children (O'Connor, Jago, Baranowski, 2009).

Other longitudinal research shows that support from family members may reduce girls' natural decline in physical activity during high school (Dowda et al., 2007). Self-efficacy was stable in that study and moderated the relation between changes in physical activity and perceived social support (Dishman et al., 2009). Girls who maintained a perception of strong social support had less of a decline in physical activity if they also had high self-efficacy. However, girls having high self-efficacy had a greater decline in physical activity if they perceived declines in social support (Dishman et al., 2009).

It makes sense that some social and physical environments can make it very difficult for people to be physically active for transportation or leisure. However, it seems less likely that merely having a family that supports physical activity or living in an environment where it is easy and pleasant to be active will directly translate into more activity unless people are otherwise motivated to be active. So, regardless of people's opportunities, their choice to be physically active must be a high priority. Identifying social and physical environmental factors in exercise behavior demonstrates the need to look beyond the individual and small group in developing interventions. The target of interventions should include policy and facility planning at the international, national, and community level and should include educational-behavioral applications in schools, churches, and health care and recreational settings (Blair et al., 1996; Dishman & Sallis, 1994; Heath et al., 2012; King, 1994).

Physical activity dimensions.   Identifying specific aspects of physical activity (e.g., frequency, intensity, duration) that enhance adoption and adherence is especially important to practitioners prescribing exercise (Dishman & Buckworth, 1996; Kahn et al., 2002). For example, Jakicic, Winters, Lang, and Wing (1999) randomized sedentary, overweight women to three exercise interventions: long bouts, multiple short bouts, or multiple short bouts at home using a treadmill. After 18 months, women in the last group reported better adherence that those in the other groups, but weight loss and improved fitness was similar regardless of intervention type. Both adoption and maintenance of exercise programs are inversely associated with exercise intensity (Dishman & Buckworth, 1996; Pollock et al., 1991; Trost et al., 2002), so it is possible that prescriptions based on preferred intensities might increase adherence to exercise programs (Dishman, 1994b).

Interventions

Physical activity is a health behavior that encompasses complex behavioral demands. It requires more time and effort than other health behaviors. However, interventions (particularly those based on behavior modification delivered to healthy people in community groups using telecommunication, print mailings, and motivating signage and targeting low-intensity, leisure-time physical activity) can be effective in changing exercise behavior at least in the short term, increasing adherence from 50 percent without intervention to about 85 percent after intervention (Dishman & Buckworth, 1996). Sustained benefits haven't been shown or examined in most studies, though. Planning for participation, initial adoption of physical activity, continued participation or maintenance, and overall periodicity of participation (e.g., relapse, resuming activity, and seasonal variation) are characteristics of physical activity that may involve different mediators warranting different interventions.

Studies using behavioral economics have demonstrated the strong influence of environmental context on sedentary choices made by children and adolescents (Epstein & Roemmich, 2001; Epstein et al., 2004). An emerging focus promotes environmental manipulations that increase opportunities and decrease barriers to physical activity. Informational interventions (e.g., "point-of-decision" prompts to encourage stair use and communitywide campaigns), school-based physical education (e.g., Pate et al., 2005; 2007), social support in community settings, and environmental or policy intervention to create or enhance access to places for physical activity have had some short-term success (Kahn et al., 2002).

Examples of behavioral strategies

Stimulus control involves manipulating antecedent conditions, or cues, that can prompt a behavior. Prompts can be verbal, physical, or symbolic. The goal is to increase cues for the desired behavior and decrease cues for competing sedentary behaviors. Examples are posters, slogans, posted notes, placement of exercise equipment in visible places, recruitment of social support, and performance of exercise at the same time and place every day (Knapp, 1988). Exercising first thing in the morning is an example of timing exercise to avoid the risk of distracting cues that can accumulate later in the day.

Reinforcement control involves understanding and controlling the consequences of physical activity to increase or decrease its occurrence. An example of positive reinforcement is an aerobics instructor praising a participant for finishing an especially hard routine. In other words something positive (praise) is added during or immediately after the target behavior to increase its frequency. Contracts with consequences, positive feedback, tokens, participation-based prizes, and group lotteries are other examples of reinforcement control.

Goal setting is used to attain a specific task in a prescribed period of time. Goals can be as simple and time limited as doing a 10-minute walk three times in the upcoming week or as complex as participating in a triathlon. Goals serve as immediate regulators of human behavior, providing direction, mobilizing effort, and fostering persistence in completing a task. Specific, measurable and time-limited goals make it easier to monitor progress, make adjustments, and know when the goal has been accomplished. Goals should be challenging but also reasonable and realistic. A goal might be achievable, but personal and situational constraints can make it unrealistic. For example, losing two pounds (1 kg) a week through diet and exercise is reasonable, but almost impossible for the working mother of three who has minimal time for exercise and cooking. Unrealistic goals set the participant up to fail, which can damage self-efficacy and adherence to the behavior-change program (Shilts, Townsend, & Dishman, 2013). Environmental and social supports and barriers also should be evaluated and modified to promote the new behaviors.

Relapse prevention can help keep individuals from dropping out of an exercise program. Relapse prevention is based on the premises that the impact of interruptions and life events on exercise can be diminished if the individual anticipates and plans for their occurrence, recognizes them as only temporary obstructions (rather than falsely catastrophizing a slip as a total failure), and develops self-regulatory skills (e.g., stimulus control, reinforcement management, and self-monitoring of progress) for preventing relapses to inactivity (Knapp, 1988). Movement from the action phase to the maintenance phase follows a decrease in the risk of relapse and an increase in self-efficacy.

Interventions will be more effective if they involve reevaluation of rewards and goals and promote strategies to cope with potential lapses from relocation, travel, or medical events. Social support, self-motivation, self-regulatory skills, and interventions such as relapse prevention seem necessary to maintain or resume exercise. Table 24-2 summarizes these tools.

Research Issues in Exercise Behavior

Over 50 different correlates of physical activity have been reported among youths and adults (Dishman & Sallis, 1994; Trost et al., 2002; Van Der Horst et al., 2007). Our understanding of how these factors influence physical activity continues to be hindered by (1) the frequent use of cross-sectional, correlational designs rather than longitudinal studies of change, (2) poorly validated measures of the moderators and mediators, (3) self-report, rather than objective, measures of

physical activity, and (4) limited use of statistical procedures that permit multilevel (i.e., personal and group level variables) modeling of direct, indirect (i.e., mediated), and moderated (i.e., interactions of mediators with external factors) relations of physical activity with theoretical networks of determinants, including personality, personal history, and genetic factors.

Longitudinal studies are also needed to determine whether perceived and objectively measured features of social and physical environments have direct relations with change in physical activity and/or indirect relations moderated or mediated by social-cognitive factors such as social support and efficacy beliefs about overcoming barriers to physical activity (Dowda et al., 2009).

Measurement of physical activity.   Most studies have used self-reports of physical activity. Fewer, more recent studies have used standardized observational systems or objective monitoring by accelerometry or global positioning devices. Studies of moderators and mediators of physical activity should increasingly compare results using both subjective and objective measures to enhance convergence of methods.

Measurement of change using multilevel models. Conceptual models should include variables measured at the individual level (e.g., personal motivation), including the family and home

---

Table 24-2 Applying Behavioral Skills for Physical Activity Promotion

- **Self-Monitoring**—Have individuals keep a tangible record of progress; use exercise logs to set goals, review progress, and identify areas for improvement.

- **Stimulus Control**—Use cues and prompts to promote exercise behaviors; identify and control psychosocial and environmental cues that have a negative impact on physical activity.

- **Goal Setting**—Have individuals set specific, realistic, but challenging, and measurable short- and long-term goals; use appropriate reward strategies when goals are achieved.

- **Problem Solving**—Identify potential barriers and apply stepwise problem-solving strategies to overcome them; encourage clients to write down their barriers and brainstorm solutions before selecting the best solution to apply.

- **Social Support**—Few goals in life are achieved in isolation; encourage individuals to identify where they need support and identify specific people who can help.

- **Cognitive Restructuring and Relapse Prevention**—Recognize unhelpful thought patterns such as negative or all-or-nothing thinking; plan ahead for high risk times and prepare for potential lapses.

environment, but also measured at the community level (e.g., neighborhoods, churches, schools). Complex models are needed to describe the independent and interactive contributions of key variables at each level to change in physical activity. Advanced techniques such as structural equation modeling and latent class growth modeling provide optimal precision for multi-level, theoretically derived analysis of change in physical activity. Three or more measurement periods are needed to examine change and to assess inter-individual variation in initial status (i.e., baseline) and inter- and intra-individual variation in change.

Gene-environment interactions. Little is known about how genes, the environment, and their interactions influence the brain's regulation of physical activity behavior or mental health outcomes of physical activity (De Moor, Boomsma, Stubbe, Willemsen, & de Geus, 2008). Family and twin studies have reported that 30–70 percent of the variation in human physical activity is inherited (e.g., Stubbe et al., 2006), and a few studies have implicated candidate genes that might explain small, but significant, portions of that variation (e.g., Rankinen et al., 2006). Most candidate genes for physical activity suggested by correlational studies were selected for study based on understanding of energy intake pathways that influence energy balance more so than models of otherwise motivated behavior (Simonen et al., 2003). However, some genes that have been studied (e.g., those related to dopamine, serotonin, and Orexin A) might be involved in regulation of motivation systems for both feeding and physical activity (Dishman, 2008).

Summary

Population studies using prospective epidemiological designs have reported that self-rated symptoms of depression, anxiety, and feelings of distress and fatigue are lower among people who are physically active regardless of gender, age, and race, although minority groups have been understudied. Randomized controlled trials of varying quality show that small-to-moderate decreases in self-rated anxiety and depression and improvements in sleep quality accompany both acute and chronic exercise. A few studies were on patients diagnosed with depression and anxiety disorders using clinical diagnostic and rating criteria and show favorable results. Prospective cohort studies and randomized controlled trials also suggest that physical activity is useful for enhancing cognitive performance in children, slowing cognitive decline associated with adult aging, and slowing the onset of dementia. More application of methodologies from behavioral and cognitive neuroscience is needed to help explain how physical activity and exercise affect the brain.

Most of the exercise training programs lasted about three to six months, but without behavior modification nearly 25–50 percent of people drop out of an exercise program within that time period. So, much of the potential benefits of exercise are lost because people quit. Clarifying the factors that affect physical activity habits over time is a major focus in exercise psychology. A lot of research has been conducted over the past 30 years to identify determinants of exercise adoption and adherence and to apply interventions to increase physical activity. However, effects have been modest for sustaining increases in physical activity. Recent research has focused on environmental factors that may be associated with physical activity in children and adults, such as the impact of the built environment on transportation and access to physical activity settings.

The modest success in sustaining increases in physical activity within the U.S. population can be attributed to the complexity of physical activity and gaps and weaknesses in the research discussed earlier. Experimental evidence verifying how interventions change putative mediators of physical activity (e.g., goals, intentions and efficacy beliefs about overcoming barriers to physical activity) or how environmental or social factors (e.g., access and social support) modify the effectiveness of interventions are needed. Also, research must consider multilevel (i.e., personal and group) influences within dynamic theories that explain the interaction of personal motivation with social and physical environments. The origin and time course for intrinsic reinforcement of physical activity remain unknown, so persistent interventions at the personal and population level, including community, school, worksite, and clinical settings, are required along with national policy initiatives that provide better social and environmental infrastructures to promote and support physical activity.

Study Questions

1. What is meant when we talk about the dose response for decreases in depression or anxiety after exercise?

2. List and discuss three plausible explanations or mechanisms for changes in mental health with exercise training.

3. What is executive control function and what evidence suggests that regular exercise affects it?

4. What features of social and physical environments seem most influential on physical activity?

5. List the three major research areas in exercise psychology, and discuss public health implications of each.

6. List and discuss three behavioral strategies that can be used to influence exercise participation. Give applied examples of each.

7. Describe the major components of transtheoretical model and their weaknesses for understanding maintenance of physical activity change. Why is it important to consider stage-specific interventions?

8. What are the three general categories of physical activity correlates? Give examples of moderators or mediators in each category. Discuss why it is important to consider how different correlates might interact.

9. A sedentary friend wants to "get in shape" and started walking after work two weeks ago. He missed walking for the past three days and asked for your help to restart his program and keep it going. What exercise stage is he in? How could relapse prevention theory help?

10. Describe cues that prompt you to exercise and some of the ways your exercise is reinforced.

References

Abrantes, A. M., McLaughlin, N., Greenberg, B. D., Strong, D. R., Riebe, D., Mancebo, M., . . . & Brown, R. A. (2012). Design and rationale for a randomized controlled trial testing the efficacy of aerobic exercise for patients with obsessive-compulsive disorder. *Mental Health and Physical Activity, 5,* 155–165.

Ajzen, I. (2002). Perceived behavioral control, self-efficacy, locus of control, and the theory of planned behavior. *Journal of Applied Social Psychology, 32,* 1–20.

Allender, S., Foster, C., Scarborough, P., & Rayner, M. (2007). The burden of physical activity–related ill health in the UK. *Journal of Epidemiology and Community Health, 4,* 344–348.

Angevaren, M. G., Aufdemkampe, H. J. J., Verhaar, A., Aleman, L., & Vanhees, L. (2008). Physical activity and enhanced fitness to improve cognitive function in older people without known cognitive impairment. *Cochrane Database of Systematic Reviews.* Issue 3. Art. No.: CD005381. doi: 10.1002/14651858.CD005381.pub3.

Asmundson, G. J., Fetzner, M. G., Deboer, L. B., Powers, M. B., Otto, M. W., & Smits, J. A. (2013). Let's get physical: a contemporary review of the anxiolytic effects of exercise for anxiety and its disorders. *Depression and Anxiety, 30,* 362–373.

Bandura A. (1997). *Self-efficacy: The exercise of control.* New York: W.H. Freeman and Company.

Baranowski, T., Anderson, C., & Carmack, C. (1998). Mediating variable framework in physical activity interventions: How are we doing? How might we do better? *American Journal of Preventive Medicine, 15,* 266–297.

Barnes, P. (2007). *Physical activity among adults: United States, 2000 and 2005.* Hyattsville, MD: US Department of Health and Human Services, CDC. Available at http://www.cdc.gov/nchs/products/pubs/pubd/hestats/physicalactivity/physicalactivity.htm.

Bauman, A., & Craig, C.L. (2005). The place of physical activity in the WHO Global Strategy on Diet and Physical Activity. *International Journal of Behavioral Nutrition and Physical Activity, 2,* 10.

Bauman, A. E., Reis, R. S., Sallis, J. F., Wells, J. C., Loos, R. J., & Martin, B. W. (2012). Correlates of physical activity: why are some people physically active and others not? *Lancet, 380,* 258–271.

Beard, J. R., Heathcote, K., Brooks, R., Earnest A., & Kelly, B. (2007). Predictors of mental disorders and their outcome in a community based cohort. *Social Psychiatry and Psychiatric Epidemiology, 42*(8), 623–630.

Berge, J. M., Wall, M., Loth, K., & Neumark-Sztainer, D. (2010). Parenting style as a predictor of adolescent weight and weight-related behaviors. *Journal of Adolescent Health, 46,* 331–338.

Blair, S. N., Booth, M., Gyarfas, I., Iwane, H., Marti, B., Matsudo, V., & Shephard, R. (1996). Development of public policy and physical activity initiatives internationally. *Sports Medicine, 21,* 157–163.

Blumenthal, J. A., Babyak, M. A., Doraiswamy, P. M., Watkins, L., Hoffman, B. M., Barbour, K. A., . . . & Sherwood, A. (2007). Exercise and pharmacotherapy in the treatment of major depressive disorder. *Psychosomatic Medicine, 69,* 587–596.

Blumenthal, J. A., Babyak, M. A., Moore, K. A., Craighead, W. E., Herman, S., Khatri, P.,. . . & Tolle T. R. (2008, February 21). The runner's high: Opioidergic mechanisms in the human brain. *Cerebral Cortex. 18*(11), 2523–2531.

Brenes, G. A., Williamson, J. D., Messier, S. P., Rejeski, W. J., Pahor, M., Ip, E., & Penninx W. J. H. (2007). Treatment of minor depression in older adults: a pilot study comparing sertraline and exercise. *Aging & Mental Health, 11,* 61–68.

Broocks, A., Bandelow, B., Pekrun, G., George, A., Meyer, T., Bartmann, . . . & Rüther, E. (1998). Comparison of aerobic exercise, clomipramine, and placebo in the treatment of panic disorder. *American Journal of Psychiatry, 155,* 603–609.

Buckworth, J., Dishman, R. K., O'Connor, P. J., & Tomporowski, P. D. (2013). *Exercise Psychology.* 2nd Ed. Champaign, IL: Human Kinetics.

Centers for Disease Control and Prevention. (2007). Prevalence of regular physical activity among adults—United States, 2001 and 2005. *Morbidity and Mortality Weekly Report, 56,* 1209–1212.

Chambliss, H. O., Huber, R. C., Finley, C. E., McDoniel, S., & Kitzman-Ulrich, H. (2011). Computerized self-monitoring and email feedback for weight loss. *Patient Education and Counseling, 85*(3), 375–382.

Chambliss, H. O., Van Hoomisen, J. D., Holmes, P. V., Bunnell, B. N., & Dishman, R. K. (2004). Effects of chronic activity wheel running and imipramine on masculine copulatory behavior after olfactory bulbectomy. *Physiology & Behavior, 82*(4), 593–600.

Chodzko-Zajko, W. J., & Moore, K. A. (1994). Physical fitness and cognitive functioning in aging. *Exercise and Sport Sciences Reviews, 22,* 195–220.

Colcombe, S. J., Erickson, K. I., Scalf, P. E., Kim, J. S., Prakash, R., McAuley, E., . . . & Kramer, A. F. (2006). Aerobic exercise training increases brain volume in aging humans. *The Journals of Gerontology. Series A, Biological Sciences and Medical Sciences, 61*(11), 1166–1170.

Colcombe, S. J., Kramer, A. F., Erickson, K. I., Scalf, P., McAuley, E., Cohen, N. J., Webb, A., Jerome, G. J., Marquez, D. X., & Elavsky, S. (2004). Cardiovascular fitness, cortical plasticity, and aging. *Proceedings National Academy of Sciences U S A, 101*(9), 3316–3321.

Conn, V. S. (2010). Anxiety outcomes after physical activity interventions: meta-analysis findings. *Nursing Research, 59,* 224–231.

Cotman C. W., & Berchtold, N. C. (2002). Exercise: A behavioral intervention to enhance brain health and plasticity. *Trends in Neuroscience, 25*(6), 295–301.

Crabbe, J. B., & Dishman, R. K. (2004). Brain electrocortical activity during and after exercise: A quantitative synthesis. *Psychophysiology, 41,* 563–574.

Crabbe, J. B., Smith, J. C., & Dishman, R. K. (2007). Emotional & electroencephalographic responses during affective picture viewing after exercise. *Physiology & Behavior, 90*(2–3), 394–404.

Craig, C. L., Bauman, A., & Reger-Nash, B. (2010). Testing the hierarchy of effects model: ParticipACTION's serial mass communication campaigns on physical activity in Canada. *Health Promotion International, 25,* 14–23.

Craggs C., Corder K., van Sluijs, E. M., & Griffin, S. J. (2011). Determinants of change in physical activity in children and adolescents: a systematic review. *American Journal of Preventive Medicine 40*, 645–658.

Davis, C. L., Tomporowski P. D., Boyle, C. A., Waller, J. L., Miller, P. H., Naglieri, J. A., & Gregoski, M. (2007). Effects of aerobic exercise on overweight children's cognitive functioning: a randomized controlled trial. *Research Quarterly for Exercise and Sport, 78*, 1–10.

DeBoer, L. B., Powers, M. B., Utschig, A. C., Otto, M. W., & Smits, J. A. (2012). Exploring exercise as an avenue for the treatment of anxiety disorders. *Expert Review of Neurotherapeutics, 12*, 1011–1022.

Deci, E. L., & Ryan, R. M. (1985). *Intrinsic motivation and self-determination in human behavior.* New York: Plenum.

De Moor, M. H., Boomsma, D. I., Stubbe, J. H., Willemsen, G., & de Geus, E. J. (2008). Testing causality in the association between regular exercise and symptoms of anxiety and depression. *Archives of General Psychiatry, 65*(8), 897–905.

Desharnais, R., Jobin, J., Cote, C., Levesque, L., & Godin, G. (1993). Aerobic exercise and the placebo effect: A controlled study. *Psychosomatic Medicine, 55*, 149–154.

Dishman, R. K. (1991). Increasing and maintaining exercise and physical activity. *Behavior Therapy, 22*, 345–378.

Dishman, R. K. (Ed.). (1994a). *Advances in exercise adherence.* Champaign, IL: Human Kinetics.

Dishman, R. K. (1997). Brain monoamines, exercise and behavioral stress: Animal models. *Medicine and Science in Sports and Exercise, 29*, 63–67.

Dishman, R.K. (2008). Gene-physical activity interactions in the etiology of obesity: Behavioral considerations. *Obesity,* 16 Suppl 3, 560–565.

Dishman, R. K., Berthoud, H. R., Booth, F. W., Cotman, C. W., Edgerton, V. R., Fleshner, M., . . . & Zigmond, M. J. (2006). Neurobiology of exercise. *Obesity (Silver Spring), 14*(3), 345–56.

Dishman, R. K., & Buckworth, J. (1996). Increasing physical activity: A quantitative synthesis. *Medicine and Science in Sports and Exercise, 28*, 706–719.

Dishman, R. K., Dunn, A. L., Sallis, J. F., Vandenberg, R. J., & Pratt, C. A. (2010). Social-cognitive correlates of physical activity in a multi-ethnic cohort of middle-school girls: two-year prospective study. *Journal of Pediatric Psychology, 35*, 188–198.

Dishman, R. K., Hales, D., Pfeiffer, K., Felton, G., Saunders, R., Ward, D. S., . . . & Pate, R. R. (2006). Physical self-concept and self-esteem mediate the association of physical activity with depression symptoms in adolescent girls: a cross-sectional study. *Health Psychology, 25*(3), 396–407.

Dishman, R. K., Jackson, E. M., Nakamura, Y., & Ray, C. A. (2013 Augmented limb blood flow during neurovascular stress in fit women. *Psychophysiology, 50*(9), 831–840

Dishman, R. K., McIver, K., Dowda, M., Saunders, R., & Pate, R. R. (2013). Intrinsic motivation and self-regulation of physical activity in middle-school boys and girls. *Developmental Psychology,* in press.

Dishman, R. K., Motl, R. W., Saunders, R., Felton, G., Ward, D. S., Dowda, M., & Pate, R. R. (2004). Self-efficacy partially mediates the effect of a school-based physical-activity intervention among adolescent girls. *Preventive Medicine, 38,* 628–636.

Dishman, R. K., Nakamura, Y., Jackson, E. M., & Ray, C. A. (2003). Blood pressure and sympathetic nerve activity during cold pressor stress: Fitness and gender. *Psychophysiology, 40,* 370–380.

Dishman, R. K., & O'Connor, P. J. (2009). Lessons in exercise neurobiology: the case of endorphins. *Mental Health and Physical Activity,* published online, 31 January 2009. *doi: 10.1016/j.mhpa.2009.01.002*

Dishman, R. K., Renner, K. J., Youngstedt, S. D., Reigle, T. G., Bunnell, B. N., Burke, K. A.,. . . & Meyerhoff, J. L. (1997). Activity wheel running reduces escape latency and alters brain monoamine levels after footshock. *Brain Research Bulletin, 42*(5), 399–406.

Dishman, R. K., & Sallis, J. F. (1994). Determinants and interventions for physical activity and exercise. In C. Bouchard, R. J. Shephard, & T. Stephens (Eds.), *Physical activity, fitness and health: International proceedings and consensus statement* (pp. 214–238). Champaign, IL: Human Kinetics.

Dishman, R. K., Saunders, R., Dowda, M., Felton, G., Ward, D., & Pate, R. R. (2006). Goals and intentions mediate efficacy beliefs and declining physical activity in girls. *American Journal of Preventive Medicine, 31*(6), 475–483.

Dishman, R. K., Saunders, R. P., McIver, K. L., Dowda, M., & Pate, R. R. (2013). Construct validity of selected measures of physical activity beliefs and motives in fifth and sixth grade boys and girls. *Journal of Pediatric Psychology, 38*(5), 563–576.

Dishman, R. K., Saunders, R. P., Motl, R. W., Dowda, M., & Pate, R. R. (2009). Self-efficacy moderates the relation between declines in physical activity and perceived social support in high school girls. *Journal of Pediatric Psychology, 34,* 441–451.

Dowda, M., Dishman, R. K., Porter D., Saunders, R. P., & Pate, R. R. (2009). Commercial facilities, social cognitive variables, and physical activity of 12th grade girls. *Annals of Behavioral Medicine, 37,* 77–87.

Dishman, R. K., Sui, X., Church, T. S., Hand, G. A., Trivedi, M. H., & Blair, S. N. (2012). Decline in cardiorespiratory fitness and odds of incident depression. *American Journal of Preventive Medicine, 43,* 361–368.

Dishman, R. K., Thom, N. J, Rooks, C. R., Motl, R. W, Horwath, C., & Nigg, C. R. (2009). Failure of post-action stages of the transtheoretical model to predict change in regular physical activity: a multiethnic cohort study. *Annals of Behavioral Medicine, 37,* 280–293.

Dishman, R. K., Vandenberg, R. J., Motl, R. W, & Nigg, C. R. (2010). Using constructs of the Transtheoretical Model to predict classes of change in regular physical activity: a multi-ethnic longitudinal cohort study. *Annals of Behavioral Medicine, 40,* 150–163.

Dowda, M., Dishman, R. K., Pfeiffer, K. A., & Pate, R. R. (2007). Family support for physical activity in girls from 8th to 12th grade in South Carolina. *Preventive Medicine, 44*(2):153–159.

Dunn, A. L., Reigle, T. G., Youngstedt, S. D., Armstrong, R. B., & Dishman, R. K. (1996). Brain norepinephrine and metabolites after treadmill training and wheel running in rats. *Medicine and Science in Sports and Exercise, 28,* 204–209.

Dunn, A. L., Trivedi, M. H., Kampert, J. B., Clark, C. G., & Chambliss, H. O. (2005). Exercise treatment for depression efficacy and dose response. *American Journal of Preventive Medicine, 28,* 1–8.

Dunn, A. L., Trivedi, M. H., & O'Neal, H. A. (2001). Physical activity dose-response effects on outcomes of depression and anxiety. *Medicine and Science in Sports and Exercise, 33,* S587–S597.

Ekeland, E., Heian, F., Hagen, K. B., Abbott, J., & Nordheim, L. (2004). Exercise to improve self-esteem in children and young people. *Cochrane Database of Systematic Reviews, 1:* CD003683.

Epstein, L. H., & Roemmich, J. N. (2001). Reducing sedentary behavior: Role in modifying physical activity. *Exercise and Sport Sciences Reviews, 29*(3), 103–108.

Epstein, L. H., Roemmich, J. N., Saad, F. G., & Handley, E. A. (2004). The value of sedentary alternatives influences child physical activity choice. *International Journal of Behavioral Medicine, 11*(4), 236–242.

Etnier, J. L., Nowell, P. M., Landers, D. M., & Sibley, B. A. (2006). A meta-regression to examine the relationship between aerobic fitness and cognitive performance. *Brain Research Reviews, 52*(1), 119–30.

Etnier, J. L., Salazar, W., Landers, D. M., Petruzzello, S. J., Han, M., & Nowell, P. (1997). The influence of physical fitness and exercise upon cognitive functioning: A meta-analysis. *Journal of Sport and Exercise Psychology, 19,* 249–277.

Faulkner, G. E. J. & Taylor, A. H. (2005). *Exercise, health and mental health,* pp. 1–233. New York: Routledge.

Ferreira, I., van der Horst, K., Wendel-Vos, W., Kremers, S., van Lenthe, F. J., & Brug, J. (2006). Environmental correlates of physical activity in youth—a review and update. *Obesity Reviews, 8,* 129–154.

Fortier, M. S., Duda, J. L, Guerin, E, & Teixeira, P. J. (2012). Promoting physical activity: development and testing of self-determination theory-based interventions. *International Journal of Behavioral Nutrition and Physical Activity,* 9:20. Published online 2012 March 2. doi: 10.1186/1479-5868-9-20

Fox, J. H., Hammack, S. E., & Falls, W. A. (2008). Exercise is associated with reduction in the anxiogenic effect of mCPP on acoustic startle. *Behavioral Neuroscience, 122,* 943–948.

Fox, K. R. (2000). Self-esteem, self-perceptions and exercise. *International Journal of Sport Psychology, 31,* 228–240.

Fulcher, K. Y., & White, P. D. (1997). Randomised controlled trial of graded exercise in patients with the chronic fatigue syndrome. *BMJ, 314*(7095), 1647–1652.

Garcia, C., Chen, M. J., Garza, A. A., Cotman, C. W., & Russo-Neustadt, A. (2003). The influence of specific noradrenergic and serotonergic lesions on the expression of hippocampal brain-derived neurotrophic factor transcripts following voluntary physical activity. *Neuroscience, 119,* 721–732.

Godin, G. (1994). Social-cognitive models. In R. K. Dishman (Ed.), *Advances in exercise adherence* (pp. 113–136). Champaign, IL: Human Kinetics.

Goodwin, R. D. (2003). Association between physical activity and mental disorders among adults in the United States. *Preventive Medicine, 36*(6), 698–703.

Greenwood, B. N., & Fleshner, M. (2011). Exercise, stress resistance, and central serotonergic systems. *Exercise and Sport Sciences Reviews, 39,* 140–149.

Groves-Chapman, J. L., Murray, P. S., Stevens, K. L., Monroe, D. C., Koch, L. G., Britton, S. L., . . . & Dishman, R. K. (2011). Changes in mRNA levels for brain-derived neurotrophic factor after wheel running in rats selectively bred for high- and low-aerobic capacity. *Brain Research, 1425,* 90–97.

Hagger, M. S., & Chatzisarantis, N. L. (2009). Integrating the theory of planned behavior and self-determination theory in health behavior: A meta-analysis. *British Journal of Health Psychology, 14,* 275–302.

Hamer, M, & Chida Y. (2009). Physical activity and risk of neurodegenerative disease: a systematic review of prospective evidence. *Psychological Medicine, 39,* 3–11.

Heath, G. W., Parra, D. C., Sarmiento, O. L., Andersen, L. B, Owen, N., Goenka, S., . . . & Brownson, R. C. (2012). Evidence-based intervention in physical activity: lessons from around the world. *Lancet, 380,* 272–281.

Herring, M. P., Jacob, M. L., Suveg, C., Dishman, R. K., & O'Connor, P. J. (2012). Feasibility of exercise training for the short-term treatment of generalized anxiety disorder: A randomized controlled trial. *Psychotherapy and Psychosomatics, 81,* 21–28.

Herring, M. P., O'Connor, P. J., & Dishman, R. K. (2010). The effect of exercise training on anxiety symptoms among patients: A systematic review. *Archives of Internal Medicine, 170,* 321–331.

Herring, M. P., O'Connor, P. J., & Dishman, R. K. (2013). Physical self-concept and self-esteem mediated associations between physical activity and anxiety in college women. Unpublished observations, University of Georgia.

Herring, M. P., Puetz, T. W., O'Connor P. J., & Dishman, R. K. (2012). Effect of exercise training on depressive symptoms among patients with a chronic illness: a systematic review and meta-analysis of randomized controlled trials. *Archives of Internal Medicine, 172,* 101–11.

Heydari, M., Boutcher, Y. N., & Boutcher, S. H. (2013). The effects of high-intensity intermittent exercise training on cardiovascular response to mental and physical challenge. *International Journal of Psychophysiology, 87,* 141–146.

Heyn, P., Abreu, B. C., & Ottenbacher, K. J. (2004). The effects of exercise training on elderly persons with cognitive impairment and dementia: a meta-analysis. *Archives of Physical Medicine and Rehabilitation, 85*(10), 1694–1704.

Hunsberger, J. G., Newton, S. S., Bennett, A. H., Duman, C. H., Russell, D. S., Salton, S. R., & Duman, R. S. (2007). Antidepressant actions of the exercise-regulated gene VGF. *Nature Medicine, 13*(12), 1476–1482.

Hutchison, A. J., Breckon, J. D., & Johnston, L. H. (2009). Physical activity behavior change interventions based on the transtheoretical model: a systematic review. *Health Education & Behavior, 36,* 829–845.

Ivy, A. S., Rodriguez, F. G., Garcia, C., Chen, M. J., & Russo-Neustadt, A. A. (2003). Noradrenergic and serotonergic blockade inhibits BDNF mRNA activation following exercise and antidepressant. *Pharmacology, Biochemistry, and Behavior, 75,* 81–88.

Jackson, E. M., & Dishman, R. K. (2002). Hemodynamic responses to stress among black women: Fitness and parental hypertension. *Medicine and Science in Sports and Exercise, 34,* 1097–1104.

Jackson, E. M., & Dishman, R. K. (2006). Cardiorespiratory fitness and laboratory stress: a meta-regression analysis. *Psychophysiology, 43*(1), 57–72. Erratum in: *Psychophysiology, 43*(1) (2006, January), 126.

Jakicic, J. M., Winters, C., Lang, W., & Wing, R. R. (1999). Effects of intermittent exercise and use of home exercise equipment on adherence, weight loss, and fitness in overweight women: A randomized trial. *Journal of the American Medical Association, 282,* 1554–1560.

Jazaieri H., Goldin, P. R., Werner, Ziv, M., & Gross, J. J. (2012). A randomized trial of MBSR versus aerobic exercise for social anxiety disorder. *Journal of Clinical Psychology, 68,* 715–731.

Jonsdottir, I. H., Rodjer, L., Hadzibajramovic, E., Borjesson, M., & Ahlborg, Jr., G. (2010). A prospective study of leisure-time physical activity and mental health in Swedish health care workers and social insurance officers. *Preventive Medicine 51*(5), 373–377.

Kahn, E. B., Ramsey, L. T., Brownson, R. C., Heath, G. W., Howze, E. H., Powell, K. E., et al. (2002). The effectiveness of interventions to increase physical activity. A systematic review. *American Journal of Preventive Medicine, 22,* 73–107.

Kessler, R. C., Berglund, P., Demler, O., Jin, R., Merikangas, K. R., & Walters, E. E. (2005a). Lifetime prevalence and age-of-onset distributions of DSM-IV disorders in the National Comorbidity Survey Replication. *Archives of General Psychiatry 62*(6), 593–602.

Kessler, R. C., Chiu, W. T., Demler, O., Merikangas, K. R., & Walters, E. E. (2005b). Prevalence, severity, and comorbidity of 12-month DSM-IV disorders in the National Comorbidity Survey Replication. *Archives of General Psychiatry 62*(6), 617–627.

King, A. C. (1994). Community and public health approaches to the promotion of physical activity. *Medicine and Science in Sports and Exercise, 26,* 1405–1412.

King, A. C., Oman, R. F., Brassington, G. S., Bliwise, D. L., & Haskell, W. L. (1997). Moderate-intensity exercise and self-rated quality of sleep in older adults. A randomized controlled trial. *Journal of the American Medical Association, 277,* 32–37.

King, A. C., Pruitt, L. A., Woo, S., Castro, C. M., Ahn, D. K., Vitiello, M. V., . . . & Bliwise, D. L. (2008). Effects of moderate-intensity exercise on polysomnographic and subjective sleep quality in older adults with mild to moderate sleep complaints. *Journals of Gerontology: Series A: Biological Sciences & Medical Sciences, 63,* 997–1004.

Knapp, D. N. (1988). Behavioral management techniques and exercise promotion. In R. K. Dishman (Ed.), *Exercise adherence: Its impact on public health* (pp. 203–236). Champaign, IL: Human Kinetics.

Koltyn, K. F., & Morgan, W. P. (1992). Influence of underwater exercise on anxiety and body temperature. *Scandinavian Journal of Medicine, Science and Sports, 2,* S41.

Kriemler, S., Meyer, U., Martin, E., van Sluijs, E. M., Andersen, L. B., & Martin, B. W. (2011). Effect of school-based interventions on physical activity and fitness in children and adolescents: a review of reviews and systematic update. *British Journal of Sports Medicine, 45,* 923–930.

Krogh, J., Nordentoft, M., Sterne, J. A., & Lawlor, D. A. (2011). The effect of exercise in clinically depressed adults: Systematic review and meta-analysis of randomized controlled trials. *Journal of Clinical Psychiatry, 72,* 529–538.

Lambourne, K., & Tomporowski, P. D. (2010). The effect of acute exercise on cognitive task performance: A meta-regression analysis. *Brain Research Reviews, 1341,* 12–24.

Landers, D. M., & Petruzzello, S. J. (1994). Physical activity, fitness, and anxiety. In C. Bouchard, R. J. Shephard, & T. Stephens (Eds.), *Physical activity, fitness and health: Proceedings and consensus statement* (pp. 868–882). Champaign, IL: Human Kinetics.

Lange, G., Cook, D. B., & Natelson, B. H. (2005). Rehabilitation and treatment of fatigue. In J. DeLuca (Ed.), *Fatigue as a Window to the Brain.* Cambridge, MA: MIT Press.

Lawlor, D. A., & Hopker, S. W. (2001). The effectiveness of exercise as an intervention in the management of depression: Systematic review and meta-regression analysis of randomized trials. *British Medical Journal, 322,* 1–8.

Lopez, A. D., Mathers, C. D., Ezzati, M., Jamison, D. T., & Murray, C. J. (2006). Global and regional burden of disease and risk factors, 2001: Systematic analysis of population health data. *Lancet, 367*(9524), 1747–1757.

Loy, B., O'Connor, P. J., & Dishman, R. K. (2013). The effect of a single bout of exercise on energy and fatigue mood states: a systematic review and meta-analysis. *Fatigue: Biomedicine, Health and Behavior,* published online October 11, 2013, http://dx.doi.org/10.1080/21641846.2013.843266.

Luban, D. R., Foster, C., & Biddle, S. J. H. (2008). A review of mediators of behavior in interventions to promote physical activity among children and adolescents. *Preventive Medicine, 47,* 463–470.

MacKinnon D. P., Fairchild A. J., Fritz M. S. (2007). Mediation analysis. *Annual Review of Psychology, 58,* 593–614.

Marcus, B. H., Pinto, B. M., Simkin, L. R., Audrain, J. E., & Taylor, E. R. (1994). Application of theoretical models to exercise behavior among employed women. *American Journal of Health Promotion, 9,* 49–55.

Marcus, B. H., & Simkin, L. R. (1994). The transtheoretical model: Applications to exercise behavior. *Medicine and Science in Sports and Exercise, 26,* 1400–1404.

Mark, T. L., Levit, K. R., Coffey, R. M., McKusick, D. R., Harwood, H. J., King, . . . & Ryan, K. (2007). National Expenditures for Mental Health Services and Substance Abuse Treatment, 1993–2003: SAMHSA Publication SMA 07-4227. Rockville, Md, Substance Abuse and Mental Health Services Administration.

Marks, B. L., Madden, D. J., Bucur, B., Provenzale, J. M., White, L. E., Cabeza, R., & Huettel, S. A. (2007). Role of aerobic fitness and aging on cerebral white matter integrity. *Annals of the New York Academy of Sciences, 1097,* 171–174.

Marshall, S. J., & Biddle, S. J. H. (2001). The transtheoretical model of behavior change: A meta-analysis of applications to physical activity and exercise. *Annals of Behavioral Medicine, 23,* 229–246.

Mathers, C. D., & Loncar, D. (2006). Projections of global mortality and burden of disease from 2002 to 2030. *PLoS Medicine, 3*(11), e442.

McAuley, E., & Blissmer, B. (2000). Self-efficacy determinants and consequences of physical activity. *Exercise and Sport Sciences Reviews, 28,* 85–88.

McAuley, E., Kramer, A. F., & Colcombe, S. J. (2004). Cardiovascular fitness and neuro-cognitive function in older adults: A brief review. *Brain Behavior and Immunity, 18*(3), 214–220.

Mead, G. E., Morley, W., Campbell, P., Greig, C. A., McMurdo, M., & Lawlor, D. A. (2009). Exercise for depression. *Cochrane Database of Systematic Reviews,* (3): CD004366.

Merom, D., Phongsavan, P., Wagner, R., Chey, T., Marnane, C., Steel, Z., Silove, D., & Bauman, A. (2008). Promoting walking as an adjunct intervention to group cognitive behavioral therapy for anxiety disorders—A pilot group randomized trial. *Journal of Anxiety Disorders, 22,* 959–968.

Metcalf, B., Henley, W., & Wilkin, T. (2012). Effectiveness of intervention on physical activity of children: systematic review and meta-analysis of controlled trials with objectively measured outcomes (EarlyBird 54). *British Medical Journal, Sep 27, 345,* e5888. doi: 10.1136/bmj. e5888.

Michaud, C. M., McKenna, M. T., Begg, S., Tomijima, N., Majmudar, M., Bulzacchelli, M. T., . . . & Murray, C. J. (2006). The burden of disease and injury in the United States 1996. *Population Health Metrics, 4,* 11.

Moore, J. B., Mitchell, N. G., Bibeau, W. S., & Bartholomew, J. B. (2011). Effects of a 12-Week Resistance Exercise Program on Physical Self-Perceptions in College Students. *Research Quarterly for Exercise and Sport, 82,* 291–301.

Morgan, K. (2003). Daytime activity and risk factors for late-life insomnia. *Journal of Sleep Research, 12,* 231–238.

Morgan, W. P. (1994). Physical activity, fitness, and depression. In C. Bouchard, R. J. Shephard, & T. Stephens (Eds.), *Physical activity, fitness and health: International proceedings and consensus statement* (pp. 851–867). Champaign, IL: Human Kinetics.

Moss-Morris, R., Sharon, C., Tobin, R., & Baldi, J. C. (2005). A randomized controlled graded exercise trial for chronic fatigue syndrome: outcomes and mechanisms of change. *Journal of Health Psychology, 10*(2), 245–259.

Motl, R. W., Birnbaum, A., Kubik, M., & Dishman, R. K. (2004). Naturally occurring changes in physical activity are inversely related to depressive symptoms during early adolescence. *Psychosomatic Medicine, 66*(3), 336–342.

Motl, R. W., Konopack, J. F., McAuley, E., Elavsky, S., Jerome, G. J., & Marquez, D. X. (2005). Depressive symptoms among older adults: long-term reduction after a physical activity intervention. *Journal of Behavioral Medicine, 28,* 385–394.

Nader, P. R., Bradley, R. H., Houts, R. M., McRitchie, S. L., & O'Brien, M. (2008). Moderate-to-vigorous physical activity from ages 9 to 15 years. *JAMA, 300,* 295–305.

Ntoumanis, N. (2012). A review of self-determination theory in sport and physical education. In G.C. Roberts & D.C. Treasure (Eds.), *Advances in Motivation in sport and exercise* (3rd ed., pp. 91–128). Champaign, IL: Human Kinetics.

O'Connor, T. M., Jago, R., & Baranowski, T. (2009). Engaging parents to increase youth physical activity: A systematic review. *American Journal of Preventive Medicine, 37,* 141–149.

O'Connor, P. J., Petruzzello, S. J., Kubitz, K. A., & Robinson, T. L. (1995). Anxiety responses to maximal exercise testing. *British Journal of Sports Medicine, 29,* 97–102.

O'Neal, H. A., Van Hoomissen, J. D., Holmes, P. V., & Dishman, R. K. (2001). Prepro-galanin messenger RNA levels are increased in rat locus coeruleus after treadmill exercise training. *Neuroscience Letters, 299*(1–2), 69–72.

Passos, G. S., Poyares, D., Santana, M. G., Garbuio, S. A., Tufik, S., & Mello, M. T. (2010). Effect of acute physical exercise on patients with chronic primary insomnia. *Journal of Clinical Sleep Medicine, 6,* 270–275.

Pate, R. R., Saunders, R., Dishman, R. K., Addy, C., Dowda, M., & Ward, D. S. (2007). Long-term effects of a physical activity intervention in high school girls. *American Journal of Preventive Medicine, 33*(4), 276–280.

Pate, R. R., Ward, D. S., Saunders, R. P., Felton, G., Dishman, R. K., & Dowda, M. (2005). Promotion of physical activity among high-school girls: a randomized controlled trial. *American Journal of Public Health, 95*(9), 1582–1587.

Peppard, P. E., & Young, T. (2004). Exercise and sleep disordered breathing: An association independent of body habitus. *Sleep, 27,* 480–484.

Petruzzello, S. J., Hall, E. E., & Ekkekakis, P. (2001). Regional brain activation as a biological marker of affective responsivity to acute exercise: Influence of fitness. *Psychophysiology, 38*(1), 99–106.

Physical Activity Guidelines Advisory Committee. (2008). Physical Activity Guidelines Advisory Committee Report, 2008. Washington (DC): U.S. Department of Health and Human Services.

Pinchasov, B. B., Shurgaja, A. M., Grischin, O. V., & Putilov, A. A. (2000). Mood and energy regulation in seasonal and non-seasonal depression before and after midday treatment with physical exercise or bright light. *Psychiatry Research, 94*(1), 29–42.

Pollock, M. L., Carroll, J. F., Graves, J. E., Leggett, S. H., Braith, R. W., Limacher, M., & Hagberg, J. M. (1991). Injuries and adherence to walk/jog and resistance programs in the elderly. *Medicine and Science in Sports and Exercise, 23,* 1194–1200.

Pressman, S. D., & Cohen, S. (2005). Does positive affect influence health? *Psychological Bulletin, 131,* 925–971.

Prochaska, J. O., & Marcus, B. H. (1994). The transtheoretical model: Applications to exercise. In R. K. Dishman (Ed.), *Advances in exercise adherence* (pp. 161–180). Champaign, IL: Human Kinetics.

Puetz, T. W. (2006). Physical activity and feelings of energy and fatigue: epidemiological evidence. *Sports Medicine, 36*(9), 767–780.

Puetz, T., O'Connor, P. J., & Dishman, R. K. (2006). Effects of exercise on feelings of energy and fatigue: a quantitative synthesis. *Psychological Bulletin, 132*(6), 866–876.

Pugliese, J., & Tinsley, B. (2007). Parental socialization of child and adolescent physical activity: a meta-analysis. *Journal of Family Psychology, 21,* 331–343.

Quan, S. F., O'Connor, G. T., Quan, J. S., Redline, S., Resnick, H. E., Shahar, E., . . . & Sherrill, D. L. (2007). Association of physical activity with sleep-disordered breathing. *Sleep & Breathing* [Schlaf & Atmung] *11,* 149–157.

Rankinen, T., Bray, M. S., Hagberg, J. M., Perusse, L., & Roth, S. M., Wolfarth, B., & Bouchard, C. (2006). The human gene map for performance and health-related fitness phenotypes: the 2005 update. *Medicine and Science in Sports and Exercise, 38*(11), 1863–1888.

Rhodes, R. E., & Pfaeffli, L. A. (2010). Mediators of physical activity behaviour change among adult non-clinical populations: A review update. *International Journal of Behavioral Nutrition and Physical Activity, 7*, 37. doi:10.1186/1479-5868-7-37

Rhodes R. E., Smith N. E. (2006). Personality correlates of physical activity: a review and meta-analysis. *British Journal of Sports Medicine, 40*(12), 958–965.

Rodgers, W. M., & Murray, T. C. (2007). Distinguishing among perceived control, perceived difficulty, and self-efficacy as determinants of intentions and behaviours. *British Journal of Social Psychology, 47*(4), 607–630.

Rolland, Y., Abellan van Kan, G., & Vellas, B. (2010). Healthy brain aging: role of exercise and physical activity. *Clinical Geriatric Medicine, 26*, 75–87.

Rolland, Y., Pillard, F., Klapouszczak, A., Reynish, E., Thomas, D., Andrieu, S.,. . . & Vellas, B. (2007). Exercise program for nursing home residents with Alzheimer's disease: a 1-year randomized, controlled trial. *Journal of the American Geriatric Society, 55*, 158–165.

Rooks, C. R., McCully, K. K., & Dishman, R. K. (2011). Acute exercise improves endothelial function despite increasing vascular resistance during stress in smokers and nonsmokers. *Psychophysiology, 48*, 1299–1308.

Rooks, C. R., Thom, N. J., McCully K. K., & Dishman, R. K. (2010). Effects of incremental exercise on cerebral oxygenation measured by near-infrared spectroscopy: a systematic review. *Progress in Neurobiology, 92*, 134–150.

Rosen, C. S. (2000). Is the sequencing of change processes by stage consistent across health problems? A meta-analysis. *Health Psychology, 19*, 593–604.

Royall, D. R., Lauterbach, E. C., Cummings, J. L., Reeve, A., Rummans, T. A., Kaufer, D. I., . . . & Coffey, C. E. (2002). Executive control function: A review of its promise and challenges for clinical research. A report from the Committee on Research of the American Neuropsychiatric Association. *Journal of Neuropsychiatry and Clinical Neuroscience, 14*(4), 377–405.

Russo-Neustadt, A. (2003). Brain-derived neurotrophic factor, behavior, and new directions for the treatment of mental disorders. *Seminar in Clinical Neuropsychiatry, 8*, 109–118.

Ryan, R. M., & Deci, E. L. (2007). Active human nature: Self-determination theory and the promotion and maintenance of sport, exercise, and health. In M. S. Hagger & N. L. D. Chatzisarantis (Eds.), *Intrinsic motivation and self-determination in exercise and sport* (pp. 1–19). Champaign, IL: Human Kinetics.

Sallis, J. F., & Owen, N. (1999). *Physical activity and behavioral medicine.* Thousand Oaks, CA: Sage Publications.

Sanchez-Villegas, A., Ara, I., Guillen-Grima, F., Bes-Rastrollo, M., Varo-Cenarruzabeitia, J. J., & Martinez-Gonzalez, M. A. (2008). Physical activity, sedentary index, and mental disorders in the SUN cohort study. *Medicine & Science in Sports & Exercise 40*(5), 827–834.

Sciolino, N. R., Dishman, R. K., & Holmes P. V. (2012). Voluntary exercise offers anxiolytic potential and amplifies galanin gene expression in the locus coeruleus of the rat. *Behavioural Brain Research, 233*, 191–200.

Secher, N. H., Seifert, T., & Van Lieshout, J. J. (2008). Cerebral blood flow and metabolism during exercise: implications for fatigue. *Journal of Applied Physiology, 104*(1), 306–314.

Shilts, M., Townsend, B., & Dishman, R. K. (2013). Using goal setting to promote health behavior change: diet and physical activity. In E. Locke and G. Latham (Eds.), *New developments in goal setting and task performance* (pp. 415–438). New York: Routledge Taylor & Francis.

Sibley, B. A., & Etnier, J. L. (2003). The relationship between physical activity and cognition in children: A meta-analysis. *Pediatric Exercise Science, 15,* 243–256.

Simonen, R. L., Rankinen, T., Perusse, L., Leon, A. S., Skinner, J. S., Wilmore, J. H., . . . & Bouchard, C. (2003). A dopamine D2 receptor gene polymorphism and physical activity in two family studies. *Physiology & Behavior, 78,* 751–757.

Singh, N. A., Clements, K. M., & Fiatrone, M. A. (1997). A randomized controlled trial of the effect of exercise on sleep. *Sleep, 20,* 95–101.

Singh, N. A., Stavrinos, T. M., Scarbek, Y., Galambos, G., Liber, C., & Singh, M. A. (2005). A randomized controlled trial of high versus low intensity weight training versus general practitioner care for clinical depression in older adults. *Journals of Gerontology Series A: Biological and Medical Sciences, 60*(6), 768–776.

Smith, J. C., O'Connor, P. J., Crabbe, J. B., & Dishman, R. K. (2002). Emotional responsiveness after low- and moderate-intensity exercise and seated rest. *Medicine and Science in Sports and Exercise, 34*(7), 1158–1167.

Soares, J., Holmes, P. V., Renner, K., Edward, G., Bunnell, B. N., & Dishman, R. K. (1999). Brain noradrenergic responses to footshock after chronic activity wheel running. *Behavioral Neuroscience, 113,* 558–566.

Sonstroem, R. J. (1998). Physical self-concept: Assessment and external validity. *Exercise and Sport Sciences Reviews, 26,* 133–164.

Sonstroem, R. J., & Morgan, W. P. (1989). Exercise and self-esteem: rationale and model. *Medicine and Science in Sports and Exercise, 21*(3), 329–337.

Spence, J. C., McGannon, K. R., & Poon, P. (2005). The effect of exercise on global self-esteem: a quantitative review. *Journal of Sport & Exercise Psychology, 27,* 311–334.

Spencer, L., Adams, T. B., Malone, S., Roy, L., & Yost, E. (2006). Applying the transtheoretical model to exercise: a systematic and comprehensive review of the literature. *Health Promotion Practice, 7,* 428–443.

Standage, M., Gillison, F. B., Ntoumanis, N., & Treasure, D. C. (2012). Predicting students' physical activity and health-related well-being: a prospective cross-domain investigation of motivation across school physical education and exercise settings. *Journal of Sport and Exercise Psychology, 34,* 37–60.

Stansfield, S. A., & Marmot, M. G. (Eds.). (2002). *Stress and the heart: Psychosocial pathways to coronary heart disease.* London: BMJ Books.

Stranahan, A. M., Mattson, M. P. (2012). Recruiting adaptive cellular stress responses for successful brain aging. *Nature Reviews: Neuroscience, 13,* 209–216.

Strine, T. W., Chapman, D. P., Kobau, R., & Balluz, L. (2005). Associations of self-reported anxiety symptoms with health-related quality of life and health behaviors. *Social Psychiatry and Psychiatric Epidemiology, 40,* 432–438.

Ströhle, A., Hofler, M., Pfister, H., Muller, A. G., Hoyer, J., Wittchen, H. U., & Lieb, R. (2007). Physical activity and prevalence and incidence of mental disorders in adolescents and young adults. *Psychological Medicine, 37*(11), 1657–1666.

Strong, W. B., Malina, R. M., Blimkie, C. J., Daniels, S. R., Dishman, R. K., Gutin, B., . . . & Trudeau, F. (2005). Evidence based physical activity for school-age youth. *Journal of Pediatrics, 146*(6), 732–737.

Stubbe, J. H., Boomsma, D. I., Vink, J. M., Cornes, B. K., Martin, N. G., Skytthe, . . . & de Geus, E. J. (2006). Genetic influences on exercise participation in 37,051 twin pairs from seven countries. *PLoS ONE, 1*, e22.

Taylor, M. K., Pietrobon, R., Pan, D., Huff, M., & Higgins, L. D. (2004). Healthy people 2010 physical activity guidelines and psychological symptoms: Evidence from a large nationwide database. *Journal of Physical Activity and Health, 1*, 114–130.

Teixeira, P. J., Carraça, E. V., Markland, D., Silva, M. N., & Ryan, R. M. (2012). Exercise, physical activity, and self-determination theory: A systematic review. *International Journal of Behavioral Nutrition and Physical Activity, 9*, 78. http://www.ijbnpa.org/content/9/1/78

Thom, N. J., Holmes, P. V., & Dishman, R. K. (2009). Effects of exercise on male copulatory behavior after beta-adrenoreceptor blockade. *Brain Research Bulletin, 79*, 414–417.

Thorsen, L., Nystad, W., Stigum, H., Dahl, O., Klepp, O., Bremnes, R. M., . . . & Fosså, S. D. (2005). The association between self-reported physical activity and prevalence of depression and anxiety disorder in long-term survivors of testicular cancer and men in a general population sample. *Supportive Care in Cancer, 13*, 637–646.

Tieman, J. G., Peacock, L. J., Cureton, K. J., & Dishman, R. K. (2001). Acoustic startle eyeblink response after acute exercise. *International Journal of Neuroscience, 106*, 21–33.

Tomporowski, P. D., Davis, C. L., Miller, P. H., & Naglieri, J. A. (2008). Exercise and Children's Intelligence, Cognition, and Academic Achievement. *Educational Psychology Review, 20*, 111–131.

Tomporowski, P. D., & Ellis, N. R. (1986). The effects of exercise on cognitive processes: A review. *Psychological Bulletin, 99*, 338–346.

Trivedi, M. H., Greer, T. L., Grannemann, B. D., Chambliss, H. O., & Jordan, A. N. (2006). Exercise as an augmentation strategy for treatment of major depression. *Journal of Psychiatric Practice, 12*(4), 205–213.

Troiano, R. P., Berrigan, D., Dodd, K. W., Mâsse, L. C., Tilert, T., McDowell, M. (2008). Physical activity in the United States measured by accelerometer. *Medicine and Science in Sports and Exercise, 40*, 181–188.

Trost, S. G., Owen, N., Bauman, A., Sallis, J. F., & Brown, W. J. (2002). Correlates of adults' participation in physical activity: Review and update. *Medicine and Science in Sports and Exercise, 34*, 1996–2001.

U.S. Department of Health and Human Services. (2010). *Healthy people 2020: Improving the health of Americans.* Washington, DC: U.S. Government Printing Office.

Van Der Horst, K., Paw, M. J., Twisk, J. W., & Van Mechelen, W. (2007). A brief review on correlates of physical activity and sedentariness in youth. *Medicine and Science in Sports and Exercise, 39*, 1241–1250.

Van Hoomissen, J. D., Chambliss, H. O., Holmes, P. V., & Dishman, R. K. (2003). Effects of chronic exercise and imipramine on mRNA for BDNF after olfactory bulbectomy in rat. *Brain Research, 974,* 228–235.

Van Hoomissen, J. D., Holmes, P. V., Zellner, A. S., Poudevigne, A., & Dishman, R. K. (2004). Effects of beta-adrenoreceptor blockade during chronic exercise on contextual fear conditioning and mRNA for galanin and brain-derived neurotrophic factor. *Behavioral Neuroscience, 118,* 1378–1390.

van Praag, H. (2008). Neurogenesis and exercise: past and future directions. *Neuromolecular Medicine, 10,* 128–140.

van Sluijs, E. M., Kriemler, S., & McMinn, A. M. (2011). The effect of community and family interventions on young people's physical activity levels: a review of reviews and updated systematic review. *British Journal of Sports Medicine, 45,* 914–922.

Wallace, L. S., & Buckworth, J. (2003). Longitudinal shifts in exercise stages of change in college students. *Journal of Sports Medicine and Physical Fitness, 43,* 209–212.

Wallman, K. E., Morton, A. R., Goodman, C., Grove, R., & Guilfoyle, A. M. (2004). Randomised controlled trial of graded exercise in chronic fatigue syndrome. *Medical Journal of Australia, 180*(9), 444–448.

Wendel-Vos, W., Droomers, M., Kremers, S., Brug, J., & van Lenthe F. (2007). Potential environmental determinants of physical activity in adults: a systematic review. *Obesity Reviews, 8,* 425–440.

Wessely, S., Hotopf, M., & Sharpe, M. (1998). *Chronic fatigue and its syndromes.* Oxford: Oxford University Press.

Williamson, J. W., McColl, R., & Mathews, D. (2003). Evidence for central command activation of the human insular cortex during exercise. *Journal of Applied Physiology, 94*(5), 1726–1734.

Yoo, H. S., Tackett, R. L., Crabbe, J. B., Bunnell, B. N., & Dishman, R. K. (2000). Antidepressant-like effects of physical activity versus imipramine: Neonatal clomipramine model. *Psychobiology, 28*(4), 540–549.

Youngstedt, S. D., Dishman, R. K., Cureton, K. J., & Peacock, L. J. (1993). Does body temperature mediate anxiolytic effects of acute exercise? *Journal of Applied Physiology, 74,* 825–831.

Youngstedt, S. D., & Kline, C. E. (2006). Epidemiology of exercise and sleep. *Sleep and Biological Rhythms, 4*(3), 215–221.

Youngstedt, S. D., O'Connor, P. J., & Dishman, R. K. (1997). The effects of acute exercise on sleep: A quantitative synthesis. *Sleep, 20,* 203–214.

Youngstedt, S. D., O'Connor, P., Crabbe, J. B., & Dishman, R. K. (2000). Effects of acute exercise on caffeine-induced insomnia. *Physiology & Behavior, 68,* 563–570.

INDEX

AASP. *See* Association for Applied Sport Psychology (AASP)
AASP certification, 8–9, 332
Abbreviated active progressive relaxation (PR), 223
ABC cognitive restructuring, 293–295
"About Smocks and Jocks" (Martens), 6
Account-making, 501
Achievement drive, 343
Achievement goal orientations, 365
Achievement goal theory, 365
Achievement goals, 58–65
ACT
   attention control training, 306
   attentional control theory, 215
Activation, 209
Active listening, 149–150
Activity theory, 492
Adaptive commitment, 449
Adlington, Rebecca, 207
Advice seeking (stress management), 217
Affect/mood, 282–283
Affective cues, 282
Affirmations, 295
African Americans. *See* Race and ethnicity
Ali, Muhammad, 386–387
All-or-none syndrome, 179–180
All-or-nothing thinking, 292
Allen, George, 359
Alzado, Lyle, 424, 426, 430
Amaechi, John, 391
American Sport Education Program, 373
Amotivation, 66, 67f
Anabolic steroids, 423–424
Anecdotes, inspirational, 113
Anger and aggression control, 414
Antecedents, 41
Anti-fat bias, 393
Anti-inflammatories, 425
Antonelli, Ferrucio, 3
Anxiety, 511
Anxiety Rating Scale (ARS-2), 211
Anxiolytic drugs, 415
Applied sport psychology, 1
Armstrong, Lance, 421
Arousal and activation, 209
Arrogant listening, 149

ARS-2. *See* Anxiety Rating Scale (ARS-2)
Ashe, Arthur, 288
Assertiveness, 151
Assertiveness training, 151–152
Assessment instruments, 339–340
Association for Applied Sport Psychology (AASP), 7
Associative phase of learning, 21–23, 25t
Athlete. *See* Student-athlete
Athlete-athlete communications, 149–150
Athlete awareness. *See* Awareness
Athlete burnout, 444–461
   athlete-team congruence, 452
   case studies, 453–456
   defined, 445–446
   depression, contrasted, 446
   dropout, contrasted, 446
   emotional and physical exhaustion, 445t
   individual-organization fit, 450–452
   need thwarting, 68
   overtraining, 446–447, 451t
   preventing burnout, 453
   psychosocial sport stress, 447–448, 451t
   reduced sense of accomplishment, 445t
   SDT, 67, 448–449, 451–452t
   sport devaluation, 445t
   sport entrapment, 449–450, 452t
Athlete Career and Education (ACE) Program (Australia), 491
Athlete leader, 110–115
Athlete motivation. *See* Motivation
Athlete stigma, 90
Athlete-team congruence, 452
Athletes' Retirement Decision Inventory, 502
Athletic Coping Skills Inventory-28, 339
Athletic injuries. *See* Injuries
Athletic motivation inventory, 3
Athletic retirement, 493–495. *See also* Career transition
Attention control, 282
Attention control training (ACT), 306
Attentional control theory (ACT), 215
Attentional cues and triggers, 317–318

Attentional focus. *See* Concentration
Attentional styles, 307f
Attribution, 83
Australian Athletes Career Transition Inventory, 502
Authentic leadership, 106
Autogenic training, 225, 238–239
Autogenic training with visualization, 225
Automating preperformance routines, 256
Automatized buffers, 166
Autonomous motivation, 66, 67, 520
Autonomous phase of learning, 23–24, 25t
Autonomy-supportive coaching, 68, 71
Autonomy-supportive interpersonal style, 91
Aversive control, 42, 43
Aversive punishment, 42, 43–44
Awareness, 176–187
   all-or-none syndrome, 179–180
   awareness training, 179
   blindfold run, 180
   feedback sheets, 181f, 183
   focus, 177
   group discussion, 184
   imagery, 184
   monitoring physiological systems, 184
   performing skills *vs.* experiencing skills, 178
   playing the edge of peak performance, 180
   psychological questionnaires, 183
   the R's, 177–178, 183
   scouting report, 178
   signal light analogy, 182, 183f
   sport journal, 183, 186–187
   stress, and, 180–182
Awareness training, 179
Awfulizing, 291

Baddour, Dick, 102
Bandwidth feedback, 31
Banned substances, 423–427
Bannister, Roger, 276
Basic mental training program (Unestahl), 317
Basketball, 200f
Baumann, Alex, 247

Bay Area Laboratory Co-Operative (BALCO), 421
Behavior modification, 520
Behavioral contracting, 436
Behavioral feedback, 373
Behavioral signatures, 47
Behavioral theories of leadership, 104*t*
Behaviorally based information, 80
"Being in the cocoon," 160
Belichick, Bill, 477
Berra, Yogi, 40, 45
BET (TAIS), 309*t*
Beta-blockers, 425
Biogenesis, 421, 428
Bioinformational theory, 247–248
Biosocial hypothesis, 87
Bird, Larry, 244
BIT (TAIS), 309*t*
Blaming, 292
Bledsoe, Drew, 477
Blindfold run, 180
Blocked practice, 27, 28*f*
Blood doping, 425
Body image, 412, 413
Bracing, 209
Brady, Tom, 477
Brain biofeedback, 319
Brain-derived neurotropic factor (BDNF), 517
Brain opioids, 516
Breathing exercises, 221–223, 230
British Athletes Lifestyle Assessment Needs in Career and Education, 502
Broad-external drills, 313
Broad-internal drills, 313
Burnout. *See* Athlete burnout

Caffeine, 425
Cammalleri, Mike, 241
Canadian Society for Psychomotor Learning and Sport Psychology (SCAPPS), 4
Candrea, Mike, 110
Capability, 19
Captain selection policies, 110
Captain's weekly monitoring sheet, 115
Career transition, 490–509
    athletes' entourages and organizational culture, 499
    athletes' retirement decision-making process, 495
    causes of career termination, 493–495
    conceptual model, 492, 493*f*
    coping strategies, 498
    developmental experiences, 495–496

history and background, 490–491
    inventories/questionnaires, 502
    perceived control, 496–497
    preretirement planning, 499–500
    retirement as transition, 492
    self-identity, 496
    social gerontology, 492
    social identity, 497
    social support, 498–499
    socioeconomic status, 497
    sport psychologists' role, 500–502
    thanatology, 491–492
Carril, Pete, 104, 113
Carron and Spink team building approach, 132–133
Case studies
    burnout, 453–456
    imagery, 262–264
    injuries, 463, 472
    instruction and feedback, 52
    positive reinforcement/ shaping, 46
    psychological skills training program, 347
    skill development, 33–35
    stress, 228, 229
Catastrophe model, 214–215
Catastrophizing, 291–292
CBAS. *See* Coaching behavior assessment system (CBAS)
CBQ. *See* Coaching behavior questionnaire (CBQ)
CBT. *See* Cognitive behavioral therapy (CBT)
Centering, 318
Central nervous system (CNS) stimulants, 424
CET. *See* Coach effectiveness training (CET)
Champion, Robert, 125
Change-oriented behaviors, 109
Changing negative thoughts to positive thoughts, 287–289
Changing the Game: The GLSEN Sports Project, 391
Charismatic, visionary and transformational leadership theories, 104*t*
Choking, 216, 309–311
Chronic fatigue syndrome, 514
Clarify, 145, 150
Clear expectations, 380
Closed skills, 22, 259
Closeness, 110
CMRT. *See* Cognitive motivational relational theory (CMRT)
Coach-athlete communications, 145–148

Coach-athlete relationship
    importance, 111
    sustainable and effective relationship, 110
Coach-coach communications, 145
Coach effectiveness training (CET), 363–364
Coach self-report form, 382
Coaching
    associative phase of learning, 22–23, 25*t*
    autonomous phase of learning, 23–24, 25*t*
    autonomy-supportive behaviors, 68, 71
    best-liked *vs.* least-liked coaches, 47
    cognitive phase of learning, 21, 25*t*
    credible coaches, 109, 142, 143
    expectancy effects. *See* Self-fulfilling prophecy theory
    goal setting, 198–199
    interpersonal style, 91
    learning situation, 40
    negative approach, 43–44
    peak performance, 168–169
    perceptual flexibility/inflexibility, 81, 93*t*
    positive approach. *See* Positive approach to coaching
    psychological skills training program, 346–351
    "psychology of," 41
    reacting to athlete behaviors, 380
    self-monitoring, 350–351
    self-report form, 382
    social environment, 40–41
    teach by example, 350
    training the coaches. *See* Evidence based coach-training programs
Coaching behavior assessment system (CBAS), 361–363
Coaching behavior questionnaire (CBQ), 109–110
Cognitive anxiety, 209
Cognitive behavior modification, 520
Cognitive-Behavioral Consultation Model, 331
Cognitive behavioral therapy (CBT), 294
Cognitive distortions, 291–293
Cognitive function, 515–516
Cognitive motivational relational theory (CMRT), 208
Cognitive phase of learning, 20–21, 25*t*
Cognitive restructuring, 293–295, 478

Cognitive Sport Psychology (Straub/
   Williams), 6
Cognitive theory of goal setting, 192
Collective ethos, 114
Collins, Jason, 391
Commitment, 449
Communication, 140–156
   assertiveness training, 151–152
   athlete-athlete communications,
      149–150
   coach-athlete communications,
      145–148
   coach-coach communications, 145
   contextual factors, 141
   credibility, 142, 143
   defined, 141
   dynamic process, 142
   empathy, 150–151
   groups, 131, 144–149
   Johari window, 149
   listening, 149–150
   misunderstandings, 144
   respect, 143
   sport psychologist, 152–153
   trust, 142
Competition novelty effect, 315
Competitive anxiety, 209–210
Competitive state anxiety, 128
Competitive State Anxiety
   Inventory-2 (CSAI-2), 183,
   211, 339
Competitive stressors, 208
Complementary roles, 118
Complete breath, 221–222
Concentration, 304–326
   attention control training
      principles, 306
   attentional styles, 307f
   choking, 309–311
   expandable awareness exercise,
      312–314
   here and now, 305
   individual differences, 308
   major component, 304
   minimizing external distractions,
      315–317
   optimal, 305
   playing to one's attentional
      strength, 308–309
   process *versus* outcome, 311–312
   shifting attention, 307–308
   strategies to stay focused, 317–320
   TAIS, 308, 309t
Concentration breathing, 222–223
Condoms, 412
Confidence, 274–303
   defined, 275
   explanatory style, 278–279
   guiding principle, 277
   imagery, 257
   mental toughness, 275–276
   misconceptions, 276–277
   optimism, 276
   psychology of excellence, 279–280
   self-awareness, 278
   self-efficacy, 276
   self-talk. *See* Self-talk
   thinking habits, 275
   thought-performance link,
      277–278
Confidence management, 227
Conscious processing hypothesis
   (CPH), 216
"Conservative strategy and cocky
   execution," 279
Constant conditions, 29
Constructive conflict management, 118
Contextual interference, 27
Contingencies, 41
Contingency management, 434
Continuity theory, 492
Continuous schedule of
   reinforcement, 46
Contract system, 436
Controllability, 247, 252
Controlled motivation, 66, 520
Controlling interpersonal style, 91
"Coping plan," 315
Coping strategies
   career transition, 498
   peak performance, 166
Coping tapes/files, 296
Countering, 290
CPH. *See* Conscious processing
   hypothesis (CPH)
Creatine, 426
Creativity, 167
Credibility and persuasiveness, 371–372
Credible coaches, 109, 142, 143
Critical race theory, 90
Cross-country skiing, 163f
CSAI-2. *See* Competitive State
   Anxiety Inventory-2 (CSAI-2)
Cultural awareness and
   reflexivity, 395
Cultural blindness, 396
Cultural competence, 394–397
Cultural competence continuum,
   396–397
Cultural destructiveness, 396
Cultural diversity
   cultural competence, 394–397
   race. *See* Race and ethnicity
Cultural incapacity, 396
Cultural precompetence, 396
Cultural proficiency, 397
Cultural sport psychology, 394
Culturally competent
   communication, 395
Culturally competent interventions,
   395
Culture, 384
Cusp catastrophe model, 214–215,
   214f
Cycle of Leadership, The (Tichy), 116

Deliberate practice, 24
Demeanor, 112
Dementia, 515
Depression, 405–406, 446, 512–513
DESC method, 114, 151–152
Deselection, 494
Developmental vulnerability, 88
Dewey, John, 141
Diaphragm, 221
Diaphragmatic breathing, 221–222
DiCicco, Tony, 260
Diem, Carl, 3
Differential progressive relaxation
   (PR), 223
Differential relaxation, 209
Diggins, Jessie, 132
Disabled persons, 393
Disassociate from fatigue, 230–231
Disconnected values model
   (DVM), 437
Discriminative stimuli, 41
Disengagement theory, 492
Dispositional hope, 165
Dissociation and detachment
   exercises, 317
Distorted thinking, 291–293
Distractions, minimizing, 315–317
Distress and well-being, 513
Diuretics, 425
Diverse worldviews, 395, 396
Diversification, 22
Donne, Elena Delle, 444
Donohue, Jack, 348
Doping, 423. *See also* Drug abuse
Dorrance, Anson, 102
Dress rehearsal, 315
Drive theory, 212
Drucker, Peter, 107
Drug abuse, 421–443
   banned substances, 423–427
   behavioral contracting, 436
   behavioral treatment approaches,
      434–436
   cognitive treatment approaches,
      432–434
   counseling, 433
   crisis management/plan of
      action, 435

Drug abuse—*Cont.*
  drug policies, 434–435
  DSDM, 436–437
  DVM, 437
  guest speakers, 436
  how widespread is the problem?,
      427–429
  MI, 433–434
  physical causes, 429–430
  psychological causes, 430–431
  random testing, 435–436
  rationale for antidrug policy, 427
  signs of drug use, 433*t*
  social causes, 431
  support groups, 436
Drug holiday, 424
Drug policies, 434–435
Drugs in sport deterrence model
    (DSDM), 436–437
Dryden, Ken, 249
Dumb-jock stereotype, 90, 411
DVM. *See* Disconnected values
    model (DVM)
Dynorphin, 516

Eating disorders, 412–413
Educational Model, 331
EEG. *See* Electroencephalography (EEG)
Ego-approach goal, 61, 62
Ego-avoidance goal, 61, 62
Ego-involved athlete, 59, 60, 64
Ego involvement, 49
Ego-involving climate, 63, 366
Ego-oriented motivational
    climate, 49
Ego-oriented people, 365
Electroencephalography (EEG), 319
Elway, John, 490
EMDR. *See* Eye movement
    desensitization and
    reprocessing (EMDR)
Emotion-focused coping, 217
Emotional and physical
    exhaustion, 445*t*
Emotional intelligence, 106
Emotionally intelligent
    leadership, 106
Emotive imagery, 479
Empathetic accuracy, 151
Empathetic listeners, 151
Empathetic understanding, 150
Empathy, 150–151
Empowerment, 108, 114
Encourage, 150
Encouragement, 381
Energizing approaches to stress
    management, 230–231
Energizing imagery, 230

Energizing verbal cues, 230
Energy Room (imagery exercise), 257
Engagement, 450
Enjoyment, 167
Enkephalin, 516
Ennis, Jessica, 57
Entity theorists, 91
Entrapment, 449–450, 452*t*
EPO, 425–426
Error correction, 24, 29–33
Error identification and diagnosis,
    30–31
Errors in performance, 30, 30*f*
Erythropoietin (EPO), 425–426
Ethics, 9, 351
Ethnicity. *See* Race and ethnicity
European Federation of Sport
    Psychology (FEPSAC), 4
Evaluative feedback, 146
Evert, Chris, 159, 246
Evidence based coach-training
    programs, 359–382
  achievement goal theory, 365
  behavioral guidelines, 369–370
  CBAS, 361–363
  CET, 363–364
  coach training as commercial
      enterprise, 373
  coach's self-awareness, 373
  credibility and persuasiveness,
      371–372
  effective presentations, 370–371
  likeability, 372
  MAC, 366–367
  modeling, 372
  motivational climate, 365–366
  philosophy of winning, 368–369
  positive learning environment,
      367–368, 381
  presenting empirical results, 369
  role playing, 372–373
Exchange and path goal models
    of leadership, 104*t*
Exchange theory, 492
Executive control, 515
Exercise psychology, 510–540
  correlates of physical activity,
      521–522
  gene-environment interactions, 525
  growth of field of, 10
  interventions, 523–524, 524*t*
  major focus, 510–511, 525
  mental health, 511–516, 518*t*
  plausible mediators/mechanisms,
      516–517
  research issues, 517, 524–525
  theories of exercise behavior,
      518–521

Expandable awareness exercise,
    312–314
Expectancy effects. *See* Self-fulfilling
    prophecy theory
Expectancy-performance process,
    79–86
Expected sensory consequences, 22
Explanatory style, 278–279
External focus, 32
External imagery perspective, 243
External locus of control, 71, 201
External-oriented behaviors, 109
External regulation, 66, 67*f*
External world, 347
Extinction, 42
Extrinsic motivation, 48, 66, 67*f*
Extrinsic rewards, 70–71
Eye movement desensitization and
    reprocessing (EMDR), 501

Faded feedback, 31
Failure-oriented athletes, 192, 201
Fairness, 292
"Fake honesty," 146
Fallacy of fairness, 292
Family relationship issues, 414–415
Faris, G. J., 477
Fear, 43
Fear-of-failure syndrome, 291
Feedback
  associative phase of learning, 22–23
  athlete leadership development, 115
  coach-athlete communication, 146
  coach's self-awareness, 373
  goal setting, 197, 199, 200*f*
  motor skill learning, 31–33
  positive approach to coaching,
      50–53
  psychological strengths/
      weaknesses, 340
  role clarity, 118
  self-fulfilling prophecy
      theory, 82–83
Feedback sheets, 181*f*, 183
Feelings of fatigue/low energy, 514
Females
  expectancy bias, 87
  women coaches, 387
  See also Gender
FEPSAC. *See* European Federation
    of Sport Psychology (FEPSAC)
5-to-1 count (rhythmic breathing),
    222
Fixation, 22
Flow, 161–162
Focus
  awareness, and, 177
  external, 32

here and now, on, 282
imagery, and, 255–256
internal focus, 32
mental toughness, and, 276
strategies to stay focused, 317–320
Focus training, 319–320
Ford, Bob, 246
Ford, Henry, 274
Formal role, 129
Foundation skills, 343
Four Olves, 152
FREEZE, 313
Frontiers of Knowledge in Sleep &
Sleep Disorders: Opportunities
for Improving Health and Quality
of Life, 513
Functional equivalence, 248

Gallwey, Tim, 281
Gamma-hydroxybutyrate (GHB), 427
Garrido, Augie, 179
Gay, Tyson, 428
Gender
defined, 384
eating disorders, 412
sexual harassment, 391–392
sport opportunities, 386
stereotypes, 89, 389
Title IX, 386
See also Females
Gender-biased coaches, 87
Gender-related stereotypes, 89, 389
Gender scholarship, 389
Generalization, 337
Generalized muscle tension, 464
Geron, Ema, 4
GHB, 427
Goal, 188–189
Goal achievement card, 200f
Goal orientations, 365
Goal setting, 188–206, 523, 524t
coaches, 198–199
cognitive theory, 192
common problems, 199–202
contract, 197
feedback, 197, 199, 200f
goal-achievement strategies, 197
goal staircase, 195f
group goals, 189, 198
importance, 189–190
injury rehabilitation, 480
life skills goal-setting programs, 193
log book/notebook, 197
mechanistic theory, 192
moderately difficult but realistic
goals, 194
outcome goals, 189, 194
performance goals, 189, 194

performance-oriented *vs.* failure-
oriented athletes, 192, 201
positive goals, 196
practice goals, 196
process goals, 189, 194
short-range/long-range goals, 194
stress management, and, 227
support from significant others,
197–198
supportive goal-setting
atmosphere, 202
target dates, 197
time commitment, 201–202
Goal staircase, 195f
Golden circle, 102
Goleman, Daniel, 106
Golf Is a Game of Confidence
(Rotella), 282
Good plays, coach's reaction to, 380
Grid concentration exercise, 320, 321f
Grief stage model, 474
Griffith, Coleman, 2–3
Griner, Brittney, 391
Group cohesion, 125–132. *See also*
Sport team
Group goals, 189, 198
Group goals and rewards, 131
Group integration, 126
Group norms, 130–131
Groupness, 125
Guidelines for Psychological Practice
with Girls and Women, 384

Hacker, Colleen, 246
Hallucinogens, 424
Hamilton, Tyler, 428
Hamm, Mia, 475
Hardiness, 466
Harrington, Padraig, 286
Harris, Dorothy, 5
Hazing, 125
Healing imagery, 479
Helton, Todd, 241
Heterosexism, 390
HGH, 426–427
Highlight tapes/videos, 260, 296
Holtz, Lou, 116
Homophobia, 390
Horton, Tim, 471
Human growth hormone (HGH),
426–427
Humor, 372

IAMS. *See* Immediate Anxiety
Measurement Scale (IAMS)
Ice hockey, 163f
"Ideal conditions," 292
Ideal self-image (ISI), 257

Idealized influence, 105
Identified regulation, 66, 67f
Identity issues, 410–411
Identity *versus* role confusion, 412
Imagery, 240–273
automating preperformance
routines, 256
basic training, 251
bioinformational theory, 247–248
case studies, 262–264
controllability, 247, 252
defined, 240
energizing, 230
energy management, 257
evaluation questionnaire, 270–273
functional equivalence, 248
individual imagery program, 262
injuries, 258–259, 479–480
internal/external perspectives, 243
ISI exercise, 257
mental focus, 255–256
mental readiness, 248
mental training tool, 242
mistakes, 255
negative aspects of, 249
polysensory experience, 241
practicing performance
strategies, 255
preparatory strategy, as, 244–245
sample imagery script, 269
self-awareness, 253, 258
self-confidence, 257
self-talk, 285
setting up imagery training
program, 249–254
strategies to enhance imagery
practice, 259–261
stress management, 225, 257–258
symbolic images, 254
team imagery program, 261–262
technology, and, 260
verbal triggers, 254
vividness, 247, 251–252
when to use it, 259
Imagery pair distraction exercise, 316
Imagery tapes, 260
Immediate Anxiety Measurement
Scale (IAMS), 211
Impart, 145
Inappropriate praise, 89
Inattentive listening, 149
Incremental theorists, 91
Individual imagery program, 262
Individual-organization fit, 450–452
Individualized consideration, 105
Individualized zone of optimal
functioning (IZOF), 162–164,
214, 331

Infidelity, 415
Informal role, 129
Information gathering (stress management), 217–218
Injuries, 462–489
  athletic retirement, 494
  case studies, 463, 472
  cognitive appraisal models, 470–474
  drug abuse, 429
  goal-setting, 480
  history of stressors, 465
  imagery, 258–259, 479–480
  interventions, 467–469
  personality and coping resources, 465–467
  potentially dangerous attitudes, 474–475
  psychological reactions to, 469–470
  rehabilitation strategies, 478–481
  relaxation, 480–481
  risk factors, 462–465
  social support, 476–477
  stress-injury model, 462–463, 463f
  thought stoppage/cognitive restructuring, 478–479
  whole-person philosophy, 475–477
Inspirational anecdotes, 113
Inspirational motivation, 105
Inspire, 145
Intellectual stimulation, 105
Intentions, 314
Interactionism paradigm, 5
Internal dialogue. See Self-talk
Internal focus, 32
Internal imagery perspective, 243
Internal locus of control, 201
Internal motivation, 67f
Internal world, 347
International Society of Sport Psychology (ISSP), 3
Interpersonal conflict, 144
Intersex, 390
Intimacy versus isolation, 412
Intrinsic motivation, 48–49, 66, 67f
Introjected regulation, 66, 67f
Inverted-U hypothesis, 212–213, 213f
Invisible knapsack, 388
Invisible whiteness, 388
Irrational beliefs, 291
ISI exercise, 257
IZOF. See Individualized zone of optimal functioning (IZOF)
IZOF iceberg profile, 163f

James, William, 510
Job-person fit model of burnout and engagement, 450

Johari window, 149
Johnson, Ben, 428
Jones, Bobby, 288
Jones, Marianne, 421
Jordan, Michael, 304
Journal of Sport Psychology, 5
Journaling, 183, 186–187
Judgmental labeling, 292

Kahneman, Daniel, 359
Kinesiology, 5
Kinesthetic sense, 241
King, Billie Jean, 58
Kleiber, Carlos, 305
Kompany, Vincent, 124
Krzyzewski, Mike, 101
Kypreos, Nick, 462

Labeling, 292
Lack of attention, coach's reaction to, 380
Latent class growth modeling, 525
Leadership, 101–123
  athlete leadership development, 110–115
  authentic, 106
  captain's weekly monitoring sheet, 115
  CBQ, 109–110
  coach leadership development, 107–110
  emotionally intelligent, 106
  leadership partnership, 111
  multidimensional model (MML), 106
  optimal leadership behaviors, 108
  overview of theories, 104t
  seven secrets of successful coaches, 109
  team captains leadership model, 112, 112f
  team leadership development, 116–119
  transformational, 105–106
  what it "is"/"is not," 107
Leadership in learning organizations, 104t
Leadership of self, 115
Leadership partnership, 111
Learner-regulated feedback, 31
Lehigh wrestling covenant, 117, 117f
Lendl, Ivan, 295
Lesbian, gay, bisexual, and transsexual (LGBT) people, 390–391, 411
Lesgaft, P. F., 10
Lethargy, 406
LGBT people, 390–391, 411

Life Development Intervention, 331
Life skills goal-setting programs, 193
Lifestyle Program (Ireland), 491
"Like playing possessed, yet in complete control," 160
Likeability, 372
Lilly, Kristine, 246
Lindros, Eric, 471
Listening, 149–150
Locus of control, 71, 201
Long distance runners, 231
Louganis, Greg, 318

MAC. See Mastery approach to coaching (MAC)
Mandel, Arnold, 5
Manipulating task/practice variables, 33
Mantra, 224
Marcus, Mitchell, 124
Martens, Rainer, 6
Mastery approach to coaching (MAC), 134, 366–367
Mastery climate, 365–366
Mastery imagery, 479
Mastery-oriented motivational climate, 49–50
Mastery-oriented team climate, 92
Mastery tapes/files, 296
MAT. See Multidimensional anxiety theory (MAT)
Mauresmo, Amelie, 391
McEnroe, John, 311
McGuire, Mark, 426
Mechanistic theory of goal setting, 192
Meditation, 224, 319
Meichenbaum's stress inoculation training program, 466
Mental focus, 255–256. See also Focus
Mental health, 511–516, 518t
  anxiety, 511
  cognitive function, 515–516
  depression, 512–513
  distress and well-being, 513
  feelings of fatigue/low energy, 514
  self-esteem, 514–515
  sleep, 513–514
  See also Referral for counseling
Mental links to excellence, 165
Mental practice, 243–244. See also Imagery
Mental preparation, 169
Mental Readiness Form (MRF), 211
Mental rehearsal, 316–317
Mental toughness, 167–168, 275–276
Mental toughness pyramid, 168f

Mental training program. *See*
    Psychological skills training
    program
Messi, Lionel, 66
Metaphor self-generation method, 164
MI. *See* Motivational interviewing (MI)
Mickelson, Phil, 246
Military programs, 12
Mind-to-muscle techniques, 219
Mindfulness, 162
Mindfulness exercise, 319
Mindfulness training, 162
Minimizing external distractions,
    315–317
Misbehavior, coach's reaction
    to, 380
Mistakes, 44, 53, 255, 380
Misunderstandings, 144
Mitchell, Michele, 320
Mitchell Report (steroid use), 431
MML. *See* Multidimensional model
    of leadership (MML)
Modeling, 372, 431, 519
Models of sport psychology
    delivery, 330–331
Momentary muscle relaxation
    exercises, 224
Momentary relaxation, 220–221
Monitor, 145
Mood congruence, 47
Morgan, Bill, 5, 7
Moses, Edwin, 427
Motivation, 57–77
    achievement goals, 58–65
    autonomous *vs.* controlled, 66, 67f
    autonomy supportive *vs.* socially
        supportive coaching, 68, 71
    ego approach *vs.* ego avoidance,
        61, 62
    extrinsic, 66, 67t
    extrinsic rewards, 70–71
    intrinsic, 66, 67t
    motivational climate, 62–63, 65t
    SDT, 66–68
    TARGET structures/strategies, 65t
    task involvement *vs.* ego
        involvement, 59, 60, 64, 65t
Motivational climate, 49–50, 62–63,
    65t, 365–366
Motivational interviewing (MI),
    433–434
Motor program, 20
Motor skill learning, 19–37
    associative phase, 21–23, 25t
    autonomous phase, 23–24, 25t
    cognitive phase, 20–21, 25t
    error correction, 24, 29–33
    feedback, 31–33

    manipulating task/practice
        variables, 33
    motor learning, defined, 19–20
    overview, 20f
    practice. *See* Practice
Movement-related feedback, 32
MRF. *See* Mental Readiness Form (MRF)
Multicultural competence, 394
Multicultural psychology, 384
Multidimensional anxiety theory
    (MAT), 214
Multidimensional model of
    leadership (MML), 106
Multimodal mental training
    interventions, 245
Multimodal stress management
    techniques, 225
Multiple identities, 384
Murphy, Shane, 6
Murphy's law, 370
Muscle tension, 464
Muscle-to-mind techniques, 219
"Must" statements, 293

NAR (TAIS), 309t
Narcotic analgesics, 425
Narrow-external drills, 312–313
Narrow-internal drills, 313
Narrow-to-broad external drills, 313
Narrow-to-broad internal drills, 313–314
Narrowing of peripheral vision, 464
National Center for Cultural
    Competence, 397
National Institute on Drug Abuse
    Research Report Series, 424
National Youth Sports Coaches
    Association program, 373
NCAA CHAMPS/Life Skills
    program, 471
Neck and shoulder check, 224
Need thwarting, 68
Needs assessment, 339, 340, 342
Negative identity, 411, 414
Negative norms, 131
Negative perfectionism, 430–431
Negative performance-enhancing
    emotion, 163
Negative performance-impairing
    emotion, 163
Negative reinforcement, 42
Neurofeedback, 319
Nightmare Season, The (Mandel), 5
Nonverbal communication, 147
Norepinephrine, 516
Norms, 130–131
North American Society for the
    Psychology of Sport and
    Physical Activity (NASPSPA), 4

Novelty, 372
Number-one affirmation, 295

Obesity, 393
Objective performance feedback, 51
OET (TAIS), 309t
Off-season norms, 130
Office of Minority Health, 397
Ogilvie, Bruce, 3
Oglesby, Carole, 5
OIT (TAIS), 309t
OMSAT-3. *See* Ottawa Mental Skill
    Assessment Tool (OMSAT-3)
On Death and Dying (Kübler-Ross), 470
One Minute Drill, 146
"One pointing" exercise, 319–320
1:2 ratio (rhythmic breathing), 222
One-trial generalizations, 292–293
Open-door policy, 146, 148
Open-ended questions, 150
Open skills, 22
Oppression, 385
Optimal performance. *See* Peak
    performance
Optimism, 276, 466
Optimistic explanatory style, 279
Organization stressors, 208
Organizational stress, 169
Other-referenced, 49
Ottawa Mental Skill Assessment Tool
    (OMSAT-3), 165, 340
Outcome expectancy, 519
Outcome goals, 189, 194
Overreaching, 446–447
Overtraining, 446–447, 451t
Overtraining syndrome, 447
Oververbalization, 281

Paralysis by analysis, 216, 281
Paraphrase, 150
Part practice, 24–26, 26f
Partial schedule of reinforcement, 47
ParticipACTION, 521
Passive progressive relaxation (PR),
    223–224
Pavlovian conditioning, 315
PDMS. *See* Personal-disclosure
    mutual-sharing (PDMS)
Peak performance, 159–175
    coaching, 168–169
    coping strategies, 166
    defined, 159
    flow, 161–162
    goal setting, 188–206. *See also*
        Goal setting
    IZOF, 162–164
    mental links to excellence, 165
    mental preparation, 169

Peak performance—*Cont.*
   mental skills, 171*t*
   mental skills training, 170, 346
   mental toughness, 167–168
   metaphor self-generation
      method, 164
   mind and body, 159
   mindfulness, 162
   organizational stress, 169
   parents and family members, 169
   psychological profile, 171*t*
   questionnaires, 164–165
   sport intelligence, 166
   team chemistry, 168
Peak performance dyad, 160–161
Pedroia, Dustin, 421
Peer leadership, 110–115
Perceptual flexibility/inflexibility,
      81, 93*t*
Perfectionism, 291, 430–431
Performance accomplishments, 519
Performance contract, 436
Performance edge, 180
Performance errors, 30, 30*f*
Performance evaluation card, 200*f*
Performance feedback, 50–53.
      See also Feedback
Performance feedback sheet, 181*f*
Performance goals, 189, 194
Performance Lifestyle Program
      (UK), 491
Performance-oriented team
      climate, 92
Performance-oriented *vs.* failure-
      oriented athletes, 192, 201
Performance profiling, 340–342
Performance rituals, 320
Performance skills, 344
Performance success, 131–132
Performing skills *vs.* experiencing
      skills, 178
Periodization of Mental Training, 331
Peripheral narrowing, 464
Permanence, 278
Person cues, 80
Personal development skills, 344
Personal-disclosure mutual-sharing
      (PDMS), 134
Personal highlight videotapes,
      260, 296
Personal problems. *See* Drug abuse;
      Mental health; Referral for
      counseling
Personal sports stories, 371
Personal stressors, 209
Personalization, 278, 292
Persons with disabilities, 393
Pervasiveness, 278

PET. *See* Processing efficiency
      theory (PET)
PETTLEP approach to motor
      imagery, 266
Phelps, Michael, 57, 240, 246,
      274, 281, 304
Philosophy of winning, 368–369
Physical activity, 387. *See also*
      Exercise psychology
Physical activity behavior change,
      517–525
Physical activity dimensions, 522
Physical inactivity, 510
Physicality, 393
Pinella, Lou, 177
Pitino, Rick, 475
Planning, 218
Play It Smart, 12
Polarized thinking, 291, 292
Popovich, Greg, 71
Positive action-oriented
      self-statements, 295
Positive approach to coaching
   cornerstone, 44
   performance feedback, 50–53
   practical guidelines, 53
   reinforcement. *See* Positive
      reinforcement
Positive Coaching Alliance, 373
Positive control, 42
Positive goals, 196
Positive internal self-evaluation, 49
Positive learning environment,
      367–368, 381
Positive performance-enhancing
      emotion, 162
Positive performance-impairing
      emotion, 163
Positive reinforcement, 44–50
   case study, 46
   defined, 42
   intrinsic motivation, and, 48–49
   motivational climate, 49–50
   practical guidelines, 53
   reinforcers, 45
   reinforcing effort/desirable
      behaviors, 48
   schedules and timing of
      reinforcement, 46–48
   shaping, 45
   target behaviors, 45
Positive sandwich technique, 108
Positive social influence
      techniques, 147
Potential reinforcers, 45
Practice, 24–29
   blocked *vs.* random, 26–28
   deliberate, 24

   variable, 28–29
   whole *vs.* part, 24–26
Practice goals, 196
Praise, inappropriate, 89
Pre-competition plan, 218, 218*f*
Precompetition and competition
      plans, 347–348
Preparatory imagery, 244–245
Preperformance routine, 256,
      311, 320
Prerace mental preparation
      plan, 337*t*
Preretirement planning, 499–500
Presentations, 370–371
"Previous experience" strategy, 315
Privilege, 385
Proactive behavior, 219
*Problem Athletes and How to Handle
      Them* (Ogilvie/Tutko), 3
Problem-focused stress management
      strategies, 217–219
Problem solving, 219
Process cues, 312
Process goals, 189, 194
Processes of change, 520
Processing efficiency theory
      (PET), 215
Productive perfectionism, 165
Productive thinking, 343
Professional associations, 3–4, 7
Professional Athletes Career
      Transition Inventory, 502
Progressive-part practice, 24, 26*f*
Progressive relaxation (PR), 223–224,
      235–237
Proprioceptive control, 21
PSIS. *See* Psychological Skills
      Inventory for Sport (PSIS)
Psychic self-regulation, 10
Psychological characteristics of peak
      performance, 159–175. *See also*
      Peak performance
Psychological distress, 513
Psychological identity foreclosure, 411
Psychological interventions, 1
Psychological Skills Inventory for
      Sport (PSIS), 165
Psychological skills objectives and
      outcomes, 344*t*
Psychological skills training program,
      329–358
   analyze demands of the sport, 342
   assess psychological strengths/
      weaknesses, 338–342
   case study, 347
   discuss the approach, 337–338
   effectiveness of interventions,
      330–331

emphasize importance of mental training, 338
ethical considerations, 351
evaluation of program effectiveness, 345–346
nonsport applications, 348–349
potential problem areas, 351–352
practical pointers for coaches, 346–351
precompetition and competition plans, 347–348
prerace mental preparation plan, 337t
self-regulation, 336–337
skills included in program, 342–345
summary/review, 352
time commitment, 335–336
when should athletes practice the skills?, 334–335
when to implement the program?, 334
who benefits?, 331–332
who should conduct the training?, 332–333
Psychology of Athletics (Griffith), 3
"Psychology of coaching," 41
Psychology of Coaching (Griffith), 3
Psychology of excellence, 279–280
Psychopharmacology, 415
Psychosocial sport stress, 447–448, 451t
Psychosocial stress, 447
Puni, A. Z., 3
Punishment
    aversive, 42, 43–44
    negative reinforcement, compared, 42
    negative side effects, 43–44
    response cost, 42, 44
"Pygmalion in the Classroom" (Rosenthal/Jacobson), 78
Pygmalion-prone vs. non-Pygmalion-prone coaches, 79, 92–93t
Pyramiding, 424

Questioning, 150
Questioning approach (feedback), 32
Quick body scan, 224–225

Race and ethnicity, 392–393
    athlete-athlete communication, 149
    athletic directors, 387
    college coaches, 387
    health disparities, 392
    stereotypes, 88–89
    white privilege, 386–387
Racial and Gender Report Card, 387
Radomski, Kirk, 428

RAE. See Relative age effect (RAE)
Raja yoga meditation, 319
Random drug testing, 435–436
Random practice, 27, 28f
Rational emotive behavior therapy (REBT), 226, 293
REBT. See Rational emotive behavior therapy (REBT)
Reciprocity, 372
Recovery, 447
RED (TAIS), 309t
Reduced sense of accomplishment, 445t
Reduction stress management strategies, 219–226
Referral for counseling, 405–420
    alcohol and substance abuse, 413–414. See also Drug abuse
    anger and aggression control, 414
    eating disorders, 412–413
    factors to consider, 407, 408
    how to start the referral process, 408–409
    identity issues, 410–411
    professional development tasks for practitioners, 415–416
    romantic and family relationship issues, 414–415
    sex- and health-related issues, 411–412
    sexual orientation, 411
    when referral doesn't go well, 409–410
Reflect, 150
Reflective listening, 150
Refocusing plan, 348, 349t
Reframing, 290–291
Rehearsal of simulated competition, 315–316
Reinforce, 145
Reinforcement
    good plays, 380
    negative, 42
    positive. See Positive reinforcement
    schedules of, 46–47
    team participation, 380
Reinforcement contingencies, 45
Reinforcement control, 523
Reinforcement schedules, 46–47
Relapse prevention, 523–524
Relations-oriented behaviors, 109
Relative age effect (RAE), 87
Relaxation response, 224
Relaxation techniques
    autogenic training, 225, 238–239
    breathing exercises, 221–223
    injuries, 480–481
    meditation, 224

momentary muscle relaxation exercises, 224
momentary relaxation, 220–221
progressive relaxation, 223–224, 235–237
visualization, 224–225
Repeated blocked practice, 28, 28f
Repetitive-part practice, 24–25, 26f
Resonance Performance Model, 331
Respect, 143
Response characteristics, 247
Response cost, 42, 44
Restructuring stress management strategies, 226–227
Retirement, 493–495. See also Career transition
Retirement Sports Survey, 502
Retrospection, 284–285
Reward power, 45
Rhetorical questions, 372
Rhythmic breathing, 222
Rickey, Branch, 50
Roadmap, 108
Rock of Gibraltar, 254
Rodriguez, Alex, 421, 428
Roid rage, 414, 423
Role, 129–130
Role acceptance, 118, 130t
Role ambiguity, 129, 130t
Role clarity, 118
Role conflict, 130t
Role efficacy, 130t
Role identity, 118
Role overload, 130t
Role performance, 130t
Role playing, 372–373
"Role restricted," 497
Role satisfaction, 130t
Romantic and family relationship issues, 414–415
Rondo, Rajon, 23
Rose, Russ, 146
Rotella, Bob, 281
Ruminating on a failed event, 319
Rupp, Galen, 68
Rydze, Richard, 428

Sandusky, Jerry, 392
Sandwich approach (feedback), 32
SAS-2. See Sport Anxiety Scale-2 (SAS-2)
Scale, Athlete Retirement Questionnaire, 502
SCAPPS. See Canadian Society for Psychomotor Learning and Sport Psychology (SCAPPS)
Schedules of reinforcement, 46–47
Schema theory, 29
Schilling, Curt, 474

Schlossberg's model of human adaptation to transition, 492
Scouting report, 178
SDT. *See* Self-determination theory (SDT)
Self-awareness, 106, 253, 258, 278, 343. *See also* Awareness
Self-confidence, 166, 343. *See* Confidence
Self-defeating thoughts, 289*t*
Self-determination continuum, 67*f*
Self-determination theory (SDT), 66–68, 448–449, 451–452*t*, 519–520
Self-determined extrinsic motivation regulations, 67
Self-efficacy, 51, 276, 283–284, 519
Self-enhancing thoughts, 289*t*
Self-esteem, 281, 363, 430, 514–515
Self-esteem list, 295
Self-fulfilling prophecy theory, 78–100
    attribution, 83
    behavioral recommendations for coaches, 93–95
    coach-athlete interactions, 82
    coach's expectations, 80–81
    coach's interpersonal style, 91
    entity *vs.* incremental perspective, 91
    expectancy-performance process, 79–86
    feedback, 82–83
    maturation rates, 86–88
    performance-oriented *vs.* mastery-oriented team climate, 92
    Pygmalion-prone *vs.* non-Pygmalion-prone coaches, 79, 92–93*t*
    quantity/quality of instruction, 82
    RAE, 87
    stereotyping, 88–90
Self-handicapping, 63
Self-identity, 496
Self-monitoring, 182, 373, 524*t*
Self-regulation, 336–337, 373
Self-regulation theory, 474
Self-regulation training, 10
Self-talk, 280–296
    ABC cognitive restructuring, 293–295
    affect/mood, 282–283
    affirmation statements, 295
    attention control, 282
    changing bad habits, 282
    changing negative thoughts to positive thoughts, 287–289
    coping tapes/files, 296
    countering, 290

exercise behavior, 284
    highlight tapes/videos, 296
    imagery, 285
    injuries, 478–479
    mastery tapes/files, 296
    reframing, 290–291
    retrospection, 284–285
    self-confidence, 284
    self-efficacy, 283–284
    self-talk log, 285
    skill acquisition, 281–282
    stress, and, 226
    thought stoppage, 286–287
Self-talk log, 285, 288
Semi-structured interview, 339
"Sensation seekers," 414
Serotonin, 516
Seven secrets of successful coaches, 109
Sex, 384
Sexual behaviors, 412
Sexual harassment, 391–392
Sexual orientation, 389–391, 411
Sexual prejudice, 390
Sexuality, 389
Sexually transmitted diseases (STDs), 412
Shaping, 45
Shared knowledge, 110
Shared perspectives, 110
Shared understanding, 110
Shared vision, 144
"She Got Game: A Celebration of Women's Sports" (Hall), 392
"Should" statements, 293
Sighing with exhalation, 222
Signal light analogy, 182, 183*f*
Silva, John, 7
Simulated competition experiences, 315–316
Situational theories of leadership, 104*t*
Skill, 22
Skill analysis, 30
Skill development. *See* Motor skill learning
Slatter-Hammel, Arthur, 4
Sleep, 513–514
Slogans, 295
Social breakdown theory, 492
Social death, 491–492
Social gerontology, 492
Social identities, 384
Social identity, 497
Social loafing, 128
Social reinforcers, 45
Social support
    career transition, 498–499
    injuries, 476–477

physical activity behavior change, 524*t*
    stress management, 217
Socially supportive coaching, 68, 71
SOLER, 150
Solomon expectancy sources scale (SESS), 80
Somatic anxiety, 209–210
Speedskater, 349*t*
Spink and Carron team building approach, 132–133
Spiritual/authentic leadership, 104*t*
Sport Anxiety Scale-2 (SAS-2), 211, 339
Sport Competition Anxiety Test, 339
Sport-confidence model, 275
Sport devaluation, 445*t*
Sport dropout, 446
Sport entrapment, 449–450, 452*t*
Sport imagery evaluation, 270–273
Sport injuries. *See* Injuries
Sport intelligence, 166
Sport journal, 183, 186–187
Sport muscle check, 224
Sport opportunities, 386
Sport psychologist
    AASP certification, 8–9, 332
    career transition, and, 500–502
    communication skills, 152–153
    counseling competencies, 333
    cultural competence, 394–397
    referrals. *See* Referral for counseling
    required characteristics, 333
Sport psychology
    applied, 1
    Eastern Europe, 10–11
    ethical standards, 9
    functions, 1
    future directions, 11–12
    historical overview, 2–11
    job market, 9–10
    professional associations, 3–4, 7
    women trailblazers, 8
Sport Psychology Academy (SPA), 4
Sport psychology books, 8
Sport Psychology Service Delivery Heuristic, 331
Sport team, 124–139
    cohesion, 125–132
    communication, 131, 144–149
    competitive state anxiety, 128
    environmental factors, 127–128
    example (Toronto Maple Leafs), 134–135
    group integration, 126
    group processes, 131
    groupness, 125
    imagery, 261–262
    leadership, 116–119, 128–129

norms, 130–131
overview, 126t
performance outcome, 131–132
personal factors, 128
proximity, 127
roles, 129–130
satisfaction, 128
social loafing, 128
team building, 132–133
team leadership development,
   116–119
team size, 127–128
Stacking, 424
Stages of change model, 520
State anxiety, 211
STDs. *See* Sexually transmitted
   diseases (STDs)
Stereotype
   African American athletes, 88–89
   dumb-jock, 90
   gender, 89, 389
   Pygmalion-prone coach, 92t
Stereotype threat theory, 90, 392
Steroids, 412, 414, 423–424
Stimulants, 424
Stimuli, 315
Stimulus characteristics, 247
Stimulus control, 41, 523, 524t
Storey, John, 104
Strahan, Michael, 277
Stress, 207–239
   ACT, 215
   arousal and activation, 209
   awareness, and, 180–182
   burnout, and, 447–448, 451t
   case studies, 228, 229
   causes, 208–209
   CMRT, 208
   competitive anxiety, 209–210
   CPH, 216
   cusp catastrophe model, 214–215,
      214f
   drive theory, 212
   emotion-focused coping, 217
   energizing approaches to stress
      management, 230–231
   imagery, 257–258
   inverted-U hypothesis, 212–213, 213f
   MAT, 214
   measuring stress-related
      symptoms, 211–212
   PET, 215
   problem-focused stress management
      strategies, 217–219
   reduction stress management
      strategies, 219–226
   restructuring interventions, 226–227
   ZOF, 213–214

Stress-injury model, 462–463, 463f
Stress inoculation training, 225, 466
Stress management training, 225–226
Structural equation modeling, 525
Student-athlete
   athlete-athlete communications,
      149–150
   athlete leadership development,
      110–115
   burnout. *See* Athlete burnout
   coach-athlete communications,
      145–148
   drug use, 422
   external world, 347
   internal world, 347
   mental skills, 343t
   personal problems. *See* Drug
      abuse; Mental health;
      Referral for counseling
   stress. *See* Stress
Student-athlete leadership
   development, 110–115
Subculture theory, 492
Success list, 295
Suicide, 406
Summarize, 150
Summitt, Pat, 19, 118
Superficial listening, 149
Swoops, Sheryl, 391
Symbolic images, 254
Sympathomimetic amines, 424

TAIS. *See* Test Attentional and
   Interpersonal Style (TAIS)
TARGET structures/strategies, 65t
Task approach goal, 62
Task avoidance goal, 62
Task-involved athlete, 59, 60, 64, 65t
Task-involving coach-created
   environment, 63
Task-oriented behaviors, 109
Teacher expectations. *See* Self-
   fulfilling prophecy theory
Team, 125. *See also* Sport team
Team building, 117–119, 132–133,
   144, 184
Team captains leadership model,
   112, 112f
Team commitment contract (Lehigh
   wrestling covenant), 117, 117f
Team confidence, 344
Team goal-setting sessions, 118
Team imagery program, 261–262
Team leadership development,
   116–119
Team skills, 344
Technical instruction, 381
Tension sensation, 220

Terminating your career, 493–495.
   See also Career transition
Test Attentional and Interpersonal
   Style (TAIS), 308, 309t
Test of Attentional and Interpersonal
   Style, 339
Test of Performance strategies
   (TOPS), 165
Thanatology, 491–492
The First Tee, 12
The R's, 177–178, 183
Theory of Planned Behavior (Ajzen), 519
Thermogenic hypothesis, 516
Thought stoppage, 286–287, 478
Thoughts-feelings-behavior link, 274,
   277–278
Tianlang, Guan, 20
TIC-TOC exercise, 318
Tichy, Noel, 116
Title IX (Educational Amendments
   Act), 386
Tittel, Kurt, 10
TOPS. *See* Test of Performance
   strategies (TOPS)
Toronto Maple Leafs (team values),
   134–135
Total relaxation, 220
Tough jock identity, 411
Track and field, 218f
Traffic signal light analogy, 182, 183f
Trait anxiety, 211, 465
Trait-State Sport Confidence
   Inventory, 339–340
Trait theories of leadership, 104t
Transfer, 27
Transferring energy, 230
Transformational leadership,
   105–106, 129
Transtheoretical model, 520
Troyan, Sue, 116
Trust, 142
Trust gap, 102
"Turning failure into success"
   exercise, 318–319
Tutko, Tom, 3
2×2 achievement goal model, 62
Tygart, Travis, 436

Uncertainty, 147
Unfairness, 292
United States Army, 12
United States Olympic Committee
   (USOC), 6
Unproductive perfectionism, 165

Variable practice, 29
Verbal persuasion, 519
Verbal reinforcement, 45

...ng (of failed event), 319
...ers, 254
..., 370

...s experiences, 519
...games (focus training), 320
...ar, Peter, 256
...alization, 224–225
...vidness, 247, 251–252
...onn, Lindsey, 240, 246

Walsh, Erica, 146
Ware, Kevin, 475, 476
Weight bias, 393

Weiss, Don, 430
White, Kelli, 427, 436
White privilege, 386–387
Whole-person philosophy, 475–477
Whole practice, 24
Wilberg, Robert, 4
Wilhout, Julie, 178
Williams, Jean, 7
Williams, Roy, 188
Williams-Anderson stress-injury
    model, 462–463, 463f
Winning, philosophy of, 368–369
Wooden, John, 40, 43, 44, 48–50,
    119, 359

Woods, Tiger, 57
Word cues, 282, 283
Worker burnout. *See* Athlete
    burnout

Yates, Dorothy, 3
Ye Quiobo, 428
Young, Steve, 58
Yow, Kay, 110

Zero-activation, 220
Zone of optimal functioning (ZOF),
    213–214